PAINTINGS FROM BOOKS

THE PAINTINGS ON THE WALLS, THE BOOKS ON THE SHELVES The library at Cragside, Northumberland, the home of the inventor and industrialist Sir William (later Baron) Armstrong, in the 1870s. (Photograph: National Monuments Record.)

PAINTINGS FROM BOOKS

Art and Literature in Britain, 1760–1900

BY RICHARD D. ALTICK

OHIO STATE UNIVERSITY PRESS : COLUMBUS

Designed by Harold M. Stevens

Text and illustrations layout by Harold Franklin

Library of Congress Cataloging in Publication Data

Altick, Richard Daniel, 1915–
Paintings from books.

Bibliography: p.
Includes index.
1. Art and literature—Great Britain—History.
2. English literature—Illustrations. 3. English literature—Appreciation. 4. Great Britain—Popular culture. 5. Books and reading—Great Britain. 6. Painting, British. I. Title.
PR408.A68A48 1985 700'.941 85-21737
ISBN 0-8142-0380-9

To My Colleagues, 1945–1982
With Gratitude and Affection

CONTENTS

PART THREE: THE REST OF THE GALLERY

ILLUSTRATIONS

ACKNOWLEDGMENTS

In calling the roll of the institutions and persons to whose support and encouragement I owe so much, I must first single out the Ohio State University, which through a generous research grant paid my travel, photographic, and word-processing bills. Once more, I have made heavy use of the university library's book and periodical collections. Clara Goldslager was tireless in obtaining additional books on inter-library loan, and for several years the ever helpful Susan E. Wyngaard and her staff provided what was virtually a second home for me at the university's Jacqueline Sisson Fine Arts Library. I am also grateful for the resources and assistance I enjoyed at three major art libraries, the Yale Center for British Art, the library of the Victoria and Albert Museum, and the library of the Courtauld Institute, University of London, where Dr. Catherine Gordon, herself the author of a dissertation on paintings from Sterne, Scott, and Dickens, generously gave me much guidance in the early stage of my research.

For joining me in the necessary but taxing drudgery of finding art criticism in the long files of British periodicals, I thank Elizabeth Isaac and (especially) Joan Samuelson. John Clubbe, Robert A. Colby, David Frantz, E. D. H. Johnson, Dianne Macleod, and Christian Zacher readily answered my appeals for information and advice. As always, my wife assisted with the proofs and index.

For giving me an opportunity to talk about my favorite subject, either in words without illustrations or in the form of an itinerant raree show, I am obliged to the Departments of English at DePaul University, the University of Kentucky, the State University of New York at Binghamton (the Miriam Leranbaum Lecture), the University of Toledo, and Indiana University of Pennsylvania; and to the Midwest Victorian Studies Association, the Victorians Institute, and the Yale Center for British Art.

I am particularly pleased that this book appears under the imprint of the Ohio State University Press, with which I have been associated for many years as a member of the editorial board. To its first director (now emeritus), Weldon A. Kefauver, I owe countless insights into the mixed delights and difficulties of scholarly publishing. The patience and expertise of the acting director, Richard Rose, and my editor, Robert Demorest, were more than equal to the challenges offered by an illustrated manuscript laden with an uncommon number of problems.

Finally, I owe thanks to all the art galleries and private owners in the following list who have consented to the reproduction in this book of paintings in their possession. (Asterisks designate owners who generously waived the customary permission fees.)

*By the gracious permission of Her Majesty the Queen (copyright reserved): 107, 146, 237, 250, 260, 265, 278, 279, 311, 326

Aberdeen Art Gallery and Museums: 81, 196

Ashmolean Museum, Oxford: 23, 121, 160, 174, 313

By courtesy of Birmingham Museums and Art Gallery: 13, 56, 71, 108, 132, 133, 162, 177, 187, 204, 205, 206, 256, 264, 295, 331

*Bristol Museum and Art Gallery: 126, 203, 306, 321

*Courtauld Institute of Art (crown copyright): 8, 106, 143, 310, 314

*Lord Egremont (photographs: Photographic Survey): 15, 99, 104, 114, 246, 261, 287, 319

*Reproduced by permission of the Provost and Fellows of Eton College (photograph: Courtauld Institute of Art): 347

The Faringdon Collection Trust, Buscot Park (photographs: Photographic Survey): 76, 166

Fitzwilliam Museum, Cambridge: 17, 225

From the art collection of the Folger Shakespeare Library: 180, 198

*Forbes Magazine Collection: 58, 61, 131, 191, 201, 220, 235, 249, 317

*The Garrick Club (photographs: ET Archive Ltd.): 10, 12, 110, 156

Glasgow Art Gallery and Museum: 65, 128, 179, 247, 271, 284, 290, 308, 324, 329

Guildhall Art Gallery, City of London: 69, 210, 234, 238, 269, 281, 333, 344

Reproduced by kind permission of the Harris Museum and Art Gallery, Preston, Lancashire: 52, 89, 141

*The Huntington Library, Art Gallery, and Botanical Gardens: 32, 226

From the collection of the Laing Art Gallery, Newcastle upon Tyne, England. Reproduced by permission of the Tyne and Wear County Council Museums Service: 298, 350

*Lady Lever Art Gallery (Merseyside County Council): 88, 134, 140, 164, 165, 263, 275, 289

Leicestershire Museums and Art Galleries: 49, 95, 150, 175

*City of Manchester Art Galleries: 80, 84, 86, 97, 103, 129, 130, 138, 167, 183, 213, 215, 223, 296, 330, 332, 338

National Galleries of Scotland, Edinburgh: 37, 72, 74, 85, 101, 148, 199, 227, 231, 283, 291, 316, 318, 323

From Petworth House, a property of the National Trust (photographs: Photographic Survey): 19, 224, 230, 253

Royal Commission on Historical Monuments (England): frontispiece

The Governors of the Royal Shakespeare Theatre (photographs: University of Warwick, History of Art Department): 11, 22, 26, 27, 30, 54, 70, 105, 111, 113, 118, 119, 154, 155, 159, 176, 189, 200, 207, 208, 209, 239, 241

Permission of Sheffield City Art Galleries: 50, 282, 286, 322, 337, 352

The Trustees of Sir John Soane's Museum: 14, 112, 214, 232, 259

Southampton Art Gallery: 36, 75, 87, 142, 274, 300

Tate Gallery, London: 1, 3, 4, 7, 18, 20, 21, 28, 33, 35, 39, 41, 45, 47, 48, 51, 57, 59, 60, 62, 64, 67, 82, 91, 93, 98, 100, 117, 127, 137, 139, 149, 158, 161, 168, 170, 178, 182, 184, 190, 192, 195, 211, 216, 219, 222,

229, 233, 236, 251, 252, 254, 255, 266, 267, 270, 272, 276, 277, 297, 299, 301, 325, 327, 335, 339, 342, 343, 348, 353, 354, 356

Victoria & Albert Museum (crown copyright): 25, 40, 43, 44, 46, 55, 66, 68, 78, 79, 83, 90, 94, 96, 102, 115, 136, 144, 145, 151, 152, 153, 163, 185, 218, 242, 268, 280, 288, 292, 302, 303, 304, 307, 309, 312, 320, 328, 355

*Victoria Art Gallery, Bath City Council: 125

*Walker Art Gallery (Merseyside County Council): 2, 34, 38, 42, 63, 77, 120, 123, 124, 147, 169, 186, 188, 193, 197, 212, 217, 243, 245, 248, 262, 273, 285, 305, 334, 336, 340, 345, 346, 349, 351

*Reproduced by permission of the Trustees, the Wallace Collection, London: 135

*Wolverhampton Art Gallery: 53, 122, 240, 315, 341

*Yale Center for British Art, Paul Mellon Collection: 5, 6, 9, 16, 31, 92, 157, 171, 173, 202, 257, 258, 293, 294; Paul Mellon Fund: 24, 29, 73, 109, 116, 181, 194, 221, 228, 244

PREFACE

Although this book derives most of its material from the graphic and printed records of British art, it is not meant to be either a volume of art criticism or a formal contribution to art history. It bears no direct relationship to the flourishing branch of present-day interdisciplinary scholarship that seeks to interpret pictures in detail by iconographical and other means. Nor is it a study of popular art *per se*. Instead, it explores a hitherto neglected phenomenon in the historical sociology of English literature, the interaction of middle-class literary culture and popular taste under the auspices of painted art. Paintings are not considered as autonomous objects of art but simply as primary documentation of the literary and artistic tastes that were current from the middle of the eighteenth century to the end of the nineteenth.

If any case can be made for the high aesthetic worth of most of these pictures, it will be found nowhere in these pages. They are to this book what subliterary texts—street literature, cheap fiction, large-circulation periodicals—are to a book on the history and habits of the mass reading public. To accurately describe the nature of popular culture, in whatever medium, one must assemble, confront, and resolutely consider the evidence, which in the present instance is composed of paintings most of which fall distinctly short of being masterpieces. They must be looked at just as the texts must be read, in a spirit of historical detachment.

In choosing the pictures to be used as illustrative material, I have preferred lesser known ones—a number, in fact, are reproduced here for the first time—rather than those that are familiar to every student of British art. Reproductions of the latter, if they are not found here, can be located by way of Appendix C.

I have not hesitated to quote freely from the comments of contemporary art critics. Theirs were certainly not the values nor the language of modern criticism, though the two giants among them, Hazlitt and Ruskin, must be exempted from whatever depreciation the rest of the breed may deserve. Indeed, any sustained reading of the journalistic reviews of the annual London exhibitions leads us to value Hazlitt and Ruskin all the more for their sensitive eyes, the seriousness of their standards, and the skill and polish of their prose. But, as with the paintings themselves, the banality of the common run of nineteenth-century art criticism is itself significant. It expresses, better than any paraphrase or summary would do, the true climate of people's minds, viewers' and reviewers' alike, as they looked at and judged the pictures on the walls before them. The very language the reviewers chose, to say nothing of the aesthetic assumptions underlying their words, captures the tone, as it were, of the prevailing taste: the feel of the ideas as well as their bare substance. The reviews are the authentic voices of the past, revealing just how superficial and even perfunctory was the response to most new pictures, even those that were most praised. In addition, they are the only surviving descriptive records of countless paintings that are now lost. And so, whatever their shortcomings as criticism, they are an indispensable part of the evidential package.

In arrogating to myself *de facto* adjunct membership in the guild of art historians I can claim neither formal accreditation, prior experience, nor native gifts. As one trained in a quite different field, I would have been totally helpless without the large body of information and informed professional opinion at my disposal. I hope that in helping myself so liberally to the printed and iconic evidence of British art history I have, by way of modest recompense, incidentally cast some fresh light upon it. But my only governing intention has been to illuminate, in the manner of the social historian, one aspect of the long-lasting and constantly shifting nexus between the sister arts of painting and literature.

R. D. A.

PART ONE

THE PICTURES ON THE WALLS

INTRODUCTION

Beginning in 1760, London's seasonal art exhibitions annually attracted a throng of open-pursed men and women who came to look and often to buy. More and more it became the fashion to decorate the walls of one's home with newly created art—first the mansions of the wealthy, then, from the Regency years onward, the proliferating suburban villas that were conspicuous evidence of an increasingly numerous and prosperous middle class. Prominent among the several kinds of paintings they bought were ones whose subjects were drawn from the poems, plays, and novels that lined their library or drawing-room shelves. Two territories of the English imagination thus were joined, those ruled respectively by the visual image and the printed word. The pictures whose subjects were taken from, or at least nominally associated with, English literature were, in effect, extensions of the books themselves: they were detached forms of book illustration, in which were constantly assimilated the literary and artistic tastes of the time. They combined to produce a tertium quid, a new kind of imaginative activity in which the separate experiences of reading and beholding coalesced. Readers, as the eighteenth-century painter Henry Fuseli put it, were turned into spectators.[1]

This development, of no small importance in the history of modern British culture, is the subject of the following pages. Because this book is in some ways an unusual kind of historical study, its introduction must take the equally unconventional form of a critical account of the evidence on which it is necessarily based, and which, of equal necessity, determines its limitations. Lest the reader suspect a bid for his sympathy, I have almost refrained from repeating Dickens's anguished capitals when he complained in 1854 of the trouble he had in writing *Hard Times* in the cramped space of weekly installments: "The difficulty . . . is CRUSH-

ING."[2] The difficulty here has been of another, though no less formidable, kind. It is not every day that a rash student commits himself to writing about a visual subject only to discover, early on, that most of the pertinent primary evidence is invisible.

There has also been the problem of definition, of limitation. What, within the confines of these chapters, is a "literary picture," not in the art historian's sense of a painting that in some way intimates a story, but in the more restricted sense, uniformly adopted here, of one that is somehow related to English literature? The term covers a broad, uninterrupted spectrum. At one end is the painting that transfers a scene in a poem, play, or novel from the pages of a book to canvas or a wood panel. At the other is the painting that is merely embellished with a poetic quotation meant to set or intensify the tone of the picture but whose subject has no relation to the work alluded to. Thus there are innumerable shades of literary relevance, from faithful illustration to the application of a vaguely appropriate motto. In amassing and ordering my evidence, I have drawn a wavering line across the wide expanse of literature-related art, deciding, too often on the basis of insufficient or unreliable evidence, which pictures, seen or unseen, were at least marginally illustrative and therefore should be included, and which should be set to one side, for use in chapter 9, as examples of pictures that are related to literature only through the tenuous attachment of an epigraph. In the absence of the paintings themselves, for reasons that will soon be clear, I have had no choice but to separate the eligible from the ineligible with hair-raising arbitrariness. Somewhere in the continuum, the word *from* loses its ordinary meaning; and though the formula "Picture A is *from* Literary Work B" will regularly be used for its convenience, the reader should be notified that *from* is used throughout with the broadest license ever allowed to any preposition.

Another necessarily arbitrary decision had to be made at the beginning of my research. For urgently practical reasons, its scope has been restricted to oil paintings of larger than miniature size. To have included also watercolors and drawings of literary subjects would have made an already virtually unmanageable subject truly impossible to cope with. It is reasonable to suppose that, if they had been included, their presence would not have seriously affected the generalizations based on oil paintings alone; they would merely have demonstrated the fairly obvious fact that certain kinds of literary subjects are suitable for the delicate treatment that watercolor, pencil, or pen and ink make possible, and certain other subjects are not. But it has not been possible to exclude all non-oil pictures for the simple reason that in an exasperating number of records, including some catalogues of the annual London exhibitions, the medium of a listed work is not specified. Despite initially rigid rules of exclusion, a few watercolors have been consciously admitted, and a few more have doubtless slipped in undetected.

Such a limitation has the ironical but not unwelcome effect of largely omitting the two great figures in British art who best exemplify the mingling, indeed the merging, of poetry and painting: William Blake and Dante Gabriel Rossetti. "Well, Mr. Blake," said Sir Joshua Reynolds, "I hear you despise our art of oil painting." "No, Sir Joshua," Blake replied, "I don't despise it; but I like fresco better."[3] Years later, in the catalogue of his unsuccessful one-man show (1809), Blake's view was less tactfully expressed: "Let the works of modern Artists since Rubens' time," he declared, "witness the villany of some one at that time, who first brought oil Painting into general opinion and practice: since which we have never had a Picture painted, that could shew itself by the side of an earlier production."[4] Rossetti, by contrast, had nothing against oils, though he should have favored them more than he did, because, as Ruskin advised him, "oil fetches always about six or seven times as much as water-colour. Very foolish it is, but so it is."[5] But it so happens that few of his many illustrations of literary subjects were produced in oil. In any event, the graphic oeuvres of both Blake and Rossetti, as well as their very different ways of assimilating poetry and painting, have been, and continue to be, intensively discussed elsewhere, and I have no contribution to make to the literature on those perennial topics.

Fixing the scope of the study, however, does not alter the nature of the material to be studied. Every historian of literate culture is confronted, sooner or later, by the silences of the written and printed record as it comes down to him. But one who sets out to narrate an episode in the history of the English visual imagination is constantly confronted with blank spaces on the wall where pictures should be. Much of his primary evidence is literally invisible. Although art historians may well lament the disappearance of many works they could profitably use in their studies of individual artists, they can more or less comfortably make do with what survives, with amplification as required from secondary sources such as biographies and contemporary art criticism. But when broad tendencies are in question, as in any study of widely shared and evolving artistic taste, it is the sheer quantity of material, both primary and secondary, that counts: the more there is, the more confident and illuminating can be the inferences drawn from it.

To say that a pursuit of this kind involves simultaneous feast and famine is not a paradox but a statement of the bare truth. The documents of art history provide, at once, both too much material (the all but overwhelming number of recorded paintings) and too little; for most of the surviving evidence, the actual pictures apart, is both elusive and, when found, less dependably informative than one would wish. Though copious, it is fraught with undiscoverables, imponderables, ambiguities, and deceptions. We see the pictures of which we have record but which are now lost through the cracked, sometimes virtually opaque glasses that are all that the printed documentation permits.

Considerations such as these soon extinguished whatever hopes I initially entertained that my report on the occurrence of the literary subject in British art could rest on a solid base of quantification and its academic respectability ensured by the application of computer science. Figures will be found in some abundance in Parts Two and Three, but throughout the book the arithmetic, stated or implied, is tinged with an unavoidable dash of impressionism.

The recorded oil paintings of English literary subjects produced by British artists between 1760 and 1900 that fall on the "eligible" side of the demarcation I have drawn number somewhere between ten and twelve thousand, give or take a few hundred. Of these, only some seven or eight percent are known to be in public galleries, and an undeterminable number remain in private collections. Paintings now lost or inaccessible that are represented by engravings or photographs account for another five or six percent. Therefore, of the total number of pictures individually recorded as having existed at one time or another, only about fifteen percent, at most, can be seen today in any form.

But this data base, large though it is, actually is only a generous sample of the total number of literary paintings that were turned out in those 140 years. It consists of the ones listed in the standard sources, the catalogues of the annual London exhibitions: the Royal Academy and the minor institutions that had inspired it, the [Incorporated] Society of Artists and the Free Society of Artists; the Academy's two major nineteenth-century satellites, the British Institution and the [Royal] Society of British Artists, and the [Royal] Scottish Academy; catalogues of modern exhibitions of eighteenth- and nineteenth-century artists, the printed records of sales, and biographies of individual artists and the sketchy or in a few cases exhaustive *catalogues raisonnés* sometimes appended to them. (Ideally, the catalogues of provincial art exhibitions should have been searched as well, for paintings not shown in London or Edinburgh, but the results would hardly have justified the labor involved.)

Thousands of relevant pictures, however, escaped all such nets. There were several ways, increasingly favored by artists, of bypassing the exhibitions. Many painters sold pictures directly to customers who visited their studios. Sometimes they hired rooms like the Egyptian Hall in Piccadilly for one-man shows, as did Haydon and Martin early in the century and Ford Madox Brown in 1865. Many pictures by exceptionally promising or well-established artists were commissioned and sold privately, or increasingly, as the Victorian years passed, by way of dealers; many more were submitted to the annual exhibitions but were rejected and therefore unlisted, and then disappeared from view. There is no record of this voluminous commerce except insofar as some pictures subsequently left traces in the annals of auction rooms or surfaced in present-day galleries and private collections. It is beyond question that the unrecorded ones considerably outnumbered those in the formal records. In a large exhibition of manuscripts, pictures, and memorabilia related to Robert Burns, held in 1896, forty-three paintings were shown, only eight of which had passed through any public exhibition at the time they came from the artist's easel.[6]

How large, to resort to the unsinkable cliché, was the iceberg beneath this visible tip? There is no way of telling.* The reader hot for certainties must bear in mind that the figures in Parts Two and Three are introduced solely for the purpose of rough comparison, and that the only rule of thumb to be applied in an attempt to convert the sample into the hidden totality is to multiply by a factor of *X*. The only firm guarantee that can be offered is that all such approximations are conservative—perhaps extremely so.

If more than ninety percent of the recorded pictures are lost, except for reproductions in a certain number of instances, what happened to them? One explanation is that, with the exception of a number of celebrated examples, they were not protected from neglect and oblivion by mere virtue of the names attached to them. None of the major nineteenth-century British artists made a specialty of literary paintings. Earlier, Henry Fuseli (1741–1825) had probably come closest to doing so, but his was not a name to conjure with in the sale room. The great names—Turner, Wilkie, the Pre-Raphaelites, Watts, Leighton, Burne-Jones, and the rest—painted, among them, a fair number of pictures with literary asso-

*For some notion of the over-all size of the nineteenth-century trade in paintings, see chapter 4, below.

ciations, but these figure only incidentally in their total oeuvres. The nineteenth-century artist who was most significantly affected by English literature, not only in respect to subject but in his whole conception of art, was the Frenchman Eugène Delacroix, in whose canon a severe gap would be left if his many paintings from Shakespeare, Scott, and Byron were deleted.[7] The most prolific artists in a literary way were men like William Hamilton, Thomas Stothard, and Henry Howard late in the eighteenth and early nineteenth centuries and such popular and well-paid Victorian artists as C. R. Leslie, Daniel Maclise, W. P. Frith, and E. M. Ward.

Surrounding them were a host of near-nonentities such as the virtually untraceable Alfred J. Woolmer, who exhibited no fewer than eighty-four pictures from English literature between 1827 and 1886, mostly at the unrevolutionary London equivalent of the Salon des Refusés, the Society of British Artists. Woolmer seems to have had a preternaturally shrewd instinct for the hackneyed; the list of subjects he chose is a perfect epitome of the range of literary characters and situations most painted for the market. Few examples of this indefatigable artist's output have been located, and only a handful of engravings. Like Woolmer, many of the painters of literary subjects survive only as recurrent names in the catalogues of the annual exhibitions. Their work is unrepresented even in that huge collection of iconographical records, the Witt Library of the Courtauld Institute.

Literary paintings suffered, perhaps more than most other genres, the same fates that met Victorian art in general during its worst period of devaluation in the first half of the present century. In 1930 one of Clarkson Stanfield's marine paintings, *The Abandoned,* for which Sir Thomas Baring had paid 500 guineas in 1856, was auctioned at Sotheby's for seven pounds.[8] Seven years later, Daniel Maclise's huge (ten by seven feet) *Ordeal by Touch* (1846) brought a derisory £2 12s. 6d.[9] In the most precipitous decline of all, John Martin's "Day of Judgment" canvases, equally large, which were so sensationally popular in the 1850s that they were toured in Great Britain and the United States as profit-making exhibitions, were sold in 1935 for less than seven pounds for the three.[10] (Today they occupy prominent walls in the Tate Gallery.)

Many Victorian paintings were cheap to begin with. Some artists priced their small ones ("cabinet pictures") at no more than three to ten pounds. Hence, when householders or their heirs grew tired of them or they simply passed from fashion, they were discarded without a qualm. There was a similar casualty rate among the equivalent artifacts of "popular literature"—yellowback novels, shilling shockers, penny-a-part serials, and the other ephemeral pabulum of the English mass-reading public. Most, having served their trivial purpose, were thrown out with the rubbish, and what survived became a casualty of the wastepaper drives during the two world wars. No one knows how many of their painted counterparts, large or small, recorded or unrecorded, passed through parish bazaars and dealers in secondhand goods on their way to ultimate destruction or to be bought by impecunious artists for the sake of the canvas alone, which they proceeded to overpaint with new subjects. Most of the paintings commissioned by the publishers of illustrated books—a particularly busy form of artistic activity in the last part of the eighteenth century and most of the nineteenth—were discarded once they had been engraved. Only a small portion of the thousands of designs made by such prolific illustrators as Thomas Stothard survive in their original form.

Some paintings self-destructed, thanks to the widespread use of bitumen ("Dead Sea pitch"), which added to new canvases the dark quality of age prized in Old Master paintings. The diary-keeping artist Joseph Farington once noted that one Wilder, a picture restorer, was "taking off Asphaltum [one kind of bitumen] in such quantities from Opie's picture from *Tempest—that with the child*—as to roll it up in Balls like coblers wax."[11] Scottish artists seem to have been especially devoted to the pernicious substance, with the result that many of their pictures survive only as sad, unrestorable wrecks. In addition, many eighteenth- and nineteenth-century British paintings perished in fires at the country houses to which much contemporary art gravitated. Alexander Runciman's twelve ceiling pictures on themes from Ossian (1772), for instance, were destroyed when Penicuik House burned in 1899.

As tastes changed, many pictures were valued solely for their ornate and expensive frames; and when a day of reckoning came, either the canvases were thrown away and the frames retained or sold, or picture and frame were sold together to a dealer, who might keep them in dusty stock for many years, for the sake of the frame alone. In the 1930s, a painting by the parricide artist Richard Dadd surfaced in the picture-frame department of the Army and Navy Stores in London, where, for all anybody knew, it may have been since the establishment opened in the 1870s.[12] It was subsequently owned by Sacheverell Sitwell and is now in the Tate.

Numerous run-of-the-mine nineteenth-century paintings do survive, their whereabouts unknown to the art world, in the lumber rooms of country houses, even on the walls of the few remaining homes where the Victorian period is preserved as if under a bell jar. They can be seen too in the public rooms and shadowy passages of country inns: in 1945, Evelyn Waugh came across John Martin's *Adam's First Sight of Eve* (pl. 271), in very dirty condition, in the Kilmeny Hotel, Ardrossan. The hotel's owners, the Imperial Chemical Industries, had it cleaned and presented it to the Glasgow Art Gallery.[13] Finally, hundreds of nineteenth-century canvases, rolled up or stretched inside weighty frames, rest in the cellars of public galleries in Britain and elsewhere. Most have never been photographed, and some have not even been identified or catalogued.

Apart from those that can be resurrected on request from the catacombs of museums, the only means of knowing what the recorded but now invisible paintings are—or were—like is through reproductions. Some pictures lent to exhibitions by private owners were photographed for the printed catalogue of the show, and those passing through the hands of the major London dealers nowadays are routinely photographed and copies made available in art reference libraries. But totally lost paintings can be envisioned only through the engravings made of many popular ones—an unsatisfactory resort—and, even less satisfactorily, through descriptions found in print, most often in reviews of the exhibitions where they were first seen.

Reproductions and descriptions, usually so brief as to be of little help to the imagination, exist for only a small proportion of the total number of paintings exhibited; and for all the rest, one has only the titles, often with a poetic quotation added, found during a volume-by-volume, page-by-page search of the catalogues. Here the real insufficiency and ambiguity of the evidence makes itself felt, frustrating any attempt at reasonably exact quantification. Several pictures with the same title may be attributed to a given artist over a short or extended span of years, either at a single exhibiting institution or at two or, in rare cases, even three. There is no way of knowing whether all but the first were copies, versions, replicas, repetitions, replications—whatever the terminology—efforts by the artist to exploit the vogue of a particular subject, or, indeed, the favorable reception of his own first rendering of it, or whether the later ones were so different in composition as to amount to fresh creations. The difficulty is like that of the literary scholar who must cope with the bibliographical-textual uncertainties of new editions, revisions, and reprints, and their relation to the work as the author initially delivered it to his publisher. But such textual problems can eventually be solved, because the books in question exist and can be examined. The paintings normally do not and therefore cannot. There is the further possibility, in the case of a title that turns up in two or three consecutive years, that the several entries represent the same canvas, still unsold. How should one count these apparently similar or identical compositions, often so vaguely described by their titles, that cross and recross our distant view as stage armies appear and reappear?*

In compiling lists of paintings with literary associations, by all odds the most frequent and exasperating source of uncertainty, a veritably hydra-headed problem, lies in the titles of the pictures themselves. Normally there is no such difficulty in literary or bibliographical scholarship: most printed books continue to bear the title they had when first published, no matter how often reprinted. Cases such as those of *Rasselas,* always called *The Prince of Abyssinia* in Dr. Johnson's lifetime, Clara Reeve's *The Champion of Virtue* (1777), which became *The Old English Baron* the next year, and Shelley's *The Revolt of Islam,* first published as *Laon and Cythna,* are rare in literary history (except, say, for the frequent retitling of modern books when they suffer a sea change from Britain to America or vice versa). Not so in British art, where the listings in catalogues are more in the nature of temporary descriptive labels than fixed baptismal names. Hence, for one thing, the same picture may have been hung at one exhibition under one name and at a second under another, and possibly is known at its present place of exhibition under a third. Thus:

Frith's *The Love Token / Scene from The Bride of Lammermoor*
Etty's *A Bevy of Fair Women / The Origin of Marriage /*
The World Before the Flood / The Marriage Festival Previous to the Deluge
Cope's *Scene from Goldsmith / Age and Whispering Lovers*
Ward's *Byron's Early Love / The Dance*
Mulready's *Burchell and Sophia / Haymaking*
Orchardson's *Casus Belli / The Challenge*
Paton's *Beati Mundo Corde / How an Angel Rowed Sir Galahad over Dern Mere*
Gilbert's *Scene from Henry VIII / Ego et Rex Meus*

An unknown number of paintings with literary subjects lie buried in the records because their titles do not identify them as such, and only external evidence occasionally enables them to be identified. At the Society of Artists in 1764, James Lambert showed a picture called simply *A Storm.* Horace Walpole obliged posterity by writing in his copy of the catalogue,

*Part of the answer depends on the actual practice at the time. Until 1844, pictures previously shown at the Royal Academy could be admitted to the British Institution exhibitions at the discretion of the committee on hanging, which seems to have maintained a liberal policy in this respect. After that date, there was an absolute ban on paintings that had been exhibited elsewhere. But pictures that had been hung once, but were not sold, could be rehung after several years had passed. In my computations, I have assumed, where there was no substantial evidence to the contrary, that the same title recorded in exhibitions in two successive years indicates a single canvas that went unsold the first year and that if a title is repeated in the records after a lapse of two or more years, either at the same institution or a different one, it represents a new picture. Both these assumptions are open to objection, but they probably serve as well as any others that could be adopted.

"Edgar, Lear, and Kent." Lambert also showed "It's companion." Walpole: "Ye witches meeting Macbeth and Banquo."[14] Only by accident does one discover that paintings entered in catalogues as *The Orphan and the Bird, Waiting for an Answer, Back to Back,* and *The Life's Story* were pictures from *Nicholas Nickleby, The Two Gentlemen of Verona, The Vicar of Wakefield,* and *Othello,* respectively.

On the other hand—a more frequent pitfall or source of perplexity—many pictures with titles associating them with literature prove to have subjects with no literary connection. Any picture called simply *Twelfth Night* may or may not have had a Shakespearean subject: the festival of Twelfth Night was a frequent subject with such Dutch and Flemish painters as Jan Steen and Jordaens. *Twelfth Night* paintings from their brushes were at Buckingham Palace, Woburn, and Chatsworth in early Victorian times, so it is reasonable to suppose that new English versions of the same subject, with or without Shakespearean reference, were intended to fill a demand from people who wished to emulate royalty, the Duke of Bedford, or the Duke of Devonshire. There was also the English penchant for naming sporting and domestic animals after literary figures. As early as 1762, only two years after the first volumes of Sterne's novel were published, a racehorse was named Tristram Shandy and George Stubbs painted its portrait. The Perdita shown in 1776 was not Shakespeare's heroine but a mare belonging to Sir John Lister Kaye, Bart.; Sir Peter Teazle, shown at the Royal Academy in 1789, had won the Derby *for* Lord Derby two years earlier; and—to approach the dawn of Victoria's reign itself—in 1835 the art critic for the *Literary Gazette,* having spotted the title *Tom Jones* in the Academy catalogue, "eagerly sought for the picture, wondering what lively incident in that unrivalled representation of real life Mr. C [Abraham Cooper, the well-known animal painter] had selected for his subject; when, behold! we found that Fielding's hero was merely the name of another dray-horse!"[15]

In similar fashion, John MacWhirter's *The Three Witches* (1889) was a portrayal, not of the Weird Sisters so familiar to English art-lovers for well over a century, but of three gnarled tree trunks with lightning striking what might reasonably be regarded as a blasted heath. Macbeth's witches were nowhere in sight. Pictures called *The Last Chapter in Pamela* and *Alice in Wonderland* turn out to have been examples of that perennially popular subject in English, as in European, art, studies of a girl or woman reading.

Of the various classes of ambiguous titles, the largest is the one generated by artists' practice of applying literary heroines' names to routine portraits or figure studies. To lend a touch of class, a rustic maiden could be called Phoebe or a Greek girl Haidee, though in fact the name was all the picture owed to *As You Like It* or *Don Juan.* Thus the records of Victorian painting are replete with studies titled Jessica, Nell, Dora, Helena, Viola, Elaine, Sophia, each of which may or not have had any literary reference. Some, of course, may have been the actual names of the sitters, because the English then had a habit of naming their daughters, like their animals, after literary characters. (The noticeable increase in the number of Enids pictured after 1880 may reflect the popularity of Enid as a baptismal name following the appearance of Tennyson's *Idylls of the King* in 1859.)

Even assuming that some of these names did have genuine literary reference, it is often hard to be sure what work is alluded to. With

Ophelias, Desdemonas, Mirandas, Rosalinds, and Juliets, there is seldom a problem. But which Beatrice (Dante? *Much Ado About Nothing? The Cenci?* Or the Beatrix of *Henry Esmond?*)? Which Olivia (*Twelfth Night? The Vicar of Wakefield?*)? Which Portia (*Julius Caesar? The Merchant of Venice?*)? Which Maria (*Twelfth Night? A Sentimental Journey?*)?

A picture bearing the name of a single character might actually have been a tableau with several characters, of whom the eponymous one was merely the most prominent or the one most likely to sell the picture. The tableau itself might not be specified: what, among several possibilities, was Ophelia doing in a given painting shown with merely her name—having a nervous interview with Hamlet, describing Hamlet's madness to Polonius, giving Gertrude, or later in the play Laertes, a glimpse of her own madness, or floating in the stream? The same bothersome vagueness occurs in the customary form of titles that merely designate the work without specifying the scene.

Other announced subjects may have come from alternative sources. Paintings with Titania, Puck, Oberon, and the fairies probably were derived from *A Midsummer Night's Dream,* but not necessarily so; Fuseli's numerous designs involving such figures came not only from Shakespeare but from Milton's "L'Allegro" and Wieland's *Oberon.* Pictures of biblical subjects, especially the Creation and Fall of Man, may or may not have come from *Paradise Lost.* Paintings of the Deluge not explicitly attributed to Genesis may have been derived not from Milton but from the Swiss poet-artist Salomon Gessner's *Idyllen,* which was the stated source of a number of paintings exhibited in London. Like a number of other familiar subjects in British art, moreover, those from the Bible were often traceable as much to the Old Masters as to any literary source.

Of the many paintings depicting scenes from English and Scottish history—Queen Katherine and Wolsey, the murder of the young princes in the Tower, the escape of Mary Queen of Scots from Loch Leven, Leicester and Amy Robsart—which came straight from Shakespeare or Scott (as the case may be) and which from the history books? Ordinarily this is an unanswerable question, for even if the painting was equipped with a reference to a literary source, its iconography and general treatment may well have associated it more firmly with Shakespeare's or Scott's historical source than with the play or novel cited.

Sometimes paintings were given titles intended to cash in on the current popularity of a writer, even though the subject had nothing to do with him. When James McNeill Whistler's *The White Girl* was rejected by the Royal Academy in 1862, he sent it to a dealer, who rechristened it *The Woman in White* in a patent attempt to exploit the fame of Wilkie Collins's novel, published only two years earlier. In a letter to the *Athenaeum,* the artist denied any intention of illustrating it. "It so happens, indeed," he said, "that I have never read it. My painting simply represents a girl dressed in white standing in front of a white curtain."[16] (The third name applied to it stuck: *Symphony in White, Number One.*) Three years later, a picture titled *Our Mutual Friend* was exhibited when the serialization of Dickens's novel, with which it had no connection whatsoever, was only two-thirds completed. (By a kind of reverse action, scenes of rural festivities titled *Under the Greenwood Tree,* echoing a song in *As You Like It,* and several paintings called *Far from the Madding Crowd,* echoing Gray's "Elegy," were exhibited before Hardy's novels with those titles appeared in

1872 and 1874. It is not impossible that Hardy's choice of the titles was influenced by their familiar occurrence in exhibition catalogues.)

Despite all the hazards and deceptions to be recognized and avoided as we utilize the manifold iconographic and written records of British art, an authentic notion of what actually happened when English literature and painting overlapped begins to take shape. If we are able to compensate for our imperfect vision and make allowance for the irreparable distortion inherent in the materials used, we may arrive not very far from the truth. The paintings discussed and reproduced here faithfully represent the various ways, sometimes broadly shared, sometimes idiosyncratic, in which artists envisioned English literature on behalf of the middle-class public who paid them. We can say of these literary pictures what Henry James once said of English art in general: ". . . English painting interests me chiefly, not as painting, but as English. It throws little light, on the whole, on the art of Titian and of Rembrandt; but it throws a light which is to me always fresh, always abundant, always fortunate, on the turn of the English mind. It is far from being the most successful manifestation of that mind; but it adds a good deal to our knowledge of it."[17]

CHAPTER 1

*The earliest literary pictures: Hogarth, the theater, and the novel.—*Ut pictura poesis *and the theory of history painting.—The expanding variety of literary subjects down to 1800.—Paintings from history, fancy pictures, early genre, landscape.*

English literature entered English painting through the stage door, so to speak, with timely assistance from William Hogarth. The earliest subjects were from the world of entertainment rather than that of polite literature: popular actors and actresses costumed for, and often posed in, the parts that had won them fame. In 1663–64, an artist in crayons named John Greenhill portrayed Betterton as Bajazet in Marlowe's *Tamburlaine* and Joseph Harris as Cardinal Wolsey in Shakespeare's *Henry VIII.* In a single picture from the 1670s, now at Hampton Court, Michael Wright depicted the comedian John Lacy in three roles. No less a portraitist than Sir Godfrey Kneller painted Anthony Leigh as Dominic in Dryden's *The Spanish Friar,* and an unknown artist, Betterton and Mrs. Barry in the closet scene in *Hamlet.*

Theatrical pictures, first character portraits and then representations of scenes as well, continued for more than half a century to be the chief link between the painted and the written (and in this case performed) arts of England. Hogarth was the first English artist to paint directly from the stage, beginning with two more or less Shakespearean productions of 1727: *Falstaff and His Recruits,* from the Drury Lane performance of *2 Henry IV,* and *Henry VIII Leading Anne Boleyn to Court,* from Colley Cibber's adaptation of *Henry VIII.* His first signed and dated canvas, however, was a scene from Gay's *The Beggar's Opera,* painted within months of its first performance in January 1728 (pl. 1). These pictures, so well received that he was commissioned to paint five replicas, marked the beginning of Hogarth's influential career as a narrative painter whose strongest affinity was with the theater. In an autobiographical note he recalled, ". . . I wished to compose pictures on canvas similar to representations on the stage, and further hope that they will be tried by the same test, and

1. William Hogarth, *Scene from "The Beggar's Opera"* (1728) (Tate Gallery, London). Macheath, in chains, is claimed by both his "wives," Lucy Lockit and Polly Peachum, who beseech their respective fathers to "sink the Material evidence, and bring him off at his Tryal" (act 3, scene 11). This larger, elaborated replica of the original was painted for John Rich, who hung it in his Theatre Royal, Lincoln's Inn Fields, where the play was first performed.

criticized by the same criterion. . . . I have endeavoured to treat my subjects as a dramatic writer: my picture is my stage, and men and women my players, who by means of certain actions and gestures are to exhibit a dumb show."[1]

In 1745, Hogarth returned to a theatrical subject with his picture (pl. 2) of Garrick as Richard III in Colley Cibber's adaptation of Shakespeare's play, illustrating lines that Cibber had transferred from Shakespeare's *Henry V.** In this starkly melodramatic concentration on a single figure at

2. William Hogarth, *Garrick as Richard III* (1745) (Walker Art Gallery, Liverpool). Unlike Hogarth's scene from *The Beggar's Opera,* this is more than a portrayal of an actual moment in a play (Colley Cibber's adaptation of Shakespeare's *Richard III,* act 5, scene 3: the king is visited by a succession of ghosts before the battle of Bosworth Field). It removes the murderous monarch's torment from its theatrical context and transforms it into a subject from history.

*Meanwhile, about 1738, several other scenes from the theater had been painted. Among the surviving ones are Peter Van Bleeck's scene from act 1 of Ben Jonson's *The Alchemist* and four by Philip Mercier: *Falstaff at the Boar's Head Tavern, Falstaff and Doll Tearsheet,* and scenes from Cibber's *The Careless Husband* and Farquhar's *The Recruiting Officer.*

a moment of extreme stress, Hogarth fully realized for the first time the potentialities of a graphic art that drew its inspiration from the English drama. Several other artists[2] were to paint Garrick in this role (pl. 198), his first enactment of which in October 1741 had instantly given him the celebrity he was to enjoy for the rest of his career; but no other treatment had the impact this one did on the course of literary painting, for it marked the beginning of the artist's and the actor's warm and mutually beneficial friendship. Hogarth's mature art drew inspiration from Garrick's performances, and Garrick, though his own brand of art was less susceptible to Hogarthian influence, encouraged the painter's own essays in dramatic and narrative representation.[3]

The ensuing popularity of theatrical painting was due partly to Garrick's shrewd recognition of its publicity value. Of some 282 known images of the actor,* about ninety portray him in character.[4] Many were engraved and widely distributed through the print shops, which were the chief means by which graphic art reached the public. Both as separate prints and as illustrations in editions of plays, they stimulated popular interest in the drama and especially in Shakespeare. Garrick made Shakespeare his central concern as actor and manager, and in the course of his career he produced all but eleven of the plays and took eighteen different roles himself. As the plays became more familiar to theatergoers, subjects taken from them became more popular with artists who painted for the market.[5]

Except for a scene from *The Tempest* (pl. 172), Hogarth painted no more Shakespeare subjects, but his close relationship with Garrick was one aspect of his larger role as mediator between art and literature. His self-portrait of 1745, a picture-within-a-picture in which the oval canvas bearing his image rests on the bound works of Shakespeare, Milton, and Swift, themselves flanked by his palette, is a perfect symbol of his role as he conceived it. Half a century later, Hazlitt would include him among the great English comic *writers.* In practice as in theory, he bestrode the triple worlds of painting, drama, and fiction in his time. His first literary subjects, to be sure, were from neither the theater nor fiction, but from Samuel Butler's satirical poem *Hudibras* (1663–78), a work as popular then as it is forgotten now. *Hudibras* had already supplied the subjects for a dozen paintings (pl. 3)—the first recorded oils from a nondramatic

3. Francis LePiper, *Hudibras' Discomfiture at the Hands of the Skimmington* (before 1695) (Tate Gallery, London). The earliest example of the way graphic evidence reflects the popularity of a literary work at a given time. Butler's *Hudibras,* published in 1663–78, remained a ready source of comic episodes to be illustrated by this amateur artist, who is said to have made humorous drawings for the taverns in which he spent most of his time. For evidence of the protracted endurance of *Hudibras* as a subject for artists, see pls. 282 and 283.

*He has been called "one of the most bepictured men in the whole eighteenth century," exceeding even Alexander Pope, Voltaire, and George III in number of representations (G. W. Stone, Jr., and G. M. Kahrl, *David Garrick* [Carbondale, Ill., 1979], p. xvi).

English literary source—by a raffish dilettante named Francis LePiper (or LePipre), son of a Kentish gentleman of Flemish extraction, who died in 1695. Hogarth may have known these paintings when, in 1726, he drew and engraved twelve large illustrations from *Hudibras,* to be sold as separate prints, and seventeen small ones for two separate editions.

Before he painted Garrick as Richard III, Hogarth had produced two series of narrative pictures, *A Harlot's Progress* (1733) and *A Rake's Progress* (1735), which had anticipated, on the pictorial side, the emergence of the new realistic novel with Richardson's *Pamela* (1740–41) and Fielding's *Joseph Andrews* (1742). In the same year as the Garrick picture (1745), Hogarth painted the third of his novels-in-pictures, *Marriage à la Mode.* Richardson's *Clarissa Harlowe* and Fielding's *Tom Jones* followed close after, one in 1747–48, the other in 1749. Thus, in one of the most significant conjunctions in the history of English painting and literature, artist and novelist worked together, reaching across from the parallel paths of their respective arts.[6] Hogarth spared Fielding the expense of an illustrator by providing him with the ready-made figures of Bridget Allworthy, Partridge's wife, and Thwackum in *Tom Jones*; all the novelist needed to do was to refer his readers to Hogarth's well-known engravings, a convenient form of allusive description that also served for characters in *Joseph Andrews* and *Amelia.* Meanwhile, Fielding's rival novelist, Samuel Richardson, employed Hogarth to design the frontispieces for the second edition of *Pamela*; they were completed but not used. In *Clarissa Harlowe,* he drew from the fifth and sixth plates of *A Harlot's Progress* unacknowledged but unmistakable borrowings similar to those that appeared in Fielding's novels in addition to his explicit references to Hogarth's plates.[7]

Both Hogarth and his friend and companion on convivial outings, the theatrical scene painter Francis Hayman, were involved in an enterprise that brought literary painting to an even wider audience than the one that bought Hogarth's engravings.[8] London had almost no public art such as was to be found in the churches, cathedrals, palaces, and other great buildings of France and Italy. In 1732, Jonathan Tyers—quite possibly acting on suggestions from Hogarth, to whom he sent a medallion the next year in appreciation of "your many past favours"—reopened Vauxhall Gardens, the outdoor resort across the river to which all classes of Londoners repaired on summer evenings to stroll, flirt, dine, drink, and listen to music. From the mid-thirties to the late forties, responding to Hogarth's further suggestion that decorating the buildings would constitute a "rational and elegant Entertainment" in harmony with those already provided, Tyers arranged for all fifty of Vauxhall's supper boxes as well as other buildings to be embellished with paintings. Some were as much as eight feet wide. Their subjects included rural festivals, games, old ballads—and scenes from plays and (after 1740) novels. One painting was copied from Hogarth's *Henry VIII and Anne Boleyn*; another, of "fairies dancing on the green by moonlight," with overtones—but no more—of Purcell's *The Fairy-Queen,* an adaptation of *A Midsummer Night's Dream,* has been attributed to Hogarth, but the ascription has recently been questioned on stylistic grounds.[9] Hayman, who was also occupied in designing illustrations to Sir Thomas Hanmer's edition of Shakespeare, painted most of the scenes from literature: for the supper boxes, *Falstaff in the Buck Basket, Falstaff's Cowardice Detected,* and scenes from a popular

4. Joseph Highmore, *Pamela Asks Sir Jacob Swinford's Blessing* (1744) (Tate Gallery, London). One of a set of twelve paintings engraved in 1745. When sold in 1920, they were divided among the Tate Gallery, the Fitzwilliam Museum, and the National Gallery of Victoria, Australia, each of which received four pictures. The costuming is, of course, contemporary; a century later, the same rich eighteenth-century dress would regain popularity in historical costume pieces drawn from literary biography as well as fiction.

old play, Coffey's *The Devil to Pay* as altered by Cibber, and Fielding's *The Mock Doctor*; and for the Prince's Pavilion, the play scene in *Hamlet,* the ransom scene between Montjoy and the king in *Henry V,* the storm scene in *King Lear,* and Miranda's first sight of Ferdinand in *The Tempest.*

Another artist, working in Hayman's style, painted in two other supper boxes a pair of scenes from the newly published *Pamela,* for the sixth edition of which (1742) Hayman designed a set of illustrations. Lacking precise dates for the Vauxhall scenes, we cannot tell if these were the first publicly exhibited paintings (as distinct from book illustrations) to be made from English fiction. Joseph Highmore painted a series of twelve scenes (pl. 4) from *Pamela* that were finished by February 1744 and formed the basis of a series of engravings that were advertised for sale in July of the following year. Philip Mercier's scene of a girl getting out of bed, with a letter signed "Your dutyful and ever-chaste daughter—Pamela," may have preceded the Highmore series, but there is no clue to its exact date.[10] Highmore's treatment, certainly, was—and is—the best

5. Joseph Highmore, *The Harlowe Family* (ca. 1748) (Yale Center for British Art, Paul Mellon Collection). From *Clarissa Harlowe,* letter 7: in Richardson's own words (in a private letter), "the assembled Harlowes, the accusing Brother, and the accused Sister, on her return from Miss Howes's."

known. It is likely that the success of Highmore's paintings encouraged him to project a similar series from *Clarissa Harlowe,* published in 1747–48. But seemingly no more than two pictures were completed—*The Harlowe Family* (pl. 5) and a lost portrait of Clarissa.[11]

These early events in the history of English literary painting occurred against a background that can be seen only fragmentarily, through the few pictures that survive, the brief biographies and anecdotes collected by George Vertue and Horace Walpole, and other occasional sources. But with the founding of the first exhibiting bodies in the 1760s, formal documentation begins, and the art scene begins to come into focus. The catalogues of the annual exhibitions held by the Society of Artists (1760–91), the dissident Free Society of Artists (1761–83), and, above all, the Royal Academy of Arts (beginning in 1769), comprise a full record of the works of art publicly exhibited in London, under institutional auspices, for the rest of the eighteenth century.

The walls of the exhibitions were covered with pictures of every imaginable quality* so that not a square inch of plaster or wallpaper was visible between the frames: portraits (the only dependably lucrative branch of painting, the more so as many members of the well-to-do middle class, prepared to pay well for this indulgence of vanity, entered the market), still lifes, landscapes, figure studies, a sprinkling of genre scenes, pictures of animals domestic, sporting, and wild. In the first decade of exhibitions, English literature was represented almost exclusively by paintings from dramatic sources. In the years 1760–65 inclusive, no fewer than ten of Shakespeare's plays provided subjects. Other noncontemporary but currently revived plays were sometimes drawn upon: Jonson's *The Alchemist* and *Every Man in His Humour,* Rowe's *Jane Shore,* Van Brugh's *The Provoked Wife,* Otway's *The Orphan.* In 1762 Johann Zoffany painted Gar-

*Presumably the best were at the Royal Academy, the worst at the Society of Artists. E. K. Waterhouse says of the latter, "At first anyone who sent in a picture was entitled to have it shown, and the first exhibitions, for all that they included some very distinguished pictures, were flooded with a torrent of trivialities which would hardly find admission today to a parish bazaar" (*Painting in Britain, 1530–1790,* p. 214).

rick in the actor's own *The Farmer's Return,* first performed at Drury Lane only months before the picture was exhibited (pl. 6). From this time onward, pictures from contemporary plays, especially comedies, were seen every year at one exhibition or another.

Timely and lively though they were, however, such paintings were not regarded as serious art: they were mere exercises in theatrical publicity. Pictures from novels, such as Highmore's *Pamela* illustrations, were likewise depreciated, since fiction, regarded simply as an agreeable, undemanding, time-passing amusement, had no claim to dignity as polite literature. Except for the contributors of Shakespearean subjects, who in any event painted stage tableaux and portraits rather than realizations of the poetic text, no artist in that decade responded to the suggestion a correspondent in Cork made to that difficult Irishman, the history painter James Barry, in 1763: "There is a large field for the exercise of your art in the descriptions of our three great English poets, Spenser, Shakspeare, and Milton."[12] But with the advent of the Royal Academy, the situation radically changed. This was the moment when art derived from English literature achieved what might be called official status. It seemed to conform to, or fulfill, two of the major premises on which the conventional aesthetic theory of the age was based: *ut pictura poesis* and the conviction that history painting was the loftiest kind of art.

The doctrine of *ut pictura poesis,* loosely called the sisterhood of painting and poetry, was most often associated with Horace, who used the famous phrase in his *Ars Poetica.*[13] Already possessed of a long history by the time Horace expressed it, it arrived in eighteenth-century England by way of Dryden's translation (1695) of Dufresnoy's Latin poem *De arte graphica,* which he accompanied with a theoretical essay "The Parallel of Poetry and Painting." Interpretations of the doctrine had differed from critic to critic throughout its history and continued to do so in England. The best

6. Johann Zoffany, *Garrick in "The Farmer's Return from London"* (Society of Artists 1762) (Yale Center for British Art, Paul Mellon Collection). A contemporary newspaper praised the picture as "a most accurate representation on canvas" of Garrick's comedy "as performed at Drury Lane. The painter absolutely transports us in imagination back again to the theatre. We see our favourite Garrick . . . and . . . the wife and children—as we saw them on the stage—in terror and amazement" as he relates the story of the Cock Lane ghost, a hoax which in that season fascinated all of London (Whitley [1], 1: 180).

7. James Barry, *King Lear Weeping over the Body of Cordelia* (Boydell's Shakespeare Gallery) (Tate Gallery, London). This painting from the last scene of *King Lear* typifies the way history painters adapted the grand, or heroic, style to subjects from native English literature. The portrait of Lear, his hair streaming in the wind, conspicuously suggests the influence Barry's style had on William Blake's.

known of the many formulations in poetry and prose was Alexander Pope's, in his verse epistle to his erstwhile art teacher, the painter George Jervas (1716):

> Smit with the love of Sister-arts we came,
> And met congenial, mingling flame with flame;
> Like friendly colours found them both unite,
> And each from each contract new strength and light.
> How oft' in pleasing tasks we wear the day,
> While summer suns roll unperceiv'd away?
> How oft' our slowly-growing works impart,
> While images reflect from art to art?

The nub of the *ut pictura poesis* idea was that a poem was a "mute painting" and painting was "spoken poetry": both were expressive arts, differing only in the medium chosen. The chief creative use to which this tenet was put was the warrant it gave to the poet who wished to write in "painterly" terms—to embody in his lines a series of vivid pictures. But since the relationship was a reciprocal one, it also meant that the painter should invest his own creation with "poetry." And from this it was an easy step to assuming that the actual subject matter of art might be borrowed from existing poetry, or, by a further easy extension, from literature at large.

In 1766, in his influential *Laocoön,* Lessing presented a minority report on *ut pictura poesis,* contending that the differences between the sister arts were greater than their similarities. In particular, each had a dimension the other lacked: poetry operated in time, painting in space. Subsequent critics saw further difficulties. The result was that in the last third of the eighteenth century, which coincided with the first thirty years of the Royal Academy's existence, paintings from English literature made their way into public exhibitions against a background of aesthetic debate, which, however, did nothing to inhibit the use of the supposed affinity of the arts as an unspoken rationale for the admission of English literary material into painting.

The second principle that hastened this development was the Royal Academy's espousal, tirelessly voiced by its first president, Sir Joshua Reynolds, of the supremacy of history painting. Originally, the Renaissance ideal of *istoria,* naturalized in England in the preceding century, referred to the portrayal of great events, political and military, in a nation's history. By Reynolds's time, the term "history painting" had been widened to embrace not only national (and ancient) history but classical mythology and Scripture as well, often with a heavily allegorical and didactic slant. These were the subjects the High Renaissance masters, as well as Poussin, had painted; and their heroic dignity elevated them above all others, making history painting the pinnacle of artistic ambition, the exact equivalent of the epic in the hierarchy of poetry. The most significant aspect of the first Academy exhibition in 1769 was that among the forty portraits and forty-eight landscapes there were no fewer than twenty-two paintings from history, Scripture, and poetry.

Like the concept of *ut pictura poesis,* that of history painting was interpreted with increasing liberality in the course of time, its scope being widened to include subjects from national literature. Alongside pictures of dramatic or narrative content drawn from ancient and English history, classical myth, Scripture, *Orlando Furioso,* and modern Continental literature (*Don Quixote* and *Gil Blas* were then, as they would remain for a century, the most drawn-upon European sources), hung paintings best suited to the changing tastes of the art lovers who attended the exhibitions each year. They, in common with all their countrymen, were coming to take great pride in the English literary heritage, a development associated with the rising patriotic spirit of those decades. "The Englishman," wrote Fuseli in 1765, "eats roast beef and plum pudding, drinks port and claret; therefore, if you will be read by him, you must open the portals of Hell with the hand of Milton, convulse his ear or his sides with Shakespeare's buskin or sock, raise him above the stars with Dryden's Cecilia or sink him to the melancholy of the grave with Gray."[14] The same could be said of his taste in pictures. He could accept the solemn, dramatic neoclassicism of academic art the more easily if it were applied to themes from the accepted classics of English literature.

The growing pride of proprietorship that marked the Briton's attitude toward his native literature was delightfully exemplified in an episode that lay behind the exhibition at the Society of Artists in 1775 of a painting by a Welsh artist named Thomas Jones, *A View of the House in Chaffant St. Gile's, Bucks, Where Milton Resided During the Plague of London, and Where He Wrote His L'Allegro.* Jones recorded in his journal on 5 August 1774 that he and one Dr. Bates, a friend who had commissioned the picture, went down from London to sketch the house, then occupied by a wheelwright, and dine on provisions they brought with them. As they dined "in the same room in which we fondly imagined that Milton had so often dined,"

> we indulged ourselves in the sweetest reveries, and Contemplated every old Beam, rafter and Peg with the greatest Veneration and Pleasure—On these very boards, thought we, the great Milton trod—On that very Ceiling (for he was not, at that period blind)
>
> "The Poet's Eye in a fine frenzy rolled"
>
> and pitied those poor, frigid, flegmatic Philosophers who would not have felt the same Enthusiasm as our selves—on the same Occasion—I had not long retired to my Station again to proceed with my work, but I heard the Doctor, over the second bottle, *spouting* with an elevated Voice, the L'Allegro and Il

Pensoroso to an old Woman who was spinning in One Corner of the Parlour—I could not proceed—but shutting up my portfolio hurried into the house to join him, when we drank many a bumper to the immortal Memory of that illustrious Bard.[15]

The filtration of English literary subjects into the precincts of history painting was also reflected in the fact that the gold medal for history painting in oil at the Royal Academy schools, awarded biennially, was won no fewer than eight times between 1772 and 1799 by paintings on set subjects from *Macbeth, King Lear* (John Hoppner's work), *The Tempest, Paradise Lost, Samson Agonistes,* and, on two occasions, *Coriolanus.*[16] (This last subject, to be sure, was already a staple of neoclassic art, derived as it was from Shakespeare's own source, Plutarch. But it illustrates the way in which the entry of some subjects associated with English literature into the painting of the time was facilitated by their existing art credentials.) And so, as painters mindful of the Academy's veneration of the grand subject continued, with diminishing success, to ransack Homer, Virgil, Ovid, Livy, Pliny, Plutarch and the other old treasuries for fresh subjects, they increasingly turned to English literature to find equivalent, and as yet unhackneyed, themes.

A review of the literary pictures hung at the three annual exhibitions a decade apart offers a good idea of the breadth of literary reference so far achieved. In 1770 Shakespeare was represented by pictures from five plays. There were other paintings from the drama, one, of a shipwreck, from Richard Cumberland's play *The Brothers,* produced the preceding year, and another, Johann Zoffany's portrait of Garrick as Abel Drugger in *The Alchemist.* There was a picture from *The Seasons*; Romney exhibited twin pictures, *L'Allegro* and *Il Penseroso*; and there was *A Landscape—an Autumnal Evening, with Figures. The Hint Taken from Spectator No. 425.*

By contrast, the season of 1780 saw only two Shakespearean subjects hung. At the Royal Academy, there were four pictures from *The Faerie Queene,* including Reynolds's *Una and the Lion.* Milton was represented by Fuseli's *Satan Starting from the Touch of Ithuriel's Spear* and Gray by a fresh version of what had already become a familiar subject, his poem "The Bard." But the most significant trend was represented by three "stained drawings" by Edward Burney from his cousin Fanny's popular novel *Evelina* (1778), and, most important, by three pictures of Sterne's Maria, who had first appeared in the seventh volume of *Tristram Shandy* (1765) and then, at greater length, in *A Sentimental Journey* (1768).

8. George Carter, *Nampont. A Story from "A Sentimental Journey"* (Society of Artists 1773) (Engraving, Witt Library, Courtauld Institute of Art). Apart from the flurry of paintings from *Pamela* and *Clarissa Harlowe* in the 1740s, pictures from Sterne's novels were the first to exploit the new popularity of fiction among middle-class readers. This subject, the sentimental incident of "the old man and the ass," would become an enduring favorite with artists and their clients.

Now, from the 1780s onward, the walls of the exhibitions, like the shelves of the proliferating circulating libraries, faithfully mirrored their patrons' tastes in recently published, or at any rate still read, poetry. In the next twenty years, the authors who had by then become staples in artists' repertories and were destined to remain so—Shakespeare, Milton, Spenser, Thomson—were joined by newcomers, present for only a season or two, whose names mean no more to us than do those of most of the workaday artists who scented profit in catering to the current literary interests of their clientele. Some of the works they drew from, like Beattie's *The Minstrel* and Somerville's *The Chase,* had been, or were now, bestsellers, going through edition after edition, their subjects readily identifiable when depicted in paint. But who now responds to mention of, let alone reads, John Pinkerton, Dr. Aikin, Edward Jerningham, John Langhorne, John Cunningham, or Mrs. Charlotte Smith? They were all

9. Joseph Wright of Derby, *A Dead Soldier, His Wife, and Child* (RA 1789) (Yale Center for British Art, Paul Mellon Collection). An illustration of six lines from John Langhorne's poem *The Country Justice* (1774–77), which deeply affected Burns (see text, p. 417).

represented at the exhibitions, in a few cases, such as those of Beattie and Langhorne, by artists of the stature of Joseph Wright of Derby (pl. 9).

Sometimes the exhibited pictures acquired prestige from the fact that the poets were enshrined in Dr. Johnson's *Lives of the Poets* (1779–81), which nourished, or in some instances briefly resuscitated, the fame of a mixed bag of poetic practitioners from Milton and Denham onward. Readers of Johnson's biographical-critical chapters, which served originally as introductions to the collected works of those authors, would have looked with special appreciation at the pictures inspired by such poems as Shenstone's *The School-mistress,* Prior's "Henry and Emma," Collins's *Eclogues and Odes,* Parnell's "The Hermit," Mallet's *Edwin and Emma,* and Young's *Night Thoughts.*

No one questioned the propriety of deriving subjects for paintings from the nation's poetry. But in the august rooms of the Royal Academy, and to a perhaps lesser extent at the other exhibitions, pictures from novels were another matter. No definition of the scope of history painting ever went so far as to embrace the subject matter of novels, and no definition of *poesis* included fiction; but the inexorable pressure of popular literary taste, strengthened by the example of the pictorial novels by Hogarth, the "Comic History-Painter" as Fielding called him, left the artistic establishment little choice. Though never legitimizing this bold *mélange des genres,* it had to concede its existence. Thus *Tom Jones,* first represented at the Royal Academy in 1772, would turn up half a dozen times before the end of the century. George Morland's scene from *The Vicar of Wakefield,* exhibited in 1784, was in the vanguard of hundreds of *Vicar* paintings.

Alongside the paintings from Fielding and Goldsmith were hung pictures inspired by more recent, even immediately current, fiction, and meant in some cases to be engraved as illustrations for new editions. They ran the gamut from the pert social satire of Fanny Burney (*Cecilia*) to the chilling Gothicism of Ann Radcliffe (*The Italian, The Mysteries of Udolpho*). At various times between 1780 and 1800, there were pictures from the anonymous *Adventures of a Hackney Coach,* Thomas Holcroft's translation of a German romance called *Caroline of Lichtfeld,* Edward Kimber's *Life and Adventures of Joe Thompson* (painted by Isaac Cruikshank), William Godwin's *Things As They Are* (better known by its subtitle, *The Adventures of Caleb Williams*), Mrs. Hanway's *Ellinor,* and Maria Regina Roche's sentimental *The Children of the Abbey.*

A further legacy of Hogarth was moralized fiction as represented by narrative pairs or series of pictures having only tenuous connection, if any at all, with existing novels. In 1774, Edward Penny exhibited at the Academy *The Virtuous Comforted by Sympathy and Attention* and *The Profligate Punished by Neglect and Contempt,* clearly inspired by Hogarth's *Industry and Idleness*; and the next year, at the Society of Artists, John Hamilton Mortimer, a leading history painter, presented a four-panel *Progress of Virtue.* Probably the leading example of the type was George Morland's so-called *Laetitia* series (1789) of six pictures—*Domestic Happiness, The Elopement, The Virtuous Parent, Dressing for the Masquerade, The Tavern Door,* and *The Fair Penitent*—which, not surprisingly given these titles, narrated the unhappy fortunes of a young country girl who comes to London, is seduced, and, eventually repenting, is welcomed back by her parents to their humble cottage, as was Olivia in *The Vicar of Wakefield.* Morland also produced several pairs of Hogarthian paintings that contrasted idleness and industry on the part of mechanics, laundresses, and cottagers, among other exemplars of prudential morality and its antithesis. Less didactic in intent was his narrative "Deserter" series, consisting of *Trepanning [Snaring] a Recruit, The Recruit Deserted, The Deserter Taking Leave of His Wife,* and *The Deserter Pardoned.* A little later (1796), James Northcote's series of ten pictures at the Royal Academy, titled *Diligence and Dissipation,* traced the progress of two maidservants to their morally predestined fates. The narrative picture, however direct or indirect its indebtedness to a literary source, and however faint or explicit its didactic purpose, was to ride the wave of the future in popular English art. A century later, Henry James signalized its total conquest of academic shibboleths when he announced the culmination, from his point of view, of *ut pictura poesis*: "The analogy between the art of the painter and the art of the novelist is, so far as I am able to see, complete."[17]

10. Samuel de Wilde, *Scene from "The Village Lawyer"* (RA 1793) (Garrick Club). De Wilde was for a time the in-house illustrator for *Bell's British Theatre,* a long series of reprinted plays, for which he produced, for engraving, no fewer than thirty-six theatrical portraits in the year 1791 alone. He often exhibited at the Royal Academy. "De Wilde," Edward FitzGerald was to write, "was an Artist of Genius. . . . Looking over [his engravings] is my way of going to the Play." Later, he declared to Fanny Kemble that De Wilde "never missed Likeness, Character, and Life, even when reduced to a 16mo engraving" (*Letters of Edward FitzGerald,* ed. Terhune, 3: 83–84, 4: 316). The comedian Jack Bannister (left) would later become a friend and neighbor of John Constable in Hampstead.

The mounting popularity of pictures from fiction toward the end of the eighteenth century did not detract from, but on the contrary nurtured, the fortunes of theatrical painting. Even though Garrick, the prime sponsor and subject of theatrical art, had died in 1779, Zoffany, William Hamilton, James Roberts, and others continued to paint scenes and characters in the currently performed plays of Sheridan, Colman, Holcroft, O'Keeffe, and Mrs. Cowley. The early 1790s saw the beginning of the long career of Samuel DeWilde, whose hundreds of paintings and drawings, executed for illustrated texts and separate engravings, would constitute the most valuable single graphic record of the London stage from that time to the early 1820s, when his sight began to fail. Many of his designs were among the 200 theatrical paintings that the comedian Charles Mathews collected and displayed in a purpose-built gallery at his cottage in Kentish Town and that subsequently became the property of the Garrick Club.[18]

As English literary subject matter and allusions made their way into art, no new branch of painting was established. Instead, literary pictures merged within their single frames current enthusiasms in both pictorial art and literature: the sublime or heroic, with Satan, King Lear, Macbeth, Gray's Bard; the pastoral or Georgic, as in Thomson's *The Seasons,* Gay's *The Shepherd's Week,* Ramsay's *The Gentle Shepherd*; the allegorical, as in Milton's *Comus,* "L'Allegro" and "Il Penseroso," and *The Faerie Queene*; the sentimental-domestic, as in *Pamela, Clarissa Harlowe,* and *The Vicar of Wakefield.* In addition, literary associations colored and vitalized several existing formal categories of art: the history picture, the fancy picture, genre, and landscape.

11. **John Opie,** ***The Duke of York Resigned by the Queen*** (between 1793 and 1806) (Royal Shakespeare Theatre Picture Gallery ©). The scene is from Shakespeare's *Richard III* (2. 4), but this picture was painted to be engraved not in any literary work but in Bowyer's edition of Hume's *History of England.*

The painting of English historical subjects had begun as early as 1729–30, when Queen Caroline commissioned three scenes from the life of Henry V from William Kent, the architect, landscape designer, and painter who was also an illustrator of literary works. (Between 1720 and 1751, he made designs for editions of Gay's *Poems on Several Occasions* and his *Fables,* and Thomas Birch's edition of *The Faerie Queene.*)[19] But it was not until the 1760s, when the first exhibitions were established, that this class of native subject matter, the celebration of the great events of Britain's past, joined the familiar classical themes.[20] In the first decade of the Royal Academy exhibitions (1769–79) alone, twenty paintings from medieval English history were displayed.[21] This was the time when a surge of nationalistic pride and interest in Britain's heroic past—a side effect of which, as we have seen, was increased pride in the national literature—lent special pertinence to the neoclassic ideal of history painting as the *ne plus ultra* of visual art. Painters committed to this goal found ideally appropriate subjects close at hand, because the writing of history was beginning to be regarded as a highly respectable form of polite literature. Indeed, until the time of Scott, who wrote history and fiction either separately or in combination, the historian enjoyed much greater respect than did his fellow narrator, the novelist. Between the contemporary prestige of historiography, as typified by David Hume and William Robertson, and that of history painting as typified by Mortimer, Benjamin West, and John Singleton Copley, there was a close link. The fame of Hume's history of England, competed in 1761, further encouraged painters to take up native themes themselves, as a patriotic application of the high-art ideal. Thus they turned to Hume, and to Shakespeare's history plays, as naturally as Shakespeare in his own time had turned to Holinshed's *Chronicles.* It was not accidental that many of the artists who illustrated the history plays for Boydell's Shakespeare Gallery (see chapter 2, below) also were contributors to Bowyer's illustrated edition of Hume, published in 1793–1806.[22]

Although historians were freely drawn upon, Shakespeare as a source of paintings from English history was most convenient to the artist's brush because in his plays the drama of character and scene was already fully endowed with the poetry that could now be transferred to canvas. At the Society of Artists' exhibition in 1776, for example, there were two paintings by Andrew van Rymsdyk, a native of Holland now settled at Bristol: *The Battle of Agincourt, Representing the Earl of Exeter Supporting Edward, Duke of York, Who is Expiring near the Body of his Deceased Friend, Lord Suffolk,* and *Hotspur Having Defeated Douglas at Holmden Hill,* the catalogue referring the viewer to Shakespeare's *Henry V* and *Henry IV* respectively. James

12. John Hamilton Mortimer, *Scene in "King John"* (Society of Artists 1768) (Garrick Club). Mortimer was primarily a history painter, but here he momentarily invaded the theatrical painter's territory, depicting a scene (4. 2) in an actual performance of *King John* in 1767, with three leading actors, William Powell, Robert Bensley, and William Smith, as King John, Hubert, and the Bastard respectively.

Northcote, who made a considerable name for himself as a history painter as well as a portraitist—he contributed nine pictures to the Shakespeare Gallery—specialized in episodes from the time of the Wars of the Roses. "The tragic events of these sad times," he told his fellow artist James Ward late in life, "afford fine subjects for the painter and the poet; the gloomy dungeons, and the armour, and the caparisoned horses, produce the finest picturesque effects . . . there is one family—that of Edward IV—which I may almost say I have got half my livelihood by."[23] And so Shakespeare was introduced into eighteenth-century painting by a second route, alongside the theater.

13. **Edward Penny,** *A Scene in "Jane Shore"* (Society of Artists 1762) (Birmingham City Museum and Art Gallery). Shakespeare was not the only dramatist from whom painters of subjects from English history drew. Nicholas Rowe's often-acted tragedy (1714) was based on the story of Jane Shore, the mistress of Edward IV, whom Richard III alleged to be a sorceress. Some fifteen or twenty recorded paintings, of which this is the earliest, represented incidents in the story. Here she is made to offer public penance for her supposed dealings with the devil.

Long before English artists began to fill canvases with scenes of battles and crises of state, and more private incidents of confrontation and death, history in the conventional mythological-cum-religious sense had invaded portrait painting at the Stuart court, sometimes grotesquely mismatching, in a moral sense, sitter and role. The practice was initiated on the highest possible level when Rubens painted Charles I as St. George. "This," commented Allan Cunningham, the pre-Victorian Vasari of British art, "was the common-place pedantry of painting . . . Lely and Kneller caused the giddy madams of the courts of the Stuarts to stalk like Minervas or Junos, though they had naturally the dispositions of Venus or of Danaë."[24] Van Dyck had portrayed courtly or fashionable beauties as Prudence and Fortuna; Lely had flattered them as Juno, Pallas Athena, Pomona, Diana, and St. Agnes, and cast Nell Gwyn as Venus and her son, the first Duke of St. Albans, as Cupid.

The vogue persisted, unabated. In the second of his *Moral Essays* (1735), Pope addressed Martha Blount:

> How many pictures of one Nymph we view,
> All how unlike each other, all how true!
> Arcadia's Countess, here, in ermin'd pride,

Is there, Pastora by a fountain side:
Here Fannia, leering on her own good man,
And there, a naked Leda with a Swan.
Let then the Fair one beautifully cry
In Magdalen's loose hair and lifted eye,
Or drest in smiles of sweet Cecilia shine,
With simp'ring Angels, Palms, and Harps divine;
Whether the Charmer sinner it, or saint it,
If Folly grow romantic, I must paint it.

By Gainsborough's and Reynolds's time, there was a great deal more room for "fancy" in art as typified by these impersonation, or role-playing, portraits. Indeed, fancy pictures, as they were called, formed a distinct, though very loosely defined, category of painting. Whether portraits or scenes, they were "conceits" in which the artist improved on reality by generalizing and beautifying—by treating subjects with greater refinement than they intrinsically possessed, adding poetic sug-

14. **William Hamilton,** ***Richard II's Return from Ireland*** (Boydell's Shakespeare Gallery) (Sir John Soane's Museum, London). Whatever iconological associations it may have, the figure of the brooding king (*Richard II*, 3. 3) perhaps represents the lyrical side of his self-image. Of the twenty-four paintings Hamilton contributed to the Shakespeare Gallery (chap. 2), eight were from the history plays and fourteen from the comedies and romances, to which his talent was better suited.

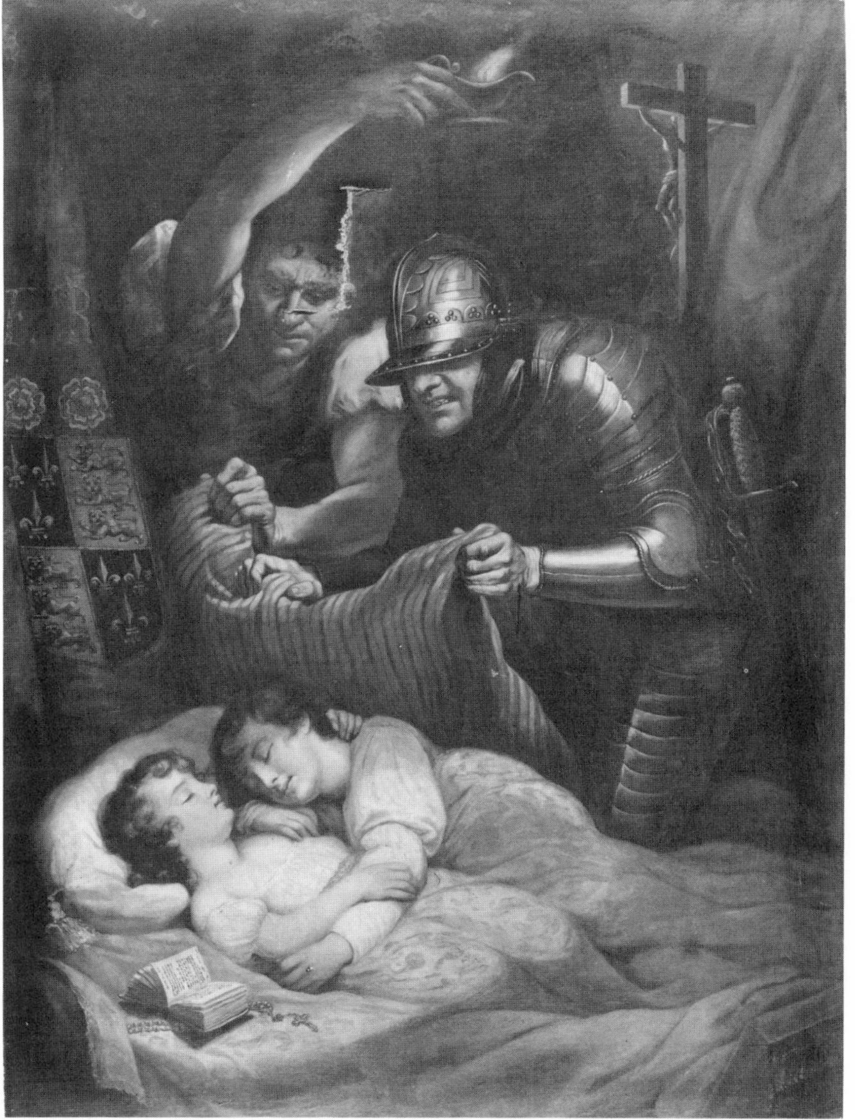

15. James Northcote, *The Murder of the Princes in the Tower* (Boydell's Shakespeare Gallery) (Petworth House). This was one of the numerous episodes in the Wars of the Roses painted by Northcote, Reynolds's assistant and a well-known portraitist and history painter in his own right. It was largely due to the celebrity of this picture and its companion, *The Burial of the Princes*, that the story of the murder of Edward, Prince of Wales, and his younger brother in Shakespeare's *Richard III* (4. 3) became one of the most popular English historical subjects in art.

gestiveness, and, where appropriate (or even inappropriate), arcadian idealization. Although Reynolds disapproved of the persisting custom of dressing sitters in the fashion of Van Dyck's time and giving them fanciful names, he was not innocent of the practice himself, for a reason that was at once practical and theoretical.[25] History paintings, despite their supremacy in the hierarchy, were notoriously hard to sell. Artists might, therefore, profitably and with benefit to their consciences channel their devotion to history paintings from large tableaux to money-making faces, "historical portraits" as Reynolds's one-time assistant Northcote called them.[26] To pose fashionable sitters in "historical" garb, with suitable identification, was to promote, in however small a way, the cause of history painting. Reynolds's studio, wrote Cunningham, was crowded with women who "wished to be transmitted as angels,"[27] and he obliged—or at least compromised—by painting Mrs. Quarrington as St. Agnes, Mrs. Crewe as St. Genevieve, and Mrs. Sheridan as St. Cecilia. In the first Royal Academy show, he depicted the Duchess of Manchester and her son as Diana disarming Cupid; at other points in his career, he cast his sitters in allegorical roles—the daughters of Sir William Montgomery as the

16. Sir Joshua Reynolds, *Mrs. Abington as Prue in "Love for Love"* (RA 1771) (Yale Center for British Art, Paul Mellon Collection). Strictly speaking, this is a theatrical portrait: Frances Abington was a popular actress in Shakespearean and non-Shakespearean roles. (Six years after this portrait was exhibited, she would create the role of Lady Teazle in *The School for Scandal* [pl. 110].) In the Drury Lane seasons of 1769–72, she played Prue; but in the picture the association with Congreve's comedy is limited to the costume she presumably wore, and the painting is actually a splendid example of a "fancy dress" picture, complete with lap dog.

17. George Stubbs, *Portrait of a Young Lady (Miss Isabella Saltonstall) in the Character of Una* (RA 1782) (Fitzwilliam Museum, Cambridge). "Impersonation pictures" were far from Stubbs's specialty, but as an animal painter he may well have been momentarily reconciled to the form as a source of bread and butter by the attractions of this familiar subject. Spenser's *The Faerie Queene* provided him with two animals to paint: an excessively tame lion (also seen in Reynolds's portrait of Mary Beauclerk as Una) and a palfrey.

Graces adorning a term of Hymen, Lady Sarah Bunbury sacrificing to the Graces, Miss Morris as Hope nursing Love, and, most memorably, Mrs. Siddons as the Tragic Muse. In effect—theoretical and practical considerations apart—Reynolds moved the contemporary love for masquerades from the assembly room to the studio. At balls put on by the Thursday Night Club to which he belonged, people came in a number of specific roles: characters in popular plays, Henry VIII, Jane Shore, Queen Elizabeth, Falstaff and the merry wives of Windsor.[28]

In introducing these grace notes of allusive costume, accessories, and pose into what were essentially portraits, it was to be expected that sooner or later the painters of Reynolds's era would seek fresh roles in English literature as it grew in prestige. There was at least a tangential reference to Milton in Reynolds's pictures of Mrs. Fortescue as La Pensiorosa and Mrs. Hale as Euphrosyne, and to Shakespeare in his portrayal of the courtesan Kitty Fisher as Cleopatra; disapproving of the latter, William Hazlitt was to write, "What can be more trifling than giving the portrait of Kitty Fisher the mock-heroic title of Cleopatra?"[29]* An explicit allusion was contained in Reynolds's well-known painting (1780) of Mary, the eldest daughter of Lady Diana Beauclerk, as Una. Shakespeare's comedies supplied the demand for suitable roles for beautiful and/or vivacious women sitters. At various times, ladies were depicted as Hermione (the Countess of Derby in Zoffany's picture), Miranda (Mrs. Tollemache in Reynolds's, and Mrs. Michael Angelo Taylor, wife of a politician, in Hoppner's), Rosalind, and Perdita.

From the very beginning of the exhibition era, artists also drew roles for their fancy pictures from more recent literary sources: Highmore from Richardson's *Sir Charles Grandison* ("Clementina"), Nathaniel Hone from Rowe's *The Fair Penitent* (Lady Stanhope as Calista), and Matthew William Peters, the only English artist of any consequence to paint lubricious pictures and then take holy orders, from *The Rape of the Lock* (Belinda).

*Hazlitt presumably did not consider as "trifling" his Titianesque portrait of Charles Lamb dressed as a Venetian senator.

18. John Opie, ***Portrait of a Lady in the Character of Cressida*** (RA 1800) (Tate Gallery, London). Pandarus (to Troilus, looking on): "Here she is now; swear the oaths now to hear that you have sworn to me." (to Cressida): "Come, draw this curtain, and let's see your picture" (Shakespeare, *Troilus and Cressida,* 3. 2). The title Opie gave to the painting implies that it was meant as an impersonation picture—though the identity of the model is not known—rather than as an illustration of literature. The pose and subject also suggest the relation of such portraits to the current fashion for "attitudes" or living representations of pictures and statues. In December following the exhibition, at the elaborate Christmas revels at William Beckford's Gothick mansion, Fonthill Abbey, Lady Hamilton, the leading exponent of this form of parlor entertainment, depicted Agrippina presenting the ashes of Germanicus before the Roman populace.

Hoppner painted Harriet, Lady Cunliffe as Sophia Western and his own wife as Sterne's Eliza. Romney portrayed the actress Miss Wallis as both L'Allegro and Il Penseroso in a single painting (pl. 19), and later painted his patron William Hayley's son, Tom, as Robin Goodfellow (Puck). As portraits of children in "fancy" or historical roles went, this probably was as inoffensive as any. On the whole, it certainly was preferable to Reynolds's painting of the four-year-old Master Crewe costumed as, of all people, Henry VIII, or a picture, exhibited at the Royal Academy in 1785 but unfortunately now lost, of a *girl* in the character of Falstaff. It was such palpable excesses as these, notwithstanding their possibly satirical point, that doubtless inspired a satire of the vogue itself in *The Vicar of Wakefield* (1776), where the role-playing portrait has been drastically demoted from London society to the humble family of a country clergyman. The Vicar has hired an itinerant "limner" to paint the family:

> We . . . at length came to an unanimous resolution of being drawn together, in one large historical family piece. This would be cheaper, since one frame would serve for all, and it would be infinitely more genteel; for all families of any taste were now drawn in the same manner. As we did not immediately recollect an historical subject to suit us, we were contented each with being drawn as independent historical figures. My wife desired to be represented as Venus, and the painter was desired not to be too frugal of his diamonds in her stomacher and hair. Her two little ones were to be as Cupids by her side, while I, in my gown and band, was to present her with my books on the Whistonian controversy. Olivia would be drawn as an Amazon, sitting upon a bank of flowers, drest in a green joseph, richly laced with gold, and a whip in her hand. Sophia was to be a shepherdess, with as many sheep as the painter could put in for nothing; and Moses was to be drest out with an hat and white feather. Our taste so much pleased the 'Squire, that he insisted on being put in as one of the family in the character of Alexander the great, at Olivia's feet. (Chap. 16)

The resulting canvas was so large that it could not be moved from the kitchen, against whose wall the limner had propped it, and it became "the jest of all our neighbours."

The itinerant limner's painting of the Primrose family in their "historical" get-ups was a *reductio ad absurdum* of the multiple fancy portrait. It was also a satire of another characteristic type of eighteenth-century painting, the conversation piece—a picture of a family or a group of friends playing cards, drinking tea, making music, conversing, or even, as in Hogarth's early picture of a children's performance of Dryden's *The Indian Emperor,* putting on amateur theatricals.[30] As time went on, and the stock of English fiction was more and more drawn upon by artists, it proved to abound with situations suitable for converting into narrative conversation pieces. The painting from *The Vicar of Wakefield* that Charles Ryley showed at the Royal Academy in 1786, for example, depicted the Primrose family's picnic interrupted by Olivia's return home after her seduction and mock marriage to Squire Thornhill. More than a century later, an occasional literary painting revived the mode. Margaret Dicksee's picture of *Sheridan at the Linleys'* (RA 1899) was a scene from literary biography, the beautiful Linley sisters singing as their father accompanied them at the harpsichord and the handsome Richard Brinsley Sheridan, who was soon to elope with Elizabeth, listened.*

Another popular form of late eighteenth-century British art was the genre picture, which also represented a human situation whether or not it had narrative content. The low place it occupied in the neoclassic hier-

*Many subjects taken from literary biography—and, for that matter, seventeenth- and eighteenth-century history—had added appeal to painters desirous of imitating well-known portraits of historical figures. In this case, the artist would have had in mind Gainsborough's charming picture of Elizabeth and Mary Linley.

19. George Romney, *Mirth and Melancholy* (1788–89) (Petworth House). "Melancholy is represented near the entrance of a gloomy cell, urged with gentle force by her sister, Mirth, to join a joyous party dancing round a maypole on a distant hill" (William Hayley's memoir of Romney). The artist seems not to have heeded his patron's advice, tendered in the second of his *Epistles to Romney* (1788): "And most, my friend, a syren's wiles beware, / Ah! shun insidious Allegory's snare!"

archy counterbalanced by the credentials acquired when the so-called little Dutch masters came into vogue at the court of Louis XIV, it was brought to English attention through engravings from Greuze. Idealized or moderately realistic portrayals of humorous or pathetic incidents, customs, and occupations in everyday life, usually rural and domestic, became something of a fashion in England before collectors' tastes turned toward the paintings of the seventeenth-century Dutch and Flemish masters themselves. It was here, and to a lesser extent in certain kinds of fancy pictures, that the eighteenth-century (pre-Romantic) penchant for sensibility—the conscious, self-indulgent exercise of the tender feelings in sympathy with pathetic or otherwise moving characters and situations, or merely representations of the supposedly enviable "simple life"—found its chief place in English art as it had earlier done in France. Greuze's *Family Bible Reading* (1755), *A Marriage Contract* (1761), and *The Father's Curse: The Ungrateful Son* and its sequel *The Father's Curse: The Punished Son* (1777–78), with their moralized narrative content, had their counterparts in Morland's *Laetitia* and Mortimer's *Progress of Virtue* series, already mentioned, and the series Francis Wheatley exhibited from year to year at the Royal Academy, *Life of a Country Girl, Maidenhood, Courtship, Marriage, Married Life,* and so on. Few English genre paintings at this time, however, borrowed their subjects from English literature, although reviewers and others sometimes attributed to a painting a source that the artist never had in mind. Thus Gainsborough's fancy picture *Young Hobbinol and Gandaretta,* supposedly from Somerville's comic pastoral poem *Hobbinol,* acquired that title only when it was engraved for Macklin's Poet's Gallery (see chapter 2, below).

Among the early genre paintings exhibited with explicit allusions to literary sources were Edward Penny's scene (Society of Artists 1764) from Swift's description of a city shower (described by Horace Walpole as "A pretty light girl, trundling a mop, and a gentleman starting back as having been wetted by it") and the same artist's *The Gossiping Blacksmith* (RA 1769), suggested by lines in Shakespeare's *King John,* "I saw a smith stand with his hammer, thus, / The whilst his iron did on the anvil cool, / With open mouth swallowing a tailor's news" (4. 2. 193–95). Paintings of beggars from, for example, Mackenzie's *The Man of Feeling* and Joseph Warton's "Ode to Fancy"; hermits from Parnell's "The Hermit" as well as "Edwin and Angelina," a ballad in *The Vicar of Wakefield*; village schoolmistresses (Shenstone's *The School-Mistress*); gleaners (Thomson's *The Seasons*); and cottagers (Gray's "Elegy"), all occasionally brought the breath of humble country life to the bustling city by way of painters collaborating with poets.

They would do so in far greater quantity—by the thousands—in years to come. But in the eighteenth century, the chief importers of poetry-flavored rusticity into art were the landscapists, who, like the history painters, gradually (though never entirely) replaced classical allusions with allusions to English literature. The extent to which any human figures could be admitted into a landscape was a lively issue during the years at mid-century when native landscape painters aspired to the manner of Claude Lorrain and Poussin. Those almost oppressively influential artists had often inserted in their classical scenes small figures or groups representing identifiable mythological or scriptural stories: Claude, *Landscape with Acis and Galatea, Landscape with Psyche at the Palace of Cupid, Land-scene with the Flight into Egypt, The Finding of the Infant Moses, Cephalus and Procris Reunited by Diana, St. George and the Dragon*; Poussin, landscapes with Orpheus and Eurydice, Orion, Polyphemus, Pyramus and Thisbe, Juno, Argus, Phocion. Just as the landscapists portrayed generalized, ideal scenes composed in their studios rather than painting from nature, so they also were not concerned to individualize their figures, refugees, as it were, from history paintings; such figures served simply to organize and add human presence to the composition, thus dignifying it as a work of art according to Aristotelian principle. The connection with a literary theme was purely nominal. If any more than a name were borrowed from the source, the conventional separation of the genres would be violated and the landscape would no longer be a landscape. Contemporary English thought on this subject was expressed by Jonathan Richardson (whom we will meet again in Part Three, in connection with Milton) in his *Account of the Statues, Bas Reliefs, Drawings and Pictures in Italy* (1722):

> Landskips are in Imitation of Rural Nature, of which therefore there may be as many Kinds, as there are Appearances, of This sort of Nature; and the Scenes may be laid in any Countrey, or Age, With figures, or Without; but if there are Any, as 'tis necessary there should be, Generally speaking, they must be Suitable, and only subservient to the landskip, to Enrich, or Animate it; Otherwise the Picture loses its Denomination, it becomes a History, a Battel-piece, &c. or at least it is of an Equivocal kind.[31]

From time to time, Richard Wilson, the first considerable English landscapist, followed this practice, as in his *Ego fui in Arcadia* (1755), *The Destruction of the Children of Niobe* (1760), *Phaeton* (1763), and *Cicero and His Friends* (1770)—not so much from any devotion to Claude as from financial necessity: a landscape without figures could command forty guineas, but one with figures might be sold at double the price. Only once, however, did Wilson portray figures from an English literary subject: *A Summer*

20. William Williams, ***A Thunderstorm, with the Death of Amelia*** (1784) (Tate Gallery, London). A tempestuous landscape reminiscent of Salvator Rosa, with the addition of an episode from English poetry. In Thomson's *The Seasons* ("Summer"), the lovers Celadon and Amelia are caught in a storm and Amelia is killed by lightning.

Storm, with the Story of the Two Lovers (Celadon and Amelia), from *The Seasons* (1765).

Gainsborough placed in his landscapes few if any figures drawn from "history" (including poetry). His people were anonymous persons, drovers, herdsmen, woodmen, milkmaids, without literary associations. They were meant to harmonize with their surroundings, not to import extra meaning into them.* A contemporary writer alleged that a landscape (so called in the catalogue) that Gainsborough exhibited at the Royal Academy in 1778 illustrated a passage in *The School-Mistress,* when at recess time

> . . . Liberty unbars her prison doors;
> And like a rushing torrent out they fly,
> And now the grassy cirque have covered o'er,
> With boisterous revel rout and wild uproar

—but the association with Shenstone was the critic's, not the artist's.[32] The very fact that it was made, however, suggests the alacrity with which spectators at this time, and thenceforward, would read into paintings literary references that the artist did not have in mind.

As other landscapists ceased to imitate the carefully composed scenes of the French masters and turned to portraying nature as it was actually observed, they associated the English countryside and woods with figures and scenes in English, not classical, literature. Besides satisfying Reynolds's criterion of suitability, they drew on the close connection that had already been established between painting and English descriptive poetry, largely through the popularity of *The Seasons.* Although Thomson did

*Wordsworth, who took pride in his artistic opinions, considered figures to be a distracting element. He told Farington that "he thought historical subjects shd. never be introduced into Landscape but where the Landscape was to be subservient to them.—Where the Landscape was intended principally to impress the mind, figures, other than such as are general, such as may a thousand times appear, and seem accidental, and not particularly to draw the attention, are injurious to the effect which the Landscape shd. produce as a scene founded on an observation of nature" (Farington [1], 8.3003 [28 April 1807]).

21. Sir George Beaumont, *Landscape, with Jaques and the Wounded Stag* (undated) (Tate Gallery, London). The wealthy and generous artist, a friend of poets and painters, remained an advocate of conventional landscape painting, complete with a familiar literary reference, at a time when Turner was beginning to develop his own idiosyncratic style. Although Beaumont favored Constable over Turner, he also had reservations about the former's quite different, but still intensely personal, way of seeing nature. This difference of opinion did not affect his friendship with Constable, whom he entertained at Coleorton, his seat in Leicestershire.

not often directly translate specific painted scenes into poetry, he was deeply affected by the art produced and inspired by the three landscape painters venerated by his generation and mentioned in his famous lines in *The Castle of Indolence,* "Whate'er Lorrain light-touched with softening Hue, / Or savage Rosa dash'd, or learned Poussin drew." The pictorialism of *The Seasons* was looked upon as a triumphant exemplification of *ut pictura poesis.*[33] The central place the poem occupies in the history of British aesthetics and landscape art down to Turner's time substantiates the remark of a modern critic that "the patrons and artists of British landscape were, not always deeply, but certainly much of the time, concerned with poetry and prose; there is a deal of truth in the notion that our art was verbally framed before becoming visually real."[34]

The prevailing associational theory of psychology, derived from Hobbes and Locke, which stressed the mind's power of finding like stimuli in disparate kinds of experience, such as poetry, scenery, and painted art, provided a philosophical rationale, if any was needed, for investing landscape painting with literary suggestion if not actual reference. It was not only the pictorialism of much eighteenth-century poetry that especially recommended it to artists; more important, perhaps, was the underlying purpose of the verbal scenery, to induce a mood that could be similarly induced by brush and pigment. The mood was made specific by the characters whom the poet—and then the painter—placed in the landscape; the picture was transformed from an exercise in ideal composition or topographical representation into painted poem. The physical setting echoed the spirit of the figure or the story, whether they were Celadon and Amelia in the pastoral setting of *The Seasons* or Gray's bard, a precursor of Romantic *Sturm und Drang,* prophesying in the mountains of Wales (pls. 297, 298). Solitaries like the bard were particularly closely associated with the scenery. Since there was no other human being to commune with, the scenery served both as an inspirer and an auditor of the feelings vented by the benighted traveler, the shipwrecked mariner, the contemplative man finding intimations of mortality among bare ruined choirs. It was only to be expected that the meditative poetry of the period—Collins's "Ode to Evening," Beattie's *The Minstrel,* Parnell's "The Hermit"—would be referred to again and again in landscape art. As Romanticism began to permeate the English atmosphere, the landscape painting that was most characteristic of the time was less descriptive than expressive. Its affinity was with the poetry that used the associative powers of the physical scene as a vehicle for impassioned thought.

In the very first years of the public exhibitions, numerous landscapes were credited in the catalogues with literary associations if not actual literary inspiration. The first was Paul Sandby's picture (Society of Artists 1761) from Gray's "The Bard," which bore the motto, "But oh! what glorious scenes, etc." Quite plainly, though the picture is lost, it was in a strenuously Salvator Rosaesque manner. Two years later, at the rival Free Society of Artists, two such pictures were hung, one *A Large Landscape, with a Scene in Shakespeare's Cymbeline,* and the other *A Landscape, with the Fable of Chamont, and the Witch, from Otway's Orphan.* In the exhibitions of 1767, there were at least four, two by Thomas Smith of Derby depicting the familiar Palemon-Lavinia and Damon-Musidora stories in *The Seasons.* The third represented the first use made of a literary source that was destined to be associated, however tenuously, with scores of paintings: *A Large Landscape, with Orlando and Oliver, as Described by Oliver, in the Last Scene of Act IV of Shakespeare's As You Like It.* It was not this scene of the play, however, but the earlier one—also described rather than enacted—of melancholy Jaques and the wounded stag that would become a staple of landscape painting. Also in the Society of Artists show in 1767 was the first landscape to invoke Macbeth, Zuccarelli's *Macbeth Meeting the Witches* (pl. 22). A precursor of innumerable Macbeth-and-witches pictures to come, it survives as one of the earliest literary landscapes extant; another is the Irish artist George Mullins's *A Cataract; a Rude Scene. Vide Thomson's Seasons, Summer, Verse 585* (pl. 23). A third is Alexander Runciman's *Landscape from Milton's L'Allegro,* a Rubensesque scene with Corydon, Thyrsis and Phyllis in the foreground and the city of Perth in the distance.

In these years also, landscapes appeared with announced allusions to the *Spectator* No. 425 ("the figures of Summer, and attendants"), Shakespeare's *Venus and Adonis, The Pilgrim's Progress, Comus, Cymbeline,* and *Paradise Lost* (a reversion to the Claudian Italian landscape by a forgotten artist: *View from Nature of the Brook of Valombrosa, Immortalized by Milton in Paradise Lost, I. 301*).

From about 1788, paintings titled in this manner disappear from the records. An entry in the 1829 Royal Academy catalogue, *Landscape from a Description in Thomson's Seasons,* had a hopelessly antiquated air. This does not mean, of course, that landscapes associated with literature themselves disappeared; quite the contrary. But the mode of titling changed in a significant way. From the beginning of the nineteenth century onward, landscapes intended *as* landscapes were usually named for the site represented or given a generic title like *Winter Scene* or *The Moonlit Strand* with a suitable quotation attached. The others adopted literary references as titles, often to the exclusion of any indication that they were, in fact, landscapes.

Two events at the turn of the century nicely summarize the progress so far made in linking landscape art with English literature. One was the appearance, over the period 1796–1816, of at least ten paintings from the Gothic romances of Ann Radcliffe, chiefly *The Mysteries of Udolpho* (1794). What lent them special interest, apart from exemplifying the way current best-selling fiction participated in the art exhibitions, was the fact that the novels themselves contained superabundant and lengthy descriptions of idyllic or wild landscapes in the manner of Claude, Poussin, and Rosa.[35] Because at the time she wrote them she had not yet been abroad to see the Italianate and Alpine scenery she described, Mrs. Radcliffe found her inspiration in engravings and the paintings she studied at the Royal Academy. As a consequence, her contemporaries admired her for her painterly prose: ". . . the Shakespeare of Romance Writers," one called her, ". . . who to the wild landscape of Salvator Rosa has added the softer graces of a Claude . . . many scenes truly terrific in their conception, yet so softened down, and the mind so much relieved, by the intermixture of beautiful description."[36] Wrote someone else, in an "Epistle in Rhyme to M. G. Lewis," who also was celebrated for his Gothic fiction (*The Monk*):

> Thou notest, like Radcliffe, with a painter's eye,
> The pine-clad mountain and the stormy sky,
> And at thy bidding, to my wondering view
> Rise the bold scenes Salvator's pencil* drew.[37]

In Radcliffe's fiction, as in *The Seasons* (which also contributed to her pictures), landscape paintings were, in effect, recycled: they suggested prose descriptions that in turn suggested new paintings to a fresh generation of artists.

By this time, when Turner's career was in its early stages and Constable was beginning his slow, painful ascent to acceptance, landscape art had acquired some prestige, even if it still did not rival history painting in the scale of artistic dignity, and one reason for its heightened respectability was its by now firmly established connection with literature. In May 1799, Turner's friend, the gifted young watercolorist Thomas Girtin, briefly brought together a sketching club that was intended to assist the establishment of "a school of Historic Landscape, the subjects being designs from poetick passages." Girtin and his fellow artists spent many evenings together, painting scenes suggested by the writings of one or another of nine authors esteemed for their natural descriptions: MacPherson's *Ossian* (selected on four occasions), Ann Radcliffe (whose *Mysteries of Udolpho* contained eight poems) and John Cunningham (both selected on three), Thomson, Mallet, Goldsmith, Cowper, Anna Seward, and John Gisborne.[38] They practiced what the true believers in *ut pictura poesis* had been preaching in England for a century, and they would have had no trouble understanding why an older member of their craft, the watercolorist Edward Dayes, in his *Essays on Painting* published in 1805, larded his technical advice with illustrative quotations from Thomson, Milton, Shakespeare, Pope, Prior, and several lesser eighteenth-century poets. The differences in medium between the sister arts—words in print as against watercolors on paper, pigments on canvas, or inked impressions of engraved plates—were minimized by all to whom pictorialism constituted the common quality, or effect, of the aesthetic experience.

By the end of the eighteenth century, literary pictures had played a substantial role in domesticating fine art and introducing it to a wider public. In Hogarth's time, the profession of painting in general had had

*"Pencil" was the old word for a (fine) brush.

to contend for public acceptance against discouraging odds. Neither George I nor George II set an example of royal patronage as had Charles I or even Charles II; upon being shown the print of Hogarth's *The March to Finchley*, which the artist proposed to dedicate to him, George II muttered, "I hate bainting and boetry, neither the one nor the other ever did any good."[39] Young men ambitious to become artists had to go to Italy to learn, and even when the Royal Academy schools were established in the most recent (and first successful) effort to provide art education at home, the canvases from which they learned their lessons, wherever found, were importations. As late as 1766, a nobleman who had an opportunity to buy one of Benjamin West's first large history paintings asked, "What could I do, if I had it? You surely would not have me hang up a modern English picture in my house unless it was a portrait?"[40]

Portraiture, indeed, was the only branch of painting to flourish commercially during the greater part of the century. Its technique could be learned at home, from the numerous portraitists, predominantly foreigners, who were attracted by the expanding market for their personalized products. And it was this growing demand for portraits, stimulated by the expansion of the affluent middle class and its members' sharpening sense of social place as well as by their sheer vanity, that was initially

22. Francesco Zuccarelli, *Macbeth Meeting the Witches* (Society of Artists 1767) (Royal Shakespeare Theatre Picture Gallery ©). One of the earliest of the many depictions of the subject, and iconographically by all odds the most eclectic. The scene is wholly unrelated to the theater. The wind-tortured landscape recalls the paintings of Gaspard Poussin and Salvator Rosa, and the horses and banner are suggestive of battle subjects in history painting as well as—in the case of the horses—the animal subjects of Stubbs and Sawrey Gilpin (pl. 92). The witches are in quasi-rural, not spectral, attire, and Macbeth's and Banquo's kilts (if that is what they are) are worn with plumed hats suggestive of the commedia dell'arte and Watteau; similar costumes will later grace characters in Boydell's Shakespeare Gallery, such as those painted by Francis Wheatley. The lightning bolt will streak the sky again in some of John Martin's apocalyptic canvases.

23. George Mullins, *A Cataract: A Rude Scene* (RA 1772) (Ashmolean Museum, Oxford). When exhibited, this painting carried a literary reference: "Vide Thomson's Seasons, Summer, verse 585" (the beginning of a twenty-line description of a waterfall). The alternative modern title given the picture, *A Fishing Party,* points to the fact that it is really a combination landscape and rustic conversation piece.

responsible for spreading interest in art to a wider public. But other factors eventually assisted the naturalization of English painting, the cause to which the pugnaciously chauvinistic Hogarth had been so energetically devoted. Subjects from English history, especially as mediated through Shakespeare, began to be painted in quantity. The characters personified in fancy, or "historical," portraits tended to be drawn more from English literary sources than mythology or hagiography. Landscapists shifted their gaze from the Continental scenes idealized by Claude, Poussin, and Salvator Rosa to indigenous vistas, especially those that could in some way be related to natural descriptions in English poetry. Early practitioners of genre like Morland and Wheatley drew their subjects, as did some poets, from the English human landscape, particularly in the countryside. It was above all in its increasing reliance on English literature—so familiar to many people, and to many a source of patriotic pride—that subject painting declared its independence of foreign models and acquired the prestige that would sustain it through the next century.

CHAPTER 2

Eighteenth-century book illustrations.—Boydell's Shakespeare Gallery.—Macklin's Poet's Gallery.—Fuseli's Milton Gallery.

By way of the illustrated editions that helped spread literary culture in eighteenth-century England, the sisterhood of the arts was brought home to a public that never visited the exhibitions.[1] In 1688 and 1709 respectively, the leading bookseller-publisher of the time, Jacob Tonson, had issued editions of *Paradise Lost,* with designs by the Flemish artist John Baptist Medina, and of Shakespeare's plays, edited by Nicholas Rowe and illustrated by the French artist François Boitard.[2] These were followed by editions of such dramatists as Beaumont and Fletcher (1711) and Dryden (1735). Plates from Tonson's Shakespeare later were sometimes used for cheap printings of the individual plays that were sold at the playhouses. In one form or another, as expensive mezzotints, cheap colored prints, or engravings bound into reading editions of the plays, these engraved representations of dramatic tableaux found an audience composed not only of the well-to-do and presumably cultivated persons who could afford the collected works of a dramatist but of the larger body of ordinary playgoers as well. The scenes, however, were "generalized theatrical constructs" inspired by the printed text.[3] At no time in the century, indeed, did book illustrations of drama often purport to be based on performances. Typically occurring on the engraved title page of a play, surrounded by an elaborate border, the scenes were usually unrelated to the play as staged or to its actors, whose portraits also accompanied the text. Only occasionally did they incorporate details that seemingly were suggested by theatrical productions.

The demand for these illustrated texts of old or currently popular dramas—in the latter case often rewritten by the playwrights before printing, so that they might be read as novels composed solely of dialogue—accounts in part for the steady increase in the production of theatrical portraits and tableaux toward the end of the century by such specialists as DeWilde and Roberts. Newly published volumes of belles lettres, however, were not usually illustrated. It has recently been pointed out that of some 1,850 poems separately published between 1704 and 1724, only a dozen had plates. Conspicuous among the latter was *The Rape of the Lock* (1714), which had five engraved tableaux and a frontispiece by Louis du Guernier. The first edition of Swift's *A Tale of a Tub* to be illustrated (with eight engravings) was the fifth (1710).[4] The first edition of *Robinson Crusoe* had only a portrait of the shipwrecked mariner and a map, but the sixth edition of the first part and the second edition of the second part (both 1722) were illustrated.[5]

Throughout the century, illustrations were so expensive an item in the initial production of a book that publishers normally commissioned them only when the success of a certain title suggested that an illustrated edition might attract additional buyers. (Once made and paid for, however, they could be, and often were, reused in subsequent editions over long periods of time.) Sometimes a publisher sought the advice of the book's author. Thus in 1727, Swift's publisher asked him to name the episodes of *Gulliver's Travels* that he thought should be illustrated in a new edition, and Swift responded with a list of twenty-two in all.[6] Some twenty years later, Sir Thomas Hanmer acted, in a sense, as Shakespeare's deputy when he gave Francis Hayman directions for twenty-seven of the illustrations he was commissioned to draw for Hanmer's new edition of the plays.[7] Hayman later contributed pictures and vignettes to a wide variety of literary works—editions of Pope, Milton, Congreve, and Addison; the *Spectator, Tatler,* and *Guardian; Roderick Random,* Christopher Smart's *Poems on Several Occasions, The Beggar's Opera,* and Young's *Night Thoughts.* In the 1760s, the first book illustrator to do so, he sent several pictures to exhibitions of the Society of Artists, of which he was the first president.

Hayman's career ended (1776) just as cheap illustrated editions of the works of standard authors, old as well as recent, began to multiply in the wake of a court decision in 1774 that, by abolishing the concept of perpetual copyright, threw into the public domain a large body of literature that certain publishers had hitherto claimed as their exclusive property. In addition to separate editions of single works and collections of individual authors' oeuvres, several enterprising publishers brought out long series of pocket-sized volumes with the same contents. Their low prices, convenient formats, and illustrations recommended them to many middle-class readers whom the generally high prices of books had barred from participating in the steady expansion of the reading public. (W. Jackson Bate has argued that "the potential audience for poetry in the period from 1770 to 1830 was greater than it had ever been since the invention of printing.")[8] The principal series in the 1770s and 1780s were John Bell's *Poets of Great Britain Complete from Chaucer to Churchill,* his *British Theatre,* and John Harrison's *Novelist's Magazine,* a "select library" of fiction issued in parts. In the 1790s, Bell reissued his two long series, along with his 1774 edition of Shakespeare, at the new low price of 6d. a volume, and another member of the trade, John Cooke, brought out his *Cheap and Elegant Pocket Library of Select Poets, Pocket Edition of Select Novels,* and *Select British Classics.* As a group, these enterprising publishers widened the public's acquaintance with scores of poets, dramatists, novelists, and essayists. Cooke's editions particularly won the affection of young students who could pay no more than a weekly sixpence for good reading.

"How I loved those little sixpenny numbers containing whole poets!" exclaimed Leigh Hunt late in life. "I doated on their type, their ornaments, on their wrappers containing lists of other poets, and on the engravings from Kirk."[9]

Thomas Kirk, who illustrated certain titles in all three of Cooke's series, and John Hamilton Mortimer, who contributed frontispieces to eight or ten volumes of Bell's edition of the poets and illustrated at least nine scenes from *The Canterbury Tales,* were two of the half-dozen prominent artists who both worked as book illustrators and sent paintings, some commissioned by publishers as designs for engraving, to the yearly exhibitions. Others whose names were familiar to gallerygoers in the last decade of the eighteenth century and the first three of the nineteenth were William Hamilton, who contributed ten plates to Bell's *Shakespeare* and illustrated, among others, the poems of Thomson and Gray; Robert Smirke, who worked for all the leading publishers and sent pictures to the Academy exhibitions from 1786 to 1813; Richard Corbould, whose designs also could be found in a number of reprint series; Richard Westall, who in his later years would be among the first to illustrate the new stars of poetry, Scott, Southey, and Byron; and the best known and most prolific of the group, Thomas Stothard. Tradition credits Stothard with some 5,000 designs, of which 3,000 were engraved.* (The scores of paintings he contributed to the exhibitions probably were both oils and watercolors.) He was the most adaptable and accommodating of artists. His admirer, the early Victorian painter Charles Robert Leslie, wrote, without exaggeration: "He was engaged in every species of composition, from illustrations of Homer and Shakespeare, to designs for spelling-books and pocket-almanacks, fashions for the *Ladies' Magazine,* portraits of popular actors and actresses in character, as well as other subjects of the day."[10] Whatever his private tastes in literature may have been, he was ready to turn his hand to whatever commission a publisher of illustrated books offered him, beginning with 148 designs for Harrison's *Novelist's Magazine.* The list solely of the works of English literature he illustrated runs to many scores of titles, far too long to reproduce here. A list of the works he did *not* illustrate would probably occupy less space.

Although each artist's style has a distinctiveness readily apparent to the specialist's eye, to the uninitiated the work of the whole group tends to blur into a general impression of mannered elegance and artificiality, of prettiness rather than strong emotion, of decoration rather than representation. For the strong rococo element in their designs they were indebted to the century's most influential engraver in the field of book illustration, Hubert François Gravelot, who illustrated about one hundred books, including Gay's *Fables* and Theobald's edition of Shakespeare, during his residence in England (1732–45). Gravelot was a student of Boucher and the teacher, in turn, of Hayman and Gainsborough, and through his association with the St. Martin's Lane Academy, he transmitted the French elegance of line to the next generation of English literary illustrators and beyond.

Hazlitt, writing of Westall, delivered an estimate that well describes the limitation of the whole group of busy literary illustrators. Westall's style, he said, was

> the elegant antithesis to the style of Hogarth, where, instead of that originality of character which excludes a nice attention to general forms, we have all that beauty of form which excludes the possibility of character; the refined essence

24. Thomas Stothard, *Oberon and Titania* (1806) (Yale Center for British Art, Paul Mellon Fund). One of sixteen illustrations Stothard designed for an edition of Shakespeare, from *A Midsummer Night's Dream* (4. 1): *Oberon:* "Come, my queen, take hands with me. / And rock the ground whereon these sleepers be."

*His commercial success somehow seems incompatible with the gentle otherworldliness attributed to him by his affectionate and admiring contemporaries. In a lecture in the mid-1840s, Benjamin Robert Haydon exclaimed, "Peace to Stothard's mild and tender spirit! It was impossible to be in Stothard's company a moment, without feeling he possessed the mind of some eternal being that was out of place on this dim spot which men call earth. . . . Stothard always impressed you as if he was trying to forget the evils of earth" (*Lectures on Painting and Design,* 2:33–34). Lamb wrote a verse tribute to him:

In my young days
How often have I, with a child's fond gaze,
Pored on the pictur'd wonders thou hadst done:
Clarissa mournful, and prim Grandison!
All Fielding's, Smollett's heroes, rose to view;
I saw, and I believed the phantoms true.
. . . . . .
Age, that enfeebles other men's designs,
But heightens thine, and thy free draught refines.
In several ways distinct you make us feel—
Graceful as Raphael, as Watteau *genteel.*
Your lights and shades, as Titianesque, we praise;
And warmly wish you Titian's length of days.

25. Francis Wheatley, *Young Marlow and Miss Hardcastle* (1791) (Victoria & Albert Museum, Crown Copyright). This scene from Goldsmith's *She Stoops to Conquer* (1773) was painted for the edition of the play published in *Bell's British Theatre* (1792). The money to be made from producing designs to be engraved in collections like Bell's often induced artists to work in veins some distance from their customary ones (compare Mortimer, pl. 12). Little of the fanciful elegance that characterizes Wheatley's work is evident here.

> and volatilized spirit of art, without any of the *caput mortuum* of nature; and where, instead of her endless variety, peculiarities, and defects, we constantly meet with the same classical purity and undeviating simplicity of idea—one sweet smile, one heightened bloom diffused over all.[11]

The fact was that the alien spirit of Watteau and the Frenchified disciples of the "little Dutch masters" presided over the illustration of English books down to the end of the eighteenth century and for several decades beyond. The endless variety of English literature was sacrificed to the featureless, derivative stylization of native artists who had not yet found an illustrative idiom of their own.

Their influence on subsequent literary art amounted almost to an incubus. In his memoir of his brother David, a painter who died young, William Bell Scott recalled that "perhaps [his] first attempts at original design were suggested by the illustrations to Cooke's edition of the British Poets, Novelists, and Essayists—a complete set of proofs of these in ten or twelve volumes being his daily companion" about 1822.[12] At the same time, however, as Scott noted many years later, this enthusiastic, absorptive study was in the long run unhealthy, for it inhibited the free exercise of the imagination, binding the reader (especially the reader who was about to become an artist) to past standards and styles of expression.[13]

It is true that book illustration in the age of Stothard and Westall was not quite all of one piece. There were idiosyncratic practitioners such as

Thomas Rowlandson, an exhibitor at the staid Royal Academy between 1791 and 1818 (one of the more surprising facts of English art history), who made colored plates for editions of Smollett, Sterne, Fielding, *Hudibras* (after Hogarth), and *The Vicar of Wakefield.*[14] At the opposite pole from Rowlandson in most respects was William Blake, who in his professional capacity engraved a number of Stothard's designs. However original his style as an independent literary illustrator, chiefly in watercolors, his choice of subjects—or that of the publishers for whom he worked—was wholly conventional: *A Midsummer Night's Dream,* Gray's poems, Young's *Night Thoughts,* Milton, *The Canterbury Tales, The Faerie Queene.* Not all of these were engraved, and some were not even meant to be published. Several Shakespearean drawings, for instance, were for an extra-illustrated copy of the second folio owned by the Reverend Joseph Thomas. Again the selection of subjects is unremarkable. By the time Blake got around to them, in 1806–9, Jaques and the wounded stag, Richard III and the ghost, and Queen Katherine's dream were staples of literary illustration. In this respect, at least, Blake was a captive of custom, not a visionary dissident remote from the everyday life of English art. But neither Blake nor Rowlandson made any impact on literary painting. It was the Stothards, Westalls, and Smirkes who determined the way English literature was to be presented in visual form to the readers of illustrated editions and, to a large extent, in the paintings offered at the exhibitions down to the Victorian era. Additionally, the wide circulation of their engravings, between the covers of books as well as separately, opened the eyes of a new generation of artists to the seemingly limitless artistic potentiality of literature.

In 1743, in his epistle complimenting Sir Thomas Hanmer on his edition of Shakespeare, the poet William Collins expressed this aspiration:

26. Mather Brown, *Romeo, Juliet, and Friar Laurence* (undated) (Royal Shakespeare Theatre Picture Gallery ©). A late example of the extreme rococo style in literary painting. The artist, born in Boston in 1761, was a pupil of Benjamin West and exhibited scores of pictures, mostly portraits, at the Royal Academy between 1782 and 1831. If this painting is, by any chance, the one titled simply *Juliet* that was shown at the British Institution in 1831, it has a melancholy association. Several months later, Brown collapsed at the Royal Academy exhibition, where two paintings of his—a portrait of a lady and a Dutch genre subject, *Boys Blowing Bladders*—were hung, and died soon afterward.

O might some verse with happiest skill persuade
Expressive Picture to adopt thine aid!
What wondrous drafts might rise from every page!
What other Raphaels charm a distant age!

Thus, generous critic, as thy bard inspires,
The sister arts shall nurse their drooping fires;
Each from his scenes her stores alternate bring,
Blend the fair tints or wake the vocal string.[15]

However acceptable they might be on their own terms, engraved frontispieces, such as those by Hayman in Hanmer's edition, were a poor substitute for what Collins had in mind, the illustration of Shakespeare in paintings so accomplished—Raphaels indeed!—as to do honor to their incomparable source and at the same time to serve as an exemplary justification of *ut pictura poesis.* But although a fair number of scenes from Shakespeare had appeared at the yearly exhibitions during their first two decades, not until the 1780s were there signs that Collins's dream might be fulfilled on the scale and with the grandeur that Shakespeare's preeminence among British poets clearly required.[16]

At that time, the growing popularity of engravings as visual realizations of dramatic texts combined with Shakespeare's popularity on the stage and, of late, in the exhibition rooms to inspire three similar projects. The first was abortive and the second completed, but neither had much influence on public interest in literary art. The third, however, conceived and financed on an opulent scale, would have a profound effect on the practice of literary illustration.

The abortive project dated from 1781, when the fifty-year-old Robert Edge Pine,[17] a portraitist whom some regarded as Reynolds's rival and a history painter who had won the Society of Arts' hundred-guinea prize for "the best historical picture painted in oil colours" (*The Surrender of Calais to Edward III*), announced that he was about to paint "some of the most interesting and pleasing scenes in the works of Shakespeare" with a view toward engraving them and selling them in pairs. The first subjects, already painted, were Ophelia's mad scene and Miranda's first sight of Ferdinand. These and three other pictures, two from *King Lear* and one from *As You Like It,* were exhibited in Spring Gardens in 1782.[18] How many paintings were added to the collection is not known, but two years later Pine emigrated to the United States with the principal intention of producing a series of historical paintings illustrating the late Revolution. (He actually made portraits of leading Revolutionary figures, including George Washington and his family, General Gates, and Baron von Steuben.) With him he brought some or all of his Shakespeare pictures, which were hung at the State House in Philadelphia, the first such art exhibition in American history. After his death in 1788, they were sold to a Boston museum keeper and were burned in 1803.

Pine's Shakespeare paintings were not engraved, despite his prospectus. But in 1783 an album of prints entitled *The Picturesque Beauties of Shakespeare, Being a Selection of Scenes, From the Works of that Great Author* began to appear. When it was completed four years later it contained forty plates, four to each of ten plays, of which thirty-two were Smirke's, seven Stothard's, and one Charles Ryley's. Although this, the first collection of original Shakespeare illustrations, seems to have made no great splash at the moment, Delacroix was later to use it as his source, first for his *Macbeth* lithograph of 1825 and later for his series of *Hamlet* lithographs in the 1830s and 1840s.[19]

It may be that the *Picturesque Beauties* also figured in the conversation at a dinner party held at his Hampstead home in November 1786 by Josiah Boydell, who was associated in the printselling trade with his uncle, Alderman John Boydell.[20] The older man, who was shortly to become lord mayor of London, had for many years supplied all of Europe with prints from his "warehouse" in Cheapside. In the course of the evening—George Romney, Benjamin West, and the watercolorist Paul Sandby were among the guests—somebody* remarked, according to Josiah, that "the French had presented the works of their distinguished authors to the world in a much more respectable manner than the English had done. Shakespeare was mentioned, and several present said they would give 100 guineas for a fine Edition of Shakespeare. Being wound up by the conversation Alderman Boydell expressed a desire to undertake it, which was warmly encouraged." Within a week, the Boydells, inspired by patriotism as well as the scent of handsome publicity and profit, announced that they proposed to "help Britain acquire what she notoriously lacked, a school of Historical painting," appropriately devoted to scenes from the playwright who had by this time, by common consent, acquired the title of the national poet. Their plan was to commission from the day's leading artists a long series of oil paintings of Shakespearean subjects. These would be exhibited in a handsome purpose-built gallery, which was to be bequeathed, along with its contents, to the nation—the latter a promise that circumstances ultimately prevented being carried out. From these paintings, Boydell would have two sets of engravings made, the large ones to be gathered in an imperial folio album without text and the small ones incorporated in a sumptuous edition of the text as established by George Steevens. (In response to subscribers' complaints that if they took both series they did not want duplicates of the same subject, this policy was altered in 1794, when Boydell commissioned a separate series of designs for the small engravings.)

In June 1789, the newly erected Shakespeare Gallery was opened at 52 Pall Mall with the first batch of thirty-four paintings on the walls. More were added each spring, the total eventually reaching 167 canvases, by thirty-three artists. The promised books appeared simultaneously between 1791 and 1805. By the latter year, however, the loss of Boydell's lucrative European market for his stock of prints and the domestic dislocations caused by the Napoleonic Wars, combined with the fact that he had unwisely tied up a reported £100,000 of capital in the gallery, brought him to the verge of bankruptcy. He got Parliament's permission to hold a lottery, an occasional device used by failing exhibitors to try to recoup their losses. The winner of the grand prize received the whole inventory of paintings, which he auctioned off soon afterward for the derisory sum of £6,182.

From the beginning, Boydell's patriotic undertaking had a mixed reception. Before the gallery opened, it was publicized (1787–88) by a pair of pamphlets collectively entitled *Imperfect Hints Towards a New Edition of Shakespeare,* whose unidentified author ventured to suggest promising subjects that Boydell's stable of artists could find in a dozen plays, ranging from *Titus Andronicus* to *A Midsummer Night's Dream.*[21] Two years after the gallery opened (1791), the poet and dramatist Edward Jerningham pub-

*The Reverend John Romney emphatically claimed the honor for his father. "The idea of it," he wrote, "originated from himself individually; he had often ruminated upon it in his solitary hours; for he had always regarded Shakspeare as an author abounding in those picturesque conceptions and representations which may be so easily transferred to the canvass by an imaginative painter. But at a dinner given by Mr. Josiah Boydell . . . , when Shakspeare became the topic of conversation (induced probably by the circumstances of Mr. Romney's being at that time engaged in painting *The Tempest* . . .), he with his usual ardour and enthusiasm, then gave utterance to his conceptions, and suggested the plan of a National Gallery of pictures from that great dramatist, which would be both honourable to the country, and to the poet, and contribute essentially to the advancement of historical painting. The idea being in unison with the feelings of the company, was received with rapture" (A. B. Chamberlain, *George Romney* [London, 1910], pp. 140–41). But Romney's patron Hayley (who modeled the figure of Caliban in the *Tempest* painting) differed from John Romney, asserting that the idea was first mooted by the Alderman himself during a conversation in the artist's house in Cavendish Square at which Hayley was present (William Hayley, *The Life of George Romney, Esq.* [Chichester, 1809], p. 106). Other candidates for the honor of originating the scheme were advanced by early writers: Fuseli, Benjamin West, and the bookseller-publisher John Nichols. For a hitherto unnoted claimant, see Appendix A.

lished a 24-page pamphlet in which, after disposing of the usual art-exhibition fare—"mawkish Portraiture," the "gewgaws" of miniature's "fairy school," and suchlike trivialities—he turned to

Scenes of higher aim,
Where Eagle-Genius soars to nobler game;
Where Fancy, Reason, Taste, in one conjoin'd,
Unfold the workings of th' impassion'd mind.
Now to the laurell'd, academic band,
To ev'ry artist's emulative hand,
Munificence upholds her sacred prize,
And bids the daring reach it from the skies.[22]

After which, in equally abominable verse, he set forth his own list of desirable subjects. The press also hailed the gallery as a monument to England's cultural progress and improving public taste, the product of enlightened commercial enterprise:

> Among the circumstances which will distinguish the present reign [said a newspaper], the most striking is the rapid improvement of the arts and sciences.—Poetry first emerged from obscurity; History followed, but at a tedious interval; and Painting, which embodies and personifies the other two, stood dubious whether to advance or retire, till a Macklin and a Boydell beckoned her from the shade. To *noble* patronage Painting owes little, to *royal* patronage, less.—The spirit of the People, as it accomplished a revolution in Government, so also in Taste.[23]

How much, if anything, Boydell had to do with these early bursts of approbation is impossible to tell; they may have been paid puffery in the manner of the time, or they may not. But, in private at least, other opinions were freely expressed. Within a week or two of the first announcement of the scheme, Horace Walpole wrote to the Countess of Upper Ossory (15 December 1786):

> For the new edition of Shakespeare, it did not at all captivate me. In the first place I did not subscribe for my heirs and executors, as it would have been, when the term of completion is twelve years hence*—but I am not favourable to sets of prints for authors: I scarce know above one well executed, Coypell's *Don Quixote*—but mercy on us! *Our* painters to design for *Shakespeare*! His commentators have not been more inadequate. Pray, who is to give an idea of Falstaffe, now Quin is dead?—and then Bartolozzi [one of Boydell's engravers], who is only fit to engrave for the *Pastor fido,* will be to give a pretty enamelled fan-mount of Macbeth! Salvator Rosa might, and Piranesi might dash out Duncan's Castle—but Lord help Alderman Boydell and the Royal Academy![24]

Of the painters Boydell commissioned, the greatest catch was Reynolds, then nearing the end of his career and suffering from failing eyesight. The artist wrote to the Duke of Rutland early in 1787:

> But the greatest news relating to virtu is Alderman Boydel's scheme of having pictures and prints taken from those pictures of the most interesting scenes of Shakespear, by which all the painters and engravers find engagements for eight or ten years; he wishes me to do eight pictures, but I have engaged only for one. He has insisted on my taking earnest money, and to my great surprise left upon my table five hundred pounds—to have more as I shall demand.[25]

Finding this a "mode of reasoning . . . not to be resisted," as Northcote put it, Reynolds painted three pictures for Boydell: the death of Cardinal Beaufort (*2 Henry VI*), for which he received, over and above the "earnest money," 500 guineas; Macbeth, Hecate, and the Witches (1,000 guineas);

*But he eventually did subscribe.

and Robin Goodfellow (Puck), for which Northcote cites no price.[26] Only two of the other Boydell artists who figure prominently in the history of British art contributed more than three pictures: Fuseli (three subjects from *A Midsummer Night's Dream,* and one each from *Hamlet, Macbeth, The Tempest, Henry IV, Henry V,* and *King Lear*) and Opie (two each from *Henry VI* and *King John,* one each from *Romeo and Juliet, Timon of Athens,* and *The Winter's Tale*). The others included Barry (*King Lear*), Benjamin West (*King Lear* and *Hamlet*), Joseph Wright of Derby (*The Tempest, The Winter's Tale*), Angelica Kauffmann (*Troilus and Cressida* and *The Two Gentlemen of Verona*), John Hoppner (*Cymbeline*), and Romney[27] (two allegorical subjects and one subject each from *The Tempest* and *Troilus and Cressida*).* The most prolific contributors were Francis Wheatley and the book illustrators Westall, Smirke, and Hamilton, who were represented by a total of ninety canvases.

One of the most curious features of the gallery was the distribution of subjects. No play was allotted a specific number of paintings, for it was thought, reasonably enough, that some plays "exhibit more interesting subjects than others."[28] The subjects each artist would treat were evidently a matter for negotiation between him and Boydell. Certainly there was no correlation between the number of scenes drawn from a given play and the popularity of that play as measured by the number of performances it had had since the middle of the century. The three parts of *Henry VI,* none of which had been seen on the London stage since early in the century, were represented by fifteen pictures. The single play most painted for the gallery, *Henry VIII* (eight pictures), ranked fifteenth in the number of performances, 1751–1800. The plays tied for next place (seven paintings each), *As You Like It, Othello, The Tempest,* the first part of *Henry IV,* and *The Winter's Tale,* ranked eighth, ninth, eleventh, twelfth, and seventeenth, respectively. All the remaining plays were represented by from three to six paintings each; in their incidence, there was no differentiation between *Romeo and Juliet, Hamlet, Richard III, Macbeth,* and *The Merchant of Venice,* which were the five most performed plays in that period, and *Julius Caesar, Timon of Athens, The Two Gentlemen of Verona,* and *Antony and Cleopatra,* which were the least often performed.[29]

Whatever else these paintings were, they were not examples of theatrical art. Little attempt was made to suggest staging, and in the case of a number of the plays, the scenes selected were not included in the "adaptations" then being performed (see Introduction to Part Two, below). Insofar as the paintings reflected current theatrical style at all, they preserved the formal classicism of the then dominant Kemble-Siddons school of acting.

Boydell's Shakespeare, then, was emphatically a book, not a theater, Shakespeare. As befitted the dignity of historical painting, the subjects were taken from the printed page—Shakespeare's nominally, but, in the case of the history plays, with some infusion from the standard histories of Britain. And the pictures' graphic rhetoric, of which there was plenty, was derived from the printed text through the eyes of men influenced by, and anxious to emulate, either the Old Masters or the more recent masters of the rococo. Some Boydell paintings, indeed, like much contemporary book illustration, showed the lengths to which the rococo style could be inappropriately stretched. The spirit of Fragonard and Watteau is not easily reconciled with Shakespeare's.

*Romney also sketched five other subjects for Boydell that he did not execute: the banquet and cavern scenes in *Macbeth,* Mrs. Ford and Mrs. Page (*The Merry Wives of Windsor*), Margery Jourdain conjuring up the fiend (*2 Henry VI*), and the Maid of Orleans (*1 Henry VI*). "He perceived, he said," wrote Allan Cunningham, "that the Boydells wished to employ the elder painters no farther than was sufficient to give an impulse to the undertaking, and then complete it with works from young artists at low prices" (*Lives of the Most Eminent English Painters,* 2:184). The prices Boydell paid ranged from £63 to £525, with two pictures commanding a higher price—Reynolds's *Macbeth* and *The Death of Cardinal Beaufort,* each of which brought him £1,000. Reportedly, it was Boydell's refusal to pay Gainsborough the same sum for each of three paintings, to be completed over a span of three years, that resulted in Gainsborough's being one of the only two considerable artists of the time—the other being Loutherbourg—not represented in the Shakespeare Gallery.

As a whole, the gallery represented an eclectic range of currently fashionable styles.* Boydell cared nothing for consistency or appropriateness: he was bent on making the gallery a showcase for every mode—the grand style, sentimental genre and pastoral, fancy pictures, and for a welcome dash of strangeness, nine of Henry Fuseli's characteristic designs, filled with neurotic intensity and preoccupied with the supernatural, the irrational, and the macabre: especially the six from *King Lear, A Midsummer Night's Dream, Macbeth,* and *The Tempest.* ("Fuseli," his patron the banker Thomas Coutts told Joseph Farington, "had Shakespere's work so completely in His memory as to be able to recollect any passage alluded to—but with all His talent He still had a sort of distortion in His mind, something similar to what is seen more or less in all His pictures.")[30] The engraver John Landseer, father of Edwin, wrote to Sir Walter Scott in 1828: "As far as my experience has gone, I have found those mercenary publishing gentry 'most ignorant of what they're most assured,' namely, the Science of adapting Fine Art to Literature. . . . If you look into Boydell's Shakspear, you find, beside much other wretched mismanagement, no coherence or consistency of parts. Every scene is performed by a fresh set of players. You have as many Hamlets and Macbeths as painters."[31]

The Boydell pictures fell far short of the ambition their visionary entrepreneur entertained for them—so much is clear. But the predominant reason for their failure was unrelated to whatever artistic merit they may or may not have possessed. Most of those who judged them were concerned by what they did with, or to, Shakespeare as the supreme English poet-dramatist. Walpole expressed in a private letter (to Lord Hailes, 21 September 1790) the widely held conviction that Shakespeare's genius transcended even that of the greatest Old Masters: "The Shakespeare Gallery is truly most inadequate to its prototypes—but how should it be worthy of them? could we recall the brightest luminaries of painting, could they do justice to Shakespeare? was Raphael himself as great a genius in his art as the author of *Macbeth*? and who could draw Falstaffe, but the writer of Falstaffe?"[32] This, however, was unfair to Boydell, who in his original preface to the catalogue of the Shakespeare Gallery, dated 1 May 1789, had warned that his elaborate scheme had its built-in limitation:

> Though I believe it will be readily admitted, that no subjects seem so proper to form an English School of Historical Painting, as the Scenes of the immortal Shakespeare; yet it must always be remembered, that he possessed powers which no pencil can reach; for such was the force of his creative imagination, that though he frequently goes beyond nature, he still continues to be natural, and seems only to do that, which nature would have done, had she o'erstepp'd her usual limits[.]—It must not then be expected, that the art of the Painter can ever equal the sublimity of our Poet. The strength of Michael Angelo, united to the grace of Raphael, would have laboured in vain.—For what pencil can give to his airy beings "a local habitation and a name?" It is therefore hoped, that the spectator will view these Pictures with this regard, and not allow his imagination, warmed by the magic powers of the Poet, to expect from Painting, what Painting cannot perform.

Obviously, none of the artists who accepted Boydell's commissions were deterred by the proclaimed impossibility of their task. Shakespeare could, in fact, be painted; the trouble lay in the choice of subject. "It was a subject of complaint," recalled Northcote, who contributed eight scenes from the

*This was a very specific part of Boydell's scheme. In 1897, a mass of documents relating to the gallery was discovered in the cellar of a leading London printseller. Among them was a copy of a speech made (by Boydell's lawyer?) in the course of a suit he had brought against a subscriber who had refused to pay. Reynolds was quoted as remarking to Edmund Burke, "I am sensible that no single school at present in Europe could produce so many good pictures, and if they did they would have a monotonous sameness; they would be all Roman or Venetian, Flemish or French: whereas, you may observe here, as an emblem of the freedom of the country, every artist has taken a different road to what he conceives to be excellence, and many have attained the goal" (Algernon Graves, "A New Light on Alderman Boydell and the Shakespeare Gallery," *Magazine of Art* 21 [1897]: 143–48). In other words, the English way of advancing art was to propel it by a harmonious combination of aesthetic pluralism, patriotism, and free enterprise.

FOUR BOYDELL STYLES. 27 (*top left*). Neoclassic "high art": Samuel Woodforde, *Titus Andronicus* (2. 3) (Royal Shakespeare Theatre Picture Gallery ©). 28 (*top right*). Italian mannerism: Henry Fuseli, *A Midsummer Night's Dream* (4. 1) (Tate Gallery, London). 29 (*bottom left*). French rococo: Johann Heinrich Ramberg, *Twelfth Night* (3. 4) (Yale Center for British Art, Paul Mellon Fund). 30 (*bottom right*). English (Dutch- and Hogarth-influenced) realism: Robert Smirke, *Measure for Measure* (2. 1) (Royal Shakespeare Theatre Picture Gallery ©).

history plays and a single one from *Romeo and Juliet,* "that we painters didn't choose the finest passages to paint from. It was a mistaken complaint, for pithy sayings are addressed to the ear, not to the eye, and they are not suitable for painting. These fine passages are proper for Shakespeare's language, but they are not fit subjects for the painter's language, which is addressed to a different organ."[33] The debate over this point, fed by hundreds of paintings from Shakespeare, would drag its weary length across the next half-century and beyond.

Northcote again: "With the exception of a few pictures by Sir Joshua and Opie, and—I hope I may add—myself, it was such a collection of slip-slop imbecility as was dreadful to look at."[34] This was possibly too severe a judgment, but it was unquestionably true that Boydell's public-spirited project never stirred much enthusiasm among art lovers. The valuation they placed on "those daubs of pictures," as Hazlitt called them,[35] was apparent enough in the prices they brought at auction, an average of no more than £20 each for the ninety canvases by Smirke, Hamilton, Westall, and Wheatley. Fuseli's went for next to nothing. A few, to be sure, were unapologetically hung in private collections. Lord Egremont acquired Reynolds's *Cardinal Beaufort* for 500 guineas, and Sir Francis Baring, the banker, furnished a room in his Hampshire house, recently altered by George Dance at a cost of £25,000, with six Boydell paintings, two each by Opie, Northcote, and Peters.[36]

The engravings had a wider impact. Increasingly worn, they were reproduced, separately and in a number of editions of Shakespeare, for many years to come. Not all lovers of the plays welcomed them. Charles Lamb's diatribe is famous:

> What injury (short of the theatres) did not Boydell's "Shakespeare Gallery" do me with Shakespeare! To have Opie's Shakespeare, Northcote's Shakespeare, light-headed Fuseli's Shakespeare, heavy-headed Romney's Shakespeare, wooden-headed West's Shakespeare (though he did the best in "Lear"), deaf-headed Reynolds's Shakespeare, instead of my, and everybody's Shakespeare. To be tied down to an authentic face of Juliet! To have Imogen's portrait! To confine the illimitable![37]

In another place, Lamb remarked that he preferred to read Shakespeare in Tonson's edition rather than in Boydell's because in the former the plates, though "execrably bad," did not pretend to represent a scene actually found in Shakespeare's text, whereas Boydell's did—and thus destroyed his precious *imaginary* conception.[38] Thackeray had grim recollections of an impressionable childhood exposed to Boydell prints. "There was," he wrote,

> Boydell's Shakespeare, black and ghastly gallery of murky Opies, glum Northcotes, straddling Fuselis! there were Lear, Oberon, Hamlet, with starting muscles, rolling eyeballs, and long pointed quivering fingers; there was little Prince Arthur (Northcote) crying, in white satin, and bidding good Hubert not put out his eyes; there was Hubert crying; there was little Rutland being run through the poor little body by bloody Clifford; there was Cardinal Beaufort (Reynolds) gnashing his teeth, and grinning and howling demoniacally on his deathhbed (a picture frightful to the present day); there was Lady Hamilton (Romney)* waving a torch and dancing before a black background—a melancholy museum indeed. Smirke's delightful Seven Ages only fitfully relieved its general gloom.[39]

Some twenty years later (1876), when the engravings were once more reproduced, a writer in the *Quarterly Review* was more judicious:

*This was the picture of *Cassandra Raving,* from *Troilus and Cressida,* one of the many Romney paintings for which Lady Hamilton posed. For whatever it may be worth—her early life is swathed in mystery, some of it scandalous—one might note that she is said to have had a distant personal connection with Boydell, having entered the service of his brother-in-law at the age of thirteen as a nursery maid (Chamberlain, *George Romney,* p. 103).

> It is . . . true . . . to say that from such a company nothing but artistic mediocrity was to be expected. . . . On examining the illustrations carefully, we are conscious of a feeling of disappointment. The volume [of engravings], on the whole, is a record of lost opportunities. Still it is interesting and valuable as a representation of the state of art in England at the time, and in one or two instances, where the painter broke away from the conventional shackles of an artificial age, we have satisfactory results.[40]

The influence the Boydell pictures had on later painters of Shakespearean subjects is not documented; almost the only evidence we have is an incidental remark by W. B. Scott: "Even to the youngest of us [aspiring artists] the ignorance of costume and other historical properties was apparent, and even dramatically the action and expression of the actors were manifestly untrue."[41] The original bound "galleries" were too costly for many artists, established or aspiring, to buy, although John Crome ("Old Crome"), the founder of the Norwich school of landscapists, is said to have possessed both sets.[42] But the later, cheaper editions reached a wider audience, and there can be no question that most artists who grew up in the first half of the nineteenth century, at least, were acquainted with the Boydell engravings, the memory of which must have subliminally affected, in one way or another, their approach to Shakespeare.*

The engraved gallery had a mixed influence on the Shakespearean subjects that would be most painted in the next century; some Boydell scenes would be represented over and over in subsequent Shakespearean art, but among the other popular subjects there were at least as many that Boydell's contributors did not paint. Among the former were *Much Ado About Nothing* 3.1 (Beatrice eavesdrops on Hero and Ursula); *Romeo and Juliet* 3.5 (the lovers' farewell), 5.3 (the tomb scene), and the several scenes with Juliet and the Nurse; *Merry Wives of Windsor* 1.1 (Slender and Anne Page and Mr. Page's offstage dinner); *A Midsummer Night's Dream* 2.1, 2; 4.1 (the fairy scenes); and *Merchant of Venice* 2.5 (Shylock leaves Jessica in charge), 3.2 (the casket scene), and 5.1 (the Lorenzo-Jessica love scene). Other subjects in the gallery, for example *Twelfth Night* 4.3 (the brief exchange of Sebastian and Olivia) and 5.1 (the long dénouement scene), and many of the scenes in the history plays, would seldom if ever be depicted again.

Most striking of all is the absence from the gallery of a number of scenes that were destined to become staples of the artist's repertoire: *Merchant of Venice* 4.1 (the trial scene); *Romeo and Juliet* 2.2 (the balcony scene) and 4.1 (Friar Laurence gives Juliet the potion); *Macbeth* 2.2 (the dagger scene outside Duncan's chamber); and *Cymbeline* 4.2 (Imogen in the cave). The popularity of some of these scenes, neglected by Boydell, was doubtless due in part to their fame on the nineteenth-century stage, when the breach between performance and artistic presentation, at its widest in the Boydell Gallery, was narrowed.

Not all the trends in Shakespearean art in the following decades could, of course, be associated with Boydell. Easel artists also had at their disposal numerous engravings from other sources, including the editions illustrated by Smirke, Stothard, Singleton, and others, to suggest subjects and compositions. It has been reported that an incomplete count of the designs of Shakespearean scenes found in editions of the plays or collections of prints published between 1780 and 1810 totals almost 650, not including the 167 Boydell prints and those published separately.[43]† One

*The iconographical evidence bearing on the point has yet to be studied, so far as I know. Another worthwhile exercise in research might be devoted to determining how far, if at all, the Boydell paintings with their groupings, rhetorical poses, and settings affected the evolving manner of Shakespearean stage mounting and performance in the early nineteenth century.

†In 1835, an enthusiast in Gloucestershire named Thomas Turner began to interleave his copy of the 1802 Boydell edition with engravings. The resulting 44-volume set, now at the Huntington Library, contains 3,000 prints. Although many of them represent actors, scenery, and historical personages in the plays, the remainder are said to constitute "a virtually complete run of the engraved book illustrations down to about 1820" (Robert R. Wark, *Drawings from the Turner Shakespeare* [San Marino, Cal., 1973], p. 7).

31. Francis Wheatley, *Scene from "The Two Gentlemen of Verona"* (5. 4) (Woodmason's New Shakespeare Gallery) (Yale Center for British Art, Paul Mellon Collection). Valentine intervenes as Proteus threatens Silvia: "I'll force thee yield to my desire." Proteus will immediately apologize, and Julia, in breeches, will swoon.

source was a direct imitation of the Boydell Gallery, undertaken while the enterprise in Pall Mall was in its first bloom of fame. In 1792, a "Society of Gentlemen" announced the establishment in Dublin of the Irish Shakespeare Gallery.[44] The only publicly mentioned member of the "society" was James Woodmason, a London stationer who had moved to Ireland sometime in the early 1780s, after his premises were destroyed by a fire in which seven of his children perished. The project's inspiration was obvious enough: it was to be an edition of Shakespeare that would include seventy-two engravings made from original paintings, two for each play. The gallery opened in May 1793 with eighteen pictures, but shortly after five more were added, it closed. Woodmason, evidently blessed with more optimism than prudence, then moved the collection to London, where he installed it in rooms belonging to the Polygraphic Society in old Schomberg House, almost directly opposite the Boydell Gallery, and opened for business in January 1794 with four additional paintings. So brazen an attempt to compete was foredoomed, particularly in view of Boydell's commanding position in the trade; the New Shakespeare Gallery, after suffering various vicissitudes, closed in the spring of 1795. Eleven of the promised plates were issued and six more were left unfinished (the edition itself never materialized). Twenty-two years later, in 1817, Woodmason's son issued all seventeen as *A Series of Engravings to Illustrate the Works of Shakespeare*. The paintings were, with a single exception, the work of artists who had already contributed to the prototype gallery or were in the process of doing so: Peters (six subjects), Fuseli and Opie (five each), Hamilton (four), and Northcote and Wheatley (three each). The selection of subjects did not slavishly follow that in the Boydell Gallery: only about ten of Woodmason's were to be seen across the road as well, and only one artist (Fuseli, with *Macbeth and the Witches*) painted the same subject for both galleries.

Another exercise in commissioning and engraving pictures illustrating English literary subjects was that of Thomas Macklin, a printer and publisher in Fleet Street.[45] In 1787, some months after Boydell had announced his plan, Macklin issued a prospectus in which he proposed to commission one hundred paintings, to be hung in a permanent exhibition

32. Thomas Gainsborough, *Young Hobbinol and Gandaretta* (Macklin's Poet's Gallery) (Huntington Library and Art Gallery). The only (tenuous) connection this rural idyll has with the poem it purportedly illustrated, William Somerville's *Hobbinol, or the Rural Games, A Burlesque Poem, in Blank Verse* (1740) is the fleeting mention, early on, of Hobbinol and Gandaretta—the king and queen of the May in the poem—playing together as children.

and engraved and sold in groups of four (but not included in an edition, as Boydell's were). Since he did not erect a special building, as Boydell did, Macklin was able to open his gallery a year earlier, in 1788. Only twenty-four of the projected hundred paintings were included in the series of engravings, and several others were issued separately. The poets illustrated in the series itself were Shakespeare, Collins, Gray, Pope, Shenstone, Thomson, Somerville, Spenser, Chaucer, Mrs. Barbauld, Gay, Jerningham, Mallet, Prior, and Goldsmith. An "Ode to Meditation," by a writer of almost desperate obscurity, Dr. George Gregory, was represented by Reynolds's *Tuccia, the Vestal Virgin,* engraved outside the series. The selection of subjects faithfully conformed to the range of poets represented in the annual exhibitions, and so did the selection of artists, all but a handful of whom—not including Gainsborough—also labored for Boydell.

Macklin's gallery, though its scale was reduced, seems to have been moderately successful; at least it did not ruin its owner, as Boydell's eventually did. But the next such project, and as it proved the last, was not so fortunate. It came at a time when the Boydell Gallery had already creamed off the market, and to follow a Shakespeare Gallery with a Gallery of the Miltonic Sublime (its official title), even if it contained less than one-third of the number of paintings Boydell commissioned, required more confidence than the state of the fine book and art trade, depressed by the wars, justified.

Henry Fuseli, the projector, was not among Britain's most fashionable artists, active and prominent though he had been in London for two decades.[46] Along with Hogarth and Blake, who engraved several of his designs, Fuseli well symbolized the increasingly closer association of painting and literature that we have traced in chapter 1. He produced more pictures from English literature in several media—oil, watercolor, pencil, sepia, ink-and-wash—than did any other important artist of his time. But whereas Hogarth was the prototypical beef-and-beer Englishman and Blake also was a Londoner born and bred, however odd, the Swiss-born Fuseli was an alien. Despite his long residence in England and his close connection with the Royal Academy, he remained, culturally, temperamentally, and artistically, an outsider. His was the first English oeuvre, and as it proved the only considerable one, to be produced by the free exercise of a feverish imagination on the literary text.

A product of the *Sturm und Drang* movement in Switzerland and a disciple of Johann Jakob Bodmer, whose mission in life was to revivify German literature by setting before it the example of English poetry, as a young man Fuseli steeped himself in Milton, Pope, Gray, Thomson, Young, and above all Shakespeare. His first ambition had been to be a poet, and he actually translated some of Shakespeare into German. But he discovered that his dominant talent was for painting—specifically, painting that had its inspirational origin in sublime or dramatic poetry. While he nurtured this ambition, he made a living by accepting commissions to illustrate books. In 1769, for example, he designed frontispieces for the fourth edition of Smollett's *Peregrine Pickle.* (His own favorite among contemporary novelists, however, seems to have been Sterne, whom he never illustrated. Farington wrote that he "spoke with raptures of Sterne's Sentimental Journey, saying He preferred a page of it to the whole Spectator [or] Rambler," considering it a "spontaneous, true effusion" in opposition to John Hoppner's opinion that it was "the effect of labour.")[47]

During a long stay in Rome (1770–78), Fuseli was overpowered by the Sistine Chapel ceiling, which suggested to him the scale and magnificence with which a national monument to Shakespeare might be erected—a grandiose project in the spirit of the Shakespeare Jubilee of 1769 that his friend Garrick had produced at Stratford as a lavish exercise in Bardolatry. "He saw in imagination," wrote one of his early biographers,

> a long and shadowy succession of pictures. He figured to himself a magnificent temple, and filled it as the illustrious artists of Italy did the Sistine with pictures from his favourite poet. All was arranged according to character. In the panels and accessories were the figures of the chief heroes and heroines; on the extensive walls were delineated the changes of many-coloured life—the ludicrous and the sad, the pathetic and the humorous, domestic happiness and heroic aspirations—while the dome which crowned the whole exhibited scenes of higher emotion, the joys of heaven, the agonies of hell, all that was supernatural and all that was terrible.[48]

Nothing came of this vision of a Michelangelesque Pantheon dedicated exclusively to Shakespeare, but John Boydell, whose own vision was supported, as Fuseli's was not, by many years of business experience and large amounts of capital, accomplished the same end more prosaically in the Shakespeare Gallery. The nearest Fuseli himself came to realizing the dream he had in the Sistine Chapel was a celebration not of Shakespeare but of Milton, his second literary deity. In 1790, when he was finishing his paintings for Boydell, he was engaged by the publisher Joseph Johnson to provide thirty designs for an edition of Milton to be annotated by William Cowper, who would also translate the Latin and Italian poems: "a Milton that is to rival, and, if possible, to exceed in splendor Boydell's Shakespeare," Cowper wrote to a friend.[49] The venture was attractive to Fuseli, who counted Cowper as his favorite contemporary poet and had recently gone through the manuscript of his translation of Homer with a friendly but critical eye. Cowper, however, went into one of his periods of mental breakdown and, as a further deterrent, Boydell announced his own forthcoming (but never realized) edition of Milton; so Johnson dropped his plan. Fuseli then committed himself to a project he had thought of the year before, "a series of Pictures for *Exhibition,* Such as Boydells and Macklins."[50] "*Satan, Sin and Death,*" he wrote to his patron, the Liverpool banker-scholar William Roscoe, alluding to a Miltonic subject hitherto most notably treated by Hogarth, "would not Suffer me to think of any thing mortal or immortal till I had flung them into picturesque Existence on a Miniature-Canvas thirteen feet by ten."[51]

This was in 1791, when Fuseli was in the process of more than doubling his original goal of twenty pictures. As the years passed, his mood alternated between despair and exhilaration. Early in 1793, he told Roscoe that "Milton is Likely to eat me up before I Shall be able to dine once with him."[52] But the next year he wrote that the scheme would "*make me*. . . . The plan . . . exceeds in magnificence and I hope in execution, as far as it is gone . . . most Schemes that went before me."[53] "Unlimited applause and fresh green hopes of Success are indeed poured out before my pictures, by all who See them," he reported to Roscoe in 1795, adding, "even Americans seem to be Struck by them."[54] The next year he passed the halfway mark, with twenty-three canvases finished.

His megalomania grew apace. By this time, he was referring to the

Milton Gallery as "a monument of myself" (hence his refusal of offers from Lawrence and Opie to contribute pictures)[55] and declaring that even Michelangelo, "great as he was would in my Situation perhaps not have dared to undertake" the colossal task.[56] His hope that he could complete the whole collection by March or April 1797—"the Largest room in London will not perhaps be capacious enough to hold what I have finished advanced or begun"—was, not surprisingly, unfulfilled.[57] The Gallery of the Miltonic Sublime finally opened in May 1799, in the Royal Academy's former rooms in Pall Mall. Forty-seven paintings were on display, some of them, in the true spirit of history painting, as wide as the canvas he had described to Roscoe eight years before, and two feet taller. The first month's receipts were only £117, and they dwindled thereafter. Despite his net loss that season, Fuseli reopened the gallery the next year, but with no better luck. "All who go, praise," he complained to Roscoe, "but Milton Can not stand the competition of *Seringapatam* [a panorama then drawing crowds] and the posies of Portraits and Knickknacks of Sommerset-house [the Royal Academy's new home]—my exhibition must be broke up, and the Question now remains what am I to do?"[58] After four months, the show closed for good. "The greater part of my exhibition," Fuseli told another friend, "the rejected Family of a silly Father, are now again rolled up, Or packed together against the Walls of my Study to be Seasoned for dust, the worm, and oblivion."[59]

Short of a lottery, which evidently could not be arranged to rescue Fuseli as it was a few years later in behalf of Boydell's failed fortune, how could his "Enormous Miltonic Lumberstock," as he called it, be profitably liquidated? "I have often imagined that it might be possible to bring about a Milton-Society who might unite to do Something for me, in order to perpetuate His Ideas: but at present my Mind is so occupied with academic Nonsense"—he had entered upon his duties as professor of painting the year before—"that I Can neither form nor properly digest a Scheme of that kind."[60] Roscoe solved the problem to the extent of taking eleven

33. Henry Fuseli, *Figure from a Simile . . . of the Spirits Assembled in the New-Raised Hall of Pandemonium* (Milton Gallery) (Tate Gallery, London).

. . . faery elves,
Whose midnight revels, by a forest-side
Or fountain, some belated peasant sees,
Or dreams he sees, while overhead the Moon
Sits arbitress and nearer to the Earth
Wheels her pale course: they, on their mirth and dance
Intent, with jocund music charm his ear . . .

Paradise Lost, bk. 1, ll. 781–87

paintings to decorate his dining room, in part repayment of the £700 in direct "loans" he had given the painter.[61]* Fuseli did manage to sell a few others. Thomas Coutts bought *The Vision of the Lazar House,* which he left to his daughter the Countess of Guilford, at whose home Fuseli was to die. Lord Rivers took *Satan Calling His Legions,* which later went to the Duke of Wellington, and Sir Thomas Lawrence bought three more.[62] But in 1801, when the young American artist Washington Allston, who had seen and admired engravings of several of the pictures back home in Charleston, South Carolina, visited the studio, most of the paintings were still there, hanging on the walls or cluttering the floor. Allston singled one out as having "made a great impression on him." "No, you don't like that," the momentarily humbled Fuseli exclaimed. "You can't like that; it's bad; it's damned bad!"[63]

Fuseli would undoubtedly have revived his former high estimate of his Miltonic oeuvre if the gallery had been a commercial success. Some of his fellow artists thought better of his work than he did. "O Society for Encouragement of Art!" exclaimed Blake. "O King & Nobility of England! Where have you hid Fuseli's Milton? Is Satan troubled at his Exposure?"[64] Later, Benjamin Robert Haydon, a fellow megalomaniac and aspirant to the grand style, would write in the *Encyclopaedia Britannica,* "Fuzeli [*sic*] was undoubtedly the greatest genius of that day. His Milton Gallery showed a range of imagination equal to the poet's."[65]

After the Milton Gallery closed, Fuseli continued to illustrate books—editions of Cowper, Gray, Thomson, *Paradise Lost* once again, and two of Shakespeare. Living until 1825, he was the last survivor of the major eighteenth-century painters of literary subjects, a conspicuous but unappreciated original in an era when convention, tameness, and sentimentality dominated the portrayal of themes from English poetry. His devotion to Milton never wavered. At dinner at his fellow academician Farington's home, years after the Gallery of the Miltonic Sublime had ended in fiasco, "Fuseli," as his host wrote, "spoke with tears in His eyes of a passage in Milton as excelling in beauty, & sublimity, and feeling, all that He had read."[66]

34. **Henry Fuseli,** ***Milton as a Boy, with His Mother*** (1799–1800) (Walker Art Gallery, Liverpool). A copy of a painting designed for the Milton Gallery. As a relief from the oppressive "sublimity" that characterized most of the pictures in this ambitious but unsuccessful enterprise, Fuseli chose a few domestic subjects nominally from Milton's life. But there is nothing in the biographical record to make this conventional mother-and-child portrait particularly applicable to the poet.

*The novelist Maria Edgeworth visited Roscoe's mansion on 6 April 1813. "Turning from the drawings of Michael Angelo to a room full of Fuseli's horribly distorted figures," she wrote in a letter, "I could not help feeling astonishment not only at the bad taste but at the infinite conceit and presumption of Fuseli! How could this man ever make himself a name? I believe he gave Mr. Roscoe these pictures, else I suppose they would not be here sprawling their fantastic lengths, like misshapen dreams" (*Maria Edgeworth: Letters from England 1813–1844,* ed. Christina Colvin [Oxford, 1971], pp. 12–13).

CHAPTER 3

A period of lethargy (1800–1830): Ut pictura poesis *reinterpreted; the disappearance of the first generation of literary artists.—The "fortunate fall" of history painting.—The rise of genre, with subjects from literature.—Wilkie and the debate over Crabbe's realism.—Landscape and Scott.*

From the end of the eighteenth century, which was ushered out by the Milton Gallery, to the beginning of Victoria's reign in 1837, with few exceptions (though, since they included Turner and Constable, and the subject painters Wilkie and Martin, they were important ones), British art went through a period of lethargy. The whole basis of thinking about art gradually changed. The campaign to establish a school of history painting had suffered twin setbacks with the failure of Boydell's and Fuseli's bold attempts. The inherited aesthetic doctrine that had governed judgment in artistic matters lost its authority, and no comparable body of theory emerged to take its place. Criticism, largely in the hands of the reviewers of the annual exhibitions, tended to be *ad hoc* and pragmatic rather than theoretical, though among the critics was the dominating figure of William Hazlitt, a trained painter who had exhibited miniature portraits at the Royal Academy in 1802 and 1805 and made (unexhibited) ones of Wordsworth and Coleridge in 1803. With the advent of a large and influential bourgeois audience for painting, to be described in the next chapter, the emphasis in everyday art discussion shifted from the aesthetic to the social and moral: new buyers, new ideals.

Nothing better illustrates this change in the cultural orientation of art than the fortunes of the *ut pictura poesis* concept.[1] After the appearance of Lessing's *Laocoön,* with its crucial distinction between the spatial and temporal arts, Reynolds, formerly a true believer, recanted somewhat, in his thirteenth discourse. Another painter in the neoclassic mode, James Barry, declared in one of his Royal Academy lectures, delivered 1794–98, that "painting is not, as has been said, a silent poem, and poetry a speaking picture; but, much more truly, that painting is poetry realised, and that full, complete, and perfect poetry is indeed nothing more than an animated account or relation of the mere conception of a picture."[2] Fuseli, writing in the *Analytical Review* in those same years, reversed his anti-Lessing position and lamented that "from long bigotted deference to the old maxim that poetry is painting in speech, and painting dumb poetry, the two sisters, marked with features so different by nature, and the great masters of composition, her oracles, have been constantly confounded with each other by the herds of mediocrity and thoughtless imitation."[3] John Opie, still another professor of painting at the Royal Academy, told his students in 1807 that "the most striking beauties, as presented to one sense, being frequently wholly untranslateable into the language of another, it necessarily results, that many interesting passages in history and poetry are incapable of affording more than a bald and insipid *representation on canvas.*"[4]

These various affirmations that the parallel between poetry and painting was less marked and mutually productive than the adherents of *ut pictura poesis* for a century had believed were echoed by Romantic literary critics who strengthened the growing anti-pictorialist tradition in poetry. "What are deemed fine descriptions," wrote Coleridge, "produce their effects almost purely by a charm of words, with which & with whose combinations, we associate *feelings* indeed, but no distinct *Images.*"[5] Like Barry in his own time and Ruskin half a century later, Coleridge subsumed both of the sister arts under the single encompassing ideal of Poetry, which was now defined not as expression specifically in language but as expression regardless of the medium employed. There were, it is true, some diehard believers in the old notion of poetic pictorialism. Leigh Hunt, for one, declared, "To say . . . that the poet does not include the painter in his more visible creations, is to deprive him of half his privileges, nay, of half his very poems."[6] But it was in the new, Coleridgean form that the Horatian tenet persisted, although it ceased to be the subject of much profitable debate.

The concept of the mutual attraction of the two arts, however, was too deep-seated and convenient to be cast aside, and if it languished as an aesthetic principle, it flourished on a more demotic level as a statement of a demonstrable fact, the joining of painting and the written word in practice. The conjunction that led to the invocation of the "sisterhood" as an ever handy cliché took several forms, the most notable of which, in terms of popular culture, was the increasing popularity—for it was nothing new—of the illustrated book in the publishing trade at large. For our purposes, the physical conjunction was most evident at every annual exhibition of art, where the subjects of poetry and other kinds of literature were placed within the frames of paintings. The literary painting was in fact the culmination, in English middle-class culture, of *ut pictura poesis,* though in a form that no eighteenth-century theorist could have anticipated.

During this transition period, most of the excitement at the annual exhibitions, aside from short-lived bursts of interest in one now-forgotten painter or another, centered on such artists as Turner and Constable the landscapists, Lawrence the portraitist, Wilkie the Scottish genre painter, and Martin the wide-canvas master of cataclysm. Most of the eighteenth-century masters who had occasionally treated literary themes, such as Reynolds and Romney, had gone from the scene. Fuseli exhibited his last pictures at the Royal Academy in the year of his death, 1825. Benjamin

West painted pictures from Pope, Gray, and Milton before his own death in 1820. Two lesser figures, Hamilton and Wheatley, had died in 1801.

Among the prolific minor artists who represented subjects from English literature in these years were a few whose names and some of whose pictures have survived because their specialties appealed to certain well-established breeds of collectors—George Clint, DeWilde's successor as the graphic recorder of contemporary English drama; the animal painters James Ward, Richard Barrett Davis, and William Barraud. But most of those whose paintings from literature were seen at the exhibitions year after year are almost totally forgotten: the Corboulds (Richard, Henry, and George), the Chalons (Alfred Edward and John James), the Stephanoffs (James and Francis Philip), Henry Singleton, Alexander Carse, John Cawse, Henry Perronet Briggs, Stephen Francis Rigaud, Samuel Drummond, William Artaud, Henry Pierce Bone, John Boaden . . .

As far as literary painting was concerned, therefore, this was not a time of giants. Instead, its interest lies in the trends these industrious artists, most of them not far above the rank of hacks, represented. After 1800, there was a sharp decline in the incidence of pictures from currently talked-about novels and poems whose fame was to prove ephemeral. Between that year and 1815, only a dozen or so paintings from contemporary fiction are recorded, mostly illustrating Gothic romances like *The Mysteries of Udolpho.* But after 1825 and extending to mid-century, there was considerably greater interest in such novelists—popular then, today universally regarded as "minor"—as Captain Marryat, William Harrison Ainsworth, and (not only minor, but utterly missing from literary history) Mrs. Samuel Carter Hall. Meanwhile, the representation of currently popular but equally evanescent poetry, so marked a phenomenon in the period 1780–1800, dwindled into insignificance. Just as subjects from Scott came to dominate the treatment of fiction in art, so Scott (again), Byron, and Moore edged out the negligible versemakers of their day, to be succeeded eventually by Tennyson above all. (A small phenomenon of 1825–50 was the persistence of several eighteenth-century favorites, among them Blair, Akenside, and Collins.) The market for pictures from the small fry of contemporary literature, as we now see them to have been, simply vanished.

It is hard to tell just what was the prevailing attitude toward pictures from English literature during the first three decades of the century. Privately, a number of painters indulged the by now well established habit of literary reference. Possibly inspired by Thomas Girtin's club mentioned in chapter 1—in the interim there had been another such group, brought together by John Sell Cotman, a member of the original club—in 1808 eight or ten artists formed the Society for the Study of Epic and Pastoral Design, informally known as the Bread and Cheese Society, who met every week to paint agreed-upon subjects from literature.[7] They would continue to do so (with changing membership) until 1851, by which time their devotion to literary themes had long since spread to the public at large. Their subjects over the years, apart from non-English literature, included Tam o' Shanter and the witches, the balcony scene from *Romeo and Juliet, The Toilet (The Rape of the Lock), Robinson Crusoe, Rasselas, The Vicar of Wakefield,* the *Spectator, The Faerie Queene, Paradise Lost, Comus,* "the sonnets and plays, *not* historical, of Shakespeare," Scott's novels and poems, *The Castle of Otranto,* the novels of G. P. R. James, and the poems of

35. Henry Singleton, *Palemon and Lavinia* (undated) (Tate Gallery, London). From Thomson's *The Seasons* ("Autumn"); one of the few surviving, or identifiable, paintings by this prolific artist. Like Fuseli's *Milton as a Boy,* it merely adopts a literary reference to embellish a cliché subject, rustic lovers in a gleaning field.

Wordsworth, Byron, Rogers, and Moore—a fairly comprehensive sample of the subjects that proved to be most popular in the first half of the century.

But the failure of the Milton Gallery and of Fuseli's attempts to sell off most of the pictures, as well as the bargain-basement prices commanded by the Boydell Shakespeare paintings when they were auctioned in 1805, suggests that the art-loving public in these early years of the century was not wildly enthusiastic about literary pictures, at least of the varieties brought into being by Fuseli and Boydell. Whatever their intrinsic worth—many were inconveniently large, and probably just as many were of undesirable subjects—the attempted sale within five years of 47 paintings from Milton and 167 from Shakespeare must have glutted the market. Modern art auction houses would never contemplate so depressant a practice.

The nineteen-year-old Charles Robert Leslie, writing to his sister back in America in 1813, may have accurately sized up the demand when he reported that "pictures from modern poets [that is, all English ones, among others] do not take, and even if they should, it is uncertain how long they may continue in vogue. To insure a picture currency, therefore,

36. John Martin, *Sadak in Search of the Waters of Oblivion* (RA 1812) (Southampton Art Gallery). Although the source of the painting was James Ridley's eighteenth-century collection of allegedly Oriental stories, *Tales of the Genii,* when an engraving of it appeared in the *Keepsake* for 1828 it accompanied a poem by Shelley (see text, p. 445). In later pictures, Martin adopted the same overwhelming mountainous settings as background for better-known figures from literature, such as Gray's Bard (pl. 298) and Byron's Manfred (pl. 331).

it is necessary that it should tell either some scriptural or classic story. Even Shakespeare, Dante, and Milton, are scarcely sufficiently canonised to be firm ground."[8] To be sure, Leslie, in that very year, exhibited at the Royal Academy a painting from *Macbeth,* suggested by the lines ". . . now wither'd Murder / Alarum'd by his sentinel, the wolf"; and soon afterward, he laid the foundations of his prosperous career as a literary artist by producing scenes from *The Merry Wives of Windsor,* as well as from Scott and the *Spectator.* But these were narrative and dramatic subjects, suited both to his own talents and to the taste of the public, and meanwhile there remained some market resistance to the portrayal of more lyrical or "poetic" subjects. It was said much later that the florid pictures of William Hilton, a specialist in *The Faerie Queene,* "met with very few purchasers."[9] This may well have been true also of the work of Henry Howard, who specialized in Milton. The frequency with which pictures with suspiciously similar titles, by Hilton and Howard and others, appear in successive catalogues of the Royal Academy and the British Institution (founded in 1806 as an important alternative exhibition place) implies that they were not necessarily repetitions to oblige a demand but the same canvases, shuttled from one exhibition to another in an attempt to find buyers. A reviewer in 1834 remarked of Howard's *The Gardens of Hesperus* (from *Comus*), which had remained unsold at both exhibitions that year, "if poetic subjects were not at a sad discount, it would soon find a purchaser."[10]

That so many subjects from the standard English poets continued to be painted, whether or not the art-buying public could absorb them all, was to some extent a reflection of the reprint publishing business, where new editions of these poets were continually being put together. Although Henry Singleton was not primarily a book illustrator, his lengthy production record, including most of the hundred literary paintings he exhibited between 1785 and 1839, was typical of that of most artists who worked for publishers: Shakespeare, Ossian, Sterne, Milton, Spenser, the *Spectator.* But Singleton also could recognize straws in the wind when he saw them, and the most significant aspect of this list was the appearance, beginning in 1814, of subjects from Byron (the first was *Conrad and Gulnare,* from *The Corsair*), and from Scott, beginning in 1820 with *Old Mortality.* The recorded oeuvres of two veterans of the book-illustration trade are equally symptomatic. In 1816 Stothard, then sixty-one, showed his first subject from Burns (*Tam o' Shanter*) at the Royal Academy, and in 1828, his first from Scott. Westall made designs for Sharpe's edition of Scott's *Marmion* in 1809; at the Academy exhibition of 1832, he exhibited *Haidee Watching Don Juan as He Sleeps* and a scene from Scott's *The Wild Huntsman.*

Burns (posthumously), Scott, Byron, Moore: these became the new golden names in the world of illustrative art, restoring the faltering fortunes of literary painting on a broader, more popular basis. And as they were appearing with ever greater frequency in the exhibition catalogues, the names of new artists with arresting new specialties were beginning to appear as well. John Martin made his first splash at the Royal Academy in 1812 with *Sadak in Search of the Waters of Oblivion* (pl. 36). Although he commanded most attention with his spectacular nightmarish visions of biblical subjects—Joshua, the fall of Babylon, and Belshazzar's Feast—in the years before Victoria came to the throne he also exhibited several pictures from Milton, Goldsmith, Gray, and Byron. Between 1821 and

1835, William Etty, whose main interest in English poetry was the occasions it provided for painting the unclothed female, showed several subjects from *Comus* and *The Faerie Queene*. But neither Martin, haunted by fantastic visions of catastrophe in monstrous natural and architectural settings, nor Etty, haunted by the nude, influenced the course that the painting of literary subjects was to take during the rest of the century. Each, in his own way, was too specialized to appeal to the domestic tastes of the new, expanding art public. Instead, the future belonged to adaptable artists who had the good fortune to discover what the public most wanted.

The most momentous event of the time that determined the future of nineteenth-century literary painting was what might be called the fortunate fall of the history picture. We saw in chapter 1 that scenes from English history had become frequent subjects of art in the last third of the eighteenth century. Their popularity increased through the first decades of the nineteenth, peaking, as Roy Strong points out, in the 1840s, when as many as twenty such paintings were hung every year at the Royal Academy.[11] Among these hundreds of pictures were many that could also be called literary paintings, because, as the entries in the catalogues show, their subjects were as closely identified with Shakespeare and Scott as with historiographers: Richard I, King John, Richard II, Henry V, the Princes in the Tower, Cardinal Wolsey, Mary Queen of Scots, Cromwell, Charles II.

By no means all pictures from English history painted in response to this developing taste conformed to Thackeray's scornful description of history paintings as "pieces of canvas from twelve to thirty feet long, representing for the most part personages who never existed, . . . performing actions that never occurred, and dressed in costumes they never could have worn."[12] Such pictures—history paintings in the old sense of the term—continued to be produced, but the market for them, governed

37. James Drummond, *The Porteous Mob* (Royal Scottish Academy 1855) (National Gallery of Scotland). A historical scene treated with dramatic chiaroscuro, the nighttime riot in Edinburgh that was touched off by the execution of a smuggler in 1735. Events in Scottish history were a staple source of nineteenth-century British art, and their appeal was enhanced by their frequent association with Scott's novels, in this case *The Heart of Mid-Lothian,* which begins with the Porteous riot (chaps. 4–7).

38. Solomon A. Hart, *King Richard and Soldan Saladin* (RA 1835) (Walker Art Gallery, Liverpool). The steady stream of medieval subjects in British art was fed from numerous sources, from Shakespeare's history plays in the late eighteenth century to Tennyson's *Idylls of the King* in the Victorian era. This painting is from Scott's *The Talisman* (chap. 9): Saladin, disguised as an Arabian physician, attends the ailing Richard Coeur de Lion.

by space considerations if nothing else, had largely vanished except for local corporations (and, in the 1840s, Parliament: see chapter 8, below) desirous of animating the wall expanses of their new public buildings with inspiring themes.

While "heroic" history painting was in irreversible decline, alongside the big outdated canvases flourished smaller pictures belonging to the new category of "sentimental" or "domestic" history. It was here that historical subjects were truly popularized. The paramount reason for their rise in esteem among the art-loving public was the fact that, as early as the Shakespeare Gallery, painters increasingly chose, not the conventional stately element of English history, but the domestic life of historical

39. John Gilbert, *Cardinal Wolsey and the Duke of Buckingham* (British Institution 1862) (Tate Gallery, London). An old, conventional subject of history painting kept alive into the mid-Victorian era: a meeting of the leaders of the court in Shakespeare's *Henry VIII* (1. 1). This is a sketch for the picture now in the Royal Shakespeare Theatre Picture Gallery.

40. Charles Landseer, *The Temptation of Andrew Marvell* (RA 1841) (Victoria & Albert Museum, Crown Copyright). A product of the swelling artistic interest in the anecdotal side of history, illustrating a story in John Dove's brief *Life of Andrew Marvell* (1832). The corrupt Lord Treasurer Danby visited Marvell, politician as well as poet, in his garret and "out of *pure affection*" left behind a treasury order for £1,000. Marvell called him back and summoned his own servant to testify that he had dined on the remains of a shoulder of mutton. "My Lord," he said, "do you hear that? Andrew Marvell's dinner is provided; there's your paper. I want it not. . . . I live here to serve my constituents; the Ministry may seek men for their purpose; *I am not one.*"

characters, their private joys and suffering—in short, the biographical side of history as imagined, in their respective ways, by Scott, Carlyle, and Macaulay. Like Thackeray, in the first paragraph of *The History of Henry Esmond,* people "would have History familiar rather than heroic." As history painting of the old kind moved toward almost total eclipse, a writer in *Blackwood's Magazine* (1850) could declare that "probably no subjects are more generally popular than those that may be styled the homely-historical; scenes in the private apartments of royalty; the personal adventures and perils of princes, whether in the palace or the prison—on the steps of the throne or the verge of the scaffold."[13]* The emphasis was on "homely" rather than "historical," and "historical" itself in practice was to be interpreted broadly, because from portraying intimate events in the lives that were the stuff of history it was a short, easy, and irresistible step to portraying similar events in the lives of fictional characters, as the mixed oeuvres of such popular practitioners of "historical genre" as Sir John Gilbert, Mr. and Mrs. E. M. Ward, John Pettie, and William Frederick Yeames (pl. 41) amply show. This is what constituted the fortunate fall of history painting. With the great expansion of dramatis personae and incident, taken more and more from English literature, history painting (in both the specialized and the broad senses) was democratized; and the boundary between it and narrative genre, whose very essence was domesticity, became ever less distinct. As history painting in the old mode disappeared, genre, by a kind of contrary action, rose to the top of the hierarchy of nineteenth-century popular art.†

This was probably the most significant and far-reaching shift of direction in the whole history of nineteenth-century English taste in painting, involving many more artists and art-buyers, not to say sheer number of paintings, than the late Victorian drift away from subject pictures in the tentative direction of Impressionism. We saw in chapter 1 that the taste

*Here British taste closely followed that in France, where "indoor scenes of familial or amorous drama, rather than outdoor scenes of military conflicts and Christian miracles," as Robert Rosenblum puts it, came to dominate history painting (*French Painting 1774–1830: The Age of Revolution* [exhibition catalogue, Grand Palais (Paris), Detroit Institute of Arts, and Metropolitan Museum of Art, 1974–75], p. 169).

†The word *genre* in the sense in which modern art historians apply it to Morland and Wilkie—scenes from the life of the humble in country and town, in the manner of the old Dutch artists—was greatly expanded in nineteenth-century usage; writers at the time were disturbed by its elastic definition, which came to include, as a writer in 1857 said, "a class of works which, taken from polite society or genteel comedy, are especially suited for the drawing-room," such as *The Vicar of Wakefield* and the writings of Sterne and Addison. By 1883, another writer recognized a *fait accompli:* the term now also included all kinds of "character and incident painting." Or, as *Blackwood's Magazine* briskly put it two years later, genre was "an art of a kind not included in any other kind." In these pages, it will be applied to nineteenth-century subject painting with judicious inclusiveness. (*Blackwood's* 82 [1857]: 167; *Fortnightly Review* n.s. 33 [1883]: 864; *Blackwood's* 138 [1885]: 15.)

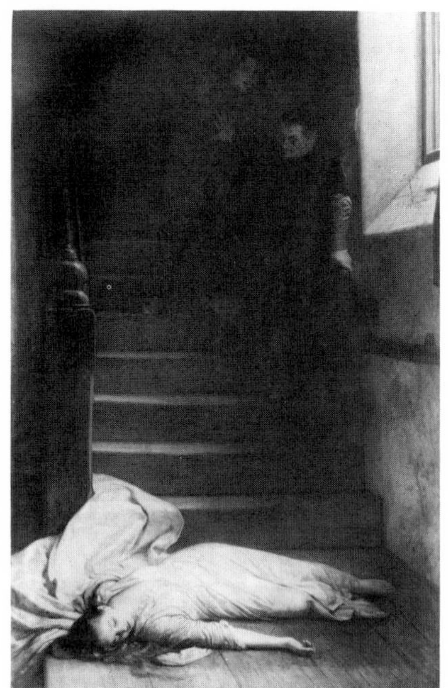

41. William F. Yeames, *Amy Robsart* (RA 1877) (Tate Gallery, London). Yeames was one of the most popular painters of historical subjects in later Victorian times. Although the painting was exhibited with a quotation from John Aubrey's *Lives*, most viewers would have identified its subject as the imaginary death scene described in Scott's *Kenilworth* (chap. 41): "'I see only a heap of white clothes, like a snow-drift,' said Foster. 'O God, she moves her arm!'"

for genre had been slowly developing in the later eighteenth century. As early as 1761, a Holborn businessman named Charles Jennens, who patronized Hogarth and Hayman, had accumulated more than 100 Dutch paintings, including, we may suppose, a substantial number of genre subjects.[14] Many more arrived at the end of the century, with the great collections that were somehow spirited out of revolutionary France. The Prince Regent himself had a notable collection of Dutch genre art, and in enthusiastic emulation so did a number of other connoisseurs—preeminently Thomas Hope and Sir Robert Peel, who were credited with the biggest collections, and also Sir Francis Bourgeois, Thomas Baring, and John Sheepshanks, who collected this kind of older art before developing his taste for its modern English equivalent. In 1815, the British Institution mounted a large exhibition of Dutch and Flemish masters borrowed from a number of private collections, and in exhibitions of wider scope held in subsequent years, this school predominated.

Thus the first decades of the century witnessed a fruitful conjunction of style and substance. The old Dutch-Flemish school of genre painting, with its concentration on domestic middle-class or rural life, was coming to preside over the taste of an influential body of connoisseurs; and its characteristic subjects, as it happened, were a particular specialty of English literature, or at least of that portion of English poetry and (especially) fiction most valued by readers who were entering the art market for the first time. The subject matter of most genre painting, as of most popular fiction from Richardson, Fielding, Sterne, and Goldsmith to Scott (the monarch of fiction at the time), was the human character in a great variety of situations and moods.

At the same time, genre painting came near to completing the task, begun by Hogarth, of widening the social reference of British art and so accommodating it to the much broader scope of fiction and the poetry that dealt with daily life. The 2,000 portraits that Reynolds and Romney painted between them seldom depicted the faces of men and women outside the world of rank and fashion. Hogarth conspicuously apart, as well as George Stubbs with his figures of grooms, farmhands, and country gentry, eighteenth-century painters had avoided contact with blunt real-

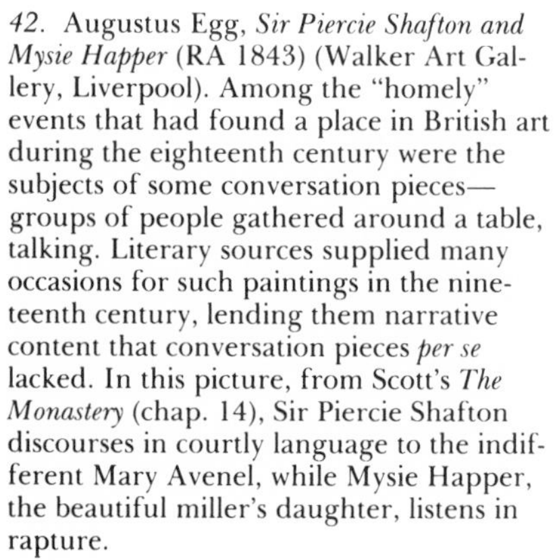

42. Augustus Egg, *Sir Piercie Shafton and Mysie Happer* (RA 1843) (Walker Art Gallery, Liverpool). Among the "homely" events that had found a place in British art during the eighteenth century were the subjects of some conversation pieces—groups of people gathered around a table, talking. Literary sources supplied many occasions for such paintings in the nineteenth century, lending them narrative content that conversation pieces *per se* lacked. In this picture, from Scott's *The Monastery* (chap. 14), Sir Piercie Shafton discourses in courtly language to the indifferent Mary Avenel, while Mysie Happer, the beautiful miller's daughter, listens in rapture.

43. Charles R. Leslie, *Queen Katherine and Her Maid* (RA 1842) (Victoria & Albert Museum, Crown Copyright). A quiet domestic interlude in a drama (Shakespeare's *Henry VIII*, 3. 1) that otherwise provided many artists with scenes of statecraft and conflict at court. This painting is a repetition of Leslie's diploma picture (1828), which, understandably in view of its sentimental appeal, was engraved for one of the giftbook annuals.

ity. Neither Gainsborough's nor Morland's rural figures, whether cottagers, artisans, children, or beggars, much resembled the real people who endured penury and squalor in the enclosed countryside. They were as untrue to fact as the graceful, expressionless figments of Stothard's imagination, which the widow of his artist-son, the novelist Anna Eliza Bray, contrasted (to his credit) with the creations of Hogarth and the "Dutch drollery" of his precursors. "He led us through the fairy ground of the picturesque and the beautiful," she wrote. His landlords and publicans "do not represent base fellows that would shock a gentlewoman," and "his gipsies, perhaps, are often too like ladies masquerading as gipsies . . . he was, as a painter, aristocratic; he could condescend gracefully to humble or rural life; but he could never descend to low life."[15] Nor did any subsequent genre painter descend, except momentarily, to "low life," by which term Mrs. Bray presumably meant a social position even more sunken than the "humble," whether rural or urban. (The lowest level of city life admitted to painting then or later was that of the picturesque street sellers made so familiar in Francis Wheatley's *The Cries of London* [1795].) But in the first decades of the nineteenth century, a mild reaction set in against the Arcadian version of country life sustained by the elegance and dreamy delicacy of Stothard's and his fellow illustrators' designs.

Three strong influences from north of the Tweed—Burns, Scott, and Wilkie—gave impetus to this promising new form of literary art between 1800 and 1820. Burns's poetry and Scott's novels provided fresh and copious sources of genre subjects. As early as 1801, Julius Caesar Ibbetson painted "Duncan Gray cam' here to woo" and "The Cotter's Saturday Night," two subjects from Burns that were destined to be painted over and over in the years to come, the latter especially being a prototypical genre subject, a kind of poor man's conversation piece. Another popular theme from Burns, "Tam o' Shanter," would join the company in 1805. A little later, the Waverley novels, the first of which appeared in 1814, began to be illustrated, the first trickle in what was to become a century-long flood of paintings from Scott's fiction. Many, perhaps the most characteristic, were domestic scenes—historical and narrative genre.

Meanwhile, David Wilkie had come down from Edinburgh with his repertory of genre subjects and his eye for the picturesque in human situations, to receive from the hand of Sir George Beaumont, patron of artists and poets and himself an amateur artist, Hogarth's mahlstick—a fine gesture of symbolic descent. Interspersed among other paintings that won him early celebrity in London, beginning with *The Village Politicians* (1806) and *The Blind Fiddler* (1807), were several subjects taken from literature: *The Refusal* (from "Duncan Gray") (pl. 44), *The Cottage Toilette* (pl. 135) and *Roger Slighted by Jenny* (from Allan Ramsay's *The Gentle Shepherd*) (pl. 291). At the peak of his career, he illustrated scenes in Scott: *The Reading of a Will (Guy Mannering),* the supper scene in *Old Mortality, Julian Peveril and the Dwarf (Peveril of the Peak),* and *Dumbiedikes and Jeanie Deans (The Heart of Mid-Lothian).*

Wilkie's literary affinities were fully appreciated in his own time; indeed, they were among the chief reasons for his popularity. Edward Bulwer, in his panoramic survey of England as it was in 1833, praised him in literary terms:

> More various, more extensive in his grasp than even Hogarth, his genius sweeps from the dignity of history to the verge of caricature itself. Humour is the prevalent trait of all minds capable of variety in character; from Shakspeare and Cervantes, to Goldsmith and Smollett. But of what shades and differences is not Humour capable? Now it loses itself in terror—now it broadens into laughter. What a distance from the Mephistophiles of Göthe to Sir Roger de Coverley of Addison, or from Sir Roger de Coverley to Humphrey Clinker! What an illimitable space from the dark power of Hogarth to the graceful tenderness of Wilkie! And which can we say with certainty is the higher of the two? . . . Wilkie is the Goldsmith of painters, in the amiable and pathetic humour, in the combination of smiles and tears, of the familiar and the beautiful; but he has a stronger hold, both over the more secret sympathies and the springs of a broader laughter, than Goldsmith himself.[16]

As it happened, Wilkie's sensational debut coincided with a revival of interest in the poetry of George Crabbe, whose poem *The Village* (1781) had been intended to confront the rosy idealization of Goldsmith's *The Deserted Village* (1770) with the hard facts of rural life. Hazlitt, writing in 1821, associated the poem with the great change he perceived as having occurred in the interim, a trend toward realism in both literary and artistic taste:

> Mr. Crabbe's earliest poem of the *Village* was recommended to the notice of Dr. Johnson by Sir Joshua Reynolds; and we cannot help thinking that a taste for that sort of poetry, which leans for support on the truth and fidelity of its imitations of nature, began to display itself much about that time, and, in a good measure, in consequence of the direction of the public taste to the subject of painting. Book-learning, the accumulation of wordy common-places, the gaudy pretensions of poetical diction, had enfeebled and perverted our eye for nature: the study of the fine arts, which came into fashion about forty years ago, and was then first considered as a polite accomplishment, would tend imperceptibly to restore it. Painting is essentially an imitative art; it cannot subsist for a moment on empty generalities: the critic, therefore, who had been used to this sort of substantial entertainment, would be disposed to read poetry with the eye of a connoisseur, would be little captivated with smooth, polished, unmeaning periods, and would turn with double eagerness and relish to the force and precision of individual details, transferred, as it were, to the page from the canvas.[17]

Crabbe's return to notice with *The Borough* (1810) provoked considerable soul-searching on the part of those who clung to the ideals of high art. The frequently observed resemblance between his poems and Dutch

44. David Wilkie, *The Refusal (Duncan Gray)* (RA 1814) (Victoria & Albert Museum, Crown Copyright). One of Wilkie's early successes, and one of the first notable pictures taken from the poems of Burns. This is a smaller version of the painting exhibited in 1814. It was painted for George Thomson, in whose *Select Collection of Original Scottish Airs* many of Burns's poems were first printed. The rising young artist William Mulready is said to have posed for the figure of Duncan Gray.

painting expanded into a discussion of the basic aesthetic theory that lay behind the rise to dominance of "realistic" genre painting.* A writer in the *Christian Observer* in 1811, the year Wilkie exhibited *The Village Festival* and was elected R.A., remarked that Crabbe was inferior to Campbell and Scott "only because his subjects keep him down." He quoted academic Scripture, one of Reynolds's *Discourses*: "The painters who have applied themselves more particularly to low and vulgar characters, and who express with precision the various shades of passion as they are exhibited by vulgar minds (such as we see in the works of Hogarth), deserve great praise; but as their genius has been employed on low and confined subjects, the praise that we give must be limited as its object."[18] In other words, the identification of "high" art with subjects from the "high" realms of society required that genre and narrative painting of low life occupy a suitably lower place in the hierarchy of kinds. This was precisely the neoclassic premise that, translated into literary terms, made Wordsworth's experiments in poetic rural genre seem so revolutionary—and unacceptable—to conservative critics.

To it, Crabbe responded in the preface to his *Tales in Verse,* published the next year:

> In this case [i.e., his own] it appears that the usual comparison between Poetry and Painting entirely fails: the Artist who takes an accurate likeness of individuals, or a faithful representation of scenery, may not rank so high in the public estimation, as one who paints an historical event, or an heroic action; but he is nevertheless a painter, and his accuracy is so far from diminishing his reputation, that it procures for him in general both fame and emolument: nor is it perhaps with strict justice determined that the credit and reputation of those verses which strongly and faithfully delineate character and manners, should be lessened in the opinion of the Public by the very accuracy, which gives value and distinction to the productions of the pencil.[19]

Assisting this transformation of subject art was the simultaneous emergence of fiction as the most popular literary form. The early presence of the novel had fostered Hogarth's purpose of adding to the inherited tradition of genre painting the twin elements of narrative and moral meaning that were largely lacking in Dutch and Flemish art, though Greuze had subsequently introduced them in France. As Fielding had said of Hogarth, the artist's task was to "express the affections of men on canvas" as the novelist expressed them on the printed page.[20] And it was the novel that now was ready at hand as new subjects were needed, not to replace the old standbys from Shakespeare, Spenser, Milton, and the other "classics," for which a steady market remained, but to enlarge the Victorian buyer's choice. Sterne and Goldsmith, whose popularity as a source of art continued to grow, were joined by Scott and Dickens.† And when novelists did not themselves supply subjects, the symbiotic relation between fiction and art still flourished. Contemporary novels were rich in the very qualities most desired in subject art: plot, dramatic or touching scenes, strong interest in character, unmistakable morality, domesticity, carefully observed "picturesque" details, gentle good-humored comedy.

As we have seen, beginning with Richard Wilson, British landscape artists sometimes inserted more or less casual literary elements in their portrayals of natural scenery. These incidental figures and references to well-known stories, introduced for compositional reasons and particularly in deference to the practice of Claude and Poussin, were, however, as

*In view of his having occasioned this debate, it is noteworthy that Crabbe himself had strong personal ties to the eighteenth-century school of academic art and aesthetic thought. Reynolds, whom he met through Edmund Burke, was an intimate friend and often entertained him at his house in Leicester Fields.

†George Eliot and Thomas Hardy, two important adapters of Dutch genre art for the purpose of fiction, appeared on the scene only when literary painting had entered its decline. For Eliot, see Part Three, below. Hardy, who studied the genre paintings in the Sheepshanks collection in 1869, was deeply influenced by genre art, and even gave *Under the Greenwood Tree* the subtitle *A Rural Painting of the Dutch School.*

far as landscape painters then went in bringing their art and that of the poet into conjunction. At the very end of the eighteenth century and the beginning of the nineteenth, Wordsworth's poems celebrated the scenery of the Lake District in imagery fresher and more vivid than the stilted pictorial language of Thomson, Dyer, and other eighteenth-century landscape poets had permitted. Meanwhile, a few artists like Wright of Derby and Farington had discovered the beauties of the region, as had William Gilpin in the course of his tours in search of the picturesque. But despite the publicity Wordsworth's poetry gave to the subjects of their paintings, no distinct school of Lake artists, comparable to Crome's Norwich school, arose alongside the school of Lake poets. The influence of the Lake poets on contemporary art was mostly confined to the inspiration and prestige they lent to landscape art at large, as with Constable.

It was Scott instead, who, almost singlehandedly among authors, touched off the century-long fashion of literary landscapes—paintings whose association with a poem or novel was not contrived and remote, as had been the case with purported pictures of the Forest of Arden in *As You Like It,* but intentional and direct. Beginning with the publication of *The Lady of the Lake* in 1810, and proceeding at an increased pace after Scott turned to fiction, English landscapists discovered in his poetry and novels a limitless reservoir of subjects. His romances, after all, were more replete with extended natural descriptions—paintings in words—than were those of any other novelist. (The incidence in Mrs. Radcliffe's fiction had been equally high, but she published only half a dozen novels whereas Scott at certain junctures was publishing three long ones in a single year.) Along with the tourists who flocked to the Highlands to enjoy for themselves the picturesque or sublime scenes Scott described came troops of professional and amateur artists bent on capturing those scenes in oil or watercolor. The engravings made from their renderings helped feed the appetite for illustrated books, and from 1811 onward, no exhibition was without paintings representing Scott topography. In addition to the hundreds explicitly identified as Scott landscapes, it is reasonable to suppose that every representation of Scottish scenery owed at least part of its saleability to its association, however faintly implicit, with the Wizard of the North.

Indeed, as had been true since English landscape painting had made its first tentative bid to evoke the feelings that the poetry of nature aroused more extensively (see chapter 1, above), association was at the very heart of the appeal such paintings possessed. Whatever intrinsic aesthetic value they had (and many had little), they almost without exception exploited the emotional content with which Scott had infused the scene. ". . . Every old ruin, hill, river, or tree," said Coleridge, "called up in his mind a host of historical or biographical associations,—just as a bright pan of brass, when beaten, is said to attract the swarming of bees. . . ."[21] Scott was his own witness. The village of Kelso, he wrote on one occasion,

> presents objects, not only grand in themselves, but venerable from their association. The meeting of two superb rivers, the Tweed and the Teviot, both renowned in song—the ruins of an ancient Abbey—the more distant vestiges of Roxburgh Castle—the modern mansion of Fleurs, which is so situated as to combine the ideas of ancient baronial grandeur with those of modern taste—are in themselves objects of the first class; yet are so mixed, united, and melted among a thousand other beauties of a less prominent description, that they

> harmonize into one general picture, and please rather by unison than by concord.[22]

Paintings inspired by Scott's descriptions in prose and verse, therefore, contained a double set of associations: the manifold ones of history and legend that had coalesced in Scott's own imagination, and those evoked by the poem or novel that had been fed by that imagination—the characters and stories to which the topography had served as a memory-laden background.

Among all the artists who sooner or later illustrated Scott, the greatest was Turner, whose watercolors of locales figuring in Scott's poetry and his prose apart from the novels marked an epoch in his career.[23] One of Turner's main links with literary painting, a retrograde one to be sure, is the way in which he gradually removed from his own form of landscape art the poetic associations he had invoked, conforming with the practice of the time, in the first phase of his career. In this phase, he had more or less regularly, and routinely, given his landscapes Poussinesque titles borrowed from mythology and tagged them with quotations from the poets, including his own purpose-made source of verses, *The Fallacies of Hope*. In addition, again like Poussin and Wilson, he had sometimes inserted tiny figures from poetry into his scenes to give the landscapes the desired literary associations. But as he moved into his "expressionist" phase, though the tags from *The Fallacies of Hope* persisted, Turner dropped the other literary trimmings except in a few canvases such as *Juliet and Her Nurse* (1836) and *A Street in Venice,* with its figure of Shylock (1837).

This was not true, however, of the numerous Victorian painters of landscape who gave literary figures a prominent place in their compositions. As recognizable characters with their own associations, who lent their names or the name of their literary source to the title of the painting, these figures now costarred with Nature. As with history painting and genre, so with landscapes and subjects from literature: the boundaries between them were largely obscured.

CHAPTER 4

The growing market for literary paintings and the shift of patronage; pictures as domestic decoration.—Books of engravings; the Art Union.—Keepsake beauties, their antecedents (fancy pictures, theatrical portraits) and descendants, the Graphic *beauties.*

Dismayed by the final passage, the night before, of the Reform Bill of 1832 and inferring from the event an odd non sequitur, Thomas Uwins wrote to his fellow artist Joseph Severn: "But whether art will ever become fashionable again is rather doubtful. The habits of the people are greatly opposed to it. Marriage is almost at an end amongst the higher and middle classes; single men have neither house nor establishment. They hire a bed-room in a garret, and live in splendour and in society, at the different club-houses."[1]

Few prophecies of the time were confounded more promptly by events, in this case the expansion of the market for art.[2] With our eyes fixed, as they usually are, on a relative handful of well-known paintings from the Victorian era, it is easy to forget that even before the age began, the production and sale of fine art had become a considerable business. When William Cobbett, the firebrand journalist then in the process of conversion from Toryism to left-wing radicalism, furnished his home in a Hampshire village in 1805, he bought the contents of one entire wall in Colnaghi's print shop. For these he paid, or undertook to pay (for Colnaghi's terms were "as long as that of a Lord or a Prince") the great, and in his case foolhardy, sum of £500.[3] Collections of art could be found in unexpected places. Five years later, when the Reverend Dr. George Tennyson moved into his rectory in a remote part of Lincolnshire, he hung in the drawing room an accumulation of paintings—perhaps inherited—known to the locals as "'eathen gods and goddesses wi'out cloäs"; yet his annual income was no more than about £450.[4]

It may well be that Carlyle expressed the sentiments of most middle-class Victorians when he growled to his friend the painter-poet William Bell Scott, "Airt, airt, what is it all about? I've never been to the Exhibition all the time that I've been in London, and don't mean to go, and more than that I believe if all art, except good portraits, faces, of great men well done, if all art but these was swept out of the world we would be all the better!"[5] The prevalent utilitarian ethos discouraged the production of art as a waste of one segment of the nation's industrial capacity. But the records of the trade assure us that there were enough bourgeois collectors of pictures to redeem the class from absolute darkness. They, along with the old-line aristocratic collectors, constituted a steadily growing market, ready to soak up much of the annual output of the studios insofar as it caught their fancy, as well as to acquire previously owned properties.

The total production down to the end of the century of the several branches of the graphic and plastic arts in Britain could be conservatively reckoned high in six figures. Unfortunately, most of the statistics found in contemporary records do not distinguish among these various types. The term most often used, "items," ordinarily referred to pictures and sculpture of all kinds, and "pictures" or "pictorial works" often comprised not only oil paintings and watercolors but engravings, miniatures, enamels, etchings, architectural drawings, and other peripheral forms of graphic art as well. But by appreciating how large the total annual output was, we can obtain a rough idea of the size of the commerce in which literary paintings participated.

At the Royal Academy, some 100,000 "items" were shown during the sixty-four Victorian years; at the British Institution during its entire career, 1806–67, more than 28,000; and at the third and least prestigious of the long-lived exhibiting institutions, the Society of British Artists, 1824–93, some 110,000.[6] (No comparable totals seem to be available for the "old" and "new" watercolor societies.) Between 1830 and 1899, the number displayed annually at the Royal Academy rose, with temporary setbacks, from 1,278 in 1830 to more than 1,500 in 1846, 1,600 in 1872, and 2,000 in 1899.[7] The average number of items at the British Institution ranged from 250 to 300 in the early years to 500 or 600 in the 1850s.[8] In both 1832 and 1858, the Society of British Artists admitted about 1,000 works.[9] To these totals must be added the undeterminable number of paintings at the various provincial exhibitions, which included much local work as well as pictures brought down from London. But, as was pointed out in the Introduction, the record of exhibited work represents only a small proportion of the whole output. Charles Robert Leslie, a newcomer to the London art scene, heard in 1813 that at the Royal Academy that year upward of 1,000 pictures were exhibited and about 500 rejected.[10] By 1848, the proportion was reversed: only a third of the works submitted were accepted, and not all of these could be hung because of the limited wall space in the Trafalgar Square building that the academy shared with the National Gallery. Even the less selective British Institution turned down a substantial number, more than 300 in 1842 as against 445 accepted.[11] And even in the more spacious quarters in Burlington House, to which it moved in 1869, the Royal Academy had room for only 18,252 out of 82,789 items submitted between 1880 and 1899; and at the very end of the century, the ratio of rejections to acceptances was about 6.5 to one.[12] There is no way of estimating the number of paintings that passed from the artist's studio to the buyer's home, either directly or by way of a dealer, and finally, the multitude of inglorious pictures that were neither submitted to an exhibition nor sold.

It is reasonable to suppose that in these categories of unrecorded pictures, paintings with literary subjects would have figured in the same proportion to the over-all total as they bore to the total listed in the exhibition catalogues. But without laborious analysis of each catalogue, one cannot obtain a dependable notion of the relative incidence of literary paintings even in the total recorded production of a given year, and even then the results would be inconclusive. A rare indication of distribution is found in the statement of Benjamin Robert Haydon's biographer that "between 1823 and 1833, 1,398 'poetical and historical works' were exhibited at the Academy, as against 5,093 portraits."[13]

The market changed rapidly in the first half of the century in respect both to the persons buying and to the products bought. Until the last decades of the eighteenth century, most serious collectors of art were aristocrats and commoners of inherited wealth. But the autocratic reign of the Old Masters in private English collections was coming to a close. Several forward-looking and patriotic patrons of the arts, Lord Mulgrave, Lord Egremont, and Sir George Beaumont, representative of an old county family, took an unprecedented interest in the advancement of young artists. Lord Egremont, who had begun collecting in 1775, gradually gave up buying Old Masters in favor of encouraging native talent, notably, in his later years, as Turner's chief patron and hospitable host.[14] The fifth Earl of Essex, the Duke of Bedford, the Marquis of Stafford, Lords Northwick, Lansdowne, and Yarborough, and Sir John Leicester, later Lord de Tabley, also were among the blue-blooded patrons of English art.

45. **Charles R. Leslie,** ***Uncle Toby and the Widow Wadman*** (RA 1831) (Tate Gallery, London). This scene, from *Tristram Shandy* (vol. 8, chap. 16), has a unique distinction: each of the three versions Leslie painted was owned by a leading collector of contemporary art, and each found its way by gift or bequest into the national collection. The first version, painted for John Sheepshanks, was among the many pictures he gave to the Victoria and Albert Museum; the second, reproduced here, was commissioned by Robert Vernon; the third was owned by Jacob Bell (see caption to pl. 48). One of these is seen hanging on the wall behind Dombey and Major Bagstock as they dine, in "Phiz's" illustration to *Dombey and Son,* chap. 26. By the 1860s, the subject had become so popular that it could even be met in advertisements and other commercial contexts. Reproduced as a polychrome print, it appeared on the lids of pots containing "Russian Bear's Grease," a kind of gentleman's hair dressing.

But everyone who commented on the English art world from the earliest Victorian days onward stressed that the chief collectors now were no longer aristocratic connoisseurs but members of the middle class, who were uninterested in the Italian and French masters so avidly collected by noblemen. They preferred instead old works painted for a bourgeois society like their own, still lifes, landscapes, and (above all, for our purposes) sentimental, anecdotal, narrative genre subjects in which art came closest to reflecting their own experience and the everyday world they lived in.

Conspicuous among this clientele were owners of the mercantile and manufacturing fortunes that had multiplied in the wake of the Napoleonic Wars, an open-pursed breed of men not unmindful of the then-surprising fact that in 1827 Lord de Tabley's collection of more than 100 modern English pictures, including half a dozen subjects from English literature, had sold for substantially more than he had paid for them.[15] Their confidence in art as a profitable investment was amply justified in the course of time. In 1863, the prices realized at the Bicknell sale represented spectacular increases over the purchase prices; and nine years later, Joseph Gillott's collection brought £164,530, far in excess of his expenditure.[16] Soon the aristocrats were far outnumbered by rich commoners in the art market: William Wells of Redleaf, shipbuilder; the elder Sir Robert Peel, cotton manufacturer; Jacob Bell, pharmaceutical chemist; Joseph Gillott of Birmingham, maker of steel pen nibs; Elhanan Bicknell, who made a fortune trading in whale oil to feed the nation's lamps; John Gibbons, Staffordshire ironmaster; Samuel Dobree, City merchant; Henry McConnell, Manchester textile magnate; Benjamin Windus, Bishopsgate coachmaker; and, most important of all because

46. Charles R. Leslie, *Catherine and Petruchio* (RA 1832) (Victoria & Albert Museum, Crown Copyright). A moment in *The Taming of the Shrew* (4. 3), commissioned by Lord Egremont. It says much for Egremont's catholicity of taste as well as his hospitality to artists that while Leslie was painting this picture at Petworth, Turner also was working there on six paintings he exhibited at the Royal Academy in 1832, including *Childe Harold's Pilgrimage—Italy* (pl. 327).

both men give their collections to the nation, to form the two most valuable concentrations of Victorian painting, John Sheepshanks, sleeping partner in a Leeds clothiers firm, and Robert Vernon, whose money came from trading in horses during the wars.[17] The appendix of the autobiography of Leslie, one of the most popular painters of subjects from English literature, contains a list of the men (and one or two women, such as the banking heiress Angela Burdett Coutts) who bought pictures from him between 1813, when he first exhibited, and 1859, the year of his death.[18] A substantial majority, among whom were some of the persons just mentioned, bore no titles of dignity.

47. Edward M. Ward, *Dr. Johnson in the Ante Room of Lord Chesterfield* (RA 1845) (Tate Gallery, London). The *Athenaeum's* comment (17 May), "It is a good, *national* picture . . . worthy a place in any contemporary gallery," helps explain the appeal such anecdotal paintings from English literature had for collectors like Robert Vernon, who gave this one to the National Gallery. "National" was not, nor is, often used as a value term, but it aptly suggests close conformity to the interests and tastes of the heart-of-the-nation middle class, and thus, by typically Victorian extension, to those of the people at large.

48. George B. O'Neill, *The Foundling* (RA 1852) (Tate Gallery, London). A narrative genre picture which was exhibited with a quotation from Crabbe's *The Parish Register* ("1. Baptisms"):

To name an infant meet our village-
sires,
Assembled all, as such event requires;
Frequent and full, the rural sages sate,
And speakers many urged the long de-
bate,—
Some harden'd knaves, who roved the
country round,
Had left a babe within the parish-bound.

The painting was in the collection of Jacob Bell, a wealthy pharmaceutical chemist who had a closer personal experience of the art world than did either Sheepshanks or Vernon. As a young man, he had simultaneously studied chemistry at the Royal Institution and painting with the Academician Henry Perronet Briggs. Before he was in his mid-twenties, he had formed the nucleus of his art collection, the best part of which he bequeathed to the nation in 1859.

One of Leslie's patrons was the celebrated engineer Isambard Kingdom Brunel, with whom the artist's son studied. In his office-cum-residence in Duke Street, St. James's, Brunel had a large dining room that he proceeded to decorate with commissioned pictures of Shakespearean subjects.[19] Leslie coordinated the project, which when completed included three of his own paintings, two from *Henry VIII* and the third from *The Winter's Tale.* Clarkson Stanfield, a marine painter somewhat out of his element, depicted the blasted heath in *Macbeth* (pl. 49); Sir Edwin Landseer, availing himself of the opportunity to paint fairies as well as the animals and human beings to which he was more accustomed, did a picture of Titania and Bottom surrounded by the cast of the Athenian wood scenes in *A Midsummer Night's Dream*; and John Callcott Horsley, Brunel's brother-in-law, presented *Launce Reproving His Dog,* from *The Two Gentlemen of Verona*—a reworking of a picture his uncle, Augustus Wall Callcott, had left unfinished at his death in 1844. These canvases, elaborately framed, hanging on walls that looked like oak paneling but were really plaster, and flanked by Venetian mirrors and red velvet curtains, looked down on a dining table "staggering like Atlas," says Brunel's modern biographer, "under the weight of monstrous silver-gilt centre and side pieces presented by the Great Western Railway Company," which was Brunel's own creation.[20] The ponderous tableware suggests the festive board of the Podsnaps, in Dickens's *Our Mutual Friend.* But we are not told that Mr. Podsnap affected a love of Shakespeare.

The unmistakable fact that the Captain of Industry and the Merchant Prince had succeeded the eighteenth-century Man of Taste as the decisive arbiters of English art aroused mixed feelings among concerned onlookers. Some interpreted the *nouveau riche* Philistine's domination of

49. Clarkson Stanfield, *Macbeth: The Blasted Heath* (RA 1850) (Leicestershire Museum and Art Gallery, Leicester). One of the few pictures with literary associations that were painted by this specialist in marine scenes; commissioned by the engineer Isambard Kingdom Brunel for his London house. Stanfield converts the witches from midnight hags to nothing more supernatural than barefoot crofters' wives resting by the wayside, and the blasted heath becomes a Scottish loch.

the market to signify the irreparable vulgarization of culture at large. Others, like a writer in the *Athenaeum* in 1849, took a longer and brighter view. "It is a striking enough feature of the times," he commented, "that to the class which in some of the best ages of Art contributed the impulse and the means on which it fed, we are again returning for the real nourishment of the eternal cause."[21]

Like the audience for books and magazines, the market for paintings had several levels and therefore different price scales. In early Victorian years, pictures by the most sought-after artists brought anywhere from £100 to £1,500 (the highest price Wilkie ever received, for his picture of *Sir David Baird Discovering the Body of Tippoo Sahib*).* Bicknell paid from 250 to 400 guineas apiece for nine Turners, £161 10s. for a pair of Thomas Webster's genre paintings, from £40 to 300 guineas for several canvases by David Roberts, and £150 for a single Clarkson Stanfield. In 1840, Leslie's scene of Victoria's coronation brought him 600 guineas. Five years later, Gillott commissioned *The Judgement of Paris* from Etty for 600 guineas. In 1850–59, Bicknell bought three Landseer paintings for between 300 and 400 guineas each; but in 1860, Frith's *The Railway Station* commanded the record sum of £5,250, surpassed later in the same year by Holman Hunt's *Christ in the Temple.*[22] The prices initially brought by literary paintings in particular were in line with the general averages, as the list given in Appendix B shows.

It was not to the mansions of the wealthy, however, but to the homes of the modestly comfortable that the great majority of new paintings gravitated. Hundreds of pictures exhibited at the British Institution and the

*The most recent rule of thumb for converting Victorian monetary sums into their approximate present-day equivalents has been to multiply by twenty-five or thirty. The appreciation in value of some select examples of British nineteenth-century art far exceeds this factor, as was sensationally demonstrated in 1984, when Turner's *Seascape: Folkstone* was sold at auction in London for the equivalent of $10,000,000. The previous record had been set by Turner's "literary" picture *Juliet and Her Nurse,* which brought $6,400,000 in New York four years earlier.

Society of British Artists were priced at only a few guineas, no more than would have bought two or three recently published books. (The conventional three-decker novel cost 31s.6d., or a guinea and a half.) It is items on this price level, ordinarily small cabinet pictures with unelaborated compositions and requiring little wall space, that swell the records of nineteenth-century British painting. This was the bargain-basement precinct of contemporary art, where the prevailing taste was reflected *en masse.*

Every artist who relied on his palette and easel for his livelihood had to defer to that taste. Wilkie, whose career, once well launched, depended as much as any artist's on his pleasing his wealthy patrons, stated the case candidly enough: ". . . Patrons visit the artist's studio, saying, 'we are not judges of the article, but we know what pleases us;' and they order a picture—be it portrait, landscape, domestic scene, or poetic painting—accordingly. To know, then, the taste of the public—to learn what will best please the employer—is to an artist the most valuable of all knowledge, and the most useful to him whose skill and fancy it calls into exercise."[23] If Wilkie, originally a poor Scottish boy whose subsequent eminence in his profession won him a knighthood and, at his death, a great memorial painting by Turner, felt such pressure, it was felt much more acutely by the undistinguished painters whose pictures constituted all but a small fraction of the yearly output. Amateur or professional, they were as much hacks as the equally motley crowd of penny-a-liners who fed the presses in this era of a portentously expanding audience for reading matter. The remark of the totally uninspired artist Henry Gowan, in *Little Dorrit,* did little credit to him (as Dickens intended) or to the idealism of his profession, but it was an accurate statement of its realities: ". . . What I do in my trade, I do to sell. What all we fellows do, we do to sell. If we didn't want to sell it for the most we can get for it, we shouldn't do it. Being work, it has to be done; but it's easily enough done. All the rest is hocus-pocus" (chap. 34). It was recognition of this manifest subservience to crass fashion, so ill comporting with the Romantic conception of the artist who follows his highest private vision and selflessly fulfills his appointed function of purifying and inspiring every human being reached by his art, that soured some of the day's art journalism. The intended destiny of most of the paintings shown at the exhibitions, it was thought, fatally corrupted contemporary art. As a reviewer of the Royal Academy show of 1843 put it, "Now, if out of these 1,530 [works] there be, peradventure, fifty, or twenty, or even five, which have not been painted for Art-Unions, or Annuals, or fashionable boudoirs, or to please the million, but for fair fame and its just reward, we may rejoice over the salvation of Art. . . ."[24]

If one commonplace of the time was that a new, demotic market for art had materialized, another, equally pervasive, was that pictures were now almost solely designed for domestic use—a fact that influenced not only the choice and treatment of subject matter, as we shall see in the next chapter, but the physical size of paintings, which had its own bearing on subject matter. From the very eighteenth-century moment when history painting began to claim the veneration of ambitious English artists, one practical objection to it was its scale: there was no place to hang pictures of such grandiose dimensions. Hogarth said, "For historical pictures there never can be a demand; our churches reject them; . . . and the generality of our apartments are too small to contain them."[25]

In the 1840s, to be sure, no less an institution than Parliament came to the rescue of artists who thought in outsize dimensions with its scheme to decorate the new Houses of Parliament with frescoes from Shakespeare, Spenser, and Milton (see chapter 8, below). The rules for the contest that was set up to discover the painters eligible for commissions required that figures in the cartoons (preliminary sketches) should be "not less than ten nor more than fifteen feet in their longest dimension."[26] If the grand style was too outdated to be wholly insisted upon, on this occasion grand size was given encouragement such as it had seldom before enjoyed in Britain. But few walls outside Westminster had space for such machines. J. C. Horsley's entry in the 1846 competition, a picture of Prince Hal taking the crown from his father's bedside, won a £200 premium, but its sheer height (twelve feet) deprived it of a home until, after the several months required to enlarge his art gallery to receive it, Sir William Armstrong, the wealthy inventor, installed it in his mansion at Newcastle.[27]

It would seem that most of the wealthy connoisseurs whose stately homes could accommodate what was properly public-monument art were already adequately supplied with it (mostly genuine or bogus Old Masters) and were not often moved to replace it with freshly painted pictures. Realization of the space problem was behind the note in the sale catalogue of the Boydell Shakespeare Gallery in 1805: "Many of the above Pictures are of the Cabinet size, and the Remainder will be found worthy objects for the large saloons of the Nobility and Gentry, or the Halls of Incorporate Bodies, or for Exhibition in distant Parts of the Kingdom." That large pictures were a drag on the market, even then, is implicit in the low prices some brought at the Boydell sale, as well as in Fuseli's failure to sell off the pictures from the Milton Gallery.

Throughout the period, there were artists such as Haydon and Martin whose ambitions and talents were firmly pointed toward the epic size, notwithstanding the commercial disadvantage of such spacious canvases. Martin's early painting of Macbeth on the blasted heath (BI 1820), for example, measured 68 by 98 inches. David Scott, dying in 1849, left behind him, among other paintings, three "ambitious, imperfect, yet grand unsold works," one of which portrayed Lady Macbeth smearing the grooms with blood from her husband's dripping dagger. In 1872, the painter James Smetham saw them in the studio of David's brother William. "There they are," he wrote; "deep in colour, blistered with the sun, mildewy, brown, in solemn, energetic, heavy epic, needing the interpretation of much knowledge and sympathy. There is scarce any one who would buy them, though many would admire and be impressed by them. They are too big to buy at random. Where are they to be put?"[28] There always was a small market for large canvases, however, if the right name were signed to them. Toward the end of the century, Burne-Jones's magnum opus *The Sleep of King Arthur in Avalon,* on which he was still working when he died, measured 21 feet 2 inches by 9 feet 3 inches. But this was one of the exceptions that proved the rule.

Since size and subject were to some extent related, as they had been historically, these twin considerations took painters in the same direction, away from subjects associated with large canvases (history pictures) and toward those associated with, and most congenial to, smaller paintings (portraits and figure studies, and dramatic and narrative genre in domestic settings). And although English literature contained many subjects well suited to large-scale pictorial treatment, especially in such poets as Shakespeare and Milton, it contained many more that were better adapted to the intimate confines of the medium- or small-size picture. Prosaic requirements of square feet and inches were not among the loftiest determinants of taste, but they undoubtedly counted.

If there was less *uninterrupted* wall space available in the houses built for the newly wealthy as well as the merely prosperous portion of the middle class, the aggregate space suitable for art was much greater than ever before. It is scarcely possible to exaggerate the degree to which Victorian art was affected by the spread of middle-class housing in cities and towns, its wall areas offering so many more millions of square feet to hang pictures on, even if the individual paintings had to be small. Seldom if ever in the history of Western art, except in seventeenth-century Holland, were paintings bought in such large quantities primarily for use as household decoration. Almost at the same moment that Uwins was declaring that art was dead because current domestic habits provided no place to put it, Bulwer, in his *England and the English* (1833), commented: "It is rather a singular fact, that in no country abroad do you see many pictures in the houses of the gentry or lesser nobles. But with us they are a necessary part of furniture. A house-agent taking a friend of mine over a London house the other day, and praising it to the skies, concluded with, 'And when, sir, the dining-room is completely furnished—handsome red curtains, sir—and twelve good "furniture pictures"—it will be a perfect nonpareil!' The pictures were as necessary as the red curtains."[29]*

This was no convenient Bulwerian fantasy; pictures were, in fact, valued for their mere contribution to décor. Sometimes this was the only consideration. In 1856, when Tennyson and his wife moved into their home at Farringford, they found that his father's pictures were insufficient to cover the stains on the wallpaper, and Emily asked their friend Thomas Woolner, the sculptor, to look out at pawnbrokers' for some paintings of "red and flesh colour and bright frames." She was partial, she said, to "oldest copies of oldest pictures to be sold for one farthing each barring the discount on ready money."[30] A few years later, Edward FitzGerald, a compulsive buyer of inexpensive (five to ten pounds) paintings he optimistically believed were from the brushes of celebrated artists, wrote to his friend George Crabbe, grandson of the poet: "I have just bought an Early Gainsboro' which Churchyard has had for years: I bought it because it was light, bright, cheerful, and making a good figure in my Room. I now have made almost the best I can of such Pictures as I have, and sit and survey my handywork with considerable Pleasure. But I must one Day oust some of the Black things and get lighter. I am sure that dark Venetian's Head you have would improve by having the edges rounded off with Gold Panel. . . ."[31]

Emily Tennyson and FitzGerald exemplified the mid-Victorian spirit insofar as the domestic usefulness of art was concerned. Two years before the latter acquired his dubious Gainsborough (1860), the pioneer historians of British art, Richard and Samuel Redgrave, wrote, using a strikingly modern phrase,

> It was soon found that pictures to suit the English taste must be *pictures to live by*; pictures to hang on the walls of that home in which the Englishman spends more of his time than do the men of other nations, and loves to see cheerful and

*It was in the same passage that Bulwer (ironically?) defended the Royal Academy's governance of contemporary art on the ground that "though it has not fostered genius, it has diffused through a large circle a respectable mediocrity, that is, it has made the standard of the Mediocre several degrees higher than it was before."

> decorative. . . . His eye, too, must be pleased before his mind, and colour is to him one of the first sources of gratification.[32] (Emphasis added.)

So long as furniture pictures were chosen for their harmony with a room's décor, their subjects, within certain agreed-upon limitations, were largely irrelevant; the colors mattered more, as the Redgraves said and as Emily Tennyson and FitzGerald implied. When such harmony was achieved, paintings could heighten the pleasures of social life. Writing of the evocations of eighteenth-century society painted by Leslie and others, a contributor to *Blackwood's Magazine* in 1857 remarked:

> How delightfully charming is a painting of silks and satins—how well, when hung in the drawing-room, it matches with the new curtains and the gay carpet—how well the elegant attitudes and manners of the people in the picture comport with the elegant trifling in society, with the graceful compliments which pass around the piano, and the *sotto voce* conversation which serves as an accompaniment to songs of conventional sentiment! Thus how complete is the accordance between art and society; and how can pictures fail of pleasing, which thus satisfy the highest needs of "evening parties?" "High Art" were an intrusion.[33]

It were indeed.

But the sensibilities of the people who lived with the pictures day in and day out had to be considered too. Art of whatever sort was depended upon to supply life and color to daily surroundings that were otherwise drab, to import the scenery and atmosphere of distant places, to widen the family circle to include men, women, and children from history and literature as well as figures in quaint genre studies. Pictures on the walls were to serve the eye as books on the shelves served the mind; both sought the same goal, the wholesome expansion of the imagination and thus the enrichment of inner lives. They often had a more intimate value as little shrines on the wall, their subjects—a face, a natural vista—conjuring up memories of departed relatives or happy occasions in the country; they served as a visual focus of private sentiment. In 1836, Wilkie described

50. Edward M. Ward, *The Disgrace of Clarendon* (signed and dated 1861) (Sheffield City Art Galleries). One of several versions Ward painted of this scene, beginning in 1846. As a populous costume piece, it would have met the specification of the *Blackwood's* writer four years earlier (see text): "a painting of silks and satins . . . elegant attitudes and manners." Supposedly, too, the people who trifled below it at evening parties were unaware of, or unperturbed by, the story behind the scene: the departure from Charles II's frivolous court of Lord Clarendon, a high official of comparative probity, brought low by the failure of the Dutch War and the intrigue of the court. Ward's widow wrote (*Memories of Ninety Years* [New York, 1925], p. 46) that the picture was based on an incident described by Pepys, but here her memory misled her, though it is true that Pepys did chronicle, day by day, the prolonged drama of Clarendon's decline and fall. Macaulay threw additional light on the scene: "On the vices of the young and gay [Clarendon] looked with an aversion almost as bitter and contemptuous as that which he felt for the theological errors of the sectaries. He missed no opportunity of showing his scorn of the mimics, revellers, and courtesans who crowded the palace" (*History of England,* chap. 2).

51. Frederick Goodall, *Village Festival* (RA 1847) (Tate Gallery, London). A typical "picture to live by." Its spirit—that of a *fête champêtre* with selective suggestions of Brueghel—was epitomized in the quotation from Milton's "L'Allegro" that accompanied it:

> When the merry bells ring round,
> And the jocond rebeks sound
> To many a youth and many a maid
> Dancing in the chequered shade;
> And young and old come forth to play
> On a sunshine holyday.

what he conceived, no doubt rightly, art meant to the average picture-lover:

> The possessor of a picture regards it not in reference to the hand which produces it, nor as one whose view of it has been hasty and fleeting: he thinks alone of the sentiment and feeling of the work, and the lasting impression which it makes on his mind; and regards it as possessing matter for thought, as a companion for the leisure hour, holding up in its solemn stillness an image which he loves, perpetuating the vanishing smile and the never-to-be-forgotten glance of one perhaps long since passed and gone, or the hue of the changing foliage, or the lustre of the fleeting cloud, beauteous
>
> "As if an angel, in his upward flight,
> Had left his garment floating in mid air:"
>
> all of which, and much more, arrested and rendered abiding by the sorcery of art, are kept treasured in the reflecting mind, affording to the possessor materials of pleasure, and a permanent source of pure enjoyment.[34]

Art therefore (one must never forget that this was the age of Ruskin) had a definable moral mission to a society built around mills and mines. To believe that it actually succeeded in ministering to people's hearts was to reaffirm one's faith in both art and industry. "It is pleasant for me," said Tom Taylor, Leslie's biographer,

> to think that so many of Leslie's pictures should have found a home among the mills of Lancashire and the smoking forges and grimy workshops of Birmingham. They are eminently calculated to counteract the ignobler influences of industrial occupation by their inborn refinement, their liberal element of loveliness, their sweet sentiment of nature, *their literary associations,* and their genial humour. I can speak from personal observation to the real appreciation of these pictures in such places, not on the part of their possessors only, but

> among the many, both masters and workmen, to whom these galleries are so liberally opened.[35] (Emphasis added.)

Of course, nowhere are generalizations more suspect than in the history of taste. Was it true that rich merchant kings and small businessmen shared the same expectations and the same gratifications in art? Certainly they agreed on broad moral and aesthetic principles. Some distinction should be made, no doubt, between those who treasured paintings as trophies of material success, as status symbols—and therefore favored large (within the confines of their rooms) and imposing canvases—and those who merely had wall space for a few five-guinea pictures to be "lived with." Various portions of the art-loving public might also be differentiated by their literary allegiances, a distinction made by a reviewer of John Knowles's biography of Fuseli in 1831:

> Shakespeare is the poet of all ranks; the theatre has familarized us with the creatures of his fancy; we see them again on canvass, as old acquaintances, and delight to compare the ideas of the artist with our own; but Milton is the poet of the scholar, and the man of refinement, to many almost unknown, familiar only to very few. He appeals too little to ordinary sympathies, and confines himself too exclusively to the elevated and the terrible to be the favourite of the crowd.[36]

There probably was also a difference between the taste of the old-line patrons of art, who were accustomed to buying works by Old Masters and their lesser contemporaries and therefore were more receptive to subjects found there, and that of newcomers to the market, whose preferences were more decisively influenced, and their range of choice narrowed, by the Victorian bourgeois ethos. But, such considerations apart, it seems likely that there was no major difference between the subjects of pictures chosen by the wealthy connoisseur and the suburbanite. In addition, there was the powerful force of emulation: middle-class picture-buyers who had ambitions beyond their present station wanted the same kind of art that their betters bought. The fact that artists often painted smaller replicas of their successful canvases points to the profit to be had in obliging budget buyers with mini-copies of the rich man's original.*

In earlier Victorian years—the evidence is less strong for the later ones—the pictures on the wall "illustrated" the middle-class family's fireside activities. Paintings from Shakespeare or Scott witnessed the readings-aloud from plays or novels that were so memorable a part of domestic entertainment. Some of the favorite ballads and elocution pieces that were recited in the course of an evening's family gathering, poems by Burns or Hood's "The Dream of Eugene Aram," for example, were also favorite subjects for artistic treatment. And furniture pictures of a literary cast complemented two other pieces of furniture, pianos and drawing-room tables, and the household activities associated with them.

On the music racks shown in such well-known Victorian pictures as Holman Hunt's *The Awakening Conscience* and Redgrave's *The Governess* would have been found the sheet music of songs taken from artists' customary literary sources. In such a domestic setting, the sister arts became a trio.[37] Moore's *Irish Melodies,* written to be sung to piano accompaniment, were represented by numerous paintings and engravings. Popular novels were as fertile a source of parlor balladry as they were of parlor art.

*The taste of Victorian collectors can be inferred most comprehensively from the pictures they commissioned or bought at the exhibitions. But we are fortunate to have private testimony from one such collector, John Gibbons, the Staffordshire ironmaster, whose letters in the mid-1840s to W. P. Frith, one of the artists he patronized, offer the only oasis in the drear wasteland that is the third volume of Frith's autobiography. On the whole, Gibbons's preferences would seem to have been those of most of his art-loving contemporaries, although he was more thoughtful and more articulate in expressing them. (See also Kathryn Moore Heleniak, "John Gibbons and William Mulready: The Relationship between a Patron and a Painter," *Burlington Magazine* 124 [1982]: 136–41.)

Dickens inspired songs about Little Nell and at least one duet between Paul and Florence Dombey; from Bulwer-Lytton came songs like one from *The Last Days of Pompeii* ("The wind and the beam loved the rose"); from Charles Kingsley, a rich selection including the popular "The Three Fishers." One John Blockley ransacked the best-loved poetry of the day in search of lyrics. Like artists, he found texts in the sentimental works of Felicia Hemans, Caroline Norton, Eliza Cook, and other writers of keepsake verse, and above all in Tennyson. From "Enoch Arden" alone came the germs (not the actual words) of a whole cycle of affecting songs, "The Fisherman's Boat," "The Golden Lock of Hair," "Enoch's Farewell," and "Enoch Arden's Dream."

Many of these songs had no more substantial relation to their literary sources than did the equivalent pictures. But in spirit they were completely harmonious. Both modes were laden with mawkish sentiment expressed in imagistic clichés. They shared common themes, such as the suffering and death of children, home sweet home (the sentiment of innumerable domestic genre paintings), and the perils of the sea.

52. William P. Frith, *Nora Creina* (British Institution 1846) (Harris Museum and Art Gallery, Preston). The heroine of "Lesbia Hath a Beaming Eye," a popular song by Thomas Moore:

Oh, my Nora Creina, dear,
My gentle, bashful Nora Creina,
Beauty lies
In many eyes,
But Love in yours, my Nora Creina.

On the drawing-room table, meanwhile, could be found volumes or portfolios of engravings, a fourth component in the home experience of literature and art. Alongside, and to a certain extent overlapping, the public that bought original paintings at whatever price was the larger public that formed a market for engravings made from paintings, the market liberally served in the latter half of the eighteenth century by Alderman Boydell and his lucrative warehouse in Cheapside. Collecting prints and displaying them, either framed on the walls or in portfolios to be leafed through on rainy days for the entertainment of guests (including daughters' suitors, who found the examination of prints side by side on a sofa the closest one could get to one's beloved) was an agreeable, undemanding, and relatively inexpensive custom. No matter that even the most elegantly produced engravings were a poor substitute for paintings, lacking, as Hazlitt said, "the size of life, the marble flesh, the rich tones of nature" and being "for the most part but hints, loose memorandums, outlines in little of what the painter has done."[38] Inadequate though black-and-white reductions were by their very nature, they still brought pictures into many households where no other art existed. The engraved, if not precisely graven, image was admissible to neo-Puritan homes where scruples against sensuousness barred pictures in color, no matter how unexceptionable their subjects.

But much more important was the role of engravings in widening the public interest in fine art. Press reports of the current exhibitions at the Royal Academy and the British Institution meant more to readers when they could look forward to the most popular, if not necessarily the best, paintings hung there being engraved and thus available for hanging, by surrogate, on domestic walls. Moreover, far from being mere substitutes for a superior kind of art, engravings had a long tradition of connoisseurship of their own, with aesthetic criteria as strict as those that applied to painting. The tastes and trends reflected in literary paintings were fully operative when the pictures were reproduced and distributed to a market many times greater than that for the paintings themselves, a still more democratic middle-class public most of whose members never attended an exhibition.

As early as Hogarth's time, engravings had conveyed his and other artists' designs to a public far removed from the connoisseurs who bought expensive prints of Old Masters. More than 300 of Morland's pictures had been engraved in his lifetime, selling between 3s.6d. and 21s., and innumerable ones of Stothard's. Some 500 families—normally the maximum number of copies that could be made from a copper plate without reengraving—could possess a reproduction of an original oil or watercolor picture.[39]

Down to near the middle of the century, the sale record for prints was held by Stothard's famous *Canterbury Pilgrims,* engraved by Luigi Schiavonetti and James Heath in 1807 (see Part Three, below, under Chaucer). Meanwhile, the whole engraving industry had been undergoing a revolution.[40] Lithography, mezzotint, and aquatint, with their capacity for tonal effects, imitated, as line engraving could not, the "painterly" qualities of pictures.* And, most important, the number of copies that could be struck off in a single edition sharply increased. Steel engraving, introduced about 1822, combined with the electrotyping process, perfected about 1845, to allow as many as 20,000 to 30,000 prints to be made from a single plate without excessive loss of quality. For mass-production work, however, the old process of engraving on wood, now improved, was found capable of even more efficient and economical results, so that as cheap illustrated magazines increased in popularity after mid-century, it began to supersede the metal process.

Distribution of these prints was chiefly in the hands of a growing branch of the art and publishing industry, the printsellers, 126 of whom were registered with their trade organization between 1847 and 1894. In that span of time, these successors of Boydell and Macklin claimed property rights in nearly 5,000 engravings, a due proportion of which had literary subjects.[41] The most influential, and for that reason the most controversial, single distributor of engravings was the nonprofit Art Union, established in 1837.[42] Each subscriber—there were 12,000 by 1841—was entitled to receive a copy of an engraving the union produced each year. But the heart of the operation was the annual lottery, each of whose winners could choose, up to the amount of his prize, a currently exhibited painting. The first prize was a picture costing no more than £200, a figure that, as we have seen, was considerably lower than the level at which works by the most popular artists were then selling. Most of the prizes were valued at no more than ten or twenty pounds, a limitation, ostensibly meant to encourage "recruits rather than veterans," which in practice simply encouraged artists to paint pictures to the taste of people who had no more than that to spend on art. This accounts, in part, for the plethora of paintings tagged at five or ten guineas at the British Institution and the Society of British Artists. To publicize its mission, the Art Union held an annual exhibition of the works selected by the prize winners and, for a time, published annual volumes with engravings of these paintings. In 1842, it gave a special boost to literary painting by urging its prize winners to "give a preference to Historical pictures illustrative of the Bible, British History, or British Literature," in anticipation of the coming Westminster frescoes competition.[43] Seven years later, it issued a well-received album of thirty woodcuts illustrating "L'Allegro" and "Il Penseroso."

Predictably, this hopeful, and initially very successful, operation in behalf of disseminating the arts among "the people"—one of many exam-

*Several processes, of course, existed by which actual color could be introduced into prints. Besides hand-coloring, there were chromoxylography (printing from woodcuts) and, later, chromolithography. Familiar though "chromos" were in domestic circles, however, they seldom represented literary subjects.

ples of the burst of interest in improving popular taste that marked the 1830s and 1840s—had its critics.* "The Art Union," grumbled Samuel Rogers, the octogenarian collector of Old Masters, at one of his famous breakfast levees, "is a perfect curse: it buys and engraves very inferior pictures, and consequently encourages mediocrity of talent; it makes young men, who have no genius, abandon the desk and counter, and set up for painters."[44] In 1844, when the union ran temporarily afoul of the law that prohibited lotteries and its treasury was confiscated, Thackeray put the case against it more expansively and half ironically:

> . . . One cannot but deplore the fate of the poor fellows who have been speculating upon the Art-Unions; and yet in the act of grief there is a lurking satisfaction. The poor fellows can't sell their pieces; that is a pity. But why did the poor fellows paint such fiddle-faddle pictures? They catered for the *bourgeois,* the sly rogues! They know honest John Bull's taste, and simple admiration of namby-pamby, and so they supplied him with an article that was just likely to suit him. In like manner savages are supplied with glass beads; children are accommodated with toys and trash, by dexterous speculators who know their market. Well, I am sorry that the painting speculators have had a stop put to their little venture, and that the ugly law against lotteries has stepped in and seized upon the twelve thousand pounds, which was to furnish many a hungry Raphael with a coat and a beefsteak. . . . [A] vast number of frame-makers will look wistfully at their carving and gilding as it returns after the exhibition to Mr. Tinto, Charlotte Street, along with poor Tinto's picture from the *Vicar of Wakefield* that he made sure of selling to an Art-Union prizeman. . . . But . . . the enemies of Art-Unions have had some reason for their complaints, and I fear it is too true that the effect of those institutions, as far as they have gone hitherto, has not been mightily favourable to the cause of art. One day, by custom, no doubt, the public taste will grow better. . . .[45]

In Scotland, meanwhile, the Art Union's prototype flourished.[46] The Association for the Promotion of the Fine Arts in Scotland ("Royal Association" after 1850, when it was chartered) had been founded in 1833 by David Octavius Hill, a painter who would achieve more lasting fame as one of the pioneers of photography. Though its membership was smaller than that of the London Art Union (728 in 1834, more than 6,000 in 1839) it seems to have attracted a superior class of subscribers, perhaps less interested in winning a prize than in furthering the cause of fine art. A witness before the select committee of Commons that met in 1846 to consider exempting the London Art Union from the lottery act stated that nearly all the 10,000 members then on its books were "of the lower middle classes." The Scottish union, by contrast, was composed largely of solid members of the professional and business classes. Of the ninety-two winners in 1838, more than half were titled, landed, or professional men, or bankers. In Dundee, eighty of ninety-two identifiable members were from the wealthy and educated class.

In addition to distributing prizes and donating ten percent of the subscription money to the National Gallery of Scotland's purchase fund for contemporary art (a form of patronage not practiced by the London Union), the Scottish union commissioned paintings to be included in a lengthy series of annual portfolios of engravings, beginning with John Faed's illustrations to "Tam o' Shanter." One poem or novel was selected for each album, and it is no ground for surprise that nearly all the poems were by Burns and nearly all the novels were by Scott.[47] This form of tribute to the two national literary heroes undoubtedly helps account for the swelling totals of recorded pictures from Burns and Scott. A few of

*During its long life (it was finally wound up in 1911), the Art Union distributed over half a million prints and spent half a million pounds in indirect patronage of the arts by way of the prizes earmarked for the purchase of paintings and other objects.

them were shown at the annual exhibitions, but most seem to have passed directly from the studio to the engraver's shop.

The technical advances that made engravings more available, coinciding as they did with the broadening of the literate populace, had a similarly stimulating effect on the production of illustrated books.[48] Here, on the level of everyday cultural commerce, the linkage between art and literature—the graphic design reflecting the verbal picture within the covers of a single book—was exploited afresh, *ut pictura poesis* being converted to a profitable fact of Victorian economic life. In the first issue of the *Illustrated London News* (14 May 1842), an extraordinarily florid prefatory address to the reader reviewed the progress of book illustration, of which the paper's own debut served as a fresh inspirational landmark:

> It began in a few isolated volumes—stretched itself next over fields of natural history and science—penetrated the arcanae of our own general literature—and made companionship with our household books. At one plunge it was in the depth of the stream of poetry—working with its every current—partaking of the glow, and adding to the sparkles of the glorious waters—and so refreshing the very soul of genius, that even Shakspeare came to us clothed with a new beauty, while other kindred poets of our language seemed as it were to have put on festive garments to crown the marriage of their muses to the arts.

We saw in chapter 2 that illustrations in eighteenth-century literary works were largely confined to reprinted poetry, fiction, and essays. First editions of novels were not illustrated even in the first third of the nineteenth century—a particular irony in the case of Scott, the friend of such artists as Wilkie, Allan, and Haydon, whose novels would supply a livelihood to eventually scores of artists who made designs for subsequent editions or painted Scott subjects to hang on the walls. Only with the dazzling success in 1836–37 of *Pickwick Papers,* its monthly parts illustrated by Hablôt K. Browne ("Phiz"), did publishers other than specialists in such confections as drawing room–table albums realize the commercial value of pictures accompanying the newly written text; and even so, the ordinary three-decker novel of the period continued to boast, by way of illustration, no more than an occasional frontispiece. But the part-issue of fiction in the Dickens manner, a practice later taking the form of magazine serialization, led readers to expect pictures along with the narrative.[49] It was not accidental that the expanded use of illustrations in new books after *Pickwick* coincided with the spreading popularity of literary paintings. At the very least, illustrated books must have enlarged the market for the paintings that often portrayed the same literary subjects.

Nowhere in the art of the time was the effect of the engraving more pronounced than in portraits of women, especially literary heroines. The "Keepsake beauty," indeed (a generic name whose origin will be made clear in a moment), was, by common agreement among all persons professionally interested in art except those who profited from her popularity, an offense against all judicious taste. Her cloyingly malign influence persisted from the late Regency almost to the end of the Victorian era; her person, as represented by countless paintings and drawings and the engravings that disseminated those images, was the quintessence of the age's notorious sentimentality, in which the preceding century's *sensibilité,* a prized affectation of the élite, was coarsened for, and by, the middle classes. It would not be too daring to suggest that pictures of her were icons secularized for Protestant homes, hung and reproduced in places where, in Roman Catholic societies, images of the Madonna and female saints could be found. They were the most familiar visual manifestation of the Victorian cult of woman worship.

The Keepsake beauty's lineage is clear enough, and to compare her with, for instance, Lely's Windsor Beauties is to have a revealing measure of the changed condition of art, not to say the role of women, in English society between the late seventeenth century and the mid-nineteenth. Insofar as she purported to represent a literary character, she was the offspring of the fashionable ladies who had impersonated figures from religion, myth, allegory, and literature for Reynolds, Romney, and other artists. These fancy, or role-playing, portraits had faded from fashion when their chief practitioners had laid down their brushes. Only on a few occasions during the first third of the nineteenth century did paintings identified as Miss X in the role of Y appear in the exhibitions. One or two ladies posed as Una (1806, 1821) or as Ellen in *The Lady of the Lake* (1811, 1815), two sisters as Hermia and Helena in *A Midsummer Night's Dream* (1806), and the Honorable Mrs. Norton, beauty, poet, and wit, as the lady in St. Swithin's chair in Scott's *Waverley* (1829). After 1830, there were virtually no pictures so styled; Millais's painting of the Honorable Caroline Roche as Diana Vernon in *Rob Roy* (1880) was most anachronistic.

53. Arthur W. Devis, *Belvidera: A Chamber in the House of Aquilina, a Greek Courtesan* (British Institution 1816) (Wolverhampton Art Gallery). The model is Eliza O'Neill, who had made a hit as Juliet at Covent Garden in 1814 and subsequently in other tragic roles such as Belvidera in Otway's *Venice Preserved.* Three years after this picture was painted, O'Neill married a member of Parliament (later a baronet) and retired from the stage.

The theatrical counterparts of these impersonation pictures, however, continued in demand. Artists, no doubt encouraged by theater managers, competed to induce currently starring actresses to pose for them in their most popular roles. In 1816, a newspaper reported in authentic press-agent's prose that "Miss [Eliza] O'Neill had no less than seven pressing solicitations from eminent painters to sit to them in her elegant and natural character of Lady Teazle, for the Royal Academy exhibition; but we understand that Sir T. Lawrence is likely to be the artist selected to give a graceful representation of this charming actress."[50] It appears that Sir Thomas lost his bid, if it was ever tendered. Miss O'Neill was, in fact, painted as Lady Teazle, but by an unknown artist. Her appearance that year at the Academy exhibition, as Juliet, was under the auspices of the lesser portraitist George Dawe.

Although such paintings testified to the continuing strength of the star system in the early nineteenth-century theater, there was a growing tendency to play down the identity of the model and to focus, instead, on the character she impersonated. Theatrical portraiture shaded into a new mutation of the fancy picture, the female portrait whose connection with, say, Shakespeare was confined to the name of the character and an appropriate quotation. The fact that the model was (or was not) an actress ceased to be an important consideration, and the role portrayed, far from remaining a distinctive link between the play and the picture, faded away also, being retained only in the name applied to the portrait and the presence of a readily identifiable attribute, such as a garland of flowers in the case of Ophelia or a shepherdess' crook in that of Celia in *As You Like It.* Complaint was seldom made, though it should have been, that the lady's costume, which usually was taken straight from the fashion books of the moment, and her hairdo, which ran to corkscrew curls when these were the vogue, diminished the authenticity of the impersonation.

These portraits were engraved for wide distribution, both separately and as illustrations in the coffee-table books of the period—insipid,

54. Daniel Maclise, *Miss Priscilla Horton as Ariel* (ca. 1838) (Royal Shakespeare Theatre Picture Gallery ©). Macready's Covent Garden production of *The Tempest,* which opened in October 1838 to such acclaim that it was performed fifty-five times during the season, began with a "magnificent moving picture" in the course of which Priscilla Horton, as Ariel, sang as she was flown on wires in the manner of fairies in a Cinderella pantomime.

pricey concoctions in watered silk with gilt edges that were called, individually as well as generically, keepsakes, gift books, albums, or annuals.[51] They were explicitly meant to capitalize upon the sisterhood of the arts by juxtaposing engravings of a sentimental cast with texts from literature (stretching the term to its limits)—milk-and-water verse, vapid short stories, vignettes of false-elegant prose. Thackeray described them with devastating accuracy:

> Take the standard "Album" for instance—that unfortunate collection of deformed Zuleikas and Medoras (from the "Byron Beauties"), the Flowers, Gems, Souvenirs, Caskets of Loveliness, Beauty, as they may be called; glaring caricatures of flowers, singly, in groups, in flower-pots, or with hideous deformed little Cupids sporting among them; of what are called "mezzotinto" pencil-drawings, "poonah-paintings," and what not. "The Album" is to be found invariably upon the round rosewood brass-inlaid drawing-room table of the middle classes, and with a couple of "Annuals" besides, which flank it on the same table, represents the art of the house. . . .

He begged artists to "never more draw a single 'Forsaken One,' 'Rejected One,' 'Dejected One' "—the standard moods to be represented, along with the more abstract depiction of something called "soulfulness"—"at the entreaty of any publisher, or for the pages of any Book of Beauty, Royalty, or Loveliness whatever."[52] Of course, no artist with publishing connections listened: like Thackeray himself, a failed painter turned journalist and art critic, all had their living to make. But unlike Thackeray, they could paint reasonably plausible faces of beautiful women.*

In one category of these female portraits and figure studies, the interest was simply that of the old Reynolds-Gainsborough picture, the flattering realization of fashionable, if not necessarily beautiful, women. The fictitious Galaxy Gallery of British Beauty in *Bleak House,* which contained an engraving of Lady Dedlock, had its real-life counterpart in such luxury items as *The Court Album* (1853–56).

Alongside the art-cum-text albums in the fashionable bookshops were displayed larger, costlier ones that were devoted entirely to engravings, with perhaps a brief literary quotation to help explain and add cultural tone to each plate. During their heyday from the 1820s to the late 1840s, these two related types of illustrated volumes for the carriage trade gave profitable employment to many artists and engravers. The latter type were often commissioned from artists and craftsmen by entrepreneurs, today's "book packagers," who would have the finished engravings bound up and then turned the product over to publisher-booksellers for retail distribution. Among the opulent volumes thus produced were several that illustrated the heroines of literature: Charles Heath's *The Shakespeare Gallery: Containing the Principal Female Characters in the Plays of the Great Poet* (1836–37) and *The Heroines of Shakespeare* (1848), with the same cast of forty-five characters but a different lineup of artists; *A Gallery of Byron Beauties* (1838?), the one Thackeray mentioned; *The Waverley Gallery* (1840); and *The Beauties of Thomas Moore* (1846).

Occasionally, the originals of the engravings would be displayed at the annual exhibitions either before or after the appearance of the albums they graced. Thus in 1833, at the British Institution (housed since its inception, suitably enough, in the former Boydell Shakespeare Gallery), William Boxall, the future director of the National Gallery, showed sever-

*Although no one thought the less of Wordsworth, Tennyson, or Browning for having contributed a few poems to such books, the involvement of serious painters was sometimes held against them, not only by fellow artists but by their patrons. Mentioning William Boxall to W. P. Frith in a letter in 1843, the collector John Gibbons remarked, "When you talk of him, [Frank] Stone, etc., as the painters of 'mere prettiness,' you must be thinking of the things that they were fools enough to do for the 'annuals.' I daresay that both are heartily ashamed of themselves for it; indeed, I know that Boxall is . . . " (Frith, *Autobiography,* 3:203). On the other hand, John Martin, celebrated then as now for the extra-large canvases on which he portrayed equally huge events, found a bread-and-butter occupation contributing twenty-seven designs to various annuals between 1826 and 1837. They could hardly be accused of "mere prettiness," dealing as they did with such subjects as the Crucifixion, the repentance of Nineveh, the destruction of Babel, and Caius Marius mourning over the ruins of Carthage (Balston, *John Martin,* pp. 91–93; Feaver, *The Art of John Martin,* pp. 103, 110–12, 125).

A Garland of Keepsake Beauties: the literary division of what Dickens called "The Galaxy Gallery of British Beauty." 55 (*top left*). Charles R. Leslie, *Griselda* (1836) (Victoria & Albert Museum, Crown Copyright). 56 (*top right*). Henry Wyatt, *Juliet. "O Romeo, Romeo, Wherefore Art Thou Romeo?"* (RA 1832) (Birmingham City Museum and Art Gallery). 57 (*bottom left*). Charles Eastlake, *Haidee: A Greek Girl* (painted 1827; RA 1831) (Tate Gallery, London). 58 (*bottom right*). John Bostock, *Rose Bradwardine* [Scott's *Waverley*] (RA 1845) (formerly Forbes Magazine Collection).

al of his designs that were engraved three years later for Heath's long-running *Book of Beauty.* As Graham Reynolds has observed, "Ephemera these Keepsake albums may be, but they embodied, even created, a standard of female beauty."[53] Certainly they influenced, to an unwholesome extent, the way serious artists treated literary heroines, who seemed too often to come from the pages of a gift book rather than from the poetic text. Represented in such a manner, it could hardly be expected that the figures whom painters named after literary characters, except perhaps Tennyson's made-to-order ones (see Part Three, under Tennyson), would bear any resemblance to their namesakes. Whatever situation in a play or poem might be dimly implied in the model's expression or pose, or accessories such as an opened letter, a nosegay, or a slim volume turned face down before her, was sacrificed to the still more vague suggestion of a mood. But no matter what her image was meant to convey, if a literary name was bestowed on her, she was credible enough, and no further explanation was needed.

Although the fashion for Keepsake books themselves subsided toward the middle of the century, the incidence of such pictures in the exhibitions sharply increased. They became, in fact, one of the most oppressive clichés of this era of painting. A reviewer of the British Institution show of 1864 wearily remarked,

> The beauty which blooms on these walls is of the complexion which years ago faded in the page of annuals, souvenirs, keepsakes, and scrapbooks. There is, it must be confessed, something too sickly sentimental and commonplace in this endless succession of damsels of pink or pallid cheeks, as the case may be, of soft rosy lips, of shoulders downy as velvet, tresses black as raven, and tortuous as Medusa's snakes—girls who, by their simpering smiles, would wish to win and flirt with every visitor in the gallery.[54]

The next year, the *Times*'s failure to locate any passage in *The Rape of the Lock* to justify Valentine Prinsep's calling his new picture *Belinda* stirred it to a shrill exasperation found in innumerable similar complaints in the sixties and seventies:

> The sacque of flowered brocade, the Japan cabinet, and something of pout and pet in the face, seem rather to have suggested the title than Pope's poem to have suggested the picture. This is neither the nymph at the fatal moment when the lock was severed, "and flashed the living lightning from her eyes"; nor as Umbriel found her sunk in Thalestriss's arms, "her eyes dejected and her hair unbound"; nor as she flew raging to Sir Plume; nor in her beauteous grief, "her eyes half languishing, half drowned in tears," though nearer this point of the poem, perhaps, than any of the others.[55]

But these snide remarks had little effect on the taste of the art-buying public. What less offensive subject could be hung on the wall of a church-going Victorian family's home, especially if the title it bore was from an approved work of English literature?

The staying power of the Keepsake-beauties branch of literary art was revealed once more toward the end of the century, when the *Graphic,* an illustrated weekly with a circulation running into hundreds of thousands, commissioned leading artists to paint a series of pretty faces of the kind generally popular with "the enormous public which sees illustrated papers."[56] The resulting engravings found their way to the ends of the earth as free supplements to the paper. An African explorer reported that "when he once fell into the power of a savage African potentate, he appeased the autocrat by daily presenting him with a 'Graphic' Type of Beauty, to adorn his tent; receiving in return one day a cow, another a goat, and so on." Besides proving that a touch of (nineteenth-century Caucasian, specifically English) female comeliness made the whole world kin, the effect on the *Graphic*'s sales was such that the editor drew up a list of Shakespeare's heroines and allotted them to a similarly eminent panel of artists for the further expression of their ideals of womanly beauty. Some of the better-remembered contributors were Luke Fildes, who drew Jessica, Frederic Leighton (Desdemona), Edward Poynter (Cressida), Alma-Tadema (Portia, wife of Brutus), and Valentine Prinsep (Mariana). Their conceptions were published in the form of colored lithographs distributed with the paper and subsequently gathered in an album, and the original paintings were exhibited as a group in 1888 prior to being sold at Christie's. The album contained letterpress by William Ernest Henley, who was prevented by the publishers from specifying the scene each picture represented. "We think," said the *Art Journal,* "his share in the work would have been more interesting had he had access to the painters, and given us their ideas upon the subject." But it is probable that they did, in fact, have few ideas, or at best they would have had to supply them retrospectively; for as the *Art Journal* also said, "an artist of talent cannot conjure up his visions at will, or upon the spur of the moment say that such and such are the lineaments with which he would portray his Julia or his Cordelia; hence it is that one so often finds that the result is merely a dressing up in a new garb of the most attractive model obtainable at the moment."[57]

Thus from their inception in the late 1820s as an ornament to the luxurious life of the drawing room to their final Victorian incarnation late in the era as a circulation-stimulant for an illustrated paper, engravings of young women exemplified the way in which artistic taste was standardized by the sheer repetition of subject and style. Nowhere was this more true than in the realm of literary illustration. Where romantic, or sentimentalized, women were concerned, and the customary situations in which their authors had placed them, an artist had an inventory of previous treatments to refer to, and, in view of the well-known popular preference for the familiar rather than the original, he had little choice but to paint one more version of the same tried-and-true subject.

CHAPTER 5

The taste of the new collectors: moral content valued over execution; taboos (nudity, "disturbing" subjects, political and social comments).—The tyranny of conventional sources and subjects; "standard" authors and "beauties" anthologies; the influence of engravings on popular demand; examples of neglected subjects and authors.

Paintings from literature reached the height of their popularity between 1830 and the 1850s, when as many as one hundred such paintings were hung each year in the London exhibitions alone. It was a sign of things to come that the first three of the annual fifty-pound prizes awarded by the Liverpool Academy (1830–32) went to literary paintings: a scene from *The Bride of Lammermoor* by Robert Scott Lauder, William Boxall's *Cordelia Receiving an Account of Her Father's Suffering,* and Daniel Maclise's *Mokanna Unveiling His Features to Zelica,* from Moore's *Lalla Rookh.*[1]

There were other manifestations of the intensified artistic interest in English literature. About 1840, when the long-lived Sketching Club (see chapter 3, above) was entering its last years, a similar coterie of young artists calling themselves "The Clique" gathered for the same purpose. Richard Dadd, W. P. Frith, Edward M. Ward, Henry Nelson O'Neil, John Phillip, Alfred Elmore, and others met weekly to compete in drawing extempore subjects "chiefly literary with a preponderance from Byron and Shakespeare."[2] One of the newly founded Art Union's projects was a competition for outline designs in the manner of John Flaxman or, more recently, the German illustrator of Shakespeare, Moritz Retzsch. Thirty sets of drawings were submitted, including a series from Shelley's *Prometheus Unbound* by Joseph Noel Paton, the Chaucerian story of Griselda by John Tenniel, and *Comus* by F. R. Pickersgill. The winner was H. C. Selous's *Pilgrim's Progress* series. The second contest was won by William Rimer's illustrations of Thomson's *The Castle of Indolence.*[3]

Both of the large collections of modern British art that were given to the nation in these years included numerous literary pictures, some commissioned by the collectors. There were seventeen in Robert Vernon's gift of 157 canvases to the National Gallery in 1847 and thirteen in John Sheepshanks's collection of 233 that the new South Kensington Museum, later renamed the Victoria and Albert, received in 1857.[4] When Francis Palgrave published in 1869 his album of color reproductions from woodcuts, *Gems of British Art,* no fewer than six of the twenty-four originals, all in the Vernon and Sheepshanks collections, were from English literature.

Far from being a merely incidental variety of subject pictures, paintings on literary themes now were valued by the new public for art as highly as landscapes and genre (into which formal categories many of them fell) and much more so than the Old Masters that had dominated the commerce in painting when noble collectors made up most of the market. Apart from their dislike of the darkened colors of the Old Masters, the new collectors failed to share the mystique, still promoted by the Royal Academy, that had hitherto determined correct English taste in painting. As far as middlebrow literary taste was concerned, the long-drawn-out critical debate over the relative merits of the ancients and the moderns had been decisively settled in favor of the latter. And just as book collectors in the preceding era had ceased to be obsessed with Greek and Roman classics, turning instead to early English and Elizabethan literature, newcomers to the art market were indifferent to the appeal of antiquity and the Renaissance and of epic themes—a fact most readily apparent, on the lowest level, in the absence of high-art (historical, mythological, religious) subjects from the Society of British Artists exhibitions, where the low-budget collector was likely to get most of his paintings.* Even subjects from Spenser and Milton, and the more heroic kinds of Shakespeare pictures, were in short supply there. As Palgrave, a relatively perceptive observer of the mid-Victorian art scene, commented, "'No demon,' in Pope's phrase, 'whispered to them to have a taste:' nor indeed was it likely that men educated in business, and ignorant of foreign lands, would appreciate very keenly the Carraccis, Guidos, Carlo Marattis, or the restored rubbish of Roman excavations, held up to them by the learned as the great examples of high art, and sole objects of enlightened admiration."[5] Few of these men, irrespective of their wealth or social position, had had more than a smattering of classical education, if any at all, and they possessed no formal knowledge of art. "They brought to their judgement of a painting, not Lemprière's classical dictionary and the academic rules, but their own experience."[6]

These collectors' indifference to the traditional subject matter of high art was compensated for by at least a nodding acquaintance with the English classics. If people with money to spend were to be interested in art at all, pictures from familiar English literature were prominent among the kinds of art they would be interested in. The stories such pictures told were well known, needing no explanation and equipped with private associations that could readily be transferred to the picture. Buyers could always feel comfortable with such art, not least—perhaps most of all—with the most hackneyed subjects.

One more consideration recommended literary paintings to that portion of the public which harbored a residual Puritan suspicion of art in general: literature, with the exception of fiction among the more rigorous Evangelicals and Dissenters, was respectable. A picture from an approved work of literature was, on principle, itself approved. Although the encouragement of morality and proper feelings, however defined, had been the primary function that English critics had generally required of liter-

*The society's exhibitions were much disparaged; in 1846 *Punch* called them "insufferably bad," and Thackeray referred to them as "deserts." On the other hand, Walter Sickert, from the long perspective of 1928, recalled the society's "position of honourable rivalry with the Royal Academy . . . in the 30s & 40s & 50s & 60s." The most bizarre episode in its long history as "the Suffolk Street gallery" occurred in the 1880s, when it invited James McNeill Whistler, whom the Royal Academy had passed by, to become a member. Before long, he was elected president, a decision everyone soon came to regret. He lasted in the office only until 1888, but before he left, he prepared on behalf of the society a "ceremonious address" to the Queen on the occasion of her golden jubilee that elicited the command that the stunned Society of British Artists might add "Royal" to its title. (Denys Sutton, *Walter Sickert: A Biography* [London, 1976], p. 222; Elizabeth R. Pennell and Joseph Pennell, *The Life of James McNeill Whistler* [London, 1908], 2:55–74.)

ature ever since the Renaissance, seldom was it more insisted upon than in the early and middle nineteenth century. In 1840 Thackeray extended the doctrine to art:

> The best paintings address themselves to the best feelings of it [the heart]; and a great many very clever pictures do not touch it at all. Skill and handling are great parts of a painter's trade, but heart is the first; this is God's direct gift to him, and cannot be got in any academy, or under any master. Look about, therefore, for pictures, be they large or small, finished well or ill, landscapes, portraits, figure-pieces, pen-and-ink sketches, or what not, that contain sentiment and great ideas. He who possesses these will be sure to express them more or less well. Never mind about the manner. He who possesses them not may draw and colour to perfection, and yet be no artist.[7]

This criterion, elevating content over execution, was never more satisfactorily met than when the chosen subject was from "moral" literature. It was the orthodoxy that governed Victorian criticism of literary painting as well as every other kind of subject art.

The whole trend away from the subjects of classical art and literature to those drawn from English sources was epitomized in the fortunes of Thomson's *The Seasons* as a favorite provider of themes for illustration. In the eighteenth century, many artists found in it attractive subjects for allegorical groups and mythological representations of the progress of the seasons—two categories closely associated with neoclassic art, as the poem itself was with Virgil and the classical tradition of pastoral poetry. But at the beginning of the nineteenth century, *The Seasons* came to be valued far more as a series of stories illustrating the domestic and social virtues, and the artists altered their perspective and emphasis accordingly. In response to the changing audience and atmosphere, they converted the poem, as they did other English literary works, into a repository of currently dominant moral ideals and "messages" that would win their paintings instant acceptance in the home.[8]

This hospitality to English literature did not mean, however, that every subject from a given work was equally approved for home viewing. Sometimes critics, delivering their dicta without offering reasons, flatly declared that a subject was unfitted for art: Gulliver's introduction to the Queen of Brobdingnag (1835 [pl. 287]: "utterly at variance with all good feeling"); Lady Macbeth's deathbed (1838: an example of "one of [Nature's] most distorted aspects, with which Art . . . has but little concern"); the old man lamenting the death of his ass in Sterne's *Sentimental Journey* (1850: "We lament such subjects, and never could feel gratification in looking upon the glazed eyes and wasted limbs of a creature like this, however ably painted"); Beatrix greeting Henry Esmond (1857 [pl. 169]: "There is nothing attractive in this subject"); Falstaff and his ragged regiment (1867: "We are sorry to see such ability devoted to what all the painter's humour and invention cannot make a pleasant subject").[9]

Some comments of this kind no doubt sprang more from individual reviewers' crotchets than from any broad laws of what constituted paintable subjects.* But it certainly can be said that the tastes, ideals, prejudices, mores, and taboos of the nineteenth-century English family dictated criteria far removed from those that determined the kind of art that had been produced for Italian princes and cardinals or German dukes. The violence and bloodshed, the battles and martyrdoms that, for example, characterized much French academic painting had little place on

*Nearly all quotations from contemporary criticism in this book are taken from major general-circulation periodicals, not, as might sometimes be suspected, from religious or didactic publications whose biases were not necessarily shared by the art-loving public at large.

59 (*top*). Thomas Stothard, *Cleopatra Dissolving the Pearl* (*Intemperance*) (RA 1810) (Tate Gallery, London). A sketch for the mural Stothard painted, 1799–1803, on the Roman staircase of Burghley House, seat of the Marquis of Exeter, joining vast murals painted there by Antonio Verrio in 1694–97. 60 (*bottom*). William Collins, *Sunday Morning* (RA 1836) (Tate Gallery, London). A contrast between the old aristocratic taste in art and the new and dominant bourgeois preference. The intemperance theme in Stothard's painting nominally had a moral aim, but pictorial allegory, even when imposed on a scene from literature, had become so heavily conventional as to be devoid of much force; like the bacchanalian scene it represents, it was an increasingly enfeebled survivor from an older time. The lesson of Collins's pious genre scene, however, was unmistakable and directly applicable to everyday life. It was exhibited with a motto from George Herbert's "Sunday": "O day most calm, most bright,/The fruit of this, the next world's bud. . . ."

English walls. The difference between the two schools struck Richard Redgrave forcibly when he visited the 1855 Paris exhibition of loaned art. "Our subjects," he noted in his diary, "are undoubtedly of a less elevated, and of a lower and more familiar character in England, but they are works a man can live with, and love to look on, obtruding no terrors on his sleeping or waking fancies."[10]

Few households, of course, required unbroken cheer on the walls; much room was reserved for, among other moods, representations of gentle pathos or melancholy, agreeable sentiments poles removed from revulsion and indispensable to a well-rounded emotional existence. Nor was there any unanimity on the score of sensuousness, which after all is a matter of degree. Modern eyes detect in Victorian paintings much latent eroticism of which contemporaries were serenely unaware. Outright sexuality in art was prohibited in every pure-minded family's home, but in respect to nudes there was considerable variance of opinion. Moral disapproval contended with aesthetic delight, and the scales decisively shifted as the nineteenth century progressed. At the time the Reverend George Tennyson installed in his rectory his collection of "'eathen gods and goddesses wi'out cloäs" (1810), Dorothea Brooke's uncle, in *Middlemarch*, had already brought home from his travels on the Continent a gentleman's collection of casts and pictures. "To poor Dorothea," wrote George Eliot, suggesting a change of taste that was evident no more than twenty years later, when Dorothea compared her uncle's collection with Casaubon's, "these severe classical nudities and smirking Renaissance-Correggiosities were painfully inexplicable, staring in the midst of her Puritanic conceptions: she had never been taught how she could bring them into any sort of relevance with her life" (chap. 9).

Tolerance of the paintings of William Etty, the pre- and early Victorian specialist in the undraped female figure, was a reliable indication of men's character. No doubt there was a touch of professional jealousy in Constable's remark, after seeing Etty's *Venus and Cupid* at the British Institution in 1830, that "I recollect nothing in the Gallery but some women's bums by Etty R. A."[11] Twenty years later, the self-righteous Thomas Uwins, deploring the influence of "railroad speculators, iron mine men, and grinders from Sheffield, &c." on contemporary art, exclaimed, "The voluptuous character of Etty's works suits the degree of moral and mental intelligence of these people, and therefore his success!"[12] But even one of Uwins's own "iron mine men," John Gibbons, had his mild doubts about the propriety of Etty's work. "I fancy, from what I have heard of it," he wrote Frith apropos of a painting that he did not identify, "that it is fitter for the antechamber of a gay young bachelor than the walls of a *family* man whose head is gray."[13] Thackeray, though unreservedly admiring Etty for his ability to paint flesh with the skill of Titian and Rubens, came down solidly on the side of morality: "A great, large curtain of fig leaves should be hung over every one of this artist's pictures," he declared in 1839, "and the world should pass on, content to know that there are some glorious colours painted beneath."[14]*

Dickens seized upon an artistic taste that ran to "voluptuousness" as an indicator of morality in his description of the home of the villainous businessman Carker, in *Dombey and Son:*

> And yet amidst this opulence of comfort, there is something in the general air that is not well. Is it that the carpets and the cushions are too soft and noiseless, so that those who move or repose among them seem to act by stealth? Is it that

*Two comments on Etty's *Phaedria and Cymocles on the Idle Lake* (pl. 61) illustrate the range of critics' disapproval. *Fraser's Magazine* (12 [1835]: 52) was relatively restrained, taking refuge in uneasy jocularity: "The amorous pair who are so closely entwined together in their tiny mother-of-pearl boat—perhaps the better to preserve its balance, seem to be altogether denizens of a holiday world, where people can live most jollily without any more substantial fare than transports and kisses. Etty is apt to *poetise* with his pencil much after the fashion that [Erasmus] Darwin piqued himself upon *painting* with his pen, rather too flowerily and lusciously: they cloy us with sweets till we feel surfeited and out of conceit with them." The *Times* (23 May 1835), on the other hand, condemned the picture as sheer pornography: "A most disgusting thing, and we wonder that in these times the people who have the direction of this exhibition venture to permit such pictures to be hung. Phaedria is the true representative of one of the Nymphs of Drury Lane [not the actresses within, but their fallen sisters on the pavement outside], and Cymocles looks like an unwashed coal-porter. The Love at the end of the boat is a sort of May-day climbing boy, his cheeks, 'touched up,' as Charles Lamb has it, 'with rose-pink;' and the boat is of the worst kind of Colebrookdale crockery. Such pictures are as shocking to good taste as they are offensive to common decency; they are only fit for the contemplation of very old or very young gentlemen, and ought to be reserved for the particular delectation of those classes of persons."

61. William Etty, *Phaedria and Cymocles on the Idle Lake* (RA 1835) (Forbes Magazine Collection). Etty's unabashed delight in flamboyant sensuousness tried the tolerance even of critics who had to concede his exceptional talent as a colorist. The subject is from Spenser's *The Faerie Queene* (bk. 2, canto 6).

the prints and pictures do not commemorate great thoughts or deeds, or render nature in the poetry of landscape, hall, or hut, but are of one voluptuous cast—mere shows of form and colour—and no more? Is it that the books have all their gold outside, and that the titles of the greater part qualify them to be companions of the prints and pictures? (Chap. 22)

Dickens here expresses the close connection between the paintings on the wall and the books on the shelves. The implication in Carker's case, supposing that he favored the canvases of contemporary artists, is that the pictures are Etty's in spirit if not in fact, and that the books are overheated to match: Carker would seem to have had the same tastes that his noble contemporary Richard Monckton Milnes, later Lord Houghton, indulged in his celebrated library and museum of erotica.*

But nudes also could carry, somewhere on their persons, highly respectable credentials. It had long been a commonplace that the unclothed human figure displayed in classical painting, especially Old Master pictures on mythological or even biblical themes, might be looked upon with unembarrassed eyes but the same figure in a modern context could not. Similarly, it was felt that nudity in a painting derived from a respectable source in English literature could not be all that bad. That was why scores of painters, for a century and more, offered their customers studies of the nude (or nearly so) Musidora, from *The Seasons*—the nation's Venus, discovered by an English stream. (See Part Three below, under Thomson.) Her acceptability extended, on the same grounds of literary cachet, to such figures as Spenser's Serena, when she was being rescued by Sir Calepine, and Lady Godiva, who had been painted as a Coventry legend long before Tennyson celebrated her, but whose entrée to domestic walls was facilitated by his poem.† Etty sought opportunities for painting the nude in such impeccable sources as Spenser and Milton (Eve and the bacchanalian figures in *Comus*), and this is one reason why other artists were so partial to these and other poets' treatments of classical myth. Late Victorian academic painters, though they replaced Etty's warm flesh with

*But only four years earlier, in his description of the art owned by the Lancashire industrialist Millbank in *Coningsby* (1844), the more liberal Benjamin Disraeli had seen no harm in his possessing, among groups of animals by Landseer ("as full of speech and sentiment as if they were designed by Aesop") and "the household humour and homely pathos of Wilkie," "some specimens of Etty worthy of Venice when it was alive" (bk. 4, chap. 4).

†As a subject of art, Lady Godiva was in need of the respectability Tennyson's poem (1842) provided; she then had a somewhat risqué reputation. In 1826, there was a wild rumor that the king wanted to buy for 10,000 guineas (a huge sum that in itself should have discredited the report) a life-size painting of Godiva then on view in a Pall Mall gallery. To encourage patronage, the proprietor seized upon the old show business device of advertising that notwithstanding criticism in the press—which he conceivably could have planted, along with the rumor—the painting could be viewed without embarrassment in mixed company (Whitley [3], pp. 109–10). On Lady Godiva and *tableaux vivants*, see Part Three, under Tennyson.

62. William Etty, *The Bather. "At the Doubtful Breeze Alarmed"* (RA 1843) (Tate Gallery, London). Given his fascination with the nude, it was inevitable that Etty should have returned several times to English poetry's archetypal female nude, Musidora, in Thomson's *The Seasons,* from which the motto is taken.

marble, sometimes took their nudes from the same sources. Edward Poynter, for example, relished the chance to paint nude subsidiary figures (nereids) when he was commissioned to make six designs for a sumptuous edition of Keats's *Endymion* in 1873.

There was less tolerance of the "disturbing" quality of some literary subjects. As Redgrave said, no terrors should be allowed to obtrude on one's sleeping or waking fancies.* After the time of the illustrations from Gothic fiction and, more important, of Fuseli's macabre and violent paintings (which, however, had no influence on popular art), the incidence of the horrific, of ghosts and evil spirits, markedly diminished—a strong indication of art's spreading invasion of the bourgeois home. There were a few exceptions: Macbeth and the witches still were painted in profusion, as were the goblins in Burns's "Tam o' Shanter." But the one subject was hallowed by its association with Shakespeare, and the other was no more disturbing than any supernatural tale told by the Victorian fireside.

Two macabre "Italian" stories were repeatedly painted. One was that of Ginevra, the daughter of the Orsino family, who on her wedding day (some accounts say during Christmas festivities) hid herself in a trunk by way of a prank. The lid closed over her and locked, and fifty years later her skeleton was discovered. The best known treatment at the time was in Samuel Rogers's poem *Italy* (1822–28), from which at least ten paintings of the story were derived between 1834 and 1854. The other story, actually a pair of cognate ones from the fourth book of Boccaccio's *Decameron,* was the grisly one centering on an anatomical item and a cruelly interrupted love affair. In the narrative retold by Keats in "Isabella, or, The Pot of Basil," Isabella's lover is murdered by her brothers and his body buried in a forest, where Isabella, led by a dream, finds it. She severs the head and places it in a pot of basil as a permanent souvenir; her brothers, noting her abnormal devotion to the pot, steal it and find the head. Isabella, bereft of her lover in any form, dies. From 1840, when the first artistic treatment was shown at the Royal Academy—by Keats's friend Joseph Severn—to the end of the century, no fewer than a score of paintings from the poem were exhibited. (For Millais's version, see pl. 334.) In the other Boccaccian narrative, paintings of which were sometimes attributed to Dryden's version in his *Sigismunda and Guiscardo,* Tancred, prince of Salerno, kills his daughter's lover Guiscardo and sends his heart (not head) to her in a golden cup; she takes poison and joins Isabella in the shades.

The gruesome aspects of both stories seem to have been discounted. To the Victorians, the sad fates of Ginevra, Isabella, and Sigismunda, irrespective of their circumstances, qualified them to be the subjects of sentimental portraits. The spirit in which they were painted is captured in a critic's description of H. W. Pickersgill's painting of Ginevra (RA 1848), this time from Thomas Haynes Bayley's ballad version: "Her bright look casts no shadow before, as she holds the lid up and bends to step in. Poor thing; it was a hard and dismal fate, and in her white raiment, orange flowers, and beaming countenance, the artist has imparted the glow of painting to its poetic tragedy."[15]

Though the claims of sentiment might sometimes overrule revulsion, the habit of the age was to avert one's eyes from unpleasantness. As a writer remarked in 1847, "The end of Art is pleasure; and to dwell habitually on the dark side of humanity is to miss that end." [16] The "dark side of humanity" presumably included its drinking habits; Burns's con-

*Presumably this would include John Martin's apocalyptic visions. Besides the ones he derived from the Old Testament and Milton, there was *The Last Man* (pl. 63), which, along with Loutherbourg's earlier painting of the same name, was related to a recurrent theme in late eighteenth- and early nineteenth-century thought, the vanity of human ambition confronted by the future annihilation of the race. This was the same gloomy idea that lay behind the numerous late-eighteenth-century paintings of ruins. Byron wrote a poem, "Darkness," suggested by Jean-Baptiste Grainville's *Le dernier homme.* Mary Shelley's novel *The Last Man* was published the same year that Martin painted his first version of the subject (1826). Thomas Lovell Beddoes incorporated portions of an unfinished drama on the theme in his *Death's Jest Book,* and Thomas Campbell, denying he had plagiarized from Byron, produced his own poem "The Last Man," a quotation from which accompanied Martin's third painted version. (See A. J. Sambrook, "A Romantic Theme: The Last Man," *Forum for Modern Language Studies* [St. Andrews University] 2 [1965]: 25–33.)

63. John Martin, *The Last Man* (RA 1850) (Walker Art Gallery, Liverpool). After visiting the Royal Academy exhibition, Charlotte Brontë wrote her father that Martin's was "a grand, wonderful picture . . . showing the red sun fading out of the sky, and all the soil of the foreground made up of bones and skulls" (*The Brontës: Their Lives, Friendships and Correspondence* [The Shakespeare Head Brontë, ed. T. J. Wise and J. A. Symington, Oxford, 1932–38], 3: 116).

vivial songs were illustrated by conspicuously diluted pictures that contained none of the tankard-emptying abandon one finds in carousal scenes in seventeenth-century Dutch art. In fact, the only drinking scenes from literature that were often portrayed were the Boar's Head Tavern festivities in *Henry IV* and the "cakes and ale" scene in *Twelfth Night,* and these were notably toned down. The alcoholic content of Victorian painting was concentrated, instead, in George Cruikshank's pictorial temperance tracts *The Bottle* and *The Drunkard's Children.*

Disturbing public issues, which more often than not concerned themselves with the dark side of humanity, were almost totally ignored in

64. William Hogarth, *Sigismunda Mourning over the Heart of Guiscardo, Her Murther'd Husband* (1759; Society of Artists 1766) (Tate Gallery, London). This painting was the first to allude to Dryden's version of the Boccaccian story in his *Fables.* Persistently anxious to prove his talent in history painting, Hogarth selected the subject in an effort to equal, if not surpass, the celebrated treatment by "Correggio" (actually Francis Furini).

65. John Burnet, *Tam o' Shanter* (undated) (Glasgow Art Gallery and Museum). This scene from Burns's poem represents the limit to which nineteenth-century artists went in depicting the social joys of drinking. Better remembered as an engraver, Burnet exhibited at the Royal Academy for fifty-four years (1808–62).

Victorian art except for such political overtones as might be detected in some history paintings and the numerically small group of social realist paintings after mid-century. Unlike the Romantic poets and the leading Victorian social critics (the so-called sages), nineteenth-century artists were almost totally uninterested in the issues represented by what Carlyle called "the condition of England question." Temperamentally if not ideologically, they were conservative, especially as they worked their way up in society. The Royal Academy exhibitions never were the political arena that the Paris Salon became on occasion.

It is not surprising, then, that forthright social or political comment was never seen, or at least publicly detected, in nineteenth-century literary paintings, despite the heterodox ideas and subversive tendencies so many English literary works contain. There may be political overtones, as has recently been argued,[17] in Turner's *The Bright Stone of Honour (Ehrenbreitstein) and the Tomb of Marceau,* from *Childe Harold* (RA 1835). But overtones only; and the same is true of what was perhaps the closest approach a Victorian literary painting made to explicit political statement, Holman Hunt's *Rienzi Vowing to Obtain Justice for the Death of His Young Brother* (RA 1849). Based on Bulwer-Lytton's novel, which had a topical bearing on the Italian Risorgimento, it was, by the artist's own admission, a pictorial expression of the liberal feelings roused in him by the fervor that had swept Europe in the previous year. "Like most young men," Hunt said much later, "I was stirred by the spirit of freedom of the passing revolutionary time. The appeal to Heaven against the tyranny exercised over the poor and helpless seemed well fitted for pictorial treatment. 'How long, O Lord!' many bleeding souls were crying at that time."[18]

66. Thomas Stothard, *Carousing Scene* (undated) (Victoria & Albert Museum, Crown Copyright). The literary source is not certain. One possibility is *Twelfth Night* (Sir Toby Belch with Maria in the background); a more likely one is *Henry IV* (Falstaff with Dame Quickly, though the other figures bear little resemblance to his drinking companions as portrayed on the stage).

In the large and repetitious array of pictures from Burns, there is little hint of the provocatively democratic and irreligious elements that inform such poems as "The Twa Dogs," "The Jolly Beggars," and "The Holy Fair," although all three were painted often enough. (A number of poems that Burns's first editor, Dr. James Currie, considered unsuitable for public display were suppressed in the edition he published in 1800.) It is safe to say that no Burns pictures even faintly expressed the "Jacobinism" and "infidelity" with which early critics had taxed the poet. When artists took individual vignettes of character and incident from his poems, they consistently drained the subject of its satiric or polemic element, reducing it to mere innocuous genre.

Although Hogarth was admired, it was for the morality of his "progress" stories, not his savage indictment of eighteenth-century social practices. The furthest that artists went in behalf of the "correction of manners" that had been an important aim of writers in the age of Swift and Dr. Johnson was their scenes from Addison's *Spectator* papers, but even these were sometimes relieved of their gentle satire (pl. 90). None of the paintings from *Don Juan* conveyed any hint of the poem's satirical voltage; nearly all, including Ford Madox Brown's (pl. 133), dealt with the romantic story of Don Juan and Haidee. The fairly numerous pictures from Samuel Butler's *Hudibras* (pls. 3, 282, 283) took the farcical situations and left the corrosive once-topical satire behind.

Because no one expected to find social or political criticism in contemporary art, critics seldom went out of their way to look for it. The liberal slant of Leigh Hunt's *Examiner* sometimes prompted it to find a message for the moment, as when Henry Monro's treatment of the familiar subject of Wolsey's disgrace in *Henry VIII* (BI 1814) led to the rather gratuitous observation that the picture should remind spectators of present-day royalty, most particularly the dissolute Prince Regent, in their "sensual, selfish, and time-serving acquiescence to their pleasures and appetites."[19] No such bracing note, however, was sounded by later art critics, who, when they did feel inclined to infer a propagandistic message from a new painting, found one that would sit well with their readers.

Their orientation is well defined by the nature of their responses to three literary paintings exhibited about the time that Hunt's *Rienzi* caused a stir (on Pre-Raphaelite, not political, grounds). Frith's *The Return from Labour* (RA 1846), equipped with a motto from Gray's "Elegy," was greeted as "a cheering domestic vision of rural comfort and happiness, which would get no belief on the floor of the House of Commons,"[20] then debating the cause and cure of the prevailing "agricultural distress," including the Irish famine. Frith's picture, the reviewer believed, would strengthen the confidence of those who maintained that all was well with the rural poor.

In violent contrast was a picture entitled *The Streets of London—A Female Dombey* (SBA 1848), which had no connection whatsoever with the new novel whose title it so brazenly echoed. It was a multiple-episode composition in the manner of F. M. Brown's later *Work* and Frith's *The Railway Station* and *Derby Day*. On Ludgate Hill, a soldier kissed his girl, a policeman beat a child, and selfish pride, in the person of an overdressed woman with a lapdog (the "female Dombey"), refused to succor misery in the form of a pallid beggar girl, while a sailor with his sweetheart on his arm did, in fact, relieve the "distressed female." The artist was chastised for his violation of artistic decorum. "We are sorry to see this performance," said the *Literary Gazette*. "We have enough of the stirring up of discontent in low and sordid literature; and it is painful to see the bad spirit transferred to the painter's art."[21]

The critical response to the third picture, Millais's rendering of Coventry Patmore's poem "The Tale of Poor Maud, the Woodman's Daughter" (RA 1851), is remarkable for what it failed to say. The painting was pure sentimental genre: a well-dressed little boy offering a handful of strawberries to the homespun-clad daughter of a woodman. No reviewer pointed out that in the poem the girl, once she was grown, was seduced by the grown-up son of wealth, and deserted by him, lost her mind and murdered their child. The social implications of the ballad-like story were totally overlooked.

When Richard Redgrave's *The Sempstress* was exhibited at the Royal Academy in 1844, it bore a quotation from Thomas Hood's "The Song of the Shirt," which had appeared in *Punch* six months earlier (December 1843). The poem had caused a sensation.[22] Redgrave's painting was an expression on the highest social level of a sudden wave of sympathy with downtrodden, ill-paid seamstresses that otherwise found expression in musical settings of Hood's poem (as well as versified spinoffs), printed handkerchiefs, dramatizations, and sermons. But the picture disappointed those who expected it to communicate the burning indignation of the poem. Here, for once, was a subject that the momentarily aroused critics decided should not be utterly smothered in sentimentality. Thackeray, for one, was hard on it. "Mr. Redgrave," he wrote, "has illustrated every thing except the humour, the manliness, and the bitterness of the song. He has only depicted the tender, good-natured part of it."[23]

The Sempstress initiated a steady stream of paintings—some twenty are recorded—depicting shirtmaking, dressmaking, millinery-making women; and if they did not actually get their titles from lines in the poem ("Work, work, work!" or "Stitch! stitch! stitch!"), they came equipped with those same words as a motto. Even so unlikely an artist as George F. Watts took up the subject in 1849, but like virtually all other representations, his carried no social message whatsoever. It is noteworthy that the other literary protest of the moment against the horrible conditions in which women and children worked, Elizabeth Barrett's "Cry of the Children," published in a volume of her poems the year after "The Song of the Shirt" and almost as well known, seems not to have inspired any paintings.

Even had artists possessed more of a social conscience than they did, the watchdogs of the press, echoing the conservative, don't-rock-the-boat prejudices of the art exhibitions' clientele, would have made it extremely risky for them to express their feelings in paint. Where touchy issues were even dimly involved, it was prudent to avoid them. The fact was that whatever else pictures from literature were expected to provide, social commentary was not tolerable except in the blandest possible terms. And so literary comment on the foolish if not vicious ways of mankind, and of nineteenth-century English society in particular, was transformed on canvas into inoffensive sentimental genre and biteless comedy of manners.

If there was an all but universal consensus regarding the kinds of pictures that were and were not suitable for home display, in the case of literary paintings there was no less broad an agreement on the sources to be drawn from, and, other things (such as domestic acceptability) being equal, the subjects to be selected. Custom governed the market. But what had hardened by the Victorian era into mindless habit had originated in spontaneous fashion, and in the earliest phase of literary painting, down to the end of the eighteenth century, the scope of adaptable subjects was still flexible. While characters and scenes from Shakespeare, Milton, Spenser, Thomson, and Gray quickly became staples, there was also, as we have seen, a significant representation of immediately contemporary literature, books popular in their own day but now wholly forgotten. At the same time, the choice of subjects was more often affected by personal relationships between artists and patrons than later, when, apart from commissions, it was governed by the demands of the market at large. Romney's eight or nine "Serena" pictures from Hayley's poem *The Triumphs of Temper,* which quickly went through fourteen editions after its publication in 1781, are a case in point.[24] Hayley was Romney's patron, and at least one of the pictures, it appears, was painted while Hayley was writing the poem and reading to him his daily production. Eventually the set was used to illustrate the sixth edition of 1788. (It had an additional tie-in with the bestseller list of the period, because Serena was a great reader, and in successive editions of the poem, the identity of the book Romney depicted in her hands was changed in Hayley's text to reflect the latest demand at the circulating library. In one edition, she was deep in Fanny Burney's *Evelina,* and in another, in an early novel by Mrs. Opie, wife of the artist John Opie.)[25]

In the nineteenth century, the winnowing process that selected the subjects for literary art was governed by uncannily accurate prescience. The only bestselling books that were repeatedly drawn upon were those of authors whose fame was destined to last: Scott, Byron, Dickens, Tennyson. Those that were the sensation of only a season or two were, in contrast to their predecessors in the late eighteenth century, seldom chosen. The few recorded paintings from obscure, ephemeral books can probably be accounted for by the personal taste or momentary enthusiasm of the artist or, more likely, by that of the buyer, who commissioned the work as a memento of a literary hobby or a sentimental attachment to the book.*

Unfortunately, apart from the relatively few pictures of whose occasion we have a record, it is impossible to distinguish between those that were "bespoke" from the ones that artists produced in the usual manner, on speculation as it were. But it is clear that as the nineteenth century wore on, the former element of adventurousness, responsiveness to immediate literary fashions, even downright eccentricity in choice of subject, diminished; there were decidedly fewer offbeat subjects than before. A few paintings seem to have been edged into the annual exhibitions to advertise a forthcoming book, as were Daniel Maclise's three illustrations of Bulwer's *Alice; or, The Mysteries* at the British Institution in 1838. And in the 1880s and 90s, a number of paintings were displayed with the explicit announcement that they were "illustrations" of this or that new novel. But except for these, art did not often reflect the current-book news in the weekly literary papers. Theatrical painting, as long as it held out against the encroachment of photography, was much more *au courant* with its field of interest.

Thus pictures from established authors, and from a limited range of their total repertory of subjects for painting, constituted all but a small proportion of the year's exhibited offerings. In reviews of exhibitions, especially after mid-century when the great boom in literary art began to

*In the 1850s, for example, Queen Victoria commissioned a series of watercolor sketches to remind her of the Shakespearean plays she had particularly enjoyed at the Princess' Theatre. These were assembled in an album that is still at Windsor (George Rowell, *Queen Victoria Goes to the Theatre* [London, 1978], pp. 56–57).

67. William P. Frith, *The Widow Wadman Lays Siege to My Uncle Toby* (RA 1866) (Tate Gallery, London). Another treatment of the subject made popular by Leslie (pl. 45). In the typical way of Victorian literary painters, the spirit of the source as well as the letter of the characterization was sacrificed in favor of a conventional portrait of a pair of young lovers. Little if any of Sterne's individual flavor remains, and in age, appearance, and romantic inclination the widow and the besieged veteran of Marlborough's wars bear little resemblance to his comic characters.

wane, the laments over the monotonous repetition of some subjects were so frequent as to be themselves the essence of monotony. "If [one] artist is original by accident," said the *Art Journal* in 1858, "all the others follow in Indian file. One paints Evangeline,* the Lady of Shalott, or some other conception of equal pungency, when lo! there is a creation of fifty Evangelines and Ladies of Shalott; and so it is with every new vein of thought."[26] The occasional novelty that "took" would soon become a cliché.

Even when painters bothered to look for fresh subjects, they sought them in the same books that had already served them well. Frith's daughter recalled that "Papa used to sit for half an hour after dinner, smoking and generally searching for a 'subject.' The ugliness, he said, of modern dress always appalled him, and he avoided it as long as he could, reading over and over again Goldsmith, Molière, Richardson, and in fact all the old writers, until one joyous day . . . he came across the pages of immortal Boz, and made himself happy with 'Dolly Varden' and 'Kate Nickleby,' and I think one or two other characters out of books he loved. But, these completed, he came back to the old writers."[27]

Despite this constant crossing and recrossing of already well gleaned fields, the full pictorial possibilities of a given poem, play, or novel were seldom realized. The incidents that were drawn from it were not necessarily the ones, or the only ones, that were most adapted for graphic representation; they seem merely to have been those that first caught the public fancy. By no means all of the deaths in Shakespeare, or the dramatically effective Shakespearean scenes involving the unmasking of disguised figures, were painted, or all the "discoveries" or rescues in *The Faerie Queene,* or the numerous confrontations or pathetic episodes in Shakespeare's plays or Scott's romances. Popular though *Tristram Shandy* was as a subject for anecdotal pictures, it contained many episodes that were seldom if ever depicted. The little incident of Uncle Toby and the fly might be expected to have been to the popular taste (though there might have been some difficulty painting the fly); but it seems never to have been the subject of a picture. The numerous incidents involving the fortifications were never used, apart from the presence of the sentry box in two famous Widow Wadman pictures (pls. 45, 67). Even Slawkenbergius's tale contains a number of passages seemly enough to be acceptable to Victorian buyers who, understandably, would have bridled at any illustration of the obstetrical passages.

Another instance is that of *The Vicar of Wakefield,* one of the most-painted single works of English literature. Artists repeatedly found *données* in the briefest of passages. Mulready's famous *Choosing the Wedding Gown* (pl. 304) was based on no more than the novel's first two sentences:

> I was ever of opinion that the honest man who married and brought up a large family did more service than he who continued single and only talked of population. From the moment I had scarce taken orders a year before I began to think seriously of matrimony, and chose my wife as she did her wedding gown, not for a fine glossy surface but such qualities as would wear well.

From a single page in chapter 16, Frith drew three different subjects at one time or another: "He [Squire Thornhill] usually came in the morning, and while my son and I followed our occupations abroad, he sat with the family at home, and amused them by describing the town, with every part of which he was particularly acquainted" (*The Squire Describing Some*

*Longfellow and Irving were the only American writers to figure prominently in British art.

68. (*left*). Charles R. Leslie, *Autolycus* (RA 1836) (Victoria & Albert Museum, Crown Copyright).

69. (*below*). Augustus Egg. *Autolycus* (RA 1845) (Guildhall Art Gallery, London). A good example of the manner in which popular artists who drew their subjects from literature imitated one another. The scene is the same: *The Winter's Tale,* 4. 4, in which the roguish peddler Autolycus hawks ballads (Leslie) and ribbons (Egg) to an enraptured group of stylishly clad shepherds and shepherdesses. For the companion to Leslie's painting, see pl. 242.

Passages in His Town Life, RA 1844); "The intervals between conversation were employed in teaching my daughters piquet or sometimes in setting my two little ones to box to make them *sharp*, as he called it" (*The Squire Teaching the Young Ladies Piquet and the Boys to Box,* pl. 86); "Then the poor woman would sometimes tell the 'Squire, that she thought him and Olivia extremely of a size, and would bid both stand up to see which was tallest" (*Measuring Heights,* pl. 303). Yet there are several scenes that would appear to have been equally adaptable to painting but were not touched even by Frith: the family's posing for the "limner" (see chapter 1, above), the vicar overtaking the strolling company, and the two "discovery" scenes, in one of which the actor who plays Horatio in Rowe's *The Fair Penitent* turns out to be the vicar's eldest son, and in the other, Burchell proves to be Sir William Thornhill.

Thomson's *The Seasons,* that inexhaustible reservoir of paintings for many decades, contained more hints for pictures than artists ever availed themselves of. A number of "human interest" passages went unused while Celadon and Amelia, Damon and Musidora, and Palemon and Lavinia were painted with oppressive regularity. Fashion dictated the initial choice, and convention preserved it even when outmoded. A picture from *The Seasons*, apart from landscapes and generalized rural genre, *had* to be a picture of Celadon and Amelia, Damon and Musidora, or Palemon and Lavinia; that was the way things were at the beginning, and the way things stayed. For this reason, the frequent occurrence of some subjects is less reliable an indication of the active taste of a particular moment than might be supposed. The persistence of these subjects implies inertia and indifference on the part of both artist and buyer—a kind of reflex conservatism—rather than a genuine, lively attachment to the subjects themselves.

This heavy conventionality marked, and to a large degree was dictated by, the nature of the books on the shelves of the rooms where the pictures hung. When first editions of novels were expensive, as they were throughout the century, many families with literary as well as artistic taste could not afford to buy them; in most homes, they were simply on loan from the many circulating libraries in the metropolis and the provinces that preceded and then (after the 1840s) surrendered their clientele to Mudie's famous "select" lending agency in New Oxford Street. But books that were merely borrowed could not be taken into the bosom of the family, to be reread and referred to in casual conversation for many years thereafter. So far as the interests of art were concerned, most of the significant books that were permanently housed under, or across from, the paintings were English classics or "standard authors"—a dignity Byron and Scott had traded for their earlier distinction of bestsellers by mid-century, and which Tennyson would attain in time. The English classics had a much longer shelf life in the nineteenth century than they were to have in the twentieth; they were by no means as readily displaced by new products of the press. The selection of subjects for pictures assumed a more stable popular taste, less affected by fleeting vogues, as well as a genuine devotion to the writers who had been popular several generations, if not a century or two, earlier. As Ian Jack has correctly observed, "The average reader in the year 1820 was as likely to be reading a book written in the eighteenth century as a book by one of his contemporaries."[28] Though the literary sympathies of readers a generation later may not have been quite so likely to reach back to the preceding century, they still were less touched by the passion for newness that characterizes present-day readers. Literary paintings, in short, reflected a now vanished phenomenon: the persistence of "our old authors," as they were called, "the rich deposits of earlier literature" as Jack describes them—the staples of literary experience among the commonalty of Victorian readers.

The illustrated eighteenth-century editions of Shakespeare, Spenser, and Milton and the reprint series of standard English poets, novelists, dramatists, and essayists that figure most prominently in the early history of reprint publishing and book illustration (see chapter 2, above) were only the best remembered of many such enterprises that often constituted the profitable backlist of publishers. In the third of a century before the Victorian era began, there were scores of series conceived in direct imitation of Bell's and Cooke's, some running to scores of volumes and a few to well over one hundred. Some were issued in weekly, fortnightly, or monthly parts, in pocket format and at prices as low as sixpence or a shilling, each with an engraved title page and perhaps a frontispiece. Others, meant for the well-to-do trade, were luxuriously bound according to the taste of the moment. Many were elegantly illustrated and were priced accordingly.

The standard authors figured on the shelves in another form, in the many "beauties" anthologies that are traceable ultimately to the kind of appreciative criticism Addison had popularized in his *Spectator* papers on Milton (1712): the singling out of short passages over which one was encouraged to linger and exclaim "O que c'est beau!" Even earlier, Edward Bysshe's *The Art of English Poesy* (1702) contained an assemblage of quotable excerpts; and throughout the eighteenth century, the teaching of rhetoric in schools for middle-class boys was assisted by anthologies of passages to be analyzed, memorized, and/or recited. After the middle of the century, the presses poured forth books entitled *The Beauties of Poetry Display'd, The Beauties of Shakespeare, The Beauties of the Spectator* (or the *Tatler* or the *Rambler*), *The Beauties of English Poesy* (one of Goldsmith's potboilers), *The Beauties of Fielding, The Beauties of Sterne.* A number of these anthologies, including one devoted to Dr. Johnson, were reissued through the first third of the nineteeth century.

In 1789, the publication of the first of the many editions of the Tonbridge schoolmaster Vicesimus Knox's *Extracts, Elegant, Instructive, and Entertaining, in Poetry; from the Most Approved Authors* (a similar volume of prose had appeared in 1783) added fresh vigor to the anthology business; in 1810, Wordsworth observed that the work was "circulated every where and in fact constitutes at this day the poetical library of our Schools."[29] Its popularity led to the adoption of its title as the generic term for such books. New collections competed for a share of the market as it was expanded, not only by the spread of popular education but by the fashion for gift books (see chapter 4, above), which led publishers to package the literary (textual) beauties in volumes whose formats were themselves regarded as modestly elegant. Among these anthologies were *Lyrical Gems* (1824), *Croly's British Poets, or New Elegant Extracts* (1828), *Specimens of the Lyrical, Descriptive and Narrative Poets of Great Britain* (1828), *The Juvenile Poetic Selector* (1829), and so on, down to the most popular and influential of all such works in Victorian times, Palgrave's *Golden Treasury* (1861).

The practice of singling out passages of unusual merit was a common one among reviewers, beginning in the later decades of the eighteenth century. Critical articles were often as much quotation as original text, a scarcely surprising practice when writers were working at space rates. Extracts were a favorite means of filling the unused portions of columns or pages in middle- and working-class periodicals. The custom extended also to the lectures on literary topics delivered from the 1830s onward at the hundreds of mechanics' institutes that served the cause of popular adult education; such platform performances were mainly recitations interspersed with appreciative remarks.

These several entwined conventions in popular literary culture served to focus the eys of ordinary readers on the shining high spots of poetry and fiction—the "beautiful" image or thought, the striking dash of psychological characterization or natural description, the memorable pointing of a moral—rather than the work's totality. Paintings fulfilled the same purpose. They too, by necessity, captured only fragments of the work. Engravings of literary paintings were scarcely more than elegant extracts in visual form.

The invention of the stereotype at the beginning of the nineteenth century, in addition to being an important technical advance, created a perfect metaphor to symbolize the effect of the engraving process on British art. Recalling the furor that greeted the Pre-Raphaelites' defiance of convention, Holman Hunt wrote that the assumption that "all that British art was required to display" could be seen at the annual exhibitions "was . . . indicated by the avidity with which all well-to-do homes were furnished with engravings of the favourite current pictures" at those showcases. [30] The increasing presence of such engravings in the home, that is, homogenized taste; they and their subjects became so familiar, through day-to-day experience of them, that they became the norm for aesthetic experience and standards. Engravings discouraged whatever adventurousness the art-buying public might otherwise have risked, making it more conservative, less receptive to innovation, and then enforcing its fixed taste upon the painters. If their clients were satisfied with repetitions of the same themes, why should artists whose livelihood depended on their acceptance exert themselves to find fresh subjects?

Such a persistent state of mind probably explains in large part (but not entirely, because some of these anomalies defy rational explanation) why the artistic coverage of English literature, even that portion of the literary heritage which lent itself to visual treatment, was so fragmentary despite its abundance. It was not only that artists confined themselves to a well-worn selection of subjects in the books that they most frequently drew upon; some works they simply ignored, for whatever reason.

One of the most surprising oversights was artists' neglect of Jane Austen's novels. Although she was never widely read in the nineteenth century, she had a steady following in the upper-middle class reading audience as well as genuine, however limited, critical fame. Sir Thomas Lawrence counted her as "one of his most favourite authors," and at least one Victorian painter, George Frederic Watts, was partial to her novels, though admittedly his characteristic mature style was ill adapted to the kind of subjects they suggested. He relied on them, he said, along with Scott's romances, as "the books that he turned to most often when tired or unwell."[31] Jane Austen herself was aware of the resemblance her art bore to that of the painter. In a letter to her brother Edward, dated 16 December 1816, she asked: "What should I do with your strong, manly, spirited Sketches, full of Variety and Glow?—How could I possibly join them on to the little bit (two Inches wide) of Ivory on which I work with so fine a Brush, as produces little effect after much labour?"[32] Critics repeatedly compared her art with that of the Dutch school and even (a revelation of the ease with which they could separate technique from content) with that of Hogarth. One could point to numerous episodes in Austen's novels that were perfectly adapted to be the subjects of conversation pieces, a form of painting still popular in her lifetime, or the parlor-genre pictures that were to become even more popular a generation later. But no artist picked up the hint of the *Blackwood's* reviewer of *Northanger Abbey* and *Persuasion* (1818) when he predicted that "the time, probably, will return, when we shall take a more permanent delight in those familiar cabinet pictures, than even in the great historical pieces of our more eminent masters."[33] As the search for suitable "cabinet picture" subjects was pressed, Jane Austen, the accomplished miniaturist-in-prose, was wholly overlooked.*

No pictures were suggested by Lamb's essays, and only one or two were inspired by *Pickwick Papers.* Except for Mrs. Radcliffe, few of the numerous Gothic novelists provided subjects, nor did William Beckford's *Vathek* (even when Oriental scenes were a staple of the early nineteenth-century exhibitions), or Charles Maturin's Fuseliesque *Melmoth the Wanderer.* There was, to put it mildly, an oversupply of pictures from Scott, but his fellow Scotsman John Galt, whose quiet portrayals of village life north of the Tweed would have qualified him as a source for Wilkie's genre pictures, was absent from the walls. There were no pictures from Mrs. Gaskell's novels, although *Cranford,* for one, would have provided numerous conversation pieces and genre tableaux, and none from Miss Mitford's *Our Village,* although a new edition (1835) was illustrated by the landscape artist Charles Baxter, whom the author personally conducted to the sites described. [34] (*Our Village* did figure indirectly in art, as the source of the story of Tennyson's poem "Dora," from which a number of paintings were derived.) There were no pictures from Disraeli, Wilkie Collins, or Trollope, though Millais, to be sure, supplied illustrations for editions of three of Trollope's novels.[35] Nor, despite the lavish opportunities it afforded to paint scenes in late seventeenth-century Italy in the style of the Renaissance masters, not to say the scores of dramatic moments that occur in the 21,000-line narrative poem, was Browning's *The Ring and the Book* ever drawn upon, much as it was discussed and admired when it appeared in 1868–69, one of its first critics declaring that it was "the most precious and profound spiritual treasure that England has produced since the days of Shakespeare."[36]

It is curious, and not much to their credit, that although Victorian art reviewers were forever deploring the stubborn appeal of certain hackneyed subjects, they almost never proposed fresh ones. It was left for Thackeray to ask, in his lecture on Steele in *The English Humourists,* "Could not some painter give an interview between the gallant captain of Lucas's, with his hat cocked, and his lace, and his face, too, a trifle tarnished with drink, and that poet, that philosopher, pale, proud, and poor, his friend and monitor of schooldays, of all days?" Although the subject had a triple recommendation—"interviews" were a familiar form of tab-

*The mystery is all the more tantalizing because Jane Austen once saw a picture that, on the highest possible authority—her own—might have come out of *Pride and Prejudice.* After visiting the exhibition of the Society of Painters in Oil and Water Colours in May 1813, five months after the novel was published, she wrote her sister Cassandra, "It is not thought a good collection, but I was very well pleased—particularly (pray tell Fanny) with a small portrait of Mrs. Bingley, excessively like her. I went in hopes of seeing one of her Sister, but there was no Mrs. Darcy . . . —Mrs. Bingley's is exactly herself, size, shaped face, features & sweetness; there never was a greater likeness. She is dressed in a white gown, with green ornaments, which convinces me of what I had always supposed, that green was a favourite colour with her." As R. W. Chapman, editor of the letters, commented, to identify Mrs. Bingley's portrait from the exhibition catalogue "would be indeed a triumph of research" (*Jane Austen's Letters,* ed. R. W. Chapman [Oxford, 1932], 2: 309–10, [519]).

leau, eighteenth-century settings were in demand for costume pictures, and episodes from literary biography were increasingly popular—apparently no artist undertook a picture of Addison and Steele taking their ease in a coffeehouse.

Readers did slightly better than reviewers in this regard. Thackeray's old college friend Edward FitzGerald, fresh from reading Scott's *A Legend of Montrose,* wrote in 1878, in a letter to Charles Eliot Norton: "What a fine Picture would that make of Evan Dhu's entrance into Tully Veolan Breakfast Hall, with a message from his Chief; he standing erect in his Tartan, while the Baron keeps his State, and pretty Rose at the Table. There is a subject for one of your [American] Artists. Another very pretty one (I thought the other Day) would be that of the child Keats keeping guard with a drawn sword at his sick Mother's Chamber door. Millais might do it over here; but I don't know him."[37] FitzGerald recommended the latter scene, in Monckton Milnes's life of Keats, to his friend the cartoonist Charles Keene, asking him to relay it to Millais.[38] But, if he did receive the suggestion, Millais, who was occupied at the moment with several subjects from Scott, failed to act on it. And, by that much, English literary art is doubtless the poorer.

CHAPTER 6

Subjects reflected from nonliterary art: magic, fairies, sleeping figures, dreams, amiable humorists; domestic themes.—Suffering women, femmes fatales, coquettes, the satire of women.—Horses and dogs; shipwrecks, captivity, escapes and rescues, letter scenes, partings, deaths, trials and supplications, "discoveries."

To painters, the great value of English literature lay in the wealth of examples it provided of subjects most congenial to the art of the time. Many pictures from literature were, in effect, variations on familiar themes. The patterns already existed, either in history paintings drawn from the standard sources—mythology, Scripture, classic and Renaissance literature, and history—or in genre and narrative art at large; and in attributing his subject to an English literary source, the artist simply filled in the outline.[1] In the former case, he replaced the traditional source-association with a new one; in the latter, he supplied a literary identification where none had existed before. In either event, by lending a familiar art-subject a habitation and name drawn from English literature, he added an extra element of allusion to subjects already established in the artistic repertory.

A systematic catalogue of all the conventional subjects that turned up on exhibition walls thinly disguised as literary pictures would be intolerably dull even if it were practical. A few examples, discussed in some detail, can make the point well enough. There was, for one, the supernatural theme of spirits, magicians, prophets, and witches, one often said to be especially characteristic of Romantic art but already familiar in eighteenth-century paintings drawn from such neoclassic sources as the Bible, Homer, and Dante, to say nothing of native sources like Shakespeare, Spenser, and Milton. One of Reynolds's last paintings was *Macbeth and the Three Witches* (1789). Fuseli, in some respects a harbinger of Romanticism, specialized in ghosts and witches. His *Saul and the Witch of Endor,* like Benjamin West's painting of the same subject, was taken, of course, from Scripture; but most of his witches, and they were legion, came from *Macbeth.* Beginning about the turn of the century, English literature sup-

70. Unknown artist, *The Weird Sisters* (undated) (Royal Shakespeare Theatre Picture Gallery ©). With the possible exception of Ariel in *The Tempest,* the witches in *Macbeth* were the most often painted of all the supernatural beings who people English literature, and Henry Fuseli painted them more often than did any other artist. This unattributed picture portrays a stock Fuselian subject in a less than successful effort to imitate the Fuselian style.

plied painters with most of their ghostly and magical subjects. In addition to the Weird Sisters, there were Prospero the magician, Cassandra *(Troilus and Cressida),* the furies *(2 Henry VI),* and the ghosts of Gloucester and Claudius—all in Shakespeare; Archimago and Busirane in *The Faerie Queene;* Byron's Witch of the Alps and demons in *Manfred,* Keats's Lamia, Coleridge's Geraldine in "Christabel", Vivien in *Idylls of the King;* the goblins in "Tam o' Shanter"; Milton's magic potion-dealing Comus, and the sorceress in *Paradise Lost,* book 2; the phantom knight in *Marmion,* the White Lady of Avenel in *The Monastery,* the mermaiden in *The Bride of Lammermoor.*

In the course of time, these generally formidable and *frisson*-inducing

71. Frederick Sandys, *Morgan-le-Fay* (RA 1864) (Birmingham City Museum and Art Gallery). The enchantress in Malory's *Morte Darthur,* depicted in the Pre-Raphaelite mode of sharp detail and close attention to costume and accessories. The *Times* (5 May) praised "the magic web which fills the fairy-loom, the picturesque apparatus of sorcery, and the carved and coloured furniture"; but the *Art Journal* (June, 26: 161) would have none of it: "The figure is medieval, a petrified spasm, sensational as a ghost from a grave, and severe as a block cut from stone or wood. We are happy to hear that the work is not without admirers, fit, though possibly few."

72. David Scott, *Ariel and Caliban* (Royal Scottish Academy 1838) (National Gallery of Scotland). The work of a painter who died at the comparatively early age of forty-three.

73. George Cruikshank, *The Last Scene in "The Merry Wives of Windsor"* (British Institution 1857) (Yale Center for British Art, Paul Mellon Fund). In the last phase of his long career, Cruikshank returned to the vein of fantasy and grotesquerie that had characterized some of his popular series of illustrations. The Herne's oak scene, in which Falstaff is tormented by a host of sprites, offered him a lavish opportunity for the exercise of his special gifts.

contributions of legend, myth, and folklore by way of literature were replaced by less fearsome ones: the benign, mischief-loving spirits and elves in *The Tempest, The Merry Wives of Windsor* (the Herne's oak scene), and *The Rape of the Lock.* Beginning in the early 1840s, when Mendelssohn's incidental music to *A Midsummer Night's Dream* (1842) was in the air where music from Weber's perennially popular *Oberon* also lingered, there was a burst of fairy pictures that lasted well into the sixties and seventies. A recent catalogue of nineteenth-century painters and book illustrators who specialized in these impalpable figures contains more than fifty names, dominated in the early years by Richard Dadd and Joseph Noel Paton.[2] The most fertile English literary sources in addition

74. Joseph Noel Paton, *The Quarrel of Oberon and Titania* (Royal Scottish Academy 1850) (National Gallery of Scotland). An extravaganza, based lightly on *A Midsummer Night's Dream.* A sketch for this painting was exhibited at the Royal Scottish Academy, as Paton's diploma work, in 1846; and its companion, *The Reconciliation of Oberon and Titania,* was shown there the following year. Both pictures caused something of a sensation, not least because their complexity invited spectators to indulge in the popular Victorian pastime of "reading" a painting inch by inch, thus obtaining what they unquestionably felt was good value for the admission price. Lewis Carroll, who saw the *Quarrel* in Edinburgh in 1857, recorded that "we counted a hundred and sixty-five fairies" (*Diaries,* ed. R. L. Green, 1: 122).

75. Sir Edward Burne-Jones, *The Dream of Sir Lancelot at the Chapel of the San Graal* (Fine Art Society 1896) (Southampton Art Gallery). A free treatment of a dream episode in Arthurian story. The scene is closest to that in Malory's *Morte Darthur,* bk. 13, chap. 2, where, however, the lady (angel?) does not appear. In view of Burne-Jones's infatuation with Malory, it is more likely that the picture was inspired by the *Morte Darthur* than by any scene in Tennyson's *Idylls of the King.* For another episode in the quest for the Holy Grail, see pl. 345.

to *A Midsummer Night's Dream* and *The Tempest* were Mercutio's "Queen Mab" speech in *Romeo and Juliet* and the description of Queen Mab in "L'Allegro," but some artists reached for their Titania-Oberon subjects, as Fuseli had done on occasion, into German literature, notably Wieland's *Oberon* and De la Motte Fouqué's *Undine.*

Inseparable from magic and the supernatural in the Romantic repertory of thematic interests were dreams and visions, benign or horrific, usually prophetic rather than retrospective.[3] To this stock, literature contributed Macbeth's vision of the armed heads, Clarence's dream (*Richard III*) and the much-painted vision of Queen Katherine (*Henry VIII*); the several dreams in *Paradise Lost* (Eve's and Noah's, the shepherd's, the vision of the lazar house); the spirit of Loda in Ossian (represented in French painting by Ingres's well-known *Le Songe d'Ossian*); the dreams of

76. Sir Edward Burne-Jones, *The Sleeping Beauty* (1884–90) (Faringdon Collection Trust, Buscot Park). One of the four paintings that make up Burne-Jones's series *The Legend of the Briar Rose,* to which, between brooding over the idea and the actual execution, he devoted twenty years. Although the sleeping beauty theme is an old one—the artist initially intended to illustrate Perrault's version in a set of tiles—critics naturally associated the subject with Tennyson's poem "The Sleeping Beauty," first published in 1830 and later incorporated into "The Day Dream" (1842). A more immediate literary connection, however, was with William Morris, who wrote verses for the four pictures. Those for *The Sleeping Beauty* were:

Here lies the hoarded love, the key
To all the treasure that shall be.
Come, fated hand, the gift to take
And smite the sleeping world awake.

the Red Cross Knight (*The Faerie Queene*) (pl. 261), Lancelot and Galahad (Malory's *Morte Darthur* and *Idylls of the King*), Madeline ("The Eve of St. Agnes"), Bunyan (*The Pilgrim's Progress*), Belinda (*The Rape of the Lock*), Mirza (*The Spectator,* No. 159), Nourmahal (Moore's *Lalla Rookh*), Don Roderick (Southey's *Roderick the Last of the Goths*), and Sardanapalus (Byron's tragedy). In some paintings, the focus was on the sleeping figure, whether or not a dream was involved. Artists had a special fondness for sleeping women, sometimes, if not usually, with their bosoms exposed—a subject that came closer to overt eroticism than any other in the repertory.[4] Thus there were pictures of sleeping Lucretias, Desdemonas, Titanias, Mirandas, Juliets (though here the sleep was induced by a potion), Imogens (in whose case the exposed bosom was required by the plot), and Florence Dombeys.

Madness, another expression of the irrational, held a particular fascination for painters from Fuseli onward (not forgetting the attraction it had for Goya and Géricault abroad).[5] This was an affliction visited mainly on women in the literary sources: Cowper's Crazy Kate (pl. 77), Ophelia (pls. 78, 215, 216, 217), Sterne's Maria (pl. 94), Scott's Madge Wildfire and Lucy Ashton, the Lady in Byron's "The Dream," Crabbe's Ellen Orford. But there were notable madmen too, presided over by King Lear: Byron's Manfred, for example, and Crabbe's Peter Grimes.

Except for *Idylls of the King* and Spenser's earlier epic, *The Faerie Queene,* heroes in the traditional sense were not often encountered in literary art, and those in Tennyson's poem were sometimes flawed. British painting faithfully reflected the eclipse of the hero that was occurring simultaneously in literature.[6] Even physical valor was not celebrated in art as much as one would be led to expect from its pervasive presence throughout the century in popular music; the heroic-martial strain was heard everywhere that people recited or sang. Such paintings as were devoted to heroism came from historical rather than specifically literary sources, and such battle and victory pictures as were derived from literature tended to portray Scottish rather than Sassenach episodes.

Instead, men typically were seen in literary pictures in roles that went against the grain of heroism as portrayed in conventional history paint-

77. Walter F. Bishop, *Crazy Kate* (undated) (Walker Art Gallery, Liverpool). A very late version (the artist exhibited at the Royal Academy until 1902) of a subject contributed to British painting a century earlier by William Cowper, in *The Task.* Although she never attained the popularity of her fellow madwoman Ophelia, Crazy Kate was a recurrent figure in nineteenth-century art.

78. Richard Redgrave, *Ophelia. "There Is a Willow Grows Ascaunt the Brook"* (RA 1842) (Victoria & Albert Museum, Crown Copyright). One of the better known of the innumerable Ophelia pictures; the vacancy of expression that characterized many female portraits at this moment, the heyday of the Keepsake beauties, was easily adaptable to the portrayal of gentle madness. When exhibited in 1842, this painting was hung close to Maclise's sensationally popular *Play Scene from "Hamlet"* (pl. 219). "Doubtful as seems to us the judgment of the hanging committee thus to subject it to such a juxtaposition," remarked the *Athenaeum* (7 May), "the less ambitious work suffers little."

79. Augustus Wall Callcott, *Scene from "The Merry Wives of Windsor"* (undated) (Victoria & Albert Museum, Crown Copyright). The prolific Callcott, "the English Claude," was best known in his time for his landscapes. Falstaff and Simple are shown at the opening of act 4, scene 5.

ings. One category of central male figures harmonized with that vein of Victorian culture which cherished evidences of some men's innocence in a wicked world, to which it responded with a gentle smile and affectionate chuckle. This was the type character that Stuart Tave has called "the amiable humorist," exemplified by several of the male figures most often depicted in nineteenth-century literary painting. In choice of subject and treatment, artists reflected the literary development Tave describes.[7] By the middle of the eighteenth century, the critical insistence, originating in the Restoration, that the proper function of comedy was to ridicule and satirize fools and knaves had given way to a more joyful and kindly theory of laughter, based on incongruity. "By the beginning of the nineteenth century an increasing confidence in the goodness of the free play of natural emotion and spirits made frank laughter a sign of an open and universal humanity, and even an unrestrained laughter at times a sign of a large, wise, and sympathetic heart."[8] This was the response that virtually all portrayals of Falstaff were designed to elicit from nineteenth-century

80. Ford Madox Brown, *Dr. Primrose and His Daughters* (ca. 1845) (City Art Gallery, Manchester). One of Brown's earliest works. Holman Hunt wrote of it as "a loyal and clever revival of French art before the classicalists swept away the prestige of the worn out followers of Watteau, when Fragonard held the field with his tapestry cupids and dry flower wreaths, and when Dresden china artificialities were in favour" (*Pre-Raphaelitism and the Pre-Raphaelite Brotherhood*, 1: 171). But Brown's style here owes as much to native genre painting as to any foreign influence.

81. John Pettie, *Silvius and Phoebe* (RA 1872) (Aberdeen Art Gallery). A rustic courtship scene, from *As You Like It* (3. 5). In contrast to the countless genre scenes of a lover and his lass, in which artists generally made some attempt to represent contemporary rural costume though in modified (cleaned up) form, those taken from literature made no pretense of realism. The lovers are clad in conventionalized period costume derived from earlier art, or, as here, from the current theatrical wardrobe.

readers, playgoers, and picture-buyers alike. (See Part Two, below, under *Henry IV* and *The Merry Wives of Windsor.*) The other major "amiable humorist" who dominated literary painting was Dr. Primrose, the vicar of Wakefield, who appeared so frequently on exhibition walls that he came to be denounced as a sheer nuisance. A whimsical, generous gentleman of "consummate benevolence"—a term he used in praise of Sir William Thornhill—he captivated artist after artist. Several other exemplars of amiable humor in English literature, Fielding's Parson Adams, Smollett's Commodore Trunnion and Matthew Bramble, and Scott's Dominie Sampson and Jonathan Oldbuck, seldom appeared in art; and another,

82. Charles R. Leslie, *Slender, with the Assistance of Shallow, Courting Anne Page* (RA 1825) (Tate Gallery, London). A sketch for the finished picture, one of three Leslie painted of the subject (*The Merry Wives of Windsor,* 1. 1). Compare the very different treatment of the scene, exhibited eleven years later, by Thomas Duncan (pl. 101).

83. Charles R. Leslie. *The Infant Princes in the Tower* (1830) (Victoria & Albert Museum, Crown Copyright). An interpretation of the subject (Shakespeare's *Richard III*) that illustrates the great difference between the horror admissible in paintings of such historical subjects as late as Boydell's Shakespeare Gallery (contrast Northcote's melodramatic treatment, pl. 15) and the tranquil prettiness demanded by the domesticated taste of Leslie's time. The picture was in John Sheepshanks's collection.

Sterne's Uncle Toby, occurred mainly in connection with his involvement with the Widow Wadman.*

Unheroic male figures like these fitted comfortably into the ordinary environment of the consumers of Victorian popular art, the middle-class home, in which not stalwart men but women and children were the centers of literary and artistic interest. Within this restricted domestic world resided an ample variety of themes. There were, for instance, the delights and sorrows, the contretemps and fulfillments, of love and courtship, typified by such well-known paintings without literary content as Arthur Hughes's *April Love* and *The Long Engagement,* Frederic Stephens's *The Proposal,* William Mulready's *The Sonnet: A Sketch for a Picture,* and Frank Stone's *The Tryst.* Paintings from Shakespeare alone covered almost the entire gamut of contemporary ideas and fancies on the subject, from the passionate but innocent eroticism of Romeo and Juliet (pls. 26, 147, 212) to the homely comedy of Anne Page and the bashful Slender (pls. 82, 101). On the strictly sentimental side, there were numerous contributions from Thomson (Palemon and Lavinia in *The Seasons*) (pl. 35), Burns (Duncan Gray)(pl. 44), and Ramsay's *The Gentle Shepherd* (Roger and Jenny) (pl. 291). Such paintings as those of Sir Roger de Coverley's courtship of the widow and the Widow Wadman's courtship of Uncle Toby (pls. 45, 67) must have evoked a response that lay somewhere between sympathy and amusement; other subjects, like Hudibras's wooing of the lady, were probably adopted solely for their value as harmless comedy.

Apart from what was implied in genre scenes of family life and situations like the departure and return of husbands—typified in nonliterary paintings by such paintings as O'Neil's *Eastward Ho! 1857* and *Home Again,* and Hughes's *Leaving Home* and *Home from the Sea*—the relation of wife and husband was a specific subject of pictures from literature less often than one might expect.[9] Treatments of marital tension or disillusionment and of adultery, such as eventually were—in some cases—daringly pre-

*Don Quixote's conformity to the amiable humorist pattern is the main reason that episodes from Cervantes were depicted by English artists more often than subjects from any other European source. Well over one hundred Quixote paintings were exhibited at the Royal Academy and British Institution alone.

sented to the mid- and late-Victorian public (Augustus Egg's narrative series *Past and Present,* William Quiller Orchardson's *Mariage de Convenance*), had few counterparts in literary pictures. There was no representation of any episode in Meredith's *Modern Love,* or of the situation in any of Browning's several dissections of marriage such as "James Lee's Wife." The Lancelot-Guinevere plot was conspicuously absent from the many paintings from Malory and *Idylls of the King.* To be sure, persons familiar with the context of Vivien's song in Tennyson's *Merlin and Vivien* might have deduced the situation portrayed in Arthur Hughes's picture of 1862, *The Rift in the Lute* ("It is the little rift within the lute / That by and by will make the music mute"); but it was left for Orchardson to apply the lines to the unmistakable situation he portrayed in another of his commentaries on the realities of married life, *The First Cloud* (1887). What little discord literary painters were prepared to recognize was treated comically in the source, as befitted a time of male supremacy; the prime example, of course, is *The Taming of the Shrew,* a favorite play with artists, presumably for that reason.

Children were another matter altogether. In English art, as in English literature, they did not figure prominently until late in the eighteenth century. Apart from such subjects as the Princes in the Tower (*Richard III*)[10] and Hubert's threatened torture of Prince Arthur *(King John),* the history painters had had little occasion to depict children in any but incidental roles. Reynolds, Romney, Gainsborough, and others painted portraits of some children from upper-crust families, but only as a matter of record, an expensive form of family album; and though children appeared in many conversation pieces, it was not as individuals interesting in their own right but as members of a family group. But in the wake of Rousseau's revelation of the philosophical significance of childhood, and even before Wordsworth discovered infinite wisdom in the child, boys and girls in various activities—playing games, stalking birds, being read to by a parent or making music, picnicking, sketching, being admonished

84. William F. Yeames, *Prince Arthur and Hubert* (RA 1882) (City Art Gallery, Manchester). By the time this canvas was painted, the harrowing scene in Shakespeare's *King John* (4. 1) in which Hubert threatens to blind Prince Arthur with a red-hot poker had been in artists' repertory for more than a century: see pls. 199, 200.

85. James Elder Christie, *The Pied Piper of Hamelin* (RA 1881) (National Gallery of Scotland). As a specialist in pictures of children, Christie was naturally attracted by this subject, one of the few from Browning's poems that found their way to the exhibitions. "The Pied Piper of Hamelin" was issued several times in illustrated editions, including one by Kate Greenaway (1889).

86. William P. Frith, *A Scene from "The Vicar of Wakefield": The Squire Teaching the Young Ladies Piquet and the Boys to Box* (dated 1860) (City Art Gallery, Manchester). A sketch possibly for the painting exhibited in 1876. Pictures of children being taught (see also Martineau's *Kit's Writing Lesson,* pl. 353) were characteristic of a society that placed a high priority on education, whether book learning or, as here, wholesome and sexually appropriate pastimes.

by a schoolmistress—were recurrent subjects of genre painters like Morland and Wheatley. As the Victorian era progressed, sentimentalized children were among the most dependable of all art subjects, from Webster and Mulready onward. Once more, the fund of literary examples was adequate to the demand. The Primrose children were central figures in some paintings from *The Vicar of Wakefield.* The Princes in the Tower enjoyed a new lease on life, as did other Shakespearean subjects such as Macduff's children, and Mamillius in *The Winter's Tale.* From Chaucer came Griselda's children; from Dickens, Oliver Twist, Little Nell, and Paul and Florence Dombey. Literary biography provided additional paintable subjects. Shakespeare was pictured in his childhood, as was Scott, seen with his friend Sandy Ormistoun.

Occasionally the theme of maternal or filial piety was touched upon in literary pictures, most notably in connection with King Lear and his daughters, and Lavinia and her mother in *The Seasons.* In 1804, Richard Westall exhibited companion pieces on the same theme, Sir Richard Steele and his mother (*Tatler* 181) and "the filial attention of Fidelia" (*Spectator* 449). Fifteen years later, Mary Ann Flaxman showed "Maternal Piety," inspired by a passage in Samuel Rogers's poem *Human Life.* But more frequent were the literary illustrations of another motif that was a staple of child-genre paintings, a boy or girl under instruction. A painting exhibited as early as 1791 took its subject, "Good mother instructing her children," from *The Seasons.* The literary prototype of such pictures was the familiar subject from *The Tempest,* Prospero teaching Miranda. Other artists showed the infant Izaak Walton receiving his first instruction (in fishing?) and the subject of one of Walton's *Lives,* George Herbert, of whom he wrote that he "spent much of his childhood in a sweet content," learning to read at his mother's knee. Artists found instances in modern works as well: David Deans teaching his daughters (*The Heart of Mid-Lothian*), Little Nell teaching Kit Nubbles (*The Old Curiosity Shop,* pl. 353), and Esther Summerson teaching Charlotte (*Bleak House*). Nor were all the pupils children. Robinson Crusoe taught his man Friday (as well as, in another picture, his parrot), Sir Tristram gave La Beale Isonde a harp lesson (Malory),* and Cathy taught Hareton his letters (*Wuthering*

*Recalling the instrumentalist angels and organ- or harp-playing St. Cecilias of Renaissance religious painting as well as their human counterparts in seventeenth-century Dutch art, artists sometimes credited literary heroines with musical talent. Desdemona, who sang the Willow Song, was sometimes pictured with a guitar or lute; and the Glee Maiden in Scott's *The Fair Maid of Perth* was equipped with a lute, or, in a late Victorian painting, with a full-sized violin such as Madame Norman-Neruda, later Lady Hallé, was then playing on the concert stage.

Heights—one of the very few subjects from a Brontë novel). A comic variation on the theme was Lucentio's mock lesson in the construing of Latin (*The Taming of the Shrew*).

As several recent scholars have discovered, the treasury of Victorian art is a rich source of information on the place of women in the society of the time.[11] The most revealing treatment of women is found not in the sentimental Keepsake beauty portraits (see chapter 4, above), though these have their own historical message to convey, but in paintings in which women play a significant role in an action. In literary paintings, their characters are given a narrative context, amplifying the simplistic and idealized sketches offered in keepsake art.

A reasonably full account of the various types of women represented in paintings from Shakespeare alone would require a chapter by itself, and another could profitably be devoted to those who were drawn from non-Shakespearean sources. (Some of the materials for such a study are found in Parts Two and Three below.) We behold, for instance, the Victorian affection for spirited, plucky girls like Shakespeare's Viola, Beatrice, Rosalind, and Celia. Equally attractive, and more harmonious with the current image of the ideal woman, was the fragile, suffering, victimized, persecuted heroine, typified by two historical figures who were often portrayed in the roles they had in literature: Lady Jane Grey (*3 Henry VI*) and Mary Queen of Scots (Scott's *The Abbot*).[12] Lady Jane was painted as early as 1776, when Gavin Hamilton fulfilled a commission from James Boswell; and between 1827 and 1877, at the Royal Academy alone, there were some twenty-five renderings of the crises in her unfortunate life. Shakespeare's Cordelia and Imogen presided over a literary art gallery that also included Chaucer's Griselda, Spenser's Una and Amoret, Richardson's Pamela and Clarissa Harlowe, Shelley's Beatrice Cenci, Tennyson's Oenone and Elaine.

Understandably, there were far fewer portrayals of unapproved or

87. Ford Madox Brown, *Cordelia's Portion* (exhibited, unfinished, at the Dudley Gallery 1867; completed 1875) (Southampton Art Gallery). A richly Pre-Raphaelite version of a familiar subject, Cordelia as the emblem of victimized womanhood. When Henry James saw it in the Brown retrospective exhibition at the Grafton Galleries in 1897, he wrote of it, borrowing his metaphor from the map of Lear's kingdom in the foreground, "There are other things, like his 'Cordelia's Portion,' which have a little of everything, including beauty, but which are so crammed with independent meanings as rather to be particoloured maps than pictures of his subject" (*The Painter's Eye*, p. 250). Unsympathetic critics might apply the observation more widely, to Pre-Raphaelite "literary" painting in general.

88. Edward Burne-Jones, *The Beguiling of Merlin* (Grosvenor Gallery 1877) (Lady Lever Art Gallery, Port Sunlight). Thanks to her appearance in one of the first four *Idylls of the King* (1859), the evil Vivien (Nimuë in Malory) helped shape the Victorians' conception of the *femme fatale.* This picture, however—commissioned by the shipowner-collector Frederick Leyland for his house in Prince's Gate, London—was based not on Tennyson but on the medieval French *Romance of Merlin.* It was one of the eight paintings Burne-Jones sent to the Grosvenor Gallery that year after a long self-imposed absence from public exhibitions. The stir they caused when hung on one wall led to his being recognized as one of the day's leading artists.

89. Daniel Maclise, *Wrestling Scene from "As You Like It"* (RA 1855) (detail) (Harris Museum and Art Gallery, Preston). Rosalind and Celia, here depicted watching the beginning of the match, were among the several pairs of figures in literature who were enlisted to represent sentimental attachment ("sisterhood") between two young women.

socially embarrassing types of womanhood. Although she had a lineage traceable to Eve, who was herself necessarily much depicted, as part of the Miltonic epic, the *femme fatale* appeared only in the form of such literary characters as Cleopatra and Tennyson's Vivien (never as Becky Sharp); perhaps Lady Macbeth could be said to have held an adjunct membership in their sodality.[13] Nor, once again for reasons that are clear enough when we remember the home environment in which most of these pic-

90. Thomas Stothard, *Brunetta and Phillis* (RA 1803) (Victoria & Albert Museum, Crown Copyright). Typical gentle satire of women, from Addison's *Spectator* 80: the calamitous ballroom scene in which Phillis, clad in rich brocade, has duplicitously managed for her rival Brunetta to come in a plain black silk mantua, only to faint away on discovering that Brunetta's black servant is wearing a skirt of the same pattern as Phillis's gown. The artist went Addison one better by dressing Phillis's servant in a dark mantua and lace collar almost identical with Brunetta's.

tures were destined to hang, were there many figures of "Magdalenes", the Victorians' inclusive euphemism for sexually delinquent women. Such Victorian pictures as Rossetti's *Found* and Holman Hunt's *The Awakening Conscience* had no literary reference. Thomas Hood's poem "The Bridge of Sighs," about a victim of men's lust who threw herself from a London bridge, was painted a number of times, six between 1856 and 1861 alone; but few if any artists, apart from "Phiz," Dickens's own illustrator, ventured to interpret Little Em'ly in *David Copperfield.*

A technique painters often used when depicting heroines from literature aligned Victorian art with both European painting and the practices of some major novelists. This was the device of pairing two women, to contrast two opposite kinds of beauty (blonde and brunette) or two opposite temperaments (the striving and the passive, for example) or to illustrate *Schwesterschaft,* as it was called in German art, "an overtly non-sexual expression of deep tenderness and love among members of the same gender."[14] Greuze had painted *The Two Friends* and *The Two Sisters* (or *The Comparison*), Mme Vigée-Lebrun *The Two Sisters,* and numerous French and German artists had followed suit. Alexander Welsh has called attention to Scott's pairing of light- and dark-haired heroines (both beautiful, but embodying opposite psychological traits): Rose Bradwardine and Flora in *Waverley,* Rowena and Rebecca in *Ivanhoe,* Brenda and Minna Troil in *The Pirate,* Jeanie and Effie Deans in *The Heart of Mid-Lothian.*[15] Artists naturally seized the chance such pairings afforded to paint in an already established mode. Besides Scott, there was a variety of literary sources to choose from, involving not necessarily contrasting personalities but in every instance a sympathetic relationship between two women, perhaps planning strategies to outwit parents and propriety in the delightful game of love, or commiserating with each other when the strategy has failed. Thus there were numerous pictures, either double portraits or tableaux in which the two women were the center of attention, featuring Viola and Olivia, Rosalind and Celia (pl. 89), Helena and Hermia, Sophia and Olivia Primrose, Dolly Varden and Emily Haredale *(Barnaby Rudge).* Both George Eliot and Thomas Hardy, who knew old and contemporary genre art well, practiced the same kind of pairing in their novels, but it was too late for artists once again to reciprocate; by then, literary painting was in decline, and few pictures were derived from either novelist.

91. Gilbert Stuart Newton, *Yorick and the Grisette* (RA 1830) (Tate Gallery, London). A favorite subject from Sterne's *Sentimental Journey*—flirtation over a pair of gloves. "She begg'd I would try a single pair, which seemed to be the least—She held it open—my hand slipped into it at once—It will not do, said I, shaking my head a little—No, said she, doing the same thing . . . So folding our hands within our arms, we both loll'd upon the counter—it was narrow, and there was just room for the parcel to lay between us." Yorick's face bears a strong resemblance to Reynolds's portrait of Sterne.

Not all Victorian representations of woman in her various roles and relationships were sentimental, and not all were even serious. Many pictures, like many *Punch* cartoons, were devoted to the restrained satire of women, and here once again artists utilized familiar subjects in literature. Belinda, in *The Rape of the Lock,* typified both the coquetry and the vanity that were the chief targets of a pictorial humor so facetious it scarcely deserved the name of satire. For representations of the techniques of sexual enticement and indulgence of vanity in fashionable society, artists time after time took up the *Spectator,* whose essays on the subject seemed as pertinent when Victoria was on the throne as they had when Queen Anne reigned. From Number 102, for example, came the scene in which a learned pundit instructs a class of ladies in the flirtatious management of the fan. (In one version of this subject, a young lady was shown with the correct number of the *Spectator* open before her, as a kind of pictorial footnote reference.) Some of the numerous paintings of Pepys's wife,

92. Sawrey Gilpin, *Gulliver Taking Leave of the Houyhnhnms* (Society of Artists 1771) (Yale Center for British Art, Paul Mellon Collection). One of four portrayals of Gulliver and his equine friends painted between 1768 and 1772 by Sawrey Gilpin, who, like Stubbs (his senior by nine years), specialized in animal subjects. No doubt wisely, Gilpin did not represent the farewell ceremony Gulliver describes: "I took a second leave of my master; but as I was going to prostrate myself to kiss his hoof, he did me the honour to raise it gently to my mouth." Whether the artist was justified in attributing human facial expressions to the noble horses is a matter for debate.

such as the 1849 picture suggested by a passage in his diary, "My wife this day put on her first French gown . . ." and the later one (1873) entitled *Mrs. Pepys Adopts the Latest Fashion,* combined lavish costuming with the gentle moralizing suitable to a pictorial homily on the vanity of dress. Another painting in the same vein was Abraham Solomon's treatment (RA 1858) of Goldsmith's "Elegy on That Glory of Her Sex Mrs. Mary Blaize," exhibited with the motto, "In silks and satins new, / And hoop of monstrous size: / She never slumbered in her pew / But when she shut her eyes." Transferred to a rural setting, this kind of guerrilla warfare against

93. John Frederick Herring, *Mazeppa Surrounded by Horses* (dated 1833) (Tate Gallery, London). A copy of Horace Vernet's picture, a manifestation of the surge of literary and artistic interest in the old story typified by Byron's poem *Mazeppa.* Herring, a prolific painter of race horses, who painted the St. Leger winner for thirty-two years, began as a stagecoach driver on the London-York, Wakefield-Lincoln, and Doncaster-Halifax runs. His own version of *Mazeppa* was exhibited at the Society of British Artists in 1842.

the desirable, defenseless male animal known as "village coquetry" was a recurrent subject of genre painting. For this purpose, Shakespeare supplied Audrey, Phoebe, and Anne Page, and Sterne the Widow Wadman, who besieged Uncle Toby; in art, she was to *Tristram Shandy* what the French innkeeper's daughter was in *A Sentimental Journey*.

At some risk of anticlimax, space must be found here for two other classes of beings whose frequent presence linked literary art with its wider milieu: horses and dogs. Burke cited horses as a symbol of the sublime, and, as Kenneth Clark has observed, they play "an equivocal role in the iconography of romanticism right up to the time of Picasso."[16] Many paintings of military and ceremonial occasions required them, and one of the most celebrated early nineteenth-century canvases was Benjamin West's apocalyptic *Death on the Pale Horse*. Horses in dramatic situations, fighting among themselves or being attacked by lions, were a specialty of George Stubbs, and he and his successors as animal painters were instrumental in building up a clientele for an appropriate kind of art in the stallion-breeding, riding-to-hounds segment of the British population.

The attractiveness of the literary allusion penetrated into even this unlikely area of nineteenth-century art. Wherever horses appeared in literature, they were bound sooner or later, and in some instances often, to be featured in painting. A picture of Sterne's Yorick with his steed that George LaPorte, "Animal Painter to H.R.H. the Duke of Cumberland," exhibited in 1826 at the Society of British Artists represented a not inconsiderable backwater of literary painting. Following the lead of Sawrey Gilpin, painter of four noteworthy scenes from Gulliver's voyage to the Houyhnhnms (pl. 92), several of the leading nineteenth-century horse painters—Richard Barrett Davis, James Ward, William Barraud, George LaPorte, John Frederick Herring, Abraham Cooper, Gourlay Steele—took subjects from literature. And so paintings of horses came from Shakespeare (Duncan's wild horses in *Macbeth,* Prince Hal on his charger, and of course the innumerable horses in the other history plays); Walton's *Life of George Herbert* (the poet-divine helping a poor man relieve his overburdened beast); the *Spectator* (Sir Roger de Coverley and the Spectator go hunting); Gay (the Council of Horses in his *Fables*); Goldsmith (Moses selling Blackberry at the fair); Burns ("Auld Mare Maggie" and the often-painted steed that Tam o' Shanter rode); "Monk" Lewis ("The Water King"); Byron (*Mazeppa*); and above all from Scott, whose Waverley novels are reputed to contain no fewer than thirty-seven *named* horses, to say nothing of uncounted anonymous ones.[17]

94. Charles Landseer, *Sterne's Maria* (British Institution 1836) (Victoria & Albert Museum, Crown Copyright). The presence of the dog identifies the source: *A Sentimental Journey* rather than *Tristram Shandy* (bk. 9, chap. 24), where Maria's attribute is a goat. The artist is faithful to Yorick's description: "I discovered poor Maria sitting under a poplar—she was sitting with her elbow in her lap, and her head leaning on one side within her hand—a small brook ran at the foot of the tree. . . . She was dress'd in white, and much as my friend described her, except that her hair hung loose, which before was twisted within a silk net.—She had, superadded likewise to her jacket, a pale green ribband, which fell across her shoulder to the waist; at the end of which hung her pipe."

The same authority reports that the Waverley novels include thirty-three named dogs. The large canine population in Scott, as well as elsewhere in literature, was another windfall for artists. Although dogs were often painted in eighteenth-century conversation pieces, they came into greater demand as the art market expanded. Hunting breeds apart, pictures of dogs obliged the taste of a much larger public than had a deep interest in horses, residents of an animal kingdom that belonged to the superior classes of society. Artists therefore left no literary text unturned for hints that would enable them to paint dogs, especially as personal pets indoors and faithful companions in the open air. A selling point for many portraits of Sterne's Maria was the presence of her attribute, a little dog. Not every literary passage was as generous to animal painters as the one

95. Augustus Egg, *Launce's Substitute for Proteus's Dog* (RA 1849) (Leicestershire Museum and Art Gallery, Leicester). So great was the demand for dogs in Victorian art that in scenes from literary sources they were freely added whenever their presence might reasonably be inferred even though they were not specifically mentioned. In some cases, however, they were central subjects of a scene. In *The Two Gentlemen of Verona* (4. 4), Launce describes in graphic detail the behavior of the unhousebroken dog he substituted for the one Proteus sent him to deliver to Silvia as a present (see text, p. 262). This is the scene, bowdlerized, of course, that is represented in Egg's painting.

an alert artist found in *Barnaby Rudge:* "There were a score of vagabond dogs belonging to the neighbours." (According to a reviewer in 1871, the picture gave full measure.)[18] But there were always enough to go round, thanks again, in large measure, to Scott, who supplied, among others, Wamba's dogs (*Ivanhoe*) and Dandie Dinmont's terriers (*Guy Mannering*). Scott himself figured in one of the most famous of Edwin Landseer's animal pictures, *Sir Walter Scott Seated at the Bottom of the Rhymer's Glen* (RA 1833), of which the *Times* remarked, "The dogs are perfect; the poet quite of secondary interest, and the likeness is not a very happy one."[19] All the reviewers praised the dogs. Many years later (1858), Landseer showed at the British Institution a routine dog picture given literary interest and point, such as it was, by two quotations, one from Shakespeare ("Crabbed age and youth cannot live together") and the other an "extract from my journal while at Abbotsford" (the title of the picture), in which Scott alluded to the amicable relationship that existed between Maida, his favorite old deer hound, and a collie puppy. *Twa Dogs,* a companion picture exhibited at the same time, documented the intended contrast from Burns's poem of that name: a suave, patrician Newfoundland placed side by side with a ploughman's collie, "just and faithful," honest and friendly.

Long-standing English custom justified artists' assumption that dogs were a natural appurtenance to many of the scenes drawn from literature, even if they were not mentioned. (Count the non-canonical dogs seen in the illustrations of the present book alone!) If Chaucer's Prioress could coddle a lapdog, as the poet said she did, there was no reason why a dog should not attend Griselda's wedding to the Marquis of Saluce in the Knight's Tale, though at least one critic found that Landseer's similar introduction of a dog into his painting of Lady Godiva (RA 1866) "detract[ed] very considerably from the solemnity of the work."[20] Poodles and other lapdogs appeared in the many literary costume pieces the Victorian age produced. E. M. Ward painted his wife's dog Mac in his picture of Dr. Johnson awaiting his audience with Lord Chesterfield (pl. 47), and another artist equipped Clarissa Harlowe with a spaniel.

In locales and narrative situations, as in their themes and casts of characters, literary paintings often were specialized versions of the most popular kinds of nonliterary subject art. From the neoclassic period onward, but most of all in the Victorian age, they were, in effect, simply conventional story pictures embellished with literary references. A copious example is the storm and/or shipwreck scene, a characteristic subject of Romantic art with subliminal roots in the maritime nation's psyche, the deep-seated fear of loss of life and property at sea. No subject was more tempting to an artist aspiring to melodrama if not to actual sublimity.[21] "The shivered mast is breaking," wrote the *Athenaeum* critic in describing a typical shipwreck scene, Francis Danby's interpretation (BI 1846) of the event that brought Miranda and Prospero to the enchanted isle,

> the terrified crew prostrate themselves along the slanting decks, the bell is adding its shrill clamour to that of the tempest [a permissible indulgence of the critic's imagination], and, towering over all, one gigantic wave impends, at the direction of Ariel, over the devoted [*sic:* doomed?] vessel. The break of the heavens, where the lightning flashes, is magnificently painted, and the sharp white light from the electric stream sheds its mysterious glare over the scene.[22]

The literary record of the nation naturally abounded in storms and wrecks. Artists found them in at least seven of Shakespeare's plays, and—the single source that inspired the most paintings of the kind—in *The Shipwreck* (1762), by William Falconer, a survivor of the wreck of the Levant trader *Britannia* off Cape Colonna. The poem's popularity lasted for three generations. By 1830, it had gone through twenty-four British editions, a number of which were illustrated by such artists as Westall.[23] Between 1790 and 1856, at least fourteen paintings from the poem are recorded.

Another staple Romantic subject of which literature afforded numerous illustrations was captivity. Reynolds's picture of Ugolino in the Tower

96. Thomas Stothard, *The Tempest* (RA 1798) (Victoria & Albert Museum, Crown Copyright). A number of artists painted the opening scene of *The Tempest,* but seldom with any greater success than did Stothard. Most surviving pictures from literary sources that showed shipwrecks portrayed the results of the event—the casting-up of the survivors onto the shore, as in Poole's scene (pl. 249), rather than the sinking of the vessel itself. Paintings from Falconer's *The Shipwreck,* however, may well have come closer to the conventional treatments of the subject that concentrated on the foundering vessel.

97. Ford Madox Brown, *The Prisoner of Chillon* (1843) (City Art Gallery, Manchester). Byron's poem supplied a number of artists with an occasion to depict the suffering prisoner, a recurrent type in painting. Among Brown's predecessors were Hogarth in his "progresses" (as well as the scene from *The Beggar's Opera* [pl. 1], where the situation is comic rather than pathetic) and Wright of Derby's *The Captive,* from *A Sentimental Journey.*

(from Dante) was, to many later artists, the definitive treatment of the theme, which reached back to such older scenes as Socrates drinking hemlock in his cell and the imprisoned St. Peter roused by an angel. As Lorenz Eitner has shown, the popularity of the theme in the late eighteenth century sprang from a variety of social and cultural influences—John Howard's campaign for prison reform, the art of Piranesi and Goya, the prison scene in *The Rake's Progress,* and, not least, the equivalent scenes in literary works as different as *The Beggar's Opera* (pl. 1) and *A Sentimental Journey.*[24] From Shakespeare alone came at least seven captivity scenes, including the often-painted one of the young Princes in the Tower (pls. 15, 83). From Scott came the imprisonment of Effie Deans, Edie Ochiltree, Rebecca and Isaac of York, and the Duke of Rothsay. Clarissa Harlowe was seen in the sponging house (pl. 301), the murderer Eugene Aram (Bulwer-Lytton's novel) in the condemned cell, Dr. Primrose in jail for debt. Other imprisonment subjects came from *Measure for Measure* (pl. 195), *The Pilgrim's Progress* (the man in the iron cage), Cowper's parlor poem *The Task,* Edward Moore's cautionary drama *The Gamester,* Mrs. Radcliffe's *The Mysteries of Udolpho,* Byron's "The Prisoner of Chillon" (pl. 97), *A Tale of Two Cities* and *Little Dorrit.*

In literary narratives, a frequent sequel to the captivity of a character was his or her release, often by means of rescue from outside. No standard subject in narrative art was better fitted to appeal to the popular taste for melodrama, especially when the deed was prompted by chivalry or at least had a wholesome component of derring-do. Britomart was repeatedly seen rescuing Amoret from Busirane (pl. 98), one of the several choice episodes of the kind that *The Faerie Queene* offered artists. Valentine rescued Sylvia from Proteus in *The Two Gentlemen of Verona* (pl. 177). Half a dozen rescue scenes were depicted from the Waverley novels alone.

98. William Etty, *Amoret Freed by Britomart from the Power of the Enchanter* (RA 1833) (Tate Gallery, London). Spenser's *The Faerie Queene* was a copious source of scenes of imprisonment and deliverance (see also pls. 257, 259). Here Britomart, disguised as a knight, frees Amoret from the chains of the magician Busirane (bk. 3, canto 12). Etty considered this painting to be one of his major works.

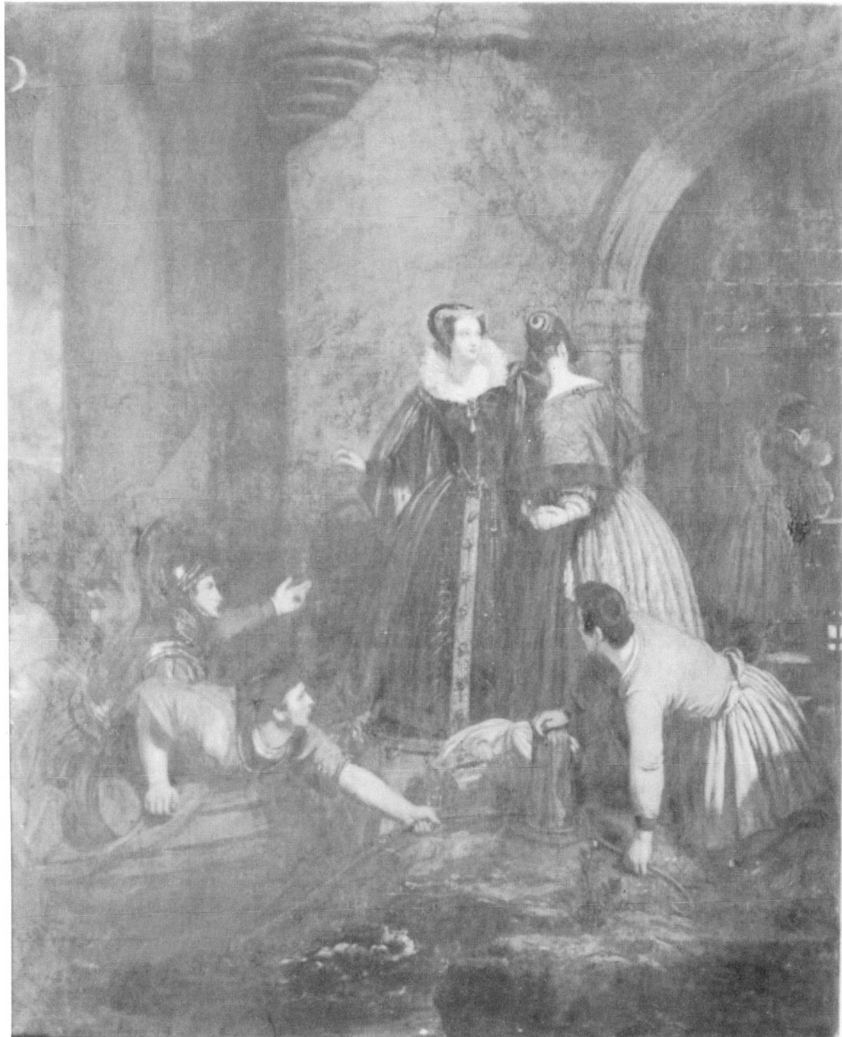

99. Edward Leahy, *Mary Queen of Scots' Escape from Loch Leven* (RA 1837) (Petworth House). One of the most frequently portrayed escape scenes in art, as well as in early nineteenth-century popular drama, was this melodramatic event in 1568, described by Scott in *The Abbot* (chap. 35).

Artists favored captivity scenes in part because their locale in cells or similar places offered agreeable problems in chiaroscuro and the portrayal of confined space. Literature offered additional occasions, without the element of enforced captivity: the witches' cave in *Macbeth,* the Cave of Spleen in *The Rape of the Lock,* the Rosicrucian Cavern in the *Spectator* (No. 379), the caverns in which lived Clonmel and Fingal (Ossian) and Belarius and his companions (*Cymbeline*) (pls. 100, 239), the ones in which King Mark surprises Tristram and Ysolt, and Haidee ministers (in some versions) to the shipwrecked Don Juan. There were also hermit's cells, as in Home's tragedy of *Douglas,* and magician's, notably Prospero's. In the same category of confined space fell the tomb at the end of *Romeo and Juliet* (pl. 213).

Although knowledge of the narrative context would have enhanced spectators' appreciation of such scenes, in some cases, at least, the instantly obvious fact of confinement would have lent sufficient force to a painting to ensure its success on its own terms. This would have been less true of eavesdropping and spying scenes, which were popular in both literary and nonliterary art. Those without a literary allusion were, or were

100. George Dawe, *Imogen Found in the Cave of Belarius* (British Institution 1809) (Tate Gallery, London). An Imogen in boy's clothing, as the plot requires (*Cymbeline,* 4. 2), would have been inadmissible in a pose modeled after neoclassic paintings, so she was allowed the flowingly draped costume conventionally assigned to a young woman in distress.

intended to be, self-explanatory. But the type was enriched when the situation represented came from an identifiable play or novel in which the occasion was an episode in an ongoing story. As early as the Vauxhall paintings in the 1740s, an unknown artist showed Mr. B., behind a screen, overhearing Pamela. But the richest source of such pictures was Shakespeare, some of whose several eavesdropping scenes were painted time after time—Lady Macbeth listening as her lord goes about his murderous business, Romeo under Juliet's balcony, Beatrice in the arbor, Othello listening to Desdemona's and Cassio's innocent but fatally misinterpreted conversation, the Polonius scenes in *Hamlet,* the *Twelfth Night* scene of Maria, Sir Toby, Sir Andrew, and Fabian listening from concealment as Malvolio makes a fool of himself. Louise and the Fair Maid of Perth were shown more than once listening at the dungeon wall, and in the 1870s there was a spate of pictures of the screen scene in *The School for Scandal.* (The first of the kind had been painted almost a century earlier [pl. 110].)

In many narrative paintings, then, the function of the literary allusion was to provide a ready-made context for genre compositions that in their pure state did no more than capture an isolated moment, forcing the spectator to infer the surrounding circumstances from the clues offered, beginning with the title. It enabled the knowledgeable spectator to break out of the time frame that, in stock treatments, boxed in the represented moment and to know exactly what happened before and what would happen next.*

A more common and straightforward means by which novelists and dramatists advanced their plots through someone's obtaining a parcel of fresh information was the arrival of news by letter or verbally, from a figure coming from outside. The letter scene, often the subject of Victorian paintings (Thomas Webster's *A Letter from Abroad,* George Smith's

*There seem, however, to have been no literary narrative pictures in series to match Highmore's now famous dozen from *Pamela.* Morland's *Laetitia* and Northcote's *Progress of an Industrious and an Idle Girl* series, as we saw (chapter 1, above), were derived more from Hogarth than from Richardson. An unnamed six-picture series by Edward Bird (RA 1813) told the story of a poacher arrested, imprisoned, and, suitably reformed, "returning home from [lawful] labour to his domestic comforts," but this claimed no literary inspiration. The handful of Victorian stories-in-pictures were belated (and updated) exercises more or less in the Hogarthian vein: Augustus Egg's in 1858, originally untitled (the *Times* called it "London Trilogy," the *Athenaeum* "The Adulteress and Her Fate," and the *Dictionary of National Biography* "The Fate of a Faithless Wife") but now generally called *Past and Present;* Frith's *The Road to Ruin* (RA 1878), and the same artist's *The Race for Wealth* (1880), each consisting of five episodes. (The entry for *The Road to Ruin* in the Academy catalogue was a sufficient synopsis: College, Ascot, Arrest, Struggles, The End.)

101. Thomas Duncan, *Anne Page Inviting Slender to Dinner* (RA 1836) (National Gallery of Scotland). Although Shakespeare provided a bountiful number of scenes in which one or more characters overheard others, these were still not enough. In this rendition of the opening scene of *The Merry Wives of Windsor,* the artist sought to enhance the comedy Shakespeare had actually written into the scene by supposing that Falstaff and his companion eavesdropped upon it.

The Morning Post, Frederick Goodall's *A Letter from Papa),* had been a favorite of seventeenth-century Dutch and Flemish artists. Its standard early form, exemplified by Vermeer, Terborch, Dirk Hals, Metsu, de Jongh, and others, was that of a girl receiving a letter from a servant, or reading it, or tearing it up after perusal. In only a few instances—one was Jan Steen's picture of Bathsheba receiving King David's letter—was the content of the missive, its place in an ongoing narrative, made explicit. But when the arrival-of-news theme was revived by nineteenth-century British artists, a story was regularly attached to it. In some cases, the visual context made the story as plain as it was in, for example, Wilkie's sensationally popular picture of the Chelsea pensioners receiving news of the Battle of Waterloo. But in pictures derived from literature, the import of the information, however transmitted, was concealed from those who had not read the book. What news did a breathless Pistol bring Falstaff? What startling information did Bassanio learn from Antonio's letter (pl. 102)?

102. Gilbert Stuart Newton, *Portia and Bassanio* (RA 1831) (Victoria & Albert Museum, Crown Copyright). An example of a conventional letter-reading scene endowed with a specific narrative context. People who had read or seen *The Merchant of Venice* would have known that the letter from Antonio began, "Sweet Bassanio, my ships have all miscarried, my creditors grow cruel, my estate is very low, my bond to the Jew is forfeit" (3. 2).

103. John Everett Millais, *Stella* (RA 1868) (City Art Gallery, Manchester). Although this painting was exhibited without any reference to Swift and reviewers did not mention it, the literary allusion is made plain by the letters (from Swift). A companion piece, *Vanessa,* in which the model also holds a letter from the two women's clerical correspondent, was exhibited the next year.

What was in Macbeth's letter to his wife? Or in the one Flora MacIvor received from her brother Fergus? Or in Swift's letters to Stella (pl. 103)?

In other paintings, the element of the story-within-a-story was more pronounced, and the loss to the nonreading spectator all the greater. He would not have known what thrilling adventures Othello was seen describing to Desdemona (pls. 143, 159, 225), or the ones Gulliver related to the Queen of Brobdingnag (pl. 287), or, if it came to that, the subheroic transaction Falstaff described upon his return to the Boar's Head tavern from Gad's Hill (pl. 104).

Another kind of episode, the emotional parting, was among the most popular themes of Victorian painting, descending from the departure and return scenes that were sometimes painted in pairs by late-eighteenth-century genre artists and typified in contemporary poetry by Tennyson's "Enoch Arden." Most such Victorian narrative pictures—Robert Martineau's *The Last Day in the Old Home,* Ford Madox Brown's *The Last of England,* J. C. Horsley's *The Soldier's Farewell*—were self-explanatory.

104. George Clint, *Falstaff Relating His Valiant Exploits at the Boar's Head, Eastcheap* (RA 1833) (Petworth House). Othello's narrative of his soldierly adventures, related to a spellbound Desdemona (pls. 143, 159), was heroic in truth; Falstaff's (*1 Henry IV,* 2. 2) heroic only in the telling. In both cases, the content of the picture could not be appreciated by anyone unacquainted with the Shakespearean play. This painting was one of three that Clint, a specialist in theatrical subjects, exhibited at the same show. The others were from *Twelfth Night:* the duel scene (4.1) and the carousing scene (2. 3).

Contemporary events, especially the mid-century wave of emigration and the Crimean War, added topicality to the stock theme. But, once again, illustrations from English literature deepened the effect, in the form of remembered dialogue, circumstantial detail, and, most important, knowledge of the characters depicted. These added elements widened the range of effects that could be produced from a single stock situation: Romeo and Juliet parting at dawn, Milton and his first wife going their separate ways, Griselda parting from her son, Burns from Highland Mary, Tom Jones from Sophia Western, Imogen from Posthumus, Leicester from Amy Robsart. La Fleur bade farewell to the girls of Montreuil, Montrose took leave of his followers, the Primroses left their

105. Thomas Stothard, *The Meeting of Othello and Desdemona* (Boydell's Shakespeare Gallery) (Royal Shakespeare Theatre Picture Gallery ©). This portrayal of Othello's return to Venice after his victory over the Turks (2. 1) is in the mode of high art that often depicted the triumphant return of warriors. The literary source added the extra element of love between the conqueror and his young wife and the threat to their happiness represented by the glowering Iago. Victorian painting would keep alive the "return" motif, but usually in domestic settings and not involving heroes except, say, for soldiers back from the Crimea.

106. Edwin Landseer, *The Death of Elspeth Mucklebackit* (ca. 1829) (Private Collection). Death in low degree: supported by the blue gown beggar Edie Ochiltree (pl. 314), the crone Elspeth dies in the fisherman's hut (Scott, *The Antiquary*, chap. 40). This is one of a number of sketches Landseer made for illustrations for the Waverley edition of Scott's novels.

cottage, and (the prototype of all such scenes) Adam and Eve turned their backs on Eden.

The irreversible parting scene, the deathbed, was a notorious specialty of Victorian fiction and biography, encapsulating much of the age's sentimental-religious spirit. This was a subject that in pre-Victorian times had encouraged the domestication of history painting, transposing what had been a recurrent subject first in religious art and more recently in neoclassic painting from the heroic mode to that of genre. In literary art, the familial, the intimate, predominated, though not to the exclusion of such violent deaths as Shakespeare, for example, provided. The bill of mortality extracted from literary sources for the edification of art lovers is a long and diversified one, mingling natural causes with an impressive array of misadventure. It includes the names of Cleopatra, Banquo, Lady Macbeth, Hotspur, Douglas, Ophelia, Romeo, Juliet, Mercutio, John of Gaunt, Richard II, Edmund, Mortimer, and Rutland, from Shakespeare alone. (By no means all of his death scenes were ever put on canvas.) From Scott were taken the deaths of, among others, Marmion, Blanche, Old

Mortality, Elspeth Mucklebackit (pl. 106), the Knight of Avenel, Old Alice, the young fisherman in *The Antiquary,* and the warrior in *Castle Dangerous.* Byron contributed at least four, Foscari (pl. 107), the Giaour, Haidee, and Medora. From other sources came the shepherd in *The Seasons,* the hermit and Matilda in Walpole's *The Castle of Otranto,* Sigismunda in Dryden's *Fables,* Arcite (Chaucer's Knight's Tale), Clarissa Harlowe, Jane Shore in Rowe's drama, Ginevra (Rogers's *Italy*), Ossian and Oscar, Palemon (Falconer's *The Shipwreck*), Arviragus (Mason's utterly forgotten drama *Caractacus*), Beverley (Moore's *The Gamester*), King Arthur and Sir Tristram. Despite the Victorians' special fondness for descriptions of the death of children, however, only two literary subjects, the Princes in the Tower and Paul Dombey, were frequently chosen. Surprisingly, the most celebrated deathbed in Victorian fiction, Little Nell's, was seldom depicted.

Some dramatic situations and actions repeatedly derived from literary (and historical) sources had few counterparts in nonliterary painting. They were more closely related to fiction and the drama than to genre art, and necessarily assumed the spectator's familiarity with the literary context. There were trial and interrogation scenes: serious ones (Queen

107. Frederick R. Pickersgill, *The Death of Foscari* (RA 1854) (Royal Collection, Copyright Reserved). Death in high estate: a vestige of the tradition of history painting. The story of the Foscari, an incident in medieval Italian history, was best known to English readers through Byron's *The Two Foscari: An Historical Tragedy.* The Prince Consort bought this painting for his wife, who was fond of Verdi's opera *I due Foscari.*

108. Henry Nelson O'Neil, *The Trial of Queen Catherine* (RA 1845) (Birmingham City Museum and Art Gallery). A small replica of the exhibited painting. In part because of the popularity of the scene (Shakespeare's *Henry VIII,* 2. 4) in the theater, this was probably the most frequently painted literary subject involving trials and supplications. See also pls. 154, 155.

Katherine [pls. 108, 154, 155], Shylock and Portia [pls. 182, 183], Rebecca, Effie Deans, Shakespeare haled before Lucy for deer stealing [pl. 118]) and comic ones (Falstaff and his reluctant recruits [pls. 204, 205], Froth and the Clown in *Measure for Measure* [pl. 30], Conrade and Borachio in *Much Ado About Nothing* [pl. 189]). There were even more scenes of supplication, sometimes representing appeals from judgments already made. Time after time, a sympathetic character—Miranda, Desdemona, Juliet, Eve, Queen Berengaria, Jeanie Deans, Lady Godiva (there were noticeably more entreating women than men)—begged a concession or a more substantial boon from a dominant figure—Prospero, Othello, Juliet's nurse, Adam, Richard Coeur de Lion, Queen Caroline, the wicked Earl of Mercia.

109. John Cawse. *Falstaff and His Recruits* (Society of British Artists 1827) (Yale Center for British Art, Paul Mellon Fund). The principal comic equivalent of the serious examination-trial scenes in Shakespeare was that involving Falstaff and his prospective ragged regiment (*2 Henry IV,* 3. 2). Cawse has added a later moment in the scene, Mouldy's and Bullcalf's successful attempt to bribe Bardolph and, through him, Falstaff.

110. James Roberts, *A Scene in "The School for Scandal"* (RA 1779) (Garrick Club). One of the most dramatic "discovery" scenes in English literature—"Lady Teazle, by all that's wonderful!" Members of the original cast of Sheridan's play, which had been first performed two years before this painting was exhibited, are shown: Thomas King as Sir Peter Teazle, William Smith as Charles Surface, John Palmer as Joseph Surface, and Frances Abington (pl. 16) as Lady Teazle.

111. Henry Thomson, *The Finding of Perdita* (ca. 1790) (Royal Shakespeare Theatre Picture Gallery ©). From *The Winter's Tale,* 3. 3. The painting was commissioned for Boydell's Shakespeare Gallery but was not engraved for inclusion in the volumes that were the end product of Boydell's scheme. Thomson made many illustrations for reprinted editions of British classics.

For their well-proved dramatic effect, artists also favored "discovery" or revelation scenes, the equivalents of the stage's dénouements. One form these took was the climax or resolution of a disguise plot: Viola, Imogen, Hermione, Rosalind and Celia, among others, in Shakespeare alone. But the most frequent kind of so-called discovery was the dramatic encounter, sometimes a confrontation, sometimes the finding of a missing person, sometimes merely a character's first sight of another. In all these categories, Scott's romances were particularly rich sources.*

Not all of these stock subjects remained in favor throughout the nineteenth century. Except for the redoubtable Ophelia and the vision of the Holy Grail in *Idylls of the King,* madness, dreams, and other manifestations of the irrational were among the themes that faded by mid-century; another was the storm-and-shipwreck. After the 1850s, also, trials were seldom depicted, as was the related subject of supplications (a rare later instance was the scene from George Eliot's *Romola* of the heroine pleading for the life of Bernardo del Nero), and the standard subjects of the arrival of news and of a character telling a story of some kind. Some subjects, it appears, had become so hackneyed—or so out of touch with contemporary interest—that they had become devalued beyond retrieval. But into the vacancy came subjects from a literary treasury that grew steadily in popularity: the lives of English writers.

*Identifiable examples of these conventional narrative subjects from literary sources total many hundreds. The list could be considerably lengthened if it were possible to know the precise subjects of paintings catalogued simply as "interviews" between named characters (Rebecca and Rowena, Jeanie Deans and her father, Dugald Dalgetty and Catherine Seyton, and Lady Ashton and her husband, to take a few instances at random from Scott alone). The term seems to have been used elastically, to designate specific scenes that spectators acquainted with the source would recognize without the aid of a more explicit title, as well as inventions of the artist who posed for himself and his fellow readers the intriguing question, "What if—?".

CHAPTER 7

Subjects from art history generate interest in subjects from literary biography.—Paintings from the lives of Shakespeare, Milton, and later authors.

The biographical part of English literature, which Dr. Johnson said he loved most, entered painting by routes both indirect (foreign) and direct (native). The flourishing Victorian commerce in pictures from the lives of English authors derived remotely from what may seem, at first glance, an irrelevant subject: Pliny's legend of the Maid of Corinth, who, to preserve in her eyes the form of her departing lover, traced his shadow on the wall. [1] According to the ancients, this was the origin of painting; and when their treatises were reexamined in the seventeenth century, the myth was repeatedly made the subject of paintings, the most famous of which was Murillo's *El Cuardo de las Sombras* (ca. 1660). The story's popularity among French artists reached its peak between 1770 and 1820, and in those years it was also retold in English art and poetry. Alexander Runciman painted it at Penicuik House in 1771, and two years later David Allan's version won a medal at the Accademia di San Luca, Rome. William Hayley wrote a poem, "The Maid of Corinth," which Wright of Derby illustrated.

In 1826, in a reduction that unfortunately would be typical of Victorian artists who had no particular scruples against debasing a noble and venerable subject, Mulready converted the theme into modern rural genre terms, moving the scene to a moonlit cottage and substituting for the Maid of Corinth a country boy sketching his father as he slept. The picture's title, significantly, was not *The Origin of Painting* but *The Origin of a Painter,* by which Mulready linked his production with a much more familiar subject of Italian and French painting, the lives of artists. Almost from the time Giorgio Vasari published his *Vite de' più eccellenti architetti, pittori e scultori italiana* in 1550, painters had memorialized true and imaginary incidents in the private and professional careers of their celebrated predecessors. This strain of biographical interest reached its climax in nineteenth-century French art.[2] Between 1804 and 1886, no single Salon was without at least one incident of art history recounted in artistic form; in the 1820s, there were as many as ten per year, and in some later years as many as twenty. There was a similar burst of interest among English artists, who, in this as in other respects, shared the academic preoccupation with the art of the golden past. The inspiration for Browning's poems about artists—"Andrea del Sarto," "Fra Lippo Lippi," "Pictor Ignotus," "Old Pictures in Florence"—came at least as much from the contemporary fashion for such paintings as from Vasari.[3] As early as 1820, Turner showed at the Royal Academy his *Raffaelle Accompanied by La Fornarina, Preparing his Pictures for the Decoration of the Loggia.* Between 1837 and 1873, scenes from the lives of Raphael, Salvator Rosa, Cimabue, Quentin Matsys, Holbein, Brunelleschi, Dürer, Titian, Michelangelo, Rubens, Rembrandt, Teniers, Correggio, Velázquez, Murillo, Veronese, Tintoretto, and Giotto were produced in English studios, in many instances by painters who were also well known for their scenes from literature: Maclise, E. M. Ward, Richard Redgrave, Eyre Crowe, Leighton, William Bell Scott, Dyce, Wallis, Henry O'Neil, Noel Paton. In 1829–33, Allan Cunningham published his six-volume *Lives of the Most Eminent British Painters, Sculptors and Architects,* whose title proclaimed its intention of being the English counterpart of Vasari, and in due course, subjects of paintings were taken from British art history. John Absolom painted *Opie When a Boy Reproved by His Mother;* Ward, *Benjamin West's First Effort in Art* and *The Foundlings Visit Hogarth's Studio;* Frith, *Hogarth at Calais;* and Charles Lucy, *The Reconciliation Between Gainsborough and Sir Joshua Reynolds.*

If painting and poetry were sister arts, it more or less followed that painters and poets (and writers in general) were brothers, and further that the lives of writers provided artists with materials as attractive as the lives of painters—the more so when the art public was also a book-reading one. Here a triad of conventional themes in Renaissance and later art supplied welcome precedent for British paintings illustrating the lives of writers—composing their greatest works (often under divine or at least allegorical inspiration), presenting them in homage to their patrons (the graphic equivalent of the literary dedication page), and reading them aloud either to patrons or to favored friends.

Thus Rembrandt had painted *The Evangelist Matthew Inspired by the Angel* and *Homer Dictating His Poetry to a Scribe;* Caravaggio, *St. Matthew and the Angel* (who is literally guiding the saint's hand in one composition, hovering over him in another) and St. Jerome writing (again, two quite different compositions). Ghirlandaio and Lucas Cranach, among others, also depicted St. Jerome; the Cranach painting, *Kardinal Albrecht von Brandenburg als heiliger Hieronymus in der Landschaft* (1527), was a fancy, or role-playing, picture showing the cardinal as scholar-saint, writing outdoors at a table set on a tree stump with his convent on a hill in the background and various animals in attendance. Poussin's companion pictures *The Inspiration of the Lyric Poet* and *The Inspiration of the Epic Poet* were in English collections early in the nineteenth century, the one at Great Cumberland Lodge, Windsor, and the other, then titled *Petrarch Composing His Odes,* in the collection of the connoisseur Thomas Hope. The Earl of Northwick owned Antonella da Messina's *St. Jerome in His Study* and

112. Richard Westall, *Milton Composing "Paradise Lost"* (RA 1802) (Sir John Soane's Museum, London). An old theme in art revived: an author in the God-given throes of composition. The appeal of the subject was doubled in the present case because it also illustrated the edifying theme of filial devotion. It was most effective on those spectators who were unaware of Dr. Johnson's statement, in his life of Milton, that "his daughters were never taught to write; nor would he have been obliged, as is universally confessed, to have employed any casual visiter in disburthening his memory, if his daughter could have performed the office."

Carlo Dolci's *St. John Writing the Apocalypse.* Paintings like these formed the lineage of the frequently depicted scene of Milton dictating *Paradise Lost* (pl. 112), as well as more distinctly genre subjects such as Burns composing "The Cotter's Saturday Night" and (twice, in 1884 and 1887) "To a Mouse."

Pictures of St. Jerome offering his translation of the Bible to the infant Jesus—examples of the subclass of paintings known as "donor portraits"—may have been in the Vicar of Wakefield's mind when he placed himself, in the wandering artist's eclectic painting, offering his learned works on the Whistonian controversy to his wife (see chapter 1, above). After the presentation (or substituting for it) came the actual recital of the work to an auditory. Homer reciting the *Iliad* to the Greeks and Virgil reading the *Aeneid* to Augustus and Octavia were repeatedly portrayed subjects of the kind in Renaissance and neoclassic art; Angelica Kauffmann painted the latter scene in 1788 and Ingres somewhat later (1812). Hazlitt knew "a common French print, in which Molière is represented reading one of his plays in the presence of the celebrated Ninon de l'Enclos, to a circle of the wits and first men of his own time," including Corneille, Racine, La Fontaine, St. Évremond, de la Rochefoucault, and Boileau.[4]

Like Pietro Longhi's *A Poet Reciting His Verses* (1770s), showing an assembly of contemporary ladies and gentlemen listening to the poet, in English hands these pictures often were a kind of conversation piece, though omitting Longhi's extraneous touch of an angel winding his long trumpet. Some scenes were as fictitious as the one showing the poet Feramorz reading "Paradise and the Peri" to Lalla Rookh in Moore's poem. It may well have been that Blind Harry, the fifteenth-century minstrel, did recite his 11,000-line poem on Sir William Wallace as he was represented as doing in a picture by James Drummond at the Royal Scottish Academy in 1846. But in degree of likelihood, there was little to choose between Spenser treating his wife and Sir Walter Raleigh to *The Faerie Queene* in manuscript or Wyclif reading his translation of the Bible to John of Gaunt, Chaucer, and Gower. There may have been a shade more plausibility in a picture of Milton reading his *Defensio Regis* to Cromwell and Allan Ramsay trying out *The Gentle Shepherd* on the Countess of Eglinton, but most paintings of the sort were the products of no more than sentimental fancy: Goldsmith reading a novel (his own *Vicar of Wakefield*?) to his "Jessamy Bride," Miss Horneck, and Burns similarly obliging Highland Mary.

In any event, all such scenes from the lives of English authors came before the picture-buying public with credentials from earlier and higher art. The displacement of Homer, Virgil, Petrarch, and the book-writing saints by native talent may have been a drastic development, but the company English authors thus joined suggests the esteem in which they were then held. No novelty was involved, therefore, when English artists came to select scenes of many kinds from literary biography to join incidents from art history on exhibition walls. Encouraging them was a popular curiosity about the lives and personalities of authors that had originated in the eighteenth century.[5] An offshoot of the prospering antiquarianism of the day, it had received particular impetus from Boswell, the tireless collector and retailer of stories about Dr. Johnson, and from Pope's early biographers, who incorporated into their books materials about the poet gathered by his friend Joseph Spence. In 1795, a year after the publication of Mrs. Thrale's *Anecdotes of the Late Samuel Johnson,* one of the several early collections of Johnsoniana, Fuseli expressed the rationale, already given currency by Johnson himself, that led his contemporaries to prize such biographical lore:

> . . . Those writers who, with intelligence, disinterestedness and taste, select the anecdotes of genius, the features of extraordinary men in their déshabille, on the spur of a great moment or when indulging in the genuine effusions of an unguarded hour, contribute, perhaps, more to a real knowledge of men and manners, open a clearer insight into the head and heart of others, than he who professedly sets out with a series of events to instruct.[6]

Fuseli was the first artist of consequence to take advantage of this interest in authors' lives. The several anecdotal paintings in the Milton Gallery, however, were not the first to draw from the poet's biography. A quarter-century earlier (1775), the Society of Artists had displayed a picture of Milton's house at Chalfont St. Giles, drawn in bibulous circumstances that have already been described (see chapter 1, above). Thus, even before Dr. Johnson published the *Life* (1779) which was responsible for acquainting a large audience with Milton's biography, the poet's personal fame had begun to figure among the literary associations that might help artists sell their pictures.

Down to the end of the eighteenth century, no similar interest in Shakespeare's life was reflected in art. The initial celebration had concentrated on the allegorical (Shakespeare as secular divinity) rather than the biographical (Shakespeare as a Stratford boy who made good in the London theater). Its tone had been set in 1769, when Garrick had virtually taken over Stratford-on-Avon to mark, five years late, the bicentenary of the Bard's birth.[7] Although the great jubilee included numerous forms of praise, such as fireworks, a masquerade ball, an oratorio (Dr. Arne's *Judith*), and a sweepstake race, the trimmings over-all were heavily emblematic. In the program—an ill-timed rainstorm forced the cancellation of the actual event—was a procession, with Shakespeare's characters, accompanied by Melpomene, Thalia, and the Graces, riding in a triumphal chariot. The odes that were recited and the songs that were sung were also allegorical. During the following theatrical season in London, two productions capitalized on the widespread publicity the Stratford celebration generated. Garrick's rival at Covent Garden, George Colman, staged *Man and Wife: or the Stratford Jubilee,* and Garrick himself produced at Drury Lane *The Jubilee,* which was performed ninety-one times during that season (the century's record) and thirty-five times in his last season (1776). Both shows, but especially the latter, featured pageants and processions of Shakespeare's characters, Bardomania bringing spectacle close to the borders of pantomime. Grouped under banners bearing the titles of the plays and carrying identifying stage properties, Garrick's cast entered the theater from the street and threaded their way through the audience. A more lasting effect of the Stratford Jubilee on the theater was seen in the drop curtains, which were often decorated with allegorical designs linking England's supreme poet with the Graces and the Muses in the best neoclassic manner.

The easel painters of the time worked in the same adulatory spirit, almost definitively expressed in Gray's "The Progress of Poesy," in which Shakespeare was himself represented as an artist:

113. George Romney, *The Infant Shakespeare Attended by Nature and the Passions* (Boydell's Shakespeare Gallery) (Royal Shakespeare Theatre Picture Gallery ©). "Nature is represented with her face unveiled to her favourite Child, who is placed between Joy and Sorrow.—On the Right-Hand of Nature are Love, Hatred, and Jealousy; on her Left-Hand, Anger, Envy, and Fear" (Boydell catalogue).

114. George Romney, *The Infant Shakespeare Nursed by Tragedy and Comedy* (Boydell's Shakespeare Gallery) (Petworth House). The companion to pl. 113; together they supplied the element of allegory that was, at that time, indispensable to any celebration of Shakespeare.

Far from the sun and summer-gale,
In thy [Albion's] green lap was Nature's darling laid,
What time, where lucid Avon strayed,
To him the mighty Mother did unveil
Her awful face; the dauntless child
Stretched forth his little arms and smiled.
"This pencil take," (she said) "whose colours clear
Richly paint the vernal year:
Thine too these golden keys, immortal boy!
This can unlock the gates of Joy;
Of horror that, and thrilling fears,
Or ope the sacred source of sympathetic tears."

In 1784, Joseph Strutt, an artist-antiquary remembered today for his pioneering researches into old English customs and sports, exhibited at the Royal Academy a group portrait of Shakespeare, Milton, and Spenser, with personified Nature dictating to Shakespeare to the rather obvious exclusion of his fellow poets. For Boydell, Romney painted companion pieces, *The Infant Shakespeare Attended by Nature and the Passions* and *The Infant Shakespeare Nursed by Tragedy and Comedy* (pls. 113, 114). Imitators followed culpably close; there was another *Infant Shakespeare Nursed by Tragedy and Comedy,* by a totally obscure artist, at the Royal Academy in 1792. Romney also projected, but did not complete, a study of *Nature Unveiling Herself to Shakespeare,* which was as clearly drawn from Gray's poem as was the poetess Helen Maria Williams's encomium on a sketch she saw: "The partial Nymph unveil'd her awful face, / And bade his colours clear her features trace."[8] Angelica Kauffmann *(The Fame and Tomb of Shakespeare)* and Stothard *(The Graces Crowning Shakespeare)* produced works in the same emblematic vein.

Another treatment inspired by neoclassic models brought the image of the poet one step closer to reality, if only by association. Without depriving him of his godlike role, they surrounded him with visually realized samples of his imaginative output—groups of characters from the plays,

115. Thomas Stothard, *Shakespeare's Characters* (RA 1813) (Victoria & Albert Museum, Crown Copyright). A composition modeled after Stothard's popular *Canterbury Pilgrims* (pl. 251). From left to right: characters from *Twelfth Night, Henry IV, As You Like It, The Tempest, King Lear, Hamlet,* and *Macbeth.* The comic characters are illuminated by a rainbow, the tragic ones clouded by a murky sky.

arranged in a procession as in a sculptural frieze, or in Garrick's productions at Stratford and Drury Lane. In 1806, Fuseli exhibited *The Nursery of Shakespeare: The Infant Nursed by Tragedy, Caressed by Comedy, Surrounded by Some of the Most Striking Characters.* Flanked by a selection of figures, the infant was literally nursed by Tragedy, while Comedy, breast bared, awaited her turn. The very next year, Stothard showed his procession of the Canterbury pilgrims (pl. 251), the sensational success of which led him to emulate Fuseli and present a group of Shakespeare's tragic and comic characters in a picture at the Royal Academy (pl. 115). With the fading of the neoclassic fashion, such pictures lost favor. One of the last was Henry Howard's *The Vision of Shakespeare* (1830), which the architect Sir John Soane, whose tastes were firmly rooted in the preceding century, bought for his museum in Lincoln's Inn Fields.

Meanwhile, the classic device of the pantheon was occasionally adopted to celebrate the English poets. This really was nothing new.[9] Portraits and sculptured busts of authors had adorned libraries in ancient Rome, and as early as the fifth century A.D., manuscripts had sometimes borne portraits of their authors. The putative images of Matthew, Mark, Luke, and John, equipped with scroll or book, embellished medieval copies of the gospels, and secular writers were so memorialized in England beginning with the portrait of Chaucer in the manuscript of Hoccleve's *Regimen of Princes* (ca. 1412). When the spirit of the Enlightenment animated English society, bibliophiles like the Earl of Halifax and Lord Oxford revived the old Roman practice. At his new mansion in Mayfair, built in 1747–49, Lord Chesterfield—the very one whose patronage Dr. Johnson eloquently declined (his library is glimpsed through the door in E. M. Ward's *Dr. Johnson in the Anteroom of Lord Chesterfield* [pl. 47])—amassed the finest such gallery of the time, twenty-two paintings in all: Chaucer, Spenser, Jonson (one genuine, one dubious), Waller and Cartwright (both erroneously identified as Milton), Butler, Denham, Cowley, Dryden, Wycherley, Otway, Prior, Swift, Congreve, Addison, Rowe, Pope, Sidney, Shakespeare, the Earl of Dorset, and the Earl of Rochester. (All but three are now in the Senate House of the University of London.) An array of such icons was, in fact, an indispensable adjunct of eighteenth-century gentlemen's libraries, lending the very word "gallery" a social cachet readily exploited when Boydell and Fuseli embarked on their Shakespeare and Milton projects.

And so William Blake was working in a long-established tradition when, in 1800, he painted in Hayley's library at Felpham a tempera frieze consisting of eighteen portraits of great poets, eight of whom were English.

Besides Shakespeare and Milton, there were Chaucer, Spenser, Dryden, Otway, Pope, and Cowper, each depicted after the traditional likenesses (the "Hoccleve" portrait of Chaucer, the Droeshout portrait of Shakespeare, and so on) and accompanied by vignettes from the poet's works, such as the Pardoner and the Wife of Bath, Macbeth, the serpent in the Garden of Eden, and scenes from Otway's *Venice Preserved* and Pope's *Eloisa to Abelard*.[10] (The set is now in the City Art Gallery, Manchester.)

But it was the more accessible, down-to-earth conception of poets as human beings with no pretensions to divinity that fed the quickening appetite for literary-biographical paintings. Beginning even before Fuseli portrayed scenes from Milton's life in his gallery, a number of compilations, some in several volumes, provided treasuries of moving, quaint, or intimate stories of authors and reports of their conversation: Isaac D'Israeli's three collections, *Curiosities of Literature* (1791–93), *Calamities of Authors* (1812), and *Quarrels of Authors* (1814), and the seventeen thick volumes of *Literary Anecdotes of the Eighteenth Century* (1812–16) and

116. George Cruikshank, *The First Appearance of William Shakespeare on the Stage with Part of His Dramatic Company in 1564* (RA 1867) (Yale Center for British Art, Paul Mellon Fund). An oil copy of the exhibited painting, which may have been a watercolor; one of the numerous by-products of the celebration in 1864 of the tercentenary of Shakespeare's birth. The scene of this whimsical extravaganza is the stage of the Globe playhouse in 1564 (thirty-five years before it was built—and it never possessed the Victorian theater's proscenium, curtains, or footlights); the date is 23 April, the approximate time when Shakespeare was born at Stratford-on-Avon. Surrounding the cradle, replacing the symbolic figures in Romney's pair, are characters from the plays, those from the comedies and romances generally on the left and those from the tragedies and histories on the right.

Illustrations of the Literary History of the Eighteenth Century (1817–58), compiled by John Nichols and his son, publishers and proprietors of the venerable *Gentleman's Magazine.* (The father is said to have been among the guests at Josiah Boydell's dinner when the Shakespeare Gallery was conceived.) In 1820, two separate editions of Spence's *Observations, Anecdotes, and Characters of Books and Men* came out the same day—the first publication of the work, which previously had circulated only in manuscript.

At the same time, Sir Walter Scott was bringing historical characters, including authors, into his romances for cameo appearances. Thus Shakespeare turned up briefly and anachronistically in *Kenilworth.* Scott's successors adopted the device to add a spurious touch of authenticity to their fictions. The success of this practice, which culminated in Thackeray's introduction of Addison, Steele, and Swift in the later pages of *The History of Henry Esmond,* encouraged genre artists on occasion to treat historical figures in the same way, inserting them into anecdotal or narrative situations—documentable, legendary, or utterly imaginary—just as novelists dropped them into their scenes.

Further encouragement came from such works as Anna Jameson's *Memoirs of the Lives of the Poets* (1829), which went through a number of editions. These romanticized excursions into poets' private lives, a genre of popular writing that was one more product of the keepsake age, offered abundant subjects for painting. Mrs. Jameson's book alone included Burns's love affair with Highland Mary, Swift's ambiguous attachment to Stella and Vanessa, and Pope's courtship of Mary Wortley Montagu—three episodes that, as treated by Mrs. Jameson and her fellow story-spinners as well as by subsequent painters, had the quality of sentimental myth rather than of sober literary biography.

Side by side on the shelves with these contributions to readers' sentimentalized visions of their favorite authors appeared another brand of popularized literary biography typified by William and Mary Howitt's indomitably chatty two-volume *Homes and Haunts of the Eminent British Poets* (1847). The coming of the railway was bringing tourism into middle-class life, and such books constituted guides, for the active excursionist and the armchair reader as well, to all the sites associated with the British poets. They usually were generously illustrated with engravings, and thus reinforced the popularity of paintings showing the same locales, either landscapes or studies of individual buildings. The appeal of association, so marked in pictures from Burns and Scott, extended to innumerable works of landscape and architectural art whose titles, if little else, referred to well-known writers.

By the late 1820s, the outworn flights of Shakespeare-devotional fancy represented by allegorical, processional, and hall-of-fame paintings were beginning to be replaced by pictures that catered to the public's growing eagerness for intimate glimpses of the Elizabethan playwright whose bust by George Dance, inscribed "We shall not look upon his like again," had presided over the entrance to Boydell's Gallery in Pall Mall. At the time of the Jubilee, Garrick had presented the citizens of Stratford-on-Avon with Benjamin Wilson's *Shakespeare in His Study,* one of the first attempts to imaginatively re-create the poet's appearance. This effort had nothing to do with the persistent attempts to discover and authenticate portraits that were claimed to be genuine likenesses. The authority on Shakespeare portraits in the early nineteenth century was James Boaden, whose treatise on the subject, with a title so long as to require eight lines in a modern book on Shakespeare's many "lives," was published in 1824.[11] Appropriately enough, the man Shakespeare, undistracted by Nature, Muses, Graces, or any other spiritual beings, was introduced into Regency exhibition rooms by Boaden's son John, a painter whose oeuvre included almost fifty pictures from English literature, none of them remarkable. One of his two contributions to the British Institution show in 1826 repeated Wilson's subject of half a century earlier, accompanied by a portrait of Queen Elizabeth, a view of the Globe playhouse, and another of Stratford church. At the same exhibition could be seen a fanciful painting by another hand, *Shakespeare, After His Return to Stratford, Entertains His Father and Mother, By Reciting the Character of Sir John Falstaff, in The Merry Wives of Windsor.* The permeation of the Shakespeare legend, already a luxuriant printed growth of legend and hearsay, by a succession of even wilder whims in pictorial form was gathering momentum.

Numerous unsupported (and in many cases totally unsupportable) anecdotes of Shakespeare had been absorbed in the eighteenth-century biographies and now were repeated, in turn, in separately published biographies both scholarly and catch-penny, and in "lives" prefixed to editions of Shakespeare's works that appeared year by year. The effect of such repetition was to increase the credibility of every nugget of supposed "fact." To these almost universally accepted tales, at this moment when painters were turning to subjects from Shakespeare lore, playwrights and novelists were adding their share of fresh fiction. At Covent Garden in 1829, Charles Kemble played Shakespeare in C. A. Somerset's *Shakespeare's Early Days,* a production soon followed by something called *Shakespeare's Dream* (1831) and other equally free conceptions of the dramatist's personal life. The novelists were not far behind. Robert F. Williams's trilogy *Shakespeare and His Friends; or, "The Golden Age" of Merry England, The Youth of Shakespeare,* and *The Secret Passion,* published between 1838 and 1844, added considerably to the store of bogus Shakespeareana.

If the artists did not absolutely outclass the dramatists and novelists in inventiveness, they gave them a good run for the money. The least removed from sober history—though even they had their share of sentimental fancy—were the many paintings that represented the topography of Shakespeare's early life. In the 1840s, a national campaign was waged to rescue his birthplace from dilapidation, refurbish it, and endow it with a permanent curatorship. One result of this effort was a growing interest in Anne Hathaway's cottage as the site of what was fondly imagined to have been an ideal courtship such as was depicted, with extravagant embellishments of floral prose, in Emma Severn's novel *Anne Hathaway; or, Shakspeare in Love* (1845). This romantic subject was so exempt from total decay that it appeared on the walls of the Royal Academy as late as 1902. In due course, many paintings of the birthplace and the cottage appeared: routine, if not actually banal domestic scenes whose only claim to more than a passing glance was their prominently announced Shakespearean association. A specialist in this line of work at one juncture was Henry Wallis. In a single Academy exhibition (1854), he hung *In Shakespeare's House, The Font in which Shakespeare was Christened,* and *The Room in which Shakespeare was Born* (pl. 117). A fourth picture in the same series, *The Parlour in Anne Hathaway's Cottage* (perhaps rejected by the Academy), was shown in the same year at the British Institution. Such pictures approached within hailing distance of historical reality; there was a certain residue of authenticity, however small. So much could not be said for such impudent attempts to borrow Shakespearean cachet for run-of-the-mine interiors as a painting catalogued ten years earlier as *The Great Hall, Hampton Court, In This Hall Many of the Plays of Shakespeare were Originally Performed.* The artist was more certain of this supposition than any scholars have been, then or now.

Against interiors or exteriors carefully contrived to suggest Elizabethan décor, Shakespeare's life story, or what passed for it, was told in paint. Since Shakespeare unquestionably married Anne Hathaway, it was reasonable to suppose that he had previously courted her. So far, the artists were on relatively solid ground. But another subject, Shakespeare's arraignment before the local magnate, Sir Thomas Lucy, on a charge of deer-stealing, had only the very tenuous authority of oral say-so: a piece of late gossip first printed by Nicholas Rowe in 1709 and subsequently assimilated without much questioning into the received narrative of Shakespeare's youth. Walter Savage Landor adopted the episode in one of his *Imaginary Conversations* (1834), and three years later, George Harvey, a leading Scottish painter, exhibited his version, the first of several by various artists, at the Scottish Academy. Like other pictures depicting apocryphal scenes from Shakespeare's biography, the engravings made of it helped distribute these legends more widely, as well as deepening people's faith in them. Pictures were as effective a disseminator of falsehood as print.

According to another story, originating with Sir William D'Avenant and then passed from one generation of Shakespearean students to the next until it was finally put into print in 1753, Shakespeare's first job when

117. Henry Wallis, *The Room in Which Shakespeare Was Born* (RA 1854) (Tate Gallery, London). The room as it was shown to tourists after the Birthplace was purchased by national subscription in the 1840s. This was one of three related paintings Wallis showed at the 1854 Academy; the others were *In Shakespeare's House* (now at the Victoria and Albert Museum) and *The Font in Which Shakespeare Was Christened.*

118. Thomas Brooks, *Shakespeare before Lucy* (International Exhibition 1862) (Royal Shakespeare Theatre Picture Gallery ©). An apocryphal event in Shakespeare's early life, his arraignment before the local magistrate on a charge of deer stealing (the evidence is seen at the left). Brooks belonged to the school of artists who were unaffected by the widespread insistence on historical authenticity (chap. 11). Here, he cheerfully ignores the differences between Elizabethan and Victorian costumes and faces, with a distinct bias toward the modern.

he arrived in London was holding horses outside the playhouse. This supposed event naturally attracted animal painters whose interest in literary biography was minimal but who knew a good subject for a horse painting when it came to their attention. Another story, recorded by that indispensable collector of sixteenth- and seventeenth-century gossip John Aubrey, inspired a picture of Shakespeare and the hostess of the Crown inn, Oxford (RA 1844). The accompanying note explained that Shakespeare sometimes stopped at the inn on his way from Stratford to London. What it failed to mention was that the source of Aubrey's statement was D'Avenant, son of the innkeeper and his beautiful and witty wife, who, in his cups, was wont to imply that Shakespeare sired him during one such layover. So, at least, his statement was interpreted, though modern opinion is that he meant to say that he considered himself to be an inheritor of Shakespeare's poetical genius rather than his natural son.

Aubrey also reported that "Ben Jonson and he [Shakespeare] did gather Humours of men dayly where ever they came"—that is, studied their characters from the life. "The Humour of the Constable in Midsomernight's Dreame," said Aubrey, confusing that play with *Much Ado About Nothing,* "he happened to take at Grendon, in Bucks (I thinke it was Midsomer night that he happened to lye there)." This was the germ of Henry Stacy Marks's painting, *How Shakespeare Studied* (RA 1863).

> Shakspeare [reported the *Athenaeum*], rather a coarse presentation, is seated in the porch of an Elizabethan inn, watching the "humours" of a knot of folks standing in the street before him. An old city legal authority, probably the original of Dogberry before he had his "losses," is enlightening an audience consisting of a vapouring knight and a swash-buckler sort of a fellow. By Shakspeare's feet is a dog, an ill-drawn animal, but an apt companion to him, not, we believe, previously suggested by any authority.[12]

The *Examiner* critic detected in the surrounding figures the roadside originals of Malvolio, Pistol, Justice Shallow, Slender, and Shylock, the last-named "in a Jew clothesman who trades under the golden sign of the 'Fleece' and is tempting Mrs. Page into a bargain."[13]

Shakespeare's largely undocumented associations with the London literati of his time offered artists an excellent chance to introduce into anecdotal paintings portraits of various Elizabethan celebrities such as might be found in Nicholas Hilliard's miniatures, thus enhancing each picture's supposed historical and literary interest. No matter if the events or juxtapositions strained credulity; it was pleasanter to imagine that they *might* have happened. In 1840, for example, visitors to the British Institution could see Shakespeare giving Ben Jonson's wife a "compliment" (present) to be given in turn to their daughter, his godchild. Also on hand: Beaumont, Fletcher, Raleigh, and Jonson himself, who was "receiving an appropriate lecture" from the young barrister John Selden. In the same year, the Royal Academy's clientele saw David Scott's populous canvas of the Globe theater the day Queen Elizabeth came—a most unlikely event in itself—to see *The Merry Wives of Windsor,* which, according to Rowe, she had commissioned. "Groundlings and balcony men, the great literary lights of the Elizabethan age, and the patrician and political notables of the time" (the words are those of Scott's brother), all were there. The "sharp wits in the Mermaid" were present too, including Ben Jonson, "in plain black, a humble dress in those gay days . . . clenching his hand, and enjoying the practical jibes of the Merry Wives."[14] Another canvas representing a kind of Tudor hall of fame was John Faed's *Shakespeare and His Contemporaries* (RSA 1851), the company including Chapman, Lyly, Florio, Drayton, Daniel, Marston, Nashe, and Jonson. Such pictures were the equivalents in literary art of the paintings of recent historical events, such as Haydon's *Meeting of the Anti-Slavery Society* and George Hayter's *The House of Lords Discussing the Bill to Divorce Queen Caroline,* which were, in effect, portrait galleries of contemporary notables assembled within single frames.

Shakespeare was repeatedly shown reading his latest production to a rapt auditor or audience. Usually it was Queen Elizabeth who was thus favored. In 1834, Stothard had him reading *The Merry Wives of Windsor* to her. The next year a lesser artist, showing the same subject, failed to specify the play; a much later one, Henry Nelson O'Neil, proposed that it was *A Midsummer Night's Dream.* The scene of the latter painting (RA 1877) was the gaily appointed royal barge floating down the Thames on a sunlit day, the monarch reclining Cleopatra-like on cushions as her favorite poet ("a reddish-haired man with a phrenologically intellectual forehead" according to one critic) sat uncomfortably before her on a stool.[15] It was George Cattermole, however, who most audaciously capped a dubious legend with an extreme unlikelihood. In 1868, he depicted Shakespeare reading a play to, of all people, his old bête noire Sir Thomas Lucy. Evidently all was forgiven.

Another of Wallis's paintings was a fanciful scene in a sculptor's workshop at Stratford the year after Shakespeare's death (pl. 119). While children in nineteenth-century dress played at the open door, a visitor watched the sculptor as he finished the "bust" (actually a half-length figure) that was to be incorporated into the monument in Holy Trinity Church. Palgrave, "reading" the picture as a modern critic might read Hogarth or Turner, professed in the *Saturday Review* to find symbolic

119. Henry Wallis, *A Sculptor's Workshop, Stratford-on-Avon, A.D. 1617* (RA 1857) (Royal Shakespeare Theatre Picture Gallery ©). A blend of two popular kinds of narrative painting, showing an artist at work in a fictitious scene suggested by literary biography. As usual, some liberty was taken with the known facts: the workshop of Gerard Johnson (Janssen), who sculpted the first Shakespeare monument, was in Southwark, not Stratford; and if he worked from a death mask, there is no record of such priceless evidence of Shakespeare's features. Reviewers were divided on the identity of the onlooker. The *Athenaeum* (9 May) said he was Ben Jonson, but the *Saturday Review* (23 May) hedged: "Burbage is it, or Southampton?"

meaning in the details: ". . . In bringing together, as accessories of this single *atelier,* the Gothic corbels and a religious statue, together with an Italian model of the human muscles, Mr. Wallis, we presume, intended to indicate that meeting of the Old Art and the New which Shakespeare himself symbolized."[16]

Milton exceeded even Shakespeare in the number of paintings that showed real or supposed events in their respective lives. About fifty are recorded, half of them in the two decades 1830–40 and 1850–60. In 1850, each of the three regular exhibitions, the Royal Academy, the British Institution, and the Society of British Artists, had at least one.

The subject most often painted was that of the blind poet dictating to his daughters, sometimes with a suggestion of celestial grace streaming down into the chamber. Dr. Johnson quoted Jonathan Richardson's report that "he would sometimes lie awake whole nights, but not a verse could he make; and on a sudden his poetical faculty would rush upon him with an *impetus* or *oestrum,* and his daughter was immediately called to secure what came."[17] Romney painted the scene in 1793, it was on the Miltonic agenda that Barry never carried beyond the point of sketches, Fuseli included it in the Milton Gallery, and Westall exhibited his version in 1802 (pl. 112). At least fifteen later treatments are recorded.* Thackeray had no praise for Haydon's interpretation of the scene at the Society of British Artists in 1840:

> A buxom wench in huge gigot sleeves stands behind the chair, another is at a table writing. The draperies of the ladies are mere smears of colour; in the foreground lies a black cat or dog, a smudge of lamp-black, in which the painter has not condescended to draw a figure. The chair of the poetical organ-player is a similar lump of red and brown; nor is the conception of the picture, to our thinking, one whit better than the execution.[18]

Other aspects of Milton's domestic life were the topics of much contro-

*Delacroix painted the subject on a small canvas, ca. 1824–28. For good measure, he placed in the background a painting of another favorite Miltonic moment, the expulsion of Adam and Eve from Eden.

120. Henry Fuseli, *The Return of Milton's First Wife* (ca. 1799) (Walker Art Gallery, Liverpool). An incident in Milton's life that was not included in the group of biographical paintings in the Milton Gallery (cf. pl. 34). "He was at a Friend's house upon a Visit; his Wife Surpriz'd him; she came into the Room and all in Tears flung her Self at his Feet. At first he seem'd Inexorable, but the Submission of a few Minutes drove away the Provocations of So Long a Continu'd Crime. He Melted, Receiv'd her, and was Reconcil'd" (Jonathan Richardson in his life of Milton, 1734). Fuseli sent this painting, along with several others, to his Liverpool patron William Roscoe, in part payment for loans Roscoe had made him.

versy and myth-making before and during the Victorian age, the most influential fiction being Anne Manning's account of *The Maiden and Married Life of Mary Powell,* the poet's first wife, first published in *Sharpe's Magazine* in 1849 and continued by a sequel, *Deborah's* [his third daughter's] *Diary* (1858). It says something for the restraint of Victorian artists that they did not draw much from these flights of sensational sentimentality, preferring on the whole to rely on scenes that could be deduced less extravagantly from the corpus of Milton biography. In Fuseli's gallery had hung, in addition to the dictating scene, a portrait of the poet as a youth with his mother (pl. 34); and in those same years (1799–1800), he had also painted the return of Milton's first wife to his bed and board (pl. 120) and his dream, later in life, of her deceased successor ("My late espousèd saint"). One Milton Gallery painting, however, represented a totally fictitious episode, that of a pair of foreign ladies coming upon the teen-aged Milton as he lay asleep under a tree near Cambridge and being so impressed by his beauty that the younger composed some extempore lines in Italian which she left in his hand. Milton, so the myth went, conceived such a passion for "the fair unknown" that he went to Italy in an unsuccessful search for her, whom he thought of to the end of his days as his own Lost Paradise. Several later artists illustrated the same scene, which they sometimes transferred to a suburb of Rome in deference to what was reported to be the local Roman version of the story.[19]

Milton also appeared in a number of the paintings from seventeenth-century history that were so popular in the Victorian era, as much for their colorful costuming and portrayals of "manners" as for whatever political overtones they may have possessed. In several, all dating from 1850 and after, he was one of the principal figures. Frederick Newenham's scene of Cromwell dictating to Milton—turnabout, the poet's daughters might have said, was fair play—the dispatch in favor of the persecuted Protestants of the Valleys of Piedmont attracted considerable notice when it was hung at the British Institution in 1850. In 1877, Ford Madox Brown painted the same episode, adding Andrew Marvell to the cast of characters. Other Milton-Cromwell paintings went further in their fancy. One, at the Royal Academy in 1854, showed Cromwell "directing Milton to prepare a copy of his Latin verses, intended to accompany the portrait of himself which he is about to send to Christina of Sweden"—the first Mrs. Milton being in attendance, as she almost certainly was not. The most improbable of all was the scene by Charles Lucy in which Milton was represented playing the organ to an appreciative Cromwell.

Since fewer people were acquainted with Chaucer than with Shakespeare and Milton, there was much less interest in the older poet's life. Little of substance was known about it in any case, and such information as was available was not conducive to free adaptation in the domestic or sentimental mode of popular art. The first painting drawn from his life was William Bell Scott's *Chaucer, with His Friend and Patron John of Gaunt, and the Two Sisters, Catherine and Philippa, Their Wives* (RA 1842), a title wisely and more descriptively shortened to *Chaucer Reading His Poem of The Flower and the Leaf to John of Gaunt* when it was shown subsequently at the Royal Scottish Academy. The half-dozen paintings representing Chaucer between 1845 and 1856 may have been inspired in part by the publication in the former year of the first biography (Sir Nicholas Harris Nicolas's) to be founded on fact rather than legend.

At the Free Exhibition of 1848, Chaucer, along with Gower and John of Gaunt, was an auditor rather than a performer in Ford Madox Brown's *Wyclif Reading His Translation of the Bible*. When this painting was shown, Brown had not yet completed a work he had begun in Rome in 1845, after his chance encounter with a passage in Sir James Mackintosh's *History of England* while reading at the British Museum. As he remembered it when writing of the event in his diary two years later, the passage ran: "And it is scarcely to be wondered at, that English about this period should have become the judicial language of the country, ennobled as it had recently been by the genius of Geoffrey Chaucer." "This at once fixed me," Brown recorded. "I immediately saw a vision of Chaucer reading his poems to knights & Ladyes fair, to the king & court, amid air & sun shine."[20] His first intention was to call the painting, a triptych with Chaucer in the center panel and Wyclif and John of Gaunt in the wings, "The Seeds of the English Language." Then (one notes that this was just half a century after Blake painted his garland of poets on the walls of Hayley's library) Brown substituted what he called "a love-offering to my favourite poëts, to my never-faithless Burns, Byron, Spenser, and Shakespeare." The finished painting (pl. 121), exhibited at Liverpool in 1853, was titled on the frame *Milton: Spenser: Shakespeare: Chaucer Reading the Legend of Constance to Edward III and His Court. An. Dom. 1375: Byron: Pope: Burns.* Chaucer occupied the central panel, flanked by three poets in each of the wings. Another version of the panel meanwhile had been exhibited, alone, at the Royal Academy in 1851.

Although Shakespeare and Milton dominated the gallery of scenes from sixteenth- and seventeenth-century English literary history, a few of their contemporaries were occasionally represented independently of them. Spenser was seen in his study in a picture (RA 1839) "from an authentic portrait." Ben Jonson was portrayed on a visit to Drummond of Hawthornden (RSA 1867). In 1862, six years after his *Death of Chatterton* (below) created a stir, Henry Wallis painted the death of Christopher Marlowe. It must have been a melodramatic presentation indeed. "The corpse," said the *Times*, disapproving of the subject (a "miserable end in a bagnio brawl"), "lies scarce seen amid the wreck of shattered chairs, upset candlesticks, flagons, and torn table-cover, by the light in the hands of the terror-stricken inmates of the foul place, who have gathered at the top of the stairs leading down to the room in which the brawl has taken place. Through the open window is seen the moonlit street with the assassins running away."[21]

Two paintings from Defoe's life are recorded. The earlier, praised as having "the true congenial and Hogarthian spirit," was E. M. Ward's *Daniel Defoe and the Manuscript of Robinson Crusoe* (RA 1849). In the shop of a publisher-bookseller, a supercilious assistant returned to the young Defoe the rejected manuscript, while the proprietor obsequiously did the honors of the establishment to a successful scandalmongering author, Mary de la Rivière Manley. The other picture, a crowded scene of London life by Eyre Crowe (RA 1862), showed the doughty journalist standing

121. Ford Madox Brown, *The Seeds and Fruits of English Poetry* (1845–53) (Ashmolean Museum, Oxford). This triptych memorializes Brown's deep attachment to nine English poets. A considerably altered version of the central panel was exhibited at the Royal Academy in 1851 (now at the Art Gallery of New South Wales, Sydney), and another, painted 1856–58, is at the Tate Gallery. The composition strikingly resembles that in an illumination of Chaucer reading aloud, found in a fifteenth-century manuscript of his *Troilus and Criseyde* (Corpus Christi College, Cambridge).

serenely in the pillory as punishment for writing his ironical pamphlet, *The Shortest Way with the Dissenters.* Grateful Whig housewives tossed bouquets to him, and a gentleman knelt before him, drinking his health. Conforming to the mid-Victorian insistence on historical accuracy in details, the painter depicted Defoe as he was described in the hue-and-cry notice: "a middle-sized spare man, about forty years old, of a brown complexion, and dark brown coloured hair, but wears a wig; a hooked nose, a sharp chin, gray eyes, and a large mole near his mouth."[22]

Sir Richard Steele figured in art most prominently, however indirectly, as the former occupant of the house in Hampstead that Constable included in his *View of London* (RA 1832). But he was also shown with his mother in a picture (1804) suggested by his essay in the *Tatler* (No. 181), and later, when Thackeray in his *English Humorists* had directed attention afresh to him as a lovably feckless husband, writing to his wife explaining why he would not be home for dinner (Eyre Crowe at the winter exhibition in Pall Mall, 1860, and another painter at the Society of British Artists, 1880).

Lady Mary Wortley Montagu, curiously enough, occasioned more paintings than did Steele. She was painted "at Belgrade" (no further clue offered) by John James Chalon (RA 1834) and as the nominal subject of a routine picture of a coquette in Turkish dress (RA 1858). When the Queen Anne period had come into fashion as a setting of costume-and-wig art, painters remembered the story of her being introduced at the age of eight or nine to her father's companions at the Kit Kat Club as "the Reigning Beauty of the Year." William Frederick Yeames depicted it in 1884. His rendition gathered inside one frame a whole constellation of popular motifs: a beautiful child in her white satin and lace, crowned with the fashionable tall head-dress of the day; the humor of the situation (grave age paying tribute to blossoming youth); colorful masculine costume; and literary-artistic allusiveness in the persons of Addison, Steele, and Kneller among others.

Lady Mary also figured in the most famous picture taken from the biography of Alexander Pope, Frith's *The Rejected Poet* (pl. 122). Based on a fragment of hearsay related in an edition of Lady Mary's letters, it showed what purported to have been the occasion of her estrangement from the physically unattractive poet, her responding with hearty laughter to his declaration of love. Frith painted it for "a collector, of a somewhat vulgar type," as he later described him, who was under the impression that Pope was a Pontiff of Rome ("The Pope make love to a married woman—horrible!").[23]

Apart from Turner's painting (1808) of the demolition of the villa at Twickenham, a house that was long a favorite subject for topographical artists, the only other picture of consequence relating to Pope was Eyre Crowe's *Pope's Introduction to Dryden, at Will's Coffee House* (RA 1858), another example of the literary portrait gallery, in which Steele, Addison, Congreve, Vanbrugh, and other writers of the day witnessed the clever Windsor lad's showing his verses to the old poet, ensconced in his favorite nook in the coffeehouse.

Jonathan Swift, an equally controversial man of letters, was more frequently painted.[24] In the forty years after his first appearance at the exhibitions in 1854, he was the subject of at least a dozen pictures, dominated by a sentimental and trivialized view of his relations with the two

122. William P. Frith, *Pope Makes Love to Lady Mary Wortley Montagu (The Rejected Poet)* (RA 1852) (Wolverhampton Art Gallery). The picture exemplifies Frith's readiness to apply imagistic formulas of proven popularity to humorous anecdotes, even at the risk of sacrificing "fidelity" or historical likelihood. Apart from the ludicrously nail-biting poet—a figure inspired by conventional theatrical gesture rather than any of the scores of genuine portraits of Pope—the "plump, buxom, bouncing hoyden, bursting with fun and frolic" as the *Athenaeum* described her (29 May) is a virtual twin of Frith's Dolly Varden (pl. 354) moved back to 1722, the date of the hypothetical putdown. The satirical comment offered by the statue of Cupid and Psyche in the background is an example of the way Frith and his fellow anecdotal artists adopted, in simplified form, Hogarth's habit of investing many accessories with symbolic or ironic meaning.

123. Edward M. Ward, *Dr. Johnson Perusing the Manuscript of "The Vicar of Wakefield"* (RA 1843) (Walker Art Gallery, Liverpool). Goldsmith has bought a bottle of wine with the guinea Johnson sent him to pay his rent, and now Johnson, searching for a chattel that will accomplish what the guinea did not, is reading the manuscript of his friend's novel, which (as readers of Boswell could predict) he will go out and sell for sixty pounds. "Suppose him [Goldsmith] to have been incarcerated and ruined, as many a noble mind has been, what would the world have lost!" exclaimed the *Literary Gazette* (27 May). But the manuscript of the *Vicar* was safe, and the world would eventually be indebted to it for some scores of paintings. The picture of the Good Samaritan on the wall is another example of symbolic iconology in Victorian anecdotal art, with a double reference: Johnson is succoring Dr. Goldsmith, who is himself a healer.

women in his life, Stella and Vanessa. Crowe's *Dean Swift at St. James's Coffee House 1710* (RA 1860) portrayed him reading a letter from Stella while a dandy received a communication of his own, a three-cornered, rose-tinted *billet doux* brought by a waitress. Four years later, Crowe showed Swift sitting in his study, this time morosely contemplating a tress of Stella's hair. Millais exhibited two subjects that were nominally from Swift, *Stella* (pl. 103) and *Vanessa* (RA 1869). But these were merely belated fancy portraits, with no attempt to individualize the two women from the clues found in Swift's letters and journal.

One of the last Swift pictures, Frith's *Swift and Vanessa* (RA 1881), was more dramatic. The subject was Swift's bursting unannounced into Vanessa's house after discovering her letter to Stella asking whether Swift was, as report had it, married to her. "Then, without speaking a word, but with a look that froze her blood, he threw the letter on to the table and left her for ever." Frith confessed in his frequently self-deprecating autobiography that he "found the subject . . . a very difficult one. I fear it required a more powerful pencil than mine to portray the crushed heart and mind of Vanessa, or the lightning fury of Swift." The *Saturday Review* agreed. The picture, it said, was "remarkable for every quality it ought not to possess."[25]

Samuel Johnson was among the first writers to be repeatedly the subject of anecdotal pictures once the fashion got under way—not surprisingly, since the several portraits his friend Reynolds had painted of him had made his physical presence, as an art critic observed in 1854, "familiar to the infancy of every beholder."[26] By the 1840s, Boswell's biography had passed through a number of editions, including John Wilson Croker's controversial one of 1831, and this classic work was supplemented by numerous collections of anecdotes, authentic or spurious, which had accumulated like barnacles on the Boswellian hull. From 1843 to 1880, at least fifteen paintings showed Johnson at various moments in his well-reported life. At the Royal Academy in 1843, E. M. Ward showed the Doctor in Goldsmith's squalid lodgings (pl. 123). Ward's second picture (pl. 47), exhibited two years later, was based on a familiar story relating to Johnson's hope of obtaining assistance from Lord Chesterfield. Thackeray found it

> . . . a very good Hogarthian work . . . representing Johnson waiting in Lord Chesterfield's ante-chamber, among a crowd of hangers-on and petitioners, who are sulky, or yawning, or neglected, while a pretty Italian singer* comes out, having evidently had a very satisfactory interview with his Lordship, and who (to lose no time) is arranging another rendezvous with another admirer. This story is very well, coarsely, and humorously told, and is as racy as a chapter out of Smollett.[27]

Johnson as a subject for biographical painting attracted an ill-assorted pair of artists toward the end of the 1850s. Eyre Crowe, who as we have seen was something of a specialist in pictures from eighteenth-century literary history (Defoe, Swift, Addison, Steele, Pope, Goldsmith, Sterne) showed a *Scene* [unidentified] *at the Mitre: Dr. Johnson, Boswell, Goldsmith* (RA 1857). Some years later he was to paint *Dr. Johnson's Penance 1784* (RA 1869), depicting him standing bareheaded in the rain in the Uttoxeter market, repenting his having once refused to tend his father's bookstall there. Another *Dr. Johnson at the Mitre* (1860) was by an artist who normally worked in a vein far removed from that of Crowe and his fellow anecdotalists. Dante Gabriel Rossetti, in a pen-and-ink sketch (Fitzwilliam Museum) and a watercolor copy (Tate Gallery), recalled Johnson's taking to the Mitre for dinner two young women from Staffordshire who had called to solicit his opinion on Methodism; after dinner, according to Boswell's informant, "he took one of them upon his knee, and fondled her for half an hour together."[28]

At the height of Frith's popularity, in 1868, he exhibited at the Royal Academy *Before Dinner, at Boswell's Lodging in Bond Street* (pl. 160), the occasion of Goldsmith's display of his stylish new coat,

> Johnson [said the *Times*], looming large in the circle, like a huge Spanish galleon, with Garrick playing, like a light English pinnace, about him; Goldsmith admiring Mr. Filby's immortal peach-blossom coat before the glass; placid Sir Joshua trying, by help of his trumpet, to catch the joke that is passing between him and Murphy and Bickerstaff; Bozzy beginning to fidget in his chair, and Tom Davies, who has been keeping dinner waiting, being ushered in at the door by the maid. . . .[29]

Frith sold this picture to the dealer Agnew for the very substantial price, for the time, of £1,200; later it was sold by Christie's for £4,567 10s., "the largest price," Frith noted, "that had been paid for the work of a living artist at that time."[30] He returned to Dr. Johnson for at least two more pictures. *Dr. Johnson and Mrs. Siddons* (RA 1884), suggested by a

*Thus Ward improved on the story, substituting for Colley Cibber, a servile dramatist and poetaster, a female figure with an unmistakable sexual innuendo.

passage in Thomas Campbell's life of the actress, merged Nollekens's bust and Reynolds's portraits in the figure of Johnson, and Gainsborough's and others' portraits in that of Mrs. Siddons. Two years later, Frith exhibited *Dr. Johnson's Tardy Gallantry* (RA 1886), in which Johnson, belatedly realizing that the French lady (Madame de Boufflers) whom Topham Beauclerk had brought to see him deserved greater honors than he had bestowed on her during their visit, overtook the pair as they reached the Temple gate and, said Beauclerk, "brushing in between me and Madame de Boufflers, seized her hand, and conducted her to her coach. His dress was a rusty brown morning suit, a pair of old shoes by way of slippers, a little shrivelled wig sticking on the top of his head, and the sleeves of his shirt and the knees of his breeches hanging loose"—a description made to order for what might be called an anticostume piece.[31]

Other Johnsonian subjects seen on Victorian walls were John Irvine's *Dr. Johnson at Tea at Mrs. Thrale's with Goldsmith, Garrick, and Reynolds* (RSA 1845) and his later pair at the same gallery (1852), *Johnson and Richard Savage Walking the Streets of London* by day and night. W. J. Grant's *Dr. Johnson Carries Home the Poor Girl He Found Deserted in the Streets* was seen at the Royal Academy in 1855, and James Drummond's *Dr. Johnson and Boswell*—incident not specified—at the Royal Scottish Academy in 1858. James Smetham painted *Mr. Robert Levett and Dr. Johnson Visiting a Poor Family* (RA 1862), and Marshall Claxton *The Last Interview between Sir Joshua Reynolds and Dr. Johnson* (SBA 1865).

During his lifetime, Johnson's friend Oliver Goldsmith had been something of a living legend in his circle of fellow writers and artists. Anecdotes of his checkered career and his charmingly irresponsible character were passed down to the Victorians in many forms. The appearance within a decade of three biographies—Sir James Prior's formless compilation of documents, down to the laundry lists that henceforth would be the standard symbol of biographical irrelevance (1837), Washington Irving's briefer narrative (1844), and John Forster's solid and readable work (1848)—wrapped the figure of Goldsmith in a thick aura of sentimental affection, at the very moment when, not accidentally, *The Vicar of Wakefield* became the favorite subject of early Victorian anecdotal painters. From the middle to the end of the century, some twenty scenes from Goldsmith's life are recorded. Most Victorians chose to minimize the faults of vanity, improvidence, and irritability Thackeray conceded in a lecture otherwise overflowing with charity, concentrating instead on his ingenuousness and amiability. It was in this spirit that the artists painted "poor Goldy" and his skimpy wig and worn knee breeches. E. M. Ward showed him earning a night's lodging at a Flemish farmhouse by playing the flute (RA 1844) and flouncing out of a fashionable house, where he was superseded as attending physician by a mere apothecary (pl. 124). Abraham Solomon's *An Awkward Position* (RA 1851) portrayed him futilely searching his pockets for money to pay for the tea to which he had treated the daughters of a respectable gentleman at Islington. There was even a rendering (SBA 1869) of the anecdote, first told by Bishop Percy in 1801 and conveyed down the chain of biographies, that while Goldsmith was writing in his squalid London room, there appeared to him "a poor ragged little girl of very decent behavior, . . . who, dropping a curtsie, said, 'My mamma sends her compliments, and begs the favour of you to lend her a chamber-pot full of coals.'"

124. Edward M. Ward, *Dr. Goldsmith and the Apothecary* (RA 1871) (Walker Art Gallery, Liverpool). A seemingly uncanonical anecdote relating to Goldsmith's failure as a physician: he finds that the lady whom he has been attending has replaced him with a mere apothecary, a member of a profession ranking below that of holders of medical degrees.

A signal contribution Washington Irving made to Goldsmith mythography was the fancy that he had been hopelessly in love with Mary Horneck, the "Jessamy bride" whom Reynolds and Hoppner painted and whom Hazlitt once met in Northcote's painting room. No episode in his life, real or imaginary, was more quintessentially Victorian in its sentimental splendor than this. Thomas F. Marshall showed him reading a manuscript to Mary and her sister (RA 1852), a subject repeated forty years later by Margaret Dicksee (RA 1894). In the interim, Eyre Crowe showed the last scene in the Goldsmith story, *Brick Court, Middle Temple, Arpil 1774* (RA 1863): the room filled, as a reviewer said, "with mourners the reverse of domestic: women without a home, without domesticity of any kind, with no friend but him they had come to weep for—outcasts of that great, solitary, wicked city, to whom he had never forgotten to be kind and charitable."[32] Extrapolating from Irving's statement that Goldsmith's coffin was opened to obtain "a lock of his hair . . . for a lady, a particular friend, who wished to preserve it as a remembrance,"[33] Crowe placed the Misses Horneck at the scene, unlikely though their presence in that squalid setting was.

Four years before Goldsmith died, not far from Brick Court, in a garret in Gray's Inn, the most-painted death scene in literary biography was enacted: the suicide of the seventeen-year-old Thomas Chatterton, precocious forger of the poems of a fifteenth-century Bristol monk named Rowley, which initiated a legend that was to have wide literary repercussions in generations to come. The pathetic glamor attached to the premature death of an adolescent (supposed) genius outweighed the fact that Chatterton was, after all, a fraud; and in contemporary opinion, he was regarded as the undeserving victim of Horace Walpole and Dr. Johnson,

125. Thomas J. Barker, *The Poet Chatterton* (RA 1860) (Victoria Art Gallery, Bath). A fairly late example of the use of Chatterton as the prototype of the Romantic starving poet in a garret. Except possibly for the rolled-up manuscripts, an allusion to the poems of a fifteenth-century monk that Chatterton claimed he had found in St. Mary Redcliffe Church, Bristol (he had actually forged them), there is little to identify the scene as belonging specifically to the Chatterton legend.

who stubbornly, and rightly, refused to believe in the authenticity of the "Rowley" poems. Some years after his death—the precise dates cannot be fixed, but the best guess is the 1780s—two painters depicted the scene: the busy Henry Singleton[34] and a very minor artist named John Cranch, who painted portraits and history pieces as well as a category of novelty art called "poker pictures" and, as a member of the Edmonton circle with whom john Constable had contact in the summer of 1796, gave the bud-

126. Mrs. Edward M. Ward, *Chatterton, 1765* (RA 1873) (Bristol Museum and Art Gallery). Hard at work on his forgeries, the boy is disturbed by his foster mother, to whom he complains (according to a fictionalizing biographer), "You are too curious and clear-sighted; I wish you would bide out of the room. It is my room." Through the window can be seen the tower of St. Mary Redcliffe.

ding artist a professional reading list.[35] In July 1782, a picture of the living Chatterton in his garret was engraved for the *Westminster Magazine* under the Hogarthian title of *The Distressed Poet;* and the design subsequently was circulated in the form of handkerchiefs on which it was printed, a rare if not absolutely unique distinction for a literature-related work of art.

But Chatterton did not come into his own as a subject of painting until well after he had become the object of the Romantic poets' adulation.[36] In "Resolution and Independence," Wordsworth celebrated him as "The marvellous Boy, / The sleepless Soul that perished in his pride"; Coleridge wrote a "Monody on the Death of Chatterton"; Keats, sensing a kinship with the "Dear child of sorrow—son of misery" that he perhaps subconsciously knew would be perpetuated by his own untimely death, not only addressed a sonnet to him but dedicated "Endymion" to his memory. Not until 1834, however, did a painter take up Chatterton again. This was a now-forgotten artist named William Proctor, who exhibited a canvas titled simply *Chatterton* at the Society of British Artists.

Between 1846 and 1886, there were half a dozen English paintings of the death of Chatterton, several accompanied by a line from Marlowe's *Dr. Faustus,* "Cut is the branch that might have grown full straight." Presiding over them was Henry Wallis's picture (pl. 127), which, by what may have been no more than a coincidence, was hung only months after the publication of a novelette called *Chatterton: The Story of a Year,* by Milton's future biographer David Masson. It had mixed reviews. "The subject," said the *Literary Gazette,* "flatters the maudlin sensibilities of many who consider themselves, like Chatterton, neglected geniuses. . . . Holiday costume and fine modeling . . . have been brought in to disguise the horrors of a scene at which true humanity shudders. . . . We object to the figure of a suicide, even of a Chatterton, being decked out in rainbow robes, and dignified with features of ideal grandeur."[37] On the other hand, Ruskin was unstinting in his praise: "Faultless and wonderful: a most noble example of the great school. Examine it well inch by inch," he urged the readers of his *Academy Notes* for the year; "it is one of

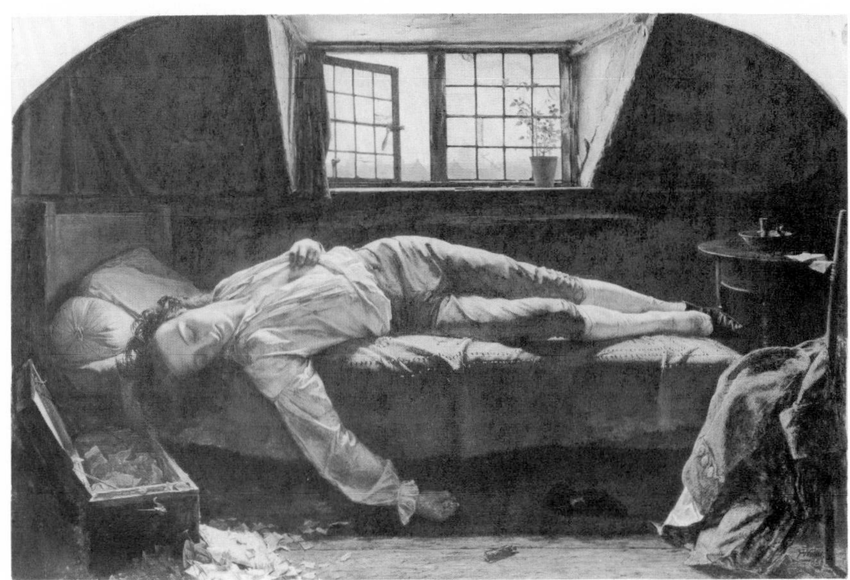

127. Henry Wallis, *Chatterton* (RA 1856) (Tate Gallery, London). The figure was modeled by George Meredith, whose wife later eloped with the artist. Within three years, the picture, bought by Augustus Egg, had become so famous that a Dublin photographer made a stereoscopic copy of it by means of a studio set-up, posing an apprentice as Chatterton. An injunction against this alleged violation of copyright was dissolved on appeal.

128. John Faed, *Burns and Highland Mary* (Royal Scottish Academy 1851) (Glasgow Art Gallery and Museum). During their long careers, John Faed and his brother Thomas turned out hundreds of paintings of Scottish life, including many from Burns and Scott. This picture typifies the sentimental harvest that artists made for many years from romanticized versions of Burns's love life.

the pictures which intend, and accomplish, the entire placing before your eyes of an actual fact—and that a solemn one. Give it much time."[38]

There were also several paintings of Chatterton while still alive and busy at Bristol. A picture of him writing the supposed poems of Rowley (1846) has been cited by his modern biographer, E. H. W. Meyerstein, as "probably one of the world's worst pictures"—an extravagant claim, considering the magnitude of the competition in Victorian England alone. The next year, W. J. Montaigne exhibited at the Royal Academy an incident in the Chatterton legend in which a local dealer, offering him a tribute in the form of a cup with "Thomas" inscribed in gold, received the haughty reply, "Paint me an angel with wings and a trumpet, that he may trumpet my name over the world."

Robert Burns was eleven years old when Chatterton died. His fame was more widespread, and the harvest of Burns pictures incomparably larger (at least sixty biographical ones). Public interest in his private life was kindled early, beginning with Dr. James Currie's piously scandalous biography prefixed to the first volume of his collected poetry (1800). Within a decade, artists were traveling to Burns country as they had already begun to travel to the land of Scott's poems. Joseph Farington and Sir Thomas Lawrence dropped by Stothard's London home in 1810 to see the sketches he had made in Scotland the previous summer. "Many of [the] sketches," Farington recorded in his diary, "were views of places from which engravings are to be made to accompany an edition of Burn's [*sic*] poems. He made a drawing of the House in which Burn's was born; the room in which He wrote, with the desk at which He wrote & the Chair on which He sat. So far is this kind of enthusiastic admiration now carried."[39] Stothard was in the vanguard of artists who were to paint every scene even tangentially related to Burns's life. There were portrayals of him in the glorious throes of composing—Sir William Allan, for instance, showed him writing "The Cotter's Saturday Night"—and reading the finished product to a patron (the Duchess of Gordon, in Edinburgh, 1785).

Burns's supposed love affair with "Highland Mary" accounted for as many pictures as were concerned with all the other occurrences of his life put together (some thirty out of the sixty). According to a story first set current by the Greenock Burns Club, shortly followed by the engraver and compiler Robert Cromek in his *Reliques of Burns* (1808), the "Highland Mary" addressed in two or three of the poems was Mary Campbell, whom legend soon idealized into his great "spiritual" love. Actually, Mary was, as a recent biographer puts it, "merely another peasant-girl beguiled into lifting her skirts by the force of Robert's personality and the urgency of his desire," who died bearing one of his illegitimate children.[40] But sober biographical fact, in Burns's case as in Shakespeare's, was no match for sentimental fancy, and Highland Mary figured in picture after picture—being courted by the earnest young peasant-poet (pl. 128), posing alone in the act of day-dreaming about him (in the best manner of the Keepsake beauties), listening to him reading his latest verses, resting on her way to visit her parents as in a Thomas Faed canvas (RA 1856) that Ruskin praised as "very lovely in its kind,"[41] and—a recurrent theme—parting from him forever. In sheer number of appearances, the fair maid of the Highlands compared well with the record scored by any other literary heroine, and she had the sanction of biographical authority—no matter that the authority was itself unreliable. The other, all too soundly documented woman in Burns's life, Jean Armour, was obviously unavailable for artistic treatment. It would have been hard to sentimentalize a heroine whom the hero married only after she produced their second pair of twins.

Burns's compatriot Sir Walter Scott was the sole nineteenth-century author to figure in more than a handful of biographical pictures. From his initial success as a poet in the first decade of the century, he was a national celebrity.[42] Devotees of his work, including such artists as Turner and Leslie, made pilgrimages to hospitable Abbotsford on pleasure or business. The periodicals of his day and for many years thereafter abounded with accounts of his genial personality, as well as with speculations on the origins of his characters and descriptions of appreciative wanderings in "Scott country." Numerous artists painted his portrait, and immediately after his death in 1832, the annual exhibitions witnessed a new phenomenon, the graphic documentation of a contemporary author's life. At the Royal Academy the next year, Edwin Landseer portrayed him sitting in the Rhymer's Glen as described in *Minstrelsy of the Scottish Border.* The publication of John Gibson Lockhart's lengthy and much praised biography in 1837–38 added fresh interest to anecdotal pictures from Scott's life. He was seen reading the manuscript of *The Lady of the Lake* to an old farmer in a painting at the Royal Academy in 1839, and at the same place in 1844 he was depicted as a young man dining with one of the blue-gown beggars of Edinburgh. The next year, at the Royal Scottish Academy, an artist portrayed an incident in the Edinburgh gang warfare of Scott's youth, recalled in his reminiscences to Lockhart, when the wounded "youthful Goth" nicknamed "Green-breeks" honorably refused to identify the assailant who had put him in the hospital. Most of the artists who repeatedly took subjects from the Waverley novels, among them the Faed and Lauder brothers and Charles M. Hardie, painted subjects from Scott's life as well. The least characteristic doubtless was J. P. Davis's entry at the Society of British Artists in 1837, described in the catalogue as *A Conference in the Shades: Bonaparte is Vindicating His Policy,*

129. Ford Madox Brown, *The Dream (Byron and Mary Chaworth)* (1875) (City Art Gallery, Manchester). At the age of sixteen, Byron fell madly, helplessly in love with Mary Chaworth, two years older than he. She derided him as "that lame boy," and in any event was already engaged to a young foxhunting country squire. Byron later idealized the one-sided affair in "The Dream." In Brown's own idealization, Mary has the standard Pre-Raphaelite profile, and Byron bears little resemblance to any known portrait.

130. Edward M. Ward, *Byron's Early Love (The Dance)* (RA 1856) (City Art Gallery, Manchester). The imagined situation into which Ward thrust Byron had already become a cliché of Victorian poetry and fiction, the lover as a jealous outsider, sometimes eating his heart out as his beloved is giddily involved in a ball (the situation in Browning's "Porphyria's Lover," for example). The *Athenaeum* (10 May) reminded its readers that Byron was "the hater of waltzes and the derider of women."

Byron Listening in Lofty Abstraction, Scott Deliberately Scrutinizing the Arguments of Napoleon. Solely as a curiosity, one regrets its disappearance more than that of most paintings from and about Sir Walter Scott.

None of the Romantic poets were represented very often in biographical art. Byron's youthful love affair with Mary Chaworth was recalled in several pictures drawn from his poem "The Dream." One of them was a landscape by Charles Eastlake (pl. 325) that, to be sure, had nothing to do with the story the poem describes; and another was Ford Madox Brown's portrayal (pl. 129) of the poet "pouring out impassioned nothings" to Mary, as the artist's grandson put it, "whilst Mary has only ears for the distant sounds of the hoofs of that sturdy Nimrod Jack Musters's horse, and eyes for that scarlet-coated gentleman himself."[43] Millais also (1856) painted *Byron's Dream.* E. M. Ward used another (imaginary?) moment from the futile courtship in his *Byron's Early Love (The Dance)* (pl. 130). One of the few surviving biographical pictures is Sir William Allan's *Lord Byron Reposing in the House of a Turkish Fisherman, After Having Swum the Hellespont* (RSA 1831).

Joseph Severn memorialized two of his friends at Royal Academy exhibitions: *Shelley Composing His Prometheus Unbound, Amidst the Ruins of Rome* (1845) and *Keats, at Hampstead, When He First Imagined his Ode to the Nightingale* (1851). Half a century later, Eyre Crowe painted *Shelley at Marlow Writing the Dedication of the Revolt of Islam* (RA 1904). Except for these isolated instances, the vein of painted "biographical illustrations" of English authors ended with Scott and Byron. Only a few formal portraits of Victorian writers were to be seen at the exhibitions. Neither during their lifetime nor later did Tennyson and Carlyle, for example, figure in anecdotal genre scenes, replete though their modern biographies are with picturesque episodes that would have tempted artists' brushes in their day.

CHAPTER 8

Artists' acquaintance with English literature.—Their adaptation of subjects from older art: the toilet of Venus, alchemist, Cymon and Iphigenia, Sigismunda, Endymion, etc.—The Westminster Palace frescoes.—The tension between artistic tradition and the "spirit" of the literary subject.

Strong though the nineteenth-century interest in English literature as a source of subjects for painting was, it owed relatively little to the literary cultivation of contemporary artists. With the possible exception of Dante Gabriel Rossetti, Pope and Reynolds had no successors who bridged the gap between the sister arts as sturdily as they had done from their opposite directions. No poet after Pope (see Part Three, below) had as many different links with painting, nor did any painter after Reynolds have as many links with literature. Reynolds, in fact, was, according to some presumably extempore verses written at the Bedford coffee-house, Covent Garden, in 1777, "th' APELLES of our modern Days," who "Shines forth superior, tho in different ways; / Has of *two* Arts attain'd the lawrel'd Heights; / Paints with a Pen, and with a Pencil Writes!"[1] The allusion was to his widely admired Royal Academy *Discourses,* the best claim he had to be considered a man of letters. But in addition to this and other published works, he left behind 2,000 manuscript pages of essays, as well as notes of various kinds he compiled for his friends, Dr. Johnson and the Shakespeare editors Malone and Steevens, among others. His closest friendships were with writers, not artists. Boswell, who dedicated his *Life of Johnson* to him, recorded that at his table were to be found "a greater group of literary men, than at any other." These included Sheridan and Goldsmith, who respectively dedicated *The School for Scandal* and *The Deserted Village* to him. The son of a book-loving parson and schoolmaster who was a former scholar of Corpus Christi College and fellow of Balliol, Reynolds was probably the most widely read of all native-born British artists;* his writings abound in references to Latin and French authors as well as to Shakespeare, Jonson, Bacon, Milton, the Augustan wits, and the best writers of his own time.

*Fuseli's acquaintance with literature was even broader, but of course he was Swiss by birth and education.

In contrast, there was Gainsborough: "I believe I shall remain an ignorant fellow to the end of my days," he wrote the Earl of Dartmouth in 1771, "because I never could have patience to read Poetical impossibilities, the very food of a Painter; especially if he intends to be KNIGHTED in this land of Roast Beef, so well do serious people love froth."[2] His friend, the Exeter cathedral organist and composer William Jackson, said that "Gainsborough avoided the company of literary men—who were his aversion[;] he was better pleased to give than to receive information . . . so far from writing he scarcely ever read a book—but, for a letter to an intimate friend, he had few equals, and no superior."[3] It is certainly true that in his letters he employs a lively, unbuttoned style with no trace of illiteracy—proof, perhaps, that sometimes one can acquire the knack of writing decent prose without the benefit of book learning.

Then there was Romney. "Mr. Romney," said Lord Thurlow, the lord chancellor, to the artist one day in a celebrated put-down, "before you paint Shakespeare, I advise you to read him";[4] and the artist's own biographer William Hayley questioned whether he "ever read, without interruption, two acts of the dramas that he most cordially admired."[5] It was notorious that George Morland detested reading, even to the point of snatching newspapers from friends who tried to read in his presence. This report has survived to the present day, but its origin in one of the four scandalous biographies of Morland published within three years of his death casts some doubt on its accuracy. It was easy enough, in such accounts of what was claimed to have been a dissolute, wastrel life, to improve the cautionary message by adding the charge that besides having been a debt-ridden alcoholic, Morland was also devoid of literary interests. As has been recently pointed out, "a closer study of his work reveals . . . a surprisingly wide acquaintance with contemporary artistic theories and literature."[6]

The lawgivers of British art at the time recommended that artists be readers of poetry in the normal routine of their occupation. In his seventh discourse, Reynolds declared that "every man whose business is description, ought to be tolerably conversant with the poets, in some language or other; that he may imbibe a poetical spirit, and enlarge his stock of ideas."[7] Another Academy lecturer, John Opie, whose biographer said he possessed "a thorough knowledge of the works of Milton, Shakespeare, Dryden, Gray, Cowper, Butler's *Hudibras,* Burke and Johnson,"[8] agreed that "drinking deep of the Pierian spring" had "the most direct tendency to exercise, warm, invigorate, and enrich the imagination, and excite noble and daring conceptions."[9] Wordsworth told Sir George Beaumont that the minor artist George Arnald, who exhibited half a dozen pictures from Gray, Shakespeare, and Milton between 1797 and 1813, "would have been a better Painter, if his Genius had led him to *read* more in the early part of his life. . . . I do not think it possible to *excel* in *landscape* painting without a strong tincture of the Poetic Spirit."[10] Beaumont in turn told his twenty-two-year-old protégé David Wilkie in 1807: "You can never read Shakespeare, Milton, and Spenser too much. Some of our best novelists, as Richardson, Fielding, and Smollett, are also worthy of your attention. Don Quixote I particularly recommend: let him lie upon your table, and read a chapter when you are fatigued with your work; it will refresh and improve your mind."[11] This counsel was based on the prevailing idea that the imagination can be fed and inspiration deliberately sought from without—in this case, from literature. By reading poetry, the artist, especially the landscapist, can put himself in the mood to paint, priming the pump, as it were.

Haydon, who pawned his studies of the Elgin marbles rather than part with his beloved books, subscribed to this notion of poetry as a stimulus to creativity in paint. It is implicit in an entry in his journal for 10 June 1839: " . . . In the evening walked up into my book-room. There they were, silent, yet teeming with thoughts, bursting with sublimity. Milton—Satan and all his rebel host filled my mind. Shakespeare—Hamlet, Lear, Falstaff, Cordelia, Imogen, Macbeth and Puck crowded my imagination. I walked about in ecstasy, but read nothing; dwelt on what I had read, and was content."[12]* John Constable, ten years older, was not as well read, but the record of the books he owned from the family collection, his allusions to writers in letters, and his use of poetic quotations as mottoes for several paintings, together suggest a catholic taste: Akenside, Bacon, Beaumont and Fletcher, Bloomfield, Boswell, Bunyan, Butler, Crabbe, Dryden, Falconer, Goldsmith, Gray, Johnson, Milton, Miss Mitford (whose *Our Village* he disliked), Shakespeare, Charlotte Smith, Smollett, Thomson.[13] He not only quoted Wordsworth, whom he knew through their common friend Beaumont, but wrote a sonnet to him beginning "Thou second Milton!"[14] (Evidently he was willing in the long run to overlook Wordsworth's habit of doling out free advice to painters. Farington recorded in 1807 that Constable "was offended with Wordsworth who offered to propose subjects to Him to paint, & gave Him to understand that when He could not think of subjects as well as paint them He wd. come to Him.")[15]† He considered "The Rime of the Ancient Mariner" the greatest modern poem and was an admirer of Cowper; but he was impervious to the glamor of Byron, commenting, on hearing of the poet's death, that "the deadly slime of his touch still remains."[16]

Turner's knowledge of poetry, though much discussed in recent years, seems to have been considerably smaller than Constable's.[17] Its range can be inferred from the titles of some of his paintings and the quotations that accompanied them to the exhibition walls: Thomson, from whose *The Seasons* he got the idea for his *Slave Ship* (*Slavers Throwing Overboard the Dead and Dying*, 1840), Pope, Churchill, Shakespeare (*The Merchant of Venice*, *Romeo and Juliet*), Spenser, and Byron. Mark Akenside's *The Pleasures of the Imagination* particularly attracted him, and in his lectures as the Royal Academy's professor of perspective, he introduced poetry by Akenside as well as by Milton and Thomson. But in the slender volume of his collected letters, there is scarcely a single allusion to anything he had read.[18]

Neither Haydon nor Constable nor Turner, however, was a literary painter, and the complaint of Allan or Peter Cunningham (it is not clear which was writing) in 1842 applied with special force, ironically, to the growing company of artists who mediated between literature and painting: "Our artists in general are the most unread of all descriptions or classes of men of genius. . . . An artist's yearly quantity of reading seems to extend over the Academy catalogue, and the cut out passage he attempts to illustrate."[19] This was an exaggeration, of course, but it had a hard kernel of truth. Young men in the "superior ranks" of society, where literary cultivation was most to be expected, seldom aspired to a career in

*The list of paintings on literary subjects that Haydon began but did not finish is larger than the list of those he completed—evidence that his absorption in English literature was deeper than the roster of finished paintings suggests. Between 1823 and his death in 1846, he made some progress on at least fourteen pictures from *Macbeth*, *Romeo and Juliet*, Milton, and Byron. His 1845 project of a representation of "Byron musing on a distant view of Harrow" constituted a variation on the theme of "Napoleon musing at St. Helena" (and elsewhere) that he had used for no fewer than twenty-three pictures to that time.

†In fairness to Wordsworth, it might be added that, according to John Opie's widow, the artist "said of Wordsworth that he talked on art more sensibly and more like an artist than any one he had met in the profession" (A. M. W. Stirling, *The Richmond Papers* [London, 1926], p. 39).

art, which had neither social prestige nor substantial promise of monetary rewards except as these were achieved by a few particularly talented or popular painters in each generation. At mid-century, about one-third of the Academicians were "sons of artisans or tradesmen; another third were sons of artists or architects, likewise moving upward, step by step, from the strata of men who took cash payment from their customers."[20] The "industrious apprentice" artist J. J. Ridley, in Thackeray's *The Newcomes,* was the son of a valet-butler. He possessed the talent and the dedication that his friend and fellow artist Clive Newcome lacked. Better-educated, better-read men, such as Clive, were discouraged from becoming artists, leaving the field more or less open to men like Ridley, in whom, despite their well-earned success (as Thackeray saw it), an extensive knowledge of books could not be expected.*

"Their history," said Cunningham, "they get from pictures, and their poetry from off the stage. Talk of Mary Queen of Scots to an artist, and the chief events he remembers in her reign are Rizzio's murder, Knox's admonition, and her escape from Lochleven; and these they know through Opie, Allan, and Sir David Wilkie."[21] Instead of reading literary sources with fresh eyes, painters consulted painters. And understandably so, because during the impressionable years in which their artistic interests were forming, the pictures in the books they read were as much of an inspiration as the texts themselves. William Bell Scott and his brother David were the sons of an engraver-painter in Edinburgh. In his *Autobiographical Notes,* William says little about the books they only read, but stresses the influence upon him and his brother of the many illustrated volumes in their home: histories and travel books, "Bible pictures from old or modern English painters," books published in numbers and sold by colporteurs, and most of all, "the portfolios and books of prints, the illustrated British poets and novelists. . . . In winter evenings our school-books were gladly thrown aside for a united and thoroughly-enjoyed examination of a large number of well-thumbed volumes of illustrations to Bell's and Cook's little editions of English poets and dramatists, Boydell's larger pictures from Shakespeare, and such performances of the generation passing or past."[22] The boys' artistic sensibilities, in other words, were attuned to existing pictorial rather than verbal representations of a literary subject; and this was probably true of many literary painters.

W. P. Frith, who used narrative literature as the sustaining subject matter of his earlier career, before the surpassing fame of *Derby Day, The Railway Station,* and *Ramsgate Sands,* was well grounded in fiction. When very young, he recalled, he "revelled in works of imagination—the novels of G. P. R. James, the romances of Mrs. Radcliffe, and, above and before all, the works of Scott† and Cooper." As a rising artist, however, he read "in books suggestive of subjects for pictures—Sterne, Goldsmith, Molière, Cervantes, and the 'Spectator' taking the lead of all others." And Shakespeare, of course, who "inspired me with terror as well as admiration." But, Frith continued, in an admission sufficiently rare among painters of literary subjects, "I have never meddled with Shakespeare without regretting my temerity, for though I have painted several pictures from different plays, I cannot recall one that will add to my reputation."[23]

From the late eighteenth century onward, most subject painters tried their hands at literary themes early in their careers. As we saw in chapter

*As is true also of English writers who grew up in the late eighteenth and early nineteenth centuries, especially if in "humble circumstances," the lists of books that artists read in childhood and youth are so similar, from person to person, as to be somewhat suspect. Unquestionably some classics, like the Bible, *Paradise Lost, The Pilgrim's Progress,* and a few revered eighteenth-century poets, notably Thomson, were more widely available and admired than most literature, but there must have been more variation than is suggested by the near uniformity of the lists given by early biographers. These lists therefore must probably be looked upon as more emblematic than literally true. In the case of painters, biographers may sometimes have inferred their reading from the literary sources they used for their pictures. Thus the assertion that the deformed, sickly Manchester artist Henry Liverseege, son of a joiner-mechanic, was "well conversant with the works of Shakespeare, Sir Walter Scott, *Don Quixote,* and *Hudibras*" (George Richardson, *The Works of Henry Liverseege, with a Memoir* [London, 1875], pp. 11–12) may be only a natural deduction from the fact that most of his pictures were derived from those works. But with such painters, largely imitative, a little learning could have gone a long way.

†Scott's readers were so numerous among artists as to call for a separate list. See Part Three, below, under Scott.

1, most of the prizes for the best historical paintings produced in the Royal Academy school between 1772 and 1799 were given for literary subjects. When Wilkie was a student at the Trustees' Academy in Edinburgh in 1800–1801, the set subject for his class was any scene from *Macbeth.* Wilkie chose to depict a relatively unhackneyed one, "Macduff's castle, with Lady Macduff defending her little son from the murderers." The prize, however, went to a pupil who painted the equally untouched murder of Banquo in the forest.[24]

It is remarkable, in fact, how many Victorian artists' oeuvres were initiated with pictures from English literature, even though some of them went on to other specialties. One more version of Sterne's dead ass was the subject of Edward M. Ward's first submission to the Royal Academy when he was nineteen. It was rejected, allegedly for lack of space.[25] Two years later (1837), the seventeen-year-old John Tenniel had better luck: his picture from Scott's *The Fortunes of Nigel, Captain Peppercul Interceding for Nigel with Duke Hildebrand,* was hung on the same walls. The future doyen of the late Victorian academic school, Frederic Leighton, began (1849–50) with paintings from *Othello* and *Romeo and Juliet.* Charles West Cope took the subject of *Iachimo Stealing Imogen's Jewels* while a student at the Royal Academy, "a very poor performance" as he admitted in his *Reminiscences.*[26] Henry Stacy Marks's first exhibited painting, rejected by the British Institution but, in a reversal of the usual traffic, hung at the Royal Academy in 1853, was of *Dogberry Examining Conrad and Borachio.*[27]

Not surprisingly, it is in the Pre-Raphaelite circle that we find the broadest scope of literary experience recorded.[28] William Michael Rossetti wrote that as small children he and his brother knew not only the Bible and Shakespeare but the poems and some of the novels of Scott, *Robinson Crusoe, Gulliver's Travels,* Gay's *Fables,* and, a little later, Byron and the *Iliad.* Later Byron was succeeded by Shelley, and Shelley in turn by Keats, Tennyson, Elizabeth Barrett, and the temporarily famous "spasmodic" poet Philip Bailey, who were themselves succeeded by Browning. "There were also a large number of romances . . . such as Scott, Bulwer, Dickens, Maturin, Thackeray."[29] At the moment the original Pre-Raphaelites were stirring a flutter in the establishment dovecot, Burne-Jones, who with William Morris had the best formal education of any nineteenth-century artist, was still at King Edward's School, Birmingham. To the early acquaintance with Shakespeare, Byron, Coleridge, and Scott that was more or less customary in his reasonably well educated social class, he was adding knowledge of Dickens (later Thackeray as well), Keats, and Tennyson, the last, apparently, from the copy in the school library.[30] The great event while at Oxford was his discovery, with Morris, of Malory's *Le Morte Darthur* (see Part Three, below).

Almost without exception, the Pre-Raphaelite artists commenced their careers with subjects derived from English literature. Among Dante Gabriel Rossetti's juvenilia were subjects from Shakespeare and Scott. At the age of twelve, John Everett Millais painted a scene from *Peveril of the Peak* (pl. 131).[31] Holman Hunt, while working for a short time in Richard Cobden's London office, decorated the walls with scenes from Dickens and Shakespeare.[32] And Morris's first picture (1857?) was a scene from *Le Morte Darthur: How Sir Tristram, After His Illness in the Garden of King Mark's Palace, was Recognised by the Dog he had Given to Iseult.*

But it was James Smetham, the minor painter befriended by both

131. John Everett Millais, *Scene from "Peveril of the Peak"* (1841) (Forbes Magazine Collection). Pictorial evidence of a precocious artist's knowledge of books, this ambitious painting, of the conventicle scene in Scott's novel (chap. 43), was created when Millais was twelve years old. It was not exhibited until his retrospective at the Royal Academy in 1898.

Rossetti and Ruskin, who, of all Victorian artists, had, if not the widest acquaintance with books, the deepest affection for them. Indeed, the contesting claims of poetry and art within his sensitive soul, already permeated with religious fervor, may well have contributed to the insanity that darkened his last twelve years. Rossetti's excepted, his letters are the most engaging, and at the same time the most revealing, of any that come down to us from the painters of his time. They contain many notes on his current reading: Boswell, Bulwer-Lytton, Dickens, Arnold, Disraeli, Browning, Carlyle, Trollope, George Eliot, Keats, and Tennyson, a copy of whose 1842 collection he bought and prized next only to the Bible. Seemingly alone among the artists of the day, Smetham read the Brontë novels as they were published, and in his letters commented at length on *Wuthering Heights.*[33]

132. James Smetham, *Imogen and the Shepherds* (ca. 1858–68) (Birmingham City Museum and Art Gallery). One of the few surviving paintings by this disciple of the Pre-Raphaelites, who had the keenest appetite for books of any Victorian artist. The subject is from *Cymbeline,* 4. 2: like Dawe (pl. 100), Smetham sacrifices the plot for pictorial effect by dispensing with Imogen's disguise as the comely boy "Fidele." Instead, he gives her the pose associated with the Sleeping Beauty (pl. 76).

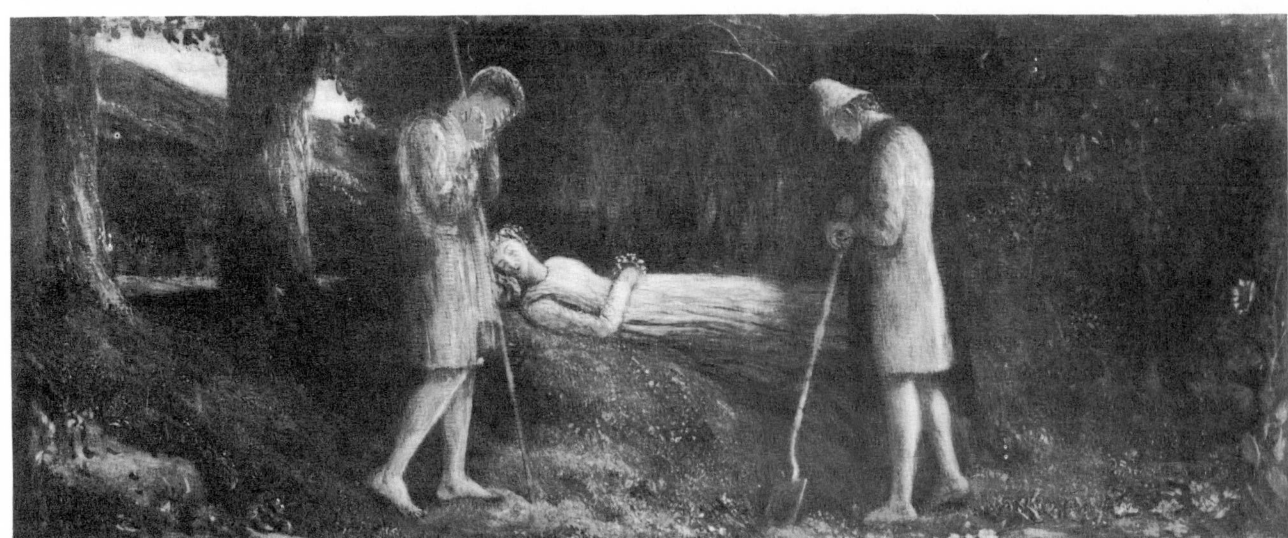

Some of the subjects chosen by artists who sought to turn to account their and their patrons' knowledge of English literature had established themselves in European painting—some even in the art of classical antiquity—long before they were given fresh expression by English poets. The lingering mystique of history painting impelled a number of artists to deliberately choose from English literature, as their predecessors had done, "elevated" themes that would enable them to pay graphic homage to, if not equal, the Old Masters.[34] Smirke, for example, took from Parnell's "The Hermit" the subject of the angel justifying Providence in order to emulate Rembrandt.[35] When Leslie attempted his first painting, he chose the subject of Timon of Athens so that he could portray a nude figure in the manner of Michelangelo.[36] (This initial choice did not accurately foreshadow his eventual preferences: his chief models during his prosperous years were to be Hogarth and the Dutch school typified by De Hooch.)

Old Masters' versions of the classical stories that made their way into English poetry were familiar to art lovers through widely circulated engravings as well as numerous paintings owned by collectors. Dr. Gustav F. Waagen, the German art historian and museum director who toured Britain's private galleries in 1835 and 1850, saw no fewer than eight versions, by Rubens, Giorgione, Domenichino, and Schiavone among others, of a familiar classical subject, the Judgment of Paris, later to be domesticated by pictures from Tennyson's treatment of the story in his poem "Oenone."[37] These included prototypes of the best-known English painting of the story, William Etty's (pl. 134), whose lineage the artist's biographer traces beyond Flaxman's series of designs from Homer (1793) to Rubens, Raphael, Mengs, and Poussin.[38] Waagen also mentions at least three Old Master versions of the expulsion of Adam and Eve, a subject painted, as from Milton, by Fuseli, Martin, and several other artists. In Waagen's time too, English collections contained a profusion of paintings

133. Ford Madox Brown, *Haidee and Don Juan* (1873) (Birmingham City Museum and Art Gallery). One of several versions of a subject from *Don Juan* (canto 2) that Brown originally painted as an illustration for Moxon's edition of Byron. The reminiscence of a *pietà* is perhaps uncomfortably obvious, involving as it does a dramatic shift of characters, from the Mother of God to the seventeen-year-old daughter of a former Greek fisherman who has struck it rich in smuggling and piracy, and from Christ (taken from the cross) to the profligate and irreverent Don Juan (saved by an oar).

of Cleopatra, especially the scene of her death: many copies of Guido Reni's, as well as treatments by Rubens, Mengs (widely known through engravings), Gerard de Lairesse. Tiepolo, Cagnacci, De Bray, Van Mieris, Vermeer, Van Orley, Claude Lorrain, Poussin, and Jan Steen. More than most such subjects, pictures of Cleopatra seem to have been customarily offered and judged as fresh treatments of an artistic theme rather than as illustrations of literature.

It was inevitable, therefore, that people with some knowledge of art should approach newly painted illustrations of some English subjects with eyes already accustomed to earlier treatments of similar, if not identical, themes. They were equipped with a kind of stereoscopic vision, half literary, half artistic. Paintings of Belinda's toilet in *The Rape of the Lock,* for example, reminded experienced picture-gazers of innumerable paintings of Venus and other beauties admiring themselves in mirrors: Titian, Velázquez, Rubens, Boucher, Carracci, Giorgione, and Watteau, among others, had contributed to this fleshly anthology, as had painters of the seventeenth-century Dutch school such as Terborch (*A Lady at Her Toilet*), who had toned down the eroticism and made the moral theme of *vanitas* more acceptable to their pious clients. It was probably the bourgeois Dutch tradition rather than the Italian and French that lay behind the versions of the theme taken from English sources: *Kenilworth* (Amy Robsart and her maid Janet Foster), the *Spectator* (Clarinda's toilet), Dickens's *Barnaby Rudge* (Dolly Varden's), Eliot's *Adam Bede* (Hetty Sorrel's), and Ramsay's *The Gentle Shepherd,* the source of Wilkie's *The Cottage Toilette* (pl. 135).

Pictures of the boar hunt in *Quentin Durward* invited comparison with paintings by Rubens, Snyders, Jan Fyt, and Albano. Pictures of the apothecary and his laboratory in *Romeo and Juliet* were, in effect, literary adaptations of a subject repeated by many Dutch and Flemish painters—the alchemist (sometimes identified as an apothecary) as depicted by Van Ostade, Van Mieris, Brueghel, and Jan Steen. Because the type was so familiar a subject in earlier painting, it is unlikely that Ben Jonson's play was alluded to in any English examples besides those that were displayed

134. William Etty, *The Judgement of Paris* (RA 1826) (Lady Lever Art Gallery, Port Sunlight). A fresh treatment of the Greek myth, a staple in Renaissance and later art (Raphael, Rubens, Poussin, Mengs, etc.). Tennyson's poem "Oenone," telling the story from the viewpoint of Paris's wife, as in Ovid, was published six years after this painting was exhibited.

135. David Wilkie, *The Cottage Toilette* (RA 1824) (Reproduced by permission of the Trustees, the Wallace Collection, London). A recurrent subject in older art transplanted to rural Scotland. The rustic figures and setting are a reasonably far cry from those found in treatments of the toilet-table-and-mirror theme in Italian, French, and Dutch painting, and the central figure has little except vanity in common with the courtesans of Giorgione, Titian, and others or with the respectable, relatively un-erotic bourgeois women seen at their mirrors in Dutch genre portraits. This picture illustrates lines in Allan Ramsay's ballad opera *The Gentle Shepherd,* act 5, scene 2:

While Peggy laces up her bosom fair,
Wi' a blew snood Jenny binds up her hair;
Glaud by his morning ingle takes a beek,
The rising sun shines motty thro' the reek,
A pipe his mouth; the lasses please his een,
And now and then his joke maun intervene.

Wilkie had painted another scene from *The Gentle Shepherd* the year before (pl. 291).

with an explicit reference to it. For a similar reason, paintings of interiors cluttered with an assortment of still-life junk, often titled *An Old Curiosity Shop,* had no substantial relation to Dickens's novel; they simply repeated another favorite subject in old genre art.

Some of these subjects not only belonged to a long pictorial tradition but had entered English literature from an earlier European literary source. The artists' choice—whether to associate a new treatment with its artistic lineage, its European literary source, or its best-known English version—seems to have followed no particular pattern. All but one of the dozen recorded English paintings of the Boccaccian tale of Sigismunda and the heart of Guiscardo made specific reference to Dryden's treatment in his *Fables.* On the other hand, only nine of the twenty recorded paintings of another subject Dryden took from Boccaccio, Cymon and Iphigenia, were displayed with a reference to Dryden or, for that matter, to Boccaccio. Their antecedents, including pictures by Rubens and Lely (whose *Cymon and Iphigenia,* also known as *Diana with Nymphs,* predated Dryden's *Fables* by some sixty years), were deemed to be artistic, and only incidentally literary.

This was true also of paintings of Endymion, notwithstanding the myth's primary association, in English minds, with Keats. Of sixteen recorded pictures, only half bore an attribution to his poem, and none to the treatments of Endymion by other poets, from Fletcher (*The Faithful Shepherdess*) to several of Keats's contemporaries and followers.[39] But the myth had come down through such painters as Carpaccio, Poussin, Tintoretto, Carracci, and Rubens; engravings of the pictures by the latter two were available to Keats, as well as of one by Anne-Louis Girodet de Roucy.

Paintings of Hero and Leander are an especially noteworthy case in point, since they included Etty's *The Parting of Hero and Leander* (pl. 139) and its companion, *Hero and Leander* ("Hero having thrown herself from

136. William Fettes Douglas, *The Alchemist* (Royal Scottish Academy 1857) (Victoria & Albert Museum, Crown Copyright). Alchemists and other practitioners of pseudo-science were a specialty of Douglas, as they were of Teniers and Thomas van Wyck. Sometimes such figures were given a literary reference, as to Ben Jonson or *Romeo and Juliet,* but Douglas did not attribute this scene to any source, unless the ghostly presence of one or more figures in the elaborate curtain implies some arcane reference.

137. Alexander George Fraser, *Figures Outside an Inn* (undated) (Tate Gallery, London). Groups of figures outside inns were familiar subjects in seventeenth-century Netherlandish painting. This nineteenth-century British example, by an artist who was for twenty years Wilkie's assistant, is based on a scene outside the Cat and Fiddle inn in Scott's *Peveril of the Peak* (chap. 21): "The horses of both guests were brought forth; and they mounted, in order to depart in company. The host and hostess stood in the doorway, to see them depart. The landlord proffered a stirrup-cup to the elder guest, while the landlady offered Peveril a glass from her own peculiar bottle. For this purpose, she mounted on the horse-block, with a flask and glass in hand; so that it was easy for the departing guest, although on horseback, to return the courtesy in the most approved manner, namely, by throwing his arm over the landlady's shoulder, and saluting her at parting."

the Tower, at the sight of Leander drowned, dies on his body") (RA 1829), Turner's *The Parting of Hero and Leander* (RA 1837), and, many years later, Leighton's *The Last Watch of Hero* (RA 1887). To gallerygoers who were equally knowledgeable in the history of painting and that of literature, such pictures were, in a way, doubly eclectic. Not only did they inspire memories of earlier pictorial treatments of the Hero and Leander legend; they recalled, in addition to its original source in Musaeus (ca. fifth century A.D.), a variety of poetic treatments, including Marlowe's poem and, more recently, poems by Leigh Hunt and Thomas Hood.

Etty, probably the most eclectic English artist of his generation, derived the subject of his *Cleopatra's Arrival in Cilicia,* also known as *The Triumph of Cleopatra* (pl. 140), from Plutarch, the source Shakespeare used, and its style was a mingling of Titian, Rubens, and contemporary French painters.[40] He chose bacchanalian scenes from poetry—*The Marriage Festival Previous to the Deluge* (*Paradise Lost,* bk. 11) (pl. 274) and the one in *Comus*—for the sake of imitating Titian and Poussin. In such a manner, pictures with a rich double heritage were equivalent to poems like Keats's, in which echoes of Shakespeare, Spenser, and Boccaccio were assimilated into new creations. The reminiscences of previous art found in the new painting were analogous to the stylistic and imagistic echoes in a poem, and when both the painting and the poem it represented contained such mingled elements, the total response of a well-read connoisseur, in theory at least, must have been complicated indeed.

Apart from a few individual paintings, not much attempt has been made as yet to identify the iconographic borrowings of nineteenth-century British art, and this is not the place to attempt anything of the sort. One such motif frequently seen in literary paintings, however, has been pointed out by more than one critic: the placement of a female model at an open window, or sometimes on a balcony, from which she gazes with whatever feelings the painter wished to ascribe to her. Artists from Rembrandt downward—notably his pupil Gerrit Dou, whose specialty it was—had portrayed women in this setting, as exemplars of wistful loneliness, amorous hope, or simple reverie. Turner's *Merchant of Venice* painting, *Shylock: "Jessica, Shut the Window, I Pray"* (RA 1830), was the most celebrated (and abused) painting of the kind in this period, followed perhaps by William Dyce's *Jessica* (or *The Signal*) (RA 1843). Some woman-in-window compositions were taken directly from a literary text; Alfred Chalon's *Rebecca,* for example, engraved for *Heath's Gallery* in 1836, bore a quotation from *Ivanhoe:* ". . . The single window [of her cell] opened

138. Sir Edward James Poynter, *Diana and Endymion* (1901) (City Art Gallery, Manchester). This painting probably alludes primarily to the Diana-Endymion story in its legendary form, as well as, by inference, to its previous treatments by Old Masters, but few persons viewing it in 1901 would have failed to associate it also with Keats's poem.

139. William Etty, *The Parting of Hero and Leander* (RA 1827) (Tate Gallery, London). One of Etty's many realizations of classical myth, this painting was exhibited without reference to the most famous English treatment of the Hero and Leander story by Christopher Marlowe. Leigh Hunt's version (1819) would have restored the tale to the consciousness of the people who saw Etty's picture, and the picture, in turn, would have added interest to Thomas Hood's version, published only months after the Academy show (August 1827) and dedicated to Coleridge, and to Tennyson's version, published three years later.

140. William Etty, *Cleopatra's Arrival in Cilicia (The Triumph of Cleopatra)* (RA 1821) (Lady Lever Art Gallery, Port Sunlight). This was the picture that made Etty famous overnight, because of its audacious eclecticism. Although Shakespeare does not mention the episode, it is described in Etty-like splendor in his source, Plutarch's life of Mark Antony; and the painting, once seen, must have colored the imagination of anyone who read the play thereafter. One wonders what effect, if any, the painting had on Clarkson Stanfield's sets for Macready's spectacular production of *Antony and Cleopatra* in 1833. The actor-manager was an admirer of Etty, whom he first met in a carriage traveling from Naples to Rome the year after the painting was exhibited.

upon an embattled space. . . ." (It would be a profitable line of research to discover how many iconographic cues of this sort occur in Scott's novels and other fiction and poetry of the time—and how many the novelists and poets, for their part, derived from pictures.) The suggestion of a votive niche in the framing of such a composition helped convey the ideal of woman as a sanctified creature, the equivalent in art of Coventry Patmore's *The Angel in the House.* In a reversal of the motif, also handed down from seventeenth-century European art, several painters, such as Millais in his well-known picture from Tennyson's "Mariana in the Moated Grange" (RA 1851), portrayed the model from the back, from a vantage point inside the room.

Iconographic "pilferings", as unsympathetic critics termed them—Blake called them outright "thievery"—were faithful to the academic tradition, and indeed were, as Horace Walpole pointed out, sanctioned in the sister art of literature; "a quotation from a great author, with a novel application of the sense, has always been allowed to be an instance of parts and taste; and may have more merit than the original."[41] Walpole was here defending the practice and principle of Reynolds, who urged painters to acquire their stylistic language from Van Dyck, Michelangelo, Raphael, Poussin, and other masters. Reynolds's own fancy pictures were full of small "quotations"—postures, expressions, and accessories borrowed from earlier mythological, religious, and allegorical pictures. Hogarth and Fuseli, as recent scholars have shown, owed extensive iconographic debts to their predecessors.[42] Fuseli's ghostly hand could sometimes be seen in the extravagant fairy paintings of the 1840s (see chapter 5, above), and Reynolds's was constantly detected elsewhere. Once in a while, an artist's servile imitation of his model was so blatant as to totally discredit the picture; both the *Times* and the *Literary Gazette* in

1836 condemned William Hilton's painting of Hotspur for its near travesty of Reynolds's *Infant Hercules.*[43]

Sometimes the new offering survived the comparison. The *Art Journal* in 1870, for instance, declared that John Pettie's *Touchstone and Audrey* "might almost have been painted by Rubens or Millais"[44]—the latter comparison being not as backhanded a compliment as one might think, because Millais's reputation by that time had been cleansed of its early Pre-Raphaelite association. But oftener than not, such measurements by previous standards were not calculated to enhance the painter's reputation. As the same journal remarked of a picture of *The Fall of the Rebel Angels* in 1853, "Every essay of this kind comes into disadvantageous comparison with versions of similar subjects by Michael Angelo and Rubens"[45]—and even, it might have added, by Fuseli.

In striving to match the "high excellencies" of inherited art, ambitious painters ran the danger, by no means always avoided, of falsifying a subject from English literature, which came to hand already endowed by its author with a spirit—its "Englishness," to borrow Sir Nikolaus Pevsner's useful word—that was inharmonious with the very nature and quality of high art: a conflict of two irreconcilable ways of looking at, and interpreting, experience. The true spirit and intentions of the literary source were misrepresented when inappropriate elements of treatment were brought into the interpretation from revered graphic sources. And so the artist was caught in a dilemma between the inherited need for allegiance to academic principles and the demonstrable and seemingly inexhaustible popularity of illustrative art—and both of these, in turn, militated against original expression. This handicap was intensified by the double vision that critics brought to his newest canvas. On the one hand, they looked at it with eyes that compared it—as the artist in his vanity intended—to the productions of the great masters that its style, if not its theme, recalled. On the other, they saw it in terms of the already existent literary story, a second kind of product originating outside the artist's mind.

The 1840s witnessed two last-ditch efforts to elicit high art from British brushes. One was a seriocomic affair, the topic of lively discussion for no more than a season or two—the Prince Consort's scheme to decorate the summer pavilion at Buckingham Palace, which, because it involved only Milton (and, very peripherally, Scott), is more conveniently described in Part Three. The other was a much more elaborate and protracted state enterprise in aid of art, which kept the potentialities of the grand history picture in the public consciousness for a number of years, until lack of progress and the sheer tiresome antiquatedness of the notion spelled the end of all such aspiration.

As Charles Barry's new Houses of Parliament rose in Westminster, replacing the ancient buildings that had burned in 1834 as Turner and Constable painted the spectacular scene, their spacious walls offered an opportunity to artists in fresco such as Britain had never before witnessed, or at least sought to take advantage of, apart from the unrealized project to decorate St. Paul's Cathedral in the 1760s. Now, at last, an art that had endowed the walls of Renaissance palaces and churches with some of the supreme productions of the Old Masters was to have its chance in London, as Parliament determined that the decoration of the

Palace of Westminster was to be placed in the hands of native artists selected through a series of competitions.[46] The subjects were to be drawn from British history or from the works of Shakespeare, Spenser, and Milton—a good indication of the prestige that English literary themes had by then acquired.

There were forebodings that the new challenge would produce a still larger surfeit of hackneyed subjects. "What numbers of Unas and lambs shall we have from Spenser," one of the Cunninghams wrote in *Fraser's Magazine;* "of Satan summoning his legions; of Hamlet with the skull in his hand; and all the often-recurring subjects of every London exhibition."[47] And so it proved. Of the 141 chalk and charcoal cartoons submitted in the first competition (1843), twelve were from Shakespeare, eleven from Spenser, and forty from Milton, and among these were many old chestnuts. Several subjects from poetry and drama won prizes: William Frost's *Una and the Satyrs,* Frank Howard's *Una Coming to Seek the Assistance of Gloriana,* E. V. Rippingile's *Una and the Red Cross Knight Led by Mercy to the Hospital of the Seven Virtues,* F. R. Pickersgill's *The Death of King Lear,* Sir William Ross's *The Angel Raphael Discoursing with Adam,* F. P. Stephanoff's *The Brothers Releasing the Lady from the Enchanted Chair (Comus),* and J. G. Waller's *The Brothers Driving Out Comus and His Rabble.* Except for the money they got, painters of scenes from *Comus* had wasted their time and talent, because Thomas Babington Macaulay, sitting as an M.P. from Edinburgh, declared that "no subject could be selected to illustrate Milton which was not taken from *Paradise Lost.*"[48] This also disqualified J. C. Horsley's combined picture of *L'Allegro* and *Il Penseroso* (pl. 279), which the Prince acquired for the royal collection.

In the second competition (1844), a number of literary pieces were singled out for special mention in the press: Ford Madox Brown's *Adam and Eve* ("an illustration of Milton after the manner of Cruikshank," said an unkind writer in the *New Monthly Magazine*),[49] William Salter's scene from *The Tempest,* Edward Armitage's *Ophelia,* and James Bridges's *Milton Dictating to His Daughters.* Thanks to parliamentary and bureaucratic shilly-shallying, however, competition succeeded competition while the Westminster walls remained blank. In 1847, the project acquired new impetus when William Dyce suggested to the Prince Consort that instead of using the *Nibelungenlied* for the paintings in the Queen's Robing Room, as had been the plan, "a suitably patriotic alternative" was available in stories from Arthurian legend.[50] The Prince liked the idea, and Dyce, who, alone among the contestants, had had experience in fresco, set to work. The first scheme, to treat the legend historically, ran afoul of the awkward fact that the most impressive part of the story, the tragic ending, lacked some of the principal characters, and moreover involved, as Dyce put it, certain incidents "which, if they are not undesirable for representation under any circumstances, are at least scarcely appropriate in such an apartment." Consequently, Dyce evaded Lancelot and Guinevere by shifting to the allegorical mode, portraying Generosity as "Arthur, Unhorsed, Spared by the Victor," Religion as "The Vision of Sir Galahad and His Companions," Mercy as "Sir Gawaine Swearing to be Merciful," and Hospitality as "Sir Tristram Admitted to the Round Table." Dyce died in 1864, one of the several victims of this quixotic project, and Courtesy and Fidelity were never painted.

Meanwhile, poetic subjects were decided upon for the Upper Waiting

Hall of the House of Lords. Between 1852 and 1854, the walls acquired J. R. Herbert's *King Lear Disinheriting Cordelia* (pl. 141), Horsley's *Satan Touched by Ithuriel's Spear,* John Tenniel's *St. Cecilia* (from Dryden), Armitage's *Personification of the Thames and of the English Rivers* (from Pope's *Windsor Forest*), the same artist's *The Death of Marmion,* C. W. Cope's *The Death of Lara,* and G. F. Watts's *The Triumph of the Red Cross Knight.* But these frescoes decayed so quickly that as early as 1868 they required wholesale rehabilitation, which had to be repeated at intervals throughout the next century. They survive only as monochrome shadows of the brilliantly colored scenes they once were, sad monuments to British artists' inability to work in a medium that had proved so successful in sunnier and drier climates.

Graham Reynolds doubtless expresses the universal modern opinion of the Westminster decorations when he says that "it is impossible to contemplate [them] without boredom verging on despair."[51] As one of the more notable fiascos of an era when elaborate projects for the public weal were more often dreamed up than brought to a triumphant conclusion, this one was doubly anachronistic. It sought to resuscitate an ideal of art that had long outlived its attraction and was, in any event, demonstrably ill suited to the English artistic temper; and it sought as well to dignify a kind of subject art, derived from native literature, for which justification was scarcely needed by the mid-forties.

141. John R. Herbert, *Cordelia Disinherited* (1850) (Harris Museum and Art Gallery, Preston). A study for the fresco Herbert was commissioned to paint in the House of Lords. Cordelia is depicted more spiritually than the typical Keepsake heroine, but it is still hard to conceive of this figure having spoken her lines in the first scene of *King Lear.*

CHAPTER 9

Literary subjects and "modern instances."—The use of literary quotations in exhibition catalogues: Turner's "The Fallacies of Hope."—Poems from pictures.

By no means all of the paintings that had some sort of literary allusion attached to them had anything to do with the content of the books to which the spectator was referred by the title or the accompanying motto. Many belonged to the popular class of Victorian art devoted to portraying what were then called "modern instances" (*As You Like It,* 2.7)—the genre studies and anecdotal scenes from contemporary life that were touched on in chapter 6.

In contemporary figural theory, which, as recent scholars have shown,[1] had a marked influence on certain kinds of Victorian paintings, episodes in the Old Testament were interpreted as prefiguring New Testament truths, and incidents in Christ's life were seen to have foreshadowed modern events. In a similar manner, episodes in literature could be interpreted as exemplars of situations, whether commonplace or crucial, in everyday modern life. In effect, the literary allusions attached to paintings without actual literary content represented a loose kind of secular Victorian typology. The "modern instance" was a realization of the prefiguration found in, or inferred from, the literary text. (Pictures from English history, especially seventeenth-century subjects, similarly could be seen to have application to current political affairs.)

A typical rural scene, of a youth in a gleaning field looking covetously at a sleeping girl, exhausted by her labors on a warm afternoon, might be called *Cymon and Iphigenia.* Viewers acquainted with the literary source in Boccaccio and Dryden, in which the youth was the handsome but boorish son of a Cyprian nobleman, would have read the picture knowing that in the *Decameron* or the *Fables,* the youth is transformed by the equally highborn maiden's love and becomes a polished gallant. If one chose to do so, one could use the recollected moral of the literary story as a means by which to reinterpret the painting: what appeared to be the prelude to a rural Victorian seduction might, in fact, be the prelude to redemption.

The relation between the "modern instance" and the literary prefiguration might not even be indicated by an explicit literary reference: it might, instead, be suggested by an iconographical resemblance. A prime example occurred in connection with the familiar humorous subject of a courtship conducted in the presence of a nominal chaperon who has dropped off to sleep. In Abraham Solomon's *First Class—The Meeting* (RA 1854), a young naval officer, riding on a train, beguiled a young woman, inferentially with tales of adventure, while her father dozed in a corner of their first-class compartment. One literary expression of this subject was the Duke of Milan's lines to Proteus in *The Two Gentlemen of Verona* (3.1. 24–25), illustrated, for example, in Alfred Elmore's painting (RA 1858): "This love of theirs myself have often seen, / Haply when they have judged me fast asleep." Solomon's picture was criticized for allowing the father to abrogate his protective duty, and so, when he painted a second version (pl. 142), he awakened the old gentleman and moved him into the center of the composition, where he listened agog as the officer addressed his stories *to him* while his daughter, busily crocheting but no less attentive, sat in the corner.[2] Now the tableau was brought into line with the equivalent scene described (not enacted) in *Othello* (1.3) in which Othello recounts the story of his soldier's life to Brabantio while Desdemona, going about her household tasks, listens enthralled. This was the subject of a number of Shakespearean paintings (see Part Two, below), from one of which, Charles West Cope's of 1853 (pl. 143), Solomon may have borrowed the composition of his revised version. The Shakespeare scenes, Elmore's and Cope's, thus represented literary prefigurations of the "modern instance" painted by Solomon.*

Literary allusion, in the form of either a title or a quotation, added resonance to a wide variety of paintings from contemporary life. Pictures of significantly empty chairs—a favorite sentimental subject; pictures of chairs vacated by Scott (Sir William Allan) and Dickens (Luke Fildes) were one expression of the national mourning that marked the death of celebrated authors—bore references to such chairs in Crabbe's *The Parish Register* and better-known poems. The canvases of Thomas Webster, the one major Victorian genre painter of contemporary subjects who seldom drew otherwise from literature, were sometimes equipped with mottoes. His pair at the Royal Academy in 1841, *The Joke* and *The Frown*, was accompanied by the familiar lines from Goldsmith's *The Deserted Village* describing the schoolmaster:

> Well had the boding tremblers learn'd to trace
> The day's disasters in his morning face;
> Full well they laugh'd, with counterfeited glee,
> At all his jokes, for many a joke had he;
> Full well the busy whisper, circling round,
> Convey'd the dismal tidings when he frown'd.

In 1858, Henry Wallis's *The Stonebreaker*, depicting the lifeless body of a road worker, came to the Royal Academy with a lengthy quotation from Carlyle's *Sartor Resartus:* "Hardly entreated, brother! For us was thy back so bent [etc., etc.] . . . thy body, like thy soul, was not to know freedom." Anecdotal paintings such as this, with at least a tinge of social concern, became more frequent in and after the 1860s; and artists continued to avail themselves of literary references, perhaps to make their disturbing message a bit more palatable and respectable. Briton Riviere's *The*

*The connection seems not to have been noticed by modern students of Victorian art, but Thackeray was aware of it, however subliminally. Conceivably fresh from seeing Solomon's first version at the Academy in 1854, and remembering Cope's picture at the previous year's exhibition, he wrote (*The Newcomes,* chap. 9), apropos of the skeletons of regretted intentions and deeds that most people conceal in their private closets, "Who, in showing his house to the closest and dearest, doesn't keep back the key to a closet or two? I think of a lovely reader laying down the page and looking over at her unconscious husband, asleep, perhaps, after dinner. Yes, Madam, a closet he hath, and you, who pry into everything shall never have the key to it. I think of some honest Othello pausing over this very sentence in a railroad carriage, and stealthily gazing at Desdemona opposite to him. . . ."

142. Abraham Solomon, *First Class: The Meeting* (after 1854) (Southampton Art Gallery). A young warrior, Othello's junior by some years, spellbinds a young lady (a modern Desdemona) and her father (Brabantio) with tales of battle and adventure. The scene has been moved from Venice (pl. 143) to a Victorian railway carriage, but that is the only substantial difference.

Poacher's Widow (RA 1879), showing "a young woman in black sunk in troubled sleep or absorbed in heartbroken thought on a copse bank, while in and out of the wood about her the pheasants and hares and rabbits, which have cost her husband his life, frisk and feed in the gloaming,"[3] bore explanatory lines from a ballad in Charles Kingsley's novel *Yeast:* "She thought of the dark plantation, / And the hares and her husband's blood." Five years earlier, a more conspicuous landmark in the progress of social realism, Luke Fildes's *Applicants for Admission to a Casual Ward,* had been hung at the Royal Academy with a more vehement quotation from a letter of Dickens: "Dumb, wet, silent horrors! Sphinxes set up against the dead wall and none likely to be at the pains of solving them until the *general overthrow.*" Attacking the picture's sordidness, the *Saturday Review* declared that Fildes's citation of Dickens was no mitigation of his offense, "inasmuch as it has for obvious reasons always been held that in written description a place may be found for horrors which become intolerable when brought into pictorial form bodily before the eye."[4]*

The Victorians' awesome penchant for turning literary references to humorous account, which can be seen lavishly if dismally displayed in any random volume of *Punch,* relied heavily on the titles of Shakespeare's plays and quotations from them, which were so available a part of the middle-class Englishman's everyday vocabulary. Pictures of *The Taming of the Shrew,* far from depicting Catherine and Petruchio, might turn out to be genial, perhaps facetious representations of the subjection of women in marital life, or, for that matter, in the animal kingdom. In 1861, Landseer exhibited *The Shrew Tamed,* which depicted a pretty equestrienne leaning in triumph against a sweat-lathered, fiery-eyed horse she has succeeded in mastering. The model was said to have been a well-known young horsewoman named Miss Gilbert, but knowledgeable men about town who happened into the exhibition would have recognized "Skittles," the most celebrated of all mid-Victorian courtesans, who was often to be seen riding in Hyde Park. ("Horsebreaker" was current slang for high-class prostitute.)[5] A painting of *Romeo and Juliet* (RA 1882) featured two

*In most cases, the quotations attached to paintings had the effect the artist intended. Occasionally, however, the spectator may have been forgiven for missing the point. Holman Hunt's *The Hireling Shepherd,* a typical picture from contemporary life showing a pair of dallying lovers, was exhibited in 1852 with lines from Edgar's song in *King Lear* (3.6. 41–44): "Sleepest or wakest thou, jolly shepherd? / Thy sheep be in the corn; / And for one blast of thy minikin mouth / Thy sheep shall take no harm." Hunt later explained that he intended a commentary on "the type of muddle-headed pastors, who, instead of performing their services to their flock—which is in constant peril—discuss vain questions of no value to any human soul" (Timothy Hilton, *The Pre-Raphaelites* [London, 1970], p. 86). No one, looking at the picture itself, would have imagined that Hunt was making a Milton-like statement on the subject of ecclesiastical negligence (and Whistonian theology?). By contrast, he made the spectator's comprehension of his purpose triply sure when he exhibited *The Awakening Conscience* the next year: it came equipped with no fewer than three biblical quotations, two in the catalogue and a third on the frame.

cats, one on top of a wall, the other looking up at it.[6] At the Society of British Artists in 1841 was seen a picture titled *A Day's Pleasure,* equipped with lines from *A Midsummer Night's Dream,* "—the reckoning, when the banquet's o'er— / The dreadful reckoning, when men smile no more." The scene was the Star and Garter inn at Richmond, where half a dozen tipsy revelers from London were haggling with a waiter over the bill.[7]

But what may well have been the nadir of this kind of foolery (though the choice is difficult) was reached in 1873, when a painting at the Royal Academy was catalogued with the quotation, "If it were done when 'tis done, then 'twere well it were done quickly." Any commonsensical expectation that the scene was from *Macbeth* was quickly dispelled. What the spectators saw, according to a reviewer, was a monkey "hopping by slow degrees towards a biscuit, the property of a large dog lying down and watching his movements. The mingled expressions of courage, covetousness and fear in the face of the monkey, and of lazy interest and astonishment in that of the dog, are given with force and skill."[8]

Innumerable pictures that were nothing more than routine treatments of banal themes were decorated with titles or quotations that related them to a favorite work of literature. Pictures titled *The Rivals* were as likely to be sentimental genre pictures of two bucolic suitors competing for one woman, or two women in envious contention, as illustrations of Sheridan's play, and many paintings called *The Cotter's Saturday Night,* or taking off from lines in Burns's poem, landed at a great distance from it. Thomas Faed's *His Only Pair* (RA 1860), for instance, bearing the motto "The mother, wi' her needle and her shears, / Gars auld claes look amaist as well's the new," was pure sentimental genre, adequately described by a reviewer: "The little owner, divested of his extreme garments, is seated on a dresser, amused by an orange, while his industrious and frugal parent is making the necessary emendations. This picture will produce many a smile of pleasure and admiration."[9] Perhaps; but it was no more a picture of a humble family living in a cottage than was Alexander John-

143. Charles W. Cope, *Othello Relating His Adventures* (RA 1853) (Engraving, Witt Library, Courtauld Institute of Art). The composition of this painting evidently provided the model for the second version of Solomon's "modern instance" of a subject familiar in literary art.

ston's *The Cotter's Saturday Night* (RA 1863), which did indeed show a family listening to pater familias reading—but the book was not necessarily the Bible (a volume of Burns?), the dress was modern-urban, and the setting suggested a comfortable middle-class home.

Artists not only enjoyed virtually absolute liberty of interpretation when appropriating a literary subject, title, or motto in this fashion: the subjects were themselves convertible. Like the wood blocks used in the early days of printing, when a generalized design of a fortification could be used interchangeably for the walls of Troy or a castle in a medieval romance, they could be painted so devoid of specificity as to serve for illustrations of any of a number of literary works. Perhaps the Keepsake beauty portraits and their descendants were the most numerous examples of this flexibility. A reviewer at the very end of the Victorian period spoke for all his impatient predecessors when he wrote of Frank Dicksee's *Yseult* (RA 1901) that it had "no particular reference to any special incident in the mythic story of King Mark's bride; with costume and other details altered it would serve almost equally for Juliet, or Hero, or Francesca, or half-a-dozen more of those passion-worn ladies that Mr. Dicksee can realise for us with such consummate skill."[10] Since these portraits of pensive, frequently insipid young women were often intended for the suburban-villa trade, it did not really matter what name was chosen to add a touch of meretricious literary gentility. This easygoing practice gave critics an irresistible opportunity for jocoseness when writing of a painting they disliked. In 1856, for example, a picture billed as Scott's Lucy Ashton moved a reviewer to remark that it "might with equal propriety be called either 'the Maid of Orleans' or 'the Witch of Endor.'"[11]*

The subjects of entire tableaux also were convertible. Charles Allston Collins's well-known *Convent Thoughts* (RA 1851) began as an illustration of Shelley's Lady in "The Sensitive Plant," "the wonder of her kind." But when he became a High Churchman, Collins also converted the girl into a nun and replaced the contemplated lines from the atheistical Shelley with mottoes from Psalm 143, "I meditate on all thy works," and *A Midsummer Night's Dream,* 1.1 ("Thrice blessèd they that master so their blood / To undergo such maiden pilgrimage"). Some years later, Arthur Hughes submitted to the Royal Academy a picture of Orlando in the forest of Arden carving Rosalind's name on a tree trunk. It was rejected, whereupon Hughes painted out Orlando, substituted "Amy" (from Tennyson's "Locksley Hall"?) on the tree, and turned the picture into a portrayal of a poor curate unable to marry the girl to whom he has been engaged for many years. Bearing a quotation from Chaucer's *Troilus and Criseyde,* "For how myghte evere swetnesse han ben knowe / To him that nevere tasted bitternesse?", it was accepted for the Academy's 1859 show.

When artists played so fast and loose with literary subject matter and allusions, it was no wonder that reviewers complained from time to time—and this was not a mere bid for a cheap laugh—that they could find no connection between the literary title of a painting and its content, or that the title had been adopted to make intelligible what was otherwise a meaningless scene. Critics' exasperation with what they deemed the misleading or inadequate labeling of so-called literary pictures sharpened, or at least was more often voiced, after mid-century, when "illustrated anecdotes" with contrived literary tie-ins had developed into a major nuisance.

*Once in a while, the transformation was effected in good faith. Early in his career, Leslie painted "a female figure with a moonlight effect" that he intended to be a Juliet but, he said, "not thinking when it was finished that it expressed her character, I gave it another name"—he did not reveal what. In Bulwer-Lytton's novel *What Will He Do With It?* (1859), the painter Vance paid the heroine three pounds to pose for a female head that he subsequently used for a series of portraits—"'variations,' as they say in music"—entitled *Titania, Beatrice Cenci, Minna [Troil], Burns's Mary in Heaven,* and *Sabrina Fair,* from *Comus* (bk. 6, chap. 1).

"Dealers only can tell us where they will be forty years hence, when the catalogue is lost and the name of the picture is forgotten," said the *Athenaeum* of one such picture—*Bruce in His Adversity,* allegedly from Scott—in 1857.[12]

The fact was that artists too often used literary allusion to lend specious value to what was undeniably bad art. "It is melancholy," said the *Saturday Review* in 1874, "to see how . . . Shakespeare and the best authors of all countries are made to pass off the worst of pictorial wares."[13] A prototypical example was a picture, shown by George Boughton at that year's Academy, which seems to have been the quintessence of Victorian popular art, *plein air* division. Evidently it had all the ingredients: "an open bit of country, with a quiet, quaint, old town beyond a white road; a holy well and cross and village maids," said one critic,[14] to which another added, "Several of the characters, forsaking the beaten path, betake themselves to the springtide meadows; the liquid air and the budding trees are of the vernal time which the poet loved so well. . . . In the foreground a pretty girl offers a draught of water to a youth whose weary journey seems likely to end in a pilgrimage of love."[15] It comes as no surprise that the painting was entitled *God Speed! Pilgrims Setting Out for Canterbury; Time of Chaucer.*

"I am not a poetically minded man," Samuel Butler, the author of *Erewhon* and *The Way of All Flesh,* once remarked. " . . . I have never read and never, I am afraid, shall read a line of Keats or Shelley or Coleridge or Wordsworth except such extracts as I occasionally see in Royal Academy Catalogues."[16] To which a writer on Scott and the visual arts has added, "Had Butler lived in Edinburgh he could have read quite extensively in Scott in the catalogues of the Royal Scottish Academy."[17]

The examples offered above of quotations used for various purposes, from the gravely didactic to the grievously humorous, represent what was, in fact, an important and revealing practice in the nineteenth-century art world. Exhibition catalogues were little *ad hoc* anthologies of elegant extracts. Charles Eastlake told the Royal Commissioners sponsoring the Westminster cartoon exhibition in 1843 that "the Catalogues in the hands of so many thousands would be the first introduction of many to an acquaintance with our best poets and writers."[18] And so the quotation-filled art catalogue may have contributed, however modestly, to the literary culture of the class it served.

But of course it served primarily as a guide book. From the painter's point of view, an apt quotation could be a ready-made alternative to writing his own prose description of a picture. Each such catalogue entry was a minuscule counterpart of the descriptive brochures that artists like Haydon and Martin provided at exhibitions of their huge, crowded canvases. Painters also used it, like the incidental printed ballads, broadsides, sheet music, newspapers, posters, and engravings that Hogarth and Victorian narrative artists such as Ford Madox Brown (*Work*) occasionally placed in their compositions, to point the picture's moral or enlarge its message. (This indication that painters could not always depend on their pictures to be self-explanatory without clues inside the scene or in the motto says something about the interpretive capacity of their clientele.) Finally, the well-chosen poetic quotation provided a means of cultivating, indeed directing, the spectator's sympathetic response to the picture, supplying mood music, so to speak, as a background for the visual experience. The hope was that under the joint auspices of the theory of the sisterhood of the arts and associationist psychology the text and the picture would merge into a single entity.

The custom of physically relating a painting with a pertinent text predated associationism. Mottoes, "haunting and now inexplicably relevant as a refrain" as David Piper has written,[19] were inscribed on miniatures and sometimes on large portraits in Elizabethan days; at Longleat, for example, hangs a portrait of Lord Thomas Seymour of Sudeley that contains, on the left side, eight lines from Sir John Harington's *Orlando.* In Hogarth's time, writing verses to accompany engravings, at half a crown per quatrain, was among the casual jobs that kept Grub Street hacks from sinking below the subsistence level. Hogarth himself patronized somewhat more reputable sources: the verses for *The Rake's Progress* and *The Four Stages of Cruelty* were written, respectively, by Dr. John Hoadly and the Reverend James Townley, both of whom were schoolmasters and dramatists prominent enough in the literary life of their period to win notice in the *Dictionary of National Biography. The Distressed Poet* bore a quotation from Pope's *The Dunciad.*

A fragment of a quotation was printed in the catalogue of the second exhibition ever held in London, that of the Society of Artists in 1761: *The Bard, from Mr. Gray's Ode. "But oh! what glorious scenes, &c."* Thirty years later, at the very moment that Archibald Alison, in his influential treatise on associationist psychology, *Essays on the Nature and Principles of Taste* (1790), was extolling the emotional value of remembered poetry when one took in a natural vista, the catalogue sold at the door of the Boydell Shakespeare Gallery contained generous quotations, sometimes as long as two or three printed pages, from the scenes the pictures illustrated. Subsequently, the catalogue of Fuseli's Milton Gallery followed the same practice, evidently out of practical necessity. A "coarse-looking" man who had probably wandered into the show by mistake and who, in any event, had not laid out sixpence for a catalogue, went up to Fuseli and asked, "Pray, Sir, what is that picture?" Instead of referring him to the guidebook, the artist obligingly answered, "It is the bridging of Chaos: the subject from Milton." "No wonder I did not know it," said the man, "for I never read Milton, but I will." "I advise you not," replied Fuseli, "for you will find it a d——d tough job."[20]

Academic doctrine was strongly against this concession to the indifferently educated. Only a few years after this encounter, Fuseli stated the principle in an Academy lecture:

> The first demand on every work of art is that it constitute one whole, that it fully pronounce its own meaning, that it tell itself; it ought to be independent; the essential part of its subject ought to be comprehended and understood without collateral assistance, without borrowing its commentary from the historian or the poet; for as we are soon wearied with a poem whose fable and motives reach us only by the borrowed light of annexed notes, so we turn our eye discontented from a picture or a statue whose meaning depends on the charity of a Cicerone, or must be fetched from a book.[21]

"I advised a painter the other day," Fuseli's fellow academician Northcote told the painter James Ward, "never to explain by words what his picture is intended to represent; I told him to endeavour by every means to find out [i.e., produce] the effect on the spectator without giving any verbal explanation. If you can talk well, persons will fancy they see in a picture what in reality has been produced by your tongue"—or, he might have added, your transcribing pen alongside an open book of poetry. But, as Ward replied, such wisdom was increasingly unheeded: "The practice of many painters of the present day is very different from what you recommend. When they exhibit their pictures to the public, they give a long descriptive account, and, not content with what prose can do for them, they introduce long quotations from the poets."[22]

This was one evidence of the age's addiction to capsulized beauty and truth, an enthusiasm to which, as we have seen (see chapter 5, above), the many collections of gems from the great authors catered.[23] From the schoolmaster's insistence on the moral and psychological benefits of memorizing passages of poetry to Matthew Arnold's magisterial doctrine that the ultimate worth of any given poem could be determined by applying the litmus test ("touchstone") of a few top-quality verses from Shakespeare or Milton, the literary temper of the time prized the small but supposedly exquisite, as well as sage, fragment: infinite riches in a couple of lines.*

The mottoes on pictures were simply the most cultivated manifestations of a phenomenon met everywhere in Victorian England: space-fillers in newspapers and cheap magazines, greeting cards, children's party crackers, "sentiments" printed, or meant to be written, in remembrance albums; scriptural texts quoted at the beginning of sermons, carved in stone or painted on the walls of churches and chapels; samplers in parlors, and framed biblical verses and prudential aphorisms on the walls of business offices, prisons, workhouses, hospitals, and orphanages. There was hardly a line in these droplets of evocation, sentiment, humor, or wisdom that did not find its way, sooner or later, into the exhibition catalogues.

In books, the equivalent of the picture motto was the printed epigraph on the title page or at the beginning of each chapter, or, as with Tennyson and others, at the head of a poem, to enrich a sentiment, express a moral, or serve as a thematic signpost. Several of the writers familiar to gallerygoers in the first half of the nineteenth century were notable users of such mottoes.[24] Crabbe prefaced each letter in *The Borough* with quotations from classical authors, Shakespeare, and other English poets. Ann Radcliffe, in *The Italian* and *The Mysteries of Udolpho,* drew upon Shakespeare, Milton, Collins, Thomson, Walpole (*The Mysterious Mother*), Mason (*Caractacus* and *Elfrida*), Goldsmith, Gray, and Beattie. By far the most persistent borrower of epigraphs was Scott, who headed 202 chapters in his novels with quotations from Shakespeare and 386 more from twenty-six other poets.[25] After Scott, numerous novelists, including Mrs. Gaskell but not Dickens or Thackeray, prefixed quotations to their chapters. For the chapter headings in her last three novels, *Felix Holt, Middlemarch,* and *Daniel Deronda,* George Eliot composed ninety-six herself, taking the rest (a larger number) from Shakespeare (thirty-one), Wordsworth (nine), Chaucer (four), Sir Thomas Browne (three), and a wide variety of other sources, English and non-English.[26]

Turner was the first painter to employ poetic quotations as a regular practice. In his very first years as an exhibitor at the Royal Academy (1798–1800), his oil and watercolor pictures were listed with extracts from Milton, Thomson, Gray, Mallet, and Langhorne. Later pictures bore quotations from Southey, Scott, Byron, and Rogers. All told, 53 of the 200 oil paintings he exhibited across the entire span of his career were so embellished.[27] Turner did not always quote accurately; the line that

*The omnipresence of those fragments of poetry, from art exhibition catalogues to collections of elegant extracts, must have had a marked though unacknowledged effect on contemporary thinking about literature, posing (among other things) the question of how parts related to the whole. In a notebook entry for 12 May 1865, Gerard Manley Hopkins recorded thoughts on the matter:

> Sometimes . . . one does imagine a quotation to be a whole when it is only a part. The effect is curious. . . . I have noticed sometimes this effect with regard to those quotations and tags of poetry and so on one sees added to the titles of pictures in the catalogue of the Academy. Suppose one saw this stanza of Shelley's chosen—
>
> Music when sweet voices die
> Vibrates in the memory
> Odours when sweet violets sicken
> Live within the sense they quicken.
>
> Now if one imagined this stanza was a single thought and the whole poem, or what, though opposite to that, would in another way be as bad, four lines namely out of some piece in the metre of his lines written among the Euganean hills, how greatly would the effect lose, unless I am mistaken, of that beauty it has when you add the next stanza—
>
> Rose-leaves, when the rose is shed,
> Are heap'd for the belovèd's bed
> And so thy thought when thou art gone
> Love himself shall slumber on.
>
> You then know the poem is complete in these two stanzas. (*The Journals and Papers of Gerard Manley Hopkins,* ed. Humphry House and Graham Storey [London, 1959], p. 98.)

served as the title of his 1830 painting, "*Shylock: 'Jessica, shut the window, I say,'*" is nowhere to be found in *The Merchant of Venice*. The line that comes closest to it is Shylock's direction to Jessica, "Lock up my doors . . . But stop my house's ears, I mean my casements." But the picture actually illustrates another direction, Launcelot's "Mistress, look out at window, for all this; / There will come a Christian by, / Will be worth a Jewess' eye" (2.5. 40–42).[28]*

Not satisfied with having the whole golden treasury of English verse to that date to choose from, Turner early began to write his own, which at first he printed in the catalogues without ascription. His frugality in this respect was notable. In 1808, he invented a long passage in verse, derived, it has been suggested, from Thomson's "An Ode on Aeolus's Harp" and Collins's "Ode Occasion'd by the Death of Mr. Thomson," to accompany his painting of the demolition of Pope's villa at Twickenham, a locale with which Thomson was also closely associated. Deciding eventually that the quotation was unnecessary, he saved the Twickenham bits and the following year attached them instead to his painting of *Thomson's Aeolian Harp* (pl. 296).[29]

Beginning with *Snow Storm: Hannibal and His Army Crossing the Alps* (1812), Turner's epigraphs were attributed to *The Fallacies of Hope,* the most famous nonexistent poem in the English language as well as the history of art, "a turbid mixture of sententious moralising and pseudo-philosophic gloom," as Peter Quennell describes it on the basis of the so-called "fragments" Turner printed in the exhibition catalogues.[30] Various sources of inspiration have been suggested for *The Fallacies of Hope,* whose title implies a more somber view of life than do those of Rogers's *The Pleasures of Memory* and Thomas Campbell's *The Pleasures of Hope.* One such source was Langhorne's poetry, in which twice occurs the phrase "fallacious hope" used in the epigraphs of three of Turner's later paintings.[31] Nobody has ever been bold enough to claim the slightest literary merit for these "excerpts," which offered additional ammunition for critics of Turner's paintings, especially the humorists among them. In 1844 Thackeray wrote for *Punch* a parody review of the Academy exhibition that quoted this supposed catalogue entry:

> TRUNDLER, R. A. A Typhoon bursting in a simoon over the whirlpool of Maelstrom, Norway, with a ship on fire, an eclipse, and the effect of a lunar rainbow.
>
> O Art, how vast thy misty wonders are,
> To those who roam upon the extraordinary deep;
> Maelstrom thy hand is here.
>
> —*From an unpublished poem.*[32]†

The following year, Thackeray contributed to *Fraser's Magazine* a review article in which he called the *Fallacies* "that sybilline book of mystic rhymes," adding, " . . . Turner is a great and awful mystery to me. I don't like to contemplate him too much, lest I should actually begin to believe in his poetry as well as his paintings, and fancy the *Fallacies of Hope* to be one of the finest poems in the world."[33] Before the essay appeared in the June *Fraser's,* Thackeray also paid his respects to Turner in *Punch* (31 May), in the form of a poem supposedly composed by the artist to accompany his *Morning—Returning from the Ball, St. Marino,* which actually had one more *Fallacies* tag appended to it:

> Oh! what a scene!—Can this be Venice? No.
> And yet methinks it is—because I see

*The poetic text was never sacrosanct. When he painted his *Haidee: A Greek Girl* (pl. 57), Charles Eastlake wrote a friend, "I would rather have found a quotation from a more respectable poem than 'Don Juan,' but it suits the picture so perfectly that it would be impossible to come nearer its impression"; but he did, in fact, alter the line in the quotation from *Don Juan* (canto 2, stanza 118), ". . . her cheek's pure dye / Like twilight rosy still with the set sun," changing "rosy" to "glowing" as being more suitable for the picture as completed (Memoir of Eastlake, compiled by Lady Eastlake, in his *Contributions to the Literature of the Fine Arts,* 2d ser. [London, 1870], p. 115).

†It was at this same exhibition (1844) that W. P. Frith saw the Duke of Wellington standing before Turner's *Rain, Steam and Speed:* "I watched the Duke's puzzled expression as he read the quotation from the 'Fallacies of Hope.' He then looked steadily at the picture, and with a muttered 'Ah! *poetry!*' walked on" (Frith, *Autobiography,* 1:120). The point of the story is not much diminished by the fact that *Rain, Steam and Speed* was exhibited without a quotation.

> Amid the lumps of yellow, red and blue,
> Something which looks like a Venetian spire.
> That dash of orange in the back-ground there
> Bespeaks 'tis Morning! And that little boat
> (Almost the colour of tomata sauce,)
> Proclaims them now returning from the ball!
> This in my picture I would fain convey,
> I hope I do. Alas! what FALLACY!

Recent students of Turner have taken the *Fallacies of Hope* fragments somewhat more seriously. Graham Reynolds points out that, like the quotations the artist took from published poems, his own verses reflected his "anxiety to find parallels between literature and his own paintings."[34]* Peter Conrad, arguing that "the image is a bland surface which can only acquire an interior by attachment to a literary context," instances Turner's use of the fragments to turn

> the images into dramatic gestures, speeches of stoic defiance or sententious contempt. The image acquires a voice, the painting becomes a soliloquy. For instance, the note to "Slaves Throwing Overboard the Dead and Dying—Typhon Coming on,"
>
> Before it sweeps your decks, throw overboard
> The dead and dying—ne'er heed their chains.
> Hope, Hope, fallacious Hope!
> Where is thy market now?
>
> with its nautical swagger and its swift change from the slave-trader's brutality to the professional fatalism of the old tar, makes the picture strike an attitude, turns it into a rudimentary dramatic monologue. Quotation supplies the absence of human characters, and makes the landscapes a continuing commentary on tragic nature.[35]

So quotations could, on occasion, be used for purposes more fundamental, and more integral to the painting, than mere embellishment or the arousal of a momentary association.

Constable too exhibited a few landscapes with appended snatches from Thomson, including *Hadleigh Castle* (1829) and *View of Salisbury Plain from the Meadows* (1831). In the letterpress of a volume of engravings from his paintings that he published in 1833 under the title *Various Subjects of Landscape, Characteristic of English Scenery,* he quoted Thomson (most frequently), Wordsworth, Milton, Crabbe, Burns, and Falconer.[36] Less famous but prolific landscapists like Thomas Cooper,[37]—scores of them, in fact—added a verbal flourish to the effect of their graphic imagery. They thus completed the process, begun by Claude Lorrain, Salvator Rosa, Poussin, and Wilson without such extraneous aid, of stimulating and guiding the individual person's response to Nature. People now looked at actual landscapes with eyes and minds freshly sensitized by Wordsworth and his fellow poets, and in due course by Ruskin; sometimes, in obedience to Alison's associationism, they even took volumes of poetry with them on their excursions in search of the sublime or the picturesque. Thanks to the poetic fragments in the exhibition catalogues, they could have the same experience indoors. As they "art-walked"—perhaps with one of their party reading the catalogue entries aloud—the quotations could heighten the emotions initiated by the paintings themselves.

It is likely that the growing use of poetic quotations had something to do with the emergence early in the nineteenth century of the so-called ideal painting, which took a mere hint from a line or two of a poetic text and developed what artist and critic alike took to be its quintessential spirit, irrespective of any literal detail. Wheatley and other popular engraved

*Kenneth Clark has observed that the quotation from *The Seasons* (beginning "Meantime refracted from yon eastern cloud") that Turner tacked onto his *Buttermere with a Rainbow* (1797–98) "specifically anticipates the theories of impressionism," as some others also reflected his preoccupation with the effects of light and atmosphere (*Landscape into Art*, rev. ed. [London, 1976], p. 189).

144 (left), 145 (right). Charles W. Cope, *L'Allegro* and *Il Penseroso* (both RA 1848) (Victoria & Albert Museum, Crown Copyright). Cope, who exhibited at the Royal Academy for forty-nine years, was prominent among the artists who supplied the mid-century demand for "ideal pictures" in the form of allegorical figures suggested by Milton's companion poems.

illustrators had often departed from the scene nominally being represented for the sake of adding graphic poetry to the language on the printed page. By the 1820s and 1830s, artists like Etty, Hilton, and Dadd were adopting a line or two from Milton (*Comus,* "L'Allegro," and "Il Penseroso") or—especially—"Come unto these yellow sands" (Ariel's song in *The Tempest,* 1.2) and developing independent compositions such as a Rubensesque circle of dancing nymphs; or, what is more likely, painting their pictures first and then adding the poetic inscription. No one would have associated designs like these with poetry without the aid of a title or quotation, although echoes of Titian or Poussin would have been audible.

Quotations were freely applied to a wide variety of pictures—genre and landscape most of all, but also animal paintings, figure studies, scenes of the Middle East, Spain, and every other exotic locale—in fact, almost every category but portraits and sporting pictures. A floral painting at the Royal Academy in 1837, for example, was embellished with a quotation from "Lycidas"; and Wilkie's *Grace Before Meat* (RA 1839), a typical genre scene, was shown with a quotation from a manuscript poem by the Countess of Blessington:

A lowly cot where social board is spread,
The simple owner seated at its head;
His bonnet lifts and doth to Heaven appeal,
To grant a blessing on the humble meal!

Probably no more than half of the mottoes in the catalogues were attributed. Some of them represented a level of versifying no higher than Valentine greetings or inscriptions on bonbon boxes. To identify all the unattributed ones would be a task beyond the aid of the largest existing batteries of concordances and dictionaries of quotations, and indeed rendered hopeless by the fact that some artists, not Turner alone, wrote their own *ad hoc* verses. (So had Scott. The many epigraphs in his romances attributed to "Old Play," "Old Ballad," and "Anonymous" were from his own pen; and it is said that a number of ascriptions to Byron, Dr. Johnson, Beaumont, Donne, Prior, Herbert, and Pope also conceal his hand.)[38] As a young man, William Quiller Orchardson exhibited at the Royal Scottish Academy a picture called *Marley Gray,* accompanied by a two-quatrain quotation from a ballad in the Scots dialect. A collector of old Scottish literature told the artist he had never seen it. "I just made the two verses myself to suit the picture," Orchardson said.[39]

Many of the genuine unlocated excerpts may have come from eighteenth-century poetasters who lingered in literary recollection as late as the first Victorian years. Among the identifiable tags most often used were two from Gray's "Elegy," "The ploughman homeward plods his weary way" and "Now fades the glimmering landscape on the sight"; two from Byron, "Ave Maria! 'Tis the hour" (*Don Juan,* canto 3, stanza 103) and "The moon is up and yet it is not night"(*Childe Harold's Pilgrimage,* canto 4, stanza 27); and, after the 1850s, "How happy I could be with either / Were t'other dear Charmer away!", a couplet from Macheath's song in *The Beggar's Opera* that was considered just the thing to attach to paintings of humorously romantic dilemmas.

In a sample of about 1,400 identified quotations, most of them accompanying pictures in the Victorian era, Shakespeare and Tennyson led the list, with some 130 each. Thomson was in third place with about 100, and at some distance behind him were Byron, Burns, and Scott, represented

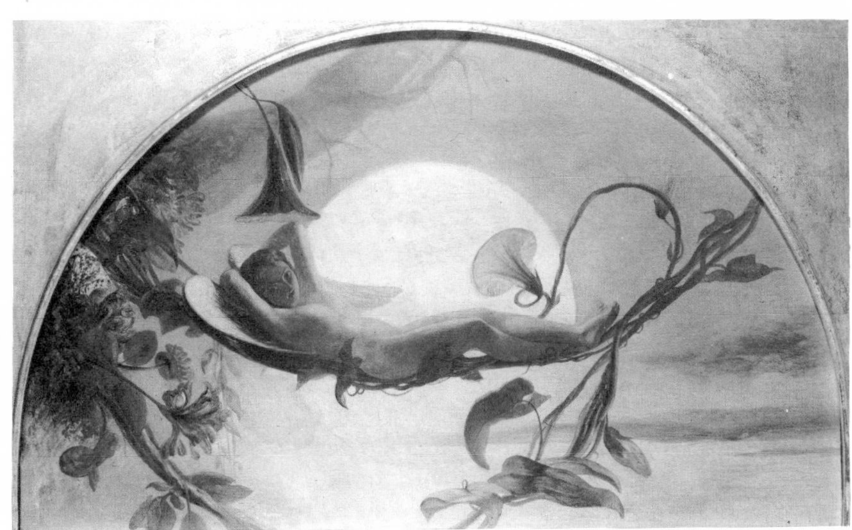

146. Henry J. Townsend, *Ariel* (RA 1845) (Royal Collection, Copyright Reserved). Although the announced subject is the sprite in *The Tempest,* the accompanying quotation from Byron ("The moon is up, and yet it is not night") reduces the picture's specificity. It is not so much an illustration of Shakespeare as an ideal picture that uses *The Tempest* merely as a point of departure.

by a range of 60 to 80 paintings each. In the third category were Moore, Rogers, Milton, and Gray, bunched quite close together. After these top ten, there was a decided gap in incidence. Among the pre-eighteenth-century poets represented by a few quotations were Fletcher, Herbert, Jonson, and Waller. The eighteenth century contributed Collins (the leader, with more than a dozen pictures), Shenstone (with 7, one as late as 1878), Addison, Akenside, Beattie, Falconer, Young, and Erasmus Darwin, from whose *The Botanic Garden* an exhibitor at the Society of British Artists in 1834 drew the motto for his picture: "Now o'er their heads the whizzing whirlwinds breathe, / And the live desert pants and heaves beneath." Perhaps something could be said for *The Fallacies of Hope,* after all. Pictures painted in the first third of the nineteenth century and later had tags from such poets as Campbell (22), Hood (16), Clare, Montgomery, Leigh Hunt, and Kirke White. The gift book set was represented by Felicia Hemans (12), Laetitia Landon, Adelaide Procter, Eliza Cook, Jean Ingelow, and Mrs. Norton. Such names are sufficiently dim today; and even more lost in oblivion are those of Swain, Bowles, Hervey, and (but for his fortuitous connection with Dr. Johnson) the forger-cleric Dr. Dodd.

Once in a while, painters indulged in what today might be called double-dipping: taking their subject (or title) from one literary source and then adorning the picture with a tag from another. The practice was similar to that employed by eighteenth- and nineteenth-century Shakespeare editors, of "illustrating" (elucidating) expressions by citing related lines in the works of other dramatists or poets. Artists seem to have meant to clarify or enhance the subject of the painting by "illustrating" it in that sense. Thus Henry Singleton's *The Taming of the Shrew* (RA 1804) quoted the *Tatler* (No. 231), and Mulready's scene from Scott's *St. Ronan's Well, Mr. Peregrine Touchwood Breaking in upon the Rev. Josiah Cargill* (RA 1832) bore an epigraph from Butler's *Hudibras.* Frith's *A Stage-Coach Adventure* (RA 1848) was based on an incident in Smollett's *Roderick Random,* but its motto was from *Macbeth:* "What! a soldier, and afeard!" A few years later (BI 1854), a figure painting illustrating a line from Moore's *Irish Melodies,* "Rich and rare were the gems she wore," was exhibited under the Keatsian title "A thing of beauty is a joy forever." To these dual references, critics once in a while chipped in a third for good measure. In 1860, Abraham Solomon showed a picture of a group of homeward bound revelers on Waterloo Bridge coming upon the body of a drowned woman just taken from the river. Although the picture was untitled, the subject, insofar as it had any literary relation, obviously was from Hood's poem "The Bridge of Sighs." Solomon, however, quoted *King Lear:* "The gods are just, and of our pleasant vices / Make instruments to scourge us." At least one critic saw, as well, "poor Ophelia."[40]

Such literary echoes as these, if legitimate and properly managed, could be effective enough. But though the assumption was that a quotation would harmonize with the picture, in practice this was by no means always true, especially if the literary context was remembered. Recent critics have pointed out that several of the poetic extracts Constable used were simply at odds with the scene depicted. The lines from Thomson's "Summer" that accompanied his *Landscape: Noon* (1827) describe "the fresher breezes of evening, not the hour of noon."[41]

The quotation was a double-edged tool: it could either amplify the painting or distort, even contradict, the artist's intention. Reviewers sometimes called attention to this discrepancy. They also suggested, only half facetiously, that some pictures, like the "convertible" ones mentioned in the first section of this chapter, were so loosely connected with the letter and spirit of their alleged literary source that the addition of a quotation from another could transform their meaning. When F. R. Pickersgill exhibited his allegorical scene from *The Pilgrim's Progress, Christian Conducted by Charity, Prudence, Piety, and Discretion into the Valley of Humiliation* (RA 1855)—a canvas filled with "knights, ladies, and attendants"—the *Athenaeum* remarked that it "would do for Spenser, if a quotation were attached to it. The Virtues pirouette and waltz round Christian, who bears it with becoming patience."[42]

Often, especially in mid-Victorian times, the quotation leaped from the catalogue to the frame of the picture itself. At today's Tate Gallery alone, Ford Madox Brown's *Lear and Cordelia* has a number of lines from *King Lear* inscribed in the upper corners of the frame, Arthur Hughes's *The Eve of St. Agnes* nine lines from Keats's poem, and Hunt's *Claudio and Isabella* two lines of dialogue from *Measure for Measure.* Pictures in other public galleries, such as Hughes's *Ophelia* and *Enid and Geraint,* Brown's *The Death of Sir Tristram,* Hunt's *Valentine and Sylvia,* and Frank Dicksee's *Juliet on the Balcony,* bear similar quotations from their respective sources. This practice, apart from putting the literary source into the closest possible juxtaposition with the painted illustration, recommended itself to artists' patrons who wanted the greatest value for their money. Contemporary frames were so ornate that they were a notorious example of conspicuous expenditure; Thackeray once described a room hung with "richly carved gilt frames (with pictures in them)."[43] The frame was the equivalent of an ostentatiously luxurious book binding. When, in addition to lavish hand carving and heavy gilt, a quotation from Shakespeare was thrown in, the buyer felt, with some justification, that he was getting his money's worth.

Unless the quotation was inscribed on the frame, or the purchaser of the painting snipped it from the catalogue and pasted it on the back, the association of picture and motto was severed when the picture was removed from the exhibition. But the association would be resumed if the painting subsequently were engraved and the motto placed at the bottom of the print, a circumstance the artist may well have had in mind when he chose the quotation in the first place.

Attractive though the custom of hanging mottoes on pictures undoubtedly was, it never lacked for critics, whose occupational wit it encouraged, as we have seen. Hazlitt seized the opportunity presented by a painting at the British Institution in 1815 to verbally slash both the picture and the source of the quotation: "We could neither understand this picture nor the lines from Lord Byron's *Corsair,* which are intended to explain the subject of it."[44] Whatever reasons may have been urged against the game of tags, painters continued to play it, and reviewers grew steadily more vigorous in their condemnation:

> This practice, we may observe [said a writer in *Fraser's Magazine* in 1860], is becoming an absolute nuisance. If a picture cannot be understood without some such clumsy aid, the wall of the Royal Academy is hardly the proper place for it. If it can, why should a quantity of superfluous prose or poetry be printed merely to afford the catalogue carrier of each party an opportunity of devolving his rounded periods as he reads the passage aloud, which he always does *in extenso,* to the infinite comfort of those bystanders who have read or don't want to read it.[45]

Sixty years after Fuseli asserted the autonomy of the picture enclosed in a frame, at least a few artists still subscribed to the principle. In 1866, the historical genre painter Henry Nelson O'Neil declared in a lecture, "It has been often said that the powers of Art commence where those of language cease; and certainly, if a picture requires any extraneous aid to make its meaning intelligible, it proves that the artist has chosen a subject which is either beyond his power, or else scarcely fitted for pictorial illustration."[46]*

If paintings could be equipped with poetry, there was no reason why traffic should not also go the opposite direction, the pictures inspiring poems that in effect served as *post hoc* mottoes. Some years before Leigh Hunt proposed a gallery of pictures from *The Faerie Queene* to be painted posthumously by a large company of Old Masters (see Part Three, below, under Spenser), Laetitia Elizabeth Landon, a versifier closely identified with the gift-book industry, published in her volume *The Troubadour: Catalogue of Pictures and Historical Sketches* (1825) a series of effusions, "Poetical Sketches of Modern Painters." These were poems inspired by a number of currently exhibited paintings, among them Henry Thomson's *Juliet after the Masquerade* (pl. 147), Stothard's *The Fairy Queen Sleeping* (RA 1825), and Henry Howard's *Fairies on the Sea Shore* (*Iris and Her Train*) (BI 1824). Ten years later, the leading poem in L.E.L.'s volume *The Vow of the Peacock, and Other Poems* was a narrative suggested by Maclise's painting of that name at the Royal Academy—a token of appreciation, no doubt, for the artist's portrait of the poet that was exhibited there in 1830.

On her unpretentious literary plane, Landon's efforts were a symptom of the revival of the old tradition of "iconic poetry"—poems inspired by particular works of art. Southey wrote a poem on a landscape of Poussin, and Lamb wrote one on Leonardo da Vinci's *The Virgin of the Rocks.* Coleridge's "The Garden of Boccaccio" was composed to accompany a plate by Stothard in the *Keepsake* for 1829. Keats, who as Ian Jack has shown was powerfully affected by all the kinds of art available to a young Londoner in the early years of the century, assimilated his memories of classic vases, seen in collections and engravings, in his "Ode on a Grecian Urn."[47]

But it was Wordsworth who most often, among the Romantics, reaffirmed this aspect of the sisterhood of the arts.[48] At various times, he composed poems on Yorkshire landscapes by Richard Westall's brother William, Haydon's often-repeated pictures of Napoleon on St. Helena and Wellington at Waterloo, a painting of Endymion by Luca Giordano that hung on the stairway at Rydal Mount, Raphael's picture of John the Baptist, and Leonardo's *The Last Supper.* None of these occasional poems represents Wordsworth at his most inspired, but his "Elegiac Stanzas Suggested by a Picture of Peele Castle, in a Storm, Painted by Sir George Beaumont" (1805) are quite another matter. This tempest landscape by the poet's steadfast friend and patron evoked and purged his deepest grief over the recent drowning of his brother in a shipwreck off Weymouth. A little later (1811), Wordsworth wrote a sonnet on another of Beaumont's landscapes and several inscriptions for stones and objects of art in the garden of his estate at Coleorton, Leicestershire. One of these was composed for an urn placed at the end of a newly planted avenue in tribute to the memory of Sir Joshua Reynolds. In 1836, nine years after Beaumont's death, Constable sent to the Royal Academy *The Cenotaph,*

*One wonders which of these interpretations O'Neil would have made of his own practice, both before and after this time. In 1839 and 1840, he exhibited paintings with quotations from Byron; and two of his later pictures, *The Night Before Waterloo* (RA 1868) and *An Incident in the Plague of London* (RA 1875) bore epigraphs from Byron and Pepys respectively.

147. Henry Thomson, *Juliet after the Masquerade* (RA 1825) (Walker Art Gallery, Liverpool). A copy of the exhibited picture, which inspired the popular keepsake poet Laetitia Elizabeth Landon to dip her pen lightly in the honorable stream of iconic verse. These lines, from the middle of her "Juliet after the Masquerade," are typical of the whole poem:

> And there the maiden leant, still in her ear
> The whisper dwelt of that young cavalier;
> It was no fancy, he had named the name
> Of love, and at that thought her cheek grew flame:
> It was the first time her young ear had heard
> A lover's burning sigh, or silver word;
> Her thoughts were all confusion, but most sweet,—
> Her heart beat high, but pleasant was its beat.

painted during a stay at Coleorton, as a graceful means of linking the memory of the two men. On that occasion, he inserted in the catalogue the "beautiful lines by Wordsworth" that made the connection explicit.[49]

Dante Gabriel Rossetti, as is well known, wrote many poems, mostly sonnets, to accompany his paintings.[50] A dozen were composed for his oils alone, ranging from *The Blessed Damozel* and *The Girlhood of Mary Virgin* to his narrative subject from contemporary life, *Found.* Rossetti's aversion to exhibiting his paintings prevented the poetry from entering the catalogues, but poems of other Pre-Raphaelites, composed under various circumstances, did appear. After seeing Whistler's *The Little White Girl* (later renamed *Symphony in White, Number Two*), Swinburne wrote a poem, "Before the Mirror," which the artist had printed on a gold label for the frame; two stanzas from the poem were quoted in the catalogue when the picture was shown at the Royal Academy in 1865. William Morris composed short poems to accompany Burne-Jones's famous Briar Rose series (pl. 76).

One of Browning's poems, "Eurydice to Orpheus: A Picture by Leighton," was first printed in the Royal Academy catalogue for 1864. In 1886, he composed four lines for another picture by Leighton, a portrait of "a little girl with golden hair and pale blue eyes," but the picture was not exhibited and the lines were not collected in any edition of Browning's works until 1981. Before their marriage, Elizabeth Barrett wrote a sonnet on Haydon's portrait of Wordsworth. No such poems written in the wake of paintings qualified for the suggestion Oscar Wilde made to Rossetti: why not take out the picture and frame the sonnet?*

*Had he possessed a readier wit, Rossetti might have beaten Wilde to the line. He told Swinburne that his poem for the Whistler painting was better than the picture itself, a judgment with which, said Swinburne, the artist enthusiastically agreed (Swinburne to Ruskin, 11 August [1865], in *The Swinburne Letters*, ed. Cecil Y. Lang [New Haven, Conn., 1959–62], 1:130).

CHAPTER 10

The quality of art criticism, including journalistic wit.—The demise of Ut pictura poesis.—*The influence of preconceptions; artists' fidelity to the literary source an occasion for praise; quibbles over departures from the text; invented scenes.*

A few years ago, it would have been chic to observe that the Victorian painters deserved the low quality of criticism they received. Today, in view of some artists' return to favor, the remark would no longer be regarded as chic. But its assessment of the prevailing level of Victorian art journalism, to use a more accurate term than "criticism," cannot be denied. The fact was that the reviews of the annual exhibitions represented cultural journalism close to its nadir. Editors were reputed to assign the least competent members of their staffs to cover the exhibitions, on the several grounds that they could do no real harm (to the papers, at least), that such assignments could give reporters who were capable of writing about nothing else something to keep them busy, and that in the state of public ignorance of the fine arts, nobody would be the wiser. In 1840, Thackeray wrote:

> The world has been imposed upon by persons calling themselves critics, who, in daily, weekly, monthly prints, protrude their nonsense upon the town. What are these men? Are they educated to be painters?—No! Have they a taste for painting?—No! I know of newspapers in this town . . . which send their reporters indifferently to a police-office or a picture-gallery, and expect them to describe [a] Correggio or a fire in Fleet Street with equal fidelity. And, alas! it must be confessed that our matter-of-fact public of England is itself but a dull appreciator of the arts, and is too easily persuaded by the dull critics who lay down their stupid laws.[1]*

The general incompetence of art critics was still notorious almost forty years later, when Sidney Colvin wrote:

> "Art-criticism" has on the whole been conducted so much at random, that a shade of ridicule and discredit has attached itself to the very word. Both before and since the days of Thackeray's genial creation, F. B. [in *The Newcomes,* 1855],

*This outburst occurred in a preliminary passage of his essay "A Pictorial Rhapsody" (*Fraser's Magazine,* June 1840), in which "Nol Yorke" (William Maginn, the magazine's editor), presiding at a staff dinner, delivered a lengthy toast to "Michael Angelo Titmarsh" (Thackeray) as he was about to make his yearly rounds of the exhibitions. In that festive context, a certain amount of satire must be allowed for. But four years later, Thackeray repeated the idea in his own person, though professing to note some improvement in the situation: "The readers of newspapers will remark this year that the leaders of public opinion have devoted an unusually large space and print to reviews of the fine arts. They have been employing critics who, though they contradict each other a good deal, are yet evidently better acquainted with the subject than critics of old used to be when gentlemen of the profession were instructed to report on a fire, or an Old Bailey trial, or a Greek play, or an opera, or a boxing-match, or a picture gallery, as their turn came" (*Fraser's,* June 1844). An irony remains, insofar as Thackeray presumably included himself among the new, "better acquainted" breed of critics. In any case, the low quality of routine art reviewing that persisted through the following decades is evidence enough that Thackeray's charge, however overstated, was not unfounded.

> the "art-critic" has been an accepted type of the person who pronounces with a light heart on matters which he has been at no pains to understand. We all know in what kind of consideration the business is usually held by artists themselves. . . . Mr. Poynter [the artist], in his volume of lectures lately published, denounces "the ordinary newspaper ignoramus;" saying that "as a rule English art-critics start on their career by criticizing the exhibitions, and trust to time and chance for learning something about art". . . . Nor can it be said that the disesteem in which newspaper criticism is thus held by artists is without warrant. . . .[2]

It says something about the increasing news value of the fine arts that whereas only some twenty journalists were at the Academy's private view in 1848, the 1892 press preview—now a separate occasion—was attended by no fewer than 300.[3] The countless columns they printed across the years are indispensable to the art historian for their descriptions of paintings that have vanished and to the historian of popular culture for their expression of contemporary taste, but as documents of aesthetic experience they have little value, simply because not much aesthetic experience of any consequence seems to have been involved; if it did occur, it was described in brief, simplistic clichés. The reviewer explained the subject of the picture, applied one or two instant tests to the artist's treatment, and passed on to the next painting. Among these critics was no Hazlitt, bringing to bear on works of art his well formulated aesthetic theory, his acute sensibility, his abhorrence of cant, and his powers of compact description.

In Hazlitt's time, one of the most prolific identifiable reviewers was Robert Hunt, who long served as art critic for his brother Leigh Hunt's *Examiner.* He had strong prejudices, but he was more readable and often more perceptive than most of his successors. He does not deserve to be remembered solely for his characterization of Blake in 1809 as "an unfortunate lunatic, whose personal inoffensiveness secures him from confinement."[4] Among the other writers whose contributions made up the annual record of the London art scene were a few whose names are not wholly forgotten today.[5] William Michael Rossetti, the nonartist member of the Pre-Raphaelite coterie, for many years wrote for the *Spectator,* the *Academy,* the *Critic,* and other papers of lesser note.[6] The playwright Tom Taylor reviewed for the *Times* from 1857 to 1880. To artists who resented his condemning, on the basis of a minute's glance, a painting on which a year's labor had been expended, he made up in pedantry what he lacked by way of artistic training and knowledge. Francis T. Palgrave, like Rossetti and Taylor a full-time civil servant, wrote for the *Saturday Review* but is said to have declined an invitation to contribute art reviews to the *Times* "on the ground that he could not conscientiously praise the work of many of the smaller contemporary artists," a scruple not shared by many of his colleagues.[7] Frederic George Stephens, another member of the Pre-Raphaelite circle (pl. 252), was the *Athenaeum*'s critic for forty years (1861–1901), being succeeded in that office by Roger Fry. His predecessors on the *Athenaeum* had included Keats's friend John Hamilton Reynolds (1828–ca.1834), Henry Fothergill Chorley, later to become widely known as a music critic (1836–41), and Frank Stone (late 1840s–mid-50s).

Whatever gifts these individual writers had as judges of pictures—several, like Stephens and Stone, were practicing artists—were suppressed by the general mediocrity that was accepted as the normal condition of art journalism. When their work was unsigned, as it was except

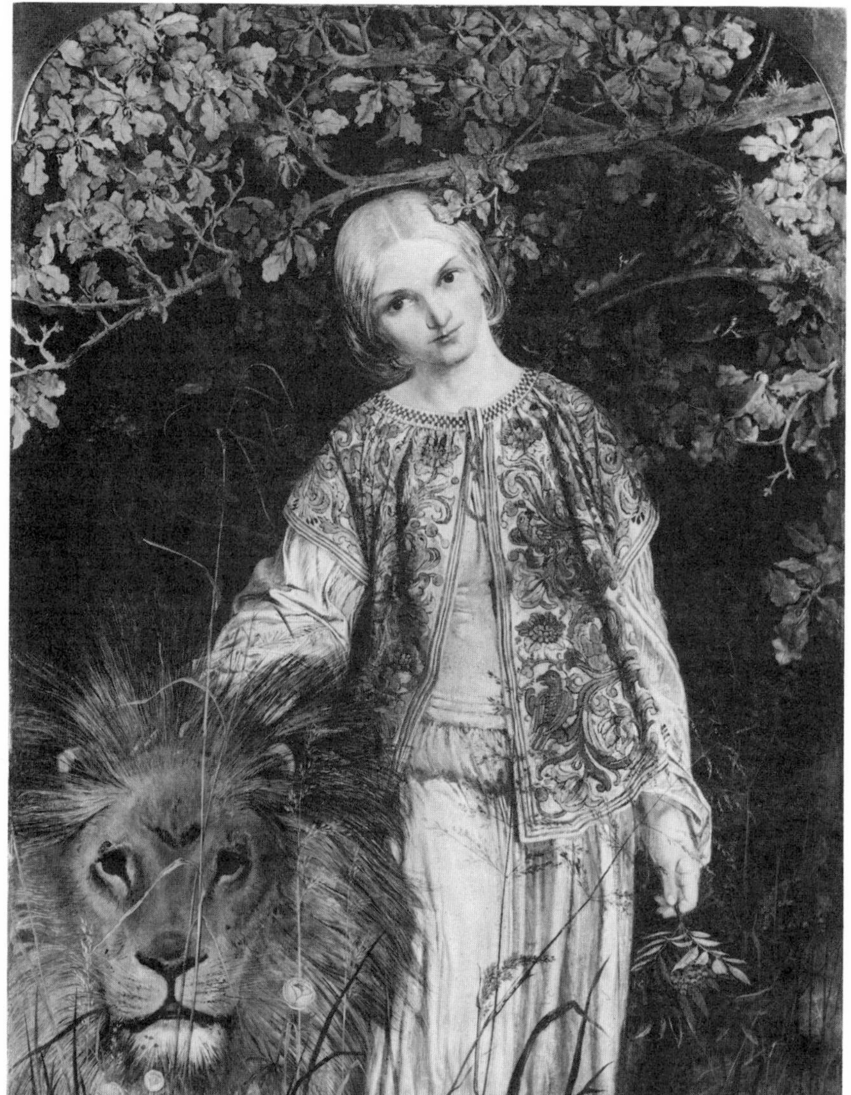

148. William Bell Scott, *Una and the Lion* (RA 1860) (National Gallery of Scotland). The reception of this painting, by a member of the Pre-Raphaelite circle, was spiced with typical "wit": "A very small Una, whose mild, not to say inane, look would astonish Spenser, leads a very large lion. This beast's mane is in a state of permanent erection, so that he looks more like a magnified porcupine with 'fretful quills' than fair Una's 'unruly page'" (*Athenaeum,* 19 May). "Una is simply a wooden lay figure with a badly-mended joint in the neck; and the lion, not to be conventional, carries a mane of electrified cocoa-fibre round his neck, and our old friend the butterfly upon his nose" (*Fraser's Magazine,* June, 61: 881). Whistler's adoption of the butterfly as his trademark was a dozen years in the future.

(sometimes) in the magazines, only the recurrence of certain pet prejudices or foibles can distinguish one man's writing from another's. One quality they did have in common, however, was levity. Although all professed to take the fine arts seriously, they could not resist the occupational impulse to hang alongside any painting they disliked a specimen of their wit. One is tempted to think that in his recital of the deficiencies of his fellow reviewers Thackeray should have added that editors often assigned the art beat to the office joker. No form of painting was immune, but pictures from literary sources were more vulnerable than most; it may have seemed particularly fitting to apply verbal humor to pictures from verbal sources. When journalists were sent to see the annual exhibitions and found literary pictures that had neither poetry nor art, they were compelled to liven up the stale commonplaces inspired by the year's crop of commonplace pictures on stale subjects by writing of them with a desperate flippancy. For this reason among others, to read much of their output at one sitting is as numbing a chore as to go through a whole volume of *Punch*—cartoons, conundrums, puns, skits, and all—without a single intermission. Although the art reviewers of the thirties and forties applied plenty of lighthearted as well as vicious remarks to paintings they disliked or failed to understand, the incidence of attempted humor increased after mid-century, when the controversial arrival of the Pre-Raphaelites made unprecedented demands on their fund of invective.

Probably the worst thing that could be said of a run-of-the-mine painting was that, to use a modern word the Victorian art viewer would have welcomed, it was nothing more than *kitsch.* In an era when the fine arts retained, or even improved on, the claim to dignity that they asserted when history painting still was vestigially regarded as the pinnacle of artistic ambition, to denounce a painting as fit only for some utilitarian or frivolous purpose or to associate it with a trivial form of art was to impute to it the ultimate vulgarity: it was a debasement of a noble art. Thus *Fraser's Magazine,* in a routine put-down, said in 1831 of a painting from Prior's poem "Henry and Emma," "We think we have met with something very much like it before, figuring as a frontispiece to a sixpenny song-book, with the only difference that here the figures are magnified to the size of life, which is not by any means an improvement on the original idea."[8] At various times, paintings were described as fit only for scented soap, bonbon, or glove boxes (Marcus Stone's scene from *Much Ado About Nothing,* 1861), or likened to a "Brummagem tea-tray" (the "iridescent rays of mother-of-pearl" in A. J. Woolmer's painting of Portia, 1868), and "sampler-work or tea-board illustration" (one William Rimer's *Ivanhoe and Rowena,* 1853).[9]

The point need not be pursued, because additional samples of comic art reviewing are necessarily scattered through these pages. They provide a convenient background against which the two most readable Victorian commentators on the annual exhibitions, Thackeray and Ruskin, may be judged. Thackeray's comments were not often concerned with literary pictures, but those that were, were wholly characteristic of the man.[10] His observations on the pictures at the exhibitions and on the art scene of his day are of a piece with his other journalism, jaunty, expansive, and good-humored. His is the manner of a literate *flâneur* who has wandered into a gallery and entertains his companions with a running commentary that is often shrewd, appreciative of the practical difficulties an artist has faced and perhaps surmounted, and invariably engaging. Even what might be, from the pens of his less gifted colleagues, nothing more than stale joking acquires a special flavor when Thackeray picks it up, if only, perhaps, because we know who wrote it. Its flavor, at the very least, is that of the fresh-voiced contributors to the early *Punch:* a parody here (the mock-Spenserian title of a fictitious painting, *Sir Botibol Rescues Una from Sir Uglimore in the Cave of the Enchantress Ichthyosaura*), a comic fancy there (" . . . the Gow Chrom [in a painting from *The Fair Maid of Perth*] is a theatre-hero, and the Glee Maiden, in pink stockings, looks as if her discomfiture arose from her vain efforts to keep her clothes on her back").[11]

Except for a possibly distinctive Thackerayan nuance, such waggeries were oppressively customary in the art criticism of the time. And the same is true of Ruskin's "remorseless contumely," to adopt his own phrase. Attention has seldom been paid to the humor in his art criticism, nor is there any special reason why it should be. But his criticism of exhibited paintings, including those from literary sources, is shot through with the kind of humor he shared with his inferiors—which shows how irresistibly contagious it was. Most of it is found in his annual series of *Academy Notes,* written the moment he returned from the private view, sped through the press, and sold just outside the Academy doors as an instructional alternative to the official catalogue.[12]

Once the foolery is strained out, what remains from the busy pens of Thackeray's and Ruskin's colleagues is an extensive body of criticism that contains some serious ideas, indispensable, however misguided they strike us as being, to our understanding of Victorian art culture. The very lack of individuality in the routine reviews has its value, because it enables us the more accurately to gauge the enlightened public taste of the time, which the critics purported to express, as contrasted with the "popular" taste they never tired of belittling even though their own approached it oftener than they admitted.

In the days before cultural journalism came to be divided among specialists, several art critics writing for newspapers and intellectual reviews were also, like Hazlitt before them, literary and/or dramatic critics. These versatile men brought to the art exhibitions a larger knowledge of English literature than the average gallerygoer possessed, an equipment that certainly affected their judgments of paintings with literary content, though how deeply or in what directions it is hard to detect. Whatever their professional interest in literature, their writings do offer a fresh way of sampling contemporary literary taste. In their roles as critics of painted literary illustration, they inadvertently reveal their opinions of scenes, characters, "atmosphere," moral content, and the other components of plays, poems, and novels. These attitudes are unstudied; it is pictures that are being reviewed, not books. And so art criticism becomes, by implication, literary criticism as well. Although there is no room in this book to explore the specific resemblances, anyone conversant with the main principles of nineteenth-century literary criticism will find striking parallels in the criteria applied to the year's output of literary paintings.

Missing from the art criticism of the Victorian era was much mention of the old *ut pictura poesis* concept, which was now a dead issue except insofar as it turned up, pro forma, in the lectures (usually that on "Invention") of painters themselves.[13] Haydon affirmed its truth on the provincial lecture circuit in 1835,[14] and so, some years later, in his Royal Academy lectures (1843), did Henry Howard, who repeated, once more, the hoary description of painting as "mute poetry" and poetry as "speaking painting" and went on to recommend that "a poetical feeling should be intermingled to the utmost possible extent in all [painters'] productions of whatever class. . . . As far as its own peculiar demands will admit, a picture should be conceived like a poem. . . . "[15] But Ruskin voiced the considered opinion of the day when he deplored the "infinite confusion" caused by "the careless and illogical custom of opposing painting to poetry, instead of regarding poetry as consisting in a noble use, whether of colours or words. . . . Poetry is the employment of either for the noblest purposes."[16]

Replacing the theoretical issue of the sisterhood of the arts (though the well-worn phrase itself continued to be too handy to retire) was the related one of illustration. Though by no means new in criticism, it came into prominence in the early Victorian years as the result of both the unprecedented popularity of subjects from literature and recent technological improvements. In their "address to readers" of the first issue (1842) of the *Illustrated London News,* already quoted in chapter 4, the editors announced:

> For the past ten years we have watched with admiration and enthusiasm the progress of illustrative art, and the vast revolution which it has wrought in the world of publication through all the length and breadth of this mighty empire. . . . It has given to fancy a new dwelling-place, to imagination a more permanent throne. . . . Art—as now fostered, and redundant in the peculiar and facile department of wood engraving—has, in fact, become the bride of literature; genius has taken her as its handmaid, and popularity has crowned her with laurels that only seem to grow the greener the longer they are worn.

To which the aged Wordsworth responded four years later, confronting pompous prose with dreadful verse, in a sonnet bearing the unpoetic title of "Illustrated Books and Newspapers":

> Now prose and verse sunk into disrepute
> Must lacquey a dumb Art that best can suit
> The taste of this once-intellectual Land.
> A backward movement surely have we here,
> From manhood,—back to childhood; for the age—
> Back towards caverned life's first rude career.
> Avaunt this vile abuse of pictured page!
> Must eyes be all in all, the tongue and ear
> Nothing? Heaven keep us from a lower stage!

At that date, Wordsworth could not have foreseen that cave drawings, far from being an emblem of man's most savage condition, would be esteemed a century later as evidence of the first glimmerings of the aesthetic impulse in prehistoric man. But his vehemence was shared by few. "Illustration," not replacing the printed word but supplementing it, was regarded all but universally as a welcome accompaniment to the contemporary March of Mind.

As it was popularly used then, "illustration" meant "to elucidate (a description, etc.) by means of drawings or pictures" (the seventh definition in the *Oxford English Dictionary*). This was the sense in which it was used by Wordsworth and the pioneers of "illustrated" journalism: the literal transformation of verbal images into visual ones, or even the employment of images to represent a subject initially, without the prior use of language or simultaneously with it, as in the reporting of news events. In art criticism, it had a more specialized meaning: the simple representation of a literary text.* Used strictly, "illustration" in this sense suggested a borrowed pictorialism that lacked any but the most minimal, unavoidable intervention of the artist.

The prior existence of the literary subject offered artists two opportunities beyond that of faithful representation, which would in itself revive the associations already present in the minds of the people who knew the literary source. They could exercise their prerogative of invention (sanctioned by all academic lecturers)† by suggesting a new reading of the familiar scene. Or, going beyond what the academic lecturers, from Reynolds down to Henry Howard, had conceived of as merely the addition of a vague, undefinable "poetic feeling" to the subject, they could invest it with a wholly new beauty, subordinating the subject, as received from the

*This definition of *illustration* differs from that offered by Martin Meisel: "interpretive re-creation" (*Realizations,* p. 32). Mine is closer to what he means by *realization.* The discrepancy is due in part to our different perspectives and to some degree, perhaps, to our reliance on different samplings of quotations.

†And rather unsatisfactorily defined by the *Oxford English Dictionary* as ". . . the devising of a subject, idea, or *method of treatment* [emphasis added], by exercise of the intellect or imagination; 'the choice and production of such objects as are proper to enter into the composition of a work of art.'"

author, to their Romantic need for self-expression. Representation might, then, turn into the expressivism that was central to the Romantic conception of art, as was the case with the great landscapists, who, once liberated from the constraints of imitating Claude or Poussin, availed themselves of that freedom to see and record nature as their temperaments prompted them to do. They *could;* but should they? This was the issue that underlay most of the criticism to which Victorian paintings from literary sources were subjected.

According to Sidney Colvin, looking back in 1874, the great flaw in eighteenth-century treatments of literary themes had been the artists' reluctance to go beyond the letter of their source, their commitment, that is, to "illustration" in the strict sense:

> It occurred to them only to follow in the wake of the narrative, and to aim at interesting the mind, through the avenue of the senses, by showing how those circumstances and incidents happened which had already been detailed to it by literature. In inspiring itself by the strict text of Shakespeare, Milton, and the poets, the arts of design had still less chance of developing their appropriate and peculiar effects. The inventors of the conceptions had fully developed them from their own side, and in connection with particular passages and junctures of incident and feeling; in this shape they had won their popularity; they were not such as the arts could go to work upon independently, and manage from the side which best suited themselves. This danger for one set of arts in becoming subordinate to the other, and inspiring itself from the works of the other, whereas both ought to inspire themselves from different aspects of the same original conception, was generally overlooked in the century. The criticism of the century had not apprehended the notion of an independent development of conceptions, as ideas in literature and as images in art. Criticism imagined quite erroneously (and it was against this error that Lessing wrote his "Laokoön") that the ancient artists had but wrought in order to illustrate the text of the ancient poets.[17]

Colvin oversimplified, of course. The early illustrators' very *lack* of servility to their sources strikes us everywhere, not least in Boydell's Shakespeare pictures, where it often led to grotesque incongruity. But the discrepancies were largely those of style, as in the persistent custom of depicting widely diversified literary subjects with the uniform elegance and unreality of the French rococo. Colvin overlooked Fuseli, for one—a not unnatural omission, because Fuseli did not loom very prominently in the retrospect of a century. But, as we now recognize, his many mannerist designs from Shakespeare or Milton—he cherished a very individual conception of *Paradise Lost*—were the expression of a strong, unique personal vision, as, even more obviously, were Blake's versions. At the end of Fuseli's life, John Martin, another illustrator of Milton, claimed the Romantic artist's privilege of freedom of interpretation. All three artists fitted the requirement laid down by a modern commentator on Miltonic illustration:

> . . . A persuasive illustration does not merely or necessarily take account of everything in the passage or conform to the conception of the critic. We cannot confine the success of the illustration to accuracy in this kind any more than we can judge the merit of Shakespeare's image of Cleopatra by his fidelity to Plutarch. The painter is to the poem as an actor is to a playwright or a performer to a composer. . . . We accept the vision of Blake and the anachronism of Martin as imaginative acts faithful to the spirit of the poem. . . . What we ask of illustrations for *Paradise Lost,* then, is something like a new poem upon an old, and in what may be called answerable style. We ask a fresh creative act in which the painter either captures the essence of his subject as we conceive it or so

> transmutes his subject that we are required to see it anew. . . . Fuseli's flamboyant nudes are not untrue to an Adam censured by Raphael for his susceptibility to an Eve fairest of her daughters and vain of her beauty. Yet they are indisputably in Fuseli's own idiom. And we must read Martin, so to speak, in awareness of the aesthetic and social currents of his time. Part of Martin's language is the sense of space and grandeur in *Paradise Lost;* and part of it is the stag, the lion, the dinosaur, the gas arc-lights. . . . *Illustration finally is illumination.*[18] (Emphasis added.)

Theoretically (again), the coming of Romanticism should have given a mighty impulse to this ideal of the creative interpretation of literature in art. "As Romanticism begins," Peter Conrad has written, "all the arts aspire to the condition of literature, the treasury of moving or ennobling subject-matter, so that painting is assigned the task of illustration"—illustration, that is, in the broad sense, as Turner "illustrated" Nature.[19]

The Romantic poets voiced their respect for their forerunners by taking old themes and making them their own in the form of new treatments, as Keats did with stories from Boccaccio, and Coleridge with ballads. A writer in *Fraser's Magazine* in 1842 urged painters to follow their example. "We once heard a Scotch poet complain that there was no more room for poets less than Shakespeare," he said.

> [But] poets create subjects; poets take up subjects already famous; and, with that rare art which belongs peculiarly to genius, give to common topics a fresh and increasing interest. A great painter will create a position; or, if he adopts a well-known attitude, will, by touch, character, and colour (the very soul of the picture), palliate the robbery by making us forget what is old in the high excellencies of what is new. A painter who will complain of a want of subjects is what Johnson would call "a barren rascal." . . . Nothing . . . but complete novelty and success can justify the taking up subjects already familiar to us all.[20]

Implicit in much criticism of Victorian literary painting was the assumption that few artists were up to the challenge presented by their recourse to literary subjects. Only the exceptional painter, it was thought, could maintain the delicate balance between the pressures and impulses generated by the literary source and those originating in the artist's sensibility. (The additional conflict between literary substance and artistic style—the simple issue of appropriateness—was seldom if ever recognized.) William Michael Rossetti was one of the rare critics who articulated the idea, and he did so rather belatedly (in the late 1850s), when the Pre-Raphaelites, whose in-house apologist he was, had defied convention by infusing a strong element of subjectivity in their paintings of literary themes:

> That line of pictorial work wherein the artist renders himself illustrator of another man's ideas is continually taken up by painters who have little of their own to draw upon, and who cling to a hint from any quarter; but it is in reality one of the most difficult of all to manage. It demands much self-abnegation on the artist's part, and earnest study of his subject-matter; and presents the double pitfall of too little originality, and too much. No common mind is required in order to enter into another mind's workings. The artist who gives too little of himself is pretty sure to be a weak man: the artist who gives too much commits the lesser fault, and one which, in the case of a superior man, carries its own palliation with it; yet it vitiates the work of art as an *illustration.*[21]

Shrewd and sympathetic though Rossetti's understanding of the literary painter's dilemma was, his phrasing seems to reflect true uncertainty on his own part. Originality, the artist's exercise of his Romantic prerogative to transform an existing literary artifact into a new creation as the poets had sometimes done, was to be valued, of course—witness the freedom claimed by the artists belonging to the Rossetti circle—but at the cost of his picture's illustrative function?

A few years later (1866), Henry Nelson O'Neil, who produced at least a score of literary pictures, carried Rossetti's idea of "self-abnegation" further, urging in a Royal Academy lecture that the artist completely efface his identity as Keats did when he entered the soul of the sparrow pecking in the gravel:

> . . . The really great artist . . . makes all the resources of his art auxiliary to the subject, into the spirit of which he throws himself, with such a power of abstraction that he becomes a spectator of the scene depicted; nay, even in delineating the varied feelings that animate the actors, he assumes, for a time, the part itself—smiling with the gay, or mourning with the sad. And he who, in depicting history or poetry, cannot so forget his own identity, whatever may be his mechanical power, never can attain success.[22]

There is no evidence that painters of literary subjects were conscious of any such tension between the claims of mimesis (illustration) and expressivism. No Victorian artist was as deeply concerned with the aesthetics of his profession as Reynolds had been, and none left any such quantity of private records as Haydon did. None, so far as the printed record reveals, seems to have been deeply introspective. We cannot tell whether, if the pressures of popular taste had not been so strong, artists would have responded more noticeably than they did to the liberating appeal of Romanticism. Nor can we tell whether they were irritably aware of the restraining influence that the use of literary sources had upon the free play of the imagination, the printed page intervening between them and the observable world about them. In practice, the theoretical conflict was resolved so decisively as to leave no doubt where the weight of popular preference, as reflected by journalism, lay. For every review objecting that an artist followed an author's description too closely (" . . . the pencil has attempted a fac-simile from the [author's] pen": the *Athenaeum* on Sir William Allan's picture from Scott's *The Fair Maid of Perth,* 1832),[23] there were a hundred that approved a painting on the ground that "the pencil of the artist has most successfully identified itself with the pen of the Scottish bard" (*Fraser's Magazine* on another picture by Allan, from Burns's "Tam o' Shanter," three years later).[24] Illustrators, no matter how eminent or how skilled, were expected to preserve the integrity of their source, at whatever cost to whatever urge they felt to indulge their private vision.

The only exception applied to the "ideal pictures" mentioned in the preceding chapter. These were of two kinds. In one, the artist candidly used the literary text, typically a line or two of evocative poetry, as the *donnée* for a free composition, more decorative than most, that did not purport to represent the content of the literary work. In the other, he simply adopted a dominant figure from a literary source—an allegorical or mythological character, for example—as the personification of an abstract moral or intellectual principle, again without reference to the text. (Eighteenth-century "role playing" paintings often belonged to this latter category, though the term "ideal picture" was not then used.)

The response of the common viewer or his surrogate, the art critic, to a literary painting, and therefore the valuation he placed on it, was dictated by his preconceptions, which amounted to an adamant reverence for what he deemed to be the "truth" of the literary text. The power of these preconceptions had long been recognized, by Reynolds in his seventh discourse (1777), by Lamb in his outbursts against Boydell's Shakespeare Gallery, and by that unofficial lawgiver to budding artists Sir George Beaumont, who told both Haydon and Wilkie that, desirable as it was for aspiring painters to acquire a "poetic feeling" from reading books, they should avoid taking actual subjects from literature, for, as he wrote Haydon, "you have always the disadvantage of having an admirable picture to contend with already formed in the minds of the circle—nay, different pictures in different minds of your spectators—and there is a chance, if yours does not happen to coincide (which is impossible in all cases) that justice will not be done you."[25]

In the lecture quoted above, O'Neil saw in the very strength of these preconceptions an equally strong challenge to the artist. He recognized, as Eagles had done,

> the difficulty to be encountered in the pictorial representation of the poet's creations, whose shadowy outlines are solely filled up according to the reader's fancy, and who, consequently, can only be satisfied in proportion as the painted image resembles the spiritual form of his own conceptions. And yet this same impossibility of satisfying all minds becomes an additional source of advantage to a great artist; for it is in his power, by the strength and beauty of his delineations, to overthrow for a time all preconceived ideas, and to make the real impression of his genius usurp the place hitherto filled by fancy alone.[26]

This is essentially what W. M. Rossetti had said a few years earlier. But the fact was that few reviewers were willing to let time reconcile an ingrained preconception with an artist's different view of the literary subject, interesting and valid though this might be. The aesthetic effect of a literary picture, indeed, was largely irrelevant (though the precise valuation placed on it differed from critic to critic), and its emotional impact was inextricably connected with the effect already associated with the scene or character depicted.

Appreciation of art, therefore, was inseparable from appreciation of literature; "in talking of the one," as a writer in 1842 put it when praising Maclise's *The Origin of the Harp* (pl. 332), "we imperceptibly glide away into pleasant remembrances of the other."[27] But this very recognition, on an everyday level, of the sisterhood of the arts carried its built-in risk to the artist. As reviewers of the exhibitions chatted on about the subjects of the pictures on display, they evinced a sternly proprietary attitude toward English literature, a sign of the great prestige it enjoyed in contemporary culture. Their message was clear: Don't tamper with our literature. Praiseworthy as a painting might be on its own terms, it was inescapably rendered vulnerable to comparison with its source. One form of mild libel that cropped up from time to time was the assertion that an artist had not actually read the book he purported to illustrate; another was that he was simply not qualified to deal with literary subjects. Good cases could have been made for both charges.

The congeniality of the artist with the author he was illustrating—a manifestation of that pearl beyond price in Romantic aesthetic theory, the faculty called "sympathy"—was always singled out for praise when it could be detected. Robert Hunt said of Stothard's portrayal (RA 1811) of the dispossessed family leaving their old cottage in *The Deserted Village,*

149. Charles R. Leslie, *Sir Plume Demands the Restoration of the Lock* (RA 1854) (Tate Gallery, London). A sketch for the exhibited painting, which was commissioned by Leslie's patron John Gibbons. Millais modeled for the head of Lord Petre; the setting is a room at Hampton Court, with details of furniture from Petworth.

"No man understands so well as Mr. Stothard the union of grace with the rustic character; he is therefore a most faithful delineator of the artless grace of Goldsmith."[28]

The self-effacing fidelity with which Leslie illustrated Sir Roger de Coverley going to church, accompanied by the Spectator, was unquestionably responsible for the acclaim that painting received when it was exhibited at the Royal Academy in 1819. Hunt may be allowed to voice the consensus:

> To excite so universal and strong a sensation as this picture does, is indeed an indubitable proof of the force and faithfulness with which he has transferred to canvass the characters mentioned in No. 112 of the *Spectator*; for interwoven with our feelings and memory as they are by the reading from infancy of that justly popular work, the pictured characters would have had but a weak effect, did they fall short of the written ones of old so much read and understood. . . .[29]

Praise of the artist's "truthfulness" sometimes took the form of a reference to previous maltreatments of the subject in art or on the stage. Thus in 1835, the *Times* welcomed another painting (not Allan's) of "Tam o' Shanter" with the comment that "it was high time" that the character

> should be represented somewhat in accordance with the notions which Burns's immortal poem has engendered. The abominable liberties which have been taken with the hero of one of the merriest and choicest poems of its size in our language (if we may call the language in which it is written ours), first, by being cut in stone-mason's work,* and next by being represented on the stage by Mr. Farren, who would seem to have as accurate a conception of Tam o' Shanter as he would have of Prester John, made it necessary that someone should rescue that King of Good Fellows from such profanation.[30]

But although critics agreed that painters should respect their literary sources, they differed on what constituted fidelity, because the individual response that "sympathy" entailed could not be wholly suppressed even at

*A self-taught sculptor named James Thom had recently carved statues of Tam o' Shanter and Souter Johnny, which, after being seen by 90,000 paying customers when they were exhibited in London, had been installed at the poet's birthplace at Alloway. Thom made sixteen replicas for various patrons, and an equally humble imitator, a Lanarkshire mason, cashed in on his success by carving eight life-sized statues representing Burns's "The Jolly Beggars."

a time when reaction to art and literature was controlled by powerful standards of public taste, and subject to the prevailing morality and rules of what was and was not admissible in art. Although the reviewers saw the same canvases, they often saw them differently, just as they retained differing recollections of the poems and plays that were illustrated. In 1831, the *Literary Gazette* said of Leslie's *Uncle Toby and the Widow Wadman* (pl. 45), "Could Sterne have beheld such an illustration of the scene he [Leslie] has so slily and humorously described, he would have hurled his wig up into the air with delight"; but the *Times* grumbled, "My uncle Toby looks too knowing by half; it is not the Uncle Toby of our fancy."[31]

In 1854, there was vehement disagreement on the fidelity to Pope of Leslie's scene from *The Rape of the Lock* (pl. 149). Ruskin, calling it "an absolute masterpiece," declared the year after it was exhibited, "Nor was it less admirable as a reading of Pope; for every subordinate character had been studied with such watchful reverence to every word in which it is alluded to throughout the poem, that it seemed to me as if the spirit of the poet had risen beside the painter as he worked, and guided every touch of the pencil."[32] The *Examiner* agreed: "It is high praise but just praise to say that the more thoroughly a man has entered into the refined spirit of Pope's mock-heroic, the more fully will he perceive the tact and skill with which Mr. Leslie has translated it into the painter's language."[33] The *Athenaeum,* on the other hand, complained, "The humour is heavy; the mock-heroic of the poem quite lost, and an air of dull seriousness thrown over the whole."[34]

The vigor with which reviewers attacked artists' supposed violation of a poet's integrity depended somewhat on who the poet was. There were, for instance, few complaints against Milton pictures on this score, apart from the tendency of Etty and his followers to stress the nudity they too eagerly inferred from the text. A writer in 1832 recommended to Etty, apropos of his picture from *Comus* (pl. 150), that he "study more attentively the dignified sobriety of style which characterizes Milton: the old

150. William Etty, *Sabrina and Her Nymphs* (1841) (Leicestershire Museum and Art Gallery, Leicester). A copy of the painting with the same title that was exhibited at the Royal Academy in 1831; one of several subjects Etty derived from *Comus* (another: pl. 275).

Puritan bard has none of those startling, unsober postures [imposed by Etty on the attendant nymphs], in all his works."[35] The authors who were most often defended against the painter's obtuseness and want of sympathy were those with whom, in the Victorian fashion, readers felt themselves to be on terms of easy personal fellowship—the Shakespeare of the comedies and romances, the genial Addison of the *Spectator,* Goldsmith, Sterne as personified by Tristram Shandy and the Yorick of *A Sentimental Journey.* Even the admired Wilkie was not exempt from censure. Although, when his late picture of *The Cotter's Saturday Night* (pl. 308) was exhibited in 1837, the *Athenaeum* observed that "Wilkie, in his *younger* works, has displayed the very genius requisite for the illustration of Burns—that genius which detects and can display the poetry and humour so closely allied in peasant life,"[36] the *Literary Gazette* lamented that his depiction of the old cotter "has nothing patriarchal in his appearance" despite Burns's specific description of the sire "Turning o'er with patriarchal grace, / The big ha' Bible."[37]

This confrontation of the artist with the plain evidence of the text on small points of detail was a favorite form of journalistic pedantry. (One can imagine a reviewer sauntering from room to room at the Academy, catalogue in one hand and a copy of Shakespeare in the other.) Early in his career, Frederic Leighton was reproved for portraying Lady Capulet as an old woman when she was, in fact, just twenty-eight years old.[38]* Henry O'Neil was told he should not portray Pericles as old and "Lear-like" when by the critic's rather shaky reckoning ("Pericles was a young and lusty knight of 20, or thereabouts, when he wedded [Mariana's] mother, and Mariana is clearly not above 18 when her father recovers her"—Q. E. D:) he was under forty.[39] Ophelia should not be shown seated on the grass in the garden, because the frightening encounter she described to Polonius took place while she was sewing in her room.[40] F. R. Pickersgill was deemed unfaithful to Milton when he painted Samson "naked to the waist" instead of being clad "in the slavish habit, ill-fitted weeds / O'er-worn and soiled," as Milton explicitly said.[41] In a picture of Byron's golden-haired Genevra, looking out at a star, the artist was half right, at any rate: "The eyelashes," said a reviewer, "are *long,* according to the quotation from Byron; but surely they are not dark, as the description would suggest."[42]†

To be sure, all but one of these examples happen to date from a span of seven years (1853–59), a time when this form of one-upmanship seems to have been especially popular. Later critics generally allowed artists a bit more license. In 1871, the *Art Journal* accepted as "pardonable" Robert Hillingford's interpretation of a passage in *The Merchant of Venice* (2.6) in which the text has Jessica addressing her speech "Here, catch this casket . . . " from an open window; the artist, instead, represented her as "having descended with it in her hand, and still carrying it, while she looks timidly and warily round, lest her movements should be watched by some concealed tale-bearer."[43] Still, even at this late date the discrepancy between text and presentation seemed sufficiently important to be called to the spectator's attention.

This literalism sometimes took another turn, when the critic professed to find no warrant whatsoever in the text for the artist's detail. A portrayal of Launce reproving his dog in *The Two Gentlemen of Verona* evoked the query, "Why is the dog blind of an eye? We know no Shakespearean authority for that and we do not think that either Mr. Collier or Mr.

*Leighton evidently was under no such pressure as the market-conscious print-publisher Charles Heath applied to artists like Kenny Meadows. When Meadows showed him drawings of Mrs. Page and her daughter in *The Merry Wives of Windsor* that he had made for one of Heath's sleek gift books, Heath insisted that the mother be portrayed as young as her child: "I don't care about her maternity, or Shakespeare, or anything else. You must not make her more than twenty or nobody will buy!" (W. B. Scott, *Autobiographical Notes,* 1:114–15.)

† The reviewer was himself no more than half right. In his "sonnet: To Genevra," Byron praised "thy eyes' blue tenderness, thy long fair hair," but said nothing about her eyelashes.

151. Charles R. Leslie, *Dinner Scene, "The Merry Wives of Windsor"* (RA 1838) (Victoria & Albert Museum, Crown Copyright). The title given this painting when first exhibited was "The Principal Characters in *The Merry Wives of Windsor,* assembled in the house of Mr. Page; a scene not in the play, but *supposed* to take place in the first act. '—There's pippins and cheese to come.'" Slender (pl. 82) remains bashful at the right.

Halliwell [two contemporary Shakespearean editors] would allow it."[44] Holding the artist strictly to the literary text was a device repeatedly adopted by Turner's malicious critics. Six years after he exhibited the "utterly incomprehensible daub"[45] that was titled with the fictitious quotation from *The Merchant of Venice*, Turner exhibited an even more controversial painting, *Juliet and Her Nurse* (RA 1836), which was really a montage of scenes from different parts of Venice. "Amidst so many absurdities," said the *Blackwood's* reviewer, "we scarcely stop to ask why Juliet and her nurse should be at Venice."[46] Surely Shakespeare never located them there.*

As if in partial compensation for being kept on a tight rein, artists were generally given leave to develop a mere hint in the text into a full-fledged exercise of literary fancy. They availed themselves of the same freedom they enjoyed when they painted legendary scenes from the lives of great artists and more or less apocryphal biblical scenes (Dyce's *St. John Leading the Blessed Virgin from the Tomb;* J. R. Herbert's *Our Saviour Subject to His Parents at Nazareth;* and, most famously as far as English painters were concerned, Millais's *Christ in the House of His Parents*). Concurrently, the same thing was happening in literature—sentimental popularizers like Mary Cowden Clarke were writing the prehistory of Shakespeare's heroines, tracing their supposed lives up to the moment when they stepped from the wings—and in the theater itself, where uncanonical scenes sometimes were interpolated into the Shakespearean text to represent what was only mentioned, developing a mere textual hint into an extra passage in the dramatic action.

There were, for one thing, scenes that took place offstage, though referred to in the dialogue. The most frequently painted scene of this sort was the dinner at Mr. Page's house in the first act of *The Merry Wives of Windsor* (pl. 151). In his portrayal, which was several times imitated, Leslie gathered Falstaff, Mrs. Page, Anne Page, Mrs. Ford, Bardolph, and others as they might have appeared had the script called for the dinner to be performed before the audience.

*Turner's moving the scene from Verona to Venice was no more culpable than Otway's moving it to Rome in his "adaptation." The latter distance is considerably greater.

152. Paul Falconer Poole, *The Death of Cordelia* (RA 1858) (Victoria & Albert Museum, Crown Copyright). The *Saturday Review* (15 May) objected to the license that the artist, "a hopeless eccentric," exercised in depicting this moment in the last scene of *King Lear:* "It is very ridiculous in Mr. Poole to introduce . . . a prominent female in a remorseful attitude, who can not be Goneril or Regan . . . for . . . both are dead by this time, . . . [and] how does Mr. Poole know that Shakespeare's Goneril or Regan would have been remorseful?" A more niggling critic would have pointed out that it should be Lear, not Edgar, who applies the feather test to Cordelia. Compare Barry's treatment of the same scene, pl. 7.

Even oftener depicted were previous actions that in the text were described retrospectively by participants or reported by breathless eyewitnesses or messengers. The scene in Brabantio's house during which, as Othello recalls in act 1, scene 3, he narrated his perilous adventures to a rapt Desdemona was painted so often that Victorians may well have come to believe it actually occurred in the play. The recurrently painted death of Ophelia no doubt encouraged a similar misapprehension: the scene is only described by Gertrude. Duncan's wild horses, a subject of animal painters, are not seen in *Macbeth,* though they are vividly described by Ross (2.4). Pictures from the history plays were especially rich in unperformed actions: the murder of the Princes in the Tower in *Richard III,* reported at secondhand by Tyrell, who had the account from the actual murderers, Dighton and Forrest; the "pouncet lord" picking his way among the corpses on the battlefield as Hotspur furiously describes him in the first part of *Henry IV;* and Bolingbroke's coronation as the groom briefly describes it to the imprisoned Richard II. Several other subjects filled up small chinks in the Shakespearean text. In 1852, for example, a minor artist showed Desdemona and Othello about to elope in a gondola, an action not specified by the playwright but legitimately inferred at any rate. Some artists, however, exercised their license too licentiously. In a picture of 1828, Lady Macbeth's deathbed, itself not shown on stage, was attended by the Weird Sisters, and a generation later another scene, equally offensive to purists, was displayed: the boy Hamlet, "joyous and frolicsome, slashing, whip in hand, poor Yorick" as he rode the court jester piggyback.

CHAPTER 11

"Theatricality" a leading issue in criticism of literary paintings; the forces joining and separating art and the stage.—Costuming and the movement toward historical authenticity.—Caricature, "coarseness," "vulgarity," the desire for "poetry."—The death of Leslie and the controversy over "realism" in Pre-Raphaelite pictures from Keats.

The critics' literal-mindedness in respect to both the literary text and the pictures made from it was a symptom of the positivistic intellectual climate that reached its peak in the mid-Victorian decades. In literary theory, the prevailing philosophical emphasis on scientific (observable) truth took the form of the belief that a modern work of imaginative literature should be judged by its fidelity to life (life selectively idealized, at any rate—not life as uncomfortably, insecurely, even brutally experienced and seen). When art critics required that painters be faithful to their sources, therefore, they were simply upholding the corollary that modern pictorial art which depicted human experience, whether or not it derived from a literary work, should itself be true. Repeatedly they cited Hamlet's admonition to the players: "O'er-step not the modesty of nature."

In effect, this was a prohibition of theatricality—a word and a concept that often figured in the charge that an inventive artist violated an author's intention and spirit. During the most prosperous years of literary painting, one of the major errors of its practitioners, as critics saw it, was an inappropriate staginess of conception and execution. The painter of dramatic subjects, said Henry Nelson O'Neil as late as 1866, "is so influenced by the theatrical presentation of the scenes he selects for illustration, that they cannot fail to modify his own conceptions; and it is for this reason that few pictures of this nature ever satisfy the judgment of those who have read the works of dramatic authors, but have never witnessed their production on the stage."[1] Although the fault was naturally detected most often in paintings derived from the drama, it was by no means limited to them. Dramatic scenes from narrative poetry and fiction were vulnerable to the same charge.

An affinity between the theatrical and painted arts had been recognized since the early eighteenth century. In 1715, Jonathan Richardson had declared that plays were a kind of "moving pictures,"[2] and this notion became something of a commonplace in the age's aesthetic thought. Even after Lessing's *Laocoön* caused adherents of the sister-art theory to have second thoughts, it was still agreed that there was a relationship, profitable to consider, between the drama (i.e., the "poetic," Shakespearean kind, not the prose plays written by modern dramatists) and history painting. In 1807, the poet laureate, Henry Pye, recommended that artists learn from stage performances, since "the Drama exhibited on the stage, exceed[s] every species of imitation short of actual deception."[3] Painting and drama alike expressed psychological truth in mimetic form, an equivalence implied in Hazlitt's art criticism and accepted by Coleridge. At the same time, as we shall see, Romantic criticism began to regard the relationship between the representational arts as a mésalliance rather than a partnership, and it was this that gave rise to the pejorative notion of "theatricality." In practice, the frequent points of contact between fine art and the working theater compromised paintings with literary subjects and significantly affected their reception.

One important link in the eighteenth century was personal. We have noted (chapter 1) the friendship of Hogarth and Garrick, each of whom was influenced by the other's *forte*. Garrick was an intimate also of Sir Joshua Reynolds, who throughout his life in London frequented the theater, in later years becoming a particular devotee of Mrs. Siddons.[4] Henry Fuseli, fresh from Switzerland, improved his knowledge of the English language by constant attendance at the playhouse, and in the process became another member of Garrick's admiring retinue of artists.[5] Sir Thomas Lawrence, according to the Victorian painter Solomon Hart, had an innate "histrionic taste" that first manifested itself in "the recitations from the drama and British poets with which the young Lawrence entertained his father's customers" (he kept an inn at Devizes, Wiltshire). This penchant, said Hart, "gave a theatrical tone not only to his portraits,

153. William P. Frith, *Mr. Honeywood Introduces the Bailiffs to Miss Richland as His Friends* (RA 1850) (Victoria & Albert Museum, Crown Copyright). The affinity between narrative painting and the theater was expressed in a practical way by several leading Victorian artists' involvement in amateur theatricals. This scene from Goldsmith's *The Good-Natured Man* originated in a production in which Frith took part, along with two other painters, Millais and Edward M. Ward, and Dickens and Wilkie Collins.

154. George H. Harlow, *The Court for the Trial of Queen Katherine* (RA 1817) (Royal Shakespeare Theatre Picture Gallery ©). Evidently not a literal representation of a performance of a scene in Shakespeare's *Henry VIII,* this painting was begun as a commissioned portrait of Mrs. Siddons but developed into an elaborate tableau composed of members of the Kemble family and several of their artistic and literary friends.

but even to his pictures, embodying a loftier theme. Thus one of his most ambitious illustrations, 'Satan calling up his Legions,' . . . savours more of the footlights than of the spirit of true poetry."[6] Lawrence had close personal ties with the Kemble family—he was successively in love with Mrs. Siddons, her two daughters Sally and Maria, and her niece Fanny—and he painted John Philip as Hamlet (p. 222), Coriolanus (pl. 238), Rolla (in Sheridan's adaptation of Kotzebue's *Pizzaro*), and Cato (in Addison's tragedy). Among the prominent early Victorian painters of narrative subjects, Wilkie, Mulready, Leslie, and Frith were known for their love of the stage. (Some of these might have seen Delacroix during his visit to London in 1825. He went every night to Covent Garden or Drury Lane and, falling under the spell of Kean as Richard III, Othello, and Shylock, discovered the power of Shakespeare's plays performed in their original language—with momentous effects on his own art.)[7]*

Meanwhile, the branch of art devoted to theatrical subjects had flourished under the brushes of Zoffany, DeWilde, Clint, and others. In the first third of the nineteenth century, portraits of actors and actresses in their popular stage roles continued in demand, especially as designs for engravings in editions of plays and, somewhat later, in magazines. Between 1800 and 1825, there were, at most, only four years when paintings from plays, both new and revived, were not exhibited at the Royal Academy. The most talked-of picture for several seasons was George Henry Harlow's *The Court for the Trial of Queen Katherine* in Shakespeare's *Henry VIII,* shown at the Royal Academy in 1817 (pl. 154). When Fanny Kemble made her debut as Queen Katherine in 1831, she was dressed in the costume made famous by the picture of her aunt in the role and the popular engraving derived from it. Many years later (1875), her friend Edward FitzGerald expressed to her his surprise that "the fine Engraving . . . —once so frequent—is scarce seen now: it has seemed strange to me to meet People who never even heard of it."[8]

*Before this visit, Delacroix, who was already well acquainted with Shakespeare in French translation, had made only a sketch, *The Ball at the Capulets.* In 1825, he completed two canvases, *Desdemona and Emilia* and *Macbeth Consulting the Witches.* Later in his career, he produced sixteen lithographs from *Hamlet* and paintings from *Macbeth, Romeo and Juliet,* and *Antony and Cleopatra.*

155. Henry Andrews, *The Trial of Queen Katherine* (ca. 1832) (Royal Shakespeare Theatre Picture Gallery ©). In contrast to Harlow's "theatrical conversation piece" in the form of an imagined performance of the trial scene, this is a belated example of a painting derived from an actual production. If, as seems probable, the production was that of Charles Kemble in his last season at Covent Garden (1831–32), the central figure is his daughter Fanny, who succeeded her aunt Sarah Siddons in the role of the queen.

The great age of theatrical portraiture, during which a certain number of pictures at each annual exhibition could be depended upon to remind critics and other spectators what honest "theatricality" was like, ended before mid-century.[9] Macready, Benjamin Webster, and Charles and Ellen Kean were painted several times in the 1840s in their popular roles, as was Samuel Phelps a little later. But the appearance of periodicals like the *Illustrated London News* had now deprived the theatrical canvas of its prime usefulness. If advertising was the motive behind many of the paintings, characters and scenes from current plays could more easily be brought to the notice of a much wider public through the printed medium. Moreover, the growing popularity of subjects from fiction diverted artists' attention from the contemporary drama as a source of paintable scenes and situations. The only recurrent subject of theatrical portraiture after the middle of the century was Ellen Terry, whom George F. Watts, briefly her husband, painted as Ophelia in 1863–64, fourteen years before she actually took the role at the Lyceum. Beginning in the 1880s, she was portrayed as Beatrice, Portia, Lady Macbeth, and Mrs. Page by such artists as John Singer Sargent (pl. 236), the Honorable John Collier, and Sir Johnston Forbes-Robertson, himself an actor as well as artist. Her longtime partner, Henry Irving, could be seen on canvas in several roles, including Benedick and Philip IV in Tennyson's *Queen Mary*.

Except for a few pictures expressly labeled as such, it is hard to determine how many nineteenth-century paintings of scenes from the drama were derived, either in total composition or in significant details, from actual performances. Unlike Harlow's more famous depiction, Henry Andrews's *Trial of Queen Katherine* (pl. 155) represented an actual production, that of 1831 with Charles and Fanny Kemble. There is some evidence that Ford Madox Brown's long-lived interest in *King Lear* had its origin in Macready's production (1838).[10] Quite untypically for the time, the presence of a proscenium arch in Dadd's *Titania Sleeping* (RA 1841) explicitly related the scene to a stage performance.

If visitors to the exhibitions sometimes detected echoes of the contemporary theater in the year's crop of paintings, theatergoers for their part also saw reflections of familiar pictures in the scenery. Both the scenic and easel arts were affected by the movement toward historical authenticity in setting and costume.[11] Until well past the middle of the eighteenth century, dramas set in some past epoch were regularly performed in modern dress, as is shown, for example, by Zoffany's painting of Garrick and Mrs. Pritchard in *Macbeth* in the 1760s (pl. 156), an easygoing indulgence of anachronism that later appeared in the mad mélange of period styles in Boydell's Shakespeare Gallery. At the turn of the century, one seldom found a picture so marked by historical realism and consistency as the trial scene from *The Merchant of Venice* (ca. 1800) by Richard Smirke, son of the better-known and more prolific Robert. Smirke actually drew his costumes from paintings of the sixteenth-century Venetian school, which was contemporary with the action of Shakespeare's play.[12]

In the theater, the antiquarian enthusiasm that was one of the products of the new historicism had begun to have its effect on staging that was becoming increasingly pictorial under the influence of such designers as P. J. Loutherbourg for Garrick and William Capon, the pioneer of histor-

156. Johann Zoffany, *Garrick and Mrs. Pritchard in "Macbeth"* (1768) (Garrick Club). A *Macbeth* in contemporary dress—the usual costuming for eighteenth-century dramas, irrespective of the time or place represented. The Gothic interior is almost equally at odds with the architecture of Scottish castles in Macbeth's time. Compare the anachronistic costuming in Zuccarelli's painting from the play (pl. 22).

ical accuracy in the theater, for John Philip Kemble. History plays were remounted according to current scholarly conceptions of what people in various epochs actually wore and the settings in which they lived. It had to be a gradual process, because, as with Kemble in the 1790s, so much money was tied up in the stock of scenery and costumes that replacements in the elaborately "authentic" style could be afforded only as old equipment was retired.

In literary and historical art, as in the theater, "authenticity" became more and more the watchword, as is demonstrated by Sir Walter Scott's worrying what Richard Westall would do in his projected illustrations for *The Lady of the Lake:* "If Westall who is really a man of talent faild in figures of chivalry where he had so many paintings to guide him what in the Devils name will he make of highland figures[?] I expect to see my chieftain Sir Roderick *Dhu* . . . in the guize of a recruiting serjaint of the Black Watch and his Bard the very model of Auld Robin Gray upon a japand tea-tray."[13]* Scott took justifiable, and timely, pride in his antiquarian expertise in matters of costume and armor, and dispensed it freely to applicants from the theater and the painting room; on the matter of kilts, he informed Haydon that the Scottish Highlanders wore them and another artist, Edward Bird, that the Scottish Borderers did not.[14] His determination to keep details straight probably exerted considerable influence on painters. When John Martin exhibited his *Macbeth on the Blasted Heath* in 1820, it was well known that he had sought and received expert advice on the tartans his accurately kilted troops wore. Eleven years later, when Scott admired the painting in Martin's studio, he presumably certified its accuracy of detail.[15]

In the theater, the issue of authenticity was fortuitously related to the advent of larger and better-equipped theaters in the age of the Keans, Macready, and Phelps. In the big houses, the old limited performance areas, well adapted for intimate acting, were enlarged to "picture" stages—a term rendered all the more apt as the action retreated from the projecting forestage to the area behind the proscenium arch that provided a ready-made frame. These picture stages were, of necessity, dominated by pictorial values and opportunities, thus giving wide scope to effects, such as massive architectural sets and crowds of colorfully costumed extras, that could be treated with large-scaled historical realism.[16] Art imitated the theater, and the theater imitated art: paintings from Shakespeare's history plays came to be laden with "authentic" details, and productions of those plays, such as Kean's *King John* (1823) and Macready's *Coriolanus* (1838) were, in effect, three-dimensional, live mountings of the pictures.

The elaboration of scenic splendor sometimes caused the drama to be engulfed by the spectacle, but this was agreeable enough to playgoers who, well acquainted with paintings of Shakespearean characters and scenes, and well educated in printed Shakespearean iconography by a steady stream of illustrated editions of the plays, brought enlarged visual expectations to Shakespearean performances. In their attempts to meet these expectations, managers may have gratified their clientele, but they also had to suffer the protestation voiced, for example, by Clement Scott in an acerb review of the Bancrofts' production of *The Merchant of Venice* in 1875, with scenery copied from Veronese's *The Marriage at Cana,* that "the stage is something more than a picture gallery."[17]

*Scott was replying to a letter from Joanna Baillie, 20 March 1810, in which she said she had seen Westall's drawings for *The Lay of the Last Minstrel* and *Marmion* and had heard that he was about to prepare a set for *Sir Lancelot.* "If he does so," she wrote, "I hope he will have the goodness to represent your stories as you tell them. His death of Marmion might be the death of any man . . . and for the broken sword he ought to brandish, if it were taken to give the artist a good rap upon the scull, it would be well employed."

It is likely that some paintings from nondramatic sources, notably but not exclusively novels, were influenced by theatrical adaptations of those works. The dramatization of novels had begun in the second half of the eighteenth century, shortly after scenes from fiction were first used as the subjects of easel paintings. This exploitation of literary material simultaneously on the stage and in art flourished throughout the first half of the nineteenth century, as hard-pressed writers for the popular theater ransacked the treasury of English fiction for subjects, even as their colleagues the artists were doing the same thing for their own popular market. Allardyce Nicoll's list of plays performed in 1800–1850 alone contains some ninety that were seemingly from literary sources, exclusive of the many from Byron and Scott (which will be discussed in Part Three) and the indeterminable number whose titles do not reveal their literary origin.[18] In the first half of the century, there were at least five plays from Burns. There were also plays from *Tristram Shandy, Tom Jones, Clarissa Harlowe, The Vicar of Wakefield, The Rape of the Lock, Robinson Crusoe,* and Gothic romances. Sir Roger de Coverley was represented on the stage, as was Izaak Walton. Several productions claimed derivation from Moore's *Lalla Rookh.* Several more dramatized novels by Bulwer-Lytton—*Rienzi, The Last of the Barons, The Last Days of Pompeii,* and *Eugene Aram.* In the second half-century, says Nicoll, there were "many hundreds" of adaptations from fiction. There was even one play whose title, if nothing else, came from *The Faerie Queene*: *Una and the Lions* (the plural suggests a connection with the circus).

A further link between the popular stage and art lay in the very nature of the entertainments offered in the contemporary theater. The great majority of plays in this era of melodrama, burletta, and farce were stitched together, ordinarily not very securely, from a series of individual episodes. They appealed to their uncritical audience not because they boasted structural craftsmanship or smooth continuity of narrative, which they seldom did, but by virtue of their separate but frequent moments of extreme emotion, suspense, or hilarity. The prescribed tableaux ("stage pictures") here and there, especially at the act curtains, were only the most obvious manifestations of this emphasis on the single moment rather than the flow of events; a play simply moved from one arresting moment to the next. The popular appeal of many literary pictures was, in this regard, precisely that of the theater. Anecdotal pictures in general had the same basic attractiveness. They were portrayals of incidents, and though a narrative may have been implied—what went before, what might come after—the immediate interest such paintings possessed resided in the single moment represented.

If literary pictures were often nothing more than graphic equivalents of theatrical tableaux, those same tableaux sometimes were overt transcriptions of existing paintings. In James Robinson Planché's melodrama *The Brigand* (1829), there were stop-action scenes after three paintings by Charles Eastlake, and in Douglas Jerrold's *The Rent Day* (1832), two tableaux after celebrated paintings by Wilkie, *The Rent Day* and *Distraining for Rent.* Hogarth's *Harlot's Progress* was recreated on the Surrey Theatre stage in a play called *The Life of a Woman* (1840), and Cruikshank's eight-part series *The Bottle* turned up in a play of the same name at the City of London Theatre (1847). In the same decade, the cobbled-together, unauthorized stage versions of Dickens's early novels often included tableaux directly modeled after the familiar engraved illustrations. Other dramatizations of literary works contained similar explicit reminiscences of well-known paintings; in Tom Taylor's first full-length drama, based on *The Vicar of Wakefield* (1850), the tableau that began the second act was designed after Maclise's picture of *Olivia and Sophia Fitting out Moses for the Fair,* shown at the Royal Academy in 1838.[19]*

In view of this steady commerce between the stage and the studio, artists perhaps should not have been censured as severely as they were—and as we shall now see—for their alleged concession to "theatricality." They may sometimes have sacrificed the dignity of their art, but that was a necessary condition of Victorian popular culture.†

Although the visual and dramatic arts retained many points of practical association, equally strong forces tended to distance one from the other, as the history of painting from the drama in the eighteenth century illustrates. When artists first took up such subjects, they retained the theatrical setting, as Hogarth did in the six versions of his *Beggar's Opera* painting in 1728–29 (pl. 1), though they did not follow Hogarth to the extreme of showing members of the audience at the edges of the composition. But as theatrical paintings proliferated, the performance framework came to be dispensed with, as it was in engraved book illustrations, notably Boydell's, and the subject was depicted as a freestanding story, like a scene from a poem or novel, rather than as an acting-out of a literary text by men and women who assumed their roles merely for the two hours' traffic of the stage.

In aesthetic theory, the separation of the performed drama and fine art was widened by the weight of Romantic critical opinion. The crucial figure here, as usual, was Shakespeare. Alderman Boydell's candid admission that painting lacked the power to adequately contain and convey Shakespeare's genius shortly had its counterpart when Romantic critics made the same disclaimer in reference to the other mimetic art. Shakespeare's plays, it was argued, were reduced in stature, their effectiveness drained, by their flesh-and-blood embodiment before an audience in a public place. They were no longer the flawless mirror of nature that they were in silent print. To perform them (not least in the current ruinous adaptations) was inescapably to distort and indeed destroy the poet's intended effect. The priceless illusion could only be maintained within the private imagination. Thus declared Lamb, in his classic essay "On the Tragedies of Shakespeare Considered with Reference to Their Fitness for Stage-Representation," in the course of which occurred the denunciation of Boydell's Gallery already quoted (chapter 2). When Hamlet, Ophelia, Othello, Macbeth, Romeo and Juliet, and above all King Lear are materialized, Lamb argued, they lose their transcendental significance, and the appurtenances of performance—elocution, gesture, costume, and setting—divert attention from the philosophical truths they express.

If the staged drama was an irreparably flawed representation of reality, it followed that paintings which emulated its physical mimesis were doubly removed from truth; and it was from this awareness that the avoidance of theatricality as a critical requirement sprang. Northcote, who contributed nine pictures to the Boydell Gallery, testified to the stage's inadequacy to mediate "reality" from the printed page to canvas. "It is,

*Another popular painting by Maclise, *The Play Scene in "Hamlet"* (RA 1842) (pl. 219), found its way onto the stage some years later. Lewis Carroll saw Kean's production of the play in January 1856 and recorded that the play scene was "evidently grouped from Maclise's picture." In July 1857, visiting the Royal Academy exhibition, he observed an example of the reverse action: of LeJeune's painting of Queen Katherine's dream in Shakespeare's *Henry VIII,* he wrote that it was "beautiful exceedingly—clearly taken from the scene at the Princess's"—that is, in Kean's unforgettable spectacular production of 1855. (*The Diaries of Lewis Carroll,* ed. Roger Lancelyn Green [New York, 1954], 1:73, 115.)

† A much later, and quite different, example of three-way interaction between literature, painting, and the stage is offered by Hardy's *Desperate Remedies* (1871). In the novel, Manston's wife, overhearing the conversation of Cythera and Owen, is described as standing "as precisely in the attitude of Imogen by the cave of Belarius, as if she had studied the position from the play." A recent critic has suggested that Hardy had in mind Helen Faucit's performance as Imogen in *Cymbeline;* the *Times,* she points out, had said of the actress's "timid approach . . . to the cave of Belarius," that "it is a study for the painter" (Grundy, *Hardy and the Sister Arts,* pp. 79–80). Imogen at the cave of Belarius was, in fact, a recurrent subject of literary pictures (pls. 100, 132, 239, 240).

surely," he said, "not the province of one art to imitate another. . . . To paint, therefore, the passions from the exhibitions of them on the stage . . . is to remove yourself one degree farther from truth."[20] Richard Westall, another fecund source of Boydell paintings, told Farington in 1806 that "he had never seen the Character of Falstaff exhibited on the stage, and should not be induced to it unless tempted by a very extraordinary account given of some one who may attempt it. At present," noted Farington, "he has in His imagination the *Character personified* & is not willing to interrupt that idea by an imperfect representation very different from it."[21] Sir George Beaumont recognized and approved such a refusal to risk an "ideal" conception by exposing it to the reductive and coarsening influence of the stage. With Shakespeare, he wrote Haydon, "you not only have the powerful productions of his mind's pencil to contend with, but also the perverted representations of the theatres, which have made such impressions on most people in early life, that I, for my part, feel it more difficult to form a picture in my mind from any scene of his that I have seen frequently represented, than from the works of any other poet."[22] Frith's level-headed patron John Gibbons agreed. Shakespeare, he wrote the artist in 1843, "is rather a dangerous fellow to meddle with. . . . In fact, it appears to me that theatrical subjects are seldom good ones. If treated theatrically, they are vile, and if not, they are almost sure to disturb some settled preoccupation, and we miss the 'old familiar faces'—the O'Neill, the Kean, the Munden—and are loth to accept of other representations."[23]

And so the practice, though not the stated policy, of Boydell's painters combined with the idealism of the Romantic critics to encourage artists, buyers, and reviewers alike to look upon pictures derived from the drama, not as representations of performances real or imaginary, but as subjects derived directly from books, the true mirror of nature. This was the atmosphere of opinion in which it came to be stipulated that paintings of dramatic subjects, whether actually from the drama or from any other form of narrative literature, be free of any suggestion of gaslights and histrionic exaggerations of real-life deportment. Literary art should never suggest the tastes of the heterogeneous audiences that filled the great barns of Covent Garden and Drury Lane and, even worse, the "minor" theaters patronized by the unruly working class. (Behind the whole aversion to theatricalism lurked an element of social disapproval. The theater was a form of public amusement avoided for virtuous reasons by considerable sections of English society; among these, it had no claim to be a legitimate form of literary expression.) Any detectable aura of the stage in a painting inescapably cheapened it, defiling the "poetry" or at the very least the truth to life that one reasonably expected to find in it.

Although no cause-effect relationship was implied, as early as 1831 a writer in *Fraser's Magazine* found a kinship between the current drama and art in the deplorable parallel courses they were following: "As on the stage itself, so likewise in painting, farce and melodrame appear to be the order of the day: whatever is not the former, partakes of the latter, till nature on the one hand, and poetry on the other, will soon be as completely banished from fashionable pictures as they already are from fashionable novels."[24] In view of the flood of literary paintings soon to come, in which farce and melodrama had their due place, the writer's lamentation was as timely (and prophetic) as it proved to be unheeded. To be sure,

157. Richard Dadd, *Scene from "Hamlet": Ghost: "Do not forget"* (British Institution 1840) (Yale Center for British Art, Paul Mellon Collection). This painting has been said to represent Charles Kean as Hamlet; if so, it was timely enough, for Kean had made a hit in the role in the 1839–40 season. Whether or not the picture records an actual performance, it illustrates, almost painfully, one aspect of what was regularly condemned as "theatricality" in art.

almost at the same moment that Gibbons was writing to Frith, the *Times*, reviewing the 1843 Royal Academy exhibition, professed to find grounds for believing that the theatricalism of which he complained was declining. The paintings from Shakespeare, it said, "represent the characters in the plays without the intervention of the actors who now-a-days undertake to play the parts. This shows an improvement in the taste of artists, and brings the spectator more immediately in connexion with the author and his meaning, than when transmitted through the insipidity or absurdity of an intermediate agency."[25]

Such optimism, however, was ill founded. By this time—the mid-1840s—the issue that had been smoldering for many years burst into flame. Looking back from the vantage point of many years, Holman Hunt recalled (with obvious exaggeration) that every episodic painting then was

> planned as for the stage, with second-rate actors to play the parts, striving to look not like sober live men, but pageant statues of waxwork. Knights were frowning and staring as none but hired supernumeraries could stare; the pious had vitreous tears on their reverential cheeks; innkeepers were ever round and red-faced; peasants had complexions of dainty pink; shepherdesses were fac-

> similed from Dresden-china toys; homely couples were ever reading a Family Bible to a circle of most exemplary children; all alike from king to plebeian were arrayed in clothes fresh from the bandbox.[26]

The gravamen of critics' assault on theatricality in painting centered on overtly histrionic gestures and poses, artificial or too fussy background, and garish lighting. Although we cannot tell how many artists consciously or unconsciously copied the appearance and postures of the stars of the day in their most popular roles, they could scarcely have escaped being affected by the attitude-striking style favored by the performing practice of the time. There was a well-known distinction between naturalistic and "formal," or rhetorical, acting, and it was this latter kind to which critics referred when they accused artists of theatricality. Sometimes the portrayals of dramatic poses and scenes, both on the stage and in easel art, may have been influenced by a common source, manuals of "iconographic language" that were to actors what such classic treatises as Charles Lebrun's *La Méthode pour apprendre à dessiner les passions* and Gerard de Lairesse's *The Art of Painting in All its Branches* had been to generations of painters. The techniques that worked on the stage seemed wholly transferable to paint; in Gilbert Austin's *Chironomia* (1806), for instance, Kemble's acting was described as "the perfection and the glory of art, so finished, that every look is a commentary, every tone an illustration, every gesture a model for the statuary, and a study for the painter."[27]

Tirelessly repeated from the 1840s onward, "theatricality" was a smear word of wide application, as "Pre-Raphaelite" became on different grounds. In 1856, a leading writer on aesthetics, E. S. Dallas, used the artistic miscalculations and deficiencies it connoted as a comprehensive means of deploring the present state of English painting. "The more narrowly we examine the sister arts," he said,

> the more nearly do we find that they assimilate. . . . Look at the walls of our exhibition-rooms, and behold the inanities that figure there, contemporary with the inanities of the theatre. This picture either displays as little action as a modern tragedy, or its action is as spasmodic as an Adelphi melodrama. In how many of these pictures do we find the artists compensating for bad drawing with gaudy colour, hiding vacancy of expression in a blaze of light, feebleness of passion in a tornado of shadows, and blundering perspective, aerial and linear, in a mist as convenient as the clouds by which the gods of Homer save their heroes from the lances of the enemy? The very faults we find in the theatre! Eternal mannerism, staginess, mimicry, trickery, grimacing, catchwords, red lights and blue lights, and the name of the perruquier mentioned in the play-bills in large letters! . . . Whether on the boards or on the canvass, incapacity and commonplace issue in virtually the same results.[28]

As was to be expected, theatricalism resided to some degree in the eye of the beholder. What smelled of gaslights to one reviewer was to another redolent with the fragrance of art lovingly studied from life. The *Times* said that Ophelia, in Frank Stone's painting of 1845, had "a certain intensity of expression, which borders on the theatrical"; but the *Examiner*, reporting on the same canvas, declared that "the madness of pure Ophelia has nothing in it affected or merely theatrical."[29] A generation later, in 1872, the *Saturday Review* was enchanted by John Pettie's *Silvius and Phoebe* (pl. 81). "The characters," it said, "are creatures of the woods and fields; Silvius looks lovesick and silly, while saucy Phebe is bewitchingly pert."[30] The *Athenaeum*, however, saw it differently:

158. George Clint, *Falstaff and Mistress Ford* (British Institution 1831) (Tate Gallery, London). *The Examiner* (20 February) called this scene from *The Merry Wives of Windsor* (3. 3) "one of the ablest dramatic pieces ever painted," in which the artist took care not to "overstep the modesty of nature"; but the *Athenaeum* (12 February) complained that "Mr. Clint renders Shakespeare too theatrically"—as well he might have, considering that he had devoted his career to theatrical pictures.

> . . . Here is the stage street; this is the stage loutish and whimpering lover, a little old for the part, and with legs which will not bear inspection in tights by daylight, yet, with a good wig, still susceptible of "dressing" surprisingly well for gaslight. Is not this Phoebe a clever actress, with the stage pout, the side-glance of the theatre? In an instant we see why the herbage and foliage of this "forest" are so vividly, so crudely green; are they not seen by gaslight?[31]

Reviewers may not always have agreed on what they saw in a given picture, but, evading the fact that Shakespeare had written his plays in the first place for the performing theater, albeit one that lacked scenic capability, they were unanimously of the opinion that a new painting from Shakespeare should contain no hint of the stage. They might even, on occasion, go so far as to urge artists to eliminate the very qualities that made Shakespeare good theater, as when Elmore's picture of Hero fainting in church, in *Much Ado About Nothing,* was censured in 1846 for being executed "with a theatrical effect somewhat too clearly akin to the theatrical nature of his subject."[32]

For the next thirty years, each season's allotment of new paintings from Shakespeare was put to the test of theatricality, and in many pictures the results were discouragingly positive. In 1848, of a picture of Lear meeting Edgar on the stormy heath: "exaggerated even beyond the stage representations."[33] In 1852, of a picture of Hortensio and Katherine in *The Taming of the Shrew:* "the contrasts are violent, and the scene seems too theatrical even for that forcible and demonstrative play."[34] In 1858, of the all too familiar parting-at-dawn scene in *Romeo and Juliet:* " . . . ghastly . . . taken, we should think, from a melodrama at the Surrey Theatre."[35] In 1864, of one of the two *Romeo and Juliet* paintings A. J. Woolmer exhibited that year: "The moon casts an opal light upon the terrace steps, against which contends the golden lustre of the lamps. In the foreground blossoms an oleander, and clustered grapes and rich rinded gourds group with Juliet and her nurse. In all this getting up we are perhaps a little too closely reminded of Vauxhall; we see the smoke and smell the rankness of the oil."[36]* In 1867, of Orchardson's *Talbot and the Countess of Auvergne (1 Henry VI):*

> . . . the very presentation of a stage-scene, from the manner in which the English lord and his followers enter the chamber by a "practicable" door to the vast extent of bare boards that form the floor of the painted theatre, and, above all, the action of the ill-favoured and excessively quaint lady who clenches her hands in dismay. The very lighting of the picture recalls the forced mode of the theatre, not less so the mean, worn-out state of the tapestries and furniture of the chamber.[37]

It will be noticed that nowhere in this sampling of contemporary comment is there any repetition of the older view, expressed by Boydell and Lamb among others, that Shakespeare was beyond the reach of mimetic art. The critics' only demand was that the Shakespearean artist place himself beyond the reach of the theater. By the 1870s, as we shall see in chapter 12, the whole question, happily, was becoming moot. As the Victorian period drew to a close, and even as Irving and Beerbohm Tree were giving new life to Shakespeare on the stage, artists' interest in the plays as a subject for painting steadily declined.

*It was bad enough for the 1858 reviewer, just quoted, to allude to the Surrey Theatre, the transpontine playhouse where low life congregated to watch blood-and-thunder melodramas, but this was the unkindest cut of all. After long service as a summer evening rendezvous for entertainment-seeking Londoners (and, not incidentally, the first place where subject art was made accessible to the general public, through the supper-box paintings by Hayman and others), the gardens had degenerated by Victorian times into a dilapidated haunt of dubious characters, including flocks of prostitutes. Vauxhall had finally closed, unlamented except by this clientele, in 1859.

One particular kind of literary painting, involving the adjacent issues of theatricality and historical authenticity, thrust art critics into a dilemma they never wholly resolved. The picture replete with period costume and accessories, whose proven popularity was among the main reasons why literary sources were so often drawn upon, elicited both admiration and censure. A play or novel, or the particular scene chosen, may have had little else to recommend it to the artist; but if it afforded him a chance to portray women in rich satins and brocades, fans in hand, and men in flowing wigs and knee breeches, swords at side, its credentials as a vendible subject for art were adequate. These were the kind of paintings favored by Sir Leicester Dedlock in Dickens's *Bleak House:* "the Fancy Ball School in which Art occasionally condescends to become a master, which would be best catalogued like the miscellaneous articles in a sale. As, . . . 'One stone terrace (cracked), one gondola in distance, one Venetian senator's dress complete, richly embroidered white satin costume with profile portrait of Miss Jogg the model, one scimetar superbly mounted in gold with jewelled handle, elaborate Moorish dress (very rare) and Othello' " (chap. 29).

This taste was but one manifestation of the enthusiasm for portrayals of history in general that spread in the time of Scott. Scenes from English life from the Middle Ages to the reign of Queen Anne, including subjects from the literature of the time, grew in demand; and as the nineteenth century progressed, the increasingly distant decades of the first Georges also qualified as a source of historical subjects. For artists, there was the additional attraction of recalling their earliest distinguished forebears on English soil, the succession of great portraitists from Holbein downward. Where seventeenth- and eighteenth-century writers had actually been painted by Kneller (Pepys, Evelyn, Congreve, Addison, Pope) and Reynolds (Boswell, Johnson, Sterne, Garrick, Sheridan, Goldsmith), there was further incentive to select biographical subjects that allowed reminiscences of well-known existing portraits to be introduced. Moreover, in the

159. Henry J. Fradelle, *Othello Relating the Story of His Life* (RA 1824) (Royal Shakespeare Theatre Picture Gallery ©). Although not all the details in Dickens's description of a "Fancy Ball School" *Othello* painting are found in this picture, it well illustrates what he meant.

160. William P. Frith, *Before Dinner, at Boswell's London Lodging in Bond Street, 1769* (RA 1868) (Ashmolean Museum, Oxford). Boswell describes at length the dinner and the lively conversation it occasioned (16 October 1769). The scene has little narrative value, apart from the fact that the company are waiting for a tardy guest; it was intended mainly as a collection of literary portraits, for which Frith sought out the extant likenesses of each man. He modeled Johnson's head after Nollekens's bust. Goldsmith, at the left, is admiring his reflection in the mirror; he is wearing his new "bloom-coloured" coat, whose tailor has asked that he mention his name whenever someone inquired who made it.

eighteenth century, long after Van Dyck finished his work, it had remained the fashion for women to affect, and be painted in, the "Van Dyck" dress indelibly associated with his many portraits. In 1741, exactly a century after the artist's death, Horace Walpole reported to Sir Horace Mann that he had seen at a masquerade at the Duchess of Norfolk's "quantities of pretty Van Dyckes and all kinds of old pictures, walked out of their frames."[38] For Victorian painters, portraying women in fashionably antiquated Van Dyck costume in scenes from the *Spectator* or *The Rape of the Lock,* or for that matter in the even more elaborate dress seen in Nicholas Hilliard's miniatures of Elizabethan men and women, had the inestimable additional appeal of sheer escapism. It was delightful to find, in the elegance of an earlier time, relief from the drabness, the almost ostentatious lack of decoration, that characterized the garb of Victorian men especially, now that the wastrel resplendence of the Regency dandy had faded away into bourgeois sobriety. Portraits and scenes from contemporary life, "hat and trousers pictures" as Frith disparagingly called them,[39] seemed to betray one of the very purposes of painted art.

Under the watchful eye of the new historic spirit, this graphic evocation of bygone English scenes, in art as on the stage, had to be achieved with dedicated regard for authenticity. At least one Victorian painter, John Faed, borrowed costumes from Madame Tussaud's, whose designers reportedly had done as much research in the area as Macready's costume-makers. On one occasion, when he asked leave to copy the dress worn by one of the waxwork wives of Henry VIII, Joseph Tussaud, who knew the value of free publicity in the form of production credits, sent him a whole trunkful of costumes from every period figuring in the famous exhibition.[40]

Many of the hundreds of literary period pieces displayed in the exhibitions received unstinted praise; men and women were dressed to the tiniest detail specified in costume books or seen in paintings and engravings from the time concerned, and the settings were furnished with a wealth of authentic accessories—an unsurpassable means of blending the pleasure of the eye with reliable instruction. Typically, E. M. Ward's *Amy Robsart and Leicester at Cumnor Hall* (RA 1866) was hailed as a triumph of visual evocation, the very curtains being as vivid as the costumes of the figures. "A picture de luxe," said the *Art Journal*.[41] "Never were silk stockings, satin and velvet robes, jewels, and dazzling orders, rendered in greater truth and lustre." "A rich sweetmeat to the eye," summed up the *Examiner*.[42]

But, echoing dramatic critics' frequent complaint against the overloading of the stage with distracting "archaeologically correct" settings, art critics often deplored the fussiness of some artists who were more concerned with historical accuracy than with capturing the true spirit of the literary subject, whatever it may have been. And, just as they relished catching one artist in the very act of deviating from the plain letter of the text (see chapter 10), so they matched another's pedantry with their own as they scrutinized his canvas for anachronisms, down to the last snuff box and shoe buckle. Reviewing the Academy show of 1855, the unusually dyspeptic *Athenaeum* critic began by commenting on the unhistorical dress and details to be seen in Frith's *Maria Tricks Malvolio* and then lighted upon Maclise's painting of the wrestling scene in *As You Like It:* "an Elizabethan house with a Victoria[n] conservatory,—a nondescript Duke with barbaric Saxon buskins and a Louis the Tenth hat,—a medieval jester,—and passion-flowers, which were first brought from South America! What a patchwork is this!" The reviewer then turned his keen and hopeful eye to a picture of John Evelyn's first meeting with Grinling Gibbons in 1671, pointing out first that the painter contravened the literary text by locating the meeting in "a sort of cool garden-house, surrounded by jars and shavings, and before a blocked-up window, festooned with cobwebs," whereas "he was found by Evelyn, if we remember rightly, in a room in the Belle Sauvage Yard." Piling Pelion on Ossa, the reviewer went on to observe that Evelyn was mistakenly clad as a Dutch peasant and that "Gibbons wears a beard, though beards were abandoned at the Restoration, and carves a crucifix, although the No Popery riots were at their height at this period."[43]*

In many such criticisms of costume pictures, the term "Wardour Street" turned up, this site of the trade in pseudo antiques linking the historical pretensions of the art gallery with those of the theater. Thus the charge of theatricality often involved this extra element of artificiality, violation of the truth-to-nature that resided in genuine historical re-creation. By 1882, the Royal Academy obsession with picturesque old-time costume and accessories, so suggestive of the overdressed pieces in the theater, stirred Harry Quilter to protest:

> It sounds like a satire, but it is really a fact, that the same ruffs, boots, and breeches re-appear year after year on the Academic walls, till their inanimate faces are as well known as those of any of the gilded youths, whose canes, flowers, and toothpicks make the glory of the Gaiety Theatre. Thus, Mr. Marks [in a picture from *2 Henry VI*] affects a long waistless medieval garment, with hanging sleeves; Mr. Horsley rarely escapes from doublet and hose; Mr. Pettie dates his costumes chiefly from the seventeenth century; Mr. Yeames takes us back to Queen Elizabeth, or perhaps to King John [the picture in question was actually from *King John*] . . .

and so on, to the specialists in late eighteenth-century, Eastern, Spanish, Roman and pre-Christian dress.[44] It was this participation in the continuing manufacture of marketable costume pieces that kept literary pictures arriving at the exhibitions long after their subjects had lost their intrinsic interest.

*This was a bad day for pedantry in art criticism. The reviewer did *not* remember rightly. For one thing, the scene of the meeting was, in Evelyn's own words, "a poore solitary thatched house, in a field in our Parish, near Sayes Court." For another, the outburst of anti-Catholic hysteria the writer presumably refers to was seven years in the future (a consequence of Titus Oates's alleged "Popish plot", 1678), and what history usually calls the "No Popery riots" did not occur until more than a century later, in 1780.

161. Charles R. Leslie, *Scene from "Twelfth Night"* (RA 1842) (Tate Gallery, London). A sketch, dated 1841, for the finished painting, commissioned by the banker Thomas Baring. The moment is in act 1, scene 3, when Sir Toby Belch instructs the bashful rustic Sir Andrew Aguecheek in the niceties of gallant courtship.

Not far distant from theatricality in untruthfulness to nature was caricature. At certain times and under certain circumstances, English popular taste ran strongly toward physical distortion as a form of satire, as the fame of Hogarth, Gillray, Rowlandson, George Cruikshank, and the *Punch* coterie of artists bears witness. Dickens was a master of verbal caricature, and comic facial exaggeration could be found even in the apparatus of children's games. But caricature was an alien element in any art that was to be taken seriously, and the suspicion of its presence in painting could not be ignored, particularly when the subject was a serious one from literature. In theatrical terms, caricature was the effect produced by "intensity of expression bordering on the theatrical" such as the *Times* noted in Stone's *Ophelia* in the review quoted above, or by the equally exaggerated bodily attitudes assumed in stop-action tableaux.

Degeneration into caricature was, of course, a hazard inherent in any work of art that attempted to convey the dynamism of strong emotion by a frozen expression or posture, and artists had before them the abundant examples of Old Masters who had successfully avoided it. It was grounds for special praise when a painter, such as Leslie in his picture of the "Accost, Sir Andrew, accost!" scene in *Twelfth Night* (pl. 161), could be said to have produced "a pure transcript of Shakespeare on canvass, without the theatrical exaggerations by which the illustrations of the great bard are deformed and distorted in the hands of artists whose only conception of his character is taken from the absurdities of the buffoons, by whom they are caricatured."[45] But once again, it depended on whose eyes looked at a picture. Commenting on Dyce's picture of *Lear and the Fool in the Storm* (RA 1851), the *Literary Gazette* began by saying that "nothing could be more trying than to paint rage so close on madness in an old man without caricature," but went on to imply, by the judicious praise it meted out, that Dyce had succeeded.[46] The *Times,* by contrast, declared bluntly that "he has converted the dignity of Lear defying the storm into the distraction of an old clothesman, and the biting jests of the Fool into a bestial caricature of humanity."[47]

Another respect in which artists sometimes were faulted for departing from the spirit of the literary original was a lapse from dignity into something variously called "coarseness" or "vulgarity." These too were epithets that were easier to fling than to define, but in a society so concerned with decorum of conduct and appearance as a sign of status, the disapproval they conveyed was a weighty one. Thus the *Athenaeum* denounced Holman Hunt's then controversial, now celebrated, painting of *Claudio and Isabella* (pl. 195): "Claudio is, after all, but a vulgar lout, and Isabella a homely creature who never could have inspired the passion of Angelo. If Mr. Hunt will not give us beauty, at least let him refrain from idealizing vulgarity."[48] Whatever "vulgarity" meant, it evidently was so conspicuous in some canvases that critics on rival papers, presumably viewing an exhibition independently, detected it at once in the same picture. On 2 April 1859, both the *Athenaeum* and the *Literary Gazette* reported on a minor artist's painting of the closet scene in *Hamlet.* "Hamlet," said one, "with his stockings down at heel, seems in a vulgar fright, and is yet running pugnaciously at his father, who seems a sort of frightened Jupiter."[49] Hamlet, said the other, "is in face, attitude, and costume, an entire misconception—coarse, vulgar, melodramatic; the Ghost is most unghostly; and the Queen thoroughly plebeian."[50]

The writer's use of "plebeian" in this context helps focus the intent of "vulgar": it meant, among other things, the artist's diminution of the character's social rank. Hamlet and the Queen were royalty, and, whatever their mental state, should be portrayed with suitable dignity or majesty, as such men and women of high degree were always depicted in high art. When they were not, they were "vulgar." So too did Shakespeare intend Petruchio to be a gentleman; Augustus Egg, according to the *Art Journal,* diminished him to a knockabout comedian in his scene from *The Taming of the Shrew* exhibited in 1860, and to that extent was untrue to Shakespeare.[51]

162. John Gilbert, *Petruchio Brings Home His Wife* (British Institution 1860) (Birmingham City Museum and Art Gallery). "It would be hard," said the *Literary Gazette* (18 February), "to express the loathing this vulgar 'effusion' excites." But it possessed no qualities that set it apart from other Victorian treatments of Shakespearean comedy, and the "vulgarity" attributed to it was the common property of hundreds of such pictures, a reflection of honest middle-class taste.

To require a painter to discriminate between the subtle physical attributes of high station and low, apart from costume and accessories, called for powers that few artists possessed enough of to satisfy the captious eye of a viewer anxious for such distinctions. But the most elusive quality critics sought in literary pictures was "poetry"; the fragile, impalpable, undefinable essence of delight that, of all the qualities literature possessed, was most tirelessly insisted upon, except in certain categories of subjects from fiction and drama. It was looked for most often in paintings from Shakespeare, especially *A Midsummer Night's Dream* and *The Tempest,* and Milton's *Comus,* the three sources from which most of the so-called ideal pictures of the period 1820–50 were taken. Here the artist was most free to stray from the letter of the text, or, more precisely, to use it simply as the point of departure for his fancy. *A Midsummer Night's Dream,* a critic wrote in 1841, "can only be illustrated when Fantasy, and not Flesh-and-Blood, holds the pencil."[52] To say of a painter, as the *Examiner* said of Maclise's picture of *Puck Disenchanting Bottom* (RA 1832), that he "has embodied the creations of Shakespeare with spirit, originality, and poetical feeling" was to award him the highest praise possible.[53]

Few iconographic figures were more "poetical" to early Victorian sensibilities than fairies and other insubstantial beings. Angels of various degrees in the celestial hierarchy had offered no difficulty to religious painters, but their secular counterparts posed a problem in this materialistic age, the suspension of disbelief being less willing in the case of literary fairies, nymphs, and sylphs than in that of supernatural agents bearing scriptural or hagiographical credentials. Admittedly, the book illustrators of an earlier generation had not hesitated to depict the incorporeal; and to judge from the esteem in which their engravings were held, they had succeeded. William Bell Scott wrote of the illustrations in Cooke's edition of the British poets:

> In point of invention these were extremely fanciful. The poet could not use a figure of speech but the artist without scruple seized upon it as a subject. If the poet said—
>
> It seemed that she had stolen all Cupid's shafts
>
> the painter forthwith represented Cupid sleeping under a tree and a nymph snatching away his quiver. Cupid played a great *role* indeed in these pretty little prints, and emblems of all the virtues and vices were freely used.
>
> Cupid claims the dart and quiver,
> But 'tis Fancy twangs the bow,
>
> were represented by a large demonstrative emblematic young lady kneeling on a cloud, and the dangerous boy skipping by her side prompting her to shoot, which she does in the most elegant attitude, not the least as if she expected to hit. At that time imitative art competed with poetry, the mistress of all the arts, in dealing with the incorporeal: it was not to be limited by the natural![54]

But now, in a new era of relative realism and toughminded critics, the painter of supernatural beings took a considerable chance, and often failed. Eastlake's contribution to the Buckingham Palace pavilion decorations (see Part Three, below, under Milton), an illustration of the epilogue of the Spirits in *Comus,* ran afoul of the *New Monthly Magazine*: "If such be Mr. Eastlake's interpretation of Milton, then the whole world has all along been at fault in its conception of those divine etherial essences. There never was conceived such a flight of spirits—such puddings of hands and

163. Joseph Severn, *Ariel: "Where the bee sucks . . . "* (RA 1838) (Victoria & Albert Museum, Crown Copyright). Possibly, but not certainly, the worst of the innumerable paintings of Ariel. "An exquisite little picture," said Thackeray of this version (*Fraser's Magazine,* June, 17: 761). Severn painted several others.

feet—such black holes for eyes—such blue wings—such vile colours of dresses—such brown rocks and woolly clouds."[55] (According to Thackeray, the spirits in the picture were better fed than the artist, who "has kept his promise, has worked the given number of hours; but he has had no food all the while, and has executed his job in a somewhat faint manner.")[56]

During the vogue for fairy pictures in the forties, most artists got off more easily than did Eastlake; nobody seems to have objected to Dadd's fairies with their gossamer wings and well rounded, fleshy bosoms. No painter's fairies were triumphs of imaginative art, but people seem to have been determined to like these excursions into the realm of Faery as a relief from the frictions and anxieties of the Chartist years. But this tolerance did not last into the fifties, when the *Times,* for example, protested that "we do not want to see Ariel and the spirits of the Enchanted Isle in the attitudes and shapes of green goblins" in Millais's much-abused *Ferdinand Lured by Ariel* (pl. 248).[57] On this score, reviewers were particularly hard on F. R. Pickersgill's rendition of several scenes in *Love's Labour's Lost* in a single picture (RA 1856). At least three complained in unison of, as one put it, "the pink, plump cupids which float bodily in the air, in defiance of gravitation."[58] Unfortunately, at this moment the theater offered a precedent for such a violation of probability when the Shakespearean productions of Charles Kean and Samuel Phelps flew angels on wires. A criticism in 1857 of one more rendition of Queen Katherine's dream in *Henry VIII* was that it "follows . . . the feeling of the representation at the Princess' Theatre, [rather] than the descriptive text of the play. We see, therefore, the angels hovering over the Queen, the nearest presenting the crown of which she speaks to Griffith."[59] Literalism in the theater or in art could hardly go further.

This, then, was the simple requirement for literary paintings during the decades when they were before the public in the largest quantities: portray what the writer described, without exaggeration, without the expressive intervention of the artist, faithful not only to the text but to life as it is observed. The criterion stemmed, in part, from the debate over the realism of Crabbe's poetry and the acceptability of genre painting in the hierarchy of kinds (see chapter 3, above) which had proved a harbinger of the moderate realism of genre art in the days of Wilkie, Mulready, and Webster. Now, more than a generation later, several events occurred that in long perspective can be seen to have marked another, equally decisive, turning point in the history of literary painting, this time away from the notion of the illustrator as subservient to the literary text.

One such event was the death of Leslie in 1859 and the revised judgment of his work that it occasioned. He had been the archetypal painter of literary subjects. As a publisher's apprentice in Philadelphia early in the century, he had acquired a pronounced taste for literature, one that was sharpened when he came to London as an aspiring painter and fell into the company of Coleridge and Washington Irving. By the 1830s, he was receiving the large sum of five hundred guineas apiece for his engaging canvases from English literature—a sure sign of the accuracy with which he estimated public taste. But he outlived his popularity.

Reviewing his career seven years after his death, the brothers Redgrave declared that the key to his success had been his adroit exploitation of Goldsmith's, Sterne's, and Shakespeare's invention by "entering into the true spirit of the poet or writer" without adding anything extraneous.[60] "Some artists of very powerful originality," echoed F. T. Palgrave, "have . . . frankly quitted the book before them to give us something of their own, widely different from their original and, perhaps (as when Turner illustrated Rogers), greatly superior to it. This, however, was not Leslie's way; it would have shocked his natural modesty to think of dealing so, even with the minor writers whom he illustrated; he keeps always within what may be called the literary side of his art; he wishes us to think, not of himself, but of Cervantes or Shakespeare; beneath their individuality he is content to sink his own."[61]

Few critics during Leslie's most prosperous years had depreciated his art on these grounds, though they occasionally faulted it on others. Clearly the temper of opinion in respect to literary illustration was changing in the 1860s. That Leslie had been the prime example of an illustrator who was wholly faithful to the letter and spirit of his source was now counted against him. The thrust of the original Pre-Raphaelites' thinking was away from the autonomy of the literary work that was implied by the mechanical concept of faithful illustration. Thus they revived and practiced a basic principle of Romanticism, reasserting, on a high level once more, the sisterhood of the arts. From their first days as a vigorously dissident coterie, the Pre-Raphaelites were distinguished for their endorsement of working back and forth between poetry and painting. Emblematized by their short-lived magazine, *The Germ,* subtitled *Thoughts Towards Nature in Poetry, Literature, and Art* and after the second issue renamed *Art and Poetry,* the principle was implemented mainly by Rossetti, whose constant aim was not merely to bring the two arts into conjunction but to blend them, the picture becoming at once a separate entity and an expression of the poem, the free-standing poem in its turn becoming a realization of the picture. In either case, he sought to fuse the two so intimately that henceforth they could not be seen as other than an expression of a single impulse or idea. Whether this was "illustration" carried to its ultimate refinement or the very antithesis of the concept depended on the relative strength of representation and subjectivism contained in a given example—as well as on which sense of the word was applied.

Although it is hard to distinguish between cause and effect, this commitment to the affinity between poetry and painting was evidenced by the earliest Pre-Raphaelites' considerable interest in literary subject matter for their art. (The oil paintings they derived from English literature were relatively few; their pen-and-ink, crayon, and pencil drawings and watercolors were much more numerous.) As early as 1844, Ford Madox Brown, who, as Christopher Wood has remarked, "was never a member of the Brotherhood, although clearly he was the one artist who should have been,"[62] executed sixteen outline drawings from *King Lear.* Rossetti, his pupil, had already counted among his very earliest juvenilia pen-and-ink sketches of a scene from *Ivanhoe,* the death of Marmion, and a scene from *King John*; and in the years before he brought the Brotherhood together (1848), he found subjects also in *As You Like It, A Midsummer Night's Dream,* Mrs. Browning's *The Romaunt of Margret,* Coleridge's "Love," Keats's "La Belle Dame Sans Merci," and Poe's "Ulalume" and "The Raven." In the next decade, he would add to the list pictures from Browning's "Pippa Passes" and "The Laboratory" and, more important, episodes from Malory's *Morte Darthur* for the Oxford Union (see Part Three, below, under Malory). Later he would turn to Shakespeare's tragedies, *Hamlet, Romeo and Juliet, Macbeth,* and *Othello.* Among them, the Pre-Raphaelites produced more than sixty illustrations from Shakespeare alone.[63]

Their impatience with the constraints imposed by the principle of literal fidelity found a sharp focus in 1857, in the affair of Moxon's Illustrated Edition of Tennyson's poems (see Part Three, below, under Tennyson).[64] Among the artists the publisher commissioned were Rossetti, Millais, and Holman Hunt, the standard-bearers of the freedom-of-interpretation principle. The poet laureate, on the other hand, turned out to be the most dedicated living representative of all the poets in whose behalf reviewers had fought the battle of artistic fidelity to the text. As the project evolved, Tennyson fiercely defended the integrity of every detail in his poems, resenting every slight novelty or departure from the verbal image that Hunt, in particular, ventured to introduce into his designs. "I didn't say her hair was blown about like that," said Tennyson, objecting to Hunt's attempt to convey, through the Lady of Shalott's disheveled coiffure, the feeling of the disaster that had overcome her. He rejected the steps Hunt inserted into his illustration for the poem of King Cophetua and the Beggar Maid: no steps were mentioned in the poem. This most unhappy collaboration, a traumatic experience for the combatants and a money-losing one for the publisher, dramatized the issue as no other single event did.[65]

But it was Keats who most engaged the pictorial fancies of the Pre-Raphaelites, and two paintings from Keats, exhibited five years apart, evoked reviews that well epitomized the widening difference of opinion on the question of the painter's right to deviate from his literary source. Here the issue was not complicated by the existence of prior treatments by well-known artists; Keats's record in art was a virtual (not total) *tabula rasa* when the Pre-Raphaelites discovered him (see Part Three, below, under Keats), and so they could realize his subjects in paint without the intervention of any predecessor. The question of fidelity was not raised in the reviews of the few Keats pictures that were produced down to 1863. But in that year, critics of Millais's *The Eve of St. Agnes* did raise it, and W. M. Rossetti promptly responded to their objections in the June issue of *Fraser's Magazine:*

> Keats places Madeline's bed behind her (a point of some importance to the incident, because Madeline "dares not look behind, or all the charm is fled"); Mr. Millais, in front of her; Keats's scene is Medieval, Mr. Millais's Jacobean; Keats's window is "triple-arched," Mr. Millais's square and square-mullioned; Keats's moonlight (we have heard even this proposed as an objection to the picture) is inaccurately like sunlight in the colours which it casts from the window; Mr. Millais's is accurately silvered down.

"All these discrepancies are truly stated," Rossetti conceded:

> What is the upshot of them with regard to Mr. Millais's picture? Simply this: that he was under no obligation to cite Keats as an authority for his picture of a girl going to bed by moonlight in a chamber with a painted window, but that he chose to do for the sake of the association and the interest thence derivable. For our own part we do not dissent from his preference: we would rather remember the picture in connexion with the lovely passage from Keats, link together in our mind Keats's Madeline and Millais's maiden, and gulp down the discrepancies for the sake of the association, than have nothing to think about except the girl and the moonlight. . . . The whole question, however, from this literal point of view, is of next to no consequence. It is as likely as not that Mr. Millais's real inspiration was not Keats's poem at all, but the moonlight which he saw, or which he thought he would like to see to paint a picture of.[66]

The critic who disapproved of Millais's moonlight, an objection of which Rossetti made more than is quoted here, was Palgrave, writing in the *Saturday Review* for 16 May. "Keats, as is well known," he said,

> poetically gave the tints of sunlight passing through gorgeous glass to the wintry moonbeams which colour his heroine with more than Venetian splendour. This was, perhaps, a just license to the artist who paints in words. He who paints in colours has, with equal justice, corrected the image, and thrown over his figure pale lurid rays, which rarely carry with them any indication of warmth. . . . But we must venture to urge, that Mr. Millais's amended version of the great Poet—and of the great Poet in his greatest work—should have stopped here.

Such literalist criticism placed the artist in a predicament from which there was no easy escape. If he followed Keats's alleged error and depicted moonlight in terms of sunlight, he was untrue to observed reality; if he corrected Keats's error and painted moonlight as moonlight, he did violence to the poetic text. And, as a matter of fact, the volatile mixing of Keatsian imagery, so specifically colorful, with the Pre-Raphaelite penchant for vivid hues could scarcely have avoided critical eruptions like Palgrave's. The loving sensuousness with which Keats described Madeline gave critics an additional pretext for denouncing the Pre-Raphaelite scheme of coloration as they applied it to her. Palgrave was distressed by "the wan face, blackened lips, and blue-stained bosom of Mr. Millais' figure;" and the *Art Journal,* finding the flesh tones "suggestive of a body rising in grave-clothes, already tainted by corruption," wound up its notice of the painting by beginning to quote "a thing of beauty" and then pointedly suppressing the next four words.[67]

The controversial moonlight and the prayerful heroine far gone in decay were not forgotten. Five years later (1868), Daniel Maclise, whom no one ever was tempted to call a Pre-Raphaelite by either sympathy or practice, showed his own version of the Keats subject (pl. 336). "Mr.

Millais," said the *Athenaeum,* "with a poetic zest that is given to few, revelled in the glory of the moonlight, painted it, and called the result after Keats's poem; Mr. Maclise painted the very idea of Keats, but would have made that lover of Endymion shudder at the lighting of his picture almost as sharply as he would wince before Mr. Millais' female figure."[68] Exhibited by the dealer Gambart at the same time that Maclise's picture hung at the Royal Academy was another subject from Keats, Holman Hunt's *Isabella and the Pot of Basil,* to which a minor journalist named Bernard Cracroft devoted an entire article in the *Fortnightly Review* that also pursued the nagging question of the artist's obligation to his poetic source. "A miracle of labour and technical resource," the painting was nevertheless "a total miscarriage in conception" before which "the impartial spectator, after he has collected his wits and recovered from his first impressions, [stands] in something like amazement." Specifically:

> Mr. Holman Hunt has painted a shrew in her teens *before* her trials, and so to speak, in the green tree. Keats has painted an exquisitely tender and headlong nature *after* a long course of heartrending frenzy, and in the fallen and disintegrating fruit. If I were to suggest the type of character that would suit the picture, I should unhesitatingly say that of the celebrated Rachelle when dying of illicit love in *Phaedra.* Mr. Hunt has painted a commonplace, violent-tempered Italian girl, with a vicious eye and a muddy brow. . . . *
>
> His Isabel is quite the girl who later in life might have cut off her *living* lover's head if he displeased her; quite capable, too, of murdering the brothers who murdered her lover; not by any means the girl whose first thought on dreaming the truth was to recover the darling head, and keep it forever, even in death, instead of being revenged upon the ruthless destroyers of her bliss. Instead of heavenly sweetness breathed upon and devastated by demon's woe, and a paradise of expression, furrowed into waste and wildness and a thousand cross channels, by the hurricane of an overwhelming calamity, we have muscularity run mad, angry health, vacant peevishness, and in the place of the actual effects of storm and tempest in the past, vague possibilities of future ill-temper.[69]

To feed his readers' indignation, Cracroft devoted two full pages to quoting Keats's "beautiful poem" against Holman Hunt's alleged travesty. The device, of course, was an old one; but by now its availability was proving a doubtful advantage, since experience had shown that it could be used with equal freedom by opposing critics. The *Art Journal* declared that "Mr. Holman Hunt has followed with literal fidelity the words of Keats, and a poem signally pathetic and passionate is here translated into a picture which few can see without emotion."[70]

But the same reviewer warned, as earlier critics had at least implied in their reception of Pre-Raphaelite art, that the "illusive realism" of such paintings would "exercise more than a legitimate spell over the vulgar public. . . . We . . . warn the spectator against taking even this miracle of manipulation for more than it is worth." The camel's nose was edging under the tent. Pejorative terms like "illusive realism" and "manipulation" could not hide the fact that formal qualities were coming more and more to present their own claims to consideration, and not merely to a "vulgar public" ready to be dazzled by superficial virtuosity while remaining indifferent to content. It might well be that an artist was disloyal to the plain sense of the literary text, and even its spirit, though this always was a matter for fruitless debate; but what of the picture *as art,* regardless of its source? The insistent question portended, then hastened, the decline of literary art.

*The picture had begun as a portrait of Hunt's wife, the distinctly un-Italian Fanny Waugh.

CHAPTER 12

The decline of literary painting: improving quality of art criticism, the developing pejorative connotation of "literary."—Conclusion: What happened when people "read" pictures?; various degrees of understanding; the relevance of literary painting to literary history, and its critical usefulness.

At the Royal Academy in 1857 appeared a painting by Millais entitled *A Dream of the Past: Sir Isumbras at the Ford* (pl. 164). Not since Turner's Venetian pictures of Shylock and Jessica (1830) and Juliet and her nurse (1836) had a literary picture by an eminent artist evoked so much indignation and ridicule. "The change in [Millais's] manner, from the years of 'Ophelia' and 'Mariana' to 1857," said Ruskin in the current edition of *Academy Notes,* "is not merely Fall—it is Catastrophe."[1] The painting inspired a burst of verbal and graphic satires, jokes, skits in the humorous papers, and serious onslaughts in the reviewing press. "An attempt on the public credulity," said the *Saturday Review;* "monstrous," said the *Athenaeum.*[2] Sir John Gilbert summed up the general reaction when, after seeing the painting six years later in the "confused, littery" study of its purchaser, the novelist Charles Reade, he wrote, "I was astonished and offended by the slovenly coarse painting, the badness of the drawing, and the entire vulgarity of the picture."[3]

In view of the large number of literary paintings to which the same discription might have been applied, it is a little hard to understand at this distance of time what all the fuss was about. But the Turner pictures and this one in 1857 are a useful way of roughly bracketing the great age of literary art, whose tide was in full flow in the 1830s and was showing signs of ebbing in the 1850s. At a time when the debate over the legitimacy and limitations of illustration was growing livelier, it was ironically fitting that Millais's painting, like each of Turner's, was a *pseudo*-literary piece, untrue to its alleged source. Turner placed Juliet and her nurse in Venice, where Shakespeare had never sent them; his "quotation" from *The Merchant of Venice* in the Shylock picture did not occur in Shakespeare's text; and though there actually was a metrical romance of Sir Isumbras, of which

164. John Everett Millais, *A Dream of the Past: Sir Isumbras at the Ford* (RA 1857) (Lady Lever Art Gallery, Port Sunlight). Lewis Carroll's judgment: "Remarkably ugly. . . . There are three people on a horse, but so much smaller than the average human stature, as to be hardly any load at all; an additional gigantic effect is given to the animal by its being partly out of the picture. The Girl's face is earnest, but coarse, and her eyes unnaturally large; the knight is good, though with an expression like an honest old gardener; the face of the boy behind is lubberley [*sic*] and wooden to a degree" (*Diaries*, ed. Green, 1: 114). When the satirical storm broke over this painting, Thackeray put his arm around Millais and said, "Never mind, my boy, go on painting such pictures." When the canvas came back from the exhibition unsold, the artist kicked a hole in it. Presumably it was repaired before Charles Reade acquired it.

several manuscripts survived, the quotation that accompanied Millais's painting was a pastiche written for the occasion by Tom Taylor. The association with literature was, once again, indirect and contrived.

From the sixties onward, the frail and inconstant assumptions on which the literary painting had rested even in the years of its greatest popularity were exposed, and critics came to agree, for a variety of reasons, that it was a blight on contemporary art.

The incidence of paintings from literary sources decreased year by year. In 1865, the usual exhibitions included twenty-five pictures from Shakespeare, ten from Tennyson, four from Moore, two each from Milton and Southey, and one each from Wordsworth, Scott, Thomson, Byron, Spenser, Burns, and Mrs. Browning—a precipitous decline from the days when more than 100 such paintings were produced each year, but still much larger than the yearly average of such pictures exhibited in the fourteen summer shows (1877–90) of Sir Coutts Lindsay's Grosvenor Gallery, the headquarters of the aesthetic movement in art and hence of one flank of the avant garde. There were only seven pictures from *Romeo and Juliet,* three Ophelias, and one picture each from half a dozen other Shakespeare plays; two or three from Tennyson; three from Spenser; four from William Morris; one each from Rossetti, Swinburne, Milton, Scott, Browning, Keats, and FitzGerald (and, incongruously, two atavistic subjects from the first days of literary painting, *The Seasons* and Ossian).[4] The exhibitions of the New English Art Club, formed in 1886 as another sector of the avant garde, were almost totally devoid of literary pictures except for a few by J. E. Christie.[5]

No longer did wealthy patrons of the arts, members of a generation quite separate from that of Vernon and Sheepshanks, commission or buy literary paintings as their predecessors had done in such numbers between 1820 and 1850. The magnates of the Midlands and the North chose instead to distribute their largesse among Pre-Raphaelites like Rossetti and Millais, who seldom turned out literary pictures for them; the new

165. Sir Frederic Leighton, *The Garden of the Hesperides* (RA 1892) (Lady Lever Art Gallery, Port Sunlight). This painting of a well-known theme from classical literature has little if anything to do with English sources (Tennyson did not reprint his early poem "The Hesperides" after it appeared in his 1832 *Poems*). It emblematizes, instead, the way classical subjects freshly attracted painters toward the end of the Victorian era as interest in English literary subjects declined. The coiled snake and skull-like apples associate the picture with the decadent poetry of *fin de siècle*.

school of classical art represented by Poynter, Leighton, and Alma-Tadema; and such purveyors of escapist dreams and vague, virtuous allegories as Burne-Jones and Watts.

Moreover, the market for cheap original paintings of literary subjects was severely affected by the proliferating editions of the English classics, which, thanks to various technical improvements, were cheaper, more replete with illustrations, and better calculated to appeal to mass taste.* The so-called golden age of book illustration in the 1860s, now generally agreed to have been the art's high-water mark, was the very time when the popularity of painted literary illustrations began to decline. The artistic distinction of many of the books produced in that decade enabled men and women possessing a certain amount of taste to discern the inferiority of the illustrations then being offered on canvas.

The diminishing demand for literary art was due as well to the sheer exhaustion of the subjects selected. From early in the century, critics had deplored the triteness of certain literary themes in art; and as the years passed, the number of those urgently recommended for retirement increased. In 1869, a writer in the *Contemporary Review* was wishing it were impossible "even to attempt universally-painted subjects any more"—the Vicar of Wakefield, Swift, Sterne, Malvolio, Dr. Johnson.[7]

By the 1870s, also, the quality of English art criticism was beginning to improve. Belatedly, jocularity posing as judgment was fading from fashion. Reviewers were becoming more judicious and responsible. On the whole, the new men were better equipped for their job and so were more

*An excellent example of the competition offered by a lavishly illustrated book was the volume, complete with blue and gilt binding, gilt edges, and ornamental headings, called *Pictures from English Literature,* by John Francis Waller, LL.D., published by Cassell in 1870. The letterpress consisted of eight- to ten-page essays pegged on specially commissioned illustrations by many of the day's leading artists. The volume constituted a veritable anthology of banal literary subjects: Griselda, Una, Falstaff, the Lady in *Comus,* Sir Roger de Coverley, Sophia Western, John Gilpin, Tam o' Shanter, Jeanie Deans, the Ancient Mariner, Gertrude of Wyoming, Haidee, Nydia (in *The Last Days of Pompeii*), and Colonel Newcome. Only Dick Dowlass (from Colman's play *The Heir-at-Law,* 1797), Sheridan's Lydia Languish, and Dickens's Pecksniff and Dora were newcomers to the all too familiar list.

effective in cultivating intelligent public interest in art. Here the influence of the magisterial Ruskin was decisive, as Sidney Colvin, one of the best of the breed, asserted in 1879, after deploring the low state of the profession down to that time (see chapter 10, above): "It has come to pass from a variety of causes, and not least from the stimulating power exercised by a master of letters, Mr. Ruskin, that a greater amount of intelligent interest is now directed to the works of art in England than was ever directed before."[8] The public now expected more of reviewers, and among the things it learned from them were reasons why literary pictures were *passé*. The fact that no new talents had arrived to reanimate the genre with fresh subjects and modes of treatment was a minor, circumstantial reason compared with the general tendency of criticism itself, which, finally rejecting whatever vestiges of *ut pictura poesis* survived, broadened to reject also the whole principle of illustration.

Though the undiscriminating public still demanded them, pictures that told stories, or captured a moment in a story, were coming into severe disrepute among critics who instead were beginning to promote the aesthetic values at the center of the art for art's sake movement. The formal

166. George Frederic Watts, *The Judgement of Paris* (Grosvenor Gallery 1887) (Faringdon Collection Trust, Buscot Park). Sixty years after Etty exhibited his version of the subject (pl. 134), the story participated in the revival of classicism under the auspices of Watts (who painted it three times), Leighton, Alma-Tadema, and Poynter. Tennyson's version ("Oenone") was familiar to everyone who owned a copy of the poet laureate's poems.

properties of a painting, its composition, color, tone, texture, now replaced moral edification, sentimental indulgence, and humorous anecdote as the artist's legitimate concerns. No longer, after a century in which the assumption was almost universally shared by the people who wrote about art and bought it, was it believed that paintings had to be "about" something.

In 1869, an appropriate year for stocktaking because it saw the Royal Academy's migration from its former quarters in a wing of the National Gallery to its present home in Burlington House, Edward Poynter, later president of the Academy as well as director of the National Gallery, declared:

Most of our popular art depends for its success almost entirely on the facts

167. Edward James Poynter, *The Ides of March* (RA 1883) (City Art Gallery, Manchester). The literary allusion in this picture was made explicit in the quotation from *Julius Caesar* (2. 2) that accompanied it: "Yet Caesar shall go forth; for these predictions / Are to the world in general as to Caesar."

168. Sir Edward Burne-Jones, *Love and the Pilgrim* (New Gallery 1897) (Tate Gallery, London). Like the artist's *Legend of the Briar Rose* series (pl. 76), this painting is a celebrated example of the presence of highly romanticized and allegorized medievalism in late Victorian art, the subject being derived loosely from the pseudo-Chaucerian *Romaunt of the Rose*. Burne-Jones dedicated it to Swinburne.

represented in the pictures and not on the art which is expended in the painting of them; a certain amount of technical skill is required no doubt by the more knowing of the public, but very little of it will go a long way. The public generally not being very profoundly instructed on the point of art, but perfectly understanding the point of a scene from Shakespeare or one of Scott's novels, the artist whose only desire is to make a popular success, does his best to amuse the public with what they can appreciate, and represents his subject without regard to the more important and nobler truths of Nature, which he knows would be thrown away upon the ignorant, only looking for just enough of reality as is sufficient to make his point obvious to them.[9]

Three years later (*Notes sur l'Angleterre,* 1872), the critic Hippolyte Taine reported an impression of the work of the most popular British artists that he had formed during several extended visits to the country beginning in 1858:

The essence . . . is the anecdote, the story, the literary attribute, the representation of some aspect of *mores* which they have chosen as a subject. The pleasure of the eye, harmony, and beauty of line and colour are all relegated to secondary roles; such is the case in the work of Maclise, Leslie, Hunt, and one of the most famous, Mulready. . . . Never has so much effort been expended in trying to address the mind by way of the senses, illustrate an idea or a truth, or in collecting a greater mass of psychological observations onto a surface twelve inches square. What patient and penetrating criticisms! What clever contrivance, and what aptitude in rendering moral values into physical terms! And what admirable vignettes these artists might have drawn to illustrate an edition of Sterne, Goldsmith, Crabbe, Thackeray or Eliot! . . . *But what a pity it is that these artists, instead of writing, took to painting!*

In the prodigious effort they have made to concentrate their entire attention on man's moral aspect, their optical sensibility has become both distorted and blunted. I do not believe that pictures so very disagreeable to look at have ever been painted. Impossible to imagine cruder effects, colour more brutal or exaggerated, more violent and gaudy discords, harder or falser juxtapositions of tones. . . .[10] (Emphasis added.)

Reviewing the Academy exhibition of 1877, Henry James joined the mounting attack on bourgeois art:

> You immediately perceive . . . that [the pictures on display] are subjects addressed to a taste of a particularly unimaginative and unaesthetic order—to the taste of the British merchant and paterfamilias and his excellently regulated family. What this taste appears to demand of a picture is that it shall have a taking title, like a three-volume novel or an article in a magazine; that it shall embody in its lower flights some comfortable incident in the daily life of our period, suggestive more especially of its gentilities and proprieties and familiar moralities, and in its loftier scope some picturesque episode of history or fiction which may be substantiated by a long explanatory extract in the catalogue.[11]

Although one might discount this observation as a mere expression of James's characteristic fastidiousness, it also manifested the way in which commentators on art in general were putting more distance between themselves and the exhibition-attending public. Their predecessors had tended to keep a foot in both the critical and the popular camps, openly sharing the public's taste even as they derided it. Now there was a sharper division, exacerbated by the steady degeneration of genre painting. Popular demand was running more and more toward triviality, toward subjects laden with vapid sentimentality or a facetiousness more appropriate to the music hall and illustrated comic papers. (It was no accident that most of the humorous adaptations of literary titles and subjects and misapplications of literary tags mentioned in the Introduction and chapter 9 occurred after the middle of the century.) The restrained realism that marked the best early Victorian genre art had given way to superficial prettiness. For this degeneration, the critics held artists as culpable as their customers. The feeling grew that art has been commercialized on a new low level of subject and treatment; that painters, more attentive to market demands than ever before, were cynically prostituting their talents in pursuit of the quick and lucrative sale.

The comfortable notion that paintings, including those from literature, were made to be "lived with," was confronted by the older doctrine that art was created for a higher purpose than interior decoration. In 1888, the critic Frederic Harrison denied that, as had often been fondly claimed, art of the kind produced for household consumption would remain companionable throughout the years:

> A picture . . . acquires or creates a certain *genius loci,* and becomes therefore part of the instinctive life of those who dwell in its presence. We cannot shut up a picture and put it away in our shelves, as we do a book; we cannot play it over and over again as the mood takes us, just as we can with a piece of music. There it stands for ever opposite to us like a Palace or Cathedral, continually reiterating the same impression. For this reason, drollery, riddles, anecdotes, novelettes, sentimentalities on canvas, are so horribly irritating. Does the painter of "Two of a Pair," "Her Favourite Flower," "How happy I could be with either" [from *The Beggar's Opera*], "Sterne and the dead Jackass," "Bugs in a Rug", "Satan addressing the Fallen Spirits in Pandemonium," "The Drunkard's Home," "Pharaoh's Daughter at Five o'Clock Tea"—do the authors of these very quaint, moral, tearful or learned compositions ever ask themselves this question,—"When the Exhibition is over, will the buyer like to sit down day by day and listen to the same jest, the same story, the same bit of sapient morality, or curious bit of learning?" A slight tale, a good anecdote, an odd incident, are all very well once in a way; in a book, over the dinner-table, in an idle hour. But to have them eternally dinned into us is maddening. "Evil communications corrupt good manners" is a grand and true saying. But who could bear to have it

> always staring at one over the fireplace, or shouted into our ears by the public bellman? Falstaff himself would drive one crazy, if we had to listen to *Henry IV* every time we took a seat at a dinner-table.[12]

Unconsciously echoing Taine's assertion that the painters of literary pictures might have done better as writers, Harrison denounced the typical subject painter of the day:

> He seems to imagine that his duty is to compose a mild original sonnet, a snippety original novel, or a watery anecdote, grave or gay. Now painters are not poets, romancers, nor literary craftsmen. . . . How can painters suppose that cultivated men and women care for their japes, their puns, their snippings from stale *Elegant Extracts,* or for their own poetical and moral maunderings on canvas? . . . Almost all the anecdotes which fill half a page of the Academy catalogues, as subjects of so-called historical pictures, scandal about Queen Elizabeth, the gallantries of some Stuart prince (understanding *gallantry* in all its various senses), the oddities of Swift, Johnson, or Walter Scott, anecdotes of the Reign of Terror, etc., are either quite unauthentic or utterly trivial; nay, not seldom they are grossly libellous and horribly mean. So long as a subject offers a medium for sheeny stuffs, quaint costume, and Wardour-Street *bric-à-brac,* none seem to be too silly, too scurrilous, or too petty for some painters. It is not the business of painters to become very minor poets and tenth-rate serial novelists.[13]

As the assaults continued on all pictures that aspired to do nothing but tell a story (the very term "literary painting" acquired a deprecatory connotation that it still retains, a century later), painting and literature steadily moved apart. Harrison, it will be noted, included several literary subjects as random examples in his diatribe; and in other commentary on the vulgarization of popular subject art, literary pictures hovered in the background even if they were not specifically mentioned. Indeed, literary subjects were the most vulnerable of all branches of currently practiced art. The awareness grew—in the past forty years it had been articulated only in reviewers' throw-away remarks—that the illustration of literary themes had been encouraged on what now appeared to be fallacious grounds. In the surge of enthusiasm for deriving artistic subjects from poetry, the limitations of the exchange had been overlooked, though these had earlier been made obvious when Lessing and his disciples had denied, or at least severely trimmed down, the pretensions of *ut pictura poesis.* There were built-in barriers to the full sisterhood of the arts. If poetry and painting could never be regarded as twins or even as siblings, it was because one could exist in the dimension of time, whereas the other could not, and because, furthermore, one depended on imagined imagery, conveyed through print or the spoken word, whereas the other froze a definite picture before the beholder's eyes, with no allowance for the expanding, enriching, and interpreting functions of the inward eye.

Paintings from literary sources had additional limitations because of the special nature of literary subject matter. They could deal only with surfaces: with appearances, situations, and actions (but with only an instant of an action). They could not fathom or represent the true depth and complexity of a literary work or even of a moment from that work, except by the sacrifice of its context, of its dependence on all that had preceded. They could not represent the special effects of language, formal structure, developing characterization, ongoing narrative. They could not reproduce dialogue. They could not represent ideas, except those that could be simplified and conveyed by a single image or set of

169. Augustus Egg, *Esmond Returns after the Battle of Wynendel* (RA 1857) (Walker Art Gallery, Liverpool). A mid-Victorian domestication of the high-art theme of the hero's return (cf. Othello, pl. 105). The scene is not actually in Thackeray's *Henry Esmond* (when Esmond returns, it is Lady Castlewood who kneels to him, not Beatrix [bk. 3, chap. 2]), but reviewers readily assumed that it was: a tribute, perhaps, to the persuasive power of Egg's sympathetic imagination. See pl. 356.

images. In short, they could only isolate, from the totality of a literary work's artistic and substantive qualities, those few that could be depicted visually and statically.

This inherent disability of the visual medium, as we have seen, was always conspicuous in the case of Shakespeare. Artists were rendered increasingly impotent as the body of nineteenth-century Shakespeare criticism grew, with its endless probings into character and motivation. The inadequacy of paint to represent what was more and more the central concern of literature from the Romantic period onward, its account of the inner life of men and women, became further evident as fiction supplied so many subjects to artists and as the psychological element in older fiction commanded the attention of critics. When artists drew from a novel, the only overt guide they had was the author's verbal description of a character's appearance and—impossible to transfer to paint—his or her speech. Beyond that lay what was the novelist's exclusive province, the whole story of the character's psychological experience, complex makeup, and interaction with other figures. As the *Times* said when describing Augustus Egg's *Esmond Returns after the Battle of Wynendel* (pl. 169), "Who could paint that mixture of fiend and fairy, of demon and Delilah, Beatrice? . . . If the writer had been under the same matter-of-fact necessity of outward embodiment which lies upon the painter, Mr. Thackeray, courageous as he is, and consummate workman, would scarcely have managed to bring the tale to its present termination."[14]

The truth was that from the beginning, the painter and the author he drew from had been linked in what was an inherently unequal partnership. The vocabulary of art, though it could in its own fashion enrich the literary subject, was inadequate to translate the full meaning of the words on the printed page. The painter had at his disposal the conventional or inventive language of posture and gesture, but the writer had the limitless, flexible language of words. To artists working in what had become, by the late Victorian era, a century-old vein of subject painting, and one dominated for most of its career by the critics' insistence that the painter be faithful to his source, the struggle against loaded odds must have seemed—if they paused to examine their professional consciences—hardly worth the expense of time and talent. Their task was unavoidably reductive, and the means at their disposal insufficient. It is conceivable that some such awareness turned the more sensitive members of the art-loving public away from literary pictures. Schooled by literary critics, they demanded more depth and subtlety in paintings from literature than, in the nature of things, artists could offer.

But how many prospective buyers of literary art were so sophisticated? At first glance, much evidence suggests that most of those who attended the annual exhibitions were equipped to understand, appreciate, and respond to a painting from a reasonably well-known literary source. The assumption was implicit in the frequency with which artists chose literary subjects and in the wide distribution of literary texts among the picture-buying public. But the premise was nevertheless open to question. The "common reader" was not all that common, even in respect to the works we assume to have been the customary possession of the literate Victorian. The pristine condition of the expensive sets of "standard authors" still to be seen in the libraries of great country houses (where many literary paintings were hung) suggests that there, at any rate, the classic English authors were not much read, though such sets may have been bought for ostentation rather than use, and other, less expensive copies served for everyday purposes. Even in less affluent households, those sets may have been put on the shelves as a form of cultural affectation rather than as a ready source of leisure-time pleasure. Reviewers sometimes expressed their doubts. One, writing of a picture from Addison's *Spectator* in 1844, remarked, "We are afraid that in these fickle days, the lucubrations of 'the short-faced gentleman' are oftener referred to than read."[15] Some years later (1858), Walter Bagehot observed, "Even standard authors exercise but slender influence on the susceptible minds of a rising generation; they are become 'papa's books'; the walls of the library are adorned with their regular volumes; but no hand touches them. Their fame is itself half an obstacle to their popularity; a delicate fancy shrinks from employing so great a celebrity as the companion of an idle hour."[16]

Such comments make it clear that former high estimates of the literary knowledge possessed by art buyers were too optimistic, and that the incidence of such knowledge was declining, partly because the social composition of the art clientele was changing (the educated patron giving way to the unschooled one) and partly because the prestige of literature itself was fading as the values of Matthew Arnold's Philistines gained wider credence. By the 1880s, the failure of the new policy of compulsory elementary education to add perceptibly to the culturally receptive and prepared population had intensified the conviction, always widespread though not always voiced in public, that most men and women in Britain were content to read on no higher a level than that of the sensational Sunday papers and froth mass-produced for the servant-girl class, and that even art lovers could not be depended upon to respond to any but the most familiar handful of literary subjects. Robert Gordon's *Lady Castlewood Visiting Henry Esmond* (New Gallery 1889) evoked this skeptical comment from the *Times:*

> It is, of course, always* a disputed point whether pictures ought to be painted in illustration of books—whether art should be content to make herself in this way the hand-maid of literature. It is a question of degree, and if the subject illus-

*"Always" at that time, perhaps, but the point was seldom "disputed" in the heyday of literary pictures.

> trated is one that has stamped itself upon the knowledge of a whole generation or of a whole country, like some scenes from Scott or Shakespeare, few would say that an artist might not spend the most elaborate pains in illustrating it. Perhaps the central scenes of "Esmond" have attained to this classical position, and if so, then Mr. Gordon's picture may be allowed as one that tells its own story clearly enough to be comprehended by educated Englishmen.[17]

The next year, the same critic raised a related question in writing of W. B. Richmond's realization of a six-line passage from Shelley's "Epipsychidion":

> . . . As it stands, the picture, like so many other works of English painters, is too complex—too much a confusion of the literary and the artistic motives; in a word, too great a tax upon the literary knowledge of the spectator. Everybody would have understood it if the poet in the corner had been painted out and if, instead of the lines from the poem, we had had a title like "An Allegory of Spring." But what is the percentage, even among educated persons, who have read "Epipsychidion"? And, among them, what is the percentage of those who understand it?[18]

One by one, the fetishes and taboos that had prejudiced criticism of literary painting throughout the Victorian era were demolished, overripe victims of a new climate of opinion. No longer could artists be held strictly accountable for their obedience to the literary text. When paintings came to be judged on their own merits as exercises in pictorial beauty, fidelity to their received subject was a tiresome and pedantic irrelevance.

In the 1870s, an equally tiresome grievance, that artists sacrificed Shakespeare in admitting to their pictures the distracting and degrading influence of the stage, came to a head and was finally disposed of in Shakespeare's favor. To the *Saturday Review,* an undistinguished painting from *The Merchant of Venice,* shown at the Royal Academy in 1872, once more proved "what by this time should be only too well known, that Shakspeare is at once the most easy and the most difficult of authors for a painter to deal with; easy because every character may be borrowed and appropriated from the theatre as if it were a stage property, and difficult because we have a right to expect from a picture more than from the stage; difficult also because Shakspeare, like nature herself, can seldom, if ever, receive full justice or adequate illustration."[19] Four years later (1876), a writer in the *Quarterly Review* settled the matter once and for all when he put into a nutshell the doctrine that had often been bandied about but seldom stated so forthrightly:

> Widely as the resources of the theatre have been enlarged in our time, there is a world beyond the reach of scenic contrivance; and it is in this world that we desire to see the painters, who would illustrate our great national poet, moving with freedom and creative power. . . . We are disposed to think that the artist who desires to illustrate Shakespeare will be safest when he visits the theatre seldom, and devotes himself to a profound and independent study of the immortal text. There are touches that defy the player's arts; there are tints of natural colour, and gleams of poetic light, that rouge and tinsel cannot simulate.[20]

By now this sage counsel was hardly necessary, because fewer and fewer painters were choosing Shakespearean subjects.

The attached literary tag also exhausted critics' patience. Within a few weeks in 1875, two different voices were raised against the old abomination and the crutch it provided to artists whose productions were at best incomplete and at worst incomprehensible without it. The *Spectator,* commenting on Mrs. E. M. Ward's picture at the Royal Academy of the "Ettrick Shepherd's" (James Hogg's) first love, said flatly that it "shares with most pictures of its kind the quality of being unintelligible without a long quotation, and superfluous after reading it";[21] and in a report to an American paper on the same exhibition, Henry James circuitously made the same point. The pictures of Burne-Jones, Rossetti, and Leighton, he said, "always seem as if, to be complete, they needed to have a learned sonnet, of an explanatory sort, affixed to the frame; and if, in the absence of the sonnet, the critical observer ventures to improvise one, as effective as his learning will allow, and to be pleased or displeased according as the picture corresponds to it, there is a certain justification for his temerity."[22]

By the later 1880s, a consensus had been arrived at. As Frederic Harrison put it, "All pictures should be exhibited under a simple title: every word of poetry, extract, Diodorus Siculus, Macaulay's *History,* puns, sentiments, and ejaculations, should be strictly forbidden, as at Paris."[23] But the Royal Academy was not yet ready to emulate the Salon. As late as the 1940s its exhibitors were still being offered space in the catalogue for a "quotation," even though few availed themselves of the ancient privilege.

The best known and most successful practitioners of subject art largely moved out of literary painting. Orchardson, Millais, and Pettie turned to portraiture, which once again was where the real money lay. Leighton, Alma-Tadema, Poynter, Watts, and Burne-Jones revived old classical themes in marmoreal unreality or immersed themselves in pretentious allegory. By 1900, the painting from English literature was a decided anachronism, a relic of a kind of art irreparably tainted by its association with what were now regarded in enlightened circles as the affectations, the intellectual vacuity, the clumsy moralism, the sheer lack of aesthetic imagination and taste that undermined the work of the most popular genre artists. In only two significant but isolated ways did the literary picture survive for a while in the new century. Some artists who could loosely be considered descendants of the Pre-Raphaelites—Waterhouse, Meteyard, Strudwick, Spencer Stanhope, Walter Crane, Byam Shaw*—continued to draw upon literary sources, particularly Tennyson, whose Lady of Shalott, as Christopher Wood has observed, remained "almost a cult subject."[24] There was also Edwin Abbey, who, like his fellow-American Charles Robert Leslie at the beginning of the century, had acquired his taste for English literature while involved in the book business, as an employee of the Harper publishing firm. In his time—he came to England in 1878 and remained there for the rest of his life, though retaining his American citizenship—he was a prolific illustrator of Shakespeare; and several of his paintings, especially his *Hamlet* and *Lear,* attracted much attention at the Royal Academy at the turn of the century. But as a Shakespearean painter, he was almost the last of his kind, for in the new century only Charles Ricketts and one or two others occasionally painted from that supreme source of literary art.

The descent into extinction of a form of painting that had flourished in Britain for over a hundred years was due, then, to a variety of causes, all having to do with the gradual replacement of Victorian aesthetic and cultural values by the spirit of modernism. But behind them all was the changing status of English literature itself, both the heritage and the creative presence. The disappearance of literary paintings from the exhi-

*Byam Shaw, to be sure, exhibited no fewer than thirty-nine small paintings from literature at a dealer's in May 1899; but the quantity is less significant than the spirit indicated by their collective title: *Thoughts Suggested by Some Passages from British Poets* (six from Clough, three from Christina Rossetti, four from Shakespeare, and the rest from a miscellany of poets ranging from Suckling to the Brownings, Tennyson, and Scott). As with "ideal" paintings, the literary sources provided only the departure point for exercises in lightweight pictorial philosophizing. This was the only vestigial usefulness that literature retained for artists in the early twentieth century.

bitions marked more than a momentous transition in British art. It suggested that literature, for whatever reasons, was no longer one of the central concerns of the increasingly complex culture that determined the content of art.

In the course of the 140 years we have traversed, English literature and art slowly came into conjunction, reached their maximum contact in the early and mid-Victorian eras, and then drifted apart to almost total separation by the end of the nineteenth century. The process, with all its intermediate shifts of direction, was part of the much larger movement, still uncompleted, from language to image that has marked the history of modern popular culture. Eventually the history of the visual part of English literary culture will have to be fitted into that broader pattern.

Meanwhile, the story told in these pages raises many questions, some of which may possibly be answered through more intensive research while others, in the absence of relevant documents, must remain material for speculation. Foremost among them is the tantalizing, truly unanswerable question of what really happened when a man, woman, or child was brought face to face with a picture that purported to represent a character or scene in a familiar book. Such mentions of exhibited paintings as we find in the letters, memoirs, and recorded conversations of the seasonal habitués of the exhibition rooms, like Victorian readers' private notes of their reaction to newly read books, are so brief and unparticularized as to be almost without value as historical evidence. But we do know that their approach to paintings and engravings with dramatic or narrative content took the recommended form of "reading"—that is, of methodically scrutinizing the details of the design in quest of its full meaning. Hogarth's "graphic representations," wrote Lamb, "are indeed books; and they have the teeming, fruitful, suggestive meaning of *words.* Other pictures we look at,—his prints we read." This seminal remark occurred at the beginning of Lamb's enthusiastic essay "On the Genius and Character of Hogarth" in which he demonstrated the art of reading a picture closely. An even more stimulating practical demonstration was to occur in Hazlitt's "On the Works of Hogarth" (significantly, one of a series on "the Comic *Writers,* Etc., of Great Britain," delivered in November 1818–January 1819).

Between them, Lamb and Hazlitt—and even more influentially in the next generation, Ruskin[25]—spread far and wide this concept of what, in twentieth-century literary criticism, would be called *explication de texte*—in this case, the text consisting of painted significant details that were fitted into a single design as words constituted a single poem. Although none of the popular Victorian genre painters even approached the Hogarthian extreme in loading their canvases with symbolic or ironic detail, they recognized and catered to the growing expectation that their pictures could be read like a book; and so, in their very different way, did the Pre-Raphaelites with their emphasis on emblems, which in many cases required of the beholder a considerable knowledge of religious symbolism and typology. Purposeful visitors to the annual exhibitions, as distinct from casual loungers, moved from painting to painting with eyes that sought out every meaningful detail, usually, to be sure, to the neglect of the whole composition.

We can be sure, then, that typical genre scenes from literature—from

Shakespeare or Scott or Goldsmith—were approached, fittingly enough, as exercises in "reading." But beyond that, our knowledge of individual spectators' responses must remain entirely hypothetical. In the nature of the case, an infinite number of possibilities were offered by the simultaneous presence of two large variables. One was the wide range of literary subjects treated, from the instantly comprehensible—often "modern instances" that were in the open stock of conventional themes, the literary reference serving as a mere embellishment—to the kind that were absolutely unintelligible without knowledge of their source or the aid of a lengthy explanation or epigraph in the catalogue. Between these two extremes lay what were probably the majority of literary pictures, those which were superficially comprehensible at first examination but whose context and nuances would have been lost on those who were unacquainted with the source.

Matching this spectrum of intelligibility was the varying degree of literary knowledge, if any, that spectators brought to a painting. The facts, as we have seen, are impossible to establish. Some spectators would have been vaguely aware of the announced subject and source; others would have been so well versed in the play or novel as to appreciate every touch the artist introduced into his conception of the scene. Assuming that most fell somewhere in the middle range, bringing to a painting from a reasonably familiar literary source at least some acquaintance with its subject, their "reading" would have involved, to begin with, a recollection or vicarious repetition of their prior experience with the book, whether dim or still vivid in memory. Embedded in their minds were preconceptions that were immediately brought into play as they were confronted with a pictorial version of a scene or character they had once, or many times, met in print. Like the reviewers, the people who paid their shillings at the door of the gallery carried inside their individual expectations of what a painting from Spenser or Tennyson should be like.

The predominant ones ordinarily would have come from the reader's own imaginative constructs, formed from the printed page itself—his instinctive notion of what the author had meant to convey by way of a picture, whether sketched in with but a few words or merely implied, as in the ivory miniatures of Jane Austen, or expansively delineated, as in the broad canvases of Mrs. Radcliffe or Scott. But if the text (Shakespeare, Milton, *The Seasons*) had been accompanied by illustrations, these would have affected the developing mental image of scene and character to a greater or small extent, depending on how impressionable—or, on the other hand, temperamentally resistant to such suggestion—the reader was. (One wonders how many readers of Dickens found themselves at odds with the strongly idiosyncratic pictorial extensions of the text provided by his original illustrators.) Furthermore, the mental conception the reader had was affected by his general visual orientation, apart from whatever book illustrations or separate previous treatments of the subject he had seen. The contents of his imagistic storehouse had been influenced not only by all his previous firsthand observation of people and places but by all his experience of pictorial art. The paintings and engravings he had seen of subjects more or less resembling that in a certain literary picture would have subtly provided some of the notions of facial features, postures, groupings, and settings that had been absorbed into the final expectation with which he approached a new picture.

The neatness or looseness of the fit when the artist's version was superimposed on the spectator's preconceived one determined the nature of the latter's imaginative experience. If the artist had, as Leslie was alleged to have done, realized in paint the very character that the author had contributed to the reader's imagination, in addition to the pleasant shock of recognition there would have been the delight that came from the inventive addition of appropriate details of expression, costume, and setting to the mental picture already formed. Expectation would have been gratified and knowledge enlarged. If, on the other hand, the pictorial realization conflicted with the settled idea, the experience was less predictable. The viewer might, like the typical critic, summarily reject the painting as inconsistent with the author's spirit and intent as he chose to interpret it, and thus dismiss it from consideration, the settled notion still intact and ready to do battle with the next challenge to be painted. But it was just as possible that the artist's deviant interpretation, his independent view of character and scene, might engage the viewer's imagination and lead him to revise his mental image. The effect of a picture would have been drastically altered if the artist happened to be one who was determined to paint in the style of a revered master—a Titian, a Poussin, a Teniers—in which case his allegiance would have been split between the book represented and the artistic mode adopted, and the viewer forced to reconcile the two in his own mind.

The literary work now meant more, and perhaps quite different, things to him than it had when confined to print; it affected him not only through its language but now, also, through its pictorial representation. And if he then returned to the book, his reading of the picture would prove to have enlarged, modified, possibly even basically altered, his former conceptions. The pervasiveness of painted and engraved illustrations certainly affected, if it did not signally enrich, readers' subsequent experience of books. If not many could say, with the poet Southey, that Fuseli's pictures "doubled the pleasure I derived from Milton,"[26] their experience in the interplay of visual and verbal impressions would at least have made them more responsive to the cues to the picture-making imagination they found in the next novels or poems they read.

From the private experience of viewers, it is only a short distance to larger questions of the literary taste their preferences in art reflect. Few if any existing studies of the critical fortunes, popularity, and influence of English writers recognize the significance of their record in art. Except for a small handful of specialized accounts of book illustration, it has been the printed testimony of literary critics, and sometimes of readers confiding their views in private letters, that has determined our idea of what constitutes the "critical heritage" of a writer and his works.

Parts Two and Three of this book ("Images from Shakespeare" and "The Rest of the Gallery") gather materials that will point out the right direction for whoever wishes to use a literary work's record in art for historical or critical purposes. Questions abound, and, within the limitations imposed by the chancy survival of the visual documents, may, in time, be cautiously answered. What correlation, if any, prevailed at a given moment between the critical standing of a work and its popularity as a subject for representation? To what extent are literary pictures, whose reflection of contemporary taste in art is obvious, also dependable indicators of changes in literary taste as regarded both the "standard" and

170. Arthur Hughes, *The Tryst* (ca. 1860) (Tate Gallery, London). Knowledge of its literary source may cause a picture to be reinterpreted; without it, the painting may seem an unremarkable repetition of a banal subject. "Trysts" were common enough in Victorian sentimental art, although the strained expressions of the man and woman in this painting are not typical of the usual lovers'-rendezvous scenes. But the fact, established a century after the picture was painted, that Hughes's source was Elizabeth Barrett Browning's novel in verse, *Aurora Leigh,* clarifies the situation: "Far from being the scene of adolescent love it appears to be, the girl is furious with the boy for criticizing her Greek verse, and he is offended by her refusal of him" (Graham Reynolds [2], p. 68). The identification was made by Rosalie Mander in *Apollo* 79 (1964): 221–23.

contemporary authors? How influential were they in determining which part of an author's canon would be most "visible" (this time in a figurative sense) and/or highly regarded in succeeding generations? Did the fact that certain works rather than others were frequently used in art, and thus became more familiar, mean that they were ranked higher; that is, did they assist in fixing the hierarchy within the canon? Or, on the other hand, did they merely reflect an order already established by critics and popular taste, thus following a trend rather than leading it?

There is also the intriguing problem of the role that literary art played in widening and sharpening the public's interest in literature. Such paintings when exhibited constituted, after all, a well publicized and constantly restocked showcase for books. They performed in their particular manner the popularizing function of writers-about-books like Lamb, Hazlitt, and Leigh Hunt and the shoal of lesser "appreciative" critics who followed in their Victorian wake. Essayists and artists in effect collaborated to advertise the attractions of books to a public of indifferently educated but potentially educable men and women. How many persons whose curiosity was whetted by paintings and engravings were included in the market served by the proliferating cheap editions of literary classics?

Questions like these carry one toward the borders of what might be called the historical sociology of literature. In another direction, the evidence of literary art can also be used to amplify our understanding of an individual work—a form of comparative criticism that, at least so far as English literature is concerned, has been unaccountably neglected. As Kester Svendsen has said, "the critical history of a great literary work is incomplete unless it incorporates inferences from the interpretation put upon the masterpiece by artists."[27] The observation can be carried a step further. It is now commonly accepted that the total work of literary art, as it stands at the present moment, embraces not only the text but the full record of what has been written about it as well as the accreted, though unrecorded, experience of all its individual readers from the day it was published. If this is so, then the history of its interpretation by artists, a graphic form of criticism, also is part of the work as it now exists. The contribution that artistic treatments made to the actual meaning of a work—illustration as illumination—was seldom recognized at the time. One rare instance was the *Examiner*'s treatment of Maclise's *Malvolio and the Countess* (pl. 192). The artist's portrayal of the cross-gartered, finger-kissing Malvolio, said the reviewer, was "as good as a criticism [of the character] by Charles Lamb," and in a second notice, a few weeks later, he enlarged the remark. Maclise's painted interpretation of Shakespeare's silly and pathetic ass, he said, clarified his own conception:

> We have a sympathy for him in the midst of all his high fantasticalness, such as lurks beneath our laughter at the far-famed knight of La Mancha. He who would paint Malvolio as a ludicrous object merely, would paint Don Quixote a buffoon. . . . We say to his Malvolio, as Olivia said to hers, "God comfort thee!" He has hit the truth of Shakspeare. In that face of Olivia, where deepest and gentlest pity suppresses the rising smile of wonder, he has written the poet's thought as it took shape within Olivia's mind. "I would not have him miscarry for half my dowry." In the roguish, arch, and sunny face of Maria, we have at the same time all the rich background of this noble comedy. . . . *Had this picture no other value, it would claim notice as a striking commentary on some characters of Shakspeare, less understood than usual.*[28] (Emphasis added.)

In the only intensive study yet made, so far as I am aware, of the usefulness of graphic evidence in the critical history of an individual work (Thomson's *The Seasons*), Ralph Cohen has brilliantly demonstrated not only that book illustrations are invaluable as mute supplements, refinements, and clarifications of contemporary printed criticism, but that they often went beyond the critical views of their time. To the extent that they were not habitual readers of literary criticism, artists were unaffected by currently voiced opinions about a given poem or drama, and so could on occasion be strikingly original. From their pictorial point of view, they could perceive emphases and meanings unnoticed by critics. Thus, as Cohen says, "Illustration can function as non-verbal criticism" as well as being "an independent work of art."[29]

There remains the question of how, and in what ways, the changing tastes in the subject matter of literary paintings symptomized changes in the nineteenth-century social and cultural climate as well. The value of painted iconography in representing the surfaces of life in a past era—physical scene, costume, significant incidental accessories—has long been recognized by social historians. More recently, literary students have begun to look at paintings for what they can tell us of the intangibles that lie beneath the surface, the attitudes and biases that contributed toward the Victorian temper. But the pictures they have used for evidence are for the most part those without avowed literary connections and therefore simply represent the spirit of the times as refracted through the artist alone. If contemporary attitudes toward love, women, family relationships, childhood, old age and death—many of the concerns that confront any generation—can be more or less simplistically inferred from nonliterary art, they may be inferred with less certainty, but with added depth, from pictures that emanate from both writer and painter. Restating in emblematic form a myth already embodied in a book, the painting may add to it, or subvert or transform it. No necessary identity between the attitude and purpose of the writer and those of the artist can be assumed. If, as has been argued, the occurrence in Dickens's novels of the King Lear theme provides a commentary on "Victorian England's state of the soul,"[30] so do the numerous paintings from *King Lear* that were seen in the exhibitions; but they may prove to tell a somewhat different tale. This is true of many of the traditional subjects of literature that were modified when they passed through the artist's mind and were tinged with contemporary application. (Here the artist's suppression of the author's intended meaning is as significant as his faithful expression of it. If a picture, such as one with an erotic potential, deviates drastically from its source, how far was the Zeitgeist, rather than the artist's conscious decision, responsible?)

Never in the history of British painting from literary sources did the sister arts speak with one voice. The work of art never wholly duplicated the work of literature. We can, if we wish, listen to the voices separately. A poem or a Shakespearean play or a Scott novel had a set of resonances to every reader, a reader who was inescapably a product of his time, thoroughly permeated by its preferences, ideals, prejudices, anxieties. But a painting of that same literary work might have stirred different responses. And in those dissonances between two media, quiet and unobtrusive though they may be, lies the value of the paintings as a new key to the way people thought and felt. The effect produced by a simultaneous awareness of a literary and an artistic treatment of the same subject necessarily resulted in a richer experience on the part of the reader-viewer than was possible if he listened to each voice separately. If we can somehow recreate for ourselves that same effect, we can enter the age's combined verbal and visual imagination and the emotions it governed with an immediacy and authenticity seldom afforded by other means. By putting the pictures side by side with the books, as did the people of late eighteenth- and nineteenth-century England in literal fact as well as in their assimilative minds, future students may find it possible to reconstruct not only an event that was itself of considerable importance in the history of the popular sensibility but one that tells much about their inner lives even when far removed from books and pictures.

PART TWO

IMAGES FROM SHAKESPEARE

INTRODUCTION

W. P. Frith, reminiscing at the age of eighty-nine: "Mrs. King, our washer-woman . . . sat to me in 'Ramsgate Sands.' One day when I was painting her I quoted some lines from Shakespeare. 'Them's lovely lines,' she said. 'I should think they are; they're Shakespeare's.' She looked rather puzzled, so I said, 'You've heard of Shakespeare, haven't you?' 'Yes, sir,' says she; 'wasn't he something in your line?'"[1]

Not surprisingly, pictures from Shakespeare accounted for about one-fifth—some 2,300—of the total number of literary paintings recorded between 1760 and 1900. They are impressive graphic evidence of the age's conviction that Shakespeare was incomparably the supreme poet of England and, many (not chauvinists alone) came to say, the world.[2] They began as a product of the developing Bardolatry that stemmed from the realization in the first decades of the eighteenth century that Shakespeare was something special, not just another "old dramatist" in the company of Marlowe, Jonson, Dekker, Beaumont and Fletcher.[3] In time, the paintings came to emblematize the Romantic critics' near-deification of Shakespeare; and in their most prosperous years, they reflected the prevalence of that same adoration, half reverent and half embarrassingly matey, in Victorian middle-class culture. In 1769, Garrick had produced a stately festival in which the trappings of neoclassic hero worship, such as allegory, predominated; the Victorians, by contrast, expressed their admiration of the Bard by buying sentimental volumes on the supposed girlhood of his heroines and edifying compilations of his wit and wisdom. The paintings from the plays faithfully mirrored each turn in the celebration of Shakespeare.

He entered art under the most dignified auspices. The doctrine of *ut pictura poesis* offered a convenient association: if Shakespeare was a great poet, the sister art of painting should respond to, and memorialize, that greatness; theoretically at least, only the brush of a Michelangelo or a Raphael could do justice to his genius, as no flood of verbal panegyric could. On a more practical level, he was the provider of numerous subjects appropriate to history painting, the highest form of art; and, as a bonus, late in the eighteenth century, his pastoral comedies and romances supplied literary tie-ins for landscapists in the Claudian tradition.

Critics, actors, and painters alike were fascinated by Shakespeare's uncanny penetration into the secrets of the human heart. As early as 1713–15, essays analyzing his characters had appeared in periodicals; the critic Joseph Warton published five papers on characters in *King Lear* and *The Tempest* in 1753; and in the 1770s appeared several whole books on the subject, typified by William Richardson's *Philosophical Analysis and Illustration of Some of Shakespeare's Remarkable Characters* (1774), with chapters on Hamlet, Macbeth, Jaques, and Imogen. Thomas Whately's *Remarks on Some of the Characters of Shakespeare,* written some years earlier, was published in 1785.[4] Meanwhile, the greatest actor of the time, David Garrick, had brought to the portrayal of many Shakespearean characters a psychological insight and physical expression that substantiated the discoveries critics and "moral philosophers" (analysts of the human mind) were making in the study. Two of Garrick's most famous roles, Macbeth (pl. 156) and Richard III (pls. 2, 198), were particularly significant to the psychological thought of the time. "By the last quarter of the century, [they] emerge as two opposite types of dramatic character and, at the same time, their 'minds' become archetypes of the human mind in its varied reactions to the impinging outside world."[5]

It was not accidental that these figures were among the most frequently depicted subjects of Shakespearean painting at the time. Psychological truth was of as much concern to painters as it was to actors like Garrick and critics like Warton. A well-known history painter, John Hamilton Mortimer, exhibited at the Society of Artists in 1775 a dozen pen drawings of Shakespearean characters, each purporting to represent the expression of an "impassioned state of mind."[6]* The age's most sought-after portrait painter, Sir Joshua Reynolds, was less interested in conveying who his sitters were or what they had done (the usual approach of portraitists down through Kneller) than in suggesting what they were as human beings. In an essay printed for the first time in 1952, his summary of the attractions Shakespeare had for painters stressed the element of character portrayal:

> To observe of Shakespeare that he observed everything that passed before him and considered it with a poetical mind, and that he took his ideas from nature herself, would be superfluous praise. I would only observe that by considering nature as a poet, he involuntarily considered it as a painter. His descriptions are pictures: Dover Cliff; "her head sometimes on one side, sometimes on t'other"; "clear sky of fame." He appears to have looked at the human face like a painter who wishes to imprint on his memory the movements of the features when any particular character was expressed: "peeping through their little eyes"; "swell their cheeks to idle merriment." The frown of the forehead, and the expression of the eyes in consequence, had been observed before, but "a napkin ill laid up"—[7]

In the very first years that Shakespearean subjects began to be painted in some quantity (the 1780s), a distinction was made between paintings derived from the literary text and those that originated in the theater. The former bore the more honored credentials. When Robert Edge Pine (see chapter 2, above) advertised his series of pictures to be engraved, he was at pains to dissociate them from mere theatrical paintings, of which he had produced a number as a young man, including several of Garrick. "These subjects, having hitherto been unattended to, but for frontispieces to the plays," he said, "it may be proper to observe, that the pictures proposed, are not meant to be representations of stage scenes; but will be treated with the more unconfined liberty of painting, in order to bring those images to the eye, which the writer has given to the mind; and which, in some instances, is not within the power of the Theatre."[8]

As persons of intellectual or imaginative bent found more and more reasons to study Shakespeare, successive editors strove to restore the printed texts of the plays to the condition in which they supposedly had left the hands of the poet. This was a critical undertaking in more than one sense, because it marked the beginning of the long process, requiring more than a century to complete, by which the "authentic" Shakespearean text was restored to the theater.[9] In the eighteenth century, the plays as their first audiences knew them, or even as editors found them in the grievously mangled folio texts, were seldom seen on the stage. Some were acted so infrequently as to have no impact whatsoever on the public; and in the second half of the century, a number—*Richard II, Titus An-*

*These were etched by the artist and issued in two batches in 1775–76 and subsequently in other forms. Many years later, beginning in 1853, Shakespeare's characters were put to a quite different psychological use. The parricidal artist Richard Dadd, a patient in Bethlem Hospital (see below, under *A Midsummer Night's Dream*), painted more than thirty "Sketches to Illustrate the Passions," including Jealousy (Othello) and Love (Romeo and Juliet). (See Allderidge, *The Late Richard Dadd*, pp. 30, 87 ff.)

171. Peter van Bleeck, *Mrs. Cibber as Cordelia* (1755) (Yale Center for British Art, Paul Mellon Collection). This scene is not in Shakespeare's play but in Nahum Tate's perversion of *King Lear.* In the so-called field scene (3. 3), Cordelia and her companion are in peril from ruffians sent by Edmund; Edgar, in the garb of "a madman" (Tom o' Bedlam in the original), rescues them. Susannah Cibber played Cordelia at Drury Lane, 23 June 1755.

dronicus, Troilus and Cressida, the three parts of *Henry VI,* and *Love's Labour's Lost*—were never performed.

With only two exceptions, *Othello* and *Twelfth Night,* in the first half of the century the Shakespearean repertory was regularly staged in versions for which the word "adaptations" is, in some instances, too generous a synonym and "improvements," the term employed at the time, an outright lie. The extreme case was that of Nahum Tate's perversion of *King Lear* (1681), discussed below.* Not until 1838 was Shakespeare's own text to be followed, by Macready. *Romeo and Juliet* was performed in Otway's adaptation entitled *The History and Fall of Caius Marius; Macbeth,* in D'Avenant's version; *The Tempest,* successively in Dryden / D'Avenant's, then Shadwell's; *The Taming of the Shrew* in four different versions, all under different titles; *Cymbeline* in D'Urfey's adaptation; *2 Henry IV* in Betterton's; and so forth. One of Garrick's signal services to the progress of the English stage was his refusal to produce some of the most egregiously pseudo-Shakespearean plays and his restoration of substantial passages of the original text in others, including Tate's *Lear,* although he performed Colley Cibber's *Richard III* as written, without any additional lines from Shakespeare. Thanks largely to Garrick's reverence for Shakespeare ("God," he said, "of my Idolatry—Shakespeare—*Him! Him! He is the Him!* there is no Other"), most of the outright "adaptations," with their blatantly non-Shakespearean material, disappeared from the stage in the second half of the century. But the true Shakespeare was restored in the theater only in imperfect form, with many cuts, rearrangements, and

*A hint of the uneasiness with which painters, and perhaps their clientele, regarded Tate's abomination as a source of *Lear* pictures is discernible in the way Romney's and Barry's paintings (Free Society of Artists 1763 and RA 1774 respectively) were listed in the catalogues: "from the play *as written by Shakespeare.*"

(sometimes) interpolations, not in the texts that meanwhile were being reconstructed from the folios and quartos by a succession of scholarly editors, Theobald, Rowe, Hanmer, Dr. Johnson, and Steevens (who provided the text for Boydell's illustrated edition).

The prevalence of these unauthentic versions on the stage crucially affects our understanding of the relation between Shakespearean painting and the contemporary theater. Although wise historians use such evidence with caution, some of the paintings are a fairly copious source of information on the manner in which a play was mounted and performed, including conventions of costume, pose, action, and business for which there is no warrant in the accepted Shakespearean text.[10] But what proportion of the paintings were derived from actual performances and what proportion from printed texts is as yet unknown. And which printed texts? Assuming that the artists customarily referred to them—a too hasty assumption, actually, because many paintings seem to have been merely reworkings of earlier designs, including engraved book illustrations, without any fresh recourse to the play—they could choose between the standard "literary" editions of the time and the texts used in the theater. Bell's much-used pocket edition of 1773-74, for example, printed the texts of twenty-four of the plays from the prompt books current in the theaters royal (eighteen from Drury Lane, six from Covent Garden), and the editions of Shakespeare in Mrs. Inchbald's *British Theatre* (1808), *Oxberry's English Drama* (1818–23) and Cumberland's (1828–30) were actually John Philip Kemble's performing scripts.[11] To add an extra twist of the screw, these printed acting texts were no more sacrosanct than the pure (in terms of that day) Shakespearean ones that they had themselves violated. A scene or action that was in one version of the adaptation may have been absent from another. In some paintings of the last scene in *Othello,* the hero smothers Desdemona, as Shakespeare's text dictates and as he also does in Kemble's script. But in others, he stabs her—as he is directed to do in Bell's edition, from which Kemble's prompt-book text was derived. To determine which paintings from *The Winter's Tale* are traceable to the Shakespearean text and which to the staged versions, it must be borne in mind that in the standard acting version from Garrick's time onward, the first two acts and most of the third were omitted, and the scenes most favored in art were those that were either omitted or severely cut and relocated in the play as then performed.

No one has yet attempted to discover the actual sources, iconographic, literary, or theatrical, of all the surviving pictures from Shakespeare's plays. Such an examination would finally establish the true relation they bore to the corrupt acting versions, some of which held the stage into the mid-Victorian era—how many, for example, represent scenes that were cut in production (or, vice versa, scenes added without textual authority). The several Shakespearean paintings by, or attributed to, Hogarth are early cases in point.[12] His Vauxhall Gardens picture, presumably copied from an engraving, of Henry VIII leading Anne Boleyn to court is not from Shakespeare's play but from Colley Cibber's production of 1727. It is "faithful neither to Shakespeare nor to history." Hogarth's scene from *The Tempest* (pl. 172) is from the literary text, not from any performance, because until 1746, a decade after the putative date of the picture, the play was performed only in the form of a Restoration opera, in which the scene does not occur. Hogarth's most famous "Shakespearean" picture,

172. William Hogarth, *Scene from "The Tempest"* (ca. 1735) (Nostell Priory). A rendering of act 1, scene 2, taken directly from the printed play, not the currently performed—operatic—version. "It is not unlike a subject by Sir Peter Lely—certainly Miranda has stepped straight from one of Lely's canvases, together with her garlanded sheep. Ferdinand's dress is obviously based on a contemporary theatrical costume, and Ariel is any Italian seventeenth-century *putto,* seated precariously on a cloud and playing a lute" (John Woodward in *The Listener,* 15 June 1950).

of Garrick as Richard III (pl. 2), is based not on Shakespeare's *Richard III* but on Cibber's *Henry V,* to which Cibber transferred lines from the Richard play. Thus the Shakespeare of painted art is not necessarily the Shakespeare of one's reading copy; it is "Shakespeare" in the marvelously elastic sense created by the wayward inventiveness of the theater, from Betterton to Irving.

How closely, if at all, did the frequency with which paintings were made from a play correspond with its popularity on the stage? For the half-century 1751–1800, the theatrical data for which have been exhaustively collected, a tentative answer can be made.[13] The five most-performed plays in London were *Romeo and Juliet, Hamlet, Richard III, Macbeth,* and *The Merchant of Venice.* The plays from which the most pictures were derived in the same period (omitting the large selection in the Boydell Gallery, which was determined by considerations having nothing to do with the theater) were *Macbeth, King Lear, As You Like It, Romeo and Juliet,* and the two parts of *Henry IV.* Obviously, no close correlation is apparent.

Until similar statistics on the relative popularity of the Shakespearean plays in the nineteenth century have been compiled, no such comparison can be made for the period when the overwhelming majority of Shakespearean pictures were painted. But some impressions based on exhibition records can be reported. The comedies and romances were much more popular with artists, and supposedly with their clientele, than the tragedies;* the recorded paintings from the former two categories of plays numbered (very roughly) 950, and from the tragedies, 550. There were approximately 200 pictures from the English history plays, but only some 60 from the Greek and Roman ones. The most popular plays (in a descending range of 170–100 each) were *Romeo and Juliet, The Tempest, Hamlet, The Merchant of Venice, As You Like It,* and *A Midsummer Night's Dream.* In the middle category (100–150 paintings) fell *Macbeth, Othello, Henry IV, Twelfth Night, The Taming of the Shrew, Cymbeline, The Merry Wives*

*Partly because of the box-office appeal of the pageantry and elaborate scenery associated with such productions, the comedies were often turned into lavishly mounted musicals. Dryden, D'Avenant, and Purcell had shown the way long before, with their operatic version of *The Tempest.* Between 1816 and 1833, not only that play but *A Midsummer Night's Dream, The Comedy of Errors, Twelfth Night, The Two Gentlemen of Verona, As You Like It, The Merry Wives of Windsor,* and *All's Well That Ends Well* were given similar treatment, often with music by Henry Bishop and settings by the busy and talented Grieve family. It is probable that the characteristics of these musical presentations—their colorful prettification, their sedulous attempts at Fancy—in turn influenced painters, whose pictures of Shakespearean romance often suggest that they wanted viewers to hear the music to which the scenes were set.

of Windsor, and *King Lear.* In the range of 50–25 paintings were *Much Ado About Nothing, Henry VIII, The Winter's Tale, The Two Gentlemen of Verona,* and *Antony and Cleopatra.* Each of the remaining plays in the Shakespeare canon was the source of fewer than 25 pictures.*

The decade-by-decade record of paintings across the whole of the nineteenth century reveals some interesting tendencies. *Macbeth* and *King Lear* were definitely the first tragedies to enlist many painters' brushes. *Hamlet* was taken up strikingly late: apart from the four subjects in the Boydell Gallery, few *Hamlet* pictures were produced before the early 1800s. Along with *Romeo and Juliet,* however, *Hamlet* retained its popularity, probably because of Ophelia, much longer than did the other tragedies, which declined in popularity after mid-century. The Falstaff plays (*1* and *2 Henry IV* and *The Merry Wives of Windsor*) virtually disappeared from the exhibitions after the 1860s.

Pictures from Shakespeare fully participated in the boom in literary paintings during the period 1830–60. The most popular plays in the art galleries then—a selection that implies pretty much about the taste of those early and mid-Victorian years—were *Romeo and Juliet, The Tempest, The Merchant of Venice, As You Like It,* and *A Midsummer Night's Dream.* The history plays, however, were unaffected by this prosperity; like that of *Twelfth Night,* the level of their popularity remained constant.

Many other conclusions may be drawn from the information presented in the following pages on the individual plays, arranged in the order adopted in the *Complete Penguin Shakespeare* (1969). Taken all together, the facts offer an ironic commentary on an opinion expressed more than once in Boydell's time, as in this statement in a newspaper in 1790:

> To speak of Paintings illustrative of SHAKESPEARE, is to misapply terms. He is a SCHOOL of Painting himself; but that art cannot illustrate him. All, and much more than the pencil can express, is conceived by the most negligent reader of his Works.—The Painter's Art is but to fix the limited degrees of Passion that the language of the Poet puts us into complete possession of: in proportion as this can, or cannot be successfully done, rises or falls the perfection of the Art. It is for the embodying images, present visibly to the mind, to gratify by their identity, to delight by their truth. . . . [We] hesitate not to say that the *finest Works* of the Art in this country are not drawn from the page of SHAKESPEARE.[14]

If Shakespeare was indeed beyond the reach of art, there were hundreds of English painters who declined to believe it.

*It should be borne in mind that all the figures cited throughout this part and Part Three are based on the sample described in the Introduction to the book, and do not in any instance refer to the *total* production of pictures on any given subject—a sum that is impossible to arrive at.

THE COMEDIES

THE COMEDY OF ERRORS

Although *The Comedy of Errors* was staged fairly often from 1741 onward, always in altered versions, it never caught on with artists. Three Boydell pictures took subjects from it, including Wheatley's portrayal of the (reported) storm scene. At the 1790 Royal Academy exhibition, John Francis Rigaud showed his study for the head of Aegeon, which was probably a sketch for his own Boydell commission, a scene from act 5, scene 1. But thereafter, *The Comedy of Errors* was represented in art only by book illustrations.

THE TAMING OF THE SHREW

After disappearing from the playhouse in the mid-seventeenth century, *The Taming of the Shrew* as Shakespeare wrote it was not performed again until (actually) 1886.[1] Instead, it was known in the theater only in Garrick's much-altered three-act version called *Catherine and Petruchio,* the name also given to numerous paintings. Hardly more than half the recorded pictures, which totaled about eighty, can be related to specific scenes; the titles of the rest give no clue to the passage supposedly represented. Moreover, the title *The Taming of the Shrew* itself in some instances did not refer to the play at all, but simply designated a comic genre subject illustrating that staple theme of Victorian humor, the unequal battle of the sexes, with man usually triumphant and woman eagerly embracing her ordained inferior position in Creation. In pictures from the play, of scenes prior to her eventual compliance, the termagant Kate may be said to represent the anti-Keepsake heroine in art; she has a mind and defiant will of her own.

Before the 1820s, there were only a handful of paintings from the play, including Benjamin Vandergucht's portrait of Woodward as Petruchio (pl. 173) and four Boydell scenes: the muddy wedding trip (4.1) and the argument about the sun and moon (4.5), both by J. C. Ibbetson; Christopher Sly in bed (Induction, 2) by Smirke; and the confrontation of Kate and Petruchio in act 3, scene 2, by Wheatley. After that time, they were seen more frequently. The only individual scene on which artists concentrated was the Induction, starring Christopher Sly; it was illustrated some ten times in all, the favorite moment being the one Smirke painted, in which the drunken tinker awakens to find his bed surrounded by people offering him every variety of sensual luxury. Whichever moment the artist chose, the comic character of Sly provided a capital opportunity to imitate Dutch alehouse painting.

Several popular early and mid-Victorian artists painted subjects from *The Taming of the Shrew:* Leslie (pl. 46), Martineau (pl. 174), Egg (pl. 175), and Gilbert (pl. 162). Pictures from the play retained their popularity to the end of the Victorian era.

173. Benjamin Vandergucht, *A Portrait in the Character of Petruchio* (RA 1774) (Yale Center for British Art, Paul Mellon Collection). The actor is Henry Woodward, a veteran specialist in comic roles, who played Petruchio in *Catherine and Petruchio,* Garrick's version of *The Taming of the Shrew,* in the autumn before this painting was exhibited.

THE TWO GENTLEMEN OF VERONA

The Two Gentlemen of Verona was a more popular subject for art than its patchy stage record might suggest. Garrick's production of Benjamin Victor's adaptation (1762) had only half a dozen performances. Shakespeare's text was spoken for the first time since the Restoration at Covent

174. Robert B. Martineau, *Catherine and Petruchio* (RA 1855) (Ashmolean Museum, Oxford). Petruchio is depicted as the standard coxcomb (compare, among many examples, Hotspur in pl. 207); Kate's tart expression suggests she is well equipped to cope with his male chauvinism in the dialogue of act 2, scene 1.

Garden in 1784. J. P. Kemble staged both Shakespeare's play (1790) and his own version of Victor's (1808), and an operatic version was performed at Covent Garden for twenty-nine nights in 1821. No celebrated actors were lastingly associated with any of the play's chief roles. Nonetheless, the comedy had a steady appeal for painters. In 1785, Henry Singleton exhibited at the Royal Academy a sketch of Julia in act 4, scene 4; and from this time onward, some fifty pictures were produced, among them the requisite number of portraits and figure studies of Julia and Silvia as Keepsake beauties.

The single most popular subject, however, was not sentimental but comic: the farcically soliloquizing Launce and his dog (2.3, 4.4). A Liverpool artist named James Campbell painted the pair some time before 1793, but they did not reappear until the mid 1830s, after which at least six treatments were exhibited. Of these, the best known was Augustus Egg's *Launce's Substitute for Proteus' Dog* (pl. 95), a particularly noteworthy case of robust Shakespearean coarseness cleaned up for early Victorian sensibilities. There is nothing in Egg's group of exceedingly spic-and-span and unagitated men and women to suggest the improprieties Launce describes the bulldog's having committed on and under the dinner table. "Did not I bid thee still mark me and do as I do?" he reproaches the errant cur in conclusion. "When didst thou see me heave up my leg and make water against a gentlewoman's farthingale? Didst thou ever see me do such a trick?" (4.4. 33–37.) The risky nature of the subject may have been discreetly implied in the *Athenaeum*'s comment, "Much of the interest of the text belongs to the whim and evocation in which it abounds

175. Augustus Egg (attributed), *The Wooing of Katharina* (RA 1847) (Leicestershire Museum and Art Gallery, Leicester). Petruchio's explosion over the burnt mutton and other culinary disasters, as Kate maintains a slightly nonplused expression (4. 1). In keeping with a developing practice among painters wishing to add modern flavor to literary costume scenes, the artist dresses the servants in ordinary Victorian clothing.

rather than to the situation; and the subject is therefore not well chosen for the painter's art."[1]

The play's other major source of art was the dénouement scene (5.4), various moments of which were depicted. The Boydell Gallery included two. Stothard painted the moment in which Julia throws off her disguise as a boy, to Proteus' consternation. But the scene's favorite moment for picturing was the tableau that Francis Wheatley painted for the New Shakespeare Gallery (pl. 31), and it was the subject also of Holman Hunt's *Valentine Rescuing Silvia from Proteus* (pl. 177), which had to endure the early wrath of the Pre-Raphaelites' detractors. "This," said the *Art Journal,* "is one of the eccentricities of the Young England school, in which after the facetious conceptions in impersonation, the most striking feature is the bird's-eye view of the forest scene. . . . What is presumed to be the Pre-Rafaellite manner is intense in this picture."[2] It was, conceded the *Examiner,* "the least repulsive work exhibited this year by the brotherhood." Still: "Even though we were prepared to grant to Mr. Hunt that there was no necessity for making Sylvia 'beautiful exceedingly,' recollecting that Valentine and Proteus saw her with 'the lover's eye,' yet assuredly there was equally little necessity for making her a hard-featured faded specimen of stale virginity. Julia is lounging in the attitude of a sulking lubberly schoolboy."[3]

176. Henry Perronet Briggs, *"The Two Gentlemen of Verona"* (British Institution 1827) (Royal Shakespeare Theatre Picture Gallery ©). A variant of the standard letter scene: with the servant Speed in attendance, Valentine holds the letter to his rival, Proteus, which Silvia has commissioned him to write and which she has now returned to him: "The lines are very quaintly writ," she says, "But since unwillingly, take them again" (2. 1).

A MIDSUMMER NIGHT'S DREAM

Few of the 135 paintings from *A Midsummer Night's Dream* demonstrably owe much to the theater. The full play as Shakespeare wrote it was not performed in the eighteenth century or in the first forty years of the nineteenth. Instead, a series of operatic versions was staged, beginning with the most famous, Henry Purcell's *The Fairy-Queen* (1692). Among its successors were Garrick's *The Fairies* (1755), which kept the lovers but

177. William Holman Hunt, *Valentine and Silvia* (RA 1851) (Birmingham City Museum and Art Gallery). One of the most famous Pre-Raphaelite paintings from English literature, both because of its central position in the initial critical controversy over the movement and because it is one of Hunt's most important works. It was sold sight unseen to a Belfast shipping agent who had read about it in the newspapers. Compare Wheatley's version of the same scene, painted sixty years earlier (pl. 31).

omitted the rude mechanicals, and the elder George Colman's in 1763, which omitted virtually the whole last act. Not until the Vestris-Mathews management's second season at Covent Garden (1840) did a production of the play revive most of the original text, though still with substantial cuts. No matter when performed, or by whom, or with what text, *A Midsummer Night's Dream* was a favorite vehicle for spectacular staging, especially the last act, which was treated much like a pantomime transformation scene. Both this play and *The Tempest* were the chief Shakespearean beneficiaries, if that is the right word, of the rage for fairies on the stage and in art which was one of the more picturesque phenomena of popular culture in the 1840s.

Since the play, as set to music, was not an outstanding starring vehicle, few theatrical portraits were made of actors and actresses in the leading roles. The only paintings that could have been influenced by the "legitimate" productions were those painted after the Vestris-Mathews revival. Most *Midsummer Night's Dream* pictures therefore were realizations in paint of the play's poetic imagery, its fairy and comic characters, and its never-never-land setting in a moonlit glade, not restricted to the Shakespearean text but drawing to themselves the assorted and scattered materials of fairy lore, including details borrowed from Mercutio's Queen Mab speech in *Romeo and Juliet* (1. 4. 53–94). Many, probably most, of the paintings that were nominally inspired by the play had, in fact, little connection with the action; they were compounds of all that went to make up the early Victorian notion of the fanciful—lush arboreal landscape, moonlight, fireflies, the flora and fauna of the woods from a rich variety of flowers to capacious toadstools, assorted hovering or reveling fairies and elves. It was the pervasive, generalized supernatural element of the play that artists sought to capture and convey, rather than dramatic moments for their own sake.

Not many of the pictures were related to the Theseus-Hippolyta-Helena-Hermia-Lysander-Demetrius plot, except that the names of Helena and Hermia, separately or as a pair, were occasionally borrowed as titles of female portraits. The paintings that were actually related to the text were devoted chiefly to episodes and themes from the fairy plot—Titania and Oberon, Bottom and the ass's head business, Puck's merry pranks, and Queen Mab's powers of enchantment. The rude mechanicals appeared fairly often, but their home-made play of Pyramus and Thisbe (3.1) no more than half a dozen times. Most of the art that can be localized came from act 2, scene 1 (the main locus for Puck), act 2, scene 2 (Titania's sleep), and act 3, scenes 1–2 and act 4, scene 1 (most of the comedy).

The first major artist* to have participated in the play's graphic tradition was Fuseli, who painted from it as often as he did from *Macbeth,* and, in part, for the same reason—its suggestions of the dark aspects of fairy lore, the hags and grotesque animals who existed side by side with the whimsical and benevolent spirits. In some of his *Midsummer Night's Dream* paintings, such as *Cobweb* (1785–86), there was as well the malign incubus, the malformed gnome with ape-like face who occurred in his most famous and fearsome work, *The Nightmare.* But such unearthly horror, though a prominent element in Fuseli's most characteristic work, did not dominate it at the expense of the more cheerfully dew-sprinkled realm of Faëry or, for that matter, Fuseli's delight in the female nude as represented in Titania. His wild inventiveness is apparent in one of the two

*Until recently, this distinction was Hogarth's, to whom the Vauxhall Gardens picture of *Fairies Dancing on the Green by Moonlight* was attributed on no very solid grounds (see Robin Simon, "Hogarth's Shakespeare," *Apollo* 109 [1979]: 213; and Alastair Smart, "Hogarth or Hayman? Another Look at the *Fairies Dancing on the Green by Moonlight,*" ibid., pp. 209–12). The attribution of the subject itself to *A Midsummer Night's Dream* or Purcell's *The Fairy-Queen* is equally questionable. In most of its details, the painting seems instead to be a realization of *Paradise Lost,* 1.781–88. The "fairies" are not those which were to figure in nineteenth-century fancy; they are very corporeal beings dressed in masque costumes. Fuseli painted the same subject (pl. 33).

Boydell pieces he painted from act 4, scene 1, *Titania and Bottom with the Ass's Head* (pl. 28), a surrealistic composition with a Titania modeled on Leonardo's Leda, fairies dressed in late eighteenth-century drawing-room fashion, a "grim, pigmy-philosopher crouched at the end of a leash" and a "curious elf with a head that metamorphoses into the body of a moth."*

Fuseli's third Boydell painting from the play was a portrayal of the naked Puck with the wings of a bat: "When I a fat and bean-fed horse beguile / Neighing in likeness of a filly foal" (2.1. 45–46). Reynolds's Boydell version of *Puck (Robin Goodfellow)* was quite different: a chubby, equally naked child in a forest setting with tousled hair and some wild flowers clutched in his fist, "an ugly little imp," thought Horace Walpole, "but with some character, sitting on a mushroom, half as big as a mill-stone."[1] This picture was an immediate hit, and in years to come it was to be engraved many times. In that form it became one of the most familiar of all British paintings, almost as well known as another picture of a child, Millais's *Bubbles,* which at the end of the century was enlisted to advertise Pears's soap. It was bought at the Boydell sale by the connoisseur Samuel Rogers, and as a porter bore it through the streets to his mansion, people called to one another, "There it is!"[2] †

Romney, who also painted Titania several times (his *Titania with Her Fairies Shooting at Bats with Bows and Arrows* was owned by Lord Egremont, and *Titania and the Indian Votaress* by William Beckford), carried on the Puck tradition with his picture of Tom Hayley, son of his future biographer William Hayley, "as Puck returning to Oberon with the magic flower with which he bewitched Titania." Puck engaged the talents of some of the better artists in the new generation. Dyce did several sketches of him, and Maclise showed *Puck Disenchanting Bottom; Oberon and Titania Reconciled; Messrs. Peasblossom, Cobweb, Moth, and Mustardseed Bringing Gifts* at the Royal Academy in 1832.‡ A less successful artist, David Scott, showed his *Puck Fleeing Before the Dawn* at the Royal Scottish Academy in 1838.

By then the vogue for fairy paintings was well under way. Among the six pictures from the play that were exhibited in 1841, two were by Richard Dadd, *Titania Sleeping* and *Puck and the Fairies.* Both contained iconographic reminiscences of Fuseli's and Reynolds's pictures, the existence of which no painter of these subjects could overlook. Dadd quickly won a reputation as a specialist in fairy scenes. Two years later, while of unhinged mind, he stabbed his father to death in the grounds of Cobham House, Kent, and was committed to Bethlem Hospital, the London lunatic asylum. In 1852, the institution got a new superintendent, Dr. William Charles Hood, an enlightened "alienist," as psychiatrists were then called, who firmly believed in occupational therapy. He gave Dadd painting materials and set him to work. In the following years, Dadd produced two strange pictures, *Contradiction: Oberon and Titania* and *The Fairy Feller's Master Stroke.* The latter fantasy, a small canvas crammed with figures in various, not always intelligible activities, is one of the most puzzling pictures the Victorian age produced; it has never been fully explicated. Dadd's art is linked nowadays with that of another recently discovered "fairy painter," Robert Huskisson, who exhibited *The Midsummer Night's Fairies* (pl. 178) and *Titania's Elves Robbing the Squirrel's Nest* at the Royal Academy in 1847 and 1854, respectively.

Meanwhile, Joseph Noel Paton, a painter of sounder mind and one

*These are the terms in which the painting is described in a recent catalogue (Hutton, *Alderman Boydell's Shakespeare Gallery,* p. 25). Compare Fuseli's own explanation (and high estimate) of the picture: "This is the creation of a poetic painter, and the scene is peculiarly his own; a glowing harmony of tone pervades the whole; and instead of being amused by mere humour, an assemblage calculated to delight the simple correct taste, which sensibility has refined, bursts on us to relax the features without exciting loud laughter. The moment chosen by the painter, when the queen, with soft languour, caresses Bottom, who humorously addresses her attendants, gave him licence to create the fanciful yet not grotesque group, which he has so judiciously contrasted as not to disturb the pleasurable emotions the whole must ever convey to a mind alive to the wild but enchanting graces of poetry. The elegant familiar attendants seem to be buoyed up by the sweet surrounding atmosphere, and the fragrant nosegay bound together with careless art, yet so light, that the rude wind might disperse the 'insubstantial pageant'. The soft and insinuating beauty, the playful graces here displayed, would, without reflection, scarcely be expected from the daring pencil that appears ever on the stretch to reach the upmost boundary of nature" (*Analytical Review,* May 1789, quoted in Mason, *The Mind of Fuseli,* p. 289).

† It was among the literary pictures that most appreciated in value as it passed from owner to owner. Boydell had paid Reynolds 100 guineas to paint it; Rogers bought it for £215 5s.; and Earl Fitzwilliam acquired it at Rogers's sale for 980 guineas. *Midsummer Night's Dream* paintings seem indeed to have been shrewd investments: the engineer Isambard Brunel commissioned Landseer's *Titania and Bottom* (RA 1851) for 400 guineas, and after his death eight years later, Lord Clinton bought it for £2,940 (Campbell Lennie, *Landseer: The Victorian Paragon* [London, 1976], p. 153).

‡ This was among the paintings that the wealthy mid-Victorian speculator "Baron" Grant bought *en bloc* to furnish his new mansion, converted from a former lunatic asylum, opposite Kensington Palace, but which he never occupied.

178. Robert Huskisson, *The Midsummer Night's Fairies* (RA 1847) (Tate Gallery, London). Although the picture was exhibited with a quotation from *A Midsummer Night's Dream* ("There sleeps Titania sometime of the night, / Lulled in these flowers with dances and delight" [2. 2]), its connection with the play is marginal. Like most of the fairy paintings produced at this time, it gathered its material from the open stock of fairy lore.

destined for considerable popular success crowned by a knighthood, had exhibited at the Royal Scottish Academy equally crowded compositions in an order the reverse of that in which their subjects occur in the play: *The Reconciliation of Oberon and Titania* (1847) and *The Quarrel of Oberon and Titania* (pl. 74). Their minuteness of delineation was imitated by lesser artists, whose work in this regard, as might have been expected, sometimes led critics to compare them, in praise or blame, with typical products of Pre-Raphaelite naturalistic art. Paton's *The Fairy Raid: Carrying Off a Changeling—Midsummer Eve* (pl. 179) marked his return to the play after he had consolidated his reputation with paintings from other sources.

179. Sir Joseph Noel Paton, *The Fairy Raid: Carrying Off a Changeling—Midsummer Eve* (RA 1867) (Glasgow Art Gallery and Museum). An extravagant potpourri of escapist themes—knights rescuing damsels in distress, moonlit glades, even a suggestion of Druidic ritual (Stonehenge in the distance?)—with greatest emphasis on the flora and fauna of the enchanted woods in *A Midsummer Night's Dream.* Paton's flourishing career, launched with his painting of the *Quarrel* (pl. 74) and *Reconciliation of Oberon and Titania,* was marked by his receiving a knighthood in this year.

LOVE'S LABOUR'S LOST

Love's Labour's Lost was not performed between 1604–5 and 1839, when the Vestris-Mathews management staged it at Covent Garden. Its history in art is almost as scanty. Three Boydell paintings drew their subjects from it, including two by Wheatley: the letter scene (4.1) (pl. 180) and a costume piece from act 5, scene 2. No more than ten pictures from the play were subsequently exhibited, and of these, only one attracted much notice: F. R. Pickersgill's montage (RA 1856) of several separate episodes.

180. Francis Wheatley, *"Love's Labour's Lost"* [4. 1] (Boydell's Shakespeare Gallery) (Folger Shakespeare Library). Jacquenetta, the illiterate country wench, gives Don Armado's letter to Nathaniel to read: she has received it from Costard, who is present along with Holofernes.

THE MERCHANT OF VENICE

Approximately one hundred and fifty paintings from *The Merchant of Venice* are recorded. The play's early iconographic history is closely linked with the actor-manager Charles Macklin, whose production in 1741, more or less adhering to the Shakespearean text, replaced *The Jew of Venice,* a farcical adaptation by George Granville, which had been played for forty years. Macklin's portrayal of Shylock as a heavy villain set the interpretation that was to be followed to the end of the century; he himself played the role, on which he had a virtual monopoly, until May 1789. Most of the paintings of Shylock from this period, including three attributed to Zoffany (a portrait, the trial scene, and Shylock and Tubal), are often said, with varying degrees of authority, to represent Macklin. At the turn of the century, George Frederick Cooke added a note of pathos to the role; and Macklin's greatest successor, Edmund Kean, whose debut as Shylock in 1814 was as sensational as Garrick's in the role of Richard III, played him as "a romantic hero, murderous but volcanically majestic in his racial fanaticism and the fury of his passion."[1] It was Kean's interpretation, praised by Hazlitt, that probably had the most influence on nineteenth-century paintings of Shylock.

Except for Falstaff, no male Shakespearean character on canvas was examined more critically than the usurer. The art reviewers habitually wrapped their verdict in a formula that dated from Macklin's first performance, when a man in the audience, reputedly Alexander Pope, rose and triumphantly declared—as he well might have, considering what Granville had done with the character—"This is the Jew that Shakespeare drew!" Thus the *Athenaeum* said of Gilbert Stuart Newton's painting of *Shylock and Jessica* (pl. 181), "The Jew is the Jew that Shakespeare drew, and that our stage artists so often unnaturally copy."[2]

181. Gilbert Stuart Newton, *Shylock and Jessica* (RA 1830) (Yale Center for British Art, Paul Mellon Fund). This literal illustration of the scene in *The Merchant of Venice* (2. 5) designated by Newton's compression of Shakespeare's text as the picture's epigraph: "Jessica, my girl, there are my keys; / Look to my House," was hung at the same exhibition in which Turner's very different version of the same subject brewed a storm of ridicule. An artist who showed some promise of rivaling Leslie as a painter of literary scenes, Newton exhibited another subject from *The Merchant of Venice* the next year (pl. 102) and was elected to the Royal Academy; but he went mad and was confined in the Chelsea Lunatic Asylum until his death in 1835.

From the mere fifty-five lines of act 2, scene 5, artists extracted at least sixteen pictures showing the moment when the clown Launcelot makes his exit as Shylock is giving Jessica last-minute instructions on securing his money bags while he is dining out. After Smirke painted it for Boydell, the subject seems to have been quiescent until 1830, when it was represented by two canvases at the Royal Academy, Newton's and Turner's *Jessica,* showing that popular heroine gazing from a window. The latter picture may be said to have inaugurated the early Victorian journalistic sport of Turner-bashing. "Surely these vagaries of Mr. Turner's must be the result of studying a kaleidoscope," said the *Literary Gazette.*[3] "A hazy old clothes-woman at a back window in Holywell-Street, would show a delicate and soft-eyed Venus, compared with this daub of a drab, libelling Shakespeare out of a foggy window of King's yellow," echoed the *Athenaeum.*[4] "It looks like a lady jumping out of a mustard-pot," added the *Morning Chronicle.* Even Lord Egremont, Turner's faithful patron, had no good word for the picture even though it hung at Petworth. "Turner," he

182. Johann Zoffany (attributed), *The Trial Scene in "The Merchant of Venice"* (1775?) (Tate Gallery, London). The earliest notable treatment of the scene. Charles Macklin produced and starred in the play at Covent Garden, October 1775; his daughter Maria was the Portia.

said later, "I want a picture painted when you have time. But remember, none of your damned nonsense" such as the *Jessica* represented.[5] Wordsworth dipped into the same fund of abuse when he visited the show at Somerset House: "It looks to me," he said, "as if the painter had indulged in raw liver until he was very unwell."[6] Despite this enthusiastic ridicule, however, the subject, in other hands, remained a popular one. Thirteen years later (1843), William Dyce exhibited a painting, subsequently renamed *The Signal,* which, like Turner's, used the long-established motif of the girl at the open window.

The popularity that pictures inspired by this brief scene enjoyed down into the 1870s may well have been due to the impression that they portrayed filial piety: the obedient young daughter listening to her father's instructions, accepting the weighty domestic responsibility indicated by the thick bunch of keys at her waist, as in Charles West Cope's painting (RA 1867). What seems to have been overlooked was the fact that at that very moment, Jessica inwardly was anything but obedient, and that the event jocosely suggested by Launcelot, the appearance of a well-to-do Christian, was already in the wind. In the very next scene, Jessica elopes with Lorenzo—an exit that was itself the subject of several pictures.*

Richard Westall's picture for Boydell seems to have been the first treatment of the casket scene (3.2), followed at some distance of time by one that the American painter Washington Allston exhibited at Bristol in 1814. Though numerous artists took up the subject between 1838 and 1884, no depiction of Bassanio's lucky draw aroused much comment. A development late in the scene, however—Bassanio's happiness clouded over by news of Antonio's ill fortune—was treated at least twice, first by Newton (pl. 102), and twenty years later by Frank Stone.

The earliest noteworthy treatment of the trial scene was Zoffany's (pl. 182), which has recently been ingeniously interpreted as having a double significance, referring to Macklin's production of the play at Covent Garden in 1775 (though it does not represent an actual performance) but also

*From the same scene, Cope derived a painting in a quite different vein (RA 1870). Shylock's reference to Launcelot as "a huge feeder, / Snail-slow in profit, and he sleeps by day / More than the wildcat" was developed into a picture, now lost, which the artist described as "Shylock and Jessica looking at L. Gobbo asleep after his dinner, a buzz of flies round his head" (Charles Henry Cope, *Reminiscences of Charles West Cope, R.A.* [London, 1891], p. 271).

to a lawsuit of the moment—the veteran actor's proceeding against a playhouse clique "for riotous conspiracy to deprive Mr. Macklin of his livelihood."[7] Macklin's verbal argument at the trial, protesting his indifference to money and revenge, it has been asserted, must forcibly have reminded those present of his Shylock in the trial scene. Though the scene was not included in the Boydell Gallery, it was the subject of more than a dozen pictures between 1819 and 1880. Its continuing popularity was attested to when Charles Hunt pictured it being rehearsed for a school performance (RA 1868).

Night—Lorenzo and Jessica was the title of a painting Isaac Taylor, Jr. exhibited at the Society of Artists in 1783. It was one of a set depicting the different times of day in a spirit diametrically opposed to Hogarth's earlier realization of the same conventional theme. (The others were *Morning—Belarius Sending the Prince to the Chace. Cymbeline,* 1777, *Noon—from the Elegy in a Country Church Yard, by Gray,* and *Evening—from Shakespeare's Twelfth Night,* both 1783.) The idyllic setting, a moonlit garden on a noble estate, made it an appealing subject for painters of landscape in the classical or Italianate mode; William Hodges's version, for Boydell, showed Lorenzo and Jessica seated on a grassy bank, with a lake and a domed and pillared temple, such as ornamented eighteenth-century country estates like Stourhead, in the background.

AS YOU LIKE IT

Replacing the distant adaptations that had been performed since the Restoration, *As You Like It,* more or less as Shakespeare wrote it, was returned to the stage in 1740, after which it had a permanent place in the repertory. As with *The Tempest,* there were several operatic versions, including two at Covent Garden in 1824. *As You Like It* was unquestionably one of nineteenth-century England's favorite Shakespearean plays.

It was also a favorite source of paintings, some one hundred fifty all

183. James C. Hook, *The Defeat of Shylock* (RA 1851) (City Art Gallery, Manchester). Comparison of this treatment of the trial scene with Zoffany's, painted three-quarters of a century earlier, indicates how far pictures of subjects from the drama were normally removed from the performing theater by mid-Victorian times.

told. From the late 1820s to the middle seventies, there were few years when at least one subject from *As You Like It* could not be seen at one of the annual exhibitions; in some years, there were three or four. But these paintings, like those from *A Midsummer Night's Dream,* seem to have had little connection with current theatrical productions. Relatively few theatrical portraits and tableaux from specific productions are recorded, although in some early pictures from the play, such as John Downman's portrayal of the wrestling scene (1.2) for Boydell, in which an overdressed Rosalind gives Orlando the guerdon chain, there are strong suggestions of the stage. The Reverend M. W. Peters once painted Mrs. Siddons as Celia, a role in which she proved that light romantic roles were not her strong suit.

Artists valued *As You Like It* mainly for its attractive ingenues, romantic leads, and amiable clowns against a forest background, rather than for specific moments. The titles of scores of paintings simply mention "Rosalind, Celia, and Touchstone" or "The Forest of Arden" without pinpointing the action represented. Only three individual passages served as the foci of numerous paintings, and of these only the earliest, the wrestling scene, had dramatic content. The other two were a scene described but not shown (Jaques and the wounded stag) and a set speech (Jaques's "All the World's a Stage," or "Seven Ages of Man," discourse).

The wrestling scene, or more precisely the moment immediately before or after the actual combat, was painted a dozen or so times, beginning with Hayman's version of about 1744 (pl. 184). The latest recorded example was the best known of all, Maclise's (RA 1855). Although it was attacked by Ruskin and deplored elsewhere in the press for its "patchwork" of setting, costumes, and accessories from several different centuries, it had a generally favorable reception.

The scene reported in act 2, scene 1, of Jaques soliloquizing over the wounded stag, was contributed to the Boydell Gallery by the landscapist William Hodges, assisted by Romney for the figure of Jaques and the animal painter Sawrey Gilpin for the deer. It was the first of at least fifteen versions down to 1850 of the subject, which offered in an irresistible combination forest scenery, philosophical sentiment, and—to some beholders, at least—a message against cruelty to animals. It was painted by,

184. Francis Hayman, *The Wrestling Scene from "As You Like It"* (ca. 1744) (Tate Gallery, London). Although Hayman was a scene designer, this painting contains little suggestion of a theatrical performance. Its Watteau-like quality links it more closely with the engravers, substantially influenced by Gravelot, for whom Hayman also worked.

185. William Mulready, *The Seven Ages of Man ("All the World's a Stage")* (RA 1838) (Victoria & Albert Museum, Crown Copyright). A typically crowded scene to be "read" as one recalled Jaques's lines in *As You Like It* (2. 7). The woodcut from which this painting was derived was Mulready's contribution to a book of illustrations of the Seven Ages of Man (1837).

among others, Sir George Beaumont (pl. 21), who had a particular affection for the play. When Constable visited him at Coleorton in the autumn of 1823, he wrote his wife, "Sir George reads a play in a manner the most delightfull—far beyond any pronounciation I ever heard—on Saturday evening it was 'As You Like It', and the 'Seven Ages' I never so heard before."[1]

Beaumont's partiality to the "Seven Ages of Man" speech (2.7) testified to the enduring appeal it had for artists, to say nothing of elocutionists and compilers of poetic-philosophic anthologies for use in homes and schools. Nowhere did the spheres of popular art, middle-class moralistic culture, and artistic tradition overlap more comfortably. The concept of man's life as falling into several phases—the precise number was never agreed upon—had long ago found visual representation, in stained glass windows (the source, it has been hazarded, of Shakespeare's inspiration), and paintings by Titian (whose *Three Ages of Life* was in the Bridgewater collection), Giorgione, Dosso Dossi, and other members of the Venetian school, and by early pietistic artists of the Netherlands as well as Van Dyck.[2] Some of these renditions were widely known through prints. From Smirke's treatment of the Seven Ages for Boydell, along with another set he showed at the Royal Academy in 1798, to Henry Stacy Marks's late in the Victorian age, the declension of man according to Shakespeare was depicted at least ten times. The most famous version was William Mulready's (RA 1838), which gathered all Seven Ages on a single canvas (pl. 185). "There they are, all together," wrote Thackeray in *Fraser's Magazine;* "the portly justice, and the quarrelsome soldier; the lover leaning apart, and whispering sweet things in his pretty mistress's ear; the baby hanging on her gentle mother's bosom; the school boy, rosy and lazy; the old man, crabbed and stingy; and the old, old man of all, sans teeth, sans eyes, sans ears, sans every thing . . . ."[3]*

186. William L. Windus, *Touchstone* (Society of British Artists 1847) (Walker Art Gallery, Liverpool). Touchstone describing the several degrees of the lie (*As You Like it,* 5. 4). The style of this painting contains little suggestion that three years later Windus, a Liverpool artist, would convert to Pre-Raphaelitism.

*The picture originated with a woodcut Mulready contributed to an album of *The Seven Ages of Man,* which also contained designs by Leslie, Wilkie, William Hilton, Landseer, and Callcott. Mulready later exhibited at the Royal Academy (1848) a set of drawings of the same subject that he had made for a projected porcelain card tray at "the earnest request of some eminent persons interested in the development of art manufacture in England." The tray failed to materialize, and the drawings were bought by the Art Union of London, which had them etched and gathered into an album distributed among its subscribers (1850) (W. Justin O'Driscoll, *A Memoir of Daniel Maclise, R.A.* [London, 1871], p. 97).

187. Walter Deverell, *The Mock Marriage of Orlando and Rosalind* (RA 1853) (Birmingham City Museum and Art Gallery). The American-born Deverell exhibited this picture the year before his death at the age of twenty-seven. He painted at least two other subjects from *As You Like It: Rosalind and Celia as Ganymede and Aliena* (formerly attributed to Millais), and *Rosalind Witnessing the Meeting of Jaques and Orlando in the Forest.*

Exemplifying as it did the perennially popular theme of rustic courtship—the built-in quaintness and condescension of the subject here enhanced by bogus literary pastoralism—the Touchstone-Audrey-Phoebe-Silvius plot was another favorite with painters. Of Leslie's *Touchstone and Audrey* (BI 1830), the *Times* said, "There is no finer specimen of village coquetry than is here to be met with: in the conscious glance of Audrey, with sun-flower in her breast, we recognize Mrs. Gibbs [a popular actress]: The artist has hit off the affected simplicity of her simper to the life."[4] (In Henry Liverseege's painting of the same subject, from about the same time, the simper seems baked in, because the figure of Audrey suggests a cheap piece of china bric-a-brac.) In 1853, Maclise painted *Phoebe and Silvius;* and in 1870–72, John Pettie exhibited companion pieces: *Touchstone and Audrey* and *Silvius and Phoebe* (pl. 81).

But of all the characters in *As You Like It,* it was Rosalind and Celia who were the most frequently represented, often simply as a pair of pretty girls, one demure, the other vivacious, engaged in an exchange of girlish confidences—a formula used innumerable times in Victorian popular painting.

The much-deplored conventionalism, indeed triteness, of such subjects did not deter the Pre-Raphaelite painters or their disciples from drawing upon *As You Like It* any more than the overabundance of Ophelias in art prevented Millais from having one more go at her. Walter Deverell exhibited *The Mock Marriage of Orlando and Rosalind* (4.1) (pl. 187) at the Royal Academy in 1853, the year before his death at the age of twenty-seven, and Arthur Hughes showed a triptych (pl. 188) from the play in 1872.

By this time, of course, the original Pre-Raphaelites had long since gone their separate ways. Like Hughes, Millais had lost much of his early commitment to Pre-Raphaelite principles and techniques. His Royal Academy painting of 1868 quoting "O Jupiter! how weary are my spirits" (2.4), showed the exhausted trio of Rosalind, Celia, and Touchstone resting under a beech tree.

MUCH ADO ABOUT NOTHING

Much Ado About Nothing has a comparatively slender stage history. The original play was revived at Covent Garden in 1739, and Garrick pro-

188. Arthur Hughes, *Three Pictures from "As You Like It"* (RA 1872) (Walker Art Gallery, Liverpool). The triptych represents, from left to right: Touchstone and Audrey (3. 3), Orlando and Adam (2. 6), and Rosalind (3. 2). A fairly late example of the way that *As You Like It* scenes provided artists—not only Pre-Raphaelites—with occasions for the meticulous painting of landscape.

duced it every year during his management of Drury Lane. The stars who played Benedick, including both Kembles, Macready, and Charles Kean, were more noteworthy than the actresses who played Bianca and Beatrice, though the latter was a sentimental favorite with the Victorian public. Few paintings, apart from the five in the Boydell Gallery, were taken from the play until the mid-1820s. A total of some sixty are recorded.

By far the most popular scene for painting was that of Beatrice overhearing Hero and Ursula in the orchard (3.1). Fuseli, who was singularly unequipped to do justice to the subject, was among the first to undertake it. When he showed his version in 1787, a newspaper remarked, "'Tis a pity Mr. Fusili [*sic*] should ever quit *fairy* ground; his *elves, wizards,* and other *super-natural beings,* are so wonderful in point of design and execution, that we must regret he is not sufficiently encouraged in that peculiar branch"—so that, inferentially, he would leave sentimental subjects alone.[1] Matthew W. Peters gave the scene a Watteau-like treatment in the Boydell Gallery. About twenty paintings of the orchard scene are recorded from 1824 to 1884, at least eight of them from the single decade 1850–60 and four more from 1863–67. In the earlier phase, it was no doubt the "sweetness" of the subject—a term used by a reviewer of Henry Howard's version of 1829[2]—that recommended it. Later, it was Beatrice's vivacity that painters were most likely to develop. This was the quality that critics most prized in Leslie's picture of 1850, painted for John Gibbons and twice repeated: " . . . a wildly-witty grace in the expression of the lady's countenance," noted the *Examiner.*[3]

Another scene, the fainting of Hero in church (4.1), was painted at least a half-dozen times, beginning with William Hamilton's version for Boydell. As the most dramatic episode in the play, it was especially subject to the accusation of "theatricalism," which reviewers held at the ready when paintings from Shakespeare were exhibited. In 1882, the scene became the subject of one of the few notable late Victorian theatrical paintings when Forbes Robertson recorded on canvas Henry Irving's elaborate staging at the Lyceum, a multi-media event that included the untransferable elements of incense and music by both organ and string orchestra.

To oblige a public that relished Falstaff's questioning his sorry soldiers, at least two artists presented the equivalent scene of the comic constable Dogberry examining Conrade and Borachio (4.2). Smirke painted the scene for Boydell (pl. 189), and Henry Stacy Marks chose it twice, first for his debut at the Royal Academy (1853) and again for another Academy offering (1859) that was bought by Mr. Mudie, of Mudie's Select Circulating Library.

TWELFTH NIGHT

Although not usually regarded as a starring vehicle (a fact that may explain the relative lack of theatrical portraits from the play), *Twelfth Night* was popular throughout the nineteenth century, both on the stage and in the galleries. Its lighthearted plot contained themes and devices of great appeal to the contemporary audience: the delight of seemingly hopeless love fulfilled in the end (Viola and Orsino), the deflation of a pompous ass (Malvolio), the pranks of a saucy maidservant (Maria) assisted by an amiable drunk (Sir Toby Belch) and an equally amiable country gull (Sir Andrew Aguecheek).

Of the one-hundred-plus pictures from the play, four scenes, or moments in them, accounted for about a dozen each. The first was act 1,

189. Robert Smirke, *The Examination of Conrade and Borachio* (Boydell's Shakespeare Gallery) (Royal Shakespeare Theatre Picture Gallery ©). *Much Ado About Nothing,* 4. 2. Smirke also painted for Boydell the equivalent scene in *Measure for Measure,* the examination of Froth and the Clown by Escalus (pl. 30).

scene 5, in the course of which Viola, disguised as a boy (Cesario), demands to see Olivia's face. The moment in which Olivia lifts her veil was custom-made for artists wishing to enhance with a dramatic context a portrait of a lovely woman:

> *Olivia.* . . . But we will draw the curtain and show you the picture. [*Unveils.*]
> Look you, sir, such a one I was this present. Is't not well done?
> *Viola.* Excellently done, if God did all.

Leslie's depiction of this little gesture was typical of a number of such representations (pl. 190).

190. Charles R. Leslie, *Viola and Olivia* (1859) (Tate Gallery, London). One of the last sketches Leslie made. The Viola is said to have been the actress Priscilla Horton, whom Maclise painted as Ariel (pl. 54).

191. Walter Deverell, *"Twelfth Night"* (National Institution for the Exhibition of Modern Art 1850) (Forbes Magazine Collection). A notably free elaboration of the garden scene (2. 4), the Pre-Raphaelite idea of luxurious leisure; note the Arab band in the background as well as the Moorish architecture, which seems to place Illyria somewhere in Spain. Dante Gabriel Rossetti modeled for Feste the jester, who is singing from a book titled *Carmina Illyriae;* Rossetti's future wife, Elizabeth Siddal, was the disguised Viola, and the artist himself was the Duke.

The veiled-confession scene (2.4), in which Viola expresses her love for the Duke in the guise of some other unappreciated woman's sad story, was another favorite. Two excerpts from this familiar speech were often used as titles or mottoes for sentimental portraits of heroines stoically bearing the consequences of unacknowledged love for a man:

> . . . *She never told her love,*
> But let concealment, like a worm i' th' bud,
> Feed on her damask cheek. She pined in thought;
> And, with a green and yellow melancholy,
> She sat like *Patience on a monument,*
> Smiling at grief. Was not this love indeed?

The most famous *Twelfth Night* painting, if one can judge from the number of modern books in which it is reproduced, came from this scene. Walter Deverell's early Pre-Raphaelite picture (pl. 191) attempted to capture both the lyricism and the luxury of Orsino's garden-court. As a band of Arab musicians discourses sweet music in the background and Feste the clown hovers by his side, the Duke lounges, engaged in the dialogue with Cesario that will culminate, after the stage is cleared of everyone else, in the "She never told her love" speech.

The garden scene (2.5), in which Malvolio reads the planted letter, seems to have been painted only once before 1849; but in the ensuing twenty years, it appeared in at least eight treatments. Frith, whose first painting to be hung at the Royal Academy (1840) was *Malvolio before the Countess Olivia* and who returned to *Twelfth Night* at the very end of his career (1898) with one more version of "Olivia unveiling," twice drew upon act 2, scene 5, in 1855 for a single-figure picture of Maria throwing down the letter, and in 1869 for a picture of the later moment when Malvolio, fatuously soliloquizing, is eavesdropped upon by Sir Toby, Sir Andrew, and Fabian.

The several phases of action in the later garden scene (3.4) inspired a number of paintings down to, but for some reason not beyond, the early Victorian years. Benjamin West's German pupil, Johann Heinrich Ramberg, painted, for Boydell, Malvolio's cross-purpose dialogue with Olivia (pl. 29), borrowing from act 2, scene 5, the added comic element of the eavesdroppers. Maclise painted two versions for the Royal Academy shows of 1829 and 1840 (pl. 192). Francis Wheatley's was the first noteworthy treatment of the subsequent duel (Society of Artists 1772), portraying the moment when Sir Andrew draws his sword against an unmistakably feminine-faced Viola, who is leaning so far to the left as to suggest that she has not yet recovered from her ordeal on the deck of a listing ship. Sixty years later (RA 1833), George Clint painted the follow-up duel in the next scene (4.1), in which Olivia intervenes between Sir Toby and Sebastian. The stances of the three main figures, recalling the stylized postures of combatants in a history picture, have a mock-heroic effect which suggests that Clint intended a parody of high art.

At the same Academy show, Clint exhibited the carousing scene (2.3) in which Sir Toby, Sir Andrew, and Maria have a high old time belowstairs. Hamilton's earlier treatment of the scene for Boydell was unapologetically reminiscent of similar scenes in Dutch painting, and there was no Malvolio, "the devil a Puritan that he is," to put a damper on the proceedings. Clint, however, painted for a more decorous age. Malvolio is prominent with his flowing night robe and holier-than-thou visage; Sir Toby's paunch is much reduced, and he has the face of a prosperous business man; the glasses from which he, Fabian, and Sir Andrew drink must contain nothing stronger than diluted wine; and Maria, at the left extremity, simpers out at the beholder. Cakes and ale have been diminished to a tea party that has gone slightly out of control.

THE MERRY WIVES OF WINDSOR

Seldom performed nowadays, when it is better known through Verdi's opera, and never the subject of much criticism apart from that having to do with Falstaff, *The Merry Wives of Windsor* was once as popular as Shakespeare's other comedies, a fact impressively documented by the record of

192. Daniel Maclise, *Malvolio and the Countess* (RA 1840) (Tate Gallery, London). This was the painting that the *Examiner* found to be "as good as a criticism by Charles Lamb" (text, p. 250). The actor Macready, who saw it in Maclise's studio before it was exhibited, wrote, "His picture of Olivia I can look at for ever; it is beauty, moral and physical, personified" (*Diaries of William Charles Macready,* ed. William Toynbee [London, 1912], 2: 53).

193. William P. Frith, *Duel Scene from "Twelfth Night"* (British Institution 1843) (Walker Art Gallery, Liverpool). One of Frith's earliest literary pictures. Three years earlier, his first painting to be exhibited at the Royal Academy was also from *Twelfth Night: Malvolio before the Countess Olivia.* It was overshadowed by Maclise's treatment of the same subject (pl. 192).

more than eighty paintings drawn from it. Revived in 1705 with Quin as Falstaff, it was kept in the repertory from Garrick down to Charles Kean. It did not escape the early nineteenth-century fashion of adding operatic embellishments to the Shakespearean text, and only in 1851 did Kean again play it straight. From the earliest days of theatrical portraiture, actresses were painted in the roles of Anne Page and Mistress Ford, and, following the usual pattern, mere pictures of pretty women subsequently had the name of Anne Page gratuitously attached to them.

One reason why *The Merry Wives of Windsor* appealed to artists and their clients was the presence of Falstaff, heavy, hearty, and humorous, without the embarrassments he offered to moral sensibilities in the *Henry IV* plays.* Another was the opportunity the play afforded painters to work in the bourgeois Dutch mode. Many of the *Merry Wives* pictures were genre scenes, sometimes portraying a small incident in everyday life (for Boydell, Smirke painted Sir Hugh Evans examining William on his grammar [4.1]), or a festive dinner with a number of well-fed male and female figures, or a robustly farcical episode. Although some of the women's costumes were inappropriately rich for rural life in Elizabethan times—the satiny texture and extravagant billows and folds of Anne Page's dress in one of Matthew Peters's Boydell paintings would have not been out of place in Gainsborough's studio—the settings and accessories uniformly were meant to convey the feel of country manners in the true genre style.

Most of the pictures from the play were inspired either by the opening scene or by the farcical plot of Falstaff and the buck basket. Act 1, scene 1, from which at least twenty pictures were drawn, was attractive both for what occurred onstage and what did not. One of Smirke's paintings for Boydell was among the first to exploit the moment in front of Page's house when Anne Page enters to announce dinner and Slender, the bashful suitor, hangs back. The offstage dinner itself, whose immediacy is emphasized in the text by the repeated invitations Slender receives from

*Eighteenth-century critics tended to regard the Falstaff of *The Merry Wives of Windsor* and the two parts of *Henry IV* as a single, seamless character, but Romantic criticism, following Hazlitt, tended to see a disjunction between the "Eastcheap" and "Windsor" Falstaffs. Hartley Coleridge dismissed the latter as "a big-bellied imposter, assuming his name and style, or at best it is Falstaff in dotage," and later Shakespeare critics shared his view. But it was not shared by picture-buyers, who delighted in this sunny rogue, not least in his eventual comeuppance. (See Jeanne Addison Roberts, "The Windsor Falstaff," *Papers on Language and Literature* 9 [1973]: 202–30).

194. John S. Clifton, *Buck Washing on Datchet Mead* (RA 1849) (Yale Center for British Art, Paul Mellon Fund). This offstage episode, reported by Falstaff (*The Merry Wives of Windsor,* 3. 5), was one of the most popular farcical scenes in artists' Shakespearean repertory. Many literary pictures were painted by obscure artists, but Clifton hovers on the edge of total oblivion. Only two pictures by him are recorded, this and another exhibited at the Academy the next year.

Anne and her father to join them, was painted at least a half-dozen times.

The artist most closely identified with the play was Leslie, whose early *Merry Wives* paintings started him on the road to fame. The first of his four renderings of "Slender's Courtship" was exhibited at the British Institution in 1819, when he was twenty-five. It was the version hung at the Royal Academy in 1825 (pl. 82), however, that initiated Leslie's popular identification with the play.

Six years later, Leslie addressed himself to the dinner scene, the company including Mr. and Mrs. Ford, Dr. Caius, the obese Falstaff, Bardolph with his flaming nose, and Slender, whom Anne Page has finally prevailed upon to join the rest. His second version of the scene (pl. 151), painted for John Sheepshanks, was exhibited in 1838.

Meanwhile, other artists, veterans and novices alike, painted the same moments in the play's first scene. The landscapist Augustus Wall Callcott, nearing the end of his career, exhibited his interpretation (BI 1834) in which, understandably, the open-air background was as prominent as the human comedy of Anne Page, costumed and coiffed as she would have been in the time of Charles I, and Slender fidgeting with his stick; the dinner party could be glimpsed inside. The Scottish painter Thomas Duncan sent his *Anne Page Inviting Slender to Dinner* (pl. 101) to the Royal Academy in 1836, and in 1843 W. P. Frith, just beginning his career, picked up the theme, posing the fourteen-year-old John Everett Millais as Page's little son. The picture was skied in the worst room of the Academy's suite at the National Gallery, but after it was sold at the Liverpool exhibition for £100, it was accorded a prominent place on the line at the British Institution's next show. The scene continued to be painted for the next thirty years, after which time the reviewers had scant patience left for it. When Charles West Cope showed his version in 1875, the *Athenaeum* irreverently demanded, "Is not such a picture as this an anachronism, even for a Royal Academician?"[1] Cope did not take the hint, because he exhibited still another Anne Page and Slender seven years later.

The opening of act 2, scene 1, in which Mistress Page and Mistress Ford compare the duplicate letters they have received from Falstaff, was painted half a dozen times, first by Peters for Boydell. The next group of scenes, involving Falstaff's trip to, and into, the Thames in a laundry basket (3.3,5; 4.2), received frequent attention from painters; there are records of some fifteen treatments, beginning with Hayman's picture for one of the Vauxhall supper boxes in the 1740s. But though pictures from other parts of the *Merry Wives* continued to proliferate, this theme disappeared after the 1850s.

The opening of the night scene at Herne's oak (5.5) offered pictorial attractions akin to those that were responsible for so many *Midsummer Night's Dream* pictures: a bevy of fairies and masqueraders and a principal character in grotesque disguise, in this case Falstaff, an overweight Bottom, wearing a huge pair of antlers. There were several treatments in the 1790s and then a hiatus until 1850–70, when several more were exhibited, among them George Cruikshank's fantastic painting (pl. 73) of Falstaff sprawled on the ground underneath the tree in the midst of the revels. Thanks to this play, and doubtless the pictures illustrating it, Herne's oak was a national monument (a painting of it, *The Tree Mentioned by Shakespeare,* was exhibited at the Royal Academy in 1790); and when it was blown down in August 1864, a picture at the next year's British Institution show commemorated the event.

ALL'S WELL THAT ENDS WELL

All's Well That Ends Well was performed from time to time, with celebrated actors in the leading roles. But, unlike *The Two Gentlemen of Verona,* for example, which had a somewhat less distinguished stage record, this comedy attracted few painters. No more than twenty pictorial treatments were exhibited. In most of them, Helena was the center of interest, alone, as in Charles Eastlake's *Helena* (RA 1849), or in a picture of "sober sadness" titled *The Pilgrim* at the British Institution the following year, or as the chief figure in a tableau. The Boydell Gallery included three scenes from the play, all by Wheatley: the Countess Rousillon and Helena engaged in earnest conversation, one of the few domestic subjects in the entire gallery (1.3); Helena and the King she has cured (2.3); and a moment in the final scene (5.3). Wheatley also painted the ambushing of Parolles (4.1) for the New Shakespeare Gallery.

MEASURE FOR MEASURE

Measure for Measure was performed fairly often in the eighteenth century, but no pictures from it are recorded earlier than the four in Boydell's Gallery. Two of these reflect the era's pleasure in the play's low comedy: Smirke painted both the examination of Froth and the Clown by Escalus and the Justice (2.1) (pl. 30) and the dialogue between Abhorson and Pompey (4.2). But there seem to have been no further paintings from the comic elements. Like the two other contributions to the Boydell Gallery and William Hamilton's two pictures for the New Shakespeare Gallery, virtually all the twenty nineteenth-century pictures recorded for *Measure for Measure* were derived from the Claudio-Isabella plot. This number does not include the paintings that, though nominally from Tennyson's "Mariana in the Moated Grange," were linked with the play through the poem's epigraph: " . . . What a merit were it in death to take this poor maid from the world! . . . There at the moated grange resides this dejected Mariana" (3.1).

The most famous painting from the play was Holman Hunt's rendering (pl. 195) of the prison scene (3.1). Like nearly all products of early Pre-Raphaelitism, it was praised by William Michael Rossetti and generally damned by reviewers whose bias ran the other way. The *Examiner* praised Isabella for her "wondrous eyes and calm fervour of expression" but declared that Claudio, "whose fear of death is represented by a look and posture of imbecile lunacy, is a distressing and exaggerated feature of the scene. If it is to be supposed that Claudio expressed, in such a way as Mr. Hunt depicts it, his distress of mind, it is a thing that we had much rather suppose than see deliberately painted."[1]

In 1870, Dante Gabriel Rossetti painted Jane Morris as Mariana working at her embroidery (pl. 196). Subsequently, the Anglo-American artist Edwin A. Abbey began his London career as a painter in oils (1889) with three subjects from the play.

195. William Holman Hunt, *Claudio and Isabella* (painted 1850; RA 1853) (Tate Gallery, London). The scene is *Measure for Measure,* 3. 1: Claudio pleads with his sister Isabella to give herself to Angelo in order that he can be released from prison. Hunt is said to have painted the picture on a panel from a "superannuated coach."

196. Dante Gabriel Rossetti, *Mariana* (1870) (Aberdeen Art Gallery). Mariana listens to the boy singing "Take, O take, those lips away" (*Measure for Measure,* 4. 1).

THE HISTORY PLAYS

HENRY VI

The three parts of *Henry VI* were seldom performed in any guise. Theophilus Cibber staged his version of Parts Two and Three in 1723, and in 1817 Edmund Kean took the role of Richard, Duke of York in his wretched adaptation of Part Two. "Imagine," said Leigh Hunt of the latter enterprise, "a selection from Rafael's pictures, put together into one picture; or an opera made out of scenes of different operas of Mozart, Paesiello, and Cimarosa. A true painter or musician would laugh in your face at such a proposal. . . . For heaven's sake, let us have no more of such anomalies. Let us see Shakspeare himself, and not a degraded composition of noble limbs, with a piece besides here and there cut from other poets—an eye from poor Chapman, and knee-pan from Webster: for such also is the case with the present!"[1] Not until 1864 was the trilogy staged intact, by an adventurous but obscure company at the minor Surrey Theatre.

Yet no fewer than fourteen pictures in the Boydell Gallery, representing the highest incidence of mediocrity in the whole long series, were taken from the play: a prime instance of the way in which Shakespearean pictorial fashion, in this case dictated by the artists' ambition to scale the heights of history painting, sometimes proceeded independently of a play's theatrical fortunes. Subsequently some twenty-five more were derived from it, as late as 1900–1903, when Edwin Abbey painted the penance of Eleanor, Duchess of Gloucester (Part Two, 2.4) and the death of the king (Part Three, 5.6).

No individual subject was treated more than four times (the number of paintings of Jack Cade's rebellion in Part Two, 4.2 and of Gloucester's death in Part Two, 3.2). The iconographical history of the *Henry VI* plays is mainly interesting for the well-known artists who at one time or another turned their hands to such pictures. Fuseli seems to have been first in the field, with a picture of Warwick taking his oath over Gloucester's body (Part Two, 3.2) (1780–82). Between them, Northcote and Hamilton contributed nine *Henry VI* canvases to the Boydell Gallery. Opie painted two subjects, one of which, the Mother Jourdain conjuring scene (Part Two, 1.4), was also chosen by Matthew W. Peters as one of his contributions to the rival New Shakespeare Gallery.

But the *Henry VI* picture that stirred the most discussion at the time—it was, indeed, one of the two or three most famous paintings in the entire Boydell Gallery—was Reynolds's *The Death of Cardinal Beaufort,* illustrating Warwick's line in Part Two, 3.3, "See how the pangs of death do make him grin." The subject was already a familiar one, having been included in most illustrated editions of the play, but Reynolds added an extra touch by stationing a fiend at the dying cardinal's head as a visible symbol of his guilty conscience. Although some acclaimed the picture generally as Reynolds's finest achievement, the fiend was widely condemned; and Reynolds painted it out before the picture was engraved, though compensating for its removal by intensifying the death's-head grin into which Beaufort's face was contorted. The canvas brought the highest price of all at the Boydell sale in 1805. A number of copies were made of it, and

197. John Pettie, *Scene in the Temple Garden* (RA 1871) (Walker Art Gallery, Liverpool). One of Pettie's many paintings from English literature and history. The scene is *1 Henry VI,* 2. 4: Richard, Duke of York (left), plucks a white rose, the Duke of Somerset (right) a red one, and each calls on his followers to pluck their own. Warwick, one of the background figures, says:

And here I prophesy: this brawl to-day
Grown to this faction in the Temple garden
Shall send, between the red rose and the white,
A thousand souls to death and deadly night.

through numerous re-issues of engravings it became familiar to every reader of Shakespeare.

Fuseli, predictably, could not resist the ghost work in the second part of the trilogy; in 1808, he exhibited at the Royal Academy *Cardinal Beaufort Terrified by the Supposed Apparition of Gloucester* (Part Two, 3.2). Less fearsome than pathetic was the death of Rutland (Part Three, 1.3), a subject undertaken early in his career by Leslie. The British Institution rejected the original canvas; but the Royal Academy hung it (1816), and John Sheepshanks commissioned a copy. Edwin Landseer, then "a curly-headed youngster, dividing his time between Polito's wild beasts at Exeter Change and the Royal Academy Schools," modeled for Rutland.[2]

More than half a century later, three successful painters, one at the end of his career and two belonging to a younger generation, took up subjects from *Henry VI.* Sir John Gilbert showed "the poor weak King . . . forced by the ruthless Warwick to look on the dead body of the murdered Gloucester" (RA 1880). William Quiller Orchardson exhibited *Talbot and the Countess of Auvergne* (Part One, 2.3) at the Royal Academy in 1867, and four years later, John Pettie showed his well-known *Scene in the Temple Garden* (pl. 197).

RICHARD III

The prosperous career of *Richard III* in the art world—some fifty paintings are recorded—was launched and sustained by the drama's steady popularity on the stage.[1] The play as Shakespeare wrote it, to be sure, was seldom performed until the middle of the nineteenth century; Macready's attempt to restore the text in 1821 was a failure, and though Phelps's production of the original play in 1845 ran a month, he also later reverted, as did Charles Kean in his spectacular production of 1850, to the adaptation in which *Richard III* had been familiar to audiences since 1700. This was Colley Cibber's version, a "vile jumble" as Hazlitt called it, which included fragments of *2* and *3 Henry VI, Henry V,* and *Richard II,* as well as Cibber's own celebrated brisk line, for which Shakespeare has

198. Nathaniel Dance, *Garrick as Richard III* (RA 1771) (Forbes Magazine Collection). Garrick in his most famous role was probably the most popular single subject in eighteenth-century theatrical art, Dance's version having been painted twenty-six years after Hogarth's (pl. 2). The scene, of course, is different: Hogarth's tormented king sees ghosts (5. 3) whereas Dance's brandishes his sword at the subsequent battle of Bosworth Field (5. 4). This is a copy of the exhibited picture, which is at the Town Hall, Stratford-on-Avon, replacing Gainsborough's destroyed painting of the same subject.

enjoyed undeserved credit, "Off with his head; so much for Buckingham."

Cibber's was the play in which Garrick dazzled his first London audience on 19 October 1741, and it was as Richard III that this most-painted eighteenth-century actor was most often painted, beginning with Hogarth's picture produced immediately after his debut (pl. 2). Hayman (Society of Artists 1760), Fuseli (ca. 1766), Nathaniel Dance (pl. 198), and Gainsborough (canvas destroyed by fire at the Stratford Town Hall, 1946) were only the most celebrated of the many artists who seized upon the subject. Later paintings traced the shifting of the mantle of the stage Richard III from one famous tragedian to another; portraits of Kemble in the role (1788) and of Edmund Kean (1814, 1816) were seen at the annual exhibitions.

Subjects from *Richard III* served especially the public's voracious appetite for pathos. It was the events described in act 4, scene 3—none are actually seen on the stage—that were most often depicted: the murder of the young princes in the Tower, "this piece of ruthless butchery" as it is called by Tyrell, and their burial.[2] Fuseli painted the heads of the murderers Dighton and Forrest about 1780–82. Northcote liked to believe that his picture of the deed, exhibited in 1786 (pl. 15), had been the inspiration of the Boydell Gallery; Boydell had bought it, and it was hanging in his Cheapside home when his nephew hosted the famous dinner at which the idea of the gallery was first mooted. Boydell ordered a companion piece from Northcote, *The Burial of the Royal Children,* to accompany the other in the gallery. Northcote produced a third painting from the play for Boydell, the scene of the princes' meeting the Lord Mayor (3.1). It is among the worst of all the Boydell commissions, which is saying a good deal. The princes in the Tower were also painted by Leslie in 1830 (pl. 83), but his source was not Shakespeare but Thomas Heywood's *The First and Second Partes of King Edward the Fourth* (1599).

The androgynous children (they were sometimes played on the stage by girls) continued to be depicted as "the petted darlings of the day"—Victoria's day, when the imperatives of "pretty and domestic art" took precedence over the horror inherent in their story. But the ultimate trivialization of this famous episode in English history was accomplished not on canvas but in a program of *tableaux vivants*—animated canvases—the royal family put on at Windsor in 1860, when the living princes posed as their ill-fated predecessors. One wonders which particular paintings the children's mentor had in mind. "The two little Boys made a beautiful picture," wrote the queen in her diary. "Unfortunately Arthur turned his head away too much." But their father, she recorded, was much pleased.[3]

Mrs. E. M. Ward treated the subject in 1864—Palgrave thought he had "seen the principal figure (the young Edward) before in a well-known work by Paul Delaroche"[4]*—but the most noteworthy of the later pictures of the doomed little princes was Millais's at the Royal Academy in 1878.

The other scene from *Richard III* that was repeatedly chosen was Richard's dream, on the eve of Bosworth Field, of the ghosts of the numerous rivals he had disposed of (5.3). This was the scene in which Garrick was most often portrayed and it was also painted by Opie, who earlier had depicted a preceding scene in the play (pl. 11), and twice by Fuseli (RA 1798, 1811).

Pictures from the play continued to be shown to the end of the nine-

*He had. Delaroche's *Les Enfants d'Edouard* was shown at the Salon of 1831 without an attribution to Shakespeare. An exercise in, among other things, antiquarian precision of costume and furnishing, it was praised by Musset and Ingres and inspired Delavigne's popular play of the same name (1833). Henry James's response to the picture when he saw it as a youth doubtless was similar to his reaction to whatever English portrayals of the same subject he might have seen: "I couldn't doubt," he wrote in *A Small Boy and Others* (New York, 1913, p. 344), "that the long-drawn odd face of the elder prince, sad and sore and sick, with his wide crimped sidelocks of fair hair and his violet legs marked by the Garter and dangling from the bed, was a reconstitution of far-off history of the subtlest and most 'last word' modern or psychologic kind. I had never heard of psychology in art or anywhere else—scarcely anyone then had; but I truly felt the nameless force at play."

teenth century. The "picture of the year" in 1896 was Edwin Abbey's elaborate canvas of Henry VI's funeral procession, with the treacherous, humpbacked new monarch holding out a ring to Lady Anne, the dead king's daughter-in-law, as she walks alone (1.2). The sensation the painting caused encouraged Abbey to paint several more scenes from the history plays in the next few years—a belated and final burst of artistic interest in the Shakespearean sequence.

Of all the pictures from *Richard III* that are lost, there is a record of one whose disappearance is especially to be regretted: John Nixon's *Richard III in a Country Theatre* (RA 1786). What echoes did it possess of Hogarth's *Strolling Actresses Dressing in a Barn?*

KING JOHN

Seldom performed today, *King John* appears often in the annals of the eighteenth- and nineteenth-century London stage, a fact that explains in part, at least, its popularity with artists; some thirty-five pictures from it are recorded. Across the years a splendid succession of tragic actors played King John, and an equally distinguished series of actresses assumed the sympathetic role of Constance. Charles Kemble's production at Covent Garden in 1823, with sets and costumes by the antiquarian James Robinson Planché, was so laden with "authentic" details that the whole play seems to have consisted of a series of old engravings, monumental effigies, and illuminated manuscripts brought to life. Significantly, almost half of the paintings were produced after this year.

The only scene that was painted more than two or three times was 4.1, in which the king's nephew, Arthur, pleads with Hubert de Burgh not to burn out his eyes. Fuseli's version appeared at the Society of Artists in 1775, and Alexander Runciman produced his five years later (pl. 199). Northcote painted the subject for Boydell, at whose sale in 1805 the painting was bought by Miss Linwood, the celebrated maker and exhibitor of needlework copies of famous paintings, who used it as a model for one of her next productions. The subject was also one of the two from the

199. Alexander Runciman, *Hubert and Arthur* (1780) (National Gallery of Scotland). Like contemporary paintings of the Princes in the Tower, this version of Prince Arthur and the sadistic Hubert (*King John,* 4. 1) sought to evoke horror through the use of a child. The subject was still viable as late as 1882: see pl. 84.

200. George H. Harlow, *Hubert and Arthur* (British Institution 1815) (Royal Shakespeare Theatre Picture Gallery ©). Apart from its having evoked Hazlitt's indignation, this picture is notable chiefly for the fact that Charles Kemble posed for the figure of Hubert.

play that John Opie painted for the New Shakespeare Gallery; the other showed the earlier scene of young Arthur being taken prisoner on the battlefield (3.2). George Henry Harlow's treatment (pl. 200), was denounced by Hazlitt: "the greatest piece of coxcombry and absurdity we remember to have seen. We do not think that any one who pleases has a right to paint a libel on Shakespeare."[1] Subsequent repetitions of the subject relieved it of much of its inherent drama. By the time William F. Yeames came to paint it (pl. 84), all the *Spectator* could say, with a yawn, of his version was that it "tells its story plainly and unmistakably, and asks nothing from the spectator but a tacit acquiescence in the interest of its story."[2]

RICHARD II

The pictorial record of *Richard II,* containing no more than a dozen items, is as scanty as its dramatic one. The play was seldom performed in the eighteenth century. Edmund Kean took the title role in his own production in 1815, and Macready, who had played it as a youth in the provinces, resumed it for a couple of performances just before he retired. The play was represented by four pictures in the Boydell Gallery and by one (Northcote's *Death of John of Gaunt)* in the New Shakespeare Gallery. Two years later (pl. 201), Wheatley painted the death of Richard II.

The record is virtually blank for the next sixty years. A painting of John of Gaunt's dying interview with Richard (2.1) was shown at the Royal Academy in 1852. One of the few other paintings related to the play was Sir John Gilbert's *The Deposition of Richard II,* exhibited "rich in colour, gold embroideries and damask" at the Royal Academy in 1876.

HENRY IV

Part One of Shakespeare's most popular history play had been constantly performed ever since the Restoration. Betterton was a famous Hotspur, and when he aged out of that part, he played Falstaff with equal success. Part Two was much less popular in both the eighteenth and nineteenth centuries, a relativity mirrored in art; there were roughly two paintings from Part One to every one from Part Two. But still, there was Falstaff in both parts.

The source of at least 115 paintings, *Henry IV* occupies a special position in the evolution of British art, because it helped undermine history painting as the most elevated, and thus the most solemn, form of art. To those who had the gift of prophecy, its potential subversiveness might have been read in the fact that it alone, of the several "Henry" plays, had been the subject of more than two or three paintings before Boydell enlisted his company of artists to glorify history painting by way of Shakespeare. To be sure, it included various staple themes of history painting—statecraft, political conspiracy, battles, personal heroism. But these were not the themes that most artists chose. They concentrated from the outset on the elements of the play that were not "historical"—neither found in the written sources nor, because of their nature, admissible in history painting—but instead were dramatic embellishments or outright farcical inventions. With the presence of Falstaff, the story of the conscience-haunted monarch and his wastrel but eventually kingly son acquired in art, as it had in the Shakespearean theater, an extra dimension, so strong an element of comedy that its genuinely historical qualities were subordinated

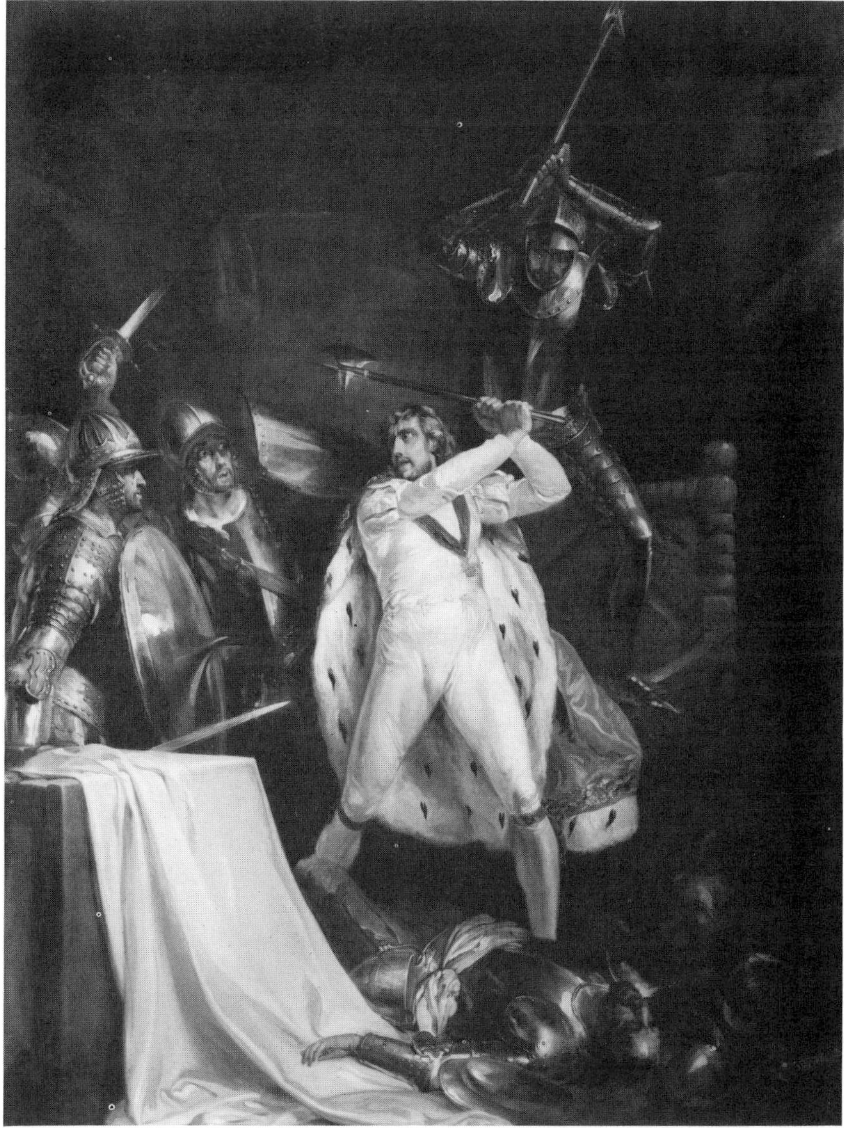

201. Francis Wheatley, *The Death of Richard II* (1795) (Forbes Magazine Collection). The violent climax of *Richard II* (5. 5). An unusual subject for Wheatley to undertake, because his Greuze-like style was better fitted for lighter scenes, such as the thirteen he painted for Boydell from Shakespeare's comedies and romances (pl. 180).

to the imagined plot of a gross old knight who had practiced impartially and with great gusto most of the seven deadly sins. When Falstaff took over a segment of English history in the art exhibitions, history painting could no longer be regarded with unmixed seriousness; cheerfulness, to say nothing of sheer exuberant riot, kept breaking in.

Falstaff was the most popular comic character on the English stage from Dryden's time onward, but the critical conception of him drastically changed in the course of the eighteenth century. Along with Sir Roger de Coverley, he was the earliest model of the "amiable humorist" type that was defined, shaped, and admired as neoclassic ideals of character gradually shaded into new Romantic ones.[1] To Dryden, he had been undoubtedly funny in his cowardice, buffoonery, and appetites but also undeniably base. From the middle of the eighteenth century, however, Falstaff was completely reinterpreted. Even Dr. Johnson, to whom he remained contemptible, conceded that his good humor redeemed him to a certain

202. Marcellus Laroon the Younger, *Scene from "Henry IV, Part 1"* (1746) (Yale Center for British Art, Paul Mellon Collection). Laroon brought to the easel a varied experience as a singer at Drury Lane and an army officer under the Duke of Marlborough. Although the figure is probably not a portrait of the actor James Quin, as has been suggested, the scene, with Bardolph in contemporary costume including a tricornered hat, has a strong flavor of the theater.

extent. In 1777, Maurice Morgann, in one of the century's most influential essays in Shakespearean criticism, devoted two hundred pages to discovering his virtues, which, to Morgann, far outweighed his numerous vices, as they did to Hazlitt as well. "Falstaff's wit," said Hazlitt in an appreciation that did much to shape the Victorians' conception of the fat rogue's character, "is an emanation of a fine constitution; an exuberance of good-humour and good-nature; an overflowing of his love of laughter and good-fellowship; a giving vent to his heart's ease, and over-contentment with himself and others."[2]

This is also the Falstaff who figures in painting. The artist's task was to overlook or at least mitigate the gluttony and coarseness and convey instead a clear and dominant impression of the character's wit: to translate Shakespeare's characterization into a kind of graphic humor acceptable to a middle-class audience with narrow and worrisome notions of personal morality and decorum. Falstaff could not be portrayed as an alcoholic, however jolly, or as a patron of whores, or as a serious threat to the stability of the kingdom through his domination of Prince Hal. Whatever lesser sins he was guilty of had to be defused by attributing to him an all-excusing geniality. There was the further difficulty that much of Falstaff's dramatic appeal lay in his verbal wit, which could not be transferred to canvas. Thus artists had somehow to depict an outsize but mute *farceur,* his sheer physical charm somehow obscuring his flirtation with sheer viciousness, a sufficiently respectable character to be admitted to the Victorian parlor. It was not a feat that every artist could manage, as reviewers repeatedly observed.

Falstaff starred in *Henry IV* paintings from the beginning. In 1728, Hogarth showed him reviewing his recruits; and about ten years later, Philip Mercier pictured him twice. One of the supper boxes at Vauxhall Gardens contained a painting by Hayman of the scene in which Hal confronts him with evidence of his late deplorable behavior at Gad's Hill. In 1746, Marcellus Laroon the younger painted Falstaff, tankard at the ready beside him, ridiculing Bardolph's incandescent nose (Part One, 3.3) (pl. 202).

No fewer than thirteen pictures from the two parts of the play were in the Boydell Gallery, including seven by Smirke. His version of the robbery at Gad's Hill was "much approved of," wrote Farington, the artist's friend, in his diary.[3] In another picture, Smirke showed the soon-to-be-robbed carriers in the Rochester Inn yard before daybreak, a crude attempt at Dutch chiaroscuro; but the subject proved not to be very popular, and only two or three subsequent treatments are recorded.

Instead, in the long run the favorite Falstaff subjects were of two kinds: the various uproarious moments at the Boar's Head Tavern in both Parts One and Two, and Falstaff's ragged regiment. Only one painting from the first tavern scene (Part One, 1.2) is recorded and that a relatively late one, William Quiller Orchardson's picture (RA 1868) of Falstaff's exit near the end of the scene. The next tavern scene (2.4) was represented a dozen times, least dramatically by Smirke in his Boydell version, a conventional group of drinkers with Falstaff in the foreground.* Three episodes were depicted. The earliest, Falstaff's fabulous narration of the late proceedings at Gad's Hill, was one of George Clint's three Shakespearean subjects at the Royal Academy in 1833 (pl. 104). It is a tableau worthy of a temperance hotel. Hal's and Poins's expressions, the slightest hint of incredulity on one face and an equally faint smile on the other, do not

*By an irony in the history of art migration, the original canvas ended up at Bob Jones University, South Carolina, where drink is anathema.

suggest that they are deeply involved in Falstaff's lusty performance, nor indeed that they care very much one way or another.

The next movement of the scene, "Falstaff's cowardice detected," was, as we saw above, portrayed by Hayman and possibly one or two others. The third movement, Falstaff's and Hal's *lèse majesté* as the old reprobate assumes the role of Hal's father, the king, in a mock parental interview, was the subject of half a dozen paintings, the best known of which was commissioned from Leslie (RA 1851). "Grimace, sensuality, and coarseness have too often made up the painter's embodiment of Falstaff," commented the *Athenaeum,* "but Mr. Leslie finds another reading" that consisted primarily of shifting the onus of disreputability from Falstaff to his companions: "The parties to the group here represented [Poins, Peto, Gadshill, and Bardolph] certainly justify the worldly castigation which the fat humourist inflicts on the Prince's associates. They are the scape-graces of the time."[4] The next tavern scene (3.3) accounted for some eight or ten paintings, most of which, illustrating Falstaff's vivid description of Bardolph's flaming nose, showed the fat knight and his companion together.

In Part Two, the chief Boar's Head scene is 2.4, presenting the swaggering silliness of Ancient Pistol and the earthy endearments of Doll Tearsheet. Half a dozen pictures illustrated one or the other. The latter was a delicate subject for nineteenth-century artists. Fuseli's version for Boydell had not evaded the plain Shakespearean sense of the moment; there was something unblushingly Rowlandsonian in his portrayal of Doll on Falstaff's lap. One wonders whether Haydon's lost painting of the same scene, exhibited at the Egyptian Hall in 1832, modified the pose somewhat in deference to the growing pre-Victorian fussiness about such matters. When Augustus Egg came to paint a moment in the scene (RA 1840), he merely had Dame Quickly place a sisterly arm around Falstaff's shoulder.

203. Edward Bird, *Falstaff* (dated 1807) (Bristol Museum and Art Gallery). The "amiable humorist" confronted by a swashbuckling Ancient Pistol (*2 Henry IV,* 2. 4). The artist was a drawing master at Bristol who first exhibited at the Royal Academy in 1809. After his election to the Academy, he served briefly as court painter to Queen Charlotte.

204. Francis Hayman, *Sir John Falstaff Raising Recruits* (Society of Artists 1761) (Birmingham City Museum and Art Gallery). The first exhibited painting of the subject; it may have been influenced by Hogarth's earlier one (ca. 1728). The 1761 show of the Society of Artists was only the second art exhibition ever held in London, and this picture brought Shakespearean farce thus early to walls which also contained, that year, scenes from *The Tempest, Every Man in His Humour,* and Gray's "The Bard."

The other favorite subject from *Henry IV* was Falstaff's ragged regiment, or rather his two regiments: the one he describes to the audience in Part One (4.2), a motley crowd of jail birds, vagrants, and cripples, and the reluctant warriors—Feeble, Bullcalf, Mouldy, and the rest—whom he recruits with the assistance of Justice Shallow in Part Two (3.2). (Paintings of which only the titles survive may have illustrated either of these two passages, although the likelihood is that most came from the latter.) In 1761 and 1765, Hayman produced two versions of the subjects, one now at Dublin and the other at Birmingham (pl. 204). From this early time onward, Falstaff's draft-board interview was a favorite with painters.

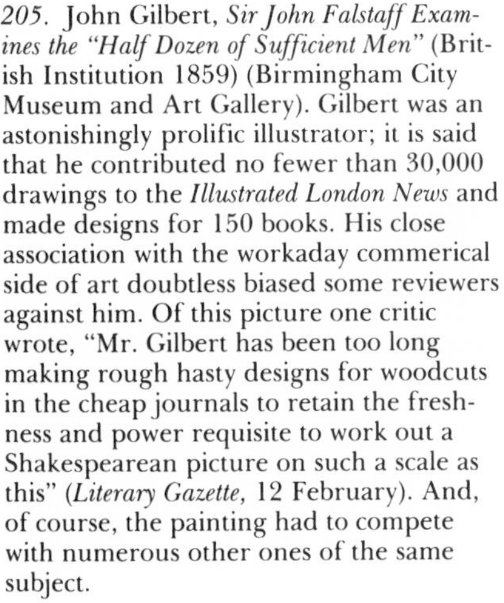

205. John Gilbert, *Sir John Falstaff Examines the "Half Dozen of Sufficient Men"* (British Institution 1859) (Birmingham City Museum and Art Gallery). Gilbert was an astonishingly prolific illustrator; it is said that he contributed no fewer than 30,000 drawings to the *Illustrated London News* and made designs for 150 books. His close association with the workaday commerical side of art doubtless biased some reviewers against him. Of this picture one critic wrote, "Mr. Gilbert has been too long making rough hasty designs for woodcuts in the cheap journals to retain the freshness and power requisite to work out a Shakespearean picture on such a scale as this" (*Literary Gazette,* 12 February). And, of course, the painting had to compete with numerous other ones of the same subject.

Thomas Durno's Boydell picture placed Falstaff in a throne-like chair, thus not only recalling the scene in Part One in which Falstaff, acting the King, used a tavern chair for his throne, but perhaps parodying history paintings that depicted real monarchs on their thrones. The version by John Gilbert (pl. 205) drew critics' fire for what they considered the repulsiveness of all the characters. One reviewer surmised that the artist had not given himself "time to glance over his text, much less to study the characters. Falstaff," he asserted, "is a mere vulgar reveller, with no humour lurking in his eye, no trace of intellect in his countenance; and Feeble, who is under examination, is almost in the last stage of senility, his bent knees shaking under him, quite unlike one who, if he would not fight, could 'run off swiftly' in a retreat."[5] The Shakespearean text was always there to confront the negligent painter.

The scene between Hotspur and his wife (Part One, 2.3), an agreeable mixture of domestic comedy and earnestness, was treated by some ten artists in quite contrasting moods. For Boydell, Smirke put Lady Percy in the conventional pose of kneeling supplication, while her dashingly mustachioed husband stood with sword resting against his foot. Painting the scene in 1836 for *Heath's Gallery,* A. E. Chalon chose instead to represent (mutely) the persiflage between the two. A picture at the Royal Academy in 1855 illustrated Lady Percy's description of Hotspur fighting battles in his sleep, as she tenderly watched over him. The artist added two details absent from Shakespeare: at the bedside also was the Percys' little boy, riding on the back of a deerhound, and his father wore armor underneath his yellow night robe.

Another scene depicting the most private moments of the protagonists is that in Part Two (4.5) in which Prince Hal tries on his father's crown for size in the presence of the sleeping King, who when he awakens accuses Hal of wishing to usurp the throne. Smirke painted it three times for Boydell, and Woodmason's rival Shakespeare Gallery had Wheatley's painting of the same moment. J. C. Horsley won a £200 prize at the Westminster Hall competition of 1846 for a huge portrayal of Hal's taking the crown.

When artists selected from *Henry IV* such conventional history-painting subjects as battlefield heroism and political deliberations or dissensions, once again they focused on the largely unhistorical, "literary" elements in the Shakespearean source. The rebellion of the dissident lords was seen in terms of the personal enmity between Hotspur and Glendower (Part One, 3.1); in 1784, Fuseli painted John Philip Kemble as Hotspur with the conspirators (pl. 206). Hotspur's feats at the battle of Holmedon, as described by Westmoreland early in Part One (1.1), went unrepresented; instead, painters chose the scene Hotspur describes in act 1, scene 3, his encounter with the pouncet-box lord picking his fastidious way among the corpses after the battle.

With but one or two exceptions, only Boydell's artists showed any interest in portraying the last scenes of the two parts. John Francis Rigaud contributed to the Shakespeare Gallery a picture of a slim if not effeminate Prince Hal, his armor-enclosed thighs suggesting an ingenue in a breeches part, standing over the downed Hotspur, with Falstaff on the ground, half hidden behind him. Smirke showed the false victor Falstaff *solus,* with the body of Hotspur on the ground instead (pl. 208). Only two pictures represented moments in the last scene of Part Two (5.5): Smirke's of a bareheaded Falstaff clutching the top of his belly in an

206. Henry Fuseli, *John Philip Kemble as Hotspur with Glendower* (1784) (Birmingham City Museum and Art Gallery). The conspiracy scene (*1 Henry IV,* 3. 1), a Shakespearean instance of a subject—the devious ways of statecraft—often depicted in history painting. Reputedly, Kemble modeled for both Hotspur and Glendower.

207. S. J. E. Jones, *Hotspur and the Fop* (British Institution 1829) (Royal Shakespeare Theatre Picture Gallery ©). The encounter Hotspur describes in *1 Henry IV,* 1. 3. The painting is a typical example of the pot-boiling literary picture. The artist exhibited fairly often at all three of the annual shows.

apparent gesture of fealty as the new king sweeps by on his way into Westminster Abbey—an obvious but foredoomed attempt to fit a familiar comic character into a conventional high-art triumphal scene—and a painting, shown at the Royal Academy in 1839, of Falstaff's being shoved aside by the outraged Lord Chief Justice.

208. Robert Smirke, *Falstaff and the Dead Body of Hotspur* (undated) (Royal Shakespeare Theatre Picture Gallery ©). Among the seven pictures from the two parts of *Henry IV* that Smirke painted for Boydell was one representing this scene (Part One, 5. 4). This painting, however, is a quite different composition. Like the Shakespearean scene it illustrates, it is a travesty of the heroic mode—an invincible warrior triumphant over the body of his adversary.

HENRY V

It was from the life of Henry V (though not from Shakespeare's dramatization) that the first known paintings from English history were taken: William Kent's three pictures of Henry at Agincourt, meeting the King of France, and marrying the French princess, commissioned by Queen Caroline in 1729–30. *Henry V* likewise was the first of Shakespeare's history plays to engage an artist; Hayman painted *Montjoy . . . Demands of Henry Whether He Will Compound for His Ransom* (4.3) for the Prince's Pavilion at Vauxhall shortly before 1745. In 1776, Andrew van Rymsdyk showed at the Society of Artists the Duke of York dying at Agincourt, supported by the Earl of Exeter.

Only two Boydell pictures were from *Henry V,* one, by Westall, showing the King at the gates of Harfleur (3.3), the other, by Fuseli, of the King telling the conspirators what was afoot (pl. 209). In 1790, at the Royal Academy, a minor artist named Benazech portrayed a minor actor named Whitfield in what must be one of the most negligible roles ever featured in theatrical painting, the common soldier Michael Williams.

The play's fortunes and, as a consequence, artists' interest in it, revived somewhat in the early nineteenth century. Macready first performed it in 1815, and gave it the full spectacular treatment, complete with a moving diorama, in 1839. Charles Kean's production in 1859, the most lavish of all, ran for eighty-four nights. Fresh paintings, accounting for most of the recorded total of twenty or so, accompanied or recalled these revivals. The heroic pictures usually depicted Henry V visiting the bivouac before Agincourt; Sir John Gilbert painted the scene as late as 1884. The comic scenes, slightly more numerous, favored the quarrel between Pistol, Nym, Bardolph, and Dame Quickly (2.1). In 1839, the Scottish painter Alexander Christie sought to have the best of both worlds, comic genre and history, when he painted Nym on the field of Agincourt. But the *Henry V* painting that one would most wish to see was a canvas that never existed except in the errant fingers (and lubricious mind?) of a typesetter engaged on a volume of Algernon Graves's record of art sales (1918–21). According to this source, a painting by Gilbert that was sold in 1877 was entitled *Pistol and Nymph:* in its bizarre way, an attractive conceit.

HENRY VIII

Of the history plays, only the two parts of *Henry IV* exceeded *Henry VIII* in the number of pictures they inspired. Although Fuseli's *Queen Katherine's Vision* (RA 1781) was virtually the only pictorial treatment before the seven commissioned by Boydell, in the ensuing century some fifty paintings were taken from the play. In marked contrast to *Henry VI,* we have here an illustration of the way in which the theatrical popularity of the play fed interest in it as a subject for art. In the wake of Betterton's productions at the beginning of the century, it had often been revived, chiefly on account of its grand ceremonial scenes; the coronation procession as performed at Drury Lane in 1762 required 140 extras. J. P. Kemble's production (1788) initiated his family's long identification with the play, Kemble himself playing first Cromwell and later Wolsey, with Mrs. Siddons as Katherine, one of her greatest roles.

Henry VIII boasted no Falstaff nor indeed much comedy of any sort, and it had no romantic love theme; but its dramatic situations and its pageantry combined to recommend it to theatergoers and art lovers alike

209. Henry Fuseli, *Henry V Discovering the Conspirators* (Boydell's Shakespeare Gallery) (Royal Shakespeare Theatre Picture Gallery ©). A few years after Fuseli painted the conspiracy scene in *1 Henry IV* (pl. 206), he took up the next one in the Shakespearean history sequence (*Henry V,* 2. 2), in which the king confronts his adversaries and arrests their three leaders on a charge of high treason.

across the whole of the nineteenth century. It was among the favorite plays of two quintessential Victorian narrative painters, C. R. Leslie and Sir John Gilbert. Leslie's interest in the fortunes of the unhappy queen dated from student days at the Academy schools. As a token of his election to the academy at the age of thirty-two, he portrayed the opening moment of act 3, scene 1, when Queen Katherine bids her waiting woman "Take thy lute, wench, my soul grows sad with troubles. . . ." In all, Leslie painted half a dozen pictures of Katherine. At the height of his fame, he painted two subjects from *Henry VIII* for Brunel's Shakespeare room. The first (1849) showed the moment when Henry reveals himself to Wolsey at the masque in York Place (1.4), and the other, exhibited at the Royal Academy the following year, the scene (4.2) in which Katherine receives Capuchius, by whom she sends her farewell to the king.

To a degree unmatched in art from the other history plays with the possible exception of *Henry IV,* painters' interest in *Henry VIII* was concentrated in two or three scenes, to various moments of which they returned time after time. The earliest of these was act 3, scene 1, which after the waiting woman's song in the first minutes develops into the passage in which the queen is brought to judgment by Cardinals Wolsey and Campeius. In all the major productions of the play, from John Philip Kemble's to those of Henry Irving and Beerbohm Tree, this was one of the great scenes. Half a dozen portrayals of it in art were to be seen in the course of the nineteenth century, of which at least three survive: George Henry Harlow's (pl. 154), Henry Andrews's (pl. 155), and Henry Nelson O'Neil's (pl. 108).

Equally popular with artists was act 4, scene 2, the scene containing both Griffith's description of the death of Wolsey and the dying Queen Katherine's dream of the troop of angels awaiting her in heaven. Wolsey's death was repeatedly pictured, by Westall for the Boydell Gallery among others. Prince Albert commissioned the same subject from Charles Cope, and near the end of his career, Gilbert included it among his several paintings from the history plays.

The queen's vision was another of the play's great moments in performance.[1] Kean's production, which ran for a record-breaking one hundred consecutive nights in 1855, was acclaimed for the long "panoramic procession" in the fifth act, which showed the journey of the lord mayor and aldermen from the City to Greenwich Palace for the christening of Elizabeth, and the "correctness and splendour" of its tableaux. The words of praise are those of the reigning Queen, who saw it on 5 June; she was especially impressed by "Queen Katherine's dream, with the angels descending on a sunbeam, waving palm branches and holding out to her a crown of the same."[2]* It is conceivable that the established fame of the scene in easel painting inspired Kean and his predecessors to these heights of pictorial splendor. Fuseli had painted at least two versions, for the Royal Academy exhibition of 1781 and Macklin's Poet's Gallery; Henry Howard had exhibited his in 1832, and Henry O'Neil still others in 1848 and 1853. It was only to be expected that artists would, in turn, immediately exploit the fame of Kean's staging. Two paintings of the scene were hung at the British Institution the next year, and another at the Royal Academy in 1857.

One other theme in the play was repeatedly chosen: the quarrel between Wolsey and Buckingham (1.2) and Wolsey's disgrace when his

*Lewis Carroll left a rapturous description of the scene, too long to quote here. It began: "But oh, that exquisite vision of Queen Catherine! I almost held my breath to watch; the illusion is perfect, and I felt as if in a dream all the time it lasted. It was like a delicious reverie, or the most beautiful poetry" (*Diaries of Lewis Carroll,* ed. R. L. Green [New York, 1954], 1:54).

210. Sir John Gilbert, *Ego et Rex Meus* (RA 1889) (Guildhall Art Gallery, London). Still another scene related to a conspiracy (*Henry VIII,* 1. 2). The King, in the toils of the duplicitous Wolsey, thanks him for warning him of Buckingham's supposed plot against him.

duplicity is revealed (3.2). Solomon Hart, for example, painted the earlier moment (RA 1834); and John Pettie was among the half-dozen, once again beginning with Westall, who painted Wolsey's disgrace (RA 1869). The Wolsey-Buckingham plot, however, was the special province of Gilbert, whose successive representations of it were landmarks in his long career. He painted Wolsey's disgrace in 1845 and again—unless it was the same picture reexhibited—in 1849. His version of Wolsey's entrance in act 1, scene 1, was exhibited in 1862 (pl. 39). But Gilbert painted his most celebrated picture from *Henry VIII*—this from the opening of act 1, scene 2—at the end of his long career as an illustrator: *Cardinal Wolsey Going in Procession to Westminster Hall* (pl. 210), better known as *Ego et Rex Meus.*

THE TRAGEDIES

TITUS ANDRONICUS

No Shakespearean play, with the exception of *Pericles,* was portrayed less often in art. There were three pictures from it in the Boydell Gallery, one by Samuel Woodforde (pl. 27) and two by Thomas Kirk. Two others were exhibited in 1792 and 1795. Opie painted Miss Talbot in the role of Lavinia (RA 1802). Though the character of Lavinia had a certain sentimental appeal, her namesake, in Thomson's *Seasons,* had a greater one, and no artist after Opie seems to have found anything worth painting in Shakespeare's bloody drama.

ROMEO AND JULIET

It has been said that in the Bodleian Library's copy of the Shakespeare first folio, the pages that bear the most conspicuous evidence of having been read by many generations of Oxford undergraduates in the seventeenth and eighteenth centuries are those occupied by *Romeo and Juliet.* In the printed text could be read the poetry that could not be heard on the stage, for in the general surrender of Shakespeare to "improvers" during the Restoration, *Romeo and Juliet* was shelved in favor of an execrable mishmash by Thomas Otway entitled *The History and Fall of Caius Marius,* in which the names of all the characters were changed and the setting moved from Renaissance Verona to republican Rome. Half a century passed before Shakespeare's voice was heard again, however faintly, in Theophilus Cibber's slightly less offensive adaptation (1744) and Garrick's own rewrite (1748). John Philip Kemble's production restored some of Shakespeare's text, but it was not until 1845–46 that the play was performed intact, by the American sisters Charlotte and Susan Cushman.

Although the total was eventually to reach two hundred, there were only a few *Romeo and Juliet* paintings before the five that Boydell commissioned. In the next forty years, however, an average of one picture per year was seen on the exhibition walls. Several of these were portraits of well-known actresses, Mrs. Wallis, Mary Ann Pope, Sarah Booth, and Eliza O'Neill, as Juliet. But it was only after Fanny Kemble's debut in the role in her father's production of 1829 that the play was firmly established in the repertory of popular art.

Juliet, of course, was the star in the large majority of the pictures taken from the play. The familiar successive lines from Romeo's speech in the balcony scene (2.2), "See how she leans her cheek upon her hand" and "O that I were a glove upon that hand," were among the most banal quotations attached to sentimental Victorian portraits. Juliets with cheek on hand, gazing dreamily into the middle distance, were as common in art exhibitions as were pining Ophelias either by streams or on dry land. And no other heroine in literary art was more critically examined to be sure the painter's portrayal was faithful to the poet's intention—or, what amounted to much the same thing, to the spectator's idea of what she should look like. Whenever a scene from the play was exhibited, reviewers looked first and most searchingly at Juliet, even before they evaluated the moonlight effect in the balcony scene. Failures were ruthlessly denounced. Fuseli's *Romeo Contemplating Juliet in the Monument* (RA 1809), a subject not especially congenial to a temperament like Fuseli's, evoked this criticism from Robert Hunt in the *Examiner:*

> In Juliet . . . though the crimson ensign of health appears in her lips and cheeks, is not "beauty's ensign." Her form has nothing of those bewitching charms which enamoured the heart of Romeo in spite of the old and rooted hatred of his family against her house. Her nose in size is like that of which Solomon so inscrutibly speaks, when, describing a beauty, he compares her nose to "the tower of Lebanon;" and her feet are actively pointed like an opera dancer presenting for a step when they should hang in the lassitude of a lethargy. . . .[1]

Was she, or was she not, Shakespeare's Juliet? The question recurred every time a new portrait was hung. Of Henry Thomson's figure of *Juliet in the Capulet Garden* (pl. 147) the *London Magazine,* quoting at length from the play to substantiate her authenticity, declared that she was "of most fascinating youthful beauty; innocent; and with large blue eyes. In short it is *the* Juliet of Shakspear."[2] But of another artist's conception eight years later, the *Examiner* said, "Mr. Hardwicke's Juliet is not Shakspeare's Juliet. . . . She is a modern fine lady, such as is too often encountered in English society,—cold and artificial in her look and air, uninventive and common-place in her dress,—a thing of etiquette and imitation,—straight-laced both in soul and body."[3] A similar complaint was lodged against Frith's *Juliet* of 1863: "If this be Shakespeare's Juliet, as the Catalogue says, the artist has more completely failed in rendering her character than in executing a not uncommon theme. Surely Juliet was not this ringletted girl, fresh from a boarding-school, clad in white satin, and posed at a window. Mr. Frith, no doubt, meant to style his picture 'Study after the Opera.'"[4]

In the seven or eight years following Fanny Kemble's debut in 1829, no fewer than eight pictures of Juliet with her nurse were exhibited; the veteran specialist in old women's roles, Mary Ann Davenport, had been a great hit as the nurse in the Kemble production. The most celebrated product of this little boom was the one in which the characters are almost undiscoverable: Turner's 1836 masterpiece, *Juliet and Her Nurse.* It was the Reverend John Eagles's attack on it in *Blackwood's Magazine* that stirred John Ruskin, aged seventeen, to Turner's defense. "It is neither sunlight, moonlight, nor starlight, nor fire-light," wrote Eagles, "though there is an attempt at a display of fireworks in one corner. . . . The scene is a composition as from models of different parts of Venice, thrown higgledy-piggledy together, streaked blue and pink, and thrown into a flour tub. Poor Juliet has been steeped in treacle to make her look sweet."[5] The chorus of journalistic billingsgate was almost deafening. "Shakespeare's Juliet?" The *Times* raised the perennial question, and answered it: "Why, it is the tawdry Miss Porringer, the brazier's daughter of Lambeth marsh, and the nurse is the twaddling old body Mrs. Mac'sneeze, who keeps the snuff-shop at the corner of Oakley-St."[6]

211. Henry Perronet Briggs, *Juliet and the Nurse* (RA 1827) (Tate Gallery, London). This painting, engraved for the 1834 *Keepsake* and in 1836 for *Heath's Gallery* and given to the National Gallery by Robert Vernon in 1847, exploited the lighter side of Shakespeare's tragedy. It was one of the *Romeo and Juliet* pictures exhibited and engraved at the time that acquired additional interest after Fanny Kemble's sensational debut as Juliet in 1829.

Concentrating as they did upon the star-cross'd lovers, the painters had little interest in the Mercutio-Tybalt plot. The *bal masqué* scene (1.5) in which Romeo and Juliet fall instantly in love and exchange their sentiments in the form of a sonnet was depicted by an obscure journeyman named William Miller, who chose for the background of his Boydell commission a stately salon where sylphs dance in the presence of other mythological figures—a decorative touch that owed more to the clichés of classical painting and early French and Italian opera than to Shakespeare. Only half a dozen later pictures portrayed the scene.

The balcony scene with Romeo in the garden and Juliet above, seems not to have been painted before 1803—it was not included in the Boydell Gallery—but once added to the repertory, it remained a stock subject throughout most of the century. Some twenty paintings are recorded, but many if not most of those that have survived are portraits of a dreaming Juliet rather than complete tableaux.

The later lyric scene in which the lovers part after their night together (3.5) was portrayed as often as the balcony scene. The subject served on occasion to contain or express the quality called "passion" in the vocabulary of the aesthetic movement. "You must expect a scene of passion," wrote Ford Madox Brown to the buyer of his picture in 1870 (as forewarning or advance recommendation?).[7] When Henry James saw the painting at the Brown retrospective in 1897, he seems to have remembered the artist's comment, quoted the preceding year in his grandson's biography, for he looked for passion and found it—in the pose of Romeo: "The motion as of a rope-dancer balancing, the outstretched, level, stiff-fingered hand of the young man who, calling time, tearing himself away in the dovelike summer dawn, buries his face in his mistress's neck and throws his ill-shaped leg over her balcony—this little gesture of reason and passion is the very making of the picture."[8] Meanwhile, the absence of the same quality was reason enough for dismissing a picture. When Frank Dicksee painted the same scene in 1884, the *Times* asserted, "Mr. Madox Brown succeeded where the young Academician [Dicksee] has not succeeded—he filled his picture with passion. Here lies the weakness of Mr. Dicksee's work: it is graceful, it is natural enough as a picture of the parting of the two young lovers; but it is not passionate—it is not Shakespeare."[9] It may not have been Shakespeare, but the embrace into which Dicksee or, some years earlier, Alfred Elmore (pl. 212) painted the lovers was the most passionate represented in any known scene from *Romeo and Juliet*.

212. Alfred W. Elmore, *Romeo and Juliet* (undated) (Walker Art Gallery, Liverpool). If warmth of embrace is any indication, this picture probably was painted no earlier than the 1870s (Elmore died in 1881). The artist availed himself of the growing freedom to depart from the letter of the literary text: the star-crossed lovers never met in a sylvan setting.

In the 1840s, artists were for some reason as devoted to the scene in which Friar Laurence gives Juliet the potion (4.1) as they had been in the immediately preceding years to Juliet and the nurse; between 1840 and 1853, at least ten examples are recorded. None of these paintings left any special mark, though the subject remained current. E. M. Ward's version was prominent in the Royal Academy show of 1867, and as late as 1896, W. P. Frith was represented by the same scene.

The later counterpart of the scene in Friar Laurence's cell, Romeo's visit to the apothecary in Mantua (5.1), was pictured less often. In 1797 the fledgling artist John Constable wrote a friend, "I have lately . . . painted two small pictures in oil, viz: a Chymist and an Alcymist; for which I am chiefly indebted to our immortal Bard. You remember Romeo's ludicrous account of an Apothecary's shop."[10] Whether or not they actually confused the two trades, artists felt at liberty to mingle them, thus merging Shakespeare and Dutch genre art. When Henry Stacy Marks exhibited a similar painting in 1876, the novelist Margaret Oliphant, writing in *Blackwood's Magazine,* called attention to the ambiguous nature of the old man's brew:

> The curious old chamber is full of curious things, drawn in their integrity from Shakespeare's list, but enriched by additions, and forming a fit background for the quaint figure in gown and skullcap, busy about some brewage. But it is

> much more probable that he is mixing the ingredients of which gold is to be made, than the potion which his poverty but not his will impelled the old starveling to sell. We have no objections; indeed we prefer, for our own part, the original creation of Mr. Marks's fancy, even to a carefully costumed shadow from Shakespeare—and do not think a bit the worse of him because, though he calls his picture the "Apothecary" and quotes from "Romeo and Juliet," he suggests the rosy cross and the philosopher's stone rather than the sleeping draught which wrought so much woe.[11]

Several paintings of the concluding tomb scene (5.3), especially early ones, represented a moment that one seeks in vain in Shakespeare's text. In his mutilation of the play, Otway rearranged the order of events so that Romeo (Marius), having swallowed the poison, managed to survive long enough to behold Juliet (Lavinia) awakening from her drugged sleep. In his production, Garrick compounded the offense by rewriting the dialogue in the form of what might be called a Drury Lane Liebestod, ending:

Romeo. . . . I thought thee dead: distracted at the sight,
(Fatal speed) drank poison, kiss'd thy cold lips,
And found within thy arms a precious grave—
But in that moment—Oh—
Juliet. And did I wake for this!
Romeo. My powers are blasted,
'Twixt death and love I am torn—I am distracted!
But death's strongest—and must I leave thee, *Juliet!*
Oh cruel, cursed fate: in sight of heav'n!
Juliet. Thou rav'st—lean on my breast—
Romeo. Fathers have flinty hearts, no tears can melt 'em.
Nature pleads in vain—Children must be wretched.
Juliet. Oh my breaking heart—
Romeo. She is my wife—our hearts are twin'd together,
Capulet forbear—*Paris,* loose your hold—
Pull not our heart strings thus—they crack—
they break—Oh *Juliet, Juliet!* [*Dies.*][12]

This was the uncanonical moment pictured in Benjamin Wilson's canvas (1753), the tomb, seen from the outside, flooded with a theatrical light, Mrs. Bellamy as Juliet sitting bolt upright and Garrick as Romeo assuming a histrionic posture and quoting his own lines. There were about a dozen subsequent pictures of the tomb scene. In Northcote's Boydell version, Juliet is in the center of a circular area of illumination that suggests a spotlight. Paris is dead, and Romeo, his assassin, almost so; at the foot of the stairs is an appalled Friar Laurence, torch held aloft. For some reason, Northcote's picture representing the scene was selected rather than that of Joseph Wright of Derby, which Boydell had also commissioned. Wright's canvas was shown instead at the Royal Academy in 1790, where it and a companion piece, a scene from *The Winter's Tale,* were, as he said, "placed in unfortunate situations." After the exhibition, he altered them and showed them at the Society of Artists the next year.

Taken all together and viewed historically, the extant pictures of *Romeo and Juliet* could document the history of decorous erotic sensibility with representations stretching from the rococo conceits of the late eighteenth century to the quasi-realism of the last Victorian years. In the course of time, the lovers were sentimentalized fulfilments of a Romantic ideal, even as they were probably vulgarized beyond recognition in amateur performances such as Robert Fox portrayed in a painting of 1862. As Robert Hunt said, in commenting on Haydon's 1811 picture of the parting scene, "The lively interest which the impassioned pen of Shakspeare

213. John Everett Millais, *Last Scene of "Romeo and Juliet"* (1850) (City Art Gallery, Manchester). A sketch made from a pen drawing dated 1848. This was one of the last pictures to be taken from the tomb scene; Leighton's elaborate *The Reconciliation of the Montagues and Capulets over the Dead Bodies of Romeo and Juliet,* now at Agnes Scott College, Georgia, was painted 1853–55.

has conferred on his description of these lovers, and the personal beauty with which he has invested them, have annexed to the mere pronunciation of their names, the idea of every grace which impresses the tender passion on the youthful heart."[13]

214. William Hilton, *Mark Antony Reading Caesar's Will* (1834) (Sir John Soane's Museum, London). Commissioned by Sir John Soane for the combination residence and museum he intended as his memorial, this painting mirrors Soane's conservative taste, formed during the declining years of neoclassic architecture and art. The kind of interest its subject represents survived, though only tenuously, into the late Victorian era, when the school of Alma-Tadema and Poynter (pl. 167) lent it a new but terminal lease on life.

JULIUS CAESAR

Two paintings from *Julius Caesar* by prominent artists in the grand style, Benjamin West's *Mark Antony Showing the Robe and the Will of Julius Caesar to the People of Rome* and Nathaniel Dance's *The Death of Mark Antony,* were shown in successive years at the Royal Academy (1775, 1776). These appearances, however, were evidence of the suitability of the Roman story to neoclassic art rather than of the play's popularity on the contemporary stage. Like Shakespeare's other Roman and Greek tragedies, it was regarded primarily as a reading, rather than a stageable, drama, though it was occasionally performed in the Garrick's time and later by J. P. Kemble and Macready.

Three paintings from *Julius Caesar,* all by Westall, were hung in Boydell's Gallery. Unlike its kindred plays, as a subject of paintings it survived the fading of the neoclassic impulse; of the dozen recorded examples, the majority were produced at intervals between 1834 and 1895. In the former year, William Hilton painted *Mark Antony Reading Caesar's Will* (pl. 214) for Sir John Soane. Half a century later (1883), Edward Poynter exhibited at the Royal Academy *The Ides of March* (pl. 167), an epitome of the late Victorian academic style. No better contrast could be found between the old classicism and the new.

HAMLET

Although *Hamlet* was the source of two early literary paintings, Francis Hayman's play scene for Vauxhall Gardens and a closet scene by the same artist, it was less often drawn upon in the eighteenth century than a number of other Shakespearean plays. It came into its own as a steady source of literary art only about the beginning of the nineteenth century, after which there were few seasons in which at least one painting from the drama was not exhibited; and in the period 1850–70, no single year passed without one or more. A principal reason for *Hamlet*'s popularity—the total of recorded pictures exceeds 150—was the long line of actors who had distinguished themselves in the title role and therefore had been painted in it, from Garrick, whom Benjamin Wilson portrayed on the battlements of Elsinore in one of the first illustrations of the play to have an exterior setting, to Henry Irving, whom Whistler painted more than a century later.

It might be said that in paintings of Hamlet himself, the character was subordinated to the actor. Contrariwise, although many celebrated Ophelias were painted, beginning with the three who played opposite Garrick (Kitty Clive, Susanna Cibber, and Maria Macklin) and ending with the last great Victorian Ophelia, Ellen Terry,* it was the character rather than the actress in whom interest centered. Whether posed by actresses or by other models, pictures of Ophelia constituted the most popular single subject of English literary painting; more than fifty are recorded, most of which were mediocre portraits or figure paintings of a supposedly beautiful young woman either in varying degrees of distress or placidly floating in a brook.[1]

Ophelia was not represented in early book illustrations of *Hamlet,* for the sufficient reason that orthodox critical opinion was against her: it deplored, on different grounds, both her madness and her death. Here, critics like Dr. Johnson maintained, Shakespeare violated the canon of decorum and the ideal of poetic justice. But beginning in the 1770s, with Fuseli's ink-and-brush drawings, the "romantic" Ophelia emerged, a figure cherished for the sheer pathos of her circumstances and destiny. In Benjamin West's contribution to the Boydell Gallery, which Robert Fulton bought in 1805 and subsequently exhibited in Philadelphia, she was (to borrow Robert Hunt's description in the *Examiner*), "robed in white; her flaxen locks hang in loose disorder over her forehead and down to her waist; with her left hand extended she carelessly strews around the rue and thyme; her eyes exhibit a wandering mind and delicious indecisiveness, yet she is gentle; rage makes no part of her character; the most beautiful and interesting of her sex. . . "[2] The description could have served for almost any of the Ophelias to be painted in the next hundred years; as it suggests, the element of overt madness was nearly always played down, artists prudently limiting her mental disturbance to a mild melancholia. Westall's picture for Boydell portrayed her at a later moment, surrounded by the luxuriant foliage that would become a standard setting for paintings of Ophelia by, or in, the fatal stream. Romney's *The Death of Ophelia* (1793), described in the catalogue of his executor's sale as showing her "leaning over Water, supported upon the Branch of a Tree; Ruined Buildings and Romantic Scenery in the Back Ground,"[3] is unfortunately lost.

Encouraged by such paintings as these, together with engraved representations in fresh editions of Shakespeare, Ophelias proliferated, to the point where any girl holding some wildflowers and having some sort of "meaningful" expression on her face was labeled Ophelia. Shakespeare offered several distinct dramatic moments to be painted. Several artists depicted the offstage encounter described by Ophelia (2.1) in which Hamlet took her by the wrist and gave a most convincing impersonation of a madman—"the very ecstasy of love," according to Polonius's instant diagnosis. The later onstage meeting (3.1), in which Ophelia gives back

*G. F. Watts's well-known picture of Ellen Terry as Ophelia was a belated example of an "impersonation" portrait, or fancy picture, rather than a theatrical portrait, because it was painted about 1863, some fifteen years before she undertook the role. He reworked it later on, presumably from a photograph.

Hamlet's presents as Polonius and the King spy on them, was one of the several Shakespearean scenes pictured by William Quiller Orchardson (RA 1865). But most Ophelia paintings came from later scenes: act 4, scene 5—the "distracted" Ophelia's performance before the king and queen, complete with snatches of pathetic-bawdy ballads, and subsequently before Laertes as well—and act 4, scene 7, in which Ophelia's death by drowning is described by the queen (not represented onstage). Because most of the pictures are lost and no descriptions survive, one cannot be sure which of the available choices was most favored by artists; some pictures titled simply *Ophelia* were so generalized that they could not be attributed to a single moment.

In the first half of the nineteenth century, at least fifteen renderings of Ophelia were exhibited, the majority by forgotten hacks but a few by well-known painters—Martin Archer Shee, the future president of the Royal Academy (a full-length picture of Mrs. Pope in the role, before 1804), William Hilton, Richard Redgrave (pl. 78), and Charles Allston Collins (RA 1848). These were all preliminary to the furor over the rival Ophelias at the Royal Academy in 1852, an early test of strength between the newly arrived Pre-Raphaelites and their critics. Evidently unaware of the coincidence until they saw each other's painting on varnishing day, both Arthur Hughes and Millais had seized on the same subject, though their compositions were quite different.

Hughes's picture (pl. 215) was skied, but Millais, whom he had not met until that day, climbed a ladder to look at it and mixed praise with tactful criticism. According to Hughes much later in life, he "said . . . that it gave him more pleasure than any picture there, but adding also very truly that I had not painted the right kind of stream. . . . He could not have

215. Arthur Hughes, *Ophelia* (RA 1852) (City Art Gallery, Manchester). This version of Ophelia has obvious resemblances to the one Richard Redgrave exhibited ten years earlier (pl. 78).

216. John Everett Millais, *Ophelia* (RA 1852) (Tate Gallery, London). The most celebrated of all the Ophelia pictures, and one of the half-dozen best-known products of the Pre-Raphaelite Brotherhood. It was this pose, rather than Redgrave's or Hughes's, that finally determined the received image of Ophelia in art. The model was Elizabeth Siddal.

done a kinder thing, for he knew I should be disappointed at the place my picture had."[4] Millais could have done with a few kind words himself, because, apart from William Michael Rossetti, few critics had anything good to say about his canvas (pl. 216). "The expression aimed at," said the *Athenaeum,* "is, that of an incapability of estimating 'her own distress'. The open mouth is somewhat gaping and gabyish,—the expression is in no way suggestive of her past tale. There is no pathos, no melancholy, no brightening up, no last lucid interval. If she die swan-like with a song, there is no sound or melody, no poetry in this strain."[5] "Certainly the least attractive and least practicable subject in the entire play," declared the *Art Journal,* in the face of fifty years' attempts to demonstrate the contrary.[6] But the worst drubbing was administered by the *Times,* whose anti-Pre-Raphaelite stance was, by this time, firmly established. "She makes us think of a dairymaid in a frolic," it said. "Mr. Millais has attempted to render the very act of drowning as if it were some freak of rude health instead of the climax of distraction."[7] Hughes's picture attracted much less attention. The third *Ophelia* of the year, that painted by the conventional Henry Nelson O'Neil, which showed the distracted girl kneeling before Laertes, was not in direct competition with the other two by virtue of its different subject.

To the end of the Victorian period, Ophelia pictures issued from the studios in a relentless stream, typified by Orchardson's and Waterhouse's

217. Henrietta Rae, *Ophelia* (RA 1890) (Walker Art Gallery, Liverpool). Unlike most paintings entitled *Ophelia,* this one depicts her in a clear dramatic context, the scene in which she reveals her madness before Gertrude and Claudius (4. 5). It underscores the fact that each generation had its own ideal of feminine beauty, which it automatically applied to the heroines of literature. This Ophelia is no Keepsake beauty but distinctively a young woman of the nineties, as comparison of her face with those in photographs of the time, not least portraits of actresses, makes plain.

218. George Clint, *Charles Young as Hamlet, Mrs. Glover as Ophelia: "I never gave you aught"* (RA 1831) (Victoria & Albert Museum, Crown Copyright). The scene (3. 1) in which Ophelia tries to return the tokens of love Hamlet has given her. Young was a well-known Hamlet of the time, and the year after this painting was exhibited, he was to choose that role for his farewell appearance. In 1831 he was fifty-four years old and Julia Glover only two years younger. It is possible that Clint knocked a few years off the apparent ages of both players in order to bring them closer to the Hamlet and Ophelia found in Shakespeare's text.

productions of 1874 and 1889 respectively. As a prime example of Victorian sentimental painting, the standard Ophelia study took a middle road, offending no one, straining no one's credulity, and making no great demands upon the artist's inventive imagination. The only conspicuous novelty that was introduced, for one appearance only, into what had become a thoroughly conventionalized treatment was seen at the International Exhibition of 1862, though it may have been painted much earlier: Joseph Severn's picture of an unmistakably sane and healthy young woman leaning against the mossy bank, on which she has spelled out Hamlet's name in flowers, as a municipal gardener would arrange a multicolored flower bed in a park or on a seaside esplanade.

No other passage in *Hamlet* came close to rivaling the Ophelia scenes in popularity. The closet scene was painted with fair regularity—some fifteen treatments are recorded, beginning with Hayman's picture of Spranger Barry as Hamlet and Mrs. Elmy as Gertrude (ca. 1751–54). No doubt some of the subject's appeal lay in its suggestion of Gothic horror, the appearance of the dead King's ghost. Fuseli painted it for Woodmason's New Shakespeare Gallery, and Richard Dadd, whose own mental tendency was in the same general direction though without much Fuselian frightfulness, exhibited his version (pl. 157) at the British Institution in 1840. Treatments of the play scene were fewer. The earliest, Hayman's for a Vauxhall supper box, was remarkable for its omission of Hamlet himself, the spectator's attention being directed, like that of the watchers in the picture, to Claudius's reaction as the "mousetrap" is sprung. Maclise's version, which dominated the Royal Academy show in 1842 (pl. 219) and was widely circulated in the form of an Art Union print, was among the most excitedly discussed of all Shakespearean paintings. "One of the most startling, wonderful pictures that the English school has ever produced" was Thackeray's accolade in *Ainsworth's Magazine.*[8] The *Athenaeum* concluded its full-column notice by asserting, supposedly without ambiguous intent, that "the whole Boydell gallery would hardly furnish so large an evidence of genius as this one picture."[9] But the most magisterial judgment of all was that pronounced by Ruskin. "Nothing, perhaps," he announced, "can more completely demonstrate the total ignorance of the public of all that is great or valuable in Shakspeare than their universal admiration of Maclise's *Hamlet*."[10] In a footnote deleted after the second edition of *Modern Painters,* Ruskin added:

> We have very great respect for Mr. Maclise's power as a draughtsman, and if we thought that his errors proceeded from weakness, we should not allude to them, but we most devoutly wish that he would let Shakespeare alone. If the Irish ruffian who appeared in "Hamlet" last year had been gifted with a stout shillelagh, and if his state of prostration had been rationally accounted for by distinct evidence of a recent "compliment" on the crown; or if the maudlin expression of the young lady christened "Ophelia" had been properly explained by an empty gin-bottle on her lap, we should have thanked him for his powerful delineation both of character and circumstance. But we cannot permit him thus to mislead the English public (unhappily too easily led by any grinning and glittering fantasy), in all their conceptions of the intention of Shakespeare.[11]

Ruskin, like everyone else who wrote about Shakespeare, had firm convictions about the poet's intention. They were probably no more valid than the others', and there is no reason to believe that his rebuke of Maclise and of the ignorant public had the slightest effect on either party.

If Keeley Halswelle, addressing himself to the same scene (pl. 220), hoped to escape the severe judgment that had been visited upon Maclise, he was disappointed, at least so far as the *Times* was concerned:

> The artist has not been well advised in choosing a subject so hackneyed, both on canvas and on the boards, as the scene in which Hamlet catches the conscience of the King. But if that scene is to be painted once more, can it be tolerated as the mere *motif* of a design like this, crowded with little figures? We desiderate

219. Daniel Maclise, *The Play Scene in "Hamlet"* (RA 1842) (Tate Gallery, London). This was the big attraction in the 1842 exhibition. Widely known through engravings, it served as a model for new stagings of the scene.

220. Keeley Halswelle, *The Play Scene in "Hamlet"* (RA 1878) (Forbes Magazine Collection). A fairly late example of a familiar subject. "The artist," said the *Times* (31 May) "has not been well advised in choosing a subject so hackneyed, both on canvas and on the boards." But the picture is, at the very least, valuable evidence of contemporary staging. *Punch*'s comment (15 June) is not far below the usual level of facetious Victorian art criticism: "Laboured: all work and no play. But 'Halswelle that ends well'—hem! Shakespere."

something more in keeping with the greatness of the play. It is impossible to interest oneself seriously with these *mannequins* in old Danish costumes.[12]

Satiety had long since set in. Yet all was not lost. At the very end of the Victorian age, two versions of the play scene demonstrated that innovation was not wholly dead in Shakespearean art. In 1897, Edwin Abbey located the players outside the picture, thus concentrating on the onlookers as they watched the mock drama seen only by themselves. Two years later, the Slade Prize was won by William Orpen's large canvas, in which attention was concentrated not on the "mousetrap" nor even on the spectators surrounding the King and Queen onstage—though they were visible—but on the audience in a small theater where *Hamlet* was being performed.

One of the few portrayals of Hamlet's interview with his father's ghost on the castle battlements was, as might be expected, that of the great

221. Charles Hunt, *"The Play's the Thing"* (RA 1863) (Yale Center for British Art, Paul Mellon Fund). One of several paintings in which Hunt portrayed schoolchildren rehearsing or performing a scene from a Shakespeare play, a throwback across more than a century to Hogarth's painting of *Children Playing Dryden's "The Indian Emperor" Before an Audience* (1731–32). Another of the kind was the one shown on the easel in Hunt's *My "Macbeth"* (pl. 235).

222. Sir Thomas Lawrence, *John Philip Kemble as Hamlet* (RA 1801) (Tate Gallery, London). This painting has an extraordinary record of migration. First it was bought by a Welsh gentleman who wanted to hang it above the altar in a church in his village. When the bishop took a dim view of this proposal, it was returned to London to be auctioned. Its buyer then resold it to the artist, who sold it, in turn, to George IV for 500 guineas. A dozen years later (1836), William IV gave it to the nation. It was then hung successively in the National Gallery and the National Portrait Gallery, finally arriving at the Tate. (Kalman Burnim, "John Philip Kemble and the Artists," *The Stage in the Eighteenth Century,* ed. J. D. Browning [New York, 1981], p. 187.)

223. Henry Liverseege, *The Grave Diggers in "Hamlet"* (Society of British Artists 1831) (City Art Gallery, Manchester). The *Times* (28 March) said that the picture "catches the humor of the characters." But only, one might add, if the spectator could supply their lines in the play—and perhaps not even then. The crudity of the painting is typical of this Manchester artist, whose pictures were hung at all three of the London exhibitions in 1831: the Royal Academy (subjects from Scott and Shakespeare), the British Institution (Gay's *Beggar's Opera*), and the Society of British Artists (this picture, and one from Scott).

specialist in ghost work, Henry Fuseli, who contributed it to the Boydell Gallery. Another dramatic encounter that was seldom pictured was Hamlet's coming upon Claudius as he was ineffectually praying: "Now might I do it pat. . . . " Orchardson ventured to depict the scene (RA 1874), and not undeservedly—because to the candid eye Hamlet looks more nonplussed than passionate—he was lambasted. "Dreadful," said the *Athenaeum;* "a more wretched prince than this painted one was never seen except in the 'counterfeit presentment' of a [puppet show] booth."[13] The *Saturday Review* offered it as "an example of the low style into which our British school is degenerating. . . . The French actor M. Fechter brought down the lofty Kemble tradition to colloquial standards, and now a Scotchman comes and reduces the noblest of Shakspeare's creations to the level of common nature."[14]

Despite all the complexity of spirit ascribed to him by critics, Hamlet was seldom painted as a psychological study; there were few if any pictures of him soliloquizing, apart from the stock theatrical portraits in which he sometimes appeared to be doing so. He usually was portrayed simply as a principal figure in a dramatic situation. He was seen at least once in his carefree youth, long before the fateful initial encounter with Claudius's ghost. Philip Hermogenes Calderon's *The Young Lord Hamlet* (RA 1868) was a literary adaptation of the popular theme of innocent childhood, with a coy intimation of future sexual love.

> Yorick [said one paper] is on his knees on the sward of the castle-garden at Elsinore, from whence one sees, over the sea, that sleeps in summer sunlight, the opposite coasts of Sweden. Sitting astride of the gentlemanly jester's shoulders, and playfully belabouring him with his own bauble, is the young Prince of Denmark. . . . To the right, and seated beneath a tree, is the mother-queen, also her maids; and with them, a girl-baby; of course, the young Ophelia.[15]

Not much of the genuine spirit of the play was retained in such a quintessentially Victorian genre scene; nor was it in the handful of pictures allegedly representing the grave diggers' scene (5.1). Henry Liverseege's *The Gravediggers in Hamlet* (pl. 223) merely showed two sturdy-looking

224. Angelica Kauffmann, *Scene from "Troilus and Cressida"* (Boydell's Shakespeare Gallery) (Petworth House). Kauffmann, one of the founding members of the Royal Academy, was the only woman contributor to the Shakespeare Gallery. In her account book, she described this scene, from act 5, scene 2: "Cressida wife of Troilus being a prisoner in the camp of the Greeks, is in the tent of Calchas the great priest and her father, she is in amorous conversation with Diomedes, Troilus comes during the period of Armistice to visit the camp, accompanied by Ulysses and another warrior. He sees his wife in loving discourse with Diomedes and he wants to rush into the tent to catch them by surprise, but Ulysses and the other keep him back by force."

chaps, one with a shovel, the other with a pick-axe, standing outside the church door; there was no sign of a funeral procession, or even of Hamlet or Horatio.

TROILUS AND CRESSIDA

Although *Troilus and Cressida* was no more popular a subject of art than most of Shakespeare's other "classical" plays, the dozen or so recorded paintings are of somewhat greater interest because of the artists involved. Two of the four Boydell scenes came from the brushes of highly esteemed artists. Angelica Kauffmann—a conspicuous presence in Boydell's catalogue of prints, some sixty of which were engraved from her designs—painted act 5, scene 2 (pl. 224). Romney's *Cassandra Raving* was one of his most famous portraits of Lady Hamilton. Like some other Boydell pieces, this painting had marked iconographical affinities with the French academic art of the moment. The laurel crown and the uplifted arm with the symbolic ax, however, need not be read as a subliminal political "statement," as they were in Revolutionary France.

One of the two *Troilus and Cressida* paintings in the New Shakespeare Gallery was Opie's scene in the Grecian camp (pl. 18). Some years later, at the Royal Academy, Opie showed another scene, of Pandarus delivering the veiled Cressida to the expectant Troilus in Pandarus' garden.

OTHELLO

Like its history on the stage, the record of *Othello* in British art is relatively uneventful. It was always performed in versions that, though often severely cut, were otherwise faithful to the Shakespearean text (there were no outright adaptations); it remained steadily in the repertory; and its three major roles, Othello, Iago, and Desdemona, were undertaken by most of the great tragic actors and actresses from Betterton's day onward. But although paintings from the play were numerous (more than one hundred are recorded), few were the work of leading artists, and even fewer achieved the fame of certain pictures drawn from Shakespeare's other great tragedies.

The most frequently painted scene was one that was never performed, but merely alluded to. In act 1, scene 3, the Moorish general Othello appears before the Venetian senate to defend himself against Brabantio's accusation of having spirited away Brabantio's daughter, Desdemona, by some kind of magic. The first treatment of the episode, if we except the picture of *Desdemona Justifying Herself to the Council* (after Othello has had his say) that Josiah Boydell painted for his uncle's gallery, was Henry Singleton's *Othello at Brabantio's Mansion* (RA 1793), depicting the scene Desdemona described to the senators. Between 1840 and 1868, several artists remembered today, as well as a number who are not, took up the subject. Frith used it for one of his first subject pictures (pl. 225). In 1857, five years after he was elected to the Royal Academy, he returned to the subject with *The Pliant Hour,* which had mixed reviews. James Smetham painted the subject in 1852, and the next year Charles West Cope exhibited his interpretation (pl. 143). Although the subject had been declared "threadbare" as early as 1854, it continued to be portrayed to the very end of the century.

A few paintings, notably Stothard's for Boydell (pl. 105), depicted Othello's triumphant arrival at Cyprus after humbling the Turkish fleet (2.2)—a theme (the hero's return) with a long high-art tradition behind it. The almost unbearable scene (3.3) in which Iago reduces Othello from a strong man serenely confident of his wife's fidelity to a groveling victim of pathological suspicion, was represented some six or eight times at intervals between 1807 and 1899. Maclise painted the handkerchief passage in 1867.

The sequence of events leading up to the final scene occasioned a few paintings. James Clarke Hook's visualization of Othello's description of Desdemona—"An admirable musician! O, she will sing the savageness out of a bear!" (RA 1852)—showed Othello listening to Desdemona singing and playing a lute; and there was a handful of pictures, one by Rossetti (1878–81), set in Desdemona's boudoir as she undresses, attended by the faithful Emilia, and sings snatches of the Willow Song. The only other scene to be represented by a fair number of pictures was the last, Othello's murder of his wife. No fewer than three Boydell paintings were devoted to the first minute.

225. William P. Frith, *Othello and Desdemona* (British Institution 1840) (Fitzwilliam Museum, Cambridge). Nothing whatsoever, except for the vague suggestion of a Venetian setting and the man's swarthy complexion, associates the scene with the play. In his late *Autobiography* (1: 81) Frith mentioned that he had used a Malay crossing sweeper as the model for Othello. The story must have been current in contemporary art circles, because in 1853–54 Thackeray, writing *The Newcomes,* a novel set in the middle and late 1830s, speaks of the painters Clive Newcome and J. J. Ridley as being "engaged in depicting a Life-Guardsman, or a muscular negro, or a Malay from a neighbouring crossing, who would appear as Othello" (chap. 22).

Like Shylock, Othello, the "thick lips," the "old black ram," was considered a difficult character to portray. "If he be represented as too heroic and handsome," said the *Examiner* in 1839, "the admirers of Shakspeare and the critics resent the impropriety; and if the artists portray him in exact accordance with the author's text, the ladies and the sentimentalists are disgusted."[1] There was also the perennial problem, expressed in a review of the same picture in the *Literary Gazette,* of Othello's race: should he be represented with "African features" or (as in the present instance) as a "half-caste"?[2]

Iago too, though for different reasons, was a hard figure to get past the critics. How could "motiveless malignity" be portrayed without turning the figure into a mere villain of gaslit melodrama? When Solomon Hart exhibited a painting of Othello and Iago in 1855, a writer in *Fraser's*

Magazine said: "Iago is too ignoble by far. He is more like a Jew pawn broker dressed for a masquerade than a Venetian in respectable society. He has r-a-s-c-a-l written legibly on his face. Even Othello could not have believed a word he said."[3]

KING LEAR

The production of pictures from *King Lear,* which began in the 1760s, remained constant for a century; there were no peaks or valleys of popularity such as one finds in the art records of some other Shakespearean dramas. Only after 1870 did the flow—there were about one hundred paintings altogether—noticeably abate. The artistic treatment of the play drew less obviously and less often from theatrical performances than did that of most of the other plays. One reason was that, of all the miserable perversions of Shakespeare that held the stage in the eighteenth century and, in some instances, down to the middle of the nineteenth, Nahum Tate's *The History of King Lear* (1681) was the most deplorable and, ironically, one of the most durable. In it, Tate had contrived a staggeringly implausible ending by concocting a love match between Cordelia and Edgar, rescuing her (by the intervention of a suddenly reinvigorated Lear) from an assassination attempt, restoring Lear for the time being to his throne and fortune, and implying, at the final curtain, that they all lived happily ever after. Lear addressed Gloucester:

> No, Gloster, Thou hast Business yet for Life.
> Thou, Kent and I, retir'd to some cool cell
> Will gently pass our short reserves of Time
> In calm Reflections on our Fortunes past,
> Cheer'd with relation of the prosperous Reign
> Of this celestial Pair

—namely, Cordelia and Edgar.[1] To comply with the decorum of his neoclassic age, Tate also deleted the Fool. Garrick, who is sometimes said to have been the greatest Lear in history, and whose near-exclusive property the play was throughout his career, did restore sizable bits of Shakespeare here and there, notably in the storm scene, while at the same time preserving Tate's outrages and adding several of his own. Tate's, however, remained the standard version. It was only in 1838 that Macready finally broke with tradition by staging the play as Shakespeare wrote it, albeit with some reordering of the scenes and casting an actress as the (newly restored) Fool.

Few artists chose to depict scenes that were in Tate's inimitable adaptation but not in Shakespeare. One who did so was Peter Van Bleeck, who painted Mrs. Cibber (pl. 171) in the so-called "field scene" in which Edgar rescued Cordelia from thugs whom Edmund had dispatched to assault her. That *King Lear* was represented by more pre-Boydellian paintings than any other Shakespearean play—more than twenty—was due partly to the belief that its "sublime" subject made it particularly amenable to the demands of history painting. Repeatedly in the literary criticism of the time, Garrick's projection of Lear's violent passions, counterpointed against his Aristotelian weakness as the victim of old age, was likened to a great painting come to life. In his *Treatise on the Passions* (1747), for example, Samuel Foote observed that Garrick's acting of the role would have

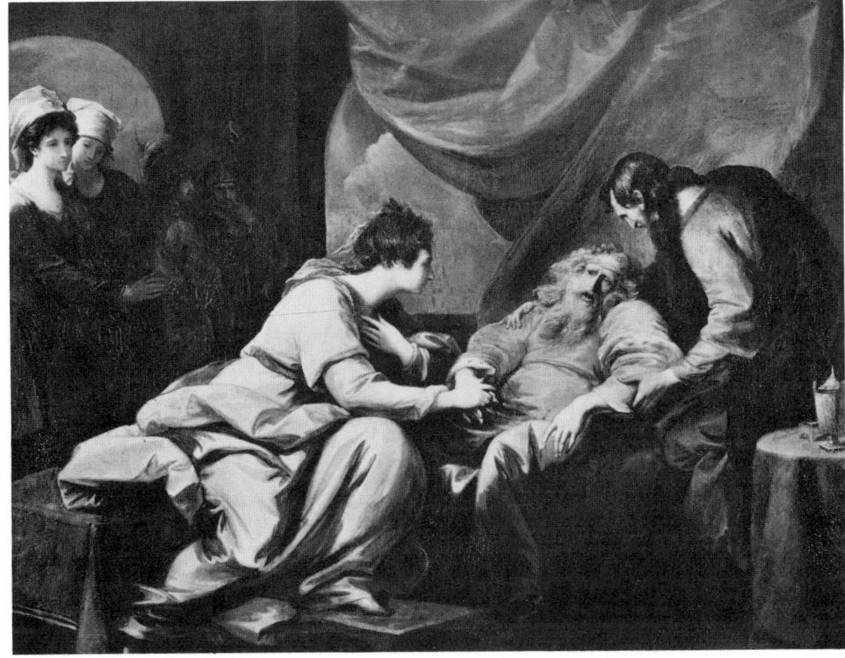

226. Benjamin West, *Lear and Cordelia* (1784) (Huntington Library and Art Gallery). A comparatively quiet early handling of a subject from *King Lear,* largely devoid of the grand-style heroics employed in the same period by Barry (pl. 7) and others. This picture was commissioned by the Empress of Russia.

honored "the Pencil of a *Rubens,* or an *Angelo.*"[2] Admiration of the Lear story as a prime subject for art in the grand style was widely reflected in practice by James Barry (pl. 7), Benjamin West (pl. 226), and Angelica Kauffmann (who decorated the reception room at Home House in Portman Square—now, suitably enough, the home of the Courtauld Institute of Art—with several subjects from the play). It was largely under the auspices of *King Lear* that artists continued to pursue the chimera of a native school of history painting. *King Lear Disinheriting His Daughters* was the subject of John Rogers Herbert's study for a fresco in the Palace of Westminster (pl. 141), and as late as 1855, a reviewer declared that the scene of Lear recovering his reason at the sight of Cordelia, treated that year by Herbert, "would tax three Raphaels to paint it,—and it deserves to be to English painters what 'The Last Supper' was to the Church decorators of the Middle Ages."[3] But no one in the by now anachronistic, if not actually moribund, school of history painters was even faintly equal to the challenge.

The stormy heath in *King Lear* was widely regarded as the very definition of sublimity. At least twenty paintings of the sequence are recorded, including those from act 3, scene 4, the scene outside the hovel involving Lear, Kent, Edgar, and (in Shakespeare's version, not Tate's) the Fool. Francis Hayman, whom Garrick advised when he was preparing the illustrations for Hanmer's edition of Shakespeare, painted the scene for Vauxhall Gardens. It was one of two *Lear* subjects—the other was Cordelia awakening Lear—that Romney, just beginning his career, completed in Kendal before moving to London in 1762.*

About this time, Benjamin Wilson painted the scene on the heath, nominally as a theatrical tableau with Garrick projecting Lear's madness in the best histrionic tradition, but the background of stormy sky and gale-whipped trees represented effects of which the contemporary theater was

*The picture of the awakening scene acquired an interesting literary history. It was raffled off at Kendal, along with twenty of Romney's other early paintings, in 1765. Many years later, a son of Adam Walker, a schoolmaster and popularizer of natural science who had become Romney's friend in Lancaster, where he was making portraits of local worthies, came upon the picture at a broker's shop in Kensington. He bought it for five shillings and took it home to his father, who recognized it at once as "an old friend." In 1804, William Blake, collecting materials for his patron William Hayley's biography of Romney, called on Walker and was shown the picture, "an incomparable production," he told Hayley, ". . . about five feet by four, and exquisite for expression, indeed, it is most pathetic; the heads of Lear and Cordelia can never be surpassed, and Kent and the other attendant are admirable . . ." (Alexander Gilchrist, *Life of William Blake,* ed. Ruthven Todd [Everyman ed., 1942], p. 184). Adam Walker said that he posed for the figure of Lear and Romney's wife for Cordelia. In view of the fact that the Romneys were estranged for most of the artist's life, being reconciled only when, at the end of his career, he became mad and destitute, her having posed as the familiar prototype of the long-suffering and forgiving woman adds irony to Tennyson's treatment of their deathbed reconciliation in his poem "Romney's Remorse."

227. John Runciman, *King Lear in the Storm* (1767) (National Gallery of Scotland). An early landmark in the development of literary painting: removing a subject from its original source, in this case a specific scene in a drama, and giving it an independent life through the artist's effort to realize the spirit rather than the literal sense of the text.

not capable. It was left for John Runciman, in his powerful canvas of 1767 (pl. 227), to complete the process by drawing instead upon the iconography of Old Master painting—Van Dyck, Rembrandt, Rubens—for his tempestuous landscape with a ship sinking and a man drowning. By these strokes of visual invention and borrowing, Runciman was among the very first painters of literary subjects to show how it was possible to enlarge a picture's reference so that, instead of illustrating a specific moment in the text, it would capture and epitomize the atmosphere of a whole passage.[4] The terrifying impact of the poet's imagery was realized in paint without the intervention of the stage, a Romantic development in art that Runciman anticipated by several decades.

In contrast, the two representations of the storm sequence in the Boydell Gallery are of little interest. Smirke's, of the hovel scene, was conventional and feeble; and Benjamin West's, of Lear on the heath, imposing and cold. By 1820, the subject was virtually exhausted: of the twenty recorded paintings, only two were produced after that year. One was William Dyce's belated version at the Royal Academy in 1851, which received a bad press, various reviewers faulting it for the Fool's "repulsive and impossible ugliness" and the artist's "entire misappreciation" of Shakespeare's meaning.[5]

The fact was that, despite the lingering dream that English Raphaels would materialize to do justice to Lear's sufferings, by mid-century it was recognized that a "primeval" British king and his barbaric age simply did not invite or tolerate the sort of treatment appropriately devoted to, say, Coriolanus or Julius Caesar. Popular taste, moreover, had decisively shifted away from the sublimity of storms—those in nature as well as in the tortured souls of tragic heroes—to the pathos of the heroine who is at once victimized by, and unshakably devoted to, an ungracious father. Cordelia was one of the most admired women in British painting, and it is significant that, except for the storm scenes, the only subjects from *King Lear* that were repeatedly painted came from scenes in which she figures:

the division of the kingdom and Lear's renunciation of her (1.1), their reconciliation (4.7), and Cordelia's death (5.3). As far as most artists were concerned, this was her play. It may be that Cordelia's demonstrable command of the market, like Ophelia's, discouraged artists from ever exploiting the many dramatic subjects in the play, apart from the storm scenes, that lie between act 1, scene 2, and act 4, scene 7, the long stretch during which she appears only once, and briefly at that (4.4).

More than a score of undescribed paintings titled either *Cordelia* or *Cordelia and Lear* cannot be attributed to any one of the scenes in which they appear together. Of the remaining number that can be identified, more than a dozen represented moments in the opening scene, among the earliest being two Boydell pictures, one, by Smirke, of the dissension among the three sisters, with Burgundy holding the white-robed, portionless Cordelia's hand, and the other, by Fuseli, of Lear starting from his throne in furious denunciation of Cordelia while his retinue and other daughters look on. William Hilton's version of 1814 seems to have been a neoclassic treatment similar to Fuseli's. Herbert, as we saw above, depicted the same scene in a study for a Westminster fresco. In 1876, he sent an entire (modified) replica of the same work to the Royal Academy, a repetition that some reviewers found gratuitous and three decades out of fashion. The *Saturday Review,* finding that the three daughters were "so little like to the creations of Shakspeare that they appear just as if they had escaped from a convent," recommended Ford Madox Brown's interpretation (pl. 87) as truer "to the text of the poet."[6] Brown had a lifelong interest in *King Lear,* particularly in the moment of Cordelia's parting from her sisters.[7]

But it was the Cordelia of the late scenes who most engaged the artists and their public. From Romney's version of about 1760 to Paul Falconer Poole's in 1867, the successive phases of "Lear asleep," "Lear awakened

228. Unknown artist, *Cordelia Championed by the Earl of Kent* (ca. 1770–80) (Yale Center for British Art, Paul Mellon Fund). In contrast to the *King Lear* paintings by West, Barry, and Runciman, from the same era, this one, formerly attributed to William Hamilton, seems to have originated in a theatrical performance. The histrionic poses and the mixture of costuming—part contemporary, part derived from old portraiture—befit the incongruity of a play most of which was written not by Shakespeare but by Nahum Tate.

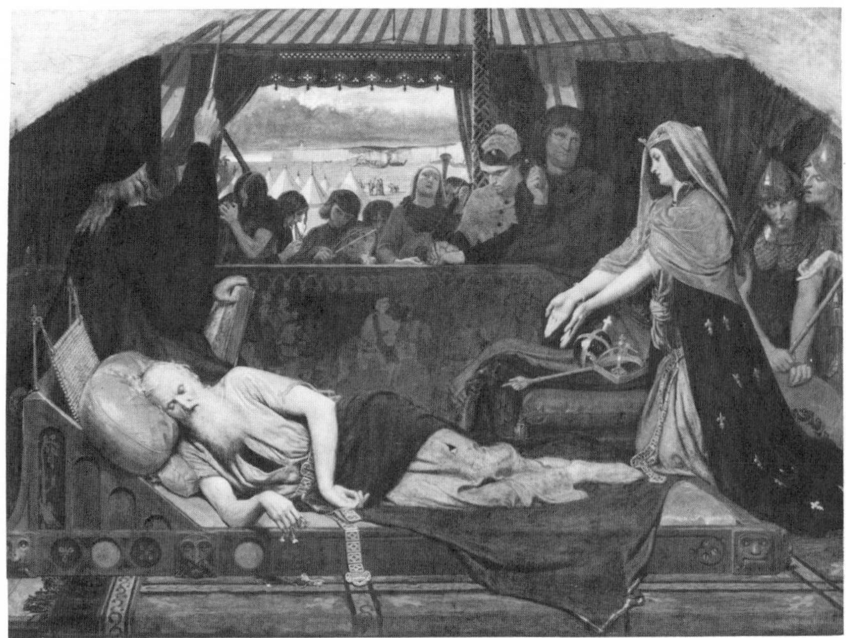

229. Ford Madox Brown, *Cordelia at the Bedside of Lear* (Free Exhibition of Modern Art 1849) (Tate Gallery, London). Like Brown's later *Cordelia's Portion* (pl. 87), an interpretation of Shakespeare notable for its luscious costuming, accessories, and setting. Brown wrote that the "Roman-pagan-British" origin of the story, which was also "medieval by external customs and habits," posed a problem in costuming. He finally chose "to be in harmony with the mental characteristics of Shakespeare's work, and have therefore adopted the costume prevalent in Europe about the sixth century, when paganism was still rife, and deeds were at their darkest. The piece of Bayeux tapestry introduced behind King Lear," he admitted, "is strictly an anachronism" (Hueffer, *Ford Madox Brown,* p. 56). But Brown did not explain how a king, or anyone else, could sleep in such a posture.

by Cordelia," and "Lear recovering his reason" were painted some twenty-five times in all. Smirke's rendition for Boydell was commonplace, as was West's lost treatment of 1794, if one can judge from the engraving. Two artists well known in their time, William Boxall and Gilbert Stuart Newton, entered rival versions at the Royal Academy in 1831. Both Millais and Ford Madox Brown (pl. 229) painted the scene in 1848–49, and Charles West Cope, a then better-known artist, not of the Pre-Raphaelite persuasion, offered his interpretation at the Royal Academy in 1850. Although its reception was mixed, the presence of "minstrels and choristers" attending the sleeping Lear, as they did also in Brown's picture (in the text there is simply offstage "music"), led the *Times* reviewer to observe, "To touch one sense by another, or, in other words, *to paint music,* is at all times a bold undertaking, and Titian and Giorgione have not always succeeded in it; but here the object was not so much to convey the direct impression of sound as the soothing effect of it on dying ears, and the burden of that melody is, as it were—Cordelia."[8]

Portrayal of the final scene (5.3), the death of Cordelia and Lear—anathema to Nahum Tate and Garrick—got off to a bad start with Barry's painting of 1774, now lost but repeated in the version for Boydell (pl. 7). A critic signing himself "Guido" in the *Public Advertiser* had a command of abuse worthy of one of his Victorian descendants in an unsentimental mood. "Had Shakespeare's Ideas been as demoniac and extravagant as Mr. Barry's," he wrote, strikingly anticipating the terms in which critics would ridicule Turner's *Shylock* and *Juliet* paintings half a century later, "we should never have enjoyed those artless Scenes which compose his inimitable *Lear.* The Artist certainly meant it as a Burlesque: Cordelia represented by a Fat Billingsgate Fish-Woman overpowered with Gin, and Lear personated by an old Cloaths-man, or Jew Rabbi picking her pocket. Even this can carry no Idea of the Extravagance of this Production."[9]

Irrespective of the virtues and defects of Barry's picture, which is interesting for its mixture of classical costume and primitive architecture if nothing else, the death scene did not appeal to many subsequent painters. No more than ten are recorded. Thomas Uwins essayed it in 1841, and F. R. Pickersgill won a prize with it in the Westminster cartoon competition two years later. The only later treatment to arouse much comment was that by Paul Falconer Poole in 1858 (pl. 152). Its reception typified the extraordinarily mixed press that Poole, "a hopeless eccentric" according to one reviewer of this picture, had to endure throughout his career.

230. Henry Fuseli, *Macbeth and the Witches* (1793–94) (Petworth House). The triplicate witches recall the larger group, mentioned in the text, which was painted ten years earlier and became the image that was to dominate Fuseli's *Macbeth* repertory.

MACBETH

D'Avenant's operatic version of *Macbeth,* originally starring Thomas Betterton, featured not only a musical score but stage machinery to fly the witches, who were given additional business. Their popularity in their expanded roles was so lasting that when Garrick staged the play more or less as Shakespeare had written it, he did not cut back D'Avenant's witches, nor did many of his successors down to Charles Kean's time. In art, the Weird Sisters' scenes were represented much oftener than any other part of the drama. The first four *Macbeth* paintings on record, from between 1760 and 1767, were of one or another of the witch scenes; and from that time down to the end of the nineteenth century, the midnight hags were the subject of at least sixty paintings out of a total of some 150. Because many of the pictures were titled merely *The Weird Sisters* or *Macbeth and the Witches,* it is impossible to determine which of the three scenes, the brief glimpse (1.1), the incantation and prophecy (1.3), or the apparitions of future kings (4.1), was most often represented.

Henry Fuseli, for whom Shakespeare might almost be said to have written his supernatural scenes,[1] painted the witches time after time in several media, the most famous of all these designs being the three serried profiles with bony-fingered hands aligned and pointing ominously to the left (RA 1783).* For Boydell, Fuseli produced the prophecy scene, Macbeth taking the form of a heroic nude figure in the Michelangelesque mode, with the witches in diaphanous veils.

> This is a sublime scene and the figure of Macbeth uncommonly grand: a character too great to be daunted by an extraordinary event betrays no sign of fear or even astonishment; the slumbering fire of ambition is roused, and the firmly-nerved hand of power raised to command those to stay and say more, from whom a dastard would have fled. . . . The figure and attitude of Banquo appear rather strained and inferior to the rest of the composition, which, like a stupendous feature in nature, seizes the whole mind, and produces the concentrated calm of admiration, instead of the various dilated pleasurable sensations which arise from contemplating grace and beauty.

The description is by Fuseli himself, anonymously commenting on his own picture in the *Analytical Review.*[2]

For Boydell's unsuccessful rival, Woodmason's New Shakespeare Gallery, Fuseli painted two *Macbeth* subjects, *Macbeth and the Witches* (pl. 230) and *Macbeth and the Armed Head.* In the latter, Fuseli gave the apparition of the armed head in act 4, scene 1, the visage of Macbeth himself, thus contriving a hallucinatory prophecy of the play's closing scene, when the tyrant's severed head is triumphantly brought onstage by Macduff. In a letter to his future biographer, John Knowles, the artist wrote, "I have endeavoured to shew a colossal head rising out of the abyss, and that head Macbeth's likeness. What, I would ask, would be a greater object of terror

*It was perhaps this picture that was the subject of an anecdote related by Farington: "Garvey [a landscape artist] sd. that when Fuseli exhibited his large picture of Macbeth at the little Royal Academy He went there with Gainsborough who on seeing it sd. He shd. not like to be in a one Horse Chaise before that picture. . . . On the contrary," Farington added, "Sir Joshua was sd. to approve it in some respects" (Farington [1], 6:2245, 15 February 1804).

to you, if, some night on going home, you were to find yourself sitting at your own table, either writing, reading, or otherwise employed? would not this make a powerful impression on your mind?"[3] It sounds suspiciously like Dickens's Fat Boy: "I wants to make your flesh creep." But Coleridge reacted otherwise when he saw another of Fuseli's paintings of the same subject at the Royal Academy in 1811. The diarist Crabb Robinson, who was with him, wrote that "he pointed out to me the 'vigorous impotence' of Fuseli, whose 'Macbeth' is, indeed, a very disgusting production. The armed head is not amiss, but Macbeth is not human, and the more prominent witch has a vulgar sneer on her lip. Coleridge said: 'She is smelling a stink.' "[4]

Reynolds's interpretation of the procession-of-future-kings scene, for Boydell, was, in Hazlitt's phrase, an "inventory of dreadful objects"[5]—skulls, toads, bats—as well as an augmented company of witches whom Macbeth harangues as the cauldron bubbles and naked babes mock his dynastic ambition.

Another notable painting of Macbeth and the witches, now lost, was by a well-known artist belonging to a later and quite different school. When the actor Macready, the supreme Macbeth of his day, came to model for Daniel Maclise in January 1836, he was disappointed by the sketch the artist had already made on his canvas. "I did not like it as a whole," he recorded in his diary; "the subject was cut in two; the group of witches was admirably imagined and in itself a picture—the figure of Macbeth was superfluous. He has not poetry enough to grasp at my idea, nor I art enough to be sanguine about his. After much discussion I yielded to his genius, which ought to have its unbridled course. Sat, and to work he went."[6] The result was exhibited at the Royal Academy in May of the same year; it was bought by John Forster, a central figure in the literary and dramatic circles of the time. Its critical reception justified Macready's doubts. "We know not how to congratulate the three Macs—Macready, Macbeth, or Maclise," wrote John Eagles in *Blackwood's Magazine*. "Did Shakspeare mean his Macbeth to look so frightened, and so undignified? No compliment to Macready—and we doubt if the witches, ludicrously horrible as they are, do not look as much scared as Macbeth."[7]

One aspect of the witch scenes that particularly recommended them to artists was the fearful storm that marked their successive appearances. (The stage direction in each case calls for "Thunder," with "lightning" added for 1.1) Convulsions of nature were always a reliable source of melodrama in the art of the age, and none were more splendid than those inspired by *Macbeth*. Zuccarelli's early treatment (pl. 22) was more or less stylized, but John Martin's Romantic conception (pl. 231) possessed the intensity typical of that specialist in cosmic-scale catastrophes. The scene was Gothic rather than Shakespearean in its "visionary awfulness"—a phrase used by the *London Magazine*'s reviewer, who then brought his readers down to prosaic earth with a thud by adding judiciously that "the army appears too numerous to be conducted against a rebellious thane of that period, in Scotland."[8] As the decades passed, however, the fury of the storm subsided, and the landscape shrank to more credible dimensions. One of the last versions, Keeley Halswelle's (1889), was tame and human-scaled, not seeking to convey any of the horror that Fuseli, Martin, and their imitators had aspired toward.

None of the actors and actresses who played the sexless sisters made a reputation out of the role, and no literal representation of the staging of

231. John Martin, *Macbeth* (British Institution 1820) (National Gallery of Scotland). A smaller copy of the lost original. There was textual authority for the lighting and the swirling vapor in which the witches rise (left), but the huge army snaking its way through the valley and the mountainscape, Himalayan rather than Highland, are Martin's own contribution.

the witch scenes, in the eighteenth century at least, could have done justice, any more than the scene designer himself could have done, to the physical atmosphere conjured up by Shakespeare's text. But the play was a vehicle for a long line of great actors and actresses, beginning (if we except Betterton in the operatic version) with Garrick and his Lady Macbeth, Hannah Pritchard, who, it is said—like Thackeray's Miss Fotheringay in *Pendennis*—was indifferently acquainted with the texts of the very dramas she starred in. Mrs. Siddons, one of the most celebrated Lady Macbeths, was repeatedly painted in the role.

Of the many "strong" scenes in which the play abounds, it was act 2, scene 2, with which the great Macbeths and Lady Macbeths were most indelibly associated, a fact wholly substantiated by the artistic record. The scene is only seventy lines long, but it evoked the most powerful acting of which anyone who assumed either role was capable. In paintings, almost every moment was depicted; and the examples, if enough survived, might be assembled in a continuous pictorial narrative, as one could be from the much longer second scene of *The Tempest.* Haydon is reported to have rendered the first moment, in which Lady Macbeth listens as her husband attempts—and as it soon transpires, bungles—his bloody deed, but the picture (1829) is untraced. Several minor artists painted the passage in the next two decades, and the better-known Alfred Elmore in 1848. Lady Macbeth's response to Macbeth's offstage cry, "Who's there? What ho?"—"Alack, I am afraid they have awaked, / And 'tis not done!"—was painted by Arthur William Devis (RA 1809).

"Hark!" she continues. "I laid their daggers ready— / He could not miss 'em. Had he not resembled / My father as he slept, I had done't." Westall painted this (reported, not enacted) scene (pl. 232). Almost eighty years later (1868), Maclise returned the subject to the Academy walls. "The idea of this action," said the *Athenaeum*, "is worthy of Rembrandt," but, though approving of the picture, it did not venture to drape Rembrandt's mantle on Maclise's aging shoulders.[9]

232. Richard Westall, *Lady Macbeth Prevented from Stabbing the King* (RA 1790) (Sir John Soane's Museum, London). The knife depicted in the very process of falling from her hand adds a stop-action immediacy to an otherwise unremarkable treatment of this familiar subject.

In 1853, Henry Selous, who served art both as an easel painter and a

233. Henry Fuseli, *Lady Macbeth Seizing the Daggers* (RA 1812) (Tate Gallery, London). This painting, a late addition to Fuseli's long series of interpretations of *Macbeth,* originated in an aquarelle the artist drew of Garrick and Mrs. Pritchard in the scene (1766). For Zoffany's theatrical version of the same subject, with the same actors, see pl. 156.

painter of panoramas, depicted the following moment, when, in staccato dialogue with his wife, Macbeth describes his ordeal in Duncan's chamber, unnerved by the drunken grooms laughing in their sleep and crying "Murder!" The next moment narrated by Macbeth, when a voice cried out "Sleep no more! / Macbeth does murder sleep," was painted by Haydon between 1809 and 1812, when he showed it at the British Institution.* The picture is now lost, but Robert Hunt, writing in his brother's *Examiner,* gave his readers some notion of what it looked like.[10] (Haydon also described it in detail, as well as noting its progress over the three years he devoted to it, in his journal.)

"Infirm of purpose!" exclaims Lady Macbeth as her husband displays his bloodstained hands. "Give me the daggers!" Zoffany painted the scene twice (1768 [pl. 156]; 1777), with Garrick and Mrs. Pritchard; and in 1794 Sir William Beechey depicted their immediate successors, John Philip Kemble and Mrs. Siddons, at the same moment. Fittingly enough, given both Fuseli's long association with the play and the theatrical fame of the passage, it was his "sketch for a large picture" of Lady Macbeth seizing the daggers that was hung at the Royal Academy in 1812, only a few weeks before Mrs. Siddons chose this role, probably her most celebrated one, for the first of her several farewell performances (pl. 233).†

Lady Macbeth, having rebuked her husband's infirmity of purpose, proposes to finish what he cravenly left undone: "If he do bleed, / I'll gild the faces of the grooms withal, / For it must seem their guilt." *Lady Macbeth Smearing the Grooms with Blood from Her Dripping Dagger* was one of David Scott's huge unsold canvases that after his untimely death hung in his brother's studio.[11] And so the scene ends. The final line, "My hands are of your colour, but I shame / To wear a heart so white," was illustrated by an exhibitor at the British Institution in 1809. Several of these passages, of course, were portrayed by a number of other artists during *Macbeth*'s long run in the exhibition galleries.

*This was the painting that Sir George Beaumont commissioned but refused to accept upon completion, thus touching off the first big quarrel of the many that would punctuate Haydon's life thereafter. The story is told in detail by Haydon in his *Autobiography* (1:98–105 et seq.), and more dispassionately by Eric George (*Life and Death of Haydon,* pp. 40–47).

†This was on the night of 29 June 1812, when the play was stopped after she made her exit in the sleepwalking scene. She returned to deliver her farewell address, the audience cheered, and the performance was not resumed. It was not until 7 June 1817, however, that she and her brother actually appeared in *Macbeth* for the last time.

234. Daniel Maclise, *The Banquet Scene in "Macbeth"* (RA 1840) (Guildhall Art Gallery, London). Thackeray's praise took the form of an imagined scene at the Royal Academy when, after the royal party has paused for (exactly) twenty-three admiring minutes before this painting, Queen Victoria borrows the Duke of Wellington's sword and knights the artist on the spot (*Fraser's Magazine,* June, 21: 723).

The banquet scene (3.4) was painted only three or four times. It was the subject of one of Westall's Boydell paintings, which showed Macbeth sitting at the edge of his throne with his arm upraised as if to fend off Banquo's ghost, which seems to be bubbling up from the floor. But the most celebrated rendition was Maclise's in 1840, a picture, painted for the Earl of Chesterfield, which was the hit of the Royal Academy show (pl. 234) and redeemed the artist's reputation from the setback it had had four years earlier with the witches' scene. (Macready praised especially the figure of Lady Macbeth, which he thought "the ideal of the character: it is a noble conception.")[12] The *Examiner* declared that "the power of the painter [has] placed us *within Macbeth's own mind*" and that Lady Macbeth held her shrinking husband down "with the sublime form and troubled beauty of a fallen angel."[13] Thackeray, writing in *Fraser's Magazine,* and John Eagles in *Blackwood's* were equally, and lengthily, enthusiastic.[14]

From the very last moment of the banquet scene came John Singer

235. Charles Hunt, *My "Macbeth"* (dated 1863) (Forbes Magazine Collection). At the Royal Academy exhibition of 1864, Hunt showed the picture seen on the easel, *The Banquet Scene: "Macbeth"* (now lost). The copy of the *Art Journal* that contained a favorable review of the painting presumably was added later. As the artist points with pride to the picture, the schoolboy witch (who, for all we know, may be his son) points back at him. The banquet scene in Shakespeare's play does not include a witch, but the Fuselian costume, evidently a tablecloth commandeered for the occasion, makes the identification certain. Schoolboys took as large liberties with the text as some painters did.

236. John Singer Sargent, *Miss Ellen Terry as Lady Macbeth* (New Gallery 1889) (Tate Gallery, London). This record of Terry's role in Irving's production was owned by Irving himself and hung in his private dining room at the Lyceum Theatre. After his death, it was bought by Joseph Duveen, who presented it to the Tate Gallery.

Sargent's famous picture (pl. 236) of Ellen Terry as Lady Macbeth, holding her crown over her head in what might be taken (wrongly) as a gesture of achievement, following the removal of the inconvenient Banquo from her husband's upward path.[15] Painted immediately after the premiere of Irving's new production (29 December 1888) and displayed to dense crowds at the New Gallery the next season, it was the eventual product of Sargent's wish to paint Terry in the splendid costume she wore when she passed between torch-lit lines of court ladies to greet Duncan as he arrived at her castle. (Oscar Wilde witnessed her arrival in Chelsea to pose: "The street that on a wet and dreary morning has vouchsafed the vision of Lady Macbeth in full regalia magnificently seated in a four-wheeler can never again be as other streets: it must always be full of wonderful possibilities.") But after making a grisaille sketch of the proposed tableau, now in the National Portrait Gallery, Sargent decided instead to portray Terry at the moment when, in Irving's production, she was left alone onstage after Macbeth's exit. The gesture with the crown, not indicated in the text but previously used by Samuel Phelps's Lady Macbeth, Miss Atkinson, in 1857, was devised to portend the darkening future. According to Terry's notes and other sources, as Macbeth departed she took off her crown, staggered to the vacated throne, held the crown in her hand, and laughed as the curtain fell.

One more famous passage, Lady Macbeth's sleepwalking scene, received half a dozen treatments, the earliest notable one being Fuseli's (RA 1784), now in the Louvre: "execrable," said Horace Walpole, tersely.[16] Lady Macbeth's death, not seen onstage but reported by Seyton, was painted by Theodor von Holst (Society of British Artists 1838). The writer who described the picture in the *Athenaeum* evidently was no admirer of, say, Fuseli's *The Nightmare*. He wrote: " . . . The dying agonies of Lady Macbeth—by the side of whose bed crouch the weird sisters [an innovation Shakespeare would have envied?]—are . . . frightfully displayed: the writhen brow—the wildly-tossed arms—the inverted eye—the foaming lip—may not, it is true, overstep what has been witnessed in nature, but belong to one of its most distorted aspects, with which Art, we think, has but little concern."[17] Von Holst, it is said, was a student of Fuseli's at the Royal Academy schools. This is barely possible (he was fifteen when Fuseli died in 1825); but in the picture, he realized Fuseli's own conception of the subject, as reported by the elder artist's friend, the eminent physiologist Charles Bell, in 1808. Fuseli, he wrote his brother, "thinks it an error in Shakspeare that when the cry of women marks the death of Lady Macbeth, she does not appear. He would have had her struggling in death among white sheets."[18] Had Von Holst lived—he died in 1844—he might well have carried out another of Fuseli's characteristic embellishments of Shakespeare. Bell continued: "And in that beautiful passage [1.6], where in the approach to the castle of Macbeth so fine a contrast is observed between the repose and softness of the scene with the horrors which are to follow, he would have had owls and bats' wings, and cobwebs and spiders, hanging from bough to bough, encircling this scene of blood."

Macbeth, alone among the great tragedies, contains no sympathetic heroine. Lady Macbeth never claimed a place in the gallery of moral beauty that was graced by innumerable Ophelias, Cordelias, and Desdemonas. When she was not modeled from actresses like Mrs. Pritchard and Mrs.

Siddons, artists tended to depict her, in conformity with the usual reading of the role at the time, as a female "heavy," overtly masculine and, as in Westall's portrait for Boydell, almost burly, with the forearms of a coal heaver. In A. E. Chalon's rendition (RA 1836), she additionally had a scowl on her face.

Like Hamlet, in art Macbeth was studied less intensively as a character than the woman who played opposite him. There was little graphic commentary on him as a study in the psychology of power hunger or as an example of a man betrayed by a too insistent imagination. Indeed, again like Hamlet, no record has been found of any painting that showed him soliloquizing, even when the phantom dagger appeared before his frantic eyes. Outside the dramatic contexts of the tableaux, he was usually seen in conventional theatrical portraits that had only limited reference to a specific situation in the play.

But with such a wealth of witchery and blood-soaked melodrama to choose from, no one seems to have missed these more thoughtful kinds of psychological studies the play offered unreceptive artists. One regal playgoer did not miss them either, but her taste was, in respect to this one literary source at least, refreshingly independent of the public as well as the painters who served them. When she saw *Macbeth* in Kean's production at the Princess' Theatre in 1853, Queen Victoria thought that the "most striking Tableaux" were two that were seldom if ever portrayed in paint: "(1) when the murder of Duncan has been discovered, and all the wild men and soldiers rush in with torches, and (2) the last scene, when Macbeth is killed and Malcolm is raised up on a shield, in the old fashion. It was really beautiful."[19]

TIMON OF ATHENS

In various adaptations, *Timon of Athens* came and went on the London stage, with little success. Kean's version, somewhat nearer the original, had seven performances in six weeks in 1816 and then was shelved. The only Victorian revivals prior to 1871 were Samuel Phelps's in 1851 (forty-one performances) and 1856.

The play was represented in book illustrations and in an occasional painting. Nathaniel Dance's rendering of act 4, scene 3—the entrance of Alcibiades, with Phrynia and Timandra—was exhibited at the Society of Artists in 1767, and is now at Hampton Court (pl. 237). The play was represented in the Boydell Gallery by three pictures, one by Opie, showing Timon digging up the gold pieces just before Alcibiades' entrance, and the other two by Henry Howard. Northcote's treatment of another moment in the scene, when Timon gives the gold to Phrynia and Timandra, was one of the two *Timon* pictures in the New Shakespeare Gallery. All told, about a dozen *Timon* paintings are recorded, including Leslie's earliest effort (ca. 1813) and one by Henry Wallis. The four dating from 1819 and after all drew their subjects from the favorite "cave" scene.

ANTONY AND CLEOPATRA

Shakespeare's play was unknown to the eighteenth-century London stage, except for a six-night run of Capell's adaptation in 1759 in which Garrick played Antony to Mrs. Yates's Cleopatra. In the theater, the Antony and Cleopatra story was known, instead, through Dryden's *All for Love,* elements of which persisted in the Shakespearean text even when

237. Nathaniel Dance, *Timon of Athens* (Society of Artists 1767) (Royal Collection, Copyright Reserved). The entrance of Alcibiades, with Phrynia and Timandra (*Timon of Athens,* 4. 3), a scene repeatedly portrayed in eighteenth-century illustrations. As a generous practitioner of conspicuous consumption, the historical Timon was invoked by Alexander Pope in his fourth *Moral Essay* ("On the Use of Riches").

the original play was revived in spectacular productions by J. P. Kemble in 1813 and Macready in 1833. It is unlikely, however, that painters of Antony and Cleopatra subjects had Dryden's tragedy in mind; not only did no such picture bear an attribution to Dryden, but apart from a picture Matthew W. Peters painted for *Bell's British Theatre* and similar designs for book illustrations, *All for Love* was unknown in the art galleries.

One cannot tell how many of the approximately forty-five pictures with "Antony and Cleopatra" or simply "Cleopatra" in their titles derived from Shakespeare or any other literary source. In the catalogue entries, only about a dozen were specifically associated with his play. The absence of explicit reference to Shakespeare is not, of course, proof that a given "Antony and Cleopatra" subject was not derived from the play. But the fact that so few Cleopatra pictures were exhibited with quotations leads one to suppose that the painters meant to relate the subject, more closely than in most such instances of a combined literary-artistic theme, to the parallel tradition in art (see above, Part One, chapter 8). In any event, the subject was one that encouraged artists to emulate the Old Masters at the same time that they might, with good conscience, endow their canvases with a fair degree of sensuousness. Henry Tresham's version of act 3, scene 7, for Boydell was extravagantly typical of the worst kind of grand-style pretension, representing Antony in naked Michelangelesque musculature and Cleopatra in the attitude of a dancing Ceres distributing seeds. The death of Cleopatra was the artists' favorite moment. In another picture for Boydell, Tresham portrayed her in a half-sitting posture, with Charmian at the head of her couch and the dead Iras at its foot, and the soldiers bursting in. A full century later (RA 1890), a huge canvas by the Honorable John Collier showed Cleopatra, according to the *Satur-*

day Review, "stretched at the feet of two gigantic gods of basalt," with Charmian, "a great fan [the *Times* man saw a harp] falling from her hand," turning away in anguish; Iras lay dead on the floor.[1]

Reynolds's portrait (1759) of the courtesan Kitty Fisher as Cleopatra dropping the pearl, an incident, not found in Shakespeare or Dryden, whose origin Leslie identified as a print in an old collection called *Jacob Cats' Book of Emblems,*[2] was the earliest of half a dozen pictures of this subject, among them Stothard's design for a painting for the great staircase at Burleigh House (pl. 59).

It is probably significant that at least half of the recorded paintings that specifically alluded to Shakespeare's play were produced in the 1880s and 90s, in the wake of the most spectacular of all productions of *Antony and Cleopatra,* staged at Drury Lane in 1873.[3] Half the text was omitted, but in its place the audience, breathing perfume supplied by something called "Rimmel's Persian Ribbon," was treated to a sight of a real barge onstage, a "Grand Roman Festival" that included "ballets, choruses, the processions of Venus, Juno, Diana, and Flora, and a 'Path of Flowers'." Such revivals of antique themes undoubtedly gave fresh inspiration and incentive to late Victorian academic painters. Alma-Tadema painted several portraits and figure studies of the cruel, sultry *femme fatale,* at least one with the asp busy upon her breast.

CORIOLANUS

Some twenty paintings, more than half of which dated from before 1800, represented scenes from *Coriolanus,* whose Plutarchan source had supplied subjects for a number of paintings by admired Continental masters, notably Poussin.[1] Its heroic action and setting in ancient Rome strongly recommended it to neoclassic taste. On the stage, a hybrid tragedy compiled by Thomas Sheridan from Shakespeare's play and one by James Thomson, the poet of *The Seasons,* provided John Philip Kemble with his greatest starring role. Mrs. Siddons played opposite him as Volumnia, and 240 extras marched across the stage in the spectacular triumphal scene. Sir Francis Bourgeois exhibited portraits of the stately Kemble in two different scenes (RA 1793, 1797), and Sir Thomas Lawrence painted him in one of his most famous canvases (pl. 238). Kean's unsuccessful revival of 1820 occasioned one or two further pictures, but neither Macready's lavish evocation of Roman antiquity in 1838 nor Phelps's remounting ten years later arrested the play's waning fortunes in art.

Of the three Boydell scenes from *Coriolanus,* Gavin Hamilton's representation of the climactic scene (5.3), in which Virgilia and Volumnia in turn plead with Coriolanus to spare Rome, was noteworthy as one of the best examples in the entire gallery of the late neoclassic style. The same scene, valued for its domestic feeling, was painted by Stothard and others. Several other canvases portrayed Coriolanus with his treacherous enemy-friend Aufidius. But the only Victorian picture of any consequence from the play was G. F. Watts's, painted for the Marquess of Lansdowne's Bowood in 1860.

238. Sir Thomas Lawrence, *John Philip Kemble as Coriolanus* (RA 1798) (Guildhall Art Gallery, London). Also called *Coriolanus at the Hearth of Aufidius* (4. 5), the painting had a mixed reception. Lawrence, it is said, "thought very well of it himself, and when questioned respecting its class, said, 'I call it a half-history picture'" (Cunningham, *Lives,* 3: 41).

THE ROMANCES

PERICLES

In the eighteenth century, there was much debate over the admission of *Pericles* to the Shakespearean canon; it was left out of most editions, including Boydell's. In 1738, the last three acts were embodied in George Lillo's *Marina,* in the belief that these were all in which Shakespeare had had a hand. There was no actual revival until 1854, when Samuel Phelps mounted a successful production laden with banquets, dances, and processions. The first recorded painting from the play predated this staging by two years: Paul Falconer Poole's scene on the deck of the Tyrian ship, when Pericles is roused by the singing of his daughter Marina (RA 1852). Urbain Bouvier's *Marina* was exhibited at the Royal Academy the year after Phelps's production, and Henry Nelson O'Neil's two paintings, one of the same scene that Poole depicted (RA 1869) and the other of Marina at the grave of her nurse (RA 1870), followed at some distance. And that is the complete history of pictures from *Pericles.*

CYMBELINE

Although *Cymbeline* is not often performed today, among playgoers and picture-lovers from the middle of the eighteenth century through the whole Victorian era it was the favorite example of what came to be called Shakespeare's "dark comedies," more than one hundred paintings being drawn from it. After Garrick revived it in 1761, replacing various drastically altered versions that had been current since the Restoration, it was kept in the Drury Lane repertory as long as he remained manager. By happy accident, the revival, so successful that for the next decade the play was performed at least five times each season, coincided with the first art exhibitions in London, and it is conceivable that Garrick immediately recognized the publicity value of having the play represented on their walls. Almost as if part of a campaign, a series of portraits of actors in the roles of Posthumus and Iachimo appeared at the Society of Artists (1762, 1765, 1768). Besides the theatrical portraits, the play was alluded to in landscapes such as one shown in 1763, *A Large Landscape, with a Scene in Shakespear's Cymbeline.* In 1788, William Hodges exhibited at the Royal Academy a similar painting with a more specific allusion: *Landscape, with the Story of Imogen and Pisanio, Taken from Shakespeare's Play of Cymbeline.* At the same time, incidents from the plot were painted without reference either to the theater or to landscape. Edward Penny's *Imogen Discovered in the Cave* (pl. 239) survives at Stratford-on-Avon, and Alexander Runciman's portrayal of Iachimo showing the horrified Posthumus the supposed proof of Imogen's adultery (2.4) (1785) is at the National Gallery of Scotland.

The great majority of the *Cymbeline* pictures executed in the next hundred years dealt with what can only be called the tribulations of Imogen. Aware of the popular appeal inherent in a combination of sexual intrigue and the flight of an injured wife through a storm, artists concentrated on only two sequences of events: the brief, tense scene in which Iachimo invades the sleeping Imogen's bedchamber (2.2) followed by his false

239. Edward Penny, *Imogen Discovered in the Cave* (RA 1770) (Royal Shakespeare Theatre Picture Gallery ©). Unlike Dawe's interpretation of the scene (pl. 100), this one, painted forty years earlier, follows Shakespeare's text, as well as current performances of the play, in disguising Imogen as a youth. Penny was a founding member of the Royal Academy as well as its first professor of painting, and the picture was hung at the Academy's second annual exhibition.

report to Posthumus of what occurred there (2.4), and the succession of scenes (3.4–4.2) in which Imogen, disguised as a page, takes refuge in a cave, is succored by the huntsmen Belarius, Guiderius, and Arviragus, and awakens from a drugged sleep to find beside her the headless body of Cloten, dressed in her husband's clothes.

Some sixteen paintings of Iachimo in Imogen's bedroom are recorded. James Barry painted one and perhaps two versions of Iachimo emerging from the chest in Imogen's chamber. Westall's version for Boydell, of Iachimo standing over her bed, could, except for Iachimo's color, have done double duty for Othello standing over the sleeping Desdemona. The subject provided Charles West Cope with his first painting as a pupil at the Royal Academy schools, "a very poor performance" as he admitted in his *Reminiscences.*[1] For some reason—there seems to have been no especially memorable staging at that moment—there was a burst of paintings from this scene in the years 1834–41, when at least eight were exhibited. F. P. Stephanoff showed *Iachimo Taking the Bracelet from Imogen* in 1834, and William Boxall's study of Imogen for the 1838 edition of *Heath's Gallery* showed her at the moment when she puts down her book and prays herself to sleep, unaware, as presumably some buyers of the elegant annual may have been as well, that Iachimo is in the trunk.

The later sequence of Imogen's adventures afield and in the cave provided subjects for more than twice as many paintings (thirty-seven) as the earlier. Three different artists toward the end of the eighteenth century portrayed Imogen about to enter the cave as the storm rages: John Hoppner and Westall for Boydell, and M. W. Peters for Woodmason's New

240. James Barnes, *The Finding of Imogen* (RA 1874) (Wolverhampton Art Gallery). The figure of the swooning Imogen is a palpable duplication of the one in Dawe's painting (pl. 100), as Dawe's, in turn, was indebted to earlier representations of suffering or dying women in classical art. Comparison of the two pictures offers an easy lesson in the persistence of iconological motifs.

Shakespeare Gallery. Some treatments of the ensuing interior scene were set, as it were, to the music of the duet Guiderius and Arviragus sing, "Fear no more the heat o' the sun."

A few other passages in *Cymbeline* engaged artists from time to time; the trio of huntsmen, for example, were depicted by G. F. Watts (RA 1842) and James Eckford Lauder (RSA 1851). But it was still Imogen who preoccupied the painters. As her presence in two editions of *Heath's Gallery* only two years apart testified—before Boxall, A. E. Chalon had depicted her in the 1836 edition brooding over Belarius's dinner table, set, for better lighting, at the mouth of the cave—she was among their favorite Shakespearean heroines, the very essence of pathos as well as moral strength, a Griselda in Roman Britain. As regularly happened with such paragons, the name became detached from the dramatic character; and Imogen, like her most celebrated Shakespearean sisters, became, as a critic of one such portrait observed, "less Imogen than any devoted wife or fiancée of our own time."[2] There was the occasional difficulty, inherent in disguise plots (cf. *Twelfth Night)*, of maintaining the graphic illusion of masculinity while assuring the spectator that the figure really was a girl. But custom could not stale Imogen's infinite appeal to the gallery-stroller.

THE WINTER'S TALE

The Winter's Tale was among the first Shakespearean plays to attract artists in any number, a fact that can be explained only in part by the popularity of Garrick's abbreviated version of 1756, which shared a double bill in the Drury Lane repertory with his similarly cut version of *The Taming of the Shrew,* renamed *Catherine and Petruchio.* Whatever knowledge the contemporary art lover possessed of the first two acts and most of the third was not acquired in the theater because Garrick, who played Leontes to Mrs. Pritchard's Hermione, totally omitted them, moving many of the best passages found there and elsewhere in the play to the sheep-shearing scene and at the same time interspersing what was left of the original text with execrable additions from his own pen. The play as Shakespeare wrote it—in general—was staged in 1802 by J. P. Kemble, and was one of those Charles Kean selected for his lavish productions in the 1850s. Billed as "an opportunity . . . of reproducing a classical era, and placing before the eyes of the spectator, *tableaux vivants* of the private and public life of the ancient Greeks," Kean's staging featured a curtain-raising feast of Leontes and his guests, followed by a "Pyrrhic Dance by 36 youths in armour" and an elaborate allegorical tableau based on Flaxman's celebrated design of the Shield of Achilles and enhanced by one of the earliest theatrical uses of an electric arc.[1]

The earliest of the sixty-odd paintings from *The Winter's Tale* typified several of the chief uses to which Shakespearean material was put in those early years. Robert Pine's theatrical portrait of Mrs. Pritchard as Hermione was hung at the Society of Artists' first exhibition in 1760, and Reynolds's of Mary Robinson as Perdita (1782) was so famous as to provide that adventurous actress, part-time author, and mistress of the Prince of Wales with a sobriquet that largely replaced her baptismal name. At the same time, *The Winter's Tale* provided characters to be assumed by ladies posing for fancy pictures. An engraving (1781) from a picture ascribed to Zoffany showed the Countess of Derby as Hermione, and in the mid-1780s, Fuseli painted several such fancy pictures of Perdita, including one of her attended by fairies and Ariel, imported from elsewhere in the Shakespearean canon.

The selection of scenes in the Boydell Gallery accurately foreshadowed, for the most part, the subsequent popular taste in *Winter's Tale* pictures. There were seven altogether, including four by Hamilton (pl. 241). Henry Thomson painted the finding of Perdita (pl. 111); but the result was not to Boydell's liking, and the canvas was not engraved. William Hodges's *Antigonus and the Bear* was similarly rejected, Boydell substituting Joseph Wright of Derby's rendering of the storm scene, with Leontes a small figure, arms outstretched, seen against a background of boiling sea and beetling cliffs. The action in act 3, scene 3—Antigonus in the storm and then pursued by the bear, and the finding of Perdita—was one of the most popular Shakespearean subjects in the eighteenth century, despite the fact that it was present only momentarily in Garrick's reworking, where it was sacrificed in favor of the shepherd's and clown's discovery of the castaway Leontes. Between 1771 and 1792, at least ten paintings were derived from the scene.

Two Boydell paintings were of the busy sheep-shearing scene (4.4, more than 820 lines), a natural choice given the popularity of rural festivals as depicted in poems like *The Seasons* and genre paintings by Greuze and Morland. The more noteworthy of the two—the other was by Hamilton—was Wheatley's, a crowded scene of merrymaking. The next noteworthy portrayals were Leslie's pair, painted for John Sheepshanks: *Autolycus* (pl. 68) and *Florizel and Perdita* (pl. 242).

Another Boydell subject, *Leontes Looking at the Statue of Hermione as It Moves and Breathes* (5.3), was painted less often than its strong dramatic quality would lead one to expect. After Hamilton represented it, it was seen only a few times. Not even the popularity of "attitudes" (the drawing-room entertainment of ladies posing as figures in fancy pictures or as

241. William Hamilton, *The Shepherd's Cot* (Boydell's Shakespeare Gallery) (Royal Shakespeare Theatre Picture Gallery ©). This painting shows how Shakespearean subjects could accommodate the late eighteenth-century taste for paintings of pastoral life and rural chivalry. The scene is *The Winter's Tale,* 4. 4 (the sheep-shearing scene), but Perdita's costume is scarcely appropriate for a "low-born lass," and the Gothic chapel is not the equivalent of a shepherd's humble cottage.

242. Charles R. Leslie, *Florizel and Perdita* (RA 1837) (Victoria & Albert Museum, Crown Copyright). Literature supplies an occasion for an exercise in a favorite early Victorian mode, the floral-sentiment painting. Leslie is faithful to the Shakespearean text (*The Winter's Tale,* 4. 4): "Give me those flowers there, Dorcas. Reverend sirs, / For you there's rosemary and rue; these keep / Seeming and savor all the winter long." This is the companion to Leslie's *Autolycus* (pl. 68), which portrays a later moment in the same lengthy scene.

243. Charles R. Leslie, *Hermione* (RA 1856) (Walker Art Gallery, Liverpool). Only a spectator acquainted with *The Winter's Tale* would have recognized this as a *pose plastique,* a popular form of theatrical entertainment in mid-Victorian England—the sculptural version of the *tableau vivant.* The model (said to have been Mrs. Charles Kean) assumes the role of a woman who is herself posing—as a statue.

celebrated statues, à la Lady Hamilton)* or, subsequently, *poses plastiques* on the stage, stimulated the production of pictures showing the Shakespearean archetype of living statuary. The last in the slender series was Leslie's (pl. 243). The *Saturday Review* was waspish:

> Mr. Leslie must be very bold, or very blind, to provoke a recurrence to Shakspeare's description of Hermione as an explanation of his picture; for many of the lines read excellently as satirical criticism on the wooden form before us. Would Paulina have prepared us "to see the life as lively mocked as ever still sleep mocked death," if she had only to show this white, uninteresting woman—more like a plaster cast than a marble statue, leaning on a stage imitation pedestal, with only three fingers to one of her hands? Or would Leontes have cried, in fixed amazement, "O royal piece! there's magic in thy majesty"? Mr. Leslie would have been kinder, and much wiser, never to have drawn the curtain.[2]

The most sensible comment was the *Literary Gazette*'s: "A representation of a lady standing so as to look like a statue, by the nature of the case excludes all expression, and leaves nothing to be admired but technical skill."[3]

THE TEMPEST

Two leading qualities of *The Tempest* recommended it to theatrical producers and painters: its opportunities for music and spectacle. The musical allusions in the text as well as the actual songs were responsible for the play's being turned into an opera as early as 1674, when Henry Purcell added a score to the adaptation of Shakespeare's drama written some years earlier by John Dryden and Sir William D'Avenant. Garrick had a frequently revived operatic version in his Drury Lane repertory, and in 1821 Macready played Prospero in still another pseudo-opera. Meanwhile, the original comedy was occasionally revived, with uneven success. It was only in 1838, when Macready staged it, that Shakespeare finally routed Dryden and D'Avenant. As theatrical technology improved, *The Tempest,* in whatever form, was a popular vehicle for showing off the latest lighting devices and stage effects. The apogee of the "spectacular" *Tempest* was reached in 1857, when Charles Kean cut large slices from the text to make room for a lavish display of theatrical beauty and wizardry. It was no accident that the highlights of the production, which received rave notices and ran for eighty-seven nights, corresponded with the subjects most favored by the painters of the period. Indeed, one might say that in this extravaganza of shipwrecks, pageantry, banquets, "visions," and transformation scenes, replete with animated scenery and props, lighting tricks, fountains, dancing naiads, fauns and satyrs, Kean moved the walls of the annual exhibitions to the Princess' Theatre.[1] His stage pictures were, in effect, a montage of the scores of *Tempest* scenes already painted (some 200 in all are recorded). And, of course, those produced after that time doubtless incorporated effects in turn from Kean's stage.

Eighteenth-century artists' strong interest in the play is nicely epitomized by a picture (1784) by two Scottish artists, Alexander Runciman and John Brown, a conversation piece in the most literal sense, since it showed them "in dispute regarding a passage in Shakespeare's *Tempest.*" Fifty years earlier, Hogarth had painted Miranda, Prospero, and Ferdinand attended by the supernatural creatures of the piece, the sprite Ariel and the anthropoid monster Caliban (pl. 172). One of Hayman's decorations in the Prince's Pavilion at Vauxhall Gardens was the scene in which Miranda is startled by the sight of Ferdinand. About 1775, Romney

*This was one of the "borrowed attitudes" performed by Gwendolen Harleth in George Eliot's *Daniel Deronda*. She modeled her pose as Hermione after Mrs. Siddons's.

244. Unknown artist, *Prospero, Miranda, and Ariel* (ca. 1770–90) (Yale Center for British Art, Paul Mellon Fund). The moment in *The Tempest,* act 1, scene 2, when Prospero summons Ariel as Miranda sleeps. "The unknown artist displays a knowledge of antique statues in Rome: the pose of Miranda is probably based on that of the abandoned Ariadne, Prospero on the Apollo Belvedere, and Ariel on the Capitoline Venus" (Ashton [1], p. 2).

painted a passage in act 1, scene 2, that Allan Cunningham, who saw the picture many years later, described in terms applicable to innumerable renditions of the same scene in years to come: "She gazes with admiration and growing tenderness on Ferdinand; her hair is loosely braided, but is too redundant to be restrained, and floats on the air; the gentle Ariel is in his ministry near, and a troop of shadowy nymphs are dancing on the 'yellow sands.' "[2] Romney was already at work on another *Tempest* scene when he attended the dinner at Josiah Boydell's that led to the founding of the Shakespeare Gallery. "The original picture," wrote Cunningham, "represented Prospero, Miranda, and Caliban, with a shipwreck in the background. Some pretender to taste declared the composition was not strictly historical [i.e., did not conform to the strict rules of academic painting], as it consisted only of three figures."[3] It was in a dutifully recomposed form that the picture was added to the Boydell Gallery. Only one fragment survives, the head of Prospero.

The Boydell Gallery had seven subjects from *The Tempest,* a number reached by only five other plays. Fuseli's contribution was *The Enchanted Isle: Before the Cell of Prospero,* and Joseph Wright's was from act 4, scene 1, with Ferdinand, Miranda, and Prospero in the cell, Caliban, Stephano, and Trinculo at a distance outside the mouth of the cave, and, glowing at the top of the composition, the masque of Iris, Ceres, Juno, and the Nymphs. Shakespeare's locale is "the still-vexed Bermoothes," presumably in Tudor times; but, like Fuseli, Wright could not have cared less about period authenticity: Ferdinand was in Van Dyck costume and Miranda in contemporary dress.

Among the various sources of the play's appeal for artists and their patrons in a period that sought to have the best of both the neoclassic and Romantic worlds were the fairy element and the perennial charm of innocent young love, especially love at first sight; Ferdinand and Miranda were Romeo and Juliet on an island, with the bonus of a happy ending. Prospero embodied two themes favored in the painting of the time, the

245. Frederick R. Pickersgill, *Prospero and Miranda* (undated) (Walker Art Gallery, Liverpool). The artist was one of a cluster of related Pickersgills who were well known in their time as painters of narrative and genre subjects, including many from literature; none have benefited much from the recent revaluation of their school. The picture may date from the early sixties, when Pickersgill exhibited two other *Tempest* paintings at the Royal Academy.

246. Henry Thomson, *Prospero and Miranda* (RA 1803) (Petworth House). A typical neoclassic treatment of Shakespearean fancy, this was Thomson's Royal Academy diploma picture.

magician (benign rather than malevolent) and that of domestic instruction, in this case a concerned father serving as moral guide and tutor to a motherless girl. While Caliban catered to the occasional taste for the Fuselian grotesque,* the play was replete with moments that obliged the more pervasive taste for graphic "prettiness": scenes by moonlit water, the suggestion of the musical qualities of the text and action through overtly rhythmical compositions, the portrayal of figures in the airy motions of dancing and floating, the expression of a pure *joie de vivre.*

In short, *The Tempest* was treasured as a prime source of "poetical" subjects, and critics vied with one another to couch their appreciation in appropriately florid terms. This is a writer in the *Gentleman's Magazine* praising William Hilton's *Miranda* (1828):

> Shakespeare's Miranda!—The lovely daughter of the instigator of *The Tempest,* and the tender and soothing love of Ferdinand, is one of the most perfectly innocent and artlessly amiable characters that were ever sketched. She is such as we might imagine the beauteous Eve in the garden of Eden, the purest specimen of her sex. And the scene chosen by Hilton for exhibiting his powers, is the most effective in this drama, some of the finest touches of nature bursting out in the language softly flowing to the heart, whose generous impulses it irrigates and cherishes."[4]

Miranda was among the favorite heroines of Shakespearean art. Reynolds painted Mrs. Tollemache in the role in 1774, and many years later the actress Priscilla Horton posed for Maclise (pl. 54). As usual with these heroines, many pictures bearing Miranda's name were, like John William Waterhouse's later in the century, nothing more than academic figure studies.

From Hogarth's treatment onward, painters used *Tempest* subjects to illustrate elementary philosophical oppositions: the flesh and the spirit,

*In 1793, Lawrence exhibited *Prospero Raising the Storm* at the Royal Academy; but the resemblance between it and Fuseli's drawing of *Macbeth, the Cauldron Sinking,* exhibited at the same time, was so striking that Lawrence subsequently painted out the picture and frugally reused the canvas for his portrait of John Philip Kemble as Rolla in Sheridan's adaptation of Kotzebue's *Pizarro.*

247. Sir Joseph Noel Paton, *Caliban* (dated 1868) (Glasgow Art Gallery and Museum). Although he often appeared in compositions that included Prospero, Miranda, and Ariel, Caliban was seldom portrayed as a single figure—understandably, because whereas Ariel could grace every home, Shakespeare's half man-half beast would have been welcome, as decoration at least, in few. This picture was equipped with a quotation from *The Tempest,* but it might well have served to illustrate the speaker in Browning's "Caliban upon Setebos," published four years earlier.

the ugly and the beautiful, youth and age, good and evil. William Bell Scott thus interpreted his brother David's design in his *Ariel and Caliban* (pl. 72): "The two impersonations . . . represent as it were, the two poles of human nature; the ascending and descending forces of mind and matter. Caliban, the brown and hairy slave, half-brute half-man, has crawled from the capture of a green snake, which he drags by the head. Ariel, long and thin, like a swift bird, touches the monster's forehead with his heel, at the same time striking into the air those sweet sounds that give delight and hurt not."[5]

But this universally popular subject in the hands of a Pre-Raphaelite painter called forth a very different response from the critical press. Millais's *Ferdinand Lured by Ariel* (pl. 248), the most celebrated of all *Tempest* illustrations, was as roughly handled as Turner's *Shylock and Jessica* had been. The *Athenaeum:* "a scene built on the contrivances of the stage manager, but with very bad success."[6] The *Times:* "We do not want to see Ariel and the spirits of the Enchanted Isle in the attitudes and shapes of green goblins, or the gallant Ferdinand twisted like a posture-maker by Albert Dürer."[7] The *Examiner:* "[Ferdinand is] bilious and dyspeptic . . . the artist has portrayed Ariel with the lineaments of Caliban."[8]

Of all the scenes in Shakespeare's plays, the first major one in *The Tempest* (1.2, following the brief one of the shipwreck) was by a considerable margin the most often pictured. It figured directly or indirectly (by the use of mottoes) in at least fifty pictures, a total that probably would be much larger if the many paintings bearing such indeterminate titles as *Miranda,* or *Prospero and Miranda,* or *Prospero and Ariel,* could be identified more specifically and some attributed to one or another of the half-dozen movements that constitute the 500-line scene. All of these were painted at one time or another, some repeatedly, so that if enough survived they might, like pictures from *Macbeth* act 2, scene 2, be assembled into a continuous narrative montage representing the entire scene from beginning to end. The most painted passage was that in which the invisible Ariel marks Ferdinand's entrance by singing

248. John Everett Millais, *Ferdinand Lured by Ariel* (RA 1850) (Walker Art Gallery, Liverpool). A sketch for the exhibited picture. Ariel (invisible in Shakespeare's text, as are the "lost fellows" the artist has supplied as accompanists) sings "Full fathom five thy father lies" (*The Tempest,* 1. 2). The artist F. G. Stephens modeled for Ferdinand.

249. Paul Falconer Poole, *Scene from "The Tempest"* (dated 1856) (Forbes Magazine Collection). Although shipwrecks were a generic subject for many years, this scene was seldom painted with the elaboration and almost too obvious attention to compositional effect that characterize Poole's version.

Come unto these yellow sands,
  And then take hands.
Curtsied when you have and kissed,
  The wild waves whist,
Foot it featly here and there;
And, sweet sprites, the burden bear.
Hark, Hark!

"Come unto these yellow sands" was an open invitation to artists to paint elaborate stylized arrangements of spirits, the Graces, nymphs, sylphs, fairies (the breeds were both indistinguishable and interchangeable) dancing by the seaside—a perfect way to lighten the drawing rooms in prosaic suburban villas with iridescent colors and compositional rhythms that were almost audible. In such an unimpeachable literary context, bevies of sleek female nudes could be introduced without qualm, and they were. Stothard, who said that Purcell's air to the words "was in my head all the time" as he painted, did several versions of the song.[9] Richard Dadd exhibited his own, first at the Royal Academy in 1842 and the next year at Liverpool, under the title *Fairies Holding their Revels on the Sea Shore by Night.*

The various phases of the final scene (5.1) were the subjects of a dozen or more paintings. Henry Singleton and Henry Howard depicted Prospero releasing Ariel from the cloven pine; Singleton also illustrated, as did Fuseli, the familiar line from Ariel's song, "On the bat's back I do fly"; and several artists portrayed the moment when Prospero discovers Ferdinand and Miranda playing chess. Francis Wheatley, who painted it for Boydell, took the permissible liberty of showing the lovers *not* playing chess. The chessboard indeed is present, but only as a mute witness to Ferdinand's bending over Miranda and holding her hand.

THE POETRY

Shakespeare's nondramatic works were seldom represented in art. Only four paintings from *Venus and Adonis* are recorded, all within the period 1805-65. Only one picture bore an explicit reference to the much-disputed sonnets, William Frost's *Disarming of Cupid* (pl. 250). The Dark Lady and other problematic aspects of the sonnets were beyond the ken and concern of the artists.

250. William E. Frost, *The Disarming of Cupid* (RA 1850) (Royal Collection, Copyright Reserved). The only recorded painting derived from a Shakespeare sonnet (No. 154):

> The little Love-god, lying once asleep,
> Laid by his side his heart-inflaming brand,
> Whilst many nymphs that vowed chaste life to keep
> Came tripping by. . . .

Frost, a *protégé* of Etty, painted the picture on commission from Prince Albert.

PART THREE

THE REST OF THE GALLERY

INTRODUCTION

Some thirty English writers were represented in painting often enough for their iconographical records to be a more or less significant part of their reputation as it developed through the years.* The following summaries of their "art histories," arranged chronologically by author but without strict attention to their birth dates, will make increasingly apparent what has already been shown in connection with individual plays of Shakespeare: though a clear correlation can often be perceived between the popular and/or critical reputation and the artistic fortunes of a given work or author, equally often the two tendencies seem to have gone their independent ways.

The correlation is evident in the case of Thomson, whose long-sustained popularity with artists and public, as reflected in the number of paintings exhibited, diminished at the very time (after 1850) that that other measure of popularity, the number of new editions published, also declined. But in other instances, a similarly neat matching of the two curves was prevented by various factors—shifting taste in art (which did not necessarily involve a similar shift in literary opinion), the varying ways in which the *content* of a literary work was embraced or rejected by the public irrespective of its author's critical status, and the discrepancy between a work's standing with the reading public and its critical reputation. Gray's popularity in art proceeded more or less independently of his fame as a poet, because the two subjects that were primarily derived from his poetry, those relating to the legend of the Welsh bard and the mood captured in the "Elegy in a Country Churchyard," were staples in the painting of the time, and it just happened that Gray had written the most familiar expressions of them. The fact that most such paintings were linked with Gray did not necessarily mean that Gray himself was still widely read.

The comparative history of Sterne's popular and critical reputation and his appearance in Victorian art represents another kind of discrepancy. Although his literary stock remained fairly high in the wake of the Romantic critics' enthusiasm for him, the spreading nervousness about his "indecency" combined with revelations of his untidy private life to reduce his readership. Thus his acceptability in art theoretically was contingent on at least two opposing forces. The situation was complicated by the fact that Sterne's two books, *Tristram Shandy* and *A Sentimental Journey*, had quite different qualities that in the Victorians' estimate made one unacceptable and the other welcome. Their respective fortunes in art clearly reflect those differences.

Similar disjunctions can be noticed in the exhibition records of Crabbe, Moore, and four of the five major Romantic poets. (The sixth, Blake, was almost never represented, for two obvious reasons—he was his own illustrator, his poems being securely locked into his engravings, and they were in any event virtually unknown to the public.) The popularity and critical standing each volume achieved during, or shortly after, the poet's lifetime seems to have had little if anything to do with its use, or neglect, by artists. Byron, incomparably the most popular of the Romantics, is the exception. Subjects from his poems were painted almost as soon as the poems were issued, and—most important—once he was established as a

*For additional references to the authors represented in this part, as well as to those who are not, see the Index.

source of pictures, his popularity in art proceeded independently of his subsequent literary reputation. When the reaction set in, in the 1830s, the production of pictures was unaffected.

Tennyson approached his first popularity as a source of art at the same time that his critical stature was being established, in the 1840s. In the next decade, reflecting the great success of *In Memoriam* (1850), more and more paintings from his earlier poems were exhibited. His critical reputation began to wane in the late 1860s, but he continued to be popular with artists, who knew very well what the wide public, who remained loyal to the laureate, wanted.

Several isolated episodes in the history of literary pictures involve poets who cannot, by any stretch of the imagination, be included among those who count. They are tiny pockets of ephemeral interest, small anterooms to the main gallery, that in their respective eccentric ways illustrate the conjunction of art and literature and the vicissitudes and vagaries of literary fame. Two typical ones may be cited. In the late eighteenth and early nineteenth centuries, as a minor but significant symptom of the Romantic temper (back to Simplicity, in poets' lives as in their poetry), attention was repeatedly directed to poets with humble origins. At the very turn of the century, the sentimental favorite among these was Robert Bloomfield, born in 1766, a poor London shoemaker and subsequently a maker of Aeolian harps, the musical symbol of Romanticism. Bloomfield wrote in 1798 (the year Wordsworth's and Coleridge's *Lyrical Ballads* appeared) and published two years later a book of poems called *The Farmer's Boy.* The strong echoes the volume contained of Thomson's *Seasons*—still, at that time, one of the most popular poems in existence—doubtless helped its fortunes. Set in Suffolk, the locale also of Crabbe's poetry, *The Farmer's Boy* celebrated rural life just as *The Village* stressed its hardships. The book went through nine editions the first six years, and fourteen in Bloomfield's lifetime.[1]

"As a painter of simple natural scenery, and of the still life of the country," wrote Hazlitt, "few writers have more undeniable and assuming pretensions than the ingenious and self-taught poet."[2] He became something of a celebrity, in token whereof Hoppner painted his portrait. There was, in fact, a Bloomfield fad, offering painters a chance to depict Thomsonian rural subjects with a fresh and, for the moment, well-known literary name attached. Most Bloomfield paintings, then and later, came from *The Farmer's Boy,* especially from the two poems "Richard and Kate" and "Walter and Jane." As early as 1802, a picture called *Richard and Kate, or Fair Day,* was shown at the Royal Academy. Sir George Beaumont painted *A Moonlight, from Bloomfield's Farmer's Boy,* which he showed to Joseph Farington in 1804.[3] Most paintings seem to have been closest in subject and treatment to Morland's genre pictures of rural life. Julius Caesar Ibbetson's *A Farm Yard* (RA 1806), for example, is said by his biographer to have been a scene on a Fellside farm, in which "the young countryman in his smock-frock is seated on a wheelbarrow basking in the sunshine, his sole occupation at the moment is to be a farmer's boy—'meek, fatherless, and poor'."[4] Two of Constable's paintings (*Ploughing Scene in Suffolk,* better known as *Dedham Vale* [RA 1814], and *A Harvest Field* [BI 1817]) were accompanied by quotations from Bloomfield.

The year the poet died (1823), the British Institution exhibited one of the several recorded paintings representing scenes in Bloomfield's life, descriptively catalogued as *View of Mr. Austen's Farm at Sapiston in Norfolk,* "where Bloomfield the Poet was first employed as a farmer's boy; the upper end window was that of his first sleeping room." Except for this tangentially related picture, there was a hiatus in Bloomfield art until 1839, when a picture of his grave was shown. Then, for mysterious reasons, the fashion revived, to persist as late as 1871 (*Lambs at Play,* at the Royal Academy) and even 1879 (*Young Poet Robert Bloomfield,* at the Society of British Artists). In this span of years, there were three illustrated editions, one with designs by the well-known artist Birket Foster (1845) and another (1871) that joined Bloomfield's poems with those of another sentimentally remembered poet from the beginning of the century, Henry Kirke White.* Altogether, some twenty paintings of actual subjects from Bloomfield's poetry and life are recorded, and, in addition, at least as many rural genre scenes that simply bore a quotation from *The Farmer's Boy* or one of the later collections. Three-quarters of the latter pictures dated from the time of his revived fame, 1839–74. The artistic record is witness enough that, however far Bloomfield disappeared into critical oblivion, his name still meant something to picture-buyers.

The case of paintings from *The Social Day* is equally a curiosity, but of art history only, since its author's protracted campaign to storm the heights of Parnassus utterly failed. Peter Coxe (?–1844) was a London art auctioneer and dealer who prospered in the early years of the nineteenth century when a number of great collections, including those of Sir William Hamilton and the French émigrés Charles Alexandre de Calonne and the Duke of Orleans, came onto the market. He sold off Macklin's Gallery in 1800–1801 and Loutherbourg's collection after that artist's death in 1812, and subsequently retired with a modest fortune. Coxe was a fairly preposterous figure, a persistent nuisance, and, worst of all, an aspiring poet. He is adequately sketched in David Wilkie's diary entry for 6 November 1808, when the young Scots artist had been in London for three years:

> Had a call from Lord Mulgrave; after he went away came Peter Coxe, who began reading to me part of a work which he had in the press against Napoleon; but was interrupted by Lord Mulgrave, who brought in his lady to look at the picture of *The Cut Finger;* his lordship went away, and I heard the remainder of the work read; we then walked out, and observing a house to let in one of the streets, we went in to inquire about it, when Mr. Coxe pulled out his MS, and began to read it to the woman who had the house in keeping. I left him, and took a look at the Elgin marbles.[5]

Coxe was also a sore trial to John Constable and his exasperated wife. " . . . That great bore Peter Cox was here nearly an hour on Saturday reading the paper & talking of himself," Mrs. Constable wrote her absent husband from their home in Charlotte Street in 1823. "I hope you will not admit him so often into your painting room." Some months later, in June 1824, Constable reported to his wife, on holiday at Brighton, that

> at tea time Peter Coxe called. Johnny [their servant] said I was at Brighton, still he came in—& we heard him talking loud in the painting room. Fisher got up and locked the parlor door. Just as Peter was going & John was letting him out, Caroline and Miss [name omitted] her friend rapped at the door—Johnny looked confused but said quite brisk, pray ladies walk in. Peter was off—and they came in.

On the next Sunday but one, "Mr. Coxe called after church—wanted to

*Kirke White (1785–1806), the son of a butcher, wrote poems abounding in evangelical piety. He died in his first year at Cambridge, where he had gone on a scholarship. A year after his death, Southey published his *Remains,* which went into a number of editions. Among the poems was an "Ode Addressed to H. Fuseli, Esq., R.A., on seeing Engravings from his designs," in which White twice addressed the artist as "Mighty Magician!" and described him also as "Genius of Horror and romantic awe, / Whose eye explores the secrets of the deep, / Whose power can bid the rebel fluids creep, / Can force the inmost soul to own its law." A handful of paintings memorialized White's brief life.

dine with me. I told him my hour was too early for him—he called for bread & butter—all went off smooth."[6]*

Unfortunately, Coxe had long harbored an ambition, very much like that of Samuel Rogers some years later, to publish his poetry in a sumptuous volume illustrated by the day's most popular artists. As early as 1814, he was soliciting subscriptions for a poem to be called *The Social Day*. For various reasons, which Coxe took pains to describe to his anxious patrons from the King on down, the poem did not appear until 1823. Housed in a portly quarto, it turned out to be a long-winded, rambling relic of a bygone fashion, its four cantos written in halting but indomitable couplets, with all the cliché baggage inherited from the age of Pope—personifications, classical allusions, periphrasis, and dusty wit, plus the usual burden of lengthy footnote commentary and irrelevant addenda. Much of the verse was on a marginally higher level than a couplet in the last canto: "Woman! superior gift of Heaven! / Thou mak'st the road of life run even." In the manner of Thomson and other eighteenth-century poets of high and low degree who were inspired by the sisterhood of the arts, Coxe combined a tribute to a living artist with an allusion to an earlier one:

> Constable, to feeling true,
> Paints Nature's freshness and her hue,
> Studious, like Hobbima, to give,
> And bid the rural landscape live.

While *The Social Day* was hanging fire, its promised appearance was amply publicized in the yearly art exhibitions. In 1817–19 alone, the Royal Academy exhibitions included at least six paintings commissioned as illustrations (the published volume would contain thirty-two).

One of these was by Wilkie himself (*The Broken China Jar, or The Ghost Laid,* 1816); two were by the animal painter Abraham Cooper (*The Deserted Child Found,* 1816; *The Turnpike Gate,* 1819); two more by Cooper's colleague in the animal line, James Ward (*The Descent of the Swan Seeking His Own Element, an Allegory,* and *The Favourite Spaniel Watching the Tomb of Her Deceased Mistress,* both 1817); and a sixth by a specialist in battle scenes, George Jones (*A Domestic Party at Cards,* 1817).† Another contribution, not exhibited until 1832, was Constable's watercolor of *Jaques and the Wounded Stag,* which Coxe had chosen from the artist's portfolio when they met at Salisbury twenty years earlier. Still another illustration, by Stothard, seems not to have been shown until a loan exhibition at the British Institution in 1894. There is no record of anyone's actually reading *The Social Day*.

*Peter Coxe had the additional distinction of being the brother of Archdeacon William Coxe, whom Constable met while visiting the Fishers at Salisbury in 1812. The archdeacon, a prebendary in that Trollopian cathedral, was also a dedicated gourmand. "Mr. Coxe," wrote Farington, "is a singular man in many respects: very little attention to others in His manners, and remarkable for His love of good eating. On His leaving Stourhead, Sir Richard Hoare said 'He is gone away well filled, and I had given Him venison every day'" (Farington [2], 7:70–71 [17 December 1811]). In 1828, Archdeacon Fisher wrote Constable, "Poor Coxe . . . is no more. He died of old age, unable to contend with two helps of Salmon & lobster sauce, washed down with large drafts of Perry [fermented pear juice]" (Constable, 6:237).

†Jones once had a substantial reputation as a painter, but his present-day fame resides in his being the subject of a celebrated anecdote. He took pride, frequently expressed, in his having (he said) once been mistaken for the Duke of Wellington. Upon hearing this, the Duke observed that it was strange, but he had never been mistaken for Mr. Jones.

THE MIDDLE AGES

CHAUCER

The audience for Chaucer's poetry was limited in the eighteenth and nineteenth centuries, mainly because of the language difficulty, although several efforts were made to popularize a judicious selection of *The Canterbury Tales* by prose paraphrases and, where required, downright bowdlerization. Whereas thousands of pictures were painted from Shakespeare, Milton, and Spenser, their forerunner, "the poet of the dawn," was only sparsely represented in gallery art.

The history painter John Hamilton Mortimer drew nine illustrations of Chaucer before his death in 1779, and in the ensuing two decades, at least two of the major book illustrators tried their hands: Stothard with fourteen frontispieces for the Chaucer volumes of Bell's multivolume set of *Poets of Great Britain* (1782–83), and William Hamilton with two scenes from the Knight's Tale, the departure for the combat and the death of Arcite, for Macklin's Poet's Gallery. Virtually the only paintings from Chaucer seen at the annual exhibitions before the end of the eighteenth century were two by John Francis Rigaud from the Clerk's Tale (RA 1785) and two by Richard Westall of an unidentified subject from the Wife of Bath's Tale (RA 1785, 1788).

It was not until 1807 that a major painting from Chaucer appeared. Stothard's procession of the Canterbury pilgrims (pl. 251), first shown in London at a perfumer's shop in the Strand, was the art sensation of the year; and subsequently it became the first painting to be toured through the provinces and Scotland as a public exhibition, admission one shilling. The engraving by Luigi Schiavonetti and James Heath was said in 1851 to have had the largest sale of any print down to that time.[1] Stothard painted three replicas, including one for Samuel Rogers; and Blake painted and engraved his own version of the subject, the coincidence leading to a bitter squabble between Blake and Stothard's publisher, Robert Cromek, the fine points of which are still being argued today. The enduring fame of Stothard's picture, if not Blake's, encouraged the production of at least eight pictures of the pilgrims down to 1892. In 1875, Henry Stacy Marks exhibited at the Royal Academy watercolor designs for two huge decora-

251. Thomas Stothard, *The Canterbury Pilgrims* (1807) (Tate Gallery, London). Thanks to the wide circulation of the engraving made of it, this was one of the most famous of all literary pictures. Not the least of its attractions was the supposed authenticity of the armor, costumes, and accessories. Stothard was said to have ransacked manuscripts from Chaucer's time in the British Museum and studied many monuments and funeral effigies in his quest for historical accuracy.

tions of the Canterbury Pilgrims that the Duke of Westminster had commissioned for the saloon at Eaton Hall, Cheshire—a project that required four years to complete.

Chaucer of course figured in the Pre-Raphaelites' fascination with the Middle Ages. As a reviewer of one of Arthur Hughes's pictures in 1859 remarked, "the P.R.B.'s all read Chaucer, or at least quote him."[2] Ford Madox Brown made him the central figure in his "love-offering to my favorite poets" (pl. 121). They did not often illustrate him, however. In 1850, Millais began, but did not finish, a picture of the pilgrims. The one devotee who memorably translated Chaucer into Pre-Raphaelite image-language was Burne-Jones, whose first work in oil (1858) was a scene from the Prioress's Tale painted on a seven-foot-high wardrobe, designed by Philip Webb, which was presented to William and Jane Morris as a wedding gift and is now in the Victoria and Albert Museum. The languorous spirit of his Chaucer interpretations possibly affected the pace of Burne-Jones's subsequent production. He began an easel picture from the Prioress's Tale in 1869 and finished it in 1898, and his painting *Love and the Pilgrim,* from *The Romaunt of the Rose,* which Chaucer claimed to have written (modern scholarship holds that he only translated a part), took twenty years to complete (pl. 168). When it was ready, in 1896, the artist dedicated it to Swinburne.

The only subject in *The Canterbury Tales* that artists repeatedly took up was the Boccaccian tale of the patient Griselda as told by the Clerk. Griselda was a familiar Victorian type-figure, the epitome of long-suffering wifehood.[3] Allusions to her abound in novels of the time, and she and her latter-day counterparts were the actual subject of novels and poems from Maria Edgeworth's *The Modern Griselda* (1804) to Edwin Arnold's *Griselda: A Tragedy* (1856). Some twenty versions of several scenes of the story are recorded. Exactly at the midpoint of the century, there was a spate of Griselda pictures, touched off, it may be, by Charles West Cope's study of Griselda's first trial that was entered in the competition for the Westminster frescoes and subsequently was shown at the Royal Academy in 1849. Two years later, Cope exhibited *The Marquis of Saluce Marries Griselda,* which he sold to the engineer I. K. Brunel. Two other Griselda pictures were shown at the Academy in 1850, Alfred Elmore's and Richard Redgrave's, and in the same year Holman Hunt and Frederic Stephens were at work on their special Pre-Raphaelite interpretations. No more is heard of Hunt's, but Stephens completed at least one, which he sent to the Royal Academy under an assumed name, only to have it rejected. This may or may not have been the canvas now in the Tate Gallery (pl. 252). Griselda occasionally joined the gallery of Keepsake beauties (pl. 55), her name being applied particularly to girls holding water pitchers.

252. Frederic George Stephens, *The Proposal (The Marquis and Griselda)* (1850?) (Tate Gallery, London). Although Chaucer does not specifically present the scene of the Marquis's proposal, Stephens's portrayal is faithful enough to the humble circumstances of Griselda and her father as described in the Clerk's Tale. Another subject he sketched at the time was Griselda's parting from her child.

There was a mere scattering of other subjects from the Chaucerian canon. Fuseli painted *The Knight Finds the Hag Transformed into a Beautiful Young Wife,* from the Wife of Bath's Tale (pl. 253), and at about the same time (1812), Stothard showed at the Royal Academy his *Canace with the Enchanted Ring* from the Squire's Tale, a picture sufficiently described by the *Examiner:*

> Poetry and enchantment to the eye and the imagination. They feast on the feminine softness, vivacity, and attractive graces of the young females, and the lofty bower that luxurious branches, and the rich crimson coloured and declin-

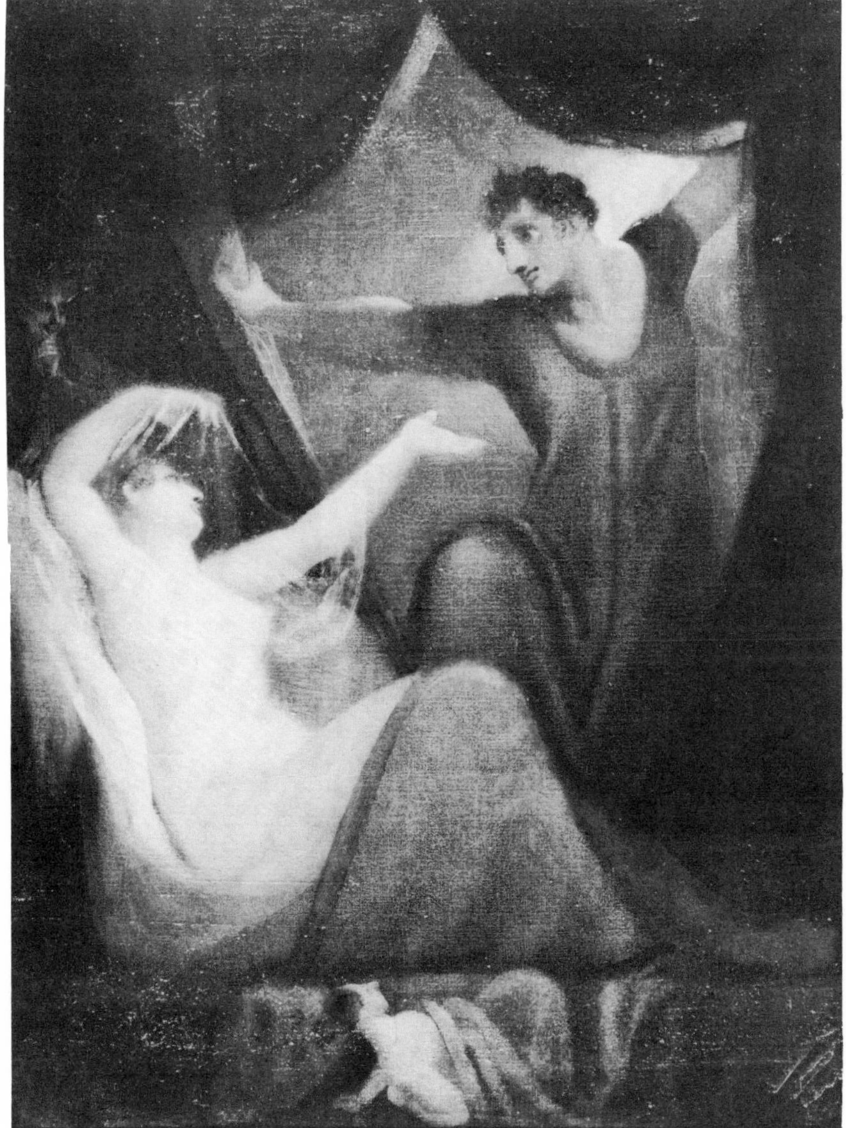

253. Henry Fuseli, *The Knight Finds the Hag Transformed into a Beautiful Young Wife* (before 1812) (Petworth House). The Wife of Bath's Tale gave Fuseli the choice of painting a hag or a beautiful woman. He could, and did, depict believable hags; he was not so expert a painter of beautiful women. On the evidence of this picture, the magical transformation fell short of complete success.

> ing sun, peeping through an interstice of the thick enclosure, as if gazing with curious and delighted eye on the rare beauties of the bower and its lovely tenants.[4]

This was the free Romantic spirit in which Chaucerian subjects were regularly treated. As typical products of the Victorian urge to make the most (if not more) of the "poetical" materials found in literary sources, none of these paintings had any apparent distinction.

MALORY AND ARTHURIAN LEGEND

Unlike two other major sources of literary art, Shakespeare's dramas and *Paradise Lost,* that had engaged painters since the 1730s, the accreted body of stories about King Arthur and the knights of the Round Table became subjects for pictures only about the middle of the nineteenth century. Until that time, they had figured sporadically in literature but never in ways that attracted artists.[1] Five editions of Sir Thomas Malory's

Le Morte Darthur Reduced into Englysshe, first printed by Caxton in 1485, had kept the Arthurian narratives alive through the English Renaissance. Spenser conceived of Prince Arthur, the hero of *The Faerie Queene,* as a Tudor-style version of Malory's figure; but his narrative never advanced beyond the knight's chivalric education, which in Malory prepared him for his mature years as sovereign of Camelot. As a young, ambitious poet, Milton considered writing an English nationalistic epic on the Arthurian theme; but political considerations intervened, and he abandoned the project in favor of a Christian epic. Dryden too, as Sir Walter Scott was to write, would have "raised the table Round again, / But that a ribald King and Court / Bade him toil on, to make them sport." Since no more editions of the *Morte Darthur* were published after 1634, people knew of King Arthur, if they knew of him at all, by way of Dryden's and Purcell's dramatic opera bearing his name (1691).

The Arthurian legend participated only faintly in the general revival of interest in the Middle Ages that accompanied the Romantic movement in literature. Southey recalled that Malory's book, in an old edition, had been "my delight since I was a school-boy"; and Scott praised Malory and his stories of Morgana's House, the Chapel Perilous, and "Sangreal's holy quest" in the introduction to the first canto of *Marmion.* Both men planned editions of Malory to bring his collection to a wider audience, but only Southey's materialized, in the form of a handsome four-volume set entitled *The Byrth, Lyf, and Actes of King Arthur* (1817). Members of three successive generations of poets, Wordsworth, Keats, and Tennyson, read this edition or the two less expensive ones published simultaneously by two different firms the previous year. Yet, apart from Scott's poem *The Bridal of Triermaine* (1813), which took "Lyulph's Tale" from Malory, Wordsworth's allegorical fantasy "The Egyptian Maid" ("The Romance of the Water Lily") (1835), which introduced names and persons from Malory, and, most important, Tennyson's short poems, "The Lady of Shalott" (1832) and "Morte D'Arthur" (1842), in contemporary English poetry no serious use still was made of Arthurian material. Instead, it reached the public through parodies and burlesques such as John Hookham Frere's *King Arthur and the Round Table* (1817) and Thomas Love Peacock's *The Misfortunes of Elphin* (1829). Popular interest in the legend was fed also in the theater through adaptations of the Arthurian part of *The Bridal of Triermain,* notably Isaac Pocock's Christmas extravaganza, *King Arthur and the Knights of the Round Table* (Drury Lane 1834), which starred Ducrow's famous troupe of trained horses.

None of this interest, however, was reflected in the art exhibitions. The history painters had long since taken to their collective bosom the Middle Ages as represented, for instance, in Shakespeare's history plays; but the one king who was conspicuously absent from their canvases was Arthur, the much earlier monarch who hovered in the shadowy realm where history dissolved into myth. As late as the 1840s, only a few paintings from any literary source portrayed incidents from the legend. R. R. McIan's *King Mark of Cornwall and His Retinue Discover Queen Ysolt and Sir Tristrem in the Cave* (Royal Scottish Academy, 1840) and William Bell Scott's *King Arthur Carried from the Battlefield to the Land of Enchantment* (RA 1847) represented no discernible trend.*

*John Martin's *Arthur and Aegle in the Happy Valley* (pl. 350) depicted a scene from a pseudo-Arthurian poem, Bulwer-Lytton's *King Arthur* (see below, under Bulwer-Lytton).

But a trend nevertheless was in the making. As we saw in chapter 8, from 1847 to 1854 William Dyce painted a series of allegorical frescoes, their subjects taken from Malory, in the Queen's Robing Room in the new Houses of Parliament. In 1855, an Oxford undergraduate, Edward Burne-Jones, discovered a copy of Southey's edition of *Le Morte Darthur* in a bookshop. Unable to afford it, he read it from day to day in the shop, placating the owner by buying a cheap book now and then. When he shared his delight with his wealthy fellow student William Morris, however, Morris at once bought the book and they took it with them to read during the long vacation. "With Edward," wrote Burne-Jones's widow, "it became literally a part of himself. Its strength and beauty, its mystical religion and noble chivalry of action, the world of lost history and romance in the names of people and places—it was his own birthright upon which he entered."[2] Burne-Jones left Oxford without a degree and became a pupil and disciple of Dante Gabriel Rossetti, who, it turned out, had discovered Malory on his own; at one time, he considered *Le Morte Darthur* and the Bible to be the world's two greatest books. The next year, Burne-Jones, Rossetti, Morris, Arthur Hughes, and several other high-spirited friends set out to paint their own frescoes, all on Arthurian subjects, on the walls of the Oxford Debating Union.[3] The subjects were:

Merlin imprisoned beneath a stone by the Damsel of the Lake
Sir Launcelot prevented by his sin from entering the Chapel of the San Graal
How Sir Galahad, Sir Bors, and Sir Perceval were fed with the San Graal
Arthur and the weeping queens (The death of Arthur)
Sir Pelleas leaving the Lady Ettarde
Sir Gawain meeting three ladies at the well
Sir Palomydes in love with the Belle Iseult (The jealousy of Sir Tristram)
King Arthur obtaining the sword Excalibur from the Damsel of the Lake

"It was simply the most unmitigated *fiasco* that ever was made by a parcel of men of genius," W. B. Scott later wrote. The pictures were "painted in water-colours on the irregular brick wall merely whitewashed!"[4] Although Dyce's paintings in London held up somewhat longer—though they too required repair within a few years—the Oxford set, lacking both priming and an adhesive medium, began to disappear a few months after completion and within a short time they were almost totally invisible. Burne-Jones's attachment to Malory, however—it might almost be called an obsession—endured to the end. Only months before he died in 1898, he wrote, "Lord! how that San Graal story is ever in my mind and thoughts continually. Was ever anything in the world beautiful as that is beautiful?"[5] His magnum opus was *The Sleep of King Arthur in Avalon,* on which he worked for seventeen years. It was not finished at his death.

254. William Morris, *La Belle Iseult (Queen Guenevere)* (1858) (Tate Gallery, London). The model was the artist's wife, the beautiful Jane Burden. He inscribed on the back, "I cannot paint you but I love you." Another who loved her, with a passion greater than her husband's, was Dante Gabriel Rossetti, who painted her as Shakespeare's Mariana (pl. 196).

Morris's first picture was *How Sir Tristram, After His Illness in the Garden of King Mark's Palace, Was Recognized by the Dog He Had Given to Iseult.* It seems not to have survived, and indeed another painting with an Arthurian subject, *La Belle Iseult* (also identified as *Queen Guinevere*), is the only easel painting by Morris now known (pl. 254). About 1860, another Pre-Raphaelite, Arthur Hughes, painted three Arthurian subjects, probably inspired by Malory though possibly by Tennyson as well: *The Death of*

Arthur (known in contemporary references as *The Knight of the Sun*), *Elaine with the Armour of Lancelot,* and *Enid and Geraint.*[6] Even one of the two nonprofessional members of the brotherhood, Frederic Stephens, had tried his hand at an Arthurian theme at the very inception of the movement (ca. 1849); his unfinished *Mort d'Arthur* is in the Tate Gallery. Malory was, in fact, near the center of the medievalist fervor that infused Pre-Raphaelite art. Not that the brethren had a complete monopoly on subjects from Malory even in those early years: the Scottish artist James Eckford Lauder, for example, showed *Sir Tristram Teaching La Beale Isonde to Play the Harp* at the National Exhibition in 1855.

By 1858, therefore, Malory's tales were being used by a significant number of artists. But the great surge of interest in stories of the Round Table, stripped of their pre-Victorian humorous adhesions, to say nothing of their violence, lechery, and other robust but un-Victorian qualities, began only in 1859, when Tennyson published *Idylls of the King,* comprising the first four of the twelve narrative poems that would eventually be gathered under that title. Although Tennyson drew from several other sources of Arthurian legend, especially Lady Charlotte Guest's translation of the Welsh *Mabinogion,* eight of the *Idylls* came substantially from Malory.

Most of the Arthurian paintings exhibited from 1860 onward were associated with the *Idylls.* But Tennyson's popularity did not wholly eclipse Malory as an artists' source, and in any case, painters took as much liberty with Arthurian subjects as they did with those from any other literary source, so that a significant number of pictures involving characters from Camelot portray situations not described in either Malory or Tennyson, or add significant details not found in the literary texts.

255. James Archer, *Le Morte d'Arthur* (RA 1861) (Tate Gallery, London). The moment before the dying Arthur is taken aboard the barge for the journey to Avilion (*Morte Darthur,* bk. 20, chap. 4), probably with some reminiscence of Tennyson's early "The Epic" ("Morte d'Arthur"). The phantom angel holding the Sangreal (upper right-hand corner) is Archer's embellishment: "too much like the clever effect by which a ghost is shown in a stereoscope," said the *Saturday Review* (25 May).

Of the approximately one hundred and forty oil paintings of Arthurian subjects recorded between 1860 and 1900, well over a score were specifically attributed to Malory. Although these were fewer than those from Tennyson, most came from the easels of artists whose reputations are alive today. This is especially true of the first decade of competition between Malory and Tennyson (1860–70), when certain artists almost ostentatiously chose Arthurian themes not present in the four *Idylls* then before the public, as if a certain snobbery were involved, their loyalty to Malory requiring them to drink Arthuriana from its pure medieval source rather than as bottled and flavored for mass consumption by Victoria's poet laureate. In successive Royal Academy exhibitions (1861–63), James Archer showed three canvases, *Le Morte d'Arthur* (pl. 255), *How King Arthur by the Means of Merlin Gate His Sword of Excalibur of the Lady of the Lake,* and *The Sancgreall, Arthur, etc.*; and in 1868, *How Sir Launcelot and His Eight Fellows of the Round Table Carried Queen Guinevere from Almesbury to Her Tomb in Glastonbury*—all subjects from Malory rather than the *Idylls* as then constituted, though the first-named may have owed something to Tennyson's early poem on the death of Arthur. At the 1863 show, Frederick Sandys had portraits of Vivien (in the *Idylls*) and La Belle Ysonde (Malory); and the next year, he exhibited Morgan-le-Fay (Malory) (pl. 71). The *Athenaeum*'s comment on this last picture presumably would not have applied to a painting from the best-selling *Idylls:* "[The picture] ought not to have been presented without explanation to a public hardly enough versed in the Arthurian cycle of legends to recognize its theme at sight."[7]

256. Ford Madox Brown, *The Death of Sir Tristram* (1864–65) (Birmingham City Museum and Art Gallery). "How shamefully that false traytour kyng Marke slew hym as he sate harpynge afore hys lady, La Beall Isode. Wyth a grounden glayve [sharpened spear] he threste hym in behynde to the harte, wyche grevyth sore me, to speke of hys dethe, for all the worlde may nat fynde such another knyght"—Launcelot's report to Sir Bors as the twilight of the heroes begins to fall over Camelot (*Morte Darthur,* bk. 20, chap. 1).

Also in 1864, Ford Madox Brown painted *The Death of Sir Tristram* (pl. 256); and at the end of the decade, Hughes produced two more Arthurian canvases, *The Brave Geraint* (RA 1869) and *Sir Galahad* (RA 1870). After that, with the notable exception of Burne-Jones, major painters' interest in Malory declined, and they joined their lesser colleagues in allegiance to the Tennysonian Arthuriad (see below, under Tennyson). But their devotion to Malory had had its effect. Thanks to them, as well as to the popular interest in the Arthurian stories that the *Idylls* stirred, *Le Morte Darthur* reappeared in nine complete editions before the end of the century and was popularized through numerous adaptations and volumes of selections.

THE ELIZABETHAN ERA

SPENSER

Joseph Spence, friend of Alexander Pope, once recorded that after he read a canto in Spenser to his—Spence's—mother, then between seventy and eighty years of age, "she said that I had been showing her a collection of pictures."[1] This seems to have been the earliest expression of a fancy that was to persist as a critical commonplace across the centuries. Like Thomson's *Seasons* on a smaller scale, *The Faerie Queene* was taken to be the quintessence of poetic pictorialism, a vivid and extensive exemplification of *ut pictura poesis,* and Spenser therefore was "the painter's poet" par excellence.[2] In 1829, Hazlitt said that he was "a poet to whom justice will never be done till a painter of equal genius arises to embody the dazzling and enchanting creations of his pen."[3] In effect, the artists' challenge was to translate *The Faerie Queene* into the visual medium to which it had such intimate affinity, and this in a period when the art of the Renaissance masters was the criterion by which the most ambitious painting was judged. It may well have been that, as a writer in the *Art Journal* observed in 1855, when Spenserianism in English art was finally declining, *The Faerie Queene* was "the most difficult poem in our classics that a painter can work from. It is more easy to paint from Shakespeare or Milton, or indeed any of our poets, than it is to work from Spenser."[4] No such painter as Hazlitt called for ever appeared, but as the record of some 175 paintings from *The Faerie Queene* suggests, there was no lack of aspirants.[5]

During the eighteenth-century decades when a revived Spenserianism served as one of the first harbingers of Romanticism in poetry, subjects from *The Faerie Queene* were regularly seen at the exhibitions and elsewhere.[6] William Kent designed engravings for the edition of 1751: "the most execrable performance you ever beheld," wrote Horace Walpole to a friend, "—the graving not worse than the drawing: awkward knights, scrambling Unas, hills tumbling down themselves, no variety of prospect, and three or four perpetual spruce firs."[7] But Walpole, whose sympathies and prejudices were deeply rooted in the neoclassicism of the time, was as unequipped to deal fairly with Spenserian subjects as Kent was unequipped, for the same reason, to portray them. Fuseli with his imaginative reach was somewhat better qualified, and two of his early watercolors (ca. 1769) were *The Appearance of the Fairy Queen to the Dreaming Arthur* and *The Cave of Despair.* Benjamin West exhibited three Spenser canvases at the Royal Academy, *Una and the Lion* (1772), *The Cave of Despair* (1773) (pl. 257), and *Fidelia and Speranza* (1777). Una was a favorite role in which ladies chose to be depicted in fancy pictures. The eldest daughter of Lady Diana Beauclerk sat to Reynolds in the character (RA 1780), Miss Isabella Saltonstall to George Stubbs (pl. 17), Miss Clark to Northcote (RA 1806), and an unnamed lady to Sir William Beechey as late as 1821. John Singleton Copley posed his three children as the Red Cross Knight, Fidelia, and Speranza (pl. 258). Four paintings from *The Faerie Queene* were commissioned for Macklin's Poet's Gallery: Richard Cosway's *Sans-Loy Killing the Lion,* Fuseli's *The Vision of Prince Arthur,* John Opie's *The Freeing of Amoret,* and the very minor artist Elias Martin's *Amoret Rapt by Greedie Lust.* Stothard made twelve Spenserian designs for Aikin's edition of Dr. Johnson's collection of the English poets (1802). He thought so much of one of

257. Benjamin West, *The Cave of Despair* (RA 1773) (Yale Center for British Art, Paul Mellon Collection). West was one of the first artists to realize the suitability of *Faerie Queene* subjects for treatment in the grand style. He had exhibited *Una and the Lion* the previous year, and in 1777 would show *Fidelia and Speranza.* In this painting, the Red Cross Knight beholds the "piteous spectacle" of Sir Terwin, captive of Despair (bk. 1, canto 9).

these, *Una Surrounded by Satyrs,* that he hung it in his drawing room in Newman Street for the remaining thirty years of his life.[8]

Spenser was one of Keats's literary enthusiasms, and among those with whom he shared it was his friend Joseph Severn, who was inspired by Keats's reciting *The Faerie Queene* to paint *Una and the Red Cross Knight in*

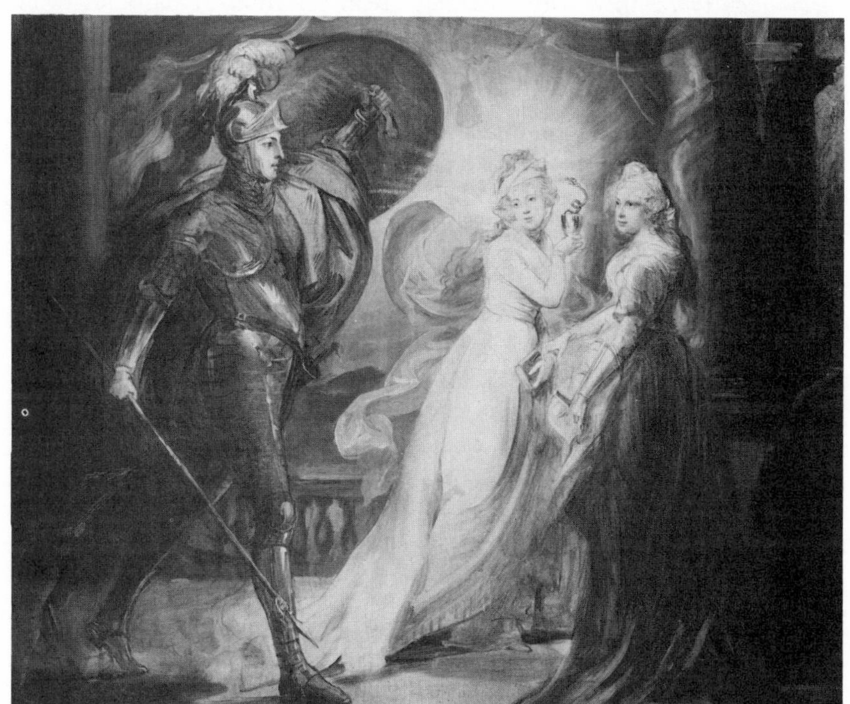

258. John Singleton Copley, *Study for the Red Cross Knight* (RA 1793) (Yale Center for British Art, Paul Mellon Collection). A sketch for the finished painting, which is at the National Gallery, Washington. The American-born artist cast his namesake son (later Baron Lyndhurst, three times lord chancellor) as the Red Cross Knight and his daughters Elizabeth and Mary as Fidelia and Speranza. The scene is *The Faerie Queene,* bk. 1, canto 10.

the Cave of Despair. The picture won the gold medal at the Royal Academy schools in 1819—the first time the prize had been awarded in eight years—and it was exhibited at the Academy the next year. At least one reviewer greeted it in the spirit in which critics at that moment were mauling the "cockney" Keats: "We despair," he said, "of this painter ever making an artist. He has [started] out by striding after Fuseli on the stilts of literature. He has overtaken every one of his faults, and has given eminent proof of his qualifications for the Presidency of the Academy at the Court of the Anthropophagi."[9]

Keats's early mentor, Leigh Hunt, was also a devoted Spenserian. Like Hazlitt, Hunt habitually thought of Spenser's poetry in terms of the Old Masters; and in the *New Monthly Magazine* for June 1833, under the title "A New Gallery of Pictures: Spenser, the Poet of the Painters," he offered an anthology of Spenserian pictorial beauties, introduced with the most extravagant praise any painter-in-words ever received:

> . . . His "Faerie Queene" contains a store of masterly, poetical pictures, as capable of being set before the eye as those in a gallery; . . . he includes in his singular genius the powers of the greatest and most opposite masters of the art, of the Titians in colouring and classical gusto, the Rembrandts in light and shade, the Michael Angelos in grandeur of form and purpose, the Rubenses in gorgeousness, the Guidos in grace, the Raphaels and Correggios in expression, and the Claudes and Poussins, and even the homely Dutch painters, in landscape. Spenser can paint a ditch, a flower-garden, an enchanted wood, a palace, a black smith's shop, an elysium. He can paint nymphs wanton or severe; warriors, satyrs, giants, ladies, courts, cottages, hermitages, the most terrible storms, the most prodigious horrors, the profoundest and loveliest tranquillity. His naked women are equal to Titian's, his dressed to Guido's, his old seers to Michael Angelo's, his matrons and his pure maidenhood to Raphael's, his bacchanals to Nicholas Poussin's; and for a certain union of all qualities in one, we know not his equal.[10]

259. Charles Eastlake, *Una Delivering the Red Cross Knight* (RA 1830) (Sir John Soane's Museum, London). The moment in the Cave of Despair immediately following the one depicted in pl. 257; another rescue scene, this time from contemplated suicide, with *putti* added to enhance the Spenserian—Renaissance—flavor. Eastlake painted it reluctantly. He received the commission from Sir John Soane in 1824, but the banality (thus early) of the specified subject discouraged him. He finally got around to it in 1828.

Eleven years later (1844), Hunt revived the conceit in his chatty anthology *Imagination and Fancy,* with a largely fresh selection of passages to be painted. The combined galleries contained thirty hypothetical canvases, excluding half a dozen duplications.

In enticing readers to *The Faerie Queene* solely on the strength of the pictures with which the poem abounded, Hunt was doing his bit to educate a steadily growing reading public whose natural taste in art ran to literary subjects more readily identified with everyday life. As Archibald Alison wrote at this time, "the Fables of Ariosto or Spencer will never rival in their influence with the great bulk of mankind the simple tales in which Burns and Scott and Shakspeare have drawn characters and awakened emotions familiar and common to all mankind."[11] Perhaps not, but there was no harm in telling them of the delights of *The Faerie Queene;* and immediately after the "New Gallery of Pictures" appeared, *Blackwood's Magazine* published (1834–35) a series of long articles by "Christopher North" (John Wilson) that supplemented Hunt's missionary efforts on another front. Archaic language apart, the multileveled allegory of *The Faerie Queene* was considered the most formidable barrier to its wider appreciation, and Wilson added to lavish encomia a patient explication that set out to teach *Blackwood's* readers more than they probably ever cared to know about allegory or Spenser. Thus instructed, however, within a few years they would have been the first to realize that Spenser's homage to Queen Elizabeth was neatly applicable to the new Gloriana who had succeeded to her throne, and that pictures from *The Faerie*

260. William E. Frost, *Una and the Wood Nymphs* (RA 1847) (Royal Collection, Copyright Reserved). The fauns and satyrs, "astonied at her beautie bright" and worshiping Una as "Goddesse of the wood," are joined by "the wooddy Nymphes, faire Hamadryades" and "all the troupe of light-foot Naiades" who "flocke all about to see her louely face" (bk. 1, canto 6).

Queene might have more contemporary significance than met the casual eye.

But comprehension of allegory was not indispensable to the appreciation of a picture from *The Faerie Queene.* As Hazlitt observed, "It might as well be pretended that, we cannot see Poussin's pictures for the allegory, as that the allegory prevents us from understanding Spenser."[12] There was, after all, the perennial attraction of chivalric themes, the many combat-and-rescue operations, the lush pictorial coloration, all of which were very much to early Victorian taste.[13] That the incidence of pictures from *The Faerie Queene,* after holding steady at one to three a year between 1800 and 1840, markedly increased in the next fifteen years is not necessarily evidence that the poem had found more readers. It was said at the time that it was "little read," except—possibly—by artists.* But there is no reason to believe that as a consequence paintings from Spenser sold any less quickly than those from other literary sources.

Throughout *The Faerie Queene*'s career in art, book 1 provided most of the subjects. (In Hunt's first dream gallery, ten picturable passages came from there, as against only four each from books 2 and 3 and none from the rest of the poem.) The main attraction was Una, who was portrayed in some forty canvases, both portraits and tableaux. William Hilton was something of a specialist in Una pictures; he showed her in a single action, seeking shelter in Corceca's cottage, at least four times between 1831 and 1835. Leading patrons of the time, especially those who did not share the developing taste for genre subjects, were partial to pictures from this book. From Richard Westall, the wealthy collector and antiquarian Richard Payne Knight commissioned (RA 1807) the scene in which the sorcerer Archimago "causes the Red Cross Knight to lust after a spirit, posing as Una." In 1824, Sir John Soane ordered from Charles Eastlake *Una Delivering the Red Cross Knight from the Cave of Despair* (pl. 259), a subject Eastlake, even then, rightly considered to be trite. Queen Victoria and the Prince Consort valued *Faerie Queene* subjects as much as they did subjects from Milton's *Comus.* In 1847, the Queen bought W. E. Frost's *Una* (pl. 260) off the wall at the Royal Academy as a gift for her husband.

*In 1848, the *Illustrated London News* (10 June, p. 378) commented that the poem was "too little read by painters but replete with fine subjects." Two years later, Thomas Uwins, replying to a remark by one of his patrons, wrote: "Nobody reads him [Spenser] but the artist; and the artist finds the 'Faery Queen' so full of the combinations which lend themselves to painting, that he loses his chance of pleasing the public in the love of pleasing himself." Uwins, however, was an embittered witness. The previous year, he had exhibited *Sir Guyon Arriving at the Bower of Bliss* (also described as *Sir Guyon . . . Destroys the Enchantments That Have Tempted His Companions from Their Duty*). "People passed by it," he complained, "as if it was so much blank wall, and went on to a mountain scene, which to my feelings was full of nothingness" (Mrs. Uwins, *A Memoir of Thomas Uwins* [London, 1858], 1:124).

261. Henry Howard, *The House of Morpheus* (RA 1821) (Petworth House). Howard, who exhibited 259 paintings at the Royal Academy alone in the course of half a century, treated all his literary subjects in the neoclassic style he had first exercised as a young contributor to Boydell's Shakespeare Gallery. This chaste scene, from the middle of his career, typifies his handling of the many Spenserian subjects he chose. It represents the "great passion of vnwonted lust," a series of dreams in the course of which the Red Cross Knight is led to believe that Una is false to him (bk. 1, canto 1).

Prince Arthur's dream vision of the Faerie Queene was the subject of six or eight paintings. A scattering of pictures was drawn from elsewhere in book 1: Abraham Cooper's *Sir Trevisan Fleeing from Despair* (1822; his Royal Academy diploma picture), Henry Howard's *The House of Morpheus* (pl. 261), Sir John Gilbert's *The Slain Dragon* (pl. 262), Charles Gere's *The Finding of the Infant St. George,* and Henry Thomson's *The Mother Finding Her Infant Playing with the Talons of the Dragon Slain by the Red Cross Knight* (RA 1806).

Paintings from book 2 were dominated by moments from the twelfth canto, set in the Bower of Bliss. This passage afforded an opportunity to paint "four naked damzells," among other delights. The best-known picture from this book, however, was Etty's (RA 1832). It depicted an earlier episode (canto 6) in which Sir Guyon encounters Phaedria as he seeks a ferry to the Floating Island, only to be attacked by his enemy Cymocles, whom Phaedria had temporarily diverted from his revenge-seeking by the application of what in Etty's time were called her "charms." When Edward FitzGerald saw the second version at the Royal Academy in 1835 (pl. 61), he reported to Thackeray, "Etty has boats full of naked backs as usual: but what they mean, I didn't stop to enquire."[14]

262. Sir John Gilbert, *The Slain Dragon* (RA 1886) (Walker Art Gallery, Liverpool). After eleven cantos and a three-day battle, the Red Cross Knight has completed his mission to slay the dragon; and Una, plucking up her courage, comes to get a closer look at the "huge and horrible mass" whose tail extends behind the tree (bk. 1, canto 11).

The first five cantos of book 3 were almost wholly neglected, except for a late painting by G. F. Watts (pl. 264). Several subjects were taken from the sixth canto, however: the birth of Belphoebe and Amoret (stanzas 1–4: W. L. Leitch's painting of this subject [pl. 265] was commissioned by the Prince Consort), *Venus in Search of Cupid, Surprising Diana at Her Bath* (stanzas 11–25; 1820 version by William Hilton), and *Venus Visiting the Body of Adonis in Secret* (stanzas 46–51). From the seventh canto came, at various times, *The Witch's Son Bringing Presents to Florimel* (stanza 17) and *Florimel Escaping from the Monster* (stanzas 22–27). Beginning with Stothard's *Britomart Taking Off Her Helmet and Revealing Her Sex* (RA 1786), there was a whole series of representations of that classic discovery

263. George Frederic Watts, *Una and the Red Cross Knight* (RA 1869) (Lady Lever Art Gallery, Port Sunlight). By the time Watts painted this picture, Una and her chivalric companion had been staple subjects of British art for almost a century. The scene, from the very opening of *The Faerie Queene,* typifies the interest Spenser's poem held for a new generation of artists, some of whom, like Watts, prized it especially for its heavy content of moral allegory.

scene in canto 9. Among them was F. R. Pickersgill's *Britomart Unarming* (RA 1855), which the *Illustrated London News,* deciding that the knight on the left resembled Sir Philip Sidney, declared was "truly Spenserian." "How exquisitely," it rhapsodized, "has Spenser painted Britomart for the pencil of Mr. Pickersgill. . . . It is said by Spenser himself that the poet's wit surpasseth painter's far in picturing parts of 'beauty daynt'; but Spenser, had he seen Pickersgill's composition from his great poem,

264. George Frederic Watts, *Britomart and Her Nurse* (RA 1878) (Birmingham City Museum and Art Gallery). Britomart's nurse describes to her the signs of the future she sees in the magic mirror: the figures of the Red Cross Knight, Sir Guyon, and Sir Aleyn (bk. 3, canto 2). This is one of the numerous paintings that featured mirrors either as literal reflections or as auguries—a frequent device in Victorian poetry as well as art.

265. William L. Leitch, *The Birth of Belphoebe and Amoret* (before 1857) (Royal Collection, Copyright Reserved). Leitch was a landscapist who taught watercolor painting to Queen Victoria and other members of the royal family. In this picture, he reverted to the old practice of placing an identifiable group of human beings in what was essentially a scene from nature. The event shown is the birth of twins to the highborn fairy Chrysogone (bk. 3, canto 6).

266. Frederick R. Pickersgill, *Amoret, Aemylia, and Prince Arthur in the Cottage of Slander* (RA 1845) (Tate Gallery, London). In this scene from *The Faerie Queene* (bk. 4, canto 8), the artist concentrates on the three figures of Amoret, Aemilia, and Prince Arthur; but in the poem, Spenser devotes most of the dozen stanzas (23–36) to a horrific description of the hag Slander. This hag is scarcely loathsome, but Pickersgill was no Fuseli, nor was he painting at a time when witches such as Fuseli depicted agreed with the public appetite.

might have admitted, without compliment, that the painter of Britomart and Amoret had done something to lessen the justice of his remark."[15] Earlier the artist had displayed two other compositions from the same series of events: *Amoret, Aemylia and Prince Arthur in the Cottage of Slander* (pl. 266), and *The Contest of Beauty for the Girdle of Florimel—Britomart Unveiling Amoret* (RA 1848). But the most frequently painted incident in book 3 was Britomart's freeing Amoret from the enchantment of Busirane in the twelfth canto. Fuseli depicted it several times, notably in 1793 (a canvas later owned by Gladstone) and 1824. Etty considered his own version (RA 1833) one of his most important works.

Book 5 supplied only a few (early) Spenserian pictures, including Mortimer's essay in the grand style, *Sir Arthegal the Knight of Justice* (pl. 267). But the sixth book, the last Spenser completed, provided several subjects, mostly of the rescues with which the cantos are studded. Calepine's second deliverance of Serena (from the salvage nation) was portrayed by both Opie (RA 1798) and Hilton (RA 1831).*

By no means all of the subjects from *The Faerie Queene* that were painted have been mentioned here. At first glance, the number of separate scenes that were portrayed is impressive. But they constitute only a small fraction of the passages in the poems—literally hundreds—that would seem equally suitable for the artist who worked with the tastes of his patrons in mind. It is curious that of the thirty subjects in Leigh Hunt's combined lists of passages he regarded as particularly eligible for painting, few were ever selected by artists, either before or after he made his choices. If artists had ranged more widely through the poem, devoting no more than one painting to a given subject, they could have filled the wall space of any of three successive locations of the Royal Academy exhibitions, Somerset House, a wing of the National Gallery, and Burlington House. The history of *The Faerie Queene* in art is a fairly impressive demonstration of the tyranny of convention.

Convention, however, cannot explain a second curious fact: that despite its pictorial suggestiveness and the contemporary taste for pastoral subjects in English settings, Spenser's *The Shepherd's Calendar* went vir-

*Hilton's canvas had a peculiar fate. In 1839, after his death, his former students presented the picture to the National Gallery in his memory. After eight months on the wall, it was realized that the asphaltum and wax that had been mixed with the pigments had never properly hardened, and, as the *Art-Union* put it in 1847, "one of the evil consequences has been that an eye of the female figure has slipped down a quarter of an inch, and there formed a perfect festoon in alto-relievo" (p. 109). The restorer John Seguier knew of no remedy. "Under these unfavourable circumstances," the *Art-Union* reported, "the picture has been for the present withdrawn, and hung upside down in one of the private apartments, in the hope that the eye may slip back to its proper position." This desirable improvement may have been accomplished when the painting was restored in 1860, but it did not bestow permanent health on the much-suffering canvas. "The work," says Robin Hamlyn, assistant keeper of the British collection, Tate Gallery, "is now classified by our Conservation Department as a 'complete wreck' and a prewar photograph shows that Serena's *mouth* has slipped somewhat, revealing a rather bituminous grin of most unpleasant proportions!" (Private letter, 27 July 1983.)

tually unrepresented in the art galleries except for a scattering of paintings that merely borrowed their mottoes from Spenser's text.

JONSON

Some twenty paintings were derived from Ben Jonson's plays, the most notable ones from *Every Man in His Humour,* which Garrick adapted in 1751. Reynolds painted him as Kitely in 1768; the artist gave the original to his friend Edmund Burke and made at least four copies. Fuseli depicted for *Bell's British Theatre* the scene between Matthew and Bobadil, and in 1848 Maclise painted a new Kitely: John Forster, friend and biographer of Dickens (pl. 268).

Peter Van Bleeck painted a scene from *The Alchemist* as early as 1738, and the play gained in popularity on the stage, and therefore in art, when Garrick assumed the role of Abel Drugger and later produced his own adaptation of Jonson's text. Zoffany's painting of the last scene of the second act (RA 1770) was famous; it is sometimes said to have laid the foundation for the artist's fame as a theatrical painter. Reynolds, in one of the first recorded transactions in British art in which the seller made a profit, bought it from Zoffany for 100 guineas and resold it to the Earl of Carlisle for £125.[1] Scenes from the play were among the favorite subjects of later theatrical artists; George Clint, for example, showed two different ones at the Royal Academy in 1816 and the British Institution the following year. Several paintings catalogued simply as *The Alchemist* probably were repetitions of a familiar subject in European art, but to viewers who knew their own English drama, they would have contained echoes of Jonson's play.

The necromancy in Jonson's *Masque of Queens* inevitably attracted Henry Fuseli, who showed at the Royal Academy in 1785 *The Mandrake: a Charm.* "Shockingly mad, madder than ever, quite mad," was Horace Walpole's equally inevitable judgment.[2] Fuseli repeated the subject for the Academy show of 1812, when Robert Hunt, declining to pass judgment on the artist's health of mind, reported receiving a *frisson* from "the squalid hag, . . . her uncouth and cowering position, her ugliness and malignant satisfaction of face peeping under a hood."[3]

267. John Hamilton Mortimer, *Sir Arthegal the Knight of Justice* (RA 1778) (Tate Gallery, London). This is one of the very few paintings drawn from book 5 of *The Faerie Queene.* No specific scene is represented.

268. Daniel Maclise, *John Forster as Kitely* (1848) (Victoria & Albert Museum, Crown Copyright). Forster, editor, biographer, and ubiquitous adviser and factotum to several leading authors, played Kitely in an amateur production of *Every Man in His Humour* performed for the benefit of Leigh Hunt. Dickens directed and played Bobadil.

THE SEVENTEENTH CENTURY

WALTON

Izaak Walton's *The Compleat Angler, or the Contemplative Man's Recreation* (1653) was one of the most frequently illustrated of the English classics.[1] The number of editions and reprints it went through, 106 in the Victorian era alone, testifies both to the size of the Walton cult and its perseverance, unaffected by changes in literary taste. Wholly apart from its piscatorial interest, it possessed a sentimental appeal that sprang from the idealized conception the reader formed of Walton himself as well as from its pervasive air of *eheu fugaces,* gentle nostalgia for times past. A large appreciative literature grew up about the book, which was a relative latecomer to the art exhibitions. Of the score of pictures derived from it, most were painted after 1850.

The first Walton paintings appeared at the Royal Academy in 1824–25, coinciding with the publication of two new editions of *The Compleat Angler,* John Major's (1823), which was subsequently reprinted fifty times, and Pickering's (1825), with plates from designs by Stothard and others, which also went through many reprints. At the Academy exhibition of 1824, a representation of Walton and his companion Venator listening to the milkmaid's song "Come live with me and be my love" was shown by the journalist and future poisoner Thomas Griffith Wainewright.* The next year, two paintings commissioned for Major's edition of Walton's *Lives* were seen: Abraham Cooper's *The Poor Man and His Distressed Horse* (from the life of Herbert) and Leslie's *Sir Henry Wotton Presenting the Countess Sabrina with a Valuable Jewel* (from the life of Wotton).

But it was Walton himself who most engaged Victorian artists, primarily for the sake of the genre subjects he offered in *The Compleat Angler:* the boy with his first rod, the grown man teaching his art to a child, Walton simply fishing on the banks of the Colne, "Walton and his companion hyeing home" with a good day's catch to Tottenham High Cross. The most celebrated painting associated with Walton, however, is one in which he does not appear. William Dyce's *George Herbert at Bemerton* (pl. 269) portrays the subject of Walton's elegiac biographical sketch walking at the edge of a stream, reciting from a book—perhaps a collection of devotional poetry, perhaps even one of his own poems, "Vertue," which Piscator quotes in *The Compleat Angler.* The artist, according to a story apparently originating in Alfred G. Temple's *The Art of Painting in the Queen's Reign* (1897), also sketched in the figure of Walton fishing from the bank of the stream. But tiresome facts intruded when someone told Dyce that the two men "lived at quite different periods, and that he must take one out." Dyce chose to delete Walton, but said, "I'm —— if I take out his basket," which remains in the painting as a token of Walton's spiritual presence. Unfortunately, tiresome facts tend to discredit Dyce's informant, if not the anecdote itself. Walton and Herbert were born the same year, 1593.

*This picture figures in a vignette communicated by the artist Samuel Palmer to Blake's early biographer, Alexander Gilchrist: "While so many moments better worthy to remain are fled, the caprice of memory presents me with the image of Blake looking up at Wainewright's picture; Blake in his plain black suit and *rather* broad-brimmed, but not quakerish hat, standing so quietly among all the dressed-up, rustling, swelling people, and myself thinking 'How little you know *who* is among you!'" (Gilchrist, *Life of Blake,* ed. Todd, p. 283.)

MILTON

In 1734, a father and son, both named Jonathan Richardson, published a squat octavo volume entitled *Explanatory Notes and Remarks on Milton's*

269. William Dyce, *George Herbert at Bemerton* (RA 1861) (Guildhall Art Gallery, London). "He succeeds . . . in representing very effectively a sort of dreamy atmosphere of devotional repose, such as may well be imagined as surrounding that mystic poet. The peaceful garden in early spring, the sluggish stream flowing by it *piscatoribus sacer,* . . . with the distant view of Salisbury spire—all are perfect. . . . The lovers of Isaac Walton and of the 'Country Parson' will see many of their inmost feelings translated visibly in this picture. But the figure of the becassocked priest spoils all. . . . That thorough gentleman, George Herbert, would never (we are sure) have been so demonstrative" (*Saturday Review,* 18 May). The creel at the foot of the tree marks the spot where the figure of Walton was originally painted in.

*"Paradise Lost."** Tucked into a corner on the last page of the book, after a "Table of the Principal Subjects in the Poem," was a little list headed "PICTURES" with page references to the following topics: The world rising out of Chaos, The rebel host ruining [*sic*] from Heaven, Satan rising out of Chaos, Satanick Host, Of angels good and evil, Fairies dancing by moon-light, Satan on his throne, and (simply) Hell. The references led to a series of exclamations in the text proper over the beauty and power of Milton's images:

> [Milton] Inriches his Poem with an Amazing Fine Picture of "These Miserable Ruining from Heaven" . . . What a Contrast! What an Inexhaustable Fund for Imagination! (1:169 ff.)
>
> Here the Poet gives a Wonderful Picture. . . . Let the Reader Attentively View every Scene, they are vastly Great, and wonderfully Painted. (1:522)
>
> What an Image! (1:565)
>
> the picture is exceeding Pretty and Delightful (1:785)
>
> Sure the most Amazing Picture that can be conceived (6:878)

And, most significant (of Satan, in book 1):

> 'tis Hard, Impossible, to Conceive a Character of Beauty proper to a Blessed Spirit; but more So to Communicate that Idea by Painting. . . . These [conceptions] are Known Only to Those who Converse with the Works of *Rafaelle, Corregio, Guido,* &c. . . . More Difficult yet is it to Imagine a proper Idea of a Ruin'd Arch-Angel; Nor *Guido,* nor *Raffaelle* has Succeeded Here, it was not a Subject Agreeable to their Kind of Genius. *Michael Angelo* was more Fit for it, and he has done Vastly beyond any other. . . .

Thus at a time when Spenser, the earlier English "painter's poet," was in eclipse, Milton's epic was admired for its word pictures.[1] In years to come, it was to provide the strongest of all literary links between British painting and the great European artistic legacy symbolized by the names the Richardsons mentioned. The subject of *Paradise Lost* was the cluster of

*The Richardsons' interests and activities made them practical exponents of the sisterhood of the arts. The father was a painter, and his *Portrait of the Artist and His Son in the Presence of Milton,* still extant, exemplifies their connection with the nascent cult of Milton, whose brow is crowned with laurel in the painting. The *Explanatory Notes* was one of the earliest influential works of Milton criticism and biography. When Richardson *père* read his preface aloud to his fellow artists assembled at Slaughter's, their favorite coffeehouse, his fulsome thanks to his son for helping him read "the Learned Languages" stirred Hogarth to dash off a quick sketch which occasioned "a great laugh" (J. F. Kerslake, "The Richardsons and the Cult of Milton," *Burlington Magazine* 99 [1957]: 23–24). The father was also a connoisseur of, and writer on, art, and it was a chance encounter with his *Theory of Painting* (1715) that reportedly determined Joshua Reynolds to become an artist. Both Richardsons were closely associated with Alexander Pope, who corrected the manuscript of the Milton book before it went to press. The father made thirty-three drawings of Pope as well as his portrait, now in the National Portrait Gallery, and the son was Pope's first annotator and textual critic (Brownell, *Pope and the Arts of Georgian England,* pp. 29–30).

themes central to the work of all illustrators of Genesis—Michelangelo, Raphael, Rubens, Masaccio, Giulio Romano, and their host of successors. By treating them as found in a Christian epic, written on English soil by a Protestant, English painters had patriotic sanction for their efforts to imitate and do homage to, if not equal, the achievements of their venerated Continental predecessors. *Paradise Lost* offered unlimited prime material for history pictures. In addition, the masque *Comus* and the short companion poems "L'Allegro" and "Il Penseroso" contained figures and scenes well known to the English public through engravings from Titian, Poussin, and the allegorical-decorative schools of art.

Propelled by Addison's frequent allusions to Milton in his pioneering series of *Spectator* essays on the imagination, and by such critical commentaries as the Richardsons', the poet's literary reputation steadily grew in the course of the eighteenth century.[2] The strength of contemporary interest in Milton was aptly indicated by a picture J. F. Rigaud exhibited at the Royal Academy in 1773, *Portrait of a Gentleman Delivering a Lecture on Milton.* Not that there was universal agreement on his stature or on the grounds for admiring him: Dr. Johnson and William Blake saw him from very different perspectives. But, whatever the reasons people had for reading him, they bought edition after edition—more than one hundred of *Paradise Lost* alone in the course of the eighteenth century and some seventy more of Milton's complete works.

Some of these editions were illustrated.[3] Each of the twelve books in the 1688 edition of *Paradise Lost* was accompanied by a plate, the majority designed by the Brussels-born John Baptist Medina, then a portrait painter resident in Edinburgh. These were reengraved several times for editions as late as 1784. Other editions down to the first years of the nineteenth century were illustrated by such artists as Hayman, Mortimer, Blake, Singleton, Westall, Kirk, and Fuseli. No one complained that these designs failed to do justice to their elevated subjects; the inadequacy of ordinary book illustrations of Milton was taken for granted. But more was expected of oil paintings, and weighty opinion held that any attempt to do justice to Milton in paint was inherently futile. *Ut pictura poesis* notwithstanding, there were transcendent effects in poetry that could not be matched in paint. In his *Philosophical Enquiry into the Origin of Our Ideas of the Sublime and Beautiful* (1756), Edmund Burke declared:

> In painting we may represent any fine figure we please, but we never can give it those enlivening touches which it may receive from words. To represent an angel in a picture, you can only draw a beautiful young man winged: but what painting can furnish anything so grand as the addition of one word, "the angel of the *Lord*"? It is true, I have here no clear idea; but these words affect the mind more than the sensible image did. . . . As a further instance, let us consider those lines of Milton, where he describes the travels of the fallen angels through their dismal habitation:
>
> O'er many a dark and dreary vale
> They passed, and many a region dolorous;
> O'er many a frozen, many a fiery Alp
> Rocks, caves, lakes, fens, bogs, dens and shades of death,
> A universe of death.
>
> Here is displayed the force of union in
>
> Rocks, caves, lakes, dens, bogs, fens, and shades;
>
> which yet would lose the greatest part of the effect, if they were not the
>
> Rocks, caves, lakes, dens, bogs, fens, and shades—of *Death.*
>
> This idea or this affection caused by a word, which nothing but a word could

> annex to the others, raises a very great degree of the sublime; and this sublime is raised yet higher by what follows, a "*universe of Death.*" Here are again two ideas not presentable but by language; and an union of them great and amazing beyond conception. . . .[4]

More succinctly, Sir Joshua Reynolds in his eighth *Discourse* (1779) also argued the inadequacy of painting confronted by the emotional power of words:

> A great part of the beauty of the celebrated description of Eve in Milton's *Paradise Lost,* consists in using only general indistinct expressions, every reader making out the detail according to his own particular imagination,—his own idea of beauty, grace, expression, dignity, or loveliness: but a painter, when he represents Eve on a canvas, is obliged to give a determined form, and his own idea of beauty distinctly expressed.[5]

In 1835, the German art historian and museum-keeper Gustav F. Waagen toured many English private galleries and, on the basis of the pictures from Milton he saw there, concluded that even if one granted that *Paradise Lost* could be adequately translated into paint, Milton's fellow countrymen were not the artists to do it. He deplored

> the twofold predilection which has long been general among English artists for Milton and Michael Angelo. This arises from the innate feeling of the English for the sublime efforts of imagination, but has produced practically, in painting, very little good. With respect to Milton, he is least of all suited to afford subjects for painting precisely where he is greatest—the representation of the characters and manners of his fallen angels. Forms and images are with him so colossal, that they must lose when they are represented to the senses. The best traits of mind are too subtilely dialectic for the painter to transfer them with success to his art. To create works of art in the spirit of Michael Angelo, the English artists are deficient in powers of invention, and in depth of scientific knowledge. So able an artist as Sir Joshua Reynolds was very sensible of this, and he therefore was contented with expressing in words only his enthusiastic admiration.[6]

But no amount of theory ever discouraged English painters. A steady demand existed for biblical art, down at least to mid-Victorian times; and beginning with Hogarth, painters set out to oblige it, with constant assistance from Milton. In 1735 or later (the date is uncertain), Hogarth, who had engraved two (unused) illustrations to *Paradise Lost* some years earlier, painted *Satan, Sin, and Death* (pl. 270), based on the description in book 2 of Satan's encounter with Sin and Death—the same passage Burke was to cite.[7] Hogarth's picture represented, as did several of his other early canvases, his participation in the attempt then barely under way to establish history painting as a mode of English art and, inseparable from this, to achieve the sublimity that Burke and Dr. Johnson later attributed to Milton. There could be no higher power in any art, said Johnson, than that he possessed, of "displaying the vast, illuminating the splendid, enforcing the awful, darkening the gloomy, and aggravating the dreadful. . . . "[8]

But Hogarth discovered that his unique genius lay in a quite different direction, and it was left for other painters to explore the riches of *Paradise Lost* as a source of history pictures. In 1771, James Barry exhibited at the Royal Academy *The Temptation of Eve,* whose "frank nudity," we are told, "shocked some of the critics."[9] His long-range ambition was to paint eighteen subjects from Milton, but its realization was prevented by the distracting circumstances of his personal life, climaxed by his expulsion from the Academy in 1799 for a truculence, excessive even by Irish stan-

270. William Hogarth, *Satan, Sin, and Death* (date indeterminate) (Tate Gallery, London). A rendering of *Paradise Lost,* book 2, lines 666–731. The style recalls that of Salvator Rosa, one of the artists whom Hogarth revered, and anticipates that of Fuseli, who also painted the subject, as did Barry, Blake and Martin.

dards, that led him to fight with everybody in that august institution. The only surviving evidence of it is in the form of several drawings and engravings.[10]*

It was left for Fuseli to produce Milton paintings in a quantity that far eclipsed Barry's projected eighteen: Fuseli, of whom Dr. Waagen was to say in 1835, a decade after the artist's death, that he was "the only man in England of considerable talents who cherished the illusion, that without profound study, and by means of a fertile but distorted imagination, he could soar to the spheres where such exalted spirits as Michael Angelo and Shakspeare, unapproachable by far mightier minds than his, pursue their eternal course."[11] Fuseli began his prolific career as an exhibited illustrator of *Paradise Lost* with *Satan Starting from the Touch of Ithuriel's Spear* (RA 1780). From then to the end of his life forty-five years later, pictures from Milton flowed from his brush, pen, and pencil. In the 1790s, as we saw in chapter 2, he painted a whole galleryful of Miltonic subjects.

Despite the failure of Fuseli's completed collection when it was thrown open to the admission-paying public in 1799–1800, Milton's poetry flourished as a source of literary art in the new century.[12] All told, about three hundred Milton pictures are recorded, the peak of production having been reached in the period 1830–60; in the 1840s alone, more than sixty canvases were displayed. But the flood subsided much more abruptly than did that of literary paintings in general and Shakespeare subjects in particular. After 1860, no more than half a dozen *Paradise Lost* pictures appeared (the total for the whole century approached one hundred); and after 1880, no more than a dozen or so from Milton's works and his biography combined.

Paradise Lost would not have been so popular with artists had its appeal been solely contingent on the uncertain fortunes of history painting. In

*Another Milton illustrator *manqué* at the time was George Romney, who early in his career (1770) had displayed a pair of pictures catalogued as *Melancholy* and *Mirth* but subsequently engraved as *Il Penseroso* and *L'Allegro.* (Lady Hamilton once sat to him as Mirth.) In 1794, he wrote William Hayley, "My plan is, if I live and retain my senses and sight, to paint six other subjects from Milton [besides the Vision of Adam with the Angel, and the flood and opening of the Ark, from *Paradise Regained*]—three where Satan is the hero, and three from Adam and Eve; perhaps six of each. I have ideas of them all, and, I may say, sketched, but alas! I cannot begin them for a year or two." He never did, and all that remain of his Miltonic aspirations are what a modern writer has described as "a vast number of drawings" (see Pointon, *Milton and English Art,* pp. 121–31). Romney had similar grandiose notions of painting from Shakespeare, but in that case he completed a few of the pictures he planned.

271. John Martin, *Adam's First Sight of Eve* (RA 1813) (Glasgow Art Gallery and Museum). This is the painting Evelyn Waugh discovered at a Scottish hotel in 1945 (see text, p. 6). Martin's vision of Milton's Eden is that of a conventional landscape artist. It is no more paradisal than the English woods and streams that served as backgrounds for Thomson's Musidora or for Jaques and the wounded stag.

the 1790s, the impact in England of the French revolutionary fever, which elevated the figure of the defiant rebel to heroic stature, merged with the growing tendency of literary criticism to regard Milton's Satan as a sympathetic hero in the mold of Prometheus. The result was a fresh concentration on the arch-fiend as a subject of art, whether or not the new interpretation affected artists' portrayal of him.[13] Again, in the years immediately preceding the Victorian period (the late 1820s and early 1830s), there was a brief visitation of turgid epics and other elaborate poetical exercises on religious themes dealing with the beginning and end of man's tenure on earth: Robert Pollok's *The Course of Time* (1827), which stretched from Creation to Doomsday, Robert Montgomery's *A Universal Prayer: Death: A Vision of Hell* and *The Omnipresence of the Deity,* which also began with Creation (both 1828), and John Abraham Heraud's *The Judgement of the Flood* (1834)—the same kind of catastrophic literature that provided a background for the appearance of Bulwer's *The Last Days of Pompeii* in 1834.[14] (See below, under Bulwer-Lytton.) These now unreadable attempts at verbal history-painting coincided with the early fruition of the career of John Martin, the great practitioner of apocalyptic, or at least richly cataclysmic, painting. Both the contemporary epic writers and Martin drew much of their inspiration from Milton, and much of their popularity—short-lived in the former case, especially after Macaulay printed a devastating article on Montgomery's poetry in the *Edinburgh Review,** somewhat longer in Martin's case—from the public's appetite for grandiose if not actually lurid expansions of Miltonic scenes, whether in bombastic verse or huge, crowded panoramic canvases. In his *Satan* (1830), Montgomery wrote of Martin as

> That second Milton, whose creative soul
> Doth shadow visions to such awful life,
> That men behold them with suspended breath
> And grow ethereal at a gaze.

Martin's first Miltonic paintings were exhibited in 1813, one at the Royal Academy (*Adam's First Sight of Eve* [pl. 271]) and one at the British Institution (*The Expulsion of Adam and Eve*). A decade later, Martin exhib-

*The attack on Montgomery appeared in the April 1830 issue of the *Edinburgh Review.* In the December 1831 issue, Macaulay delivered a commonsensical judgment on Martin as an illustrator of Milton: "He should never have attempted to illustrate *Paradise Lost.* There can be no two manners more directly opposed to each other than the manner of his painting and the manner of Milton's poetry. Those things which are mere accessories in the descriptions become the principal objects in his pictures; and those figures which are most prominent in the descriptions can be detected in the pictures only by a very close scrutiny. Mr. Martin has succeeded perfectly in representing the pillars and candelabra of Pandemonium. But he has forgotten that Milton's Pandemonium is merely the background to Satan."

ited *Adam and Eve Entertaining the Angel Raphael* in a more immediately pastoral setting (BI 1823).

In 1825–27 appeared one of the most notable illustrated books of the nineteenth century, a fit predecessor of the luxurious editions of Samuel Rogers's *Italy* and *Collected Poems,* with designs by Turner,* that were published a few years later. This was an edition of *Paradise Lost* with twenty-four mezzotints, from oil sketches by Martin, that was issued in eight different formats.[15] The critical acclaim and circulation of these volumes in influential circles added to Martin's reputation as an illustrator of Milton. In 1826, he displayed at the British Institution *The Deluge,* a larger version of which, dated 1834, won a gold medal at the Paris Salon the following year.† His *The Eve of the Deluge* (RA 1840) found its way into the Royal Collection. A further series of Martin's Milton paintings appeared at the Royal Academy in the next few years: *The Celestial City and the River of Bliss* (1841), whose precise source in Milton the artist later was unable to pinpoint; *The Fall of Man* and a pair of pictures, *Morning in Paradise* (also known as *Adam and Eve in Paradise: Morning Hymn*) and *Evening in Paradise* (all three 1844); and *The Judgement of Adam and Eve* (1845).

The subjects artists chose from *Paradise Lost* belonged to three main "movements."‡ The first consisted of the action in book 1: the war in heaven and the fall of the angels (both described in detailed flashbacks in books 5 and 6), Satan reviving on the burning lake and marshalling his fellow fiends, and the building and occupying of Pandemonium. The second portrayed Satan's collusion with Sin and Death against the background of Hell and Chaos (books 2 and 10). The third embraced the transactions in Paradise, beginning with Satan's first acquaintance with the Garden of Eden in book 3 and ending with the expulsion of Adam and Eve in book 11.

Fuseli treated the opening action of the poem twice in the Milton Gallery, with pictures of *Satan Rising from the Flood* and *Satan Calling His Legions.* But the most discussed oil painting from book 1 was Sir Thomas Lawrence's *Satan Calling His Legions.* Lawrence's canvas was indebted to Fuseli's person as well as his art. The artist said that he had conceived his image of Satan from watching Fuseli's rapture as he looked on the sea from a high rock in Pembrokeshire,[16] and many years later, he told Mrs. Jameson, the art historian, that, in addition to being inspired by the Sistine Chapel, the picture generally "owed its conception to [Fuseli's] character of composition and design"—"though rejecting (as he himself did for me) any charge of servile imitation of . . . the noblest poetically inventive genius that perhaps our modern ages have produced."[17] The picture was shown at the Royal Academy in 1797 along with Lawrence's portraits of John Philip Kemble, who had modeled for Satan's head, and Mrs. Siddons, who had posed for one of the angels in the pit (a figure later painted out). Before it was exhibited it had stirred lively gossip in artistic circles; Fuseli told Lawrence that "he had heard he was painting Satan 30 feet high."[18] (The actual dimensions were 14 feet 2 inches × 9 feet.) The picture had a mixed reception. Benjamin West told Lawrence that "the picture would immortalize him," and the Duke of Norfolk paid two hundred guineas for it.[19] But the acerb critic "Pasquin" (John Williams) said that Satan resembled "a mad German sugar-baker dancing naked in a

*Turner made seven vignettes for an edition of Milton's *Poetical Works* in 1835. They had as little to do with Milton's text as did his picture of St. Michael's Mount (RA 1834), which nominally was an illustration of "Lycidas," where the landmark is mentioned.

†The 1826 canvas, unsold, was still in Martin's studio some years later, when the distinguished scientist Baron Cuvier called to see it. Martin was not at home, but the visitor sat before the picture a long time, then rose, muttered "Mon Dieu!", placed his card and his boutonniere on Martin's palette, and departed in silence (Mary L. Pendered, *John Martin, Painter: His Life and Times* [New York, 1924], pp. 132–33).

‡Attention should be called to C.H. Collins Baker's masterly study of trends in Miltonic book illustration, in which he systematically traces the first appearance and relative popularity of each subject from *Paradise Lost.* It would be interesting to compare these tendencies with the concurrent ones in painting—an exercise that would be equally illuminating when applied to other literary works that were so often illustrated in books as well as in gallery paintings.

272. John Martin (?), *The Fallen Angels Entering Pandemonium* (undated) (Tate Gallery, London). This painting, representing the action in *Paradise Lost,* book 1, lines 757–68, is unsigned and undated, and its attribution to Martin has been made largely on stylistic grounds. In his other pictures of Pandemonium (a mezzotint published in 1825 and an oil painting signed and dated 1841), Martin's architectural interest is uppermost: the satanic palace is as huge as Belshazzar's. Here its dome looms dimly in the background.

conflagration of his own treacle."[20] Most people decided that Lawrence had aimed higher than he could reach.

In any event, between this time and the 1840s some thirty paintings were drawn from the poem's initial movement, the most celebrated of them after Lawrence's being the several Martin produced of a gigantic and lurid Pandemonium (pl. 272), the sister palace of the one he made famous in *Belshazzar's Feast.* The press' reception of a belated example, Mark Dessurne's *Fall of the Rebel Angels* (SBA 1853), suggested that mob scenes in the void were not everybody's forte—it was the lot of few to possess Fuseli's or Martin's hectic imagination—and at the same time showed how perilously close the sublime could border on the ridiculous. "The subject," said the *Times,* "is difficult no doubt, as all the rebels are head downwards, falling from the crest of heaven down a precipice, where smoke and patches of fire give tokens of hell. But there they are, legs and arms like spread eagles, conveying anything but a feeling of pleasure to the beholder, and a ray descending straight from heaven upon them, a great deal more material and solid than anything of the sort has a right to be."[21]

Hogarth's early theme of Satan, Sin, and Death appeared only a few times at the Royal Academy down to the end of the eighteenth century. The evil collaboration became almost the exclusive territory of Fuseli, who devoted no fewer than nine Milton Gallery paintings to images suggested by less than three hundred lines of book 2:

2. 662	*Lapland Orgies, the Hell-hounds round Sin . . .*
2. 752	*The Birth of Sin*
2. 771	*Sin Receiving the Key of Hell*
2. 772, 815	*Satan Encount'ring Death, Sin Interposing*

2. 781	*The Shepherd's Dream*
2. 787	*Sin Pursued by Death*
2. 927	*Satan's Ascent from Hell*
2. 943	*A Gryphon Pursuing an Arimaspian. A Comparison of Satan's Exertions to Force His Way through the Realm of Chaos*
2. 1010	*Satan Bursts from Chaos*

Still another Milton Gallery painting represented a later scene in the same chain of events: *Death and Sin Bridging the "Waste" of Chaos and Met by Satan on His Return from Earth* (10. 293, 300, 326, 352).

It was scenes in the Garden of Eden, however, especially those in the dramatic narrative reaching from book 9 to the end (part of what I have called the third movement), that predominated in the artistic repertory from *Paradise Lost.* There were several reasons for this: the opportunities they particularly afforded to echo the Old Masters; their superior fitness for domestic decoration (few households would have welcomed Satan surrounded by the fallen angels or conversing with Sin and Death, as Fuseli horribly personified them); their lush backgrounds, making them as much landscape scenes as representations of Scripture; and their symbolic value, as embodiments of perfection before the Fall of Man.* Martin seems to have painted more pictures from this movement than from the more cosmic ones, but he treated the scenes in his typical manner, the human figures almost invisible in a vast welter of natural surroundings. One can assume that most of the other artists who depicted the circumstances of original sin did so in a less Martinesque, more traditional manner; there were, after all, innumerable models in older art. Fuseli devoted two paintings in his gallery to adjoining moments in Adam's narrative: the creation of Eve (8.462, 470) and God's leading her to him (484). A dozen years later, Martin portrayed the same moment. He joined others in painting the night scene in Paradise, with Adam and Eve at prayer guarded by loyalist angels; and at least one artist, following Fuseli in the Milton Gallery, represented Eve's dream with its premonition of sin. Several artists, including Martin and Etty, who painted his version (RA 1837) for the eccentric connoisseur William Beckford, showed Adam and Eve at their morning prayers.

Five pictures in the Milton Gallery described the main events before the Expulsion:

9. 424, 523	*Satan's First Address to Eve*
9. 781	*Eve at the Forbidden Tree*
9. 848	*Adam and Eve Meeting after Her Seduction*
9. 953, 958, 990	*Adam Resolved to Share the Fate of Eve; the Guardian Angels Leaving the Garden*
10. 224, 1007	*Eve, after the Sentence and Departure of the Judge, Supported by Adam*

In the next half-century, six more artists exhibited paintings from this sequence.

The vision of the Deluge in book 11, with its suggestion of famous paintings by Giulio Romano, Carracci, and Poussin among others, was especially attractive to artists of the terrific-catastrophic school. Fuseli derived two Milton Gallery paintings from it, *The Vision of the Deluge* and *The Vision of Noah.* It inspired a picture by Turner (RA 1813) and, as we

*John Dixon Hunt has argued that the passage describing the Garden of Eden in book 4 became a "sacred text," "a prototype landscape," for eighteenth-century gardening enthusiasts (*The Figure in the Landscape,* p. 56). One wonders whether paintings of the subject were influenced in turn by those gardens at rural seats that were meant to imitate the one inhabited by "our first parents," the very definition of unspoiled Nature.

have seen, at least two by Martin. These paintings had more than a little in common with contemporaneous renderings of the "last man" theme and of Byron's "Darkness," another literary version of the same end-of-the-world nightmare. John Linnell's treatment of *The Eve of the Deluge* (RA 1848) was hailed as "one of the most magnificent effects of a foreboding sunset ever painted . . . palpably the last evening of a condemned world."[22]

Finally, there was the Expulsion from Paradise, the subject of at least a dozen recorded paintings, all but two of which were shown before the mid-1850s.[23] Fuseli painted the scene at least twice, once for the Milton Gallery and again (1802) for an engraving in DuRoveray's edition of Milton. Benjamin West left an oil sketch for a nine-by-six-foot chapel painting that evidently was not realized.

Paradise Lost contained scores of narrative and dramatic moments and, in its great array of allusions and extended similes, hundreds of borrowed images ready for painting. The likening of the numberless host of fallen angels to "faery elves, / Whose midnight revels, by a forest-side / Or fountain, some belated peasant sees" (1.781–83) inspired a number of artists, beginning with the one who painted the scene at Vauxhall Gardens (see Part Two, above, under *A Midsummer Night's Dream*) and including Fuseli (pl. 33) and David Scott. But out of the many possibilities, only a comparative handful ever were chosen; instead, favored themes were painted over and over. There was no compelling reason why a single gesture, the angel Ithuriel touching Satan with his deceit-detecting spear, a kind of moral dowsing rod, as the archfiend pours his blandishments into Eve's receptive ear (4.810–11) should have inspired more paintings than any other equally incidental moment. But there was an early series of such paintings, including Alexander Runciman's (RA 1773), Fuseli's in 1780 (and again in the Milton Gallery), and Westall's in the Academy show of 1793.

One more subject, or cluster of subjects, in *Paradise Lost* had a diversified history in British art: Satan's deception of Uriel, angel of light and "Regent of the Sun," and the ensuing description of the stars (3.648–732), which is picked up again in Milton's description of the creation of the sun and moon (7.339–86). It was a print of Fuseli's *Uriel and Satan*, which the Plymouth schoolboy Benjamin Robert Haydon saw in his father's shopwindow, that determined his career. "I stopped and gazed as if enchanted," he told lecture audiences in the 1840s, "I drank into my being its poetry with sensations in my brain unfelt before, and never forgotten since."[24] As fate would have it, this was the subject of one of Haydon's last paintings, exhibited at the Royal Academy in 1845. Although the *Times* praised it ("The face is noble and ideal, and a fine effect is produced by the golden colour of the hair. This huge commanding figure is backed by limitless space, represented by a very dark positive blue, and the whole conveys the impression of a simple vastness"),[25] its size, which required it to be hung in the anteroom at the Royal Academy, told against it. "It will not do for a chapel," said the irreverent Thackeray in *Fraser's Magazine;* "it is too big for a house: I have it—it might answer to hang up over a caravan at a fair, if a travelling orrery were exhibited inside."[26] (The buyer was later said to have had a gallery built to accommodate it.) A year later, driven to insufferable despair by notices like this, among other misfortunes, Haydon committed suicide.

Much earlier (1818), the American painter Washington Allston caused some stir at the British Institution with his *The Angel Uriel,* which Allston's pupil Leslie thought had "a harmony equal to the best pictures of Paul Veronese" but which Keats, who mistakenly thought the painting was Leslie's, confessed he could not bear.[27] The reviewers quoted copiously from *Paradise Lost* as they heaped praise on Allston's "gigantic figure," which, said the *Examiner,* "mingles the beautiful and the grand with a poetic fervor of feeling, that fixes thought not on the common place or even elegant of what is earthly, [but] upon a nobler species of beings, upon an object unearthly and celestial."[28]

The astronomical passages in books 3 and 7 particularly attracted Henry Howard, who was something of a specialist in Milton. Two of his early sketches at the Royal Academy, *Planets Drawing Light from the Sun* (1796) and *Sin and Death Passing Through the Constellations* (1797), prefigured, as his son wrote, a "ruling passion which . . . manifested its power in the production of many of his most favourite works,"[29] some thirty out of the 367 he exhibited in the course of a long career. In 1814, Howard showed *Sunrise,* better known as *The Pleiades* (*Paradise Lost,* 7.374). Unsold at the Royal Academy, the picture won a premium at the British Institution and was purchased by the Marquis of Stafford; Howard then made a copy for Sir John Leicester.* Howard's passion for "astronomical personification" as inspired by Milton surfaced again in 1823, when he exhibited *The Solar System,* a picture developed from the 1796 sketch. "The sun," said the *London Magazine,* "is represented by Apollo, who, tuning his lyre, is seated in the centre. The planets, delicately personified by nymphs, with star-light on the forehead, or illuminated lamps in their hand, are floating round and taking their light from him. The satellites of Jupiter, Saturn, &c. are sylph-like forms, with small urns of light, or streaming diadems."[30] A duplicate was painted of this picture as well, and in 1834, Howard was commissioned to paint a circular adaptation, twelve feet in diameter, for the Duchess of Sutherland's boudoir in Stafford House. He seized the opportunity to update his map of the heavens by inserting the newly discovered asteroids Juno, Pallas, Ceres, and Vesta.[31]

It was possibly with Howard's pictures in mind that Thackeray fancied Haydon's huge Uriel serving as an advertisement for a traveling orrery, for Howard was himself associated with this popular branch of education through "rational amusement." In 1797, at the request of George Romney, he painted a portrait of Adam Walker, a lecturer on scientific topics who, beginning in 1782, had toured a pictorial astronomical lecture of his invention called the Eidouranion. At some time in the device's long career (it was being exhibited as late as the 1830s by Walker's son), Howard painted the zodiacal designs surrounding the astronomical map. In some other armchair tours of the firmament offered to the public in the late eighteenth and early nineteenth centuries, lecturers often intoned Milton's majestic lines as they pointed their wands at their diagrams, slide projections, or planetarium-like models of the celestial arrangements.[32]

Milton's masque *Comus* was represented by well over seventy-five paintings. Its text was printed sixty-three times in the eighteenth century and, of course, was included in all collected editions of Milton's poetry. But it had little effect on the poetry of the time and was not much discussed by

*The success of this picture may have been one reason that Howard later exhibited another with the title *Subject from the Lost Pleiade of Miss Laetitia Elizabeth Landon* (BI 1831). This, however, had nothing to do with Milton. The poem, published ten years earlier, was a keepsake-type confection on the classical myth of Electra, "the Lost Pleiad" who vanished from Troy before its destruction because she could not bear to witness the event. It was also the subject of a sculpture by John G. Lough.

273. Joseph Wright of Derby, *A Moonlight Scene from "Comus" (The Lady in "Comus")* (1785) (Walker Art Gallery, Liverpool). One of Wright's notable experiments with light, this painting was exhibited at a London auction room in the spring of 1785 and was bought by Josiah Wedgwood, the celebrated potter. "There does a sable cloud / Turn forth her silver lining on the night, / And casts a gleam over this tufted grove."

critics. To many people, it was best known in theatrical adaptations, the texts of which were more often reprinted in the early nineteenth century than the Miltonic original.[33] Beginning in 1738, when the Reverend John Dalton's version was staged, there were few seasons through the rest of the century when *Comus* was not performed in London, either in this version or, from 1772, in George Colman's two-act version with music by Thomas Arne. The most popular afterpiece in the whole repertory, it was seen 215 times between 1776 and 1800.[34] Mrs. Siddons often played the Lady, even after increased weight and a "very evident moustache," as John Martin described her to his son,[35] would seem to have disqualified her to play the leading female role in what was essentially an allegorical fairy tale with music.

The first appearance of *Comus* at the annual exhibitions reflected this long-established association with the theater. In 1776, Francis Wheatley showed at the Society of Artists a portrait of Anthony Webster in the role of the evil magician for whom the masque was named. The most notable of the eighteenth-century *Comus* paintings was Joseph Wright of Derby's *A Moonlight Scene from Comus* (pl. 273). The Milton Gallery included two scenes, one expansively described by Fuseli's conflation, in the catalogue entry, of two of Milton's stage directions: "The palace and the rout of Comus; the lady set in the enchanted chair, to whom he offered his glass; the brothers rushing in with swords drawn, wrest the glass out of his hand; his rout flying." The other, a typically Fuselian orgiastic production, took its hint from Comus' mention of the "goddess of nocturnal sport, / Dark-veiled Cotytto, to whom the secret flame / Of midnight torches burns!" *Comus* was not especially Fuseli's Miltonic cup of tea, but he returned to it from time to time, exhibiting a subject from it in the year of his death, 1825.

Beginning in 1801, Henry Howard flooded the market with paintings from *Comus.* Few if any of these potboilers survive, but we can be sure that they served the public appetite for decorative fancy. To artists as well as theatrical producers, *Comus* was a storehouse of suggestions for "poetic" pictures, especially of the pastoral variety; it had shepherds (including Comus himself disguised as one), dryads, moonlit forests, magic (the enchanted chair, the mirror), allegory (the Lady, attended by the personified Virtues, as the captive symbol of Chastity), the *genius loci* Sabrina with her retinue of water nymphs, graceful dances with bacchanalian trimmings, numerous allusions to classical story—the themes and materials of painters from Titian to Poussin.

If Martin was the leading exponent of *Paradise Lost* after Fuseli, Etty was the most important painter (Howard not being in the same class) to derive inspiration from *Comus.* Only a few of his paintings were from *Paradise Lost,* and even they were of subjects compatible with his penchant for drawing the female figure. The principal one was *A Bevy of Fair Women* (11.582), otherwise known as *The Origin of Marriage* and *The World Before the Flood* (the title of Montgomery's ten-canto poem on the subject, 1813). Exhibited at the Royal Academy in 1828 (pl. 274), this presentation of the revels before the rains evoked from Constable the grumble, "Etty has a revel rout of Satyrs & lady bums as usual, very clear & sweetly scented with [attar] of roses—bought by an old Marquis (Ld. Stafford)—coveted by the King (from description), but too late."[36]

The sensuous, Titianesque procession of Etty's *Comus* pictures had begun seven years earlier, with *Cupid and Psyche* (pl. 275) at the British Institution. In 1828, he showed *The Dawn of Love* ("Venus now wakes and wakens love") at the same venue. "The subject," warned the *Times,* "is . . . handled in a way entirely too luscious (we might, with great propriety, use a harsher term) for the public eye."[37] *Sabrina and Her Nymphs* (pl. 150), "conspicuous," said the *Examiner,* "for the truth and beauty of the flesh colour, the graceful action and lovely forms of the Nymphs, and the appropriate scenery by which they are surrounded"[38]—terms that could have been, and were, applied to almost every literary picture Etty painted—was repeated at least once, in 1841.

274. William Etty, *A Bevy of Fair Women (The Origin of Marriage) (The World before the Flood)* (RA 1828) (Southampton Art Gallery).

A bevy of fair women, richly gay
In gems and wanton dress! to the harp they sung
Soft amorous ditties, and in dance came on.
The men, though grave, eyed them, and let their eyes
Rove without rein, till, in the amorous net
Fast caught, they liked, and each his liking chose.
And now of love they treat, till the evening-star,
Love's harbinger, appeared; then, all in heat,
They light the nuptial torch, and bid invoke
Hymen, then first to marriage rites invoked:
With feast and music all the tents resound.

Paradise Lost, bk. 9, ll. 582–92

275. William Etty, *Cupid and Psyche* (British Institution 1821) (Lady Lever Art Gallery, Port Sunlight).

Far above in spangled sheen
Celestial Cupid, her famed son, advanced,
Holds his dear Psyche sweet intranced,
After her wandring labours long,
Till free consent the gods among
Make her his eternal Bride. . . .
Comus, ll. 1003–8

An old hand at *Comus* art by this time, in 1843 Etty was caught in one of the first artistic projects sponsored by the Prince Consort.[39] This was the year in which the first competition was held to decide who would paint the frescoes in the new Palace of Westminster (see Part One, above, chapter 8). Forty of the competitors chose subjects from Milton, including a number from *Comus*. The latter were disallowed, because, as we have seen (chapter 8), Macaulay, insisting that paintings in so fanciful a vein were unsuitable for the majestic seat of government, would allow only *Paradise Lost* to be represented there.[40] But the Prince shared with the Queen pleasant memories of Macready's production the preceding year (she wrote in her diary that they were especially taken by "the first scene with the Procession of Comus, and the first Bacchante (Mme Vestris) seated in a car, drawn by tigers, who were remarkably well trained"),[41] and furthermore he had a free hand at Buckingham Palace. And so he commissioned eight of "the chief painters of the English school," including Etty, to decorate the pavilion (summer house) in the gardens with frescoes from *Comus*.

The "Milton villa," as it came to be called, was the topic of the day in London art circles: "A little Chinesey box, divided into three or four small rooms,"as the art critic Elizabeth Rigby described it in March 1844, "the centre an octagonal apartment, each side with a half circle devoted to one artist. The subjects are from Comus; Eastlake's is beautiful—he is the Raphael of England. Etty's next best in composition, and the nearest to real fresco effect."[42] Thus the future wife of Eastland, the Raphael of England; but Etty was in trouble. He had begun his subject, *Circe, Sirens, and Naiads,* also to be known as *Circe and the Sirens Three,* the preceding July, but soon found he could not adapt his skill in oil painting to the quite different requirements of fresco. Even after a six-month layoff (he had returned to work the month before Miss Rigby awarded him her judicious praise), he could not get it right. Perhaps he was more distracted than his co-workers were by the twice-daily visits of the royal family to check on their progress. He begged to be allowed to paint another subject, and to prove his competence sent to the Royal Academy of that year an oil sketch, the same size as the lunette, of the scene described in the Attendant Spirit's epilogue in *Comus:* the Hesperides dancing about a tree, flanked on one side by Venus and Adonis and on the other by Cupid and Psyche. Thackeray praised it as "one of the artist's noblest compositions, a classical and pictorial *orgy,* as it were,—a magnificent vision of rich colours and beautiful forms,—a grand feast of sensual poetry."[43] Prince Albert also said he liked the picture, but he denied Etty the chance to transfer it to the wall and, paying him off with the paltry forty pounds stipulated in the commission, appointed William Dyce in his stead.*

What they regarded as the Prince's cavalier treatment of a respected artist did not sit well with some other artists and onlookers. In those early years of his residence at the palace, still regarded as a foreign interloper, he was far from popular. Thackeray attacked his version of "Royal patronage" in *Fraser's Magazine.* "Think of august powers and principalities ordering the works of such a great man as Etty to be hacked out of the palace wall [*sic*—a rhetorical exaggeration]—that was a slap in the face to every artist in England."[44] Haydon, bitter as ever on the subject of patronage, made his way into the pavilion in November 1844 despite Eastlake's refusing him admittance. His concurrence with Miss Rigby's estimate of Eastlake's ability is a rare instance of Haydon's critical judgment prevailing over personal animosity. He wrote the American artist Seymour Kirkup:

> They were dabbing away all round the sides miserable arabesques to decorate more miserable frescoes. Ah! my dear friend, you have only got to come to

*Although Dyce's work proved satisfactory, he was scarcely happier than Etty with the rewards of painting for royalty. The considerable time and effort he devoted to his contribution netted him only £100. "I dare say," he wrote in a private letter, "you will think Her Majesty very *shabby:* and so she is. The painters are paid by her like the doctors with thanks and sometimes honours, but with very little money." But this ill-paid commission, combined with his previous experience in painting domestic decoration in fresco, helped win him the much larger and more lucrative assignment to paint the Queen's Robing Room frescoes later on (Robertson, *Eastlake,* p. 270).

276. Edwin Landseer, *The Rout of Comus and His Band* (1843) (Tate Gallery, London). Landseer's contribution to the series of Milton frescoes in the Buckingham Palace summer pavilion. No passage in Milton was better suited to the artist's specialty of animal painting than (in the poet's words) the "rout of Monsters, headed like sundry sorts of wild beasts, but otherwise like men and women" whom the Lady's brother is here dispersing.

277. Charles R. Leslie, *The Lady with the Enchanter Presenting to Her the Circean Cup* (RA 1844) (Tate Gallery, London). Another design for the Buckingham Palace frescoes. This was Leslie's only painting from Milton, and it is obviously not in his characteristic vein of literary anecdote.

> England now to lose all relish for art. Etty's, so help me Heaven! Etty's second attempt is unworthy a café chantant at Paris.* Uwin's is a poultice; Leslie's dark; Stanfield, a diminished scene from the Lyceum; Ross is not as bad as Etty's, but like a drawing of Varley's; Landseer is doing his at home [as Etty had wished to do, but he was refused permission]; and at last there is something, Eastlake's, is worthy of the very best school to be named. . . . Prince Albert should cut out all the rest, pitch them into the pond, and let Eastlake finish the whole. As it will be, and is, it must be wretched patch-work.[45]

Etty's original design was shown at the Royal Academy in 1846. Robert Browning, returning home from the exhibition, wrote Elizabeth Barrett, "Etty's picture of the *sirens* is abominable; tho' it looks admirable beside another picture of his: did I not tell you he had chosen the sirens for a subject?" Elizabeth replied by return mail:

> And now tell me. . Was there not a picture of Sirens by Etty, exhibited years ago . . which was also "abominable," as I thought when I saw it?† Is it the same picture returning like a disquieted ghoule . . much more *that,* than like a Siren at all, if it is the same, . . I remember it was scarcely to be looked at for hideousness . . though I heard some carnivorous connaisseurs praising the "colouring"!! Foreigners might refer such artistical successes to our national "beef" . . "le bifteak" ideal. The materialism of Art.[46]

Meanwhile, at the 1844 exhibition where Etty's *Comus* sketch was hung, two other designs for the pavilion were seen, Leslie's *The Lady with the Enchanter Presenting to Her the Circean Cup* (pl. 277), the painter's only Miltonic subject, which Thackeray compared unfavorably with Etty's, and Maclise's *Sabrina, the Nymph, Releasing the Lady from the Enchanted Chair.*‡

Two more summer house designs were at the Royal Academy the next year (1845). One was Eastlake's, which Miss Rigby and Haydon had impartially praised. Thackeray, Etty's partisan, was outspoken in his dislike. "The picture," he wrote,

> is prodigiously laboured, and hatched, and tickled up with a Chinese minuteness; but there is a woeful lack of *vis* in the work. . . . . This face of the

*Haydon was wrong. This was Dyce's.

†This was *The Sirens and Ulysses,* exhibited at the Royal Academy in 1837 and presented to the Manchester Institution two years later. Writing to his friend Etty from Lucca in 1849, Browning spoke nothing but the truth but something short of the whole truth when, conveying his wife's "homage," he added, "We have often remembered your grand *Sirens*" (*Letters of Robert Browning Collected by T. J. Wise,* ed. Thurman L. Hood [New Haven, Conn., 1933], p. 27).

‡Its fate decided by Father Thames, on that occasion a malign water genius who was the anti-type of Sabrina, the painting was destroyed in a flood at the Tate Gallery in 1928. In the same year, the dilapidated Buckingham Palace summer house was finally pulled down.

lady is pure and beautiful; but we have seen it at any time in these ten years, with its red transparent shadows, its mouth in which butter wouldn't melt, and its beautiful brown madder hair. She is getting rather tedious, that sweet, irreproachable creature, that is the fact. She may be an angel; but sky-blue, my wicked senses tell me, is a feeble sort of drink, and men require stronger nourishment.[47]

Thackeray found the other *Comus* painting in the 1845 show, William Edward Frost's *Nymphs Dancing*, more to his liking. It was, he said, "like a mixture of very good Hilton and Howard raised to a state of genius."[48] Frost, whose first Academy acceptance this was, was the successor, in this field of Miltonic art, of the aged Henry Howard, who was to die in 1847. Between this year and 1871 he exhibited fifteen paintings from *Comus*, "L'Allegro," and "Il Penseroso" (none from *Paradise Lost*). It did not hurt him at all that the Queen and the Prince Consort immediately took a fancy to his work. Victoria bought his Spenserian *Una and the Wood Nymphs* from the Academy show of 1847, and when the collector Elhanan Bicknell commissioned *Euphrosyne* (RA 1848), the Queen was so much taken with it that she ordered a copy of the principal group as a present for her husband (pl. 278).

Although the production of *Comus* pictures continued, the subject had exhausted its freshness by the end of the decade—not surprisingly, because of the seventy-five recorded, fully a third were painted between 1840 and 1850. "Poor Sabrina!" exclaimed the *Art Journal* in 1849. "Her Majesty's commissioners for the embellishment of the new Houses of Parliament have been instrumental in calling her too often before the curtain. But we love these hacknied subjects, because [the need for?] variety makes them so difficult."[49] It was a cheering thought.

Whereas *Comus* owed much of its popularity to its presence in the theatrical repertory, "L'Allegro" and "Il Penseroso," in their original form, figured prominently in the eighteenth-century literary imagination. A modern authority detected, perhaps a trifle too ingeniously, their influence on no fewer than 400 poems written between 1740 and 1820.[50] They were included in such anthologies as Goldsmith's *Beauties of English Poesy* and the many editions of *Elegant Extracts*. Handel set them to music and inserted them into his oratorio *Samson* (1740), in which arranged form they, like *Comus*, went through many editions. At Vauxhall Gardens, near a "Temple of Comus" in allegedly Chinese style, one of whose interior walls had a painting of Vulcan catching Mars and Venus in the net, there was a life-sized statue of Milton sitting on a rock listening to soft music, as he described himself doing in "Il Penseroso". Although, with the arrival of new tastes, poets ceased to echo their style or substance, "Il Penseroso" and "L'Allegro" were never absent from the art galleries. Well over eighty paintings were associated with them across the entire century, outlasting the vogue of *Comus* by three decades.

Although they lacked *Comus'* dramatic quality, with its choric movements and dramatic moments, like the masque they lent a literary aura to decorative and allegorical compositions involving figures, single or in groups, personifying various moral attributes. Their specific subjects, apart from occasional representations of the classical myths referred to, were sportive or meditative activities or moods.* Apart from whatever realization they contained of specific images in the text, their connection with Milton's poems, more so than that of *Comus* pictures, usually was nominal. Most of them were mood or "ideal" pictures, and a few others

*Unlike many English literary subjects, these came to artists unaccompanied by reminiscences of earlier iconography. The antecedents of "L'Allegro" and "Il Penseroso," composed ca. 1629–34, were few: the female statues representing the Vita Activa and the Vita Contemplativa that, according to Vasari, stood at corners of Michelangelo's tomb of Julius II (ca. 1542); the figure of Lorenzo de Medici, known from the sixteenth century as "Pensiero" or "Pensoso," in Michelangelo's Medici Chapel; Lucas Cranach's *Melancholy* (1528); the antithesis between "Allegrezza" and "Malinconia" in such paintings as Abraham Janssens' (1623); and Dürer's famous *Melencolia I* engraving with its numerous sixteenth- and seventeenth-century progeny. Milton's own sources seem to have been literary rather than iconographic: the "Dialogue between Pleasure and Pain" in Burton's *Anatomy of Melancholy*, songs by Nicholas Breton and Beaumont and Fletcher. But the literary tradition of contrasted moods originated with Milton, and the "L'Allegro" and "Il Penseroso" paintings derived almost wholly from it (with overtones, perhaps, of the many seventeenth- and eighteenth-century poetic treatments it inspired) rather than from any preceding or concurrent artistic tradition. (Erwin Panofsky, "The Platonic Movement and Michelangelo," *Studies in Iconology* [New York, 1939], pp. 188–209 passim; Raymond Klibansky, Erwin Panofsky, and Fritz Saxl, *Saturn and Melancholy* [London, 1964], pp. 227–29.)

departed so far from the Miltonic letter or spirit as to parody it. Two eighteenth-century pictures (1783, 1788) titled *Penseroso* were portraits of a celebrated stallion which bore that misnomer. And in 1832, Thomas Webster's *Il Penseroso* showed a village wrongdoer with his feet in the stocks, thinking things over—just as the title said.

The poems entered English art by way of such early fancy pictures as Reynolds's portrait of *Mrs. Fortescue as La Pensierosa* (1761) and Romney's pair (Society of Artists 1770), *Melancholy* and *Mirth.* Alongside these portraits developed a parallel vein of subject and landscape paintings that alluded to the twin poems. Gavin Hamilton painted a pair for a country gentleman in the 1760s, and in 1773 Alexander Runciman produced a pair of Rubenseque landscapes to which he gave the Miltonic names. *Il Penseroso* is lost, but *L'Allegro* (with Perth in the background) survives. Fuseli's Milton Gallery had four subjects from "L'Allegro" (*Faery Mab, The Friar's Lanthorn* [*Friar Tuck*], *The Lubbar Fiend* [*Puck*], and *Euphrosyne, or Mirth, with Fancy and Moderation Hovering Over Her, Tripping Forward*) and three from "Il Penseroso" (*Silence* [showing a mother with her two children], *Cremhild Meditating Revenge over the Sword of Sigfrid,* and *Melancholy Reclining on Her Throne*).

278. William E. Frost, *L'Allegro* (1849) (Royal Collection, Copyright Reserved).

But come, thou Goddess fair and free,
In heaven yclep'd Euphrosyne,
And by men, heart-easing Mirth,
Whom lovely Venus at a birth
With two sister Graces more
To ivy-crownèd Bacchus bore. . . .

A replica of the principal group in Frost's *Euphrosyne.*

In the ensuing half-century (1800–1850), there was a steady flow of "L'Allegros" and "Il Penserosos," some thirty-five in all. Female portraits with the latter title (or "La Penserosa" or "La Pensierosa") were among the leading clichés of nineteenth-century popular art. They showed women posed in attitudes suggestive of more or less deep thought, or at least engaged in the time-killing occupation, favored by Dickens's heroines, of "musing" by a fire or an open window. Judging from the few surviving examples, pictures associated with "L'Allegro" tended to be festival scenes. By one of those coincidences with which the history of English literary art is rife, two well-known pictures bearing the same quotation from the poem, "When the merry bells ring round . . .", were shown simultaneously at the Royal Academy in 1847. One was Frith's *An Old English Merry-Making,* which was so popular that the artist repeated it many times in the next sixty years. But the scene was not "from" Milton; the costumes located it in the middle of the eighteenth century. The other picture, Frederick Goodall's *Village Festival* (pl. 51), was no more Miltonic; it depicted a rural merry-making in Brittany.

Two years later (1849), the Art Union issued an album called *L'Allegro and Il Penseroso, Illustrated in a Series of Thirty Wood Engravings.* This publication combined with the publicity enjoyed by the Frith and Goodall paintings and the partiality the royal couple had for Milton's shorter works to give the poems a vigorous new lease on artistic life. Frost, having struck a profitable vein with *Comus,* continued to mine it with three paintings from "Il Penseroso" at the Royal Academy in 1850–55, and miniature replicas of the *Euphrosyne,* renamed *L'Allegro* (pl. 278) he painted for the Queen. Occasionally there were novelties of treatment. In 1851, James Digman Wingfield portrayed what a critic described as "the espousal of the two conflicting affections of the soul in one canvas," not the conventional juxtaposition of two figures but a personification of Mirth and Melancholy *en masse.* The Penserosi were depicted at the right of the composition, "a company of grave people, 'intellectually' occupied under a tree," while on the left, "a troop of young persons dancing round another tree, represent the Allegri."[51]

By this time, reviewers were growing as impatient as they had become

279. John Callcott Horsley, *L'Allegro and Il Penseroso* (RA 1851) (Royal Collection, Copyright Reserved). More "Il Penseroso" than "L'Allegro," which poem is represented only by the dancing nymphs in the background. The "pensive nun" is costumed according to Victorian notions rather than Milton's more elaborate specifications:

> All in a robe of darkest grain,
> Flowing with majestic train,
> And sable stole of cypress lawn
> Over thy decent shoulders drawn.

This is still another painting added to the royal collection during the Queen's and Prince Consort's infatuation with pictures illustrating Milton's poetry.

with *Comus* pictures. Interspersed among the customary polite phrases of approval were sharper comments. "We walk away without the slightest interest in such nonentities" said the *Literary Gazette* of John C. Horsley's study (pl. 279) of contrasting groups, shown the same year as Wingfield's—a "pensive nun, devout and pure" leading figures who might be identified, interchangeably, as Peace, Calm, and Quiet, while the background was occupied by a choir of dancing nymphs.[52] Ruskin, who yielded to none of his fellow critics in the department of wicked wit, wrote of Charles West Cope's *Penserosa* (RA 1855),

> The young lady appears to be reading, may possibly be thinking, is certainly passing under a Norman arch, and is very pretty. This *ensemble* is interesting, but had better have been put into the architectural room, as it may materially promote the erection of Norman arches in the gardens of the metropolis, for the better performance of pensive appearances to morning visitors.[53]

Vulgarization proceeded apace. By the mid-sixties, if not earlier, the name "L'Allegro" was being attached to such paintings as one of "a lady in cap and bells carrying a Punch and bells . . . a pretty picture," said the *Examiner,* "that might be taken as setting forth the L'Allegro of a nineteenth-century Milton, whose Eve giggles at slang and wears a pork-pie hat";[54] and the title "Il Penseroso" was given to a portrait of "a commonplace boarding-school girl in her night-dress, with her back hair let down, and giving her ideas of the subject preparatory for a charade performance."[55] Incongruity of source and treatment aside, the latter painting, as the *Times* pointed out, was disfigured by artificialities of style, all of which "degrade the work to a low level of art, but as surely raise it to a high level of popularity."[56] Popularity was a siren song that even one of the last painters of Milton's poems, Millais, could not resist. As late as 1887, he painted *Allegro* ("This 'Folie' of the Carnival has nought in her of Milton's lark") and *Penseroso* ("The lady is less pensieroso than misero, and has little in common with the nightingale of the poem"). The comments are those of Millais's own cataloguer, M. H. Spielmann, writing in 1898, two years after the artist's death.[57] Milton illustration had come a long way, mostly downhill, since Fuseli closed his Gallery of the Miltonic Sublime.*

THE DIARISTS: EVELYN AND PEPYS

The first publication, seven years apart (1818 and 1825), of the intimate diaries of two seventeenth-century men much involved in the events of their time, John Evelyn and Samuel Pepys, made no impact on art until the mid-1840s, with the single exception of a painting by John Cawse (SBA 1828) showing Charles II and Nell Gwyn and bearing a quotation from Evelyn. It may not have been entirely accidental that popular interest in subjects from the Commonwealth and Restoration was rising at the same time that a much enlarged edition of Pepys's diary was published in 1848–49. From this moment onward, some twenty paintings from Pepys are recorded, and about a dozen from Evelyn. The diaries had a twofold value to artists: they encouraged them to depict what were essentially public events, the subjects of modern history painting, through the eyes of private onlookers, preserved in a form of literature; and they offered occasions to create period pieces representing an epoch when costumes were especially colorful and elaborate, with staffage to match. Both diarists, happily—Pepys more then Evelyn—were not only faithful

*The remaining works in Milton's poetical oeuvre had a negligible record in art. There were no more than half a dozen paintings from *Paradise Regained. Samson Agonistes,* unrepresented in the Milton Gallery, was the source of only a dozen pictures between 1766 and 1881, including Etty's *Delilah Before the Blinded Samson* (1830s) and two pictures, both exhibited in 1859, by Frederic Leighton and F. R. Pickersgill. The *Athenaeum* (7 May, p. 618) declared that the latter was "an insult to Milton . . . as devoid of religious feeling as a bill of lading is of poetry." "Lycidas" had a considerable influence on eighteenth-century poets—greater than that of *Comus,* less than that of "L'Allegro" and "Il Penseroso"—but it did not figure conspicuously in art. There was only one Lycidas subject in the Milton Gallery, and only about a dozen are recorded from the nineteenth century; Frost's *Panope* (RA 1862), a composition of nude nymphs, was probably typical.

recorders of contemporary events but confided to their pages many events in their private lives, this at a time when anecdotal literary biography, too, was coming into its own as a staple of genre painting.

The one subject repeatedly drawn from Evelyn was his discovery of the great wood-carver Grinling Gibbons. Two artists, F. S. Cary in 1855 and Edgar Bundy in 1901, depicted the moment in January 1670/71 when Evelyn came upon him by accident in a "poore solitary thatched house in a field in our Parish, carving a crucifix after Tintoretto." At least two other painters, John Cawse in 1845 and E. M. Ward in 1869, showed the subsequent episode, narrated in detail by the disgusted diarist, when, after he had introduced Gibbons to the King and Queen at Whitehall, "a French pedling woman, one Madame de Boord, that used to bring petticoates and fanns & baubles out of France to the Ladys, began to find faults with severall things in the worke [the crucifix], which she understood no more than an Asse, or a Monky. . . ."[1]

Earlier, Ward had taken another moment (pl. 280) from the same passage in the diary, in which Evelyn recorded that while walking with the King to St. James's Park, he "both saw and heard a very familiar discourse betweene [the King] and Mrs. Nellie [Gwynne], as they cal'd an impudent Comedian, she looking out of her Garden on a Tarrace at the top of the Wall, and [the King] standing on the greene Walk under it: I was heartily sorry at this scene," Evelyn commented.[2] Ward's widow wrote long afterward that "some Early Victorians . . . were so shocked that they would hardly look at it, and were quite surprised that a man of his high principles should have immortalised this scene."[3]

Some years later (1867), Frith's picture *King Charles the Second's Last Sunday* was hung at the Royal Academy. Frith had devoted "nearly a year's incessant work" to it, and though he disliked it when he saw it on the wall, it was an immediate hit with the public and became the third of his paintings, after *Derby Day* and *The Marriage of the Prince of Wales,* to be railed round to prevent damage from too close inspection.[4] The picture portrayed a crowded and cautionary scene.

> I am never to forget [Evelyn had written] the unexpressable luxury, & prophanesse, gaming, & all dissolution, and as it were total forgetfullnesse of God (it being Sunday evening), which this day sennight, I was witnesse of; the King, sitting & toying with his Concubines Portsmouth, Cleaveland, & Mazarine: &c: a french boy singing love songs, in that glorious Gallery, whilst about 20 of the greate Courtiers & other dissolute persons were at Basset round a large table, a bank of at least 2000 in Gold before them, upon which two Gent: that were with me made reflexions with astonishment, it being a sceane of uttmost vanity; . . . six days after was all in the dust.[5]

Persons familiar with Evelyn's diary would have received the maximum impact of the painting if they remembered the earlier passage in the same entry in which he described in clinical detail the draconian measures the monarch's physicians employed a few days later in a futile effort to keep him alive. But the picture itself was sufficiently moralistic without being repellent, showing as it did "all the glittering rag-tag of that abominable Court. . . . Considering what the story is," commented the *Athenaeum,* "we are surprised to see with what subtle art and craft Mr. Frith has contrived to hide its grossness."[6]

One of the most notable, as it was among the earliest, of the paintings whose subjects were also the diarists'—though in this case a more immediate source was a contemporary biography—was Ward's *The Disgrace of*

280. Edward M. Ward, *Interview between Charles II and Nell Gwynne, as Witnessed by Evelyn* (RA 1848) (Victoria & Albert Museum, Crown Copyright). Evidently a replica (signed and dated 1859) of the exhibited painting. This scene of royal dalliance, with a disapproving Evelyn looking on, may have scandalized some Victorian art lovers, but it is more notable as an example of the visual appeal some seventeenth-century subjects had at the time for costume artists and their clients. The wall drapery and the hothouse luxuriance of the vegetation add to the richness of effect that Ward sought to produce.

Lord Clarendon (pl. 50). It too had a moral theme, and a dramatic one as well: the departure from the frivolous court, on his way to exile in France, of a high official of comparative integrity, brought low by the failure of the Dutch war and the intrigue of the court. The picture was praised both for the psychological truth with which Ward painted the central figure and for the "fantastic fashions" of the courtiers and courtesans who taunted him.

Scenes taken directly from Pepys were usually more domestic in nature. Following rather obviously, though at some distance in time, in the wake of Millais's well-received painting of a contemporary scene, a fireman's rescue of a child from a burning house (RA 1855), two popular artists painted an analogous incident recorded by Pepys (3 September 1665), the rescue of a child from a plague-stricken house. Henry O'Neil's version (RA 1875) was unenthusiastically described as "A man in nightcap handing down a child from a window to a theatrically-posed girl, another man in foreground holding a lantern; blue moonlight with 'Adelphi effects' "—that is, garish lighting associated with the cheap theaters.[7] F. W. Topham's late *Rescued from the Plague* (pl. 281) had a better reception.

A few of the more seemly episodes in Pepys's private life suggested paintings. Egg's *Pepys's Introduction to Nell Gwyn* (RA 1851) was inspired by Pepys's description (23 January 1666/67) of his and his wife's going behind the scenes at the King's Theatre to meet "Nelly, a most pretty woman . . . I kissed her, and so did my wife, and a mighty pretty soul she is."

> It is Pepys in all his glory [said the *Examiner*], fat, comfortable, self-complacent, and gorgeous as tailor can make him, in the ecstatic act of kissing Nell Gwynne, behind the scenes of the playhouse. The worthy secretary's eager enjoyment and anxiety to make the most of it, a little dashed by terror at his own audacity, and incredulity of his own felicity,—Nell's sidelong look of mockery of the awkward gallant, and her cold, half-laughing submission to him,—with the comment of Mrs. Pepys' look of unutterable horror and dismay,—tell the story as well as Pepys could have told it himself.[8]

This was as close as Victorian art came to hinting of Pepys's lecherous inclinations. Otherwise, the incidents chosen were amiable illustrations of small vanities: his dancing lesson (4 May 1663), "celebrated so often that the spectator is sated," said a reviewer of one such picture in 1862; Mrs. Pepys putting on "her first French gown, called a *Sac,* which becomes her very well" (2 March 1668/69) (RA 1849); and several linking the diarist, who like Evelyn had been painted by Kneller, with the portraiture of the time. James Noble, a prolific genre painter, whose works included *Rembrandt Painting His Father's Portrait* and *Raphael and Fornarina,* produced three versions of Pepys's seeing one of Lely's many portraits of the Duchess of York at the artist's studio (18 June 1662), adding, in the purported quotation from the diary, the uncanonical detail that subsequently Pepys "took great Pride to lead her through the Court by the Hand, she being very fine, and her Page carrying up her Train." Two years after Noble exhibited the first of these pictures, Alfred Elmore showed (RA 1852) the event of 15 February 1665/66, when Hales, the portraitist commissioned by the status-hungry Pepys, "begun [to paint] my wife in the posture we saw [in] one of my Lady Peters, like a St. Katharine." Elmore showed Pepys and two maidservants joining in a festive song; he did not depict the ensuing moment recorded by Pepys, when "comes Mrs. Pierce with my name in her bosom for her Valentine, which will cost me money," but spectators well versed in the diary would have seen it in their mind's eye.

281. Frederick W. Topham, *Rescued from the Plague, London, 1665* (RA 1898) (Guildhall Art Gallery, London). Pepys wrote (*Diary,* 3 September 1665) "of a complaint brought against a man in the town for taking a child from London from an infected house. Alderman Hooker told us it was the child of a very able citizen in Gracious-street, a saddler, who had buried all the rest of his children of the plague; and himself and wife now being shut up, and in despair of escaping, did desire only to save the life of this little child; and so prevailed to have it received stark-naked into the arms of a friend, who brought it (having put it into few fresh clothes) to Greenwich." An antiseptic treatment of historical circumstance: except for the cross on the door and the inscription "Lord have mercy upon us" above it—the healthy waif on the doorstep seems to be merely resting—there is no visual evidence of the plague. Compare Poole's picture from Defoe, pl. 286.

BUTLER

Nobody reads Samuel Butler's satirical poem *Hudibras* (1663–78) today, and it is more than a little surprising to find that so many English pictures were derived from it in the nineteenth century—some twenty altogether, from 1820 to 1884. Some people, it seems, were familiar with *Hudibras* two centuries after it was written. They had excellent critical authority for their interest. Addison had regarded the poem as the En-

282. John Pettie, *Hudibras and Ralpho in the Stocks* (Glasgow Institute 1868) (Sheffield City Art Galleries). Readers of *Hudibras* would have known that Hudibras (a Presbyterian) and Ralpho (an Independent) continued their sectarian disputes after being thrust into the stocks by the bear-baiters (part one, canto 3). But Pettie does not show them thus engaged, and the ideological content of the original scene is totally omitted in favor of the farcical discomfiture of the Don Quixote–Sancho Panza-like pair.

glish equivalent of *Don Quixote,* after which, indeed, *Hudibras* was to some extent modeled, with Ralpho playing Sancho Panza to his master's Don. Dr. Johnson had praised it in the *Idler,* as had Hazlitt in his lectures on the English comic writers, where he called it "the greatest single production of wit of this period, I might say of this country. . . . It contains specimens of every variety of drollery and satire, and those specimens crowded together into almost every page. . . . Butler is equally in the hands of the learned and the vulgar; for the sense is generally solid, as the images are amusing and grotesque. . . . Though his subject was local and temporary, his fame was not circumscribed within his own age."[1] As a schoolboy laid up with two badly scalded legs, Leigh Hunt read the poem "at one desperate plunge. . . . I did it as a sort of achievement, driving on through the verses without understanding a twentieth part of them, but now and then laughing immoderately at the rhymes and similes, and catching a bit of knowledge unawares."[2] Those same wild rhymes and similes inspired Byron to imitate them in *Don Juan,* and, in turn, Browning used them in such poems as "The Flight of the Duchess" and "Old Pictures in Florence." John Galt, the Scottish novelist, extravagantly ranked *Hudibras* not only with *Ivanhoe* but with *Hamlet, Paradise Lost,* and *The Faerie Queene.*[3] And, though Hazlitt does not reveal how he knew that "nearly one half of his [Butler's] lines are got by heart, and quoted for mottos," certain of them were common currency among nineteenth-century writers. Lecturers on the provincial mechanics' institute circuit included *Hudibras* among the comic masterpieces they described and from which they read ("the wittiest composition . . . ever penned," declared one)[4] and popular magazines ran appreciative articles on it.

But the fact that *Hudibras* was the first English poem ever to be painted in oils was forgotten. Less than two decades after its third and final part was published in 1678, Francis LePiper had painted twelve scenes from it (pl. 3). Hogarth designed a series of engravings as well as (possibly) painting a set of oil copies.[5] Sometime before 1776, John van der Gucht also took from the poem at least one picture, now lost.

The topical satirical points of *Hudibras* had largely evaporated from the poem by the time nineteenth-century artists took it up. Despite Hazlitt's opinion that it was "not virtually dramatic, or narrative," its popularity among artists of humorous bent was due to those very elements—the opportunities it offered for depicting inoffensively farcical episodes in the manner of Dutch genre art, such as Butler's own text suggested. In this respect, it ranked with the Falstaff plays, the *Twelfth Night* of Malvolio and Sir Toby, *The Vicar of Wakefield, Tristram Shandy*—and, of course, *Don Quixote,* a perennial favorite with artists—as a source of innocent merriment. The *New Monthly Magazine*'s review of F. P. Stephanoff's *The Visit of Sir Hudibras to the Lady* (BI 1820) typified the spirit, far from Butler's intention, in which episodes from the poem were painted and received: ". . . a fine grave burlesque spirit, without a particle of vulgarity or extravagance."

> Butler himself [the critic continued] could not have wished for a more lively representation of the subject. The sturdy wooer is bowing; stroking his beard with one hand, and holding his hat behind him with the other. In his amorous perturbation he has dropped one of his gloves on the floor. . . . The widow is in the flower of her age, . . . and the arch smile on her vermilion lip, might kindle a flame in any heart. . . . There is a delicious freshness in her countenance, which contrasts well with that of Hudibras.[6]

Hudibras and Ralph in the Stocks (part 1, canto 3) was a particular favorite; John Pettie painted the scene (pl. 282) and so, later on, did Sir John Gilbert. Sir William Fettes Douglas, a specialist in Scott and other historical subjects, maintained a sideline in *Hudibras* paintings. Between 1857 and 1884, he showed at the Royal Scottish Academy five pictures from the poem, *Sidrophel, Hudibras' Love Letter, Hudibras and the Lawyer, The Lady and Hudibras,* and *Hudibras and Ralph Visiting the Astrologer* (pl. 283).

BUNYAN

Popular though Bunyan's *The Pilgrim's Progress* was among the masses of people—a London bookseller once calculated that between 1678, the date of its publication, and 1792 there had been no fewer than 160 edi-

283. Sir William Fettes Douglas, *Hudibras and Ralph Visiting the Astrologer* (Royal Scottish Academy 1884) (National Gallery of Scotland). Hudibras is about to engage Sidrophel, the astrologer, in one more of the disputations of which the poem is largely composed (part two, canto 3). Douglas obviously chose this particular undramatic moment for the sake of indulging in his specialty of portraying pseudoscientists (pl. 136).

tions—as a document of Dissenting religion in the age of Deism, it had no literary standing whatsoever.[1] Such authors as did allude to it, did so with some embarrassment; Cowper, for example, said that he did not dare mention it in his verse "for fear of moving a sneer." It was decidedly a book of the people, not of the literary elite. But its readers, like other humble people to whom pictures were a particularly important part of their experience of books, prized their dilapidated copies of Bunyan's narrative not only for the text but for the illustrations they contained.[2] The third edition (1679), the first to be illustrated, had a portrait, from a pencil sketch, of the author asleep, dreaming (as the book's full title had it) of his "Progress from This World to That Which Is To Come." The fifth edition (1680–82) boasted thirteen copper plates, which were also available separately, and the twenty-second edition (1728) had twenty-two. As its constituency of Dissenter readers became more affluent toward the close of the century, new editions began to be illustrated by leading artists. Stothard made the designs for the 1788 edition, Kirk for Cooke's edition of 1796, and Westall six for an edition of 1820. Later, Blake painted from the book twenty-eight watercolor sketches, which remained unpublished. Southey's influential edition (1830) had, besides a number of wood engravings, two steel engravings from designs by John Martin, *The Valley of the Shadow of Death* and *The Celestial City*. But down to this time, *The Pilgrim's Progress* had been represented in the exhibitions by only three paintings, a Reverend Mr. Spooner's *A Landscape, with a Story from the Pilgrim's Progress* (Free Society of Artists 1773) and two of Stothard's designs for the 1788 edition (RA 1797).

284. Sir Joseph Noel Paton, *Arming Christian for the Fight* (1876) (Glasgow Art Gallery and Museum). For a century and a half after its publication in 1678, no book except the Bible was more familiar to the common people in town and country, especially the Dissenters, than *The Pilgrim's Progress.* Happily, its subject, the adventures of a Christian knight, qualified it as a source of nineteenth-century art in two popular veins that were often joined—chivalry and religion.

Meanwhile, however, as the Evangelical religion which had its roots in Dissent made its presence felt in society at large, the book was emerging from literary oblivion and sectarian obloquy. It had been a favorite childhood companion of Charles Lamb, who, apropos of the illustrations, told the Quaker poet Bernard Barton in a letter, "Nothing can be done for Bunyan but to reprint the old cuts in as honest a style as possible." Macaulay, declaring that "the allegory of Bunyan has been read by many thousands with tears," concluded that "though there were many clever men in England during the latter half of the seventeenth century, there were only two minds which possessed the imaginative faculty in a very eminent degree"—Milton and Bunyan.

The appearance in 1830 of Southey's life of Bunyan, included in his edition, together with the publicity generated by Macaulay's review in the *Edinburgh Review* and his article in the *Encyclopaedia Britannica,* gave Bunyan a wider celebrity among the cultivated reading public than he had ever enjoyed before. Beginning in 1834, when George Richmond exhibited *The Interpreter Showing Christian the Man in the Iron Cage* at the British Institution, the brisk trade in new illustrated editions of *The Pilgrim's Progress* was mirrored in the annual exhibitions. More than forty pictures are recorded down to the end of the century.

Unlike some other literary classics that supplied a few subjects to be repeatedly painted, Bunyan's was ransacked from cover to cover. Almost every episode was depicted sooner or later: Christian reasoning with Simple, Christian being armed for the fight, Christian arriving at the Palace Beautiful, Christian and his family arriving at the Slough of Despond, Christian in the house of Gaius, Christian and Pilgrim at Vanity Fair, Christian at the Valley of the Shadow of Death, Christian leaving the

City of Destruction, Christian and the Lion, Christian on the Delectable Mountain; Mercy knocking at the wicket gate, Mercy's dream; Mr. By-Ends meeting with Money-Love; Greatheart with pilgrims arriving at the porter's lodge. No set of scenes could have been more to the taste of the Nonconformist segment of the art-loving public than these. Disraeli's remark that Bunyan was "the Spenser of the People" was precisely on target: here was plain moral allegory without the classical trappings and fancy names of Spenser, embodied in figures that, though slightly idealized, were as recognizable to the unlettered commonalty as the chivalrous knights, beleaguered ladies, and fearsome beasts of *The Faerie Queene* were incomprehensible.

But it was not by *The Pilgrim's Progress* only that Bunyan was represented in art. After Southey's biography drew new attention to the tinker-preacher's experience in Bedford gaol, where he wrote *Grace Abounding*, it became the most-painted single episode from the life of any English writer, not least because it was an amalgam of elements appealing to Victorian picture-buyers: durance vile in a holy cause, an author composing a classic work under difficulties, a blind daughter selling shoelaces outside the prison. Between 1838 and the end of the century, there were at least a dozen paintings of Bunyan in prison.

285. William Huggins, *Christian and the Lions* (undated) (Walker Art Gallery, Liverpool). Christian, en route from the City of Destruction to Mount Zion, stops for the night at "a very stately palace" called Beautiful, undeterred by the lions that had previously driven Mistrust and Timorous away. The artist, known as "the Liverpool Landseer," specialized in animal subjects; needless to say, he also painted Una and the lion.

DRYDEN

As a source of literary paintings, Dryden completely dropped from view after the middle of the nineteenth century—a fairly good measure of how far his literary reputation had faded by that time. Earlier, his name had been attached to more than thirty pictures, the majority of them (ten each) from two of the *Fables:* the Boccaccian stories of Cymon and Iphigenia and of Sigismunda and Guiscardo (pl. 64), which had often been the subjects of European art. There were a few paintings from other fables, as well as from Dryden's other poems and his plays.

THE EIGHTEENTH CENTURY

DEFOE

As a tale for children, *Robinson Crusoe* was as enduringly popular as that other standard book for the chimney corner, *The Pilgrim's Progress.* The first of innumerable editions (1719) had an illustration showing the shipwrecked mariner in the home-sewn costume of skins in which he would be clothed whenever he reappeared in engravings and paintings.[1] The plates engraved from Stothard's designs for Stockdale's edition in 1790 were reused, time after time, throughout the next century. An edition of 1831 contained thirty-eight wood engravings by George Cruikshank, and nine years later a London publisher issued an English edition of the current Paris one, with notable illustrations by "Grandville" (Jean Ignace Isodore Gérard). This last, however, for some reason failed to sell; published at sixteen shillings, it was remaindered at a mere five shillings.

But, like *The Pilgrim's Progress, Robinson Crusoe* was for a long time not taken seriously by artists other than those commissioned by publishers. It became a subject of exhibited paintings only in the first decade of the nineteenth century, when Stothard showed his *Robinson Crusoe's Long Boat* at the Royal Academy (1808). The delay was due almost certainly to the low repute Defoe's narrative had as a work of literature; no book so irremediably identified with the reading fare of the humble was entitled to the dignity of easel art. But when boys who had read and reread the well-worn family copy of *Robinson Crusoe* became prosperous men and a few of them entered the market for household art, their fancy in status symbols naturally ran to paintings that depicted the subjects of fondly remembered engravings and, by no means incidentally, provided object lessons in the valuable virtue of self-help, that cornerstone of bourgeois prudential morality. The next recorded Crusoe painting following Stothard's was the work of an artist seldom associated with this kind of literary subject, William Etty, whose *Robinson Crusoe Wrecked on a Desert Island Returning Thanks to God for His Deliverance* (Etty's own title, abbreviated in practice to *The Shipwrecked Mariner*) was shown at the British Institution in 1832. Three years later, Alexander Fraser showed *Crusoe Instructing His Man Friday* (inside the hut, accompanied by Crusoe's goats, cat, and parrot, and surrounded by numerous utensils and implements testifying to the sailor's manual ingenuity). In 1845, the same artist exhibited at the Royal Academy a scene illustrating Crusoe's complacent statement, "I frequently sat down to meat with thankfulness . . ." surrounded again by his animal companions.

Some twenty-five pictures in all are recorded, more than half of them appearing between 1835 and 1863. (Two paintings shown in the seventies—Robert Collinson's *Absorbed in Robinson Crusoe* [RA 1871] and A. F. Patten's *Reading Robinson Crusoe: The Footprint on the Sand* [RA 1878]—were genre pictures testifying to the story's continuing appeal to young readers.) Besides the subjects already mentioned, artists showed Crusoe reading the Bible, having his last look at the ship, visiting the Spanish wreck and bringing stores from it, imprisoned by the Salee rover, and teaching his parrot to talk—a variety of scenes indeed, considering the brevity of Defoe's veracious narrative. In addition, there were two "factual" Crusoe paintings. One, in 1858, strained a literary connection by declaring a genre portrait to represent the "last descendant of Alexander Selkirk," the original of Defoe's mariner; the other, in 1880, depicted Selkirk's, alias Crusoe's, birthplace.

The one other of Defoe's many works that was illustrated was the *Journal of the Plague Year,* a tour de force of historical reconstruction by a journalist who never witnessed the events he described. Paul Falconer Poole's *Solomon Eagle Exhorting the People to Repentance, During the Plague of the Year 1665* (pl. 286), though its immediate source was Harrison Ainsworth's *Old St. Pauls,* a novel serialized in 1841, was ultimately indebted to the *Journal,* where the fanatical Eagle appears. The painting caused a sensation when it was hung at the Royal Academy in 1843. *Blackwood's Magazine* devoted no fewer than five columns to a review which declared that "there has not been so powerful a picture painted in this country since the days of Sir Joshua Reynolds."[2] The work was compared, not at all to its disadvantage, with Reynolds's *Ugolino in the Tower* and Poussin's *The Plague at Ashdod.* Thackeray admired the realistic execution, but raised a practical consideration:

> Figures writhe over the picture blue and livid with the plague—some are dying in agony—some stupid with pain. You see the dead-cart in the distance; and in the midst stands naked Solomon, with blood-shot eyes and wild maniacal looks, preaching death, woe, and judgment. Where should such a piece hang? It is too gloomy for a hospital, and surely not cheerful enough for a dining-room. It is not a religious picture, that would serve to decorate the walls of a church. A very dismal, gloomy conventicle might, perhaps, be a suitable abode for it; but would it not be better to tempt the public with something more good-humoured?[3]

Thackeray's fear that the picture was unsalable was justified, at least in the short run. Despite the critical acclaim and the reasonable price Poole asked for it, £400, it went unsold at the Academy and then followed the familiar route of such paintings, to the next show at the British Institution. There, or subsequently, it was bought by a picture dealer and seemingly remained in his possession until it was auctioned at Christie's in 1860 and bought in at twice the original asking price.[4] There seems to be no record of its hanging in a dining room.

286. Paul Falconer Poole, *Solomon Eagle Exhorting the People to Repentance, during the Plague of the Year 1665* (RA 1843) (Sheffield City Art Galleries). "A work of more importance than any that has, we could say ever, been exhibited upon the Academy walls. . . . Were we to look for a parallel, we must go to some of the best works of the best painters of the best ages": thus John Eagles (evidently no kin of the fanatic pictured) in *Blackwood's Magazine* (August, 54: 191). A more plausible set of parallels was still in the future: the panoramic canvases of Frith (*Derby Day, Ramsgate Sands, The Railway Station*), in which, as here, each figure and group has its own story to tell. As Eagles went on to demonstrate in his systematic explication, this was *par excellence* a painting to be "read," inch by inch.

SWIFT

One of the earliest urban genre paintings on record is Edward Penny's *Scene from Swift's Description of a City Shower,* shown at the Society of Artists in 1764. Otherwise, all pictures from Swift's works were from a single book, *Gulliver's Travels.* But although the book went through numerous editions in the eighteenth and early nineteenth centuries, unlike those other classics of popular literature, *The Pilgrim's Progress* and *Robinson Crusoe,* it did not have a strong tradition of illustration. No more than four engravings were found in any single edition until the Paris edition of 1838, with 282 illustrations by Grandville, was reissued in London two years later with one less (the episode of Gulliver extinguishing the fire in Lilliput).[1]

The most noteworthy paintings from *Gulliver's Travels* were produced early in the book's career in art. These were the four painted by Sawrey Gilpin. (Gilpin's better-known contemporary as an animal painter, George Stubbs, seems never to have taken a subject from Swift's book.) The subjects were *Gulliver Addressing the Houyhnhms, Supposing Them to Be Conjurors; Gulliver Reprimanded and Silenced by His Master, When Describing the Horrors of War; Gulliver, Taking His Final Leave of His Master, the Sorrel Nag, etc., and the Land of the Houhynhms* (pl. 92); and *Gulliver Describing Fortification to the Horses.* (The first three were exhibited at the Society of Artists, 1768–72, the last-named not until 1808, at the British Institution.) Splendid examples of horseflesh, Gilpin's Houyhnhms bore out Swift's conception of them as admirable exemplars of the virtues and powers of the reason; if the contrast he draws between them and the repulsive man-beast Yahoos was never made specific in art, it was doubtless because no one wished to own pictures of Yahoos.[2]

In the nineteenth century, critical taste leaned heavily toward the first two books, the voyages to Lilliput and Brobdingnag, which came also to be valued as children's books. Accordingly, in the 1830s several paintings moved Gulliver from the Land of the Houyhnhms to Brobdingnag. The most-discussed of these was Leslie's *Gulliver's Introduction to the Queen of Brobdingnag* (pl. 287), painted for Lord Egremont. Reviewers disapproved of the picture on various grounds. The women, they complained, were portrayed as ordinary English human beings rather than "female ogres, colossal dames," and conversely, Gulliver was not a human being but "a puppet made of wax and wire, bowing at the touch of a showwoman." The wit and satire were lost, said others, who called the subject "intractable" (the *Athenaeum*) and "trivial" (*Fraser's Magazine*).[3] Richard Redgrave's picture of another scene in the voyage to Brobdingnag, *Gulliver Exhibited to the Brobdingnag Farmer,* was shown at the British Institution the year after Leslie's picture was hung at the Royal Academy. Only a few *Gulliver* paintings were exhibited after this time, artists turning instead to Swift's life, a subject that was to account for as many pictures, about a dozen, as had his most famous work (see Part One, chapter 7, above).

THE SPECTATOR

No eighteenth- or early nineteenth-century household with any pretension to cultivation was without its leather-bound set of the *Spectator* essays.[1] Literally scores of editions were published, twelve by the time of Steele's death in 1729, twenty in the period 1783–1800 alone. Addison's

287. Charles R. Leslie, *Gulliver's Introduction to the Queen of Brobdingnag* (RA 1835) (Petworth House). Although Gulliver's description of the bodily features of Brobdingnagians seen close-up is explicit enough, he says nothing about how they were dressed. His first readers doubtless envisioned them as wearing contemporary, that is, early Hanoverian costumes. But artists were free to clothe such characters as they wished, and giving the Brobdingnagians costumes commonly associated with pictures from Shakespeare probably gratified the taste of the time.

and Steele's moral essays, their literary criticism, their pointed but inoffensive satire of the manners of the leisured class in Queen Anne's day, and above all their creation of a club of believable type-figures—a businessman, an army officer, a man-about-town—under the benevolent sovereignty of Sir Roger de Coverley, a country gentleman, were as much a part of the mental furniture of English readers as Shakespeare or Milton. Prized models of lucid prose, they were set pieces for students of rhetoric to analyze in behalf of the improvement of their own style; a leading rhetorician, Hugh Blair, asserted that Addison's chief talent lay in "describing and painting." On his first visit to London in 1763, Boswell used "Mr. Spectator" (unsuccessfully) as a role model, and the *Spectator* itself as a guide to the attitudes and activities proper to a gentlemanly Londoner.[2] Dr. Johnson's often-quoted praise was echoed in later generations by Hazlitt in his lecture on the essayists in *The English Comic Writers* and by Macaulay in the *Edinburgh Review* (1843). "In spite of the vigorous efforts of modern genius and talent to displace them," observed an art critic in 1831, "the characters and scenes of Addison still are, and will long remain to the English public, 'familiar as household words'."[3]

Some sixty paintings from the *Spectator* (few from its predecessor, the *Tatler*) were exhibited during the nineteenth century, mainly in the 1840s and 1850s, when the taste for the kind of moralized picture suggested by the character of Sir Roger de Coverley was at its peak. Derived from about 30 out of the original 555 numbers of the *Spectator,* most of them by Addison, they had more than that number of subjects—a conspicuous exception, as was *The Pilgrim's Progress,* to the general practice whereby a few passages from a given literary work were painted again and again. Even so, the *Spectator,* like *The Faerie Queene,* contained far more pictorial opportunities than artists ever availed themselves of.

288. Thomas Stothard, *Sir Roger de Coverley and the Gypsies* (RA 1803) (Victoria & Albert Museum, Crown Copyright). The gypsy reads in Sir Roger's palm that he has "a widow in his line of life who will be faithful to him and will dream of him that night." "Ah, master," she says, "that roguish leer of yours makes a pretty woman's heart ache; you have not that simper about the mouth for nothing."

Except for a pair of figure-laden allegorical landscapes by William Williams (SA 1768, RA 1770) representing the procession of the months (*Spectator* 425), and a picture at the Society of Artists (1773) called *The Levee* (Steele, No. 193), paintings from the *Spectator* were not seen at exhibitions until 1803–4, when for some reason there was a sudden spate of them, the majority representing subjects most conformable to the lingering taste for classic tales and fantasies rather than ones with satirical edge. At the Royal Academy in 1803, no fewer than eight paintings came from the *Spectator*. P. J. Loutherbourg depicted the story illustrating Dryden's lines "O cursed hunger of pernicious gold! / What bands of faith can impious lucre hold!" (Steele, No. 426). Stothard showed three canvases, each on a subject that would be repeated by later artists: *Brunetta and Phyllis* (Steele, No. 80) (pl. 90), *Sir Roger de Coverley and the Gypsies* (No. 130) (pl. 288), and *The Spectator's Club* (probably No. 1 or 2). Henry Thomson took two subjects from the Oriental tale of Fadlallah (Eustace Budgell, No. 578). Henry Tresham's contribution was *The Visionary Maraton in the World of Spirits* (No. 56), and Westall showed *Theodosius and Constantia* (No. 164) and *Sapphira Discovering the Murder of Her Husband* (Steele, No. 497).

The next year, the Royal Academy hung three paintings by Singleton: *The Cardinal Enraged at the Depositions of His Spy* (No. 439), a rendering of Addison's lively sketch of the vociferous "Trunk-maker in the upper gallery" of the playhouse (No. 235), and the annual Persian fair for the disposition of marriageable females, attributed by Steele to Herodotus (No. 511). Westall took *The Filial Attention of Fidelia* (Steele, No. 449) and Fuseli *The Rosicrucian Cavern* from No. 379, the work of Budgell.

The ensuing shift in the choice of *Spectator* subjects was evident in the ones that a minor artist named Thomas Clater picked for the canvases he sent to one or another of the annual exhibitions in the 1830s: *Sir Roger de Coverley and the Spectator in Spring Gardens* (No. 383); *Mrs. Saunter and Her Niece,* "fine women" who have reprehensibly fallen into the habit of taking snuff (Steele, No. 344); *The Transmigration of Souls Asserted by Will Honeycomb* (No. 343); and *Sempronia, the Matchmaker* (Steele, No. 437).

During the heyday of literary anecdote paintings, Sir Roger de Coverley costarred with Sterne's Uncle Toby: both were exemplars of amiability, upstanding morality, and varying degrees of quirkiness. As early as 1819, Leslie advanced his career with *Sir Roger de Coverley Going to Church, Accompanied by the Spectator,* painted for a wealthy tobacco importer and exhibited at the Royal Academy.* Near the end of his life, in 1857, he returned to *Spectator* 112 for *Sir Roger de Coverley in Church,* commissioned by a patron in Preston.

That other popular Victorian specialist in literary anecdotal art, W. P. Frith, painted scenes from the *Spectator* several times. In 1847 he exhibited *Sir Roger and the Saracen's Head,* representing the incident (No. 122) in which an old servant of Sir Roger has his master's head painted for an inn sign. The next year, Frith turned away from Sir Roger, choosing instead *The Old Woman Accused of Witchcraft* (No. 117), in which humor was replaced by a tense dramatic situation.

Frith eventually returned to Sir Roger in 1870, choosing this time the most popular subject associated with him, his courtship of the beautiful but perverse widow (Steele, No. 113)—a mirror image, in a way, of another famous subject, Sterne's Uncle Toby and the Widow Wadman (pls. 45, 67). Earlier versions of Sir Roger and the widow, by other artists, had been exhibited in 1841, 1847, and 1855.

Other artists showed Sir Roger hunting with Mr. Spectator (Budgell, No. 116), with whom he also visits Westminster Abbey (No. 329), sending the remainder of his meal at Spring Gardens to the wooden-legged waterman who had ferried him there (No. 383), and his and Will Honeycomb's little adventure with a "creature of the town," Sukey (Steele, No. 410).

Interspersed with these pictures, especially after the middle of the century, were a number of comedy-of-manners pieces bearing an affinity to the many portrayals of the rape of Belinda's lock. The delightful number (102) on "the exercise of the fan" was represented at least three times, as was Clarinda's diary of five days in the crowded and vacuous life of a fashionable *ennuyée* (No. 323).

GAY

Hogarth's picture (pl. 1) of a scene from the first production of Gay's *The Beggar's Opera* in 1728 was, after Le Piper's *Hudibras* designs, one of the very first paintings made of a subject from English literature. The play was the most popular of the century (more than a thousand perfor-

*When released from the Marshalsea debtors' prison, old Mr. Dorrit, says Dickens, "patted children on the head like Sir Roger de Coverley going to church, he spoke to people in the background by their Christian names, he condescended to all present . . ." (bk. 1, chap. 36). If this is an implied allusion to Leslie's painting, it is topically accurate, because *Little Dorrit* is set in the mid-1820s.

289. George Stubbs, *The Farmer's Wife and the Raven* (RA 1782) (Lady Lever Art Gallery, Port Sunlight). Gay's *Fable* 37. One of the very few literary subjects to be realized in an unusual medium—enamel on a ceramic tablet.

mances are recorded down to 1800), and as a full evening's entertainment or as an afterpiece, it was constantly revived down to the 1880s.[1] One out-of-the-ordinary revival occurred in 1816, when in a Covent Garden performance starring the comedian Charles Mathews, whose benefit night it was, the characters, according to the advertisements, were dressed "as on the first representation of the play in 1727[8], and taken from Hogarth's celebrated picture."[2] Though the number of paintings *The Beggar's Opera* inspired was not commensurate with its enduring popularity on the stage, scenes and characters from it appeared at least ten times down to 1875. Among them were several female portraits labeled Lucy Lockit or, oftener, Polly Peachum: Hogarth painted the originator of the latter role, Lavinia Fenton, about 1734.

Gay's *Fables* (1727) were even better known to the public at large. Some 350 editions appeared down to the end of the nineteenth century, including several with illustrations by such artists as Bewick (1779) and Blake (1794).[3] The dozen or so oil paintings from the *Fables* recorded down to 1866 were counterparts of the book illustrations, and in some instances the painting may have been the model for the illustration, or vice versa. George Stubbs's *The Farmer's Wife and the Raven* (pl. 289), one of his few literary paintings, is thought to have been copied from a design in an earlier edition by one of his predecessors as an animal painter, John Wooton. The *Fables* had a marked appeal to artists in this line. Among Landseer's early successes was *The Monkey Who Had Seen the World* (RA 1827), a typical Landseer exercise in satirical anthropomorphism in which a monkey learns the ways of the world by serving an eighteenth-century lady of fashion. James Ward, one of Stubbs's successors as an equine specialist, exhibited *The Council of Horses,* from the *Fables,* in 1848.

Eight or ten pictures were inspired by Gay's *The Shepherd's Week* (1714), a burlesque of Ambrose ("Namby-Pamby") Philips's attempts at pastoral verse that, divested of its original satirical thrust, was admired as a representation of native country life. Two pictures, exhibited at the Royal

Academy half a century apart, by Opie (1803) and one George Wells (1852), represented the same subject from the fourth pastoral: pretty Hobnelia following the May Day custom of predicting the future by watching the movements of a snail ("I search'd to find a snail, / That might my secret lover's name reveal . . ."). It was quite a reach from Captain Macheath, as depicted by such artists as Gilbert Stuart Newton (RA 1826) and Henry Liverseege (BI 1831), to domesticated Theocritan shepherdesses, but literary art could embrace them with equal enthusiasm.

RAMSAY

Allan Ramsay's *The Gentle Shepherd* (1725) was a pastoral comedy, set in the Cromwellian period, which, reportedly at the request of the pupils at the Haddington Grammar School, he converted into a ballad opera in 1728, the year Gay's *The Beggar's Opera* was produced in London. From that time to the end of the eighteenth century, except for a few years in the 1740s, it was constantly being performed somewhere in the British Isles; and after a fresh burst of popularity late in the century, an abbreviated version continued in the repertory as an afterpiece. Originally written in the Scots tongue, it was adapted in a number of English versions beginning with Theophilus Cibber's *Patie and Peggy, or The Fair Foundling* (1730). Together with *The Beggar's Opera,* Ramsay's play forged a lasting link between the stage and popular balladry; the one drew its songs from those heard in the London streets, the other from folk material.[1]

In addition to the frequent revivals on the stage, the play was printed in many cheap editions, some of which circulated among the Scottish peasantry. Thus the story (involving secret parentage, the return in disguise of an exiled landowner, and two pairs of rural lovers) and the chief characters (the lovers themselves, Patie and Peggy, and Roger and Jenny, along with old shepherds and a supposed witch) were well known to a large public. Between 1750, the date of the first recorded artistic treatment, by Paul Sandby (pl. 290), and the end of the nineteenth century, more than

290. Paul Sandby, *Scene from "The Gentle Shepherd"* (1750) (Glasgow Art Gallery and Museum). One of the earliest paintings to represent a scene in a popular contemporary work of literature. The setting, a Scottish shepherd's cottage, contrasts strongly with the upper-middle-class interiors seen in Highmore's and Hayman's pictures from Richardson's novels (pls. 4, 5) and anticipates the genre scenes from humble life derived from *The Gentle Shepherd* and Burns's poems that Wilkie would paint many years later (pls. 44, 135, 291, 308).

forty paintings depicted scenes or characters from *The Gentle Shepherd* itself or from one of the adaptations—more than came from the entire works of Chaucer, Defoe, Swift, Richardson, or Fielding, and as many as were drawn from Bunyan or Pope. Along with Burns's poems and Scott's poems and novels, Ramsay's play both stimulated and reflected the interest in Scottish themes that was a phenomenon of early nineteenth-century British painting.

Not surprisingly, many of the painters from Ramsay were themselves Scotsmen. In 1788, the warm reception of David Allan's series of aquatints illustrating *The Gentle Shepherd* encouraged him to proceed with his well-known watercolors of Scottish rural life and scenes, an early landmark in the history of Scottish art. David Wilkie made sketches from the play while he was still a student at the Trustees' Academy in Edinburgh, one of them portraying the same scene (3.2) that had been Sandby's subject in 1750.[2] The two most famous pictures from the play were by Wilkie: *Roger Slighted by Jenny,* from act 1, scene 1 (pl. 291), and *The Cottage Toilette,* from act 5, scene 2 (pl. 135). Later on, Alexander Johnston, who had come to London with a letter of introduction to Wilkie and made his own reputation as a genre and historical painter, showed two pictures from *The Gentle Shepherd* (RA 1840 and 1849).

POPE

If the sheer diversity of a poet's personal and literary ties with art had any bearing on the frequency with which artists drew upon his works, Alexander Pope should have been the most favored of all.[1] As a young man, he studied painting with the fashionable Kneller-trained portraitist Charles Jervais, in whose studio-home he lived for a year or more; he knew many of the leading painters and connoisseurs of his day; he sat for his portrait more frequently than any contemporary (the leading authority on Pope portraiture counts eighty-one distinct "types")*; his aesthetic principles were grounded in painting, and he was a leading advocate of *ut pictura poesis;* his original poems and translations are pervaded by pictorialism; and another student of Pope has said—perhaps forgetting Leigh Hunt on Spenser—that "he was, apparently, the first of our poets to explore the possibilities of colour composition in poetry, and the first whose verse might often be called a gallery of pictures in colour."[2]

Whatever forms it took, however, Pope's pictorialism did not lead to artists' selecting a wide range of subjects from his poetry, as they did from Spenser's. Their perennial choice was limited to a single poem, *The Rape of the Lock.* But this at least was a fairly durable source of literary paintings. Some forty-five pictures are recorded, distributed with unusual evenness across a hundred years. Unaffected by the vicissitudes of Pope's critical reputation, which in turn depended on succeeding generations' estimate of his private character,[3] the lighthearted story of Mistress Arabella Fermor and her stolen lock of hair, complete with attendant nymphs and other airy beings, never lost its appeal to artists and their clientele.[4] Its attractions were as numerous as its author's affinities with the art of painting. It offered a chance to paint pastiches of the many classic treatments of the toilet of Venus, localizing in an English setting the air of indolent voluptuousness that always characterized such paintings. It likewise afforded an occasion to oblige the Victorian taste for fairy pictures (the sylphs and gnomes), costume pieces, and such mild satire of social vanities and foibles as the age tolerated.

*Pope seems to have been as zealous as Garrick to disseminate pictures of himself, though for somewhat different reasons. As early as 1732, Voltaire wrote that although "the picture of the prime minister [Walpole] hangs over the chimney of his own closet . . . I have seen that of Mr. Pope in twenty noblemen's houses" (William K. Wimsatt, *The Portraits of Alexander Pope* [New Haven, Conn., 1965], pp. xv, xvii).

291. David Wilkie, *Roger Slighted by Jenny* (1823) (National Gallery of Scotland). A familiar genre subject, the rustic serenade. The appreciative attitudes of the two listeners, Jenny and Peggy, do not reflect the actual situation described in Roger's lines in Ramsay's *The Gentle Shepherd* (1. 1):

My Bawty is a cur I dearly like,
Even while he fawn'd, she [Jenny] strak the poor dumb tyke:
If I had fill'd a nook within her breast,
She wad have shawn mair kindness to my beast.
When I begin to tune my stock and horn,
With a' her face she shaws a caulrife scorn.
Last night I play'd, ye never heard sic spite,
O'er Bogie was the spring, and her delyte;
Yet tauntingly she at her cousin speer'd,
Gif she cou'd tell what tune I play'd and sneer'd.

In Victorian times, portraits of Belinda came to the galleries equipped with the inevitable motto "A heavenly image in the glass appears." Not quite a Keepsake beauty, she was still a sentimental heroine of some consequence. But by no means all, and perhaps not even most, of the paintings from *The Rape of the Lock* depicted her at her toilet. The poem contains some fifteen tableaux, and it is likely that some of the paintings listed simply as being from the poem represented these, in addition to the ones bearing explicit titles.

Among the earliest Belinda pictures was one (ca. 1776) that the authority on *Rape of the Lock* illustrations has declared to be "the most lubricious" of all.[5]* It was painted by Matthew William Peters, who had something of a reputation as the producer of pictures unfit to be viewed by respectable women in a public gallery. He became a member of the Royal Academy in 1777, the year he displayed one such painting (*A Woman in Bed*); and five years later, supposedly for prudential rather than penitential reasons, he took holy orders. From 1784 to 1790, he was the Academy's chaplain; and though he resigned both that office and his membership, he continued to paint and exhibit, his subjects now being suitably religious.[6] A decade or so later, Fuseli painted *Belinda's Awakening,* a picture identified until recently—a fairly impressive error—as *Queen Mab.* Other illustrators of *The Rape of the Lock* in these years included George Morland, whose *Belinda Billet Doux* was engraved in 1794, and William Hamilton. In the next generation, Belinda was ushered into the gift books by such specialists in keepsake art as Eliza Sharpe. Gilbert Stuart Newton, one of the most promising painters of the moment, was reported by Washington Irving to have "in hand" a picture of Belinda contemplating herself in the glass; but if it was completed, it seems to have disappeared.[7]

Despite the great surge of literary paintings between 1830 and 1850, *Rape of the Lock* pictures were then produced at a constant rather than an accelerated pace. For some reason, the rate picked up on the fifties. Of the eight or so examples exhibited in that decade, the most discussed was Leslie's *Sir Plume Demands the Restoration of the Lock* (pl. 149). "Very dingy

*Its title was *Miss Bampfylde as Belinda*—an example of what has been called, in Part One, a role-playing portrait, in which a fashionable lady is dressed and posed as a fashionable literary character. There is a possibility that some pictures exhibited simply as "Belinda," without any reference to Pope, may have been theatrical portraits; the name was a common one in Restoration and eighteenth-century comedy (e.g. Van Brugh's *The Provok'd Wife,* Shadwell's *The Fair Quaker of Deal,* and Arthur Murphy's *All in the Wrong*). Belinda was also the eponymous heroine of a novel by Maria Edgeworth (1801).

292. Joseph Severn, *Eloisa and Abelard* (undated) (Victoria & Albert Museum, Crown Copyright). A parting scene not explicitly included in Pope's "Eloisa to Abelard" but certainly to be inferred from the story. Presumably Severn did not feel himself unqualified to paint the lovers' farewell despite the poem's last lines:

> If such there be, who love so long, so well,
> Let him our sad, our tender story tell;
> The well-sung woes will soothe my pensive ghost;
> He best can paint them who shall feel them most

—a requirement which, if elevated into a general aesthetic principle, would invalidate most literary pictures with a similarly intense emotional content.

and unsatisfactory," asserted the *Athenaeum,* "—very coarse and careless in handling, very lurid in colour, and very feeble in expression. . . . Lord Petre, who dangles the heavy lock like a dead rat he is going to throw out of window, is scarcely at first observed. The humor is heavy; the mock-heroic of the poem quite lost, and an air of dull seriousness thrown over the whole."[8] Ruskin, however, had no reservations at all. "An absolute masterpiece" he called it, "and perhaps the most covetable picture of its kind which I ever remember seeing by an English artist."[9]

Pope's other poems were seldom represented in art. Maria Cosway portrayed for Macklin's Poet's Gallery a subject from *Windsor Forest,* a Musidora-like nymph named Lodona evading the embraces of Pan by dissolving into "a soft silver stream." At the same moment (1791), John Dean exhibited at the Royal Academy a didactic subject from the *Epistle to Arbuthnot, Dutiful Children Attending Their Sick Mother,* a companion piece to *A Good Mother Instructing Her Children,* from Thomson's *The Seasons.* Half a century later (RA 1855), Augustus Egg derived from Epistle III of the *Moral Essays* a pair of subjects most agreeable to the Victorian conviction that the wages of dissipation and pride is squalid death. *The Life and Death of Buckingham* (pls. 293, 294) was Hogarth's *Rake's Progress* moved back to the Restoration:

> Look on this picture, and on that [said *Fraser's Magazine*]. . . . On the left, is the Duke in gay attire, at table, with half-a-dozen men drinking, and half-a-dozen women drunk. Behind him, standing as well as he can, is, if we mistake not, his sacred Majesty Charles II, most royally tipsy—an orgie such as we never witnessed but once, and that at the Vaudeville in *La Dame aux Camélias.* On the right hand, is "the worst inn's worst room," with all the accessory meannesses invented by the poet, and on the bed is the corpse of Buckingham, just dead, in his agony and despair, gaunt, convulsed, frightful to behold. The story of the death is entirely devoid of historical foundation, but the moral is everlastingly true, and pointed here with great skill and power. No one who has ever seen these two pictures can forget them.[10]*

THOMSON

For well over a century after its publication in 1726–30, James Thomson's *The Seasons* was the most popular poem in the English language. Between 1750 and 1800, it went through at least 174 editions, and in the next half century, 270; in 1790–1810 alone, more than eighty appeared.[1] It found its way into cottages where its only companions on the shelf were the Bible and *The Pilgrim's Progress;* in elegantly illustrated format, it was on the library table of every middle-class family with any pretension to literary cultivation. When Coleridge came across a well-worn copy at a country alehouse, he exclaimed, "*That* is true fame!"[2] It was fame amplified by the widespread practice of making schoolchildren memorize passages from the poem, chiefly in behalf of the unexceptionable piety that pervaded its four books. Not surprisingly under these circumstances, the catalogues of art exhibitions contained more quotations from *The Seasons* than from the works of any other English poet except Shakespeare and Milton.

With the sole exception of *Paradise Lost,* more paintings were derived from the poem than from any other single work of English literature. There are records of more than 150 of them, beginning as early as 1765–67, when Richard Wilson exhibited his *A Summer Storm, with the Story of the Two Lovers* (Celadon and Amelia) and Thomas Smith of Derby his companion landscapes showing the stories of two other pairs of lovers, Damon

*One cannot help wondering if people viewing Egg's pictures were not reminded of the downfall of Buckingham's namesake, the second Duke of Buckingham and Chandos, who, seven years earlier (1848), had been sold up after accumulating a debt of a million pounds and was then living in penury, dependent on his son's charity. He was to die in 1861.

and Musidora and Palemon and Lavinia. No year passed without new pictures from Thomson being exhibited, and their popularity continued unabated until past the middle of the nineteenth century, when, significantly, the number of new editions also began to dwindle.

There were two reasons for Thomson's initial appeal to painters. One was that he was the first to seize upon landscape as a prime subject of English poetry, thus providing a literary context and rationale for the slowly developing native school of landscape artists. Joseph Warton wrote in his *Essay on the Genius and Writings of Pope* (1756) that Thomson "hath enriched poetry with a variety of new and original images, which he painted from nature itself, and from his own actual observations: his descriptions have, therefore, a distinctness and truth, which are utterly wanting to those of poets who have only copied from each other, and have never looked abroad on the objects themselves."[3] It was under Thomson's auspices that the English landscape school began to burgeon with Richard Wilson and bloomed with Turner and Constable, both of whom *The Seasons* served as a poetic storehouse.

At the same time, eighteenth- and early nineteenth-century artists valued the poem as much for its verbal realization of the imagery of Old Master landscapists as for its intrinsic poetic quality. Although Thomson specifically mentioned Claude, Poussin, and Salvator Rosa in a passage of verbal landscape painting in *The Castle of Indolence,* recent scholars have found a larger source of influence in the "heroic" landscapes of Renaissance and baroque art—Guido Reni, Rubens, Guercino, Carracci, Spagnoletto.[4] The landscapes in *The Seasons* invited English artists to paint nature in emulation of their great predecessors, and to fit their productions into the long tradition of art representing the progress of the seasons. Emblematic pictures of the months abounded in fifteenth- and sixteenth-century books of hours, a set of sixteenth-century tapestries in the Uffizi Gallery depicted the theme, and it was a popular subject in seventeenth-century painting. Poussin painted four seasonal landscapes for the Duke of Richelieu in the 1660s. In England, the progress of the seasons had been embedded in the poetical tradition ever since Spenser's *The Shepherd's Calendar,* and in Thomson's own time, the Duke of Beaufort owned a Roman sarcophagus whose designs illustrated the motif.

293–294. Augustus Egg, *The Life and Death of Buckingham* (RA 1855) (Yale Center for British Art, Paul Mellon Collection). These two paintings were exhibited in a single frame, which had a border of vine leaves through which a death's head protruded at each corner. They constituted a Hogarthian morality-in-paint and were based on Pope's description, in the third of his *Moral Essays,* of the high-living Buckingham's fall. The first picture shows him "Gallant and gay, in Cliveden's proud alcove, / The bower of wanton Shrewsbury and love"; the second,

> In the worst inn's worst room, with hat half-hung,
> The floors of plaster, and the walls of dung,
> On once a flock-bed, but repair'd with straw,
> With tape-tied curtains never meant to draw,
> The George and Garter dangling from that bed
> Where tawdry yellow strove with dirty red,
> . . . how changed from him,
> That life of pleasure, and that soul of whim!

Appropriately enough, the duke exhibited his treasure against a décor designed by Thomson's first illustrator, William Kent.[5] Thus the artistic association of many pictures nominally inspired by *The Seasons* was as strong as their literary heritage. As a poet, Thomson mediated between the old classical landscapists, including those who actually treated the seasons theme, and the new English ones.

The leading authority on Thomson, Ralph Cohen, has said that "*The Seasons* was for more than one hundred and fifty years the most illustrated poem in the English language."[6] The decade of the 1790s alone saw the publication of no fewer than a dozen new illustrated editions. Of the several well-known illustrators of *The Seasons* at this time, William Hamilton was the most prolific; he made designs for five editions between 1777 and 1801, the year he died. At the Academy that year and the next, he was represented by two designs for DuRoveray's deluxe edition, and Fuseli by two others (*Celadon and Amelia* and *The Dying Shepherd*).

As the subjects of these pictures indicate, *The Seasons* was valued not only for the opportunities it provided to paint landscapes *per se* but also as a source of pathetic and sentimental anecdotes—thus providing the desirable element of figures in either the foreground or the background of the landscape—and figure studies. To gallerygoers, *The Seasons* was best known as the poem from which Musidora came. The passage in "Summer" in which this stellar water nymph of British art appears had long been admired; Wordsworth said in 1815[7] that any well-thumbed copy of *The Seasons* automatically opened at the story of Musidora at the stream and Damon spying on her:

> . . . But, desperate youth,
> How durst thou risk the soul-distracting view;
> As from her naked limbs, of glowing white,
> Harmonious swell'd by Nature's finest hand,
> In folds loose-floating fell the fainter lawn,
> And fairly expos'd she stood, shrunk from herself,
> With fancy blushing, at the doubtful breeze
> Alarm'd, and starting like the fearful fawn?
>
> (Lines 1313–20)

(There is more.) Musidora appeared rather belatedly in illustrated editions of *The Seasons*.[8] The first portrayal of her testing the water before her modest bath appeared in the first edition illustrated by Hamilton (1777). Although she turned up in edition after edition, she remained a controversial figure well into the new century. The editor of Sharpe's edition (1816), whose designs by Westall included one of Musidora, was curiously defensive, though less about the figure as the artists portrayed her than about her story. "We know we shall offend common prejudice," he wrote, "in pronouncing the Tale of Musidora, which has furnished so many artists with a subject, and the publishers of so many editions of Thomson with a captivating embellishment, to be as vulgarly conceived, and to be as coarse in sentiment, though not in expression, as a Dutch painting. But Thomson is chastity and purity itself in comparison with his contemporaries."[9]*

No such scruples prevailed in the art world, however. "What a pure, virginal, shrinking, chaste, delightful creature is Musidora," marveled Benjamin Robert Haydon to his diary in 1828.[10] Irrespective of the lady's modesty, female nudity was taken for granted in imitations of Titian or

*By the end of the eighteenth century, she had already made her way to America. Washington Allston, a student at Harvard (class of 1800), painted a *Musidora* in his Cambridge room. Said his landlord, a carpenter by trade: "He has painted a woman, stark naked, going into the water to wash herself. It is as nateral as life. Mr. Allston, sir, is quite a genius" (Jared B. Flagg, *Life and Letters of Washington Allston* [New York, 1892], pp. 23–24).

Rubens and in portrayals of the two classic exemplifications of the motif, the biblical Susannah and the voyeuristic elders, and Diana and Actaeon—the young woman by the water observed by a lubricious male, or, in more general terms, the nymph under the scrutiny of a satyr. If nudity was sanctioned in painters' versions of biblical or mythological stories, it was no less permissible in an episode from a universally admired and impeccably moral English poem. The pose, the presence or absence of a voyeur, and the degree of nudity were unimportant. To ensure a freshly painted female nude's respectability, it was only necessary to provide her with a rustic English setting and call her Musidora. Thus the practice developed of labeling almost any otherwise unidentified nude-in-the-stream as Musidora. The most celebrated case of retroactive christening is an early one, Gainsborough's large oval that is now in the Tate Gallery. At his death, it was sold as *A Nymph at the Bath* but subsequently—merely because it conformed to a popular type—it was renamed *Musidora.*

295. Arthur Hughes, *Musidora* (RA 1849) (Birmingham City Museum and Art Gallery). Although he was soon to be converted to Pre-Raphaelite principles, Hughes began his career in a conventional manner, with yet another Musidora. This, his first exhibited painting, was done when he was seventeen years old.

Among the late eighteenth-century artists who named their unclothed creations Musidora were Opie (Macklin's Poet's Gallery), Smirke (RA 1792), and Hamilton (1794).* In the next generation, William Etty sent a *Musidora* to the Royal Academy in 1843 (pl. 62); it was so successful that he subsequently painted three more versions. Musidora was also the subject of Arthur Hughes's first exhibited picture (pl. 295), and at various times in these years William Frost took time off from his production of paintings from Milton's *Comus* to turn out a number of *Musidoras.* By then, the subject had become so trite that the *Literary Gazette* could say of Frost's 1850 version, with appropriately weary wit, "This lady is naturally a favourite subject for a dip of the brush, as she is going to have a dip herself . . . commonplace, not poetry nor art."[11] By that time, she was three-quarters of the way to establishing her record of some sixty exhibited pictures.

After "Summer," with its story of Damon and Musidora, the book of *The Seasons* most often represented in painting was "Autumn" with its biblically inspired (Boaz and Ruth) story of Palemon and Lavinia, the gleaner and mother who touchingly relates her misfortunes to her attentive children. About fifty pictures from "Autumn" are recorded, but the connection many of them had with *The Seasons* was as tenuous as that of pictures of Musidora. As often as not, the name Lavinia and the reference to Thomson's poem were merely hung onto routine figure studies of gleaners, either returning from the fields with their day's harvest or resting and quietly ruminating. Reynolds's *The Gleaners* (also known as *The Cottagers*) for Macklin was actually a fake-rustic conversation piece, the gleaner having been modeled by a Miss Potts, the future mother of Edwin Landseer. Gainsborough's *Lavinia* derived hardly more than the name from Thomson. It had been painted some years before the Macklin commission, and its alternative name, *Cottage Girl with a Bowl of Milk,* is a more accurate description.

The story of Amelia, who is killed by lightning, and her lover Celadon was from "Summer." It attracted fewer artists, but it was the first *Seasons* subject to be painted; and some twenty treatments are recorded down to 1850, after which the theme faded from view. Some ten paintings, none of any interest, were derived from Thomson's other major poem, *The Castle of Indolence.*

From 1736 to his death in 1748, Thomson lived in a pair of cottages in

*At the height of his prosperity as an Edinburgh portraitist, Raeburn received a commission from Lord de Tabley to paint a subject of his own choice. "His anxiety to produce a work worthy of a place in that collection," wrote a contemporary, "made him long fastidious. He at last selected Musidora, from Thomson's *Seasons,* but unfortunately he was called away before he could accomplish the object of his honourable ambition" (Whitley [3], p. 49). In view of the frequency with which Musidora had already been painted, "fastidious" does not seem quite the right word.

Kew Foot Lane, Richmond, and his admirers liked to fancy him standing on nearby Richmond Hill, awaiting inspiration. ("Heavens! what a goodly prospect spreads around" was the motto attached to a picture of *The Bard of The Seasons on Richmond Hill,* exhibited in 1863.) This was the site represented in Turner's most direct tribute to the poet, *Thomson's Aeolian Harp* (pl. 296), exhibited at his private gallery in 1809, which depicts a celebratory ritual around a monument to the poet on Richmond Hill, with the Thames in the background. The picture aptly symbolizes the considerable debt that English artists owed to the pictorial poet of *The Seasons.*

GRAY

In addition to being a poet, Thomas Gray was a fairly representative eighteenth-century man of taste; and as such, he had a greater than ordinary interest in the fine arts.[1] Like Thomson before him, he derived suggestions for his poetic imagery from the painters most revered in his age. In a footnote to his description of the Bard, in his Pindaric ode so named—"Loose his beard, and hoary hair / Stream'd, like a meteor to the troubled air"—he specifically acknowledged the inspiration of the image of God in a painting of Ezekiel's vision that Gray took to be from Raphael's brush, although Raphael is now thought to have been responsible only for the general design. His friend William Mason, however, wrote that Gray "used to say" that Parmigiano's *Moses Breaking the Tables of the Law* "came still nearer to his meaning than the picture of Raphael."[2] The image of the streaming meteor, in any case, is a striking example of the merging within small compass of a pictorial and a literary source, for it also recalls Milton's line describing Azazel's banner in *Paradise Lost* (1.537): "Shone like a meteor streaming to the wind."

296. J. M. W. Turner, *Thomson's Aeolian Harp* (Turner Gallery 1809) (City Art Gallery, Manchester). Many years earlier, Francesco Zuccarelli had painted this Claudian scene of the Thames winding around Eel Pie Island from exactly the same vantage point on Richmond Hill. Turner made what is essentially a copy of that picture, even down to the sheep grazing on the left. (In the interim, a large tree had grown in the center of the composition.) For the man, woman, and child whom Zuccarelli depicted admiring the view, Turner substituted the graceful celebrants dancing around the memorial to Thomson, which seems to have been the artist's invention.

Gray shared his age's reverence for the Italian masters as well as the great trio of seventeenth-century landscapists, Poussin, Claude, and Salvator Rosa. Jean Hagstrum has argued that the three living figures in the last section of the "Elegy in a Country Churchyard" were suggested by a painting of Poussin, *The Shepherds of Arcady,* which was well known to Gray's contemporaries through engravings and was alluded to in paintings by Reynolds, Richard Wilson, and Joseph Wright of Derby.[3] But apart from a reference in one of his letters to Paul Sandby's early picture *The Bard,* Gray virtually never evinced any interest in English painting. English artists were more partial to him than he to them. Quotations from his poems, especially the "Elegy in a Country Churchyard" and "The Bard," accompanied scores of paintings into the exhibition rooms.[4]

Down to the middle of the nineteenth century, a point at which the supply abruptly ended—only three examples are recorded after 1848—some twenty "Elegy" subject pictures were seen. From the poem's widely memorized chain of stanzas evoking the sentiment of humble rural life and death were drawn such genre and emblematic subjects as (to cite three instances from the "Elegy's" early career in art) *Rustick Happiness* (RA 1778), *Noon* (Society of Artists 1783), and *A Cottager and Family* (RA 1787). As late as 1837, artists continued to paint sets of "Morning," "Noon," and "Evening," each picture illustrating a specific scene in the poem. One of W. P. Frith's early canvases (RA 1846)—it was, at the same time, one of the last "Elegy" pictures—represented *The Return from Labour,* a cozy rural domestic scene from the poem's opening stanzas, and a slightly earlier painting by John Martin (BI 1842) was *Curfew Time.* A recurrent subject was Stoke Poges church, traditionally the site of the poet's elegiac meditation. A treatment of the scene exhibited at the Royal Academy in 1775 was bought by Gray's friend Horace Walpole for his picture gallery at Strawberry Hill.*

Paintings from "The Bard" were landmarks in the transition of English art from neoclassicism to Romanticism.[5] Between 1761 and 1820, it was the subject of at least a dozen oil paintings and numerous drawings, including a number of watercolors by Blake. The poem derived from the Welsh legend that upon his conquest of the country Edward I ordered the extinction of all bards, the repositories and mouthpieces of Welsh nationalism. The sole surviving bard, standing on the rocky slope of Mount Snowdon, pronounces a curse on the king, whose English armies are marching below. He prophesies the glories to come to Britain under the Tudors and their poets, and then hurls himself into the torrent at the base of the cliff. (The same final action was the subject of several paintings from Byron's *Manfred.*) The Bard poem, in itself and in its subsequent illustrations, aptly illustrates the interweaving of the age's arts and its culture. In painting as in poetry, it was an expression of the warming patriotism that accompanied George III's accession to the throne in 1760; and it added power to the notion, ultimately to become one of the basic articles of the Romantic creed, of the poet's high calling as prophet.

To judge from the surviving examples and descriptions of some of the lost ones (twenty are recorded altogether), paintings from "The Bard" were regularly exercises in the heroic-sublime, differing chiefly in the respective emphases they laid upon the solitary figure and the enveloping wild landscape. The earliest example was Paul Sandby's *Historical Land-*

*One famous artist's association with the "Elegy" was purely fortuitous. When Gainsborough's *Landscape* (RA 1780) was published as an aquatint after his death, it was entitled *A Country Churchyard* and bore a sixteen-line quotation from the poem. But the church was not Stoke Poges, and Gainsborough, no partisan of poetry, had no literary allusion in mind. In fact, he called Gray, the occasional poet of landscape, a "tawdry fan-Painter" (J. D. Hunt, *The Figure in the Landscape,* pp. 213–14).

297. Benjamin West, *The Bard* (RA 1809) (Tate Gallery, London). "A venerable Bard standing on the brow of a stupendous rock, agonized at the murders of his inspired brethren, and falling country, and imprecating prophetic vengeance on a sanguinary foe, is a subject partaking of the sublime, because emotions of terror, of resentment, and sorrow, are its objects. . . . The mixed feelings of grief, and an anger which pours curses on an advancing enemy, are powerfully pourtrayed in the Bard's face, turned head, and extended arm. . . . Terror, destruction, and death, hover with the Eagles who are waiting for their prey" (Robert Hunt in the *Examiner,* 21 May).

skip, Representing the Welch Bard (Society of Artists 1761), about which Mason exclaimed in a letter to Lord Nuneham, "My Lord! Sandby has made such a picture! such a bard! such a headlong flood! such a Snowdon! such giant oaks! such desert caves! If it is not the best picture that has been painted this century. . . ."[6] Thomas Jones's *The Bard* (Society of Artists 1774) seems to have stirred no equivalent rapture. Fuseli made three designs from the poem for DuRoveray's edition, two of which he exhibited at the Royal Academy in 1800. Seven years later, Richard Corbould painted *The Bard*—though somewhere in its descent the canvas lost its attribution to Gray and was sold in 1964 as *An Army Trapped in a Rocky Defile, A Wild Man Hailing Them from a Rock,* an accurate description so far as it went. In 1809, Benjamin West showed his version at the Royal Academy (pl. 297).

The catholicity of appeal "The Bard" had to pre-Victorian artists is suggested by the fact that both Martin and Etty, who had little else in common except ambition, painted it. The resemblance of Martin's (pl. 298) to Corbould's (unexhibited) canvas of ten years earlier is so marked as almost to certify that somehow Martin had seen it.[7] As usual in his treatments of literary subjects, the "central" figure is so minuscule as to be almost invisible against the massive background.* Etty forsook the usual sublime scene in favor of an allegory (pl. 299). The *Morning Chronicle* called the picture "another indulgence of what we once hoped a classical, but which we are now convinced is a lascivious, mind. If Mr. Etty continues to revel in this meretricious vein," it continued, "the labour of his anatomical studies in the school will avail him nothing—no decent family can hang such sights against their walls. The naked female may, in the severity of the antique, be modest, but it is not so in the attitudes of Mr. Etty."[8] This is probably the only case on record in which a painting from Gray was denounced as indecent.

RICHARDSON

Beginning with what is usually considered the first modern English novel, the illustration of fiction got off to an ambitious start.[1] The sixth edition of Richardson's *Pamela* (1742) contained twenty-nine plates, twelve designed by Francis Hayman and the rest by Hubert Gravelot, who etched them all. The following year, Joseph Highmore announced in the newspapers his intention of painting a series of twelve pictures from the novel and invited subscriptions to the engravings to be made from them:

1. Mr. B. finds Pamela writing
2. Pamela and Mr. B. in the summer house
3. Pamela fainting
4. Pamela preparing to go home
5. Pamela leaves Mr. B.'s house
6. Pamela shows Mr. Williams a hiding place for their letters
7. Pamela in the bedroom with Mrs. Jewkes and Mr. B.
8. Pamela greets her father
9. Pamela is married
10. Pamela and Lady Davers
11. Pamela asks Sir Jacob Swynford's blessing (pl. 4)
12. Pamela tells a nursery tale

*Twenty years later, Martin's nephew Richard exhibited *The Bard's Lament* (RA 1837). Richard was the son of John's brother Jonathan, who had set fire to York Minster. He was himself not untouched by the strain of madness in the family, and the year after the picture was exhibited, he cut his throat, firm in the belief that his breath was turning his relatives black.

The engravings seem to have sold well at first, but copies of the second issue (1762) were still listed in Boydell's catalogue as late as 1803. The original oils disappeared, to resurface only in 1920, when they were offered for sale at Christie's as being from the studio of a Dutch artist and representing scenes from *Clarissa Harlowe*. Comparison with the engravings immediately established their true identity.[2] Two other paintings from *Pamela,* said to have been in the style of Hayman, graced the supper boxes at Vauxhall: Mr. B. overhearing Pamela confessing to the housekeeper that she wishes to return home, and Pamela fleeing to the coach while Lady Davers's footmen try to stop her.[3]

The reception of these illustrations evidently was warm enough to encourage Highmore, who by then had become a friend of the novelist and the painter of his portrait (now in the National Portrait Gallery), to

298. John Martin, *The Bard* (RA 1817) (Laing Art Gallery, Newcastle upon Tyne). As he did with Macbeth (pl. 231) and Manfred (pl. 331), Martin subordinated the human figure to the terrifying mountains, rushing cascades, and tumultuous skies that obsessed him.

299. William Etty, *"Youth on the Prow, and Pleasure at the Helm"* (RA 1832) (Tate Gallery, London).

Fair laughs the morn and soft the
zephyr blows,
While, proudly riding o'er the azure
realm,
In gallant trim the gilded vessel goes,
Youth on the prow, and Pleasure at
the helm,
Regardless of the sweeping Whirlwind's
sway,
That, hushed in grim repose, expects his
evening prey.

Etty explained, rather cloudily, that Gray's lines were "a general allegory of Human life, *morally,* where what we see here portrayed in its fabulous sense, is often real" (Farr, *William Etty,* p. 158).

prepare his brushes for Richardson's next novel, *Clarissa Harlowe.*[4] It is thought that he planned a series similar to the *Pamela* one, but only two paintings emerged. One was a portrait of Clarissa, which Richardson praised in a letter to Lady Bradshaigh: " . . . He has drawn Clarissa at whole length, in the Vandyke taste and dress. He had finished the piece before I saw it, or knew of it, and before Clarissa was printed, having seen only some parts of the work in manuscript. His own imagination was his principal guide; and he has given it great intelligence, sweetness and dignity." This picture is now lost, but its companion, *The Harlowe Family,* is at Yale (pl. 5). Like the *Pamela* set, it later was grotesquely misattributed and misinterpreted. At the International Exhibition in London in 1862, it was shown as a Hogarth; and half a century later, Austin Dobson took it to be a theatrical picture set in the Drury Lane green room, with Mr. and Mrs. Pritchard, Barry, Fielding, Quin, and Lavinia Fenton, a true galaxy of contemporary stage stars. "Here we can see Hogarth at his best!" exulted Sir Charles Holmes, Slade Professor of Art.

In 1761, at the first exhibition of the Free Society of Artists, Highmore showed *A Whole Length of a Lady, in the Character of Clementina* in Richardson's last novel, *The History of Sir Charles Grandison.* Apart from this, a picture by Sir William Beechey of Clarissa Harlowe and Mr. Solmes (Society of Artists 1783) and an undated painting by Hayman, *Robert Lovelace Preparing to Abduct Clarissa Harlowe* (pl. 300), there seems to have been little further allusion to Richardson until 1796, when Northcote showed at the Royal Academy a series of ten pictures called *Diligence and Dissipation, the Progress of an Industrious and an Idle Girl.* Their dual inspiration—the industrious girl from Richardson, the idle one from Hogarth—was obvious:

300. Francis Hayman, *Lovelace Preparing to Abduct Clarissa Harlowe* (undated) (Southampton Art Gallery). The scene has strong suggestions of a theatrical performance, and Hayman had close ties with the stage as a scene painter; but, although there had been several dramatic adaptations of *Pamela,* including two immediately following the novel's publication, there would be none of *Clarissa Harlowe* until 1788.

1. The modest girl and the wanton, fellow-servants in a gentleman's house
2. The wanton revelling with her companions
3. Good advice given by an old servant
4. The wanton in her bed-chamber
5. The modest girl in her bed-chamber
6. The wanton turned out of doors for misconduct
7. The modest girl rejects the illicit addresses of her master
8. The wanton, dying in poverty and disease, visited by the modest girl
9. The modest girl receives the honorable addresses of her master
10. The modest girl, married to her master, is led to her coach; while the wanton, dead in misery, is laid in her grave

301. Charles Landseer, *Clarissa Harlowe in the Sponging-House* (Society of British Artists 1833) (Tate Gallery, London). Scenes of captivity, not least those involving hapless women, were as popular in the early nineteenth century as they had been half a century before. If Hogarth had illustrated *Clarissa Harlowe,* he would doubtless have chosen for one subject the episode in which the heroine is confined in a bawdy house. Landseer, however, was painting for a strait-laced clientele, and so he prudently selected the later passage in which Clarissa is jailed for debt, a kind of imprisonment that could offend no one's moral sensibilities.

After this, there was a hiatus of almost three decades in the representation of scenes taken directly or indirectly from Richardson, a dry spell which coincided with that in Fielding illustration. As with Fielding, one reason was the superior appeal of the newly arrived Sir Walter Scott. But, beginning in the 1830s with Charles Landseer's *Clarissa Harlowe in the Sponging-House* (pl. 301), there was a mild revival of interest in pictures from *Pamela* and *Clarissa Harlowe,* a dozen being recorded in the next fifty years, slightly fewer than were painted of *Tom Jones* alone.

It appears that what Victorian artists valued in Richardson were not dramatic situations but opportunities for costumed sentiment utilizing, once more, the venerable theme of women reading letters or books. A typical production was George D. Leslie's *Clarissa* (RA 1866): "a damsel in the costume of Richardson's heroine (that quaint, inconvenient, unpicturesque dress of the least beautiful period of Art in this country), standing in the outer walks of an old English pleasaunce, deep in the perusal of a love-letter, and evidently not likely to proceed with her walk, though the evening sets into twilight, and a pet spaniel snuffs and whimpers in front, and so shows how long his patience has been under trial."[5] Frith's *Pamela* (RA 1874) showed the heroine "in full face before us, in a black dress and a white mop cap, writing, or in an interval of writing, and, with one hand on her cheek, with eyes of meditation, looking out at nothing"[6]—in other words, one more pensive female with literary credentials.

Three paintings exhibited in 1868–71 were titled respectively *The Novel of the Day, 1753: Sir Charles Grandison*; *Reading Sir Charles Grandison* (this by Valentine Prinsep); and *A Chapter from Pamela* (by George H. Boughton). By that time, Richardson as a novelist possessed not a tithe of the lively interest he had had for Highmore's contemporaries.

FIELDING

Down to the advent of Scott in the second decade of the nineteenth century, Fielding and Richardson were commonly regarded as the two greatest novelists England had produced. But whereas Richardson's novels had attracted painters as soon as they were published, artists' recognition of *Tom Jones* (published 1749) was delayed until 1777, when *Tom Jones Rescuing Molly Seagrim* was exhibited at the Society of Artists. The three editions of a volume of extracts, *The Beauties of Fielding* (1782), must have helped sustain interest in Fielding through the rest of the century.[1] At the exhibitions, there were pictures of Tom Jones rescuing Sophia Western and confronting the schoolmaster Square almost *in flagrante delicto* with Molly, as well as other subjects, some ten pictures in all. Stothard and Smirke contributed illustrations to various editions of the novel.

The peak of critical appreciation of Fielding before the twentieth century was reached in the years 1814–32, when almost the entire company of contemporary critics, including Coleridge, Hazlitt, Lamb, Scott, Southey, and Leigh Hunt, wrote about him at greater or shorter length. While Richardson's stock declined as his moralism and his epistolary form became antiquated (and his tedium became more oppressive?), Fielding's, despite misgivings as to the propriety of some of his comic and sexual scenes, rose. And yet—a prime instance of the way the critical prestige of an author at a given time did not necessarily match his popularity among painters—it was in these same years that Fielding virtually disappeared from the galleries. Between Arthur William Devis's *Two Subjects from Tom Jones* (RA 1808) and John Massey Wright's portrayal of the moment when Jenny Jones is submitting to the taunts and jeers of Mrs. Deborah Wilson and her attendant gossips (BI 1836), no painting from *Tom Jones* seems to have been exhibited.

Then the two curves reversed themselves. As the Victorian era began, Fielding's critical stock plunged, partly because his fiction was overshadowed by the established presence of Scott, partly because his humor was too strong for the new reading audience's affectation of gentility. The coming of Dickens and Thackeray further depressed Fielding's stock, which in fact reached its lowest market value at the time of Thackeray's lectures on the English humorists (1851) in which he delivered an extensive *ad hominem* diatribe, deploring the man as well as his fiction. Yet, though people may not have read him, they were offered some fifteen paintings, admittedly always of situations that could not possibly have raised a blush to Georgiana Podsnap's susceptible cheek, for they were always sentimental love or domestic scenes. Both Leslie (RA 1850) and Frith (RA 1875) depicted Tom Jones showing Sophia her image in the glass "as a pledge of her future constancy." Sophia was seen several times at the spinet, playing the squire to sleep; in other pictures, she and Tom were saying goodbye; in still others, she was merely one more beautiful woman from stock. Frith depicted her (RA 1875) in a dark blue braided riding habit, warming her hands at an inn fire, and in an earlier portrait by A. E. Chalon (RA 1857), she was seen "reclining in an arm-chair, in deep meditation, and near her lies a muff, from which a Cupid is creeping with the evident intention of wounding her with an arrow, which he grasps in his hand"[2]—as if the artist had inadvertently picked up *The Rape of the Lock* instead of Fielding's novel.

SMOLLETT

Largely because of his earthy humor and the superior attraction of Sterne's sentimentality, Smollett's fiction seems to have had only a limited readership in the nineteenth century, and two novels, *Roderick Random* and *Peregrine Pickle,* were the sources of only about ten paintings between them, all but one produced before 1850. (There appear to have been none at all from Smollett's most famous novel, *Humphry Clinker.*) The only painting of which much notice was taken was Leslie's *Reading the Will* (RA 1846), derived from a scene in *Roderick Random.* It was well received by the critics, including Thackeray, who drew flattering comparisons with Hogarth. This was Leslie's version of a narrative genre subject already familiar in art, though based instead on a similar episode in Scott's *Guy Mannering* or, sometimes, on no literary source at all. Wilkie's *The Reading of a Will* (RA 1820), with a reference to Scott, had been preceded by at least two other treatments, William Lizars' *Reading the Will* (Edinburgh 1811), which was engraved by Turner, and Edward Bird's *The Reading of the Will Concluded* (RA 1811).

STERNE

Ironically, since *ut pictura poesis* had nothing to do with fiction, it was two novelists, Sterne and Fielding, who, after Pope, best exemplified in their different ways the affinity of literature and painting in the eighteenth century.[1] Sterne was himself an artist of no particular ability. His early memoirist, John Croft, wrote that "he chiefly copied Portraits. He had a good idea of Drawing, but not the least of mixing his colours."[2] As his many allusions to the critical and technical vocabulary of painting and to master artists and their works testify, Sterne wrote *Tristram Shandy* fully conscious of the bearing the artist's techniques and choices had upon those of the novelist. He found food for aesthetic thought in Hogarth's *Analysis of Beauty,* which he burlesqued in his description of Corporal Trim's posture as he was about to preach the sermon (volume 2, chapter 17).[3] Having had Hogarth in mind when he wrote the passage, Sterne naturally wished him to illustrate it, and in a characteristic letter wrote to a friend (8 March 1760?):

> By the Father of the Sciences (you know his Name), I would give both my Ears (If I was not to loose my Credit by it), for no more than ten strokes of *Howgarth's* witty Chissel, to clap at the Front of my next Edition of *Shandy*. . . . What Shall we do? I have the worst face in the world to ask a favour with—& besides I would not propose a disagreeable thing to one I so much admire for the whole world—but you can say any Thing—You are an impudent honest Dog & cans't set a face upon a bad Matter—prithee sally out to Leicester fields, and when You have knockd at the door (for you must knock first) and art got in—begin thus "—Mr. Hogarth, I have been with my friend Shandy this morning"—but go on yr own Way—as I shall do mine.[4]

The application was successful. Hogarth not only provided the scene desired, which formed the frontispiece of the first volume in the new edition, but threw in, as the frontispiece to the third volume, the christening of young Shandy.

While still at York, before his sudden celebrity drew him to the accolades and fleshpots of London, Sterne had a nodding acquaintance with George Romney, then an apprentice of the portraitist Christopher Steele. Scarcely had the first two volumes of *Tristram Shandy* come from the press in that town (1759) than Romney painted four illustrations, his earliest independent work: *The Death of LeFevre, Dr. Slop with Obadiah, Dr. Slop in Mr. Shandy's Parlor,* and *Uncle Toby and Obadiah in the Garden.*[5] None of these has survived, but Romney's early friend Adam Walker, a self-taught writer and lecturer on science (see above, under Milton), left a description of his treatment of the death of LeFevre, whose story, in Hazlitt's opinion, was "perhaps the finest in the English language":[6]

> The figures were about eighteen inches high, and wonderfully expressive. The dying lieutenant was looking at Uncle Toby, who sat mute at the foot of the bed; and by the motion of his hand was recommending his son to his care. The boy

> was kneeling by the bedside, and with eyes that expressed his anguish of heart, was, as it were, turning from a dying to a living father, begging protection; a most pathetic figure. Trim was standing at a distance, in his usual attitude, with a face full of grief.[7]

Despite, or perhaps because of, the *Tristram Shandy* mania of the ensuing years, when imitations, parodies, caricatures, printed handerkerchiefs, and every other manifestation of popular enthusiasm then current made the book as feverishly famous as *Pickwick Papers* was to be seventy years later, almost no other paintings followed Romney's at the time. No doubt the book's eccentricity as well as its having touched off a ludicrous fad stigmatized it in the eyes of serious artists. Even its pathos failed to recommend it; Henry Singleton's *Death of LeFevre* (1796) was virtually the only *Shandy* painting exhibited at the Royal Academy for many decades after the novel appeared.[8]

The early career of *A Sentimental Journey* in art was very different. Its appearance in 1768 touched off a vogue only a little less frenetic than the one inspired by *Tristram Shandy.* Although it had its awkward spots, on the whole it achieved a more decorous reputation than that of its frequently bawdy predecessor, thanks to its high assay of pathos and sentiment at a time when popular taste was tending more and more in that direction. The book benefited especially from the wide circulation of various anthologies called *The Beauties of Sterne,* the first of which went through twelve editions between 1782 and 1793. These consisted of passages from Sterne's works, including his sermons, "Selected for the Heart of Sensibility" and therefore providing "all his Pathetic Tales, and most distinguished Observations on Life." Three especially pathetic tales were featured, those of LeFevre, the Monk (in *Tristram Shandy;* not often pictured), and Maria (briefly in *Tristram Shandy,* at length in *A Sentimental Journey*). ("I intended to have arranged them alphabetically," wrote the editor of the third edition of the original *Beauties,* "till I found the stories . . . would be too closely connected for the *feeling reader,* and would wound the bosom of *sensibility* too deeply; I therefore placed them at a proper distance from each other.")[9]

Whereas there were few *Tristram Shandy* paintings between Romney's initial and wholly obscure early treatments and (as we shall see) the modest revival in the 1830s, pictures from *A Sentimental Journey* were seen in the galleries from the 1770s onward, without any significant interruption. Some seventy are recorded, their history falling into two phases, the first dominated by sentimental themes, the second by humorous anecdotes. Of the sentimental subjects, the most often painted, by a large margin, was the sorrowful Maria, driven from pensiveness to madness by a perfidious lover: the very prototype, along with Ophelia, of the fragile and pitiable young woman so often portrayed in English popular art (pl. 94). Contemporary and early nineteenth-century criticism abounded with florid tributes to her appeal to the reader's sensibility. Edward Mangin, the author of *A View of the Pleasures Arising from a Love of Books* (1814), said:

> [Sterne's] portrait of the forlorn and gentle Maria is complete in all the lines and tints which constitute grace and softness: her form, that of loveliness not impaired but rendered more engaging by feebleness and sorrow, than the beauty of health and happiness can ever be; her ornament, a riband of *pale* green; her attitude, sitting with her elbow in her lap, and her head leaning on *one side* within her hand: her hair streaming loose, and tears trickling down her cheek.[10]

This reads almost as if the author had a particular painting in mind. By this time, there were already plenty to choose from, and many more were to come; the total of recorded Maria pictures would eventually reach thirty. The most celebrated of those that survive are two by Joseph Wright of Derby, painted in 1777, the same year in which Angelica Kauffmann exhibited a treatment at the Royal Academy, and in 1781 (they are quite different compositions). The subject seems to have been particularly adaptable to bibelots. Wright's treatment, it has been said, "is similar to that of the figures on the jasperware products of his friend Wedgwood"; and Kauffmann's was actually transferred to articles of all sorts and sizes, from watchcases to tea-waiters.[11] Northcote painted *Sterne and Maria* (1784), and as late as 1868, Frith depicted Maria and her goat.

Two other pathetic subjects from *A Sentimental Journey* recurred from time to time before the public appetite for this sort of art was finally sated. One was the story of the captive, painted early on by three leading eighteenth-century artists, Benjamin West (ca. 1772–80), Wright (RA 1778), and John Hamilton Mortimer (pen and ink sketch, 1774). The other was the story of the pilgrim on his way to a Spanish shrine whose ass dies by the wayside. West painted it about the time he painted the captive, George Carter portrayed it at the Society of Artists in 1773 (pl. 8), and Wright left a canvas of *The Old Man and His Ass* unfinished at his death in 1797. One of the last treatments was Richard Ansdell's (BI 1850).

By this time, taste had decisively shifted from Sterne's sentimental episodes to his humorous ones. In the period 1830–60, when the fashion of anecdotal genre was at its height, there were more comic scenes from *A Sentimental Journey* than there were portrayals of Maria. All of the favorite subjects involved Yorick and one of the three flirtatious women with whom he had monetary and other transactions: the grisette (Gilbert Stuart Newton [pl. 91] and Frith [pl. 302]), the innkeeper's daughter (Frith, RA 1868), and the *femme de chambre.*

Meanwhile, the fortunes of *Tristram Shandy* in art became more closely dependent on the author's personal reputation, which was inseparable from what came to be regarded as the more dubious aspects of the novel. As a novelist whose genius fulfilled itself in idiosyncrasy, he was praised by such critics as Hazlitt, Coleridge, and Scott, and a little later by De-Quincey and Carlyle. But his personal character came under attack in the first half of the century with revelations of the full extent of his plagiarisms and of conduct that sometimes was unbecoming a parson. This moral reaction against him both as man and as artist reached its climax in Thackeray's indictment in one of his lectures on the English humorists: "He goes to work systematically and of cold blood; paints his face, puts on his ruff and motley clothes, and lays down his carpet and tumbles on it. . . . There is not a page in Sterne's writing but has something that were better away, a latent corruption—a hint, as of an impure presence."[12] One suspects that Thackeray purposely heightened the colors of his moral portraiture for the sake of a more arresting contrast with the affectionate account of Oliver Goldsmith that immediately followed. Sterne nonetheless retained many admirers.

Whatever their differences, Victorian moralists and critics agreed in deploring the Rabelaisian and satirical strains in *Tristram Shandy,* and consequently the twenty or so paintings that are recorded from between 1830 and 1885 concentrated exclusively on its pathetic and amiably hu-

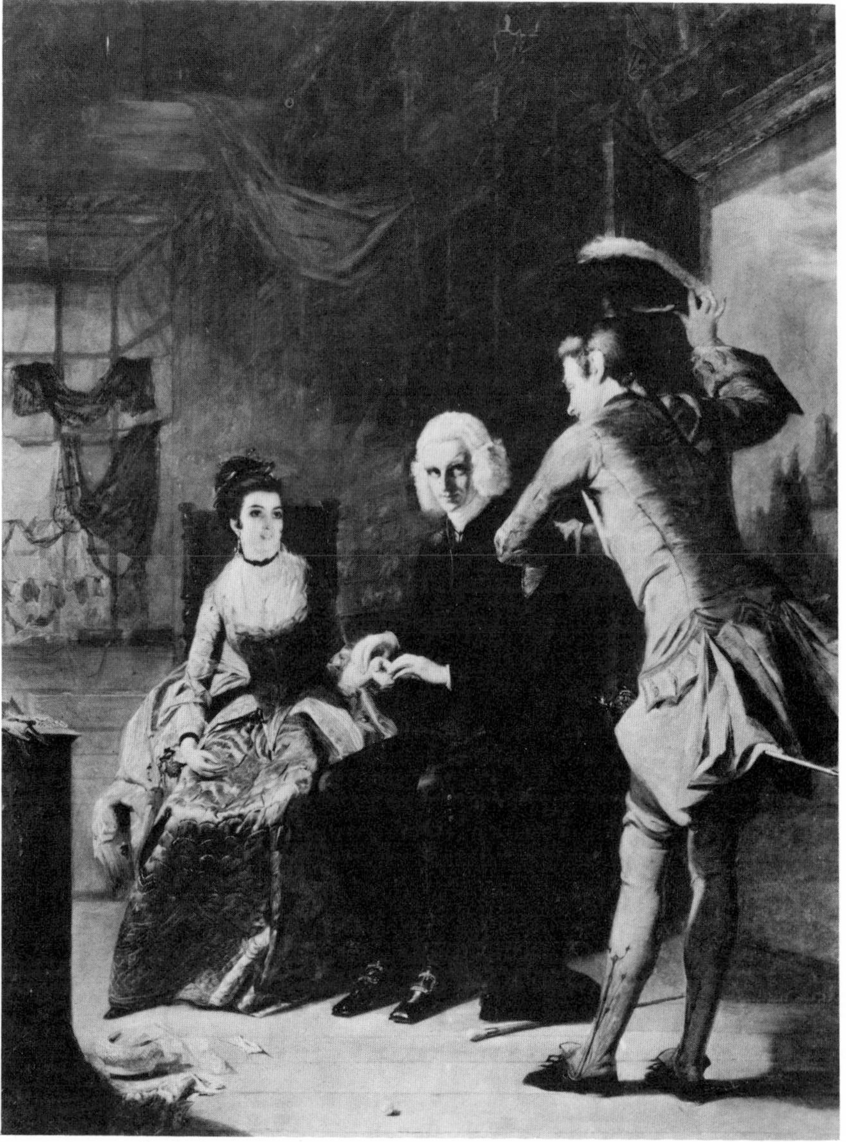

302. William P. Frith, *Feeling the Pulse* (British Institution 1842) (Victoria & Albert Museum, Crown Copyright). Parson Yorick's flirtation with the beautiful grisette was often depicted by early Victorian artists. Frith's painting represents the moment before she gets out the parcel of gloves. (See pl. 91.) "I am sure," Yorick says, "you must have one of the best pulses of any woman in the world." "'Feel it,' said she, holding out her arm. So laying down my hat, I took hold of her fingers in one hand, and applied the two forefingers of my other to the artery. . . . I had counted twenty pulsations, and was going on fast towards the fortieth, when her husband coming unexpected from a back parlor into the shop, put me a little out of my reckoning."

morous episodes. The most famous was Leslie's *Uncle Toby and the Widow Wadman in the Sentry Box* (pl. 45), of which at least three versions were painted. The remarks of Tom Taylor, Leslie's biographer, suggest the selective spirit with which Leslie painted, and contemporaries received, the scene:

> Any painter with a stain of impurity in his imagination would have risked offence in touching such a subject. There is more prurience in Sterne's pen than in Leslie's pencil. In his hands the widow becomes so loveable a person, that we overlook the fierceness of the amorous siege she is laying to Uncle Toby's heart; while Uncle Toby himself is so thoroughly the gentleman,—so unmistakeably innocent and unsuspecting, and single-hearted,—that the humour of the situation seems filtered of all its grossness.[13]

Two years later, Leslie followed up his success with *Tristram Shandy Recovering the Lost Manuscript* (RA 1833). Constable, it is said, arranged the chiaroscuro, and, because Leslie thought he resembled Sterne "very strongly," the American artist Samuel F. B. Morse sat for the Tristram figure.[14]

Subsequent artists took other subjects from *Tristram Shandy*. In 1849, Alfred Elmore showed at the Royal Academy "Mr. Shandy leaning on his cane, reading to the tailor at work on a pair of breeches 'a lecture upon the *latus clavis*, and pointing to the precise part of the waistband where he was determined to have it sewed on'."[15] In 1866, Frith ventured to revive the scene Leslie had represented with such success almost forty years earlier, Uncle Toby and the Widow Wadman in the sentry box (pl. 67), but it was received with much less enthusiasm. At least two critics, on the *Times* and the *Examiner*, complained that the widow was far too young and "bewitching" to be true to Sterne's "rather coarse" character and that the back of the stalwart male figure was equally unfaithful to Uncle Toby.[16]

The remaining *Tristram Shandy* paintings drew from the same vein of humor, sometimes tinctured with pathos. In 1879–80, for example, two artists, Sir John Gilbert and John Dawson Watson, portrayed Uncle Toby and Corporal Trim, the latter picture showing the loyal soldier laying Toby's sword and scabbard across his coffin "ere he returns to the door to take his horse by the bridle to follow his beloved master's hearse as he has directed him"[17]—an event not reached in the novel. But by this time, Sterne's appeal to the art-loving public had largely evaporated. Indeed, a full decade earlier (1869), when Francis Turner Palgrave reproduced Newton's *Yorick and the Grisette* in color, from a woodblock, in his *Gems of English Art of This Century*, he remarked, "One may doubt whether, at the present day, Sterne be not falling into the position of those authors of whose books one might say that they are supposed to be known to everybody, and practically are read by nobody."[18]

GOLDSMITH

As a token of his welcome presence in the Reynolds-Johnson coterie of artists and writers, Oliver Goldsmith held the honorary Professorship of Ancient History in the Royal Academy—a chair suggested by Dr. Johnson himself, "in order that Goldy might have a right to be at their dinners."[1] In view of the employment he was to give to artists during the next century, the honor was well earned. With the possible exception of Thomson, among art lovers Goldsmith was the most popular eighteenth-century author. The numerous early paintings suggested by the pathetic ballad of "The Hermit" ("Edwin and Angelina") were the precursors of well over one hundred canvases derived from *The Vicar of Wakefield*, in which it was first published. "We read the *Vicar of Wakefield* in youth and in age," wrote Sir Walter Scott. "We return to it again and again, and bless the memory of an author who contrives so well to reconcile us to human nature."[2] Although some good judges of literature were less enthusiastic, common readers shared Scott's opinion, and it was their taste that prevailed most dramatically in the 1840s when, in a single decade, almost as many pictures from *The Vicar of Wakefield* were exhibited (some thirty) as had been seen in the entire preceding sixty years.

Before this boom, the *Vicar* tradition in art was fed by such works as Charles Ryley's *The Sermon in Prison* and *The Return of Olivia* (both RA 1787) and John Martin's version of "The Hermit" (BI 1817), which was not at all characteristic of the artist whose *Joshua* had won a prize at the exhibition the year before and whose *The Fall of Babylon* two years later

303. William P. Frith, *Measuring Heights* (RA 1863) (Victoria & Albert Museum, Crown Copyright). A later version of a subject from *The Vicar of Wakefield* that Frith first painted in 1842. "Mrs. Primrose," explained the artist, "makes her daughter and Squire Thornhill stand up together to see which is the taller, a transparent device which, as the good old book says, she thought impenetrable" (*Autobiography,* 1: 96–97).

would cause a sensation. In 1828, Gilbert Stuart Newton hung at the Royal Academy his *The Vicar of Wakefield Reconciling His Wife to Olivia,* which was bought by the Marquis of Lansdowne for his gallery at Bowood. Wilkie, according to Haydon, was unkind enough to say that Newton's Vicar "looked like Goldsmith in a dress of Molière's. It had not got the simplicity of Goldsmith."[3]

The Vicar of Wakefield was the perfect book to ride the surge of enthusiasm for homely narrative and genre paintings that marked the period. It had everything to meet the popular taste of the moment: domestic warmth ("There is no novel in our own, or any language, that possesses more interest or pathos in all its domestic relations," said an art critic in 1839),[4] a plot studded with interesting but not agitating incidents, individualized characters such as the amiably eccentric Dr. Primrose himself, and heroines (Olivia and Sophia) admirably suited to be the subjects of sentimental figure studies. From no other novel and indeed from few if any other literary works of comparable length did artists derive so many separate episodes. The majority were strung on the main plot line: Olivia's elopement with Thornhill and her subsequent rescue and return by her father; the Vicar's imprisonment for debt; the ambiguous Mr. Burchell's courtship of Sophia. But no one scene or small group of scenes predominated, as they did, for example, in the paintings from most of Shakespeare's plays.

In 1838, Daniel Maclise was among the first to portray the comic episode of Moses going to the fair to sell the colt Blackberry and returning with the gross of green spectacles he has been paid. Then came Richard Redgrave's *The Return of Olivia to Her Parents* (RA 1839) and Maclise's *Hunt the Slipper at Neighbour Flambrough's* (RA 1841), depicting the moment just before "the 'ill-managed mirth' of the Primroses received a sudden interruption and rebuke from the stately apparition of Lady Blarney and Miss Caroline Wilhelmina Skeggs."[5]

The following year (1842), Charles Cope showed three Goldsmith subjects at the Royal Academy. But these were overshadowed by W. P. Frith's first successful painting, one that would shortly lead him to become something of a specialist in the Goldsmith repertory: *Measuring Heights* (pl. 303).

Contributing to the *Vicar* vogue at this moment was the appearance of an edition containing thirty-two wood engravings after designs by William Mulready, the climax of a series of editions illustrated by Stothard (1792), Thomas Uwins (1812), Rowlandson (1817), and George Cruikshank (1830, 1832).[6] In both 1843 and 1844, the London exhibitions contained no fewer than six *Vicar* paintings, including one by Leslie, Frith's older fellow painter of literary subjects—his only picture from Goldsmith, "whom," remarked Tom Taylor, "one would have supposed likely to be one of his favourite authors."[7] Reviewing the Academy exhibition of 1844, Thackeray said that "the editor of this Magazine [*Fraser's*] had made a solemn condition with the writer of this notice that no pictures taken from the *Vicar of Wakefield* or *Gil Blas* should, by any favour or pretence, be noticed in this review." But, he continued, the success of Mulready's contribution, *The Whistonian Controversy,* forced him to disregard the placards thus inferentially posted at the beginning of the review, as they should have been at the entrance to the exhibition: VICARS OF WAKEFIELD NOT ADMITTED.[8] The following year, doubtless taking its cue from Thackeray (unless it was Thackeray himself writing), *Punch* suggested that in the future a large room—the largest in the building except that devoted to portraits—be reserved for *Vicar* paintings.[9]

At first glance, the subject of *The Whistonian Controversy* would not seem of a kind to elicit much enthusiasm; it showed the Vicar and his old friend the Reverend Dr. Wilmot disputing a theological point, namely that a minister of the Church of England should not remarry after his first wife's death. (Wilmot was not without prejudice on the issue, since he was then courting his fourth wife.) Thackeray, however, praised the painting to the skies. "I believe this," he told *Fraser's* readers, "to be one of the finest cabinet pictures in the world . . . in drawing so admirable, in expression so fine, in finish so exquisite, in composition so beautiful, in humour and beauty of expression so delightful, that I can't but ask where is a good picture if this be not one."[10] It was no accident that the very next year, at the British Institution, a minor artist displayed a painting entitled *The Vicar of Wakefield Reading His Favourite Whiston.*

Mulready followed up the success of his Whiston painting with *Choosing the Wedding Gown* (pl. 304). Commissioned by John Sheepshanks, it was—and is—an outstanding example of early Victorian literary genre art. The next year (1847) Mulready showed still another *Vicar* subject, *Burchell and Sophia* (also known as *The Haymaking*)—the man courting the coy girl by pretending to help her glean.

Maclise returned to the Moses-at-the-fair episode with *The Gross of*

304. William Mulready, *Choosing the Wedding Gown* (RA 1846) (Victoria & Albert Museum, Crown Copyright). Suggested by the first sentences in *The Vicar of Wakefield:* "I was ever of opinion, that the honest man who married and brought up a large family, did more service than he who continued single, and only talked of population. For this motive, I had scarce taken orders a year before I began to think seriously of matrimony, and chose my wife as she did her wedding gown, not for a fine glossy surface, but such qualities as would wear well."

Green Spectacles (RA 1850). The press, with the conspicuous exception of *Blackwood's Magazine,* was unanimous in its acclaim. The *Times*'s report was typical:

> He has painted nothing more pleasant or more natural. Perhaps he has given the sheepish Moses an unwonted degree of roguishness and recklessness in that tremendous passage of his mercantile experience when it was established beyond all doubt that the price of the colt was a gross of green spectacles, *not* of silver; but the mild reproof of the vicar, the bewilderment of Mrs. Primrose, the terror of the elder brother, the sympathy of the sisters are inimitable. Everyone is in consternation but the baby—and he with more practical wisdom than his elders sees the glasses are green—and looks through them. This picture is one of Mr. Maclise's happiest efforts, and it brings us back entirely to our own English ground.[11]*

At this point—the early 1850s—Sophia and Olivia, who usually had participated in larger compositions, were singled out for attention in a brief burst of sisterly figure studies. Ford Madox Brown had somewhat anticipated the vogue a few years earlier, when he painted, as one of his first essays in literary art, *Dr. Primrose and His Daughters* (pl. 80).

Understandably, in view of the affectionate familiarity with which people regarded both the *Vicar* text and its charmingly feckless author as he figured in the biographies of the time, reviewers were unusually insistent that artists be faithful to Goldsmith's spirit and letter. This was the one criterion that could make or break each new entry in the *Vicar* competition. When a painter was judged to have succeeded, he would read, as Maclise did when he exhibited *The Gross of Green Spectacles,* that "if Goldie could himself see the amount of character embodied in this picture, he would most honestly confess himself outdone" (*Art Journal*) and "[the picture is] thoroughly imbued with the sentiment of Goldsmith" (*Examiner*).[12] On the other hand, a *Blackwood's* writer declared of the same picture, "Mr. Maclise must rely upon it that he lacks the keen perception of humour indispensable to the artist who would illustrate Goldsmith."[13] The "idealization" that art critics praised in some paintings of the period, from, say, *The Tempest* or *Comus,* was not acceptable in Goldsmith's case, critics insisting instead on fidelity to his moderate realism. The *Athenaeum* said of a minor artist's version of *Moses Going to Sell the Colt at the Fair* (1842): " . . . a work of great purity, grace, and simplicity, but with too much of the cold glazing of a china plate in its effect. All the details, too, of the cottage are flattered to a prettiness at variance with the novel. The vine-hung porch looks a perfect gate of Paradise, through which no temptations of any Squire Thornhill could have penetrated."[14]

Although there no longer was talk of *Vicar* paintings taking over the exhibitions, some twenty more were hung in the ensuing decade and another twenty-five before the end of the century. Their continuing popularity owed something to the several dramatizations of the novel that were produced in those years. Two stage versions appeared in 1850 alone. The second act of Tom Taylor's opened on a tableau based on Maclise's familiar *Dressing Moses for the Fair* (RA 1838). Another adaptation, by W. H. Wills in 1878, starred Ellen Terry as Olivia, a role for which she was long and affectionately remembered.

Nearly all of the twenty recorded paintings from Goldsmith's *The Deserted Village* were produced before 1850. The poem's career in art began in a courteous exchange of compliments between Goldsmith and his friend Sir Joshua Reynolds. Goldsmith dedicated *The Deserted Village* to

*Thackeray gently parodied appreciative notices like this, possibly including some of his own, in a review by the journalist Frederick Bayham in *The Newcomes* (1853–54): "617. 'Moses Bringing Home the Gross of Green Spectacles'. Smith, R. A.—Perhaps poor Goldsmith's exquisite little work has never been so great a favourite as in the present age. We have here, in a work by one of our most eminent artists, an homage to the genius of him 'who touched nothing which he did not adorn:' and the charming subject is handled in the most delicious manner by Mr. Smith. The chiaroscuro is admirable: the impasto is perfect. Perhaps a *very* captious critic might object to the foreshortening of Moses's left leg; but where there is so much to praise justly, the *Pall Mall Gazette* does not care to condemn" (chap. 22).

Reynolds, who responded by dedicating the engraving of his picture *Resignation* to Goldsmith. On the print were quoted these lines from the poem:

> How blest is he who crowns in shades like these
> A youth of labour with an age of ease;
> . . . .
> Sinks to the grave with unperceiv'd decay,
> While *Resignation* gently slopes the way;
> And, all his prospects brightening to the last,
> His heaven commences ere the world be past.[15]

At the Royal Academy in 1800, William Hamilton and Francis Wheatley showed a total of five paintings from *The Deserted Village* that were engraved for DuRoveray's edition of Goldsmith's poetry; and eleven years later, Stothard exhibited his *Leaving Home,* from the same poem. Probably the best-received painting, however, was Frith's *The Village Pastor* (pl. 305), commissioned by the ironmaster John Gibbons. Frith showed the beloved parson leaving the church after service surrounded by his family and his parishioners, including a timid child, a beautiful girl who is obviously the victim of a wasting illness, and in the background a group of Wilkiean village politicians. Thackeray found in the canvas "some senti-

305. William P. Frith, *The Village Pastor* (RA 1845) (Walker Art Gallery, Liverpool). A sketch, mistakenly titled *Dr. Primrose, Vicar of Wakefield,* for the painting exhibited in 1845 with these lines from *The Deserted Village:*

> The service past, around the pious man,
> With steady zeal, each honest rustic ran;
> E'en children followed with endearing wile,
> And plucked his gown to share the good man's smile.

ment of a very quiet, refined, Sir-Roger-de-Coverley-like sort—not too much of it . . . indicated rather than expressed. . . . This is the sort of picture," he concluded, "that is good to paint nowadays—kindly, beautiful, inspiring delicate sympathies, and awakening tender good-humour."[16]

A scene from *She Stoops to Conquer* was exhibited at the Royal Academy in 1774, the year following its first performance. Except for an illustration Wheatley designed for *Bell's British Theatre* (pl. 25), there were few further paintings from the play until the early Victorian years. Between 1836 and 1898, however, owing in part to the popularity of other Goldsmith subjects, *She Stoops to Conquer* was active in the artist's repertory, some fifteen paintings being recorded. In 1856–59, three different painters exhibited at the Society of British Artists—two in one year—the identical moment when Miss Hardcastle, assuming the role of a barmaid, says to the preoccupied Marlow, "Did you call, Sir? Did your honour call?" The other favorite moment, in stage revivals as well as among artists, was one that Goldsmith had thriftily repeated from *The Vicar of Wakefield:* Mrs. Hardcastle places her son Tony back to back with Miss Neville to compare their heights, and Tony seizes the opportunity to crack his thick skull against the girl's. In 1868, twenty-six years after his first *Measuring Heights* was enthusiastically received, Frith exercised a thrift of his own by repeating the subject, but this time alluding to the comedy rather than the novel.

OSSIAN

The British paintings inspired by what purported to be the "genuine remains" of a third-century Celtic bard named Ossian shared in a protracted international craze in literature and art.[1] In 1762–63, one James MacPherson published *Fingal: An Epic Poem in Six Books* and *Temora* in eight books. These proceeded to captivate the imagination of western Europe. No matter that they were mostly MacPherson's invention, though ultimately based on genuine but wholly anonymous fragments of ancient story (in most modern reference books they are branded simply as a hoax); they seemed providentially sent to satisfy the age's longing for an epic, the product of genius undefiled by civilization, to adorn Northern literature as Homer and Virgil had adorned the literatures of Greece and Rome. Wherever the developing Romantic spirit sought evidence of primitive poetic inspiration or nationalistic sentiment, as in Britain and France, a bard was required to personate either or both, and the fictitious Ossian admirably filled the bill. He was revered, translated, imitated, even dramatized; in London, between 1769 and 1793, there was a series of free stage adaptations called *The Fatal Discovery, The Captives, Comala, Oithona,* and *Oscar and Malvina* (the last-named being a pantomime, 1791).[2]

Within a few years, Ossian's putative works had kindled an enthusiasm in Germany, France, Denmark, Italy, and Russia that can only be described as a particularly bizarre episode in the history of cultivated taste. Goethe admired Ossian, whom his hero Werther, reading him on the last night of his life, preferred to Homer; the "Primitifs" in Jacques-Louis David's studio sang his praises; Napoleon, whose favorite reading was Ossian in French translation, had his house at Malmaison decorated with scenes such as Girodet's *Ossian Receiving Napoleon's Generals,* which combined his own legend, still in the making, with that of the bard. "The dream of Ossian" was the subject of the ceiling Ingres was engaged to paint for the palace Napoleon expected to occupy in Rome.

Ossian was one of the most popular sources of British art in the period 1770–1810. In those four decades, some forty-five paintings from the poems are recorded, exceeded in number only by Shakespeare and Milton (if the contents of Fuseli's Milton Gallery are included). The Ossianic materials not only provided fresh heroic themes for neoclassic artists looking beyond the customary subjects from history or Shakespeare but offered a pretext for painting landscapes in the manner of Salvator Rosa. Horace Walpole wrote to Hannah More in 1784, "The flimsy giantry of Ossian has introduced mountainous horrors. The exhibitions at Somerset House are crowded with Brobdignag ghosts."[3] While the fashion prevailed, subjects from Ossian were as popular with dyed-in-the-wool neoclassic artists as with those touched by the Romantic spirit. The incidence of Ossian paintings dropped sharply thereafter, with a marked hiatus between 1829 and 1856. The last few recorded, from 1856 to 1883, depicted not incidents in the legends but places traditionally associated with Ossian, his birthplace and grave. Insofar as Ossianic pictures were initially an expression of Scottish nationalism, they were pushed from the market by paintings from Scott, who was much more familiar to the common art lover, even in Scotland, than was MacPherson's bard; but as late as 1847, the fourteen-year-old Birmingham schoolboy Edward Jones (later Burne-Jones) shared a friend's copy of Ossian and, according to his wife, "They used to repeat it aloud when they walked about, taking parts as far as possible." "A very few years later," the artist himself recalled, "I was told it was a forgery and very deplorable even if it wasn't—bombastic and silly. But it couldn't be quite choked out of me and there was a forlorn note in it that gently broke my heart, like the blessed word 'Mesopotamia.'"[4]*

The most elaborate scheme to paint the matter of Ossian was Alexander Runciman's, who was said to have dreamed the same extravagant dream Henry Fuseli had—of painting frescoes that would rival those in the Sistine Chapel. Fuseli never achieved his transcendental tribute to Shakespeare, but Runciman realized his ambition to memorialize Ossian at Sir John Clerk's seat, Penicuik, a few miles south of Edinburgh.[5] In 1771–72, he decorated the ceiling of Penicuik's great hall with a large oval of Ossian and Malvina seated before a large crowd and surrounded it with twelve individual subjects, forming a kind of pictorial epic. Several of these subjects, such as Cormar attacking the Spirit of the Waters, Fingal encountering the spirit of Loda, and the death of Ossian, became standard choices in subsequent Ossianic art. The frescoes were destroyed by fire in 1899, but several sketches survive at the National Gallery of Scotland.

One of the panels ("Elysium") in the famous series James Barry painted in the great room of the Society of Arts in London was from Ossian. Angelica Kauffmann exhibited *Trenmore and Imbaca,* also known as *The Power of Love,* from *Fingal* book 6, at the Royal Academy in 1773 (another version was sold in 1922, disguised as *Armed Amazons*); and a decade later, Maria Cosway displayed two Ossian subjects, *Darthula Discovers Herself to Caribar her Lover* (RA 1782) and *"Althan stood in the wood alone . . ."* (RA 1783).

SHERIDAN

The School for Scandal entered art as soon as it was staged; James Roberts's depiction of the screen scene (pl. 110) was hung at the Royal

*An allusion to the reputed power of that word, sonorously pronounced by the eighteenth-century evangelist George Whitefield, to induce a state of religious ecstasy in his susceptible auditors.

Academy in 1779, two years after the first performance, and Zoffany had a portrait of Robert Baddeley as Moses in the Academy show of 1781. But of the approximately twenty-five recorded paintings from the play (by contrast, *The Rivals* was represented only three or four times), most were the result of its sensational popularity in the 1870s. It ran for more than four hundred performances at the Vaudeville Theatre in 1872–73, after which Buckstone presented it at the Haymarket; and the next year, the Bancrofts revived it at still another house, the Prince of Wales'. In 1875, E. M. Ward's *Lady Teazle Playing Her Father to Sleep* was shown at the Royal Academy, and two subjects by lesser painters were at the Society of British Artists. The popularity of *The School for Scandal* in the galleries is a late example of the two-way traffic between art and the theater. The Bancrofts' production was celebrated for its lavish, period-perfect mounting; one critic, praising the brilliant setting in general, also admired the costumes and bearing of the actors, "who wear the look, indeed, of animated portraits of Gainsborough and Sir Joshua."[1] During this period, as earlier, the most painted moment in the play was the climax of the screen scene (4.3). A number of pictures took their titles from Charles Surface's "Lady Teazle, by all that's wonderful!" as he throws down the screen.

COWPER

William Cowper's *The Task* (1785) charmed readers by its comfortable vignettes of rural retirement and quiet domesticity: the same qualities that then recommended, and would continue to recommend, *The Vicar of Wakefield,* for example. His modern bibliographer has called it "the most popular poem of its day with the reading public," noting that "the demand for his poems steadily increased during the years following his death [1800]. No other poet, with the exception of Scott and Byron, was so frequently reprinted and none had such a sustained run of popularity."[1] Cowper was an early favorite of John Constable, who wrote in 1812 to his fiancée, Maria Bicknell, "How delighted I am that you are so fond of Cowper but how could it be otherwise—for he is the poet of Religion and Nature,"[2] and he was reading Southey's newly published life of the poet a few hours before he died suddenly in April 1837. Like Bunyan's, Cowper's popularity grew with the spread of Evangelicalism in the first half of the nineteenth century. But many more pictures were derived from *The Pilgrim's Progress* than from Cowper's poems. A dozen or so, nearly all before 1850, came from *The Task* and a mere handful from the other poems.

As early as the 1790s, Thomas Barker of Bath painted two pictures from *The Task*: *The Woodman,* which he sold to Macklin for engraving (the famous artist in wool, Miss Linwood, later produced a needlework version), and *Crazy Kate,* the subject of half of the other paintings from the poem (pl. 77). The most notable exercise in illustrating Cowper was Fuseli's, for Joseph Johnson's edition of the poet's works in 1805–6. It was not a happy matching of subject and artist. Conversation pieces such as *Newsreading in the Country* (*The Task,* 4.30–33) and *Family Life in the Country* ("Retirement," lines 189–90) were not Fuseli's forte. Leigh Hunt saw in the designs

> a chaos of mingled genius and absurdity, such as, perhaps, was never before seen. . . . A student reading in a garden is all over intensity of muscle; and the quiet tea-table scene in Cowper, he has turned into a preposterous conspiracy

306. John Pettie, *Charles Surface Sells His Ancestors* (RA 1885) (Bristol Museum and Art Gallery). From *The School for Scandal,* act 4, scene 1: Careless, rolled-up pedigree in hand, auctions off "the family of the Surfaces, up to the Conquest" as Charles and Sir Oliver offer a running commentary on the originals of the portraits.

> of huge men and women, all bent upon showing their thews and postures, with dresses as fantastical as their minds. One gentleman, of the existence of whose trowsers you are not aware till you see the terminating line at the ankle, is sitting and looking grim on a sofa, with his hat on and no waistcoat.[3]

As his admirer Haydon conceded, "When Fuseli attempted the domestic, as in his illustrations of Cowper, his total want of nature [human sympathies] stares one in the face, like the eyes of his own ghosts."[4] Crazy Kate, the popeyed subject of the frontispiece to the second volume, was more in Fuseli's line.

E. M. Ward once painted *John Gilpin Delayed by His Customers* (RA 1851), a typical humorous piece showing the dandiacal Cheapside tradesman impatient to begin his journey as an elegantly dressed mother and daughter dawdle over their choice of dress materials and their escort yawns.[5]

The story of Cowper's retired life at Olney, cared for by Mrs. Unwin and devoted to writing verse as a therapy for religious mania, was well known to nineteenth-century readers, initially through his friend Hayley's biography (1803–4) and through his charming, though often enervated, letters, some of which were first published in Hayley's book. As a subject of painting, Cowper's life survived longer than did his verse. In the middle and later Victorian years, there was a small series of pictures representing him receiving his mother's picture out of Norfolk (the subject of one of his best-liked occasional poems), pricking the flowers on his mother's dress, and meditating in his garden, accompanied by his three cherished hares. A painting of this last subject by Henry Stacy Marks was sold in 1888.

CRABBE

The history of George Crabbe's poems as subjects of paintings is a rather odd one, especially because of the disjunction between his critical fame and his delayed, and, as it turned out, brief occurrence in art.[1] He established himself as "the poet of the poor," as his son called him, with

307. Thomas Stothard, *John Gilpin* (undated) (Victoria & Albert Museum, Crown Copyright). The wild ride of Cowper's Cheapside linen draper, bereft of hat and wig, past the Bell Inn, Edmonton, where he has arranged to meet his wife and family to celebrate their twentieth wedding anniversary.

At Edmonton his loving wife
  From the balcony spied
Her tender husband, wond'ring much
  To see how he did ride.

Stop, stop John Gilpin!—Here's the
    house—
  They all at once did cry,
The dinner waits and we are tir'd,
  Said Gilpin—So am I.

The Library (1781), *The Village* (1783), and *The Newspaper* (1785), but no paintings were then made from these narratives of rural life, written in thousands of relentless heroic couplets. With Goldsmith's pleasantly sentimental *Vicar of Wakefield* to draw from, and Gainsborough's and Morland's genre art to imitate, artists must have regarded Crabbe's realism as too grim to suit contemporary elegant taste; his ambition was, as he wrote in *The Village,* "to paint the cot / As truth will paint it, and as Bards will not." After an absence of two decades, Crabbe returned to the public eye with his *Poems* (1807), including revised versions of his earlier work as well as a new poem, *The Parish Register.* This was followed by *The Borough* (1810), *Tales in Verse* (1812), and *Tales of the Hall* (1819), by which time his reputation had caught fire. For a short while, among contemporary poets only Scott, Moore, and eventually Byron surpassed him in critical esteem. In 1818, the publisher John Murray paid £3,000 for the copyright of his works, the same price that Moore had received two years earlier for *Lalla Rookh.* "Crabbe's the man," Byron told Murray, despite the fact that "he has got a coarse and impracticable subject."[2] "Truth," he wrote in "English Bards and Scotch Reviewers,"

. . . sometimes will lend her noblest fires,
And decorate the verse herself inspires;
This fact in Virtue's name let Crabbe attest;
Though nature's sternest painter, yet the best.

Wordsworth, whose *Excursion,* said one reviewer, was "sketched with all the truth of Crabbe's descriptive pencil," said that Crabbe's works would "last, from their combined merits as Poetry and Truth full as long as any thing that has been expressed in Verse since they first made their appearance"[3]—including all the productions of the English Romantic poets down to 1815.

As we saw in chapter 3, the publication of Crabbe's successive volumes between 1807 and 1819 touched off a critical debate on the admissibility and limits of realism in poetry. In the course of this debate, and in other reviews, critics likened Crabbe's poetry to painting more insistently than they did, then or later, in the case of any other poet of comparable stature. It quickly became a platitude to praise him as the English poetic heir of the Dutch genre painters, as well as to link him with Hogarth. As Thomas Noon Talfourd said in 1815, "It is true that in his minute representations of hard-hearted villainy, he has often bordered on the shocking and disgustful; but there will generally be found, as in the works of Hogarth, some kind of gentle touch which sobers the whole scene. . . ."[4]

Yet despite these clear signals to artists that Crabbe's tales were a reservoir of subjects, especially now that David Wilkie was making relatively unidealized rural genre painting fashionable, only four pictures are recorded down to the late 1830s: Henry Singleton's two subjects from *The Borough, Peter Grimes* (RA 1812) and *Ellen Orford* (BI 1813), T. M. Simpson's *Edward Shore,* from *Tales in Verse* (RA 1813), and Henry Corbould's *The Parting Hour* (RA 1826, BI 1828). By that time, Crabbe's critical reputation had already declined, though in years to come Tennyson would still value him, as did Crabbe's fellow-Suffolkman, Edward FitzGerald, and still later Newman, Ruskin, Rossetti, Clough, and George Eliot. But when the eight-volume collection of his poems appeared in 1834, John Gibson Lockhart observed that despite the consensus of "every one of his eminent contemporaries" that he belonged "in the very highest rank of excellence, Crabbe has never yet become familiar to hundreds of thousands of English readers well qualified to appreciate and enjoy his merits."[5]

Only at this point, ironically, did Crabbe's fortunes in the art world improve. His fame there remained modest, but between 1838 and 1849, a dozen paintings were credited to his poems. Most of them were pictures of two heroines, Ellen Orford (*The Borough*) and Phoebe Dawson (*The Parish Register*); two portraits of the latter, indeed, were exhibited as late as 1867 (BI) and 1874 (RA). The rest were portrayals of a few sentimental or pathetic situations, including George B. O'Neill's *The Foundling,* from *The Parish Register* (pl. 48).

Why were so few pictures taken from Crabbe? Despite the applause of reviewers in his post-*Borough* years and the liberality with which they suggested subjects in his poems that awaited the artist's pencil, it is likely that, as a practical matter, too many of those subjects were "painful" or "disgusting" (both terms occurred often in the reviews). The main charge against Crabbe was that his rural realism, far from being Goldsmith-idyllic, was too brutal, unsettling, repulsive. There was nothing agreeably picturesque or sentimental in his poems, and only a few characters, notably Ellen Orford, were qualified for artistic treatment because their stories were pathetic. In Crabbe's case, as in that of a number of other English writers, many subjects presented themselves, but few, in the event, were chosen.

ROGERS

The wealthy poet-connoisseur Samuel Rogers, whose home in St. James's Place housed a famous art collection, occupies a peripheral place in the history of both literature and painting. His reputation as a poet, at first the product of genuine admiration but later kept alive by artificial means, rested on no solid grounds.[1] Fuseli expressed an increasingly common opinion when he observed in 1812, "He never wrote a line of Poetry in his life, all His good lines are *Copies* from Poets, and in His 'Pleasures of Memory' He begins with *Gray*"[2]—as if there had been no earlier poets worth mentioning. *The Pleasures of Memory* (1792), a frigid versifying of the theory of associationism laden with personifications and heroic couplets, was one of the most popular poems of its day; by 1816, some 23,000 copies, a great quantity for the time, had been sold. Mary Ann Flaxman, the half-sister of one well-known artist, and Maria Cosway, the wife of another, displayed a pair of pictures from the poem at the Royal Academy in 1800; and in 1819, Miss Flaxman exhibited a picture of *Maternal Piety* from Rogers's *Human Life,* which had just appeared.

Rogers's poetry was represented in the art exhibitions between 1830 and 1860 by some twenty-five pictures, most bearing quotations from his series of meditative and anecdotal poems published in 1822 and 1828 under the title *Italy.* Comparing unfavorably, as it did, with the fourth canto of *Childe Harold's Pilgrimage,* which was of a somewhat similar cast, *Italy* met with no success. But Rogers, as one of Stothard's biographers rather cattily wrote, "was in the happy and rare position of at once holding his own poetry in high estimation, and of possessing the means of presenting it to the world with all the added attractions which art could provide for it."[3] Burning the unsold copies of the first edition, he undertook to prepare a new one, enlarged, revised and, above all, lavishly illustrated, at a cost of £7,335—a true fortune. From Stothard, who had illustrated the fifth edition of *The Pleasures of Memory,* he commissioned twenty designs, and from Turner, twenty-four. The resulting volume (1830) was a landmark in the history of the illustrated book.[4] It sold 4,000 copies in the first fortnight, largely on the strength of Turner's small landscape vignettes; Turner, it was said, "supplied the poetry, and Rogers the prose."[5] A copy of *Italy* given him by his father's partner in the wine-importing business opened the thirteen-year-old John Ruskin's eyes to the power of the artist of whom he was soon to be the eloquent champion. "This book," he wrote toward the end of his life, "was the first means I had of looking carefully at Turner's work: and I might, not without some appearance of reason, attribute to this gift the entire direction of my life energies."[6]

In 1834, Rogers republished his 1812 volume of *Poems* in an edition embellished with thirty-three designs by Turner. *Italy* and the *Poems* together cost him £10,000, and they made their way into upper-class homes in a variety of forms, all sumptuous: octavo, quarto, or duodecimo, bound in morocco with gilt fore-edges. None of his contemporaries, says a modern student, "had a reputation so spectacularly restored to life."[7] But it was on the strength of the illustrations, not the text. When Scott praised *Italy* as "a rare specimen of the manner in which the art of Poetry can awaken the Muse of painting" and Macaulay told the aged poet that "if your 'Italy' were dug up in some Pompeii or Herculaneum two thousand years hence, it would give to posterity a higher idea of the state of the arts amongst us than anything else which lay in an equally small compass," both men evaded committing themselves on the merits of the poems.[8] As the free-spoken Lady Blessington is said to have remarked, both volumes "would have been dished if it had not been for the plates."[9]

It was the snob appeal of Rogers's poems in their luxurious packaging that was at least partially responsible for their popularity among artists. In addition to the many Italian scenes embellished with quotations from the poem, *Italy* inspired in the next two decades some dozen paintings taken directly from the text. Most of these depicted Ginevra, the girl who hides in a chest during Christmas revels and suffocates—a story familiar from sources as diverse as Schiller, balladry, and, though few picture-collectors would have been found in such an audience, plays like *The Mistletoe Bough; or, The Fatal Chest,* performed at a Whitechapel theater in 1834. Two or three other paintings portrayed the story of Bianca Capello, another "oft-told tale" of elopement and assassination to which Rogers briefly referred.

BURNS

Robert Burns's association with literary pictures began with an incident in his own lifetime. Sir Walter Scott recalled meeting the peasant-poet in Edinburgh in 1786 or 1787, a symbolic event—the fleeting conjunction of Scotland's greatest poets—commemorated in more than one Victorian painting.

> The only thing I remember which was remarkable in Burns' manner [Scott told his biographer John Gibson Lockhart], was the effect produced upon him by a print of Bunbury's, representing a soldier lying dead on the snow, his dog sitting in misery on the one side, on the other his widow, with a child in her arms. These lines were written beneath,—
>
> Cold on Canadian hills, or Minden's plain,
> Perhaps that parent wept her soldier slain;
> Bent o'er her babe, her eye dissolved in dew,
> The big drops, mingling with the milk he drew,
> Gave the sad presage of his future years,
> The child of misery baptized in tears.
>
> Burns seemed much affected by the print, or rather the ideas which it suggested to his mind. He actually shed tears. He asked whose the lines were, and it chanced that nobody but myself remembered that they occur in a half-forgotten poem of Langhorne's, called by the unpromising title of "The Justice of the Peace."* I whispered my information to a friend present, who mentioned it to Burns, who rewarded me with a look and a word, which, though of mere civility, I then received, and still recollect, with very great pleasure.[1]

"A dead soldier, his wife and child" was shortly to become the subject of a better known picture by Joseph Wright of Derby, exhibited at the Royal Academy in 1789 (pl. 9).[2]

Burns's first illustrator was the leading Scottish artist of the day, David Allan, whose designs for Ramsay's *The Gentle Shepherd* he admired. Allan

*Properly, *The Country Justice* (1774–77).

made twenty etchings for George Thomson's *Select Collection of Original Scottish Airs* (1793), which included 114 of Burns's poems, and pleased the poet by sending him the original oil sketch of one of them, the illustration to "The Cotter's Saturday Night."[3]

During Burns's lifetime, his fame was largely confined to Scotland.[4] His use of the Lowland Scots dialect, to say nothing of his irreverent spirit and populist themes, did not commend his poems to most English readers, and such notices as they received in England were only mildly appreciative. In addition, the poems had been published in chapbooks, broadsides, and scattered and obscure song collections such as Thomson's; and it was not until 1800, with the appearance of Currie's collected (but incomplete) edition, that they became conveniently available. At that point, English interest in Burns quickened; and within a year, Julius Caesar Ibbetson painted two pictures, now lost, from "Duncan Gray cam' here to woo" and "The Cotter's Saturday Night"—the latter immediately establishing itself as the most popular Burns subject in art, as it was the most popular poem among English readers. "Tam o' Shanter" and "Hallow E'en" were first drawn upon in 1805, again by Ibbetson, who exhibited paintings from them in that year's Royal Academy. Soon thereafter, the Burns cult began to develop, primarily to feast on haggis and drink his health each year on the anniversary of his birth (25 January) and eventually to spread his fame throughout the English-speaking world. "Search Scotland over, from the Pentland to the Solway," wrote Lockhart in his life of Burns (1828), "and there is not a cottage-hut so poor and wretched as to be without its Bible; and hardly one that, on the same shelf, and next to it, does not treasure a Burns."[5]

From the very beginning, Burns's poems were likened to paintings. The first influential critical notice they received, by Henry Mackenzie in *The Lounger* (1786), remarked of "To a Mountain Daisy," "Such strokes as these mark the pencil of the poet, which delineates Nature with the precision of intimacy, yet with the delicate colouring of beauty and of taste. The power of genius is not less admirable in tracing the manners, than in painting the passions, or in drawing the scenery of Nature."[6] Echoed Carlyle four decades later: "No poet of any age or nation is more graphic than Burns: the characteristic features disclose themselves to him at a glance; three lines from his hand, and we have a likeness. And, in that rough dialect, in that rude, often awkward metre, so clear and definite a likeness! It seems a draughtsman working with a burnt stick; and yet the burin of a Retzsch* is not more expressive or exact."[7]

To some critics, Burns's genius for making word pictures, like that of Shakespeare and Milton, left no room for illustration. "Let no man paint after Burns," said Hazlitt. "He held the pencil in his own hands."[8] But the admonition came too late. Alexander Carse's picture *The Borough—Market Day,* from "Tam o' Shanter" (RA 1815), which prompted Hazlitt's remark, belonged to a tide that had begun with Ibbetson's pictures a decade earlier and was destined to swell inexorably for many more. Making pictures from Burns became a prosperous cottage industry—in view of their genre subjects, the term is especially fitting—both north and south of the Tweed. In addition to easel paintings, leading artists were commissioned to illustrate edition after edition of Burns's poems, among them the ever-adaptable Thomas Stothard and, in later generations, John Faed and Sam Bough. Many of the paintings and drawings that served as

*Moritz Retzsch's Flaxman-like outline drawings, especially of Shakespearean subjects, were then popular.

originals of the printed illustrations were exhibited in the customary places. Although pictures from Burns were seen there less often in the last third of the century, a number of competent artists, notably James Elder Christie, supplied the continuing demand.

Hundreds of pictures were equipped with quotations from Burns; in fact, only Shakespeare, Tennyson, Thomson, and Byron exceeded him in the frequency of mottoes. In the course of a parody review of the 1844 Royal Academy show, Thackeray mentioned a fictitious painting entitled *The Highland Luncheon,* which he said came equipped with the epigraph,

> 'Gin a' the binks that fa' your body,
> Your bubbly Jock and winsome poddie,
> Your lilting, filting, linkum doddie,
> Should gar your ee.

"The words of the Ayrshire bard," remarked the grave critic, "were never more admirably illustrated."[9]

The two poems most discussed in the early criticism of Burns were the two that were most often painted: "The Cotter's Saturday Night" and "Tam o' Shanter." It was probably no accident that these were also the subjects of Allan's best-known illustrations. "There is in that immortal poem," wrote John Wilson of "The Cotter's Saturday Night," "a depth of domestic joy—an intensity of the feeling of home—a presiding spirit of love—and a lofty enthusiasm of religion, which are all peculiarly Scottish, and beyond the pitch of mind of any other people."[10] "Tam o' Shanter" was popular for diametrically opposed reasons. It offered opportunities to paint horses, Dutch burgher-like inebriety (pl. 65), and diablerie. "The gothic architecture of the old Kirk at Alloway," wrote someone who had seen Ibbetson's version of the subject before it disappeared into the collection of an American naval officer, "gives a sacred setting which by contrast heightens the effect of the monstrous orgies. A blaze of unearthly,

308. Sir David Wilkie, *The Cotter's Saturday Night* (RA 1837) (Glasgow Art Gallery and Museum). With this painting Wilkie returned to the Scottish genre vein that had made his reputation twenty years earlier (he was knighted in 1836). In the interim, he had drifted away from such subjects and turned to others—Spanish scenes, historical episodes—for which his special genius was less fitted.

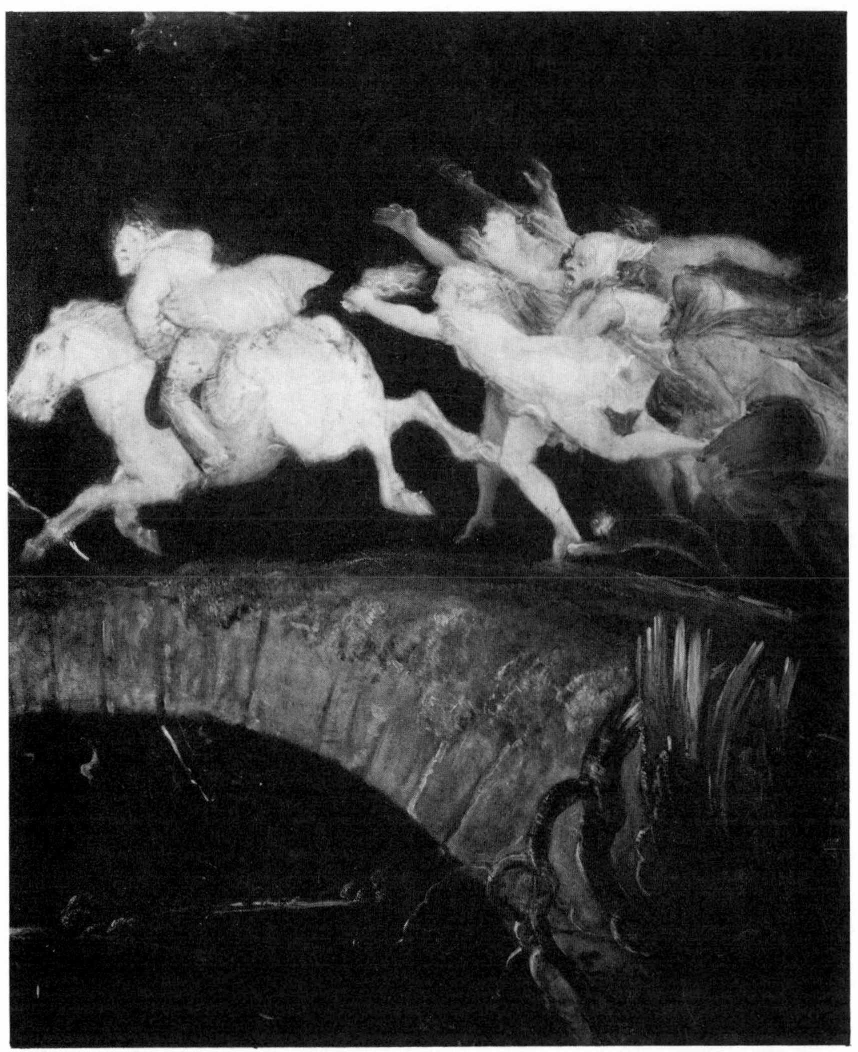

309. Thomas Stothard, *Tam o' Shanter* (RA 1816) (Victoria & Albert Museum, Crown Copyright).

For Nannie, far before the eest,
Hard upon noble Maggie prest,
And flew at Tam wi' furious ettle;
But little wist she Maggie's mettle—
Ae spring brought aff her master hale,
But left behind her ain grey tail.

ruddy light streams from the murky gloom and tinges the characters on the stage. The spectator and his steed alone are of this world. . . ."[11]

Half a century later, George Cruikshank exhibited (RA 1852) a version of "Tam o' Shanter" that must have absolutely out-Fuselied Fuseli.

> . . . The warlocks and witches, the coffins and candles, the tomahawks and scimitars, the music maker himself, "black, grim, and large" [said a reviewer], are all there; with legions of lesser imps, who stream up in the flames, swarm in the rafters, and wing the murky air, according to the well known habits of those fragmentary impersonations of evil. Conjure up what visions he will the reader's fancy . . . will be outdone by the rush and hurry, the tumult and storm, the madness and mirth of this infernal scene.[12]

In third place among the Burns subjects most favored by artists was "John Anderson, My Jo," of which a dozen or more paintings were exhibited between 1832 and 1870. Like "The Cotter's Saturday Night," it was beloved for domestic sentiment, in this case the portrayal of placid old age, marital affection preserved to the end. The appeal of such heartwarming domestic tableaux knew no boundaries; it was as compelling in London as in Edinburgh.

The most celebrated Burns painting was Wilkie's *The Refusal* (pl. 44) from "Duncan Gray." The *Literary Gazette*'s welcome was typical:

> The principal persons in this little drama of art [the 1818 version] are perfect; so much so as to produce a desire in the mind of the beholder to follow them into after-life, and to anticipate, from the disdain and coquetry so exquisitely depicted in the countenance of Maggie, and the disappointment swelling into anger in that of her lover, that their marriage state will be chequered by a few storms, at least (for we are amiable critics) will not be allowed to stagnate. . . . The story is pointed and sarcastic, with sufficient of humorous incident to correct the spirit of satire upon so *serious* a subject as *lovemaking*.[13]

Like Scott, Burns was a constant source of subjects, or at least faint tie-ins, for landscape painters. Contemporary criticism often alluded to the poetic truth of his Scottish settings, and artists like David Octavius Hill, who supplied a series of illustrations for "Christopher North's" *Land of Burns*, took advantage of the praise to offer topographical canvases with no attempt to reproduce the scenes as they were in Burns's day. Even the most tenuous association with the poet was invoked in albums and separate paintings depicting the Scottish scene. In 1838, for example, what must have been a perfectly routine landscape-cum-genre subject was described in the Royal Academy catalogue as "a scene in Glen Esk, Forfarshire, after a good day's sport. . . . On the table is the celebrated bowl, once the property of Robert Burns." (This was one of the innumerable drinking utensils, attributed on dubious authority to the poet, which were prized as hallowed relics during the nineteenth century).

Pictures from Burns were more numerous than those taken from any other poet's oeuvre of a similar size. But in proportion to their number, they probably included fewer memorable or otherwise significant paintings than did any comparable group. The Burns cult was a popular but parochial phenomenon, reflecting a grass-roots literary taste that was not much shared by the more cultivated part of the reading public. Consequently, paintings of Burns themes were not likely to be bought by the major collectors of contemporary art, whose tastes ran instead to Shakespeare, Goldsmith, and Sterne. Apart from the countless engravings, not many illustrations of Burns survive; Wilkie's *The Refusal* is one of the few Burns oils to be found on gallery walls today, however thickly they populated the exhibitions in their time.

THE ROMANTIC ERA

WORDSWORTH

Despite his central role in awakening his countrymen to the spiritual significance of nature, and therefore as a kind of patron saint to landscape painters, Wordsworth did not figure prominently in nineteenth-century art.[1] His name occurred more often as the author of the mottoes affixed to paintings than as the source of the subjects themselves. Of the approximately sixty quotations from Wordsworth in the exhibition catalogues, only a dozen appeared before 1850, the year of his death. The first appeared in the 1824 catalogue of the Society of British Artists, in connection with an Ullswater landscape by T. J. Hofland.

No more than a dozen Wordsworth poems were illustrated in the twenty or so gallery paintings recorded, and half of these came from the two editions (1798, 1800) of *Lyrical Ballads.* The poet's patron, Sir George Beaumont, illustrated five poems in landscapes: "The Thorn," exhibited at the Royal Academy in 1806; "Lucy Gray" and "Peele Castle," engraved for the 1815 collected edition of Wordsworth's poems; "The White Doe of Rylstone," engraved as the frontispiece to the volume of that name, published in the same year; and "Peter Bell," reproduced as the frontispiece to Wordsworth's 1819 volume. There were at least four later pictures from "The White Doe," which gave artists an opportunity to attach a literary reference to pictures of Bolton Abbey, the poem's setting and, as it happened, a favorite subject of painting. The most notable of these, indeed one of the very few pictures of Wordsworthian themes to survive, was John William Inchbold's (pl. 310).[2] In 1851, the year after the poet's death, Richard Redgrave added a far-fetched touch of timely literary association to a painting of a verdant copse by captioning it: *A Poet's Study. Wordsworth is Said to Have Sat for Hours in This Glen with Coleridge and Southey.*

COLERIDGE

Except for Wordsworth, whose poem "The Thorn" was illustrated by Beaumont's painting in 1806, Coleridge was the first English Romantic poet to supply a subject for art.[1] His friend George Dawe showed at the Academy in 1812, along with a portrait of Coleridge, a painting listed as *Genevieve: From a Poem by T. [sic] Coleridge,* a portrayal, said a reviewer, of a "young man on his knee singing to a Lady who is pensively and elegantly leaning on a pedestal, . . . an impassioned exemplification of . . . pleasing lines" from the poem "Love."[2] (Three other pictures from the same poem would be painted in the course of the years, one of them, in 1838, being a view of the Rhine, with a group in the foreground suggested by Coleridge's lines.) In 1817, Coleridge's "Ode to Georgiana, Duchess of Devonshire, on the Twenty-Fourth Stanza in her 'Passage over Mount Gothard'," first published in 1799, was the inspiration for Arthur Perigal's painting *Maternal Delight.*

All told, there were about thirty-five paintings from Coleridge. Surprisingly, in the light of the poem's gorgeous exotic imagery, only one from "Kubla Khan" is recorded, and that as late as 1890. It was by two other poems that Coleridge was mainly represented in the art of the century.

The title "The Ancient Mariner" was used for about a dozen recorded pictures, but some of these undoubtedly were merely genre studies of weather-beaten old salts. We do not know which scenes from the poem—the specter ship, the killing of the albatross, the encounter with the wedding guest—were depicted in the remaining paintings. Of those explicitly associated with Coleridge in the catalogues, perhaps the most noteworthy were the ones Joseph Severn painted in Rome in 1833, *Life in Death* and *Death.* It may have been one of these that Severn exhibited at the Royal Academy six years later under the title *Rhyme of the Ancient Mariner.* When David Scott saw the pictures in Rome, he recorded in his journal that *Life in Death* was "a failure in my view of the poem—he having made her beautiful; the old mariner and the ship very good."[3] Scott's eye, however, was scarcely unbiased at the time, for he was already at work on a series of illustrations of the poem, about which he had corresponded briefly with Coleridge himself. In a letter mostly taken up with complaints about his ill health and lack of friends, the poet said, "I acknowledge and duly appreciate the compliment, payed to me, in having selected a poem of mine for ornamental illustration and an alliance of the Sister Arts, Metrical and Graphic Poesy."[4] Of the twenty-five designs Scott completed and published in 1839, a recent historian of Scottish art has commented, "These interwoven elements of the descriptive and imaginative in the *Ancient Mariner* were so sympathetic to David Scott's way of thinking, that the resulting illustrations are close visual parallels to the poem. They are, as Dante Gabriel Rossetti remarked, 'in the truest Coleridgean vein.' "[5] Subsequently (1863), Joseph Noel Paton exhibited at the Royal Academy two of the twenty illustrations to the poem he produced to be engraved for the Art Union of London's subscribers.

None of the *Ancient Mariner* oil paintings seem to survive, and only one of the dozen pictures entitled *Christabel,* most of which seem actually to have had some connection with Coleridge's poem although a few may well have been routine female figure studies with a poetic label stuck on. With one exception, all of the scenes of the spell cast by the enchantress Lady Geraldine upon Sir Leoline's pious daughter were painted in the second half of the century; it was in them that the old Romantic vein of sorcery was sustained at a time when it had otherwise gone out of fashion in art. The one extant picture that represents the theme is William Dyce's *Christabel* (RA 1855), an example, Ruskin said, of "one of the false branches of PreRaphaelitism, consisting in the imitation of the old religious masters."[6]

310. John W. Inchbold, *At Bolton* (RA 1855) (Leeds Art Gallery). An illustration of Wordsworth's "The White Doe of Rylstone," canto 1. It has been pointed out that the passage actually describes the people crowding in the ruins of the old priory and their reaction to the doe; the artist dispenses with all human presence.

SOUTHEY

In his time, Robert Southey was regarded as the equal of Wordsworth and Coleridge; the three *were* the "Lake School" of English poets, though Southey eventually dropped from the trinity. The number of paintings derived from Southey in the course of the century (some twenty) was roughly the same as those from Wordsworth; from Coleridge came somewhat more. While Coleridge was represented by a number of pictures from "The Rime of the Ancient Mariner" and "Christabel" in the period 1848–1900, and post-1840 paintings from Wordsworth were spaced fairly evenly across the same years, those from Southey were concentrated in the decades 1845–65, when his reputation was drifting away from the company it had kept.

311. Franz Xavier Winterhalter, *Florinda* (RA 1852) (Royal Collection, Copyright Reserved). This picture by a court painter with an international clientele owed its existence less to the episode in Southey's poem it supposedly illustrated—the moment when Roderick, last of the Goths, loses his heart to Florinda as he meets her alone "at eve" in "bowers which overhang / The glen where Tagus rolls between his rocks"—than to the enthusiasm Queen Victoria and her husband had at the moment for luscious groups of semi-nude figures.

Half a dozen paintings came from his *Roderick the Last of the Goths* (1814), a romantic narrative poem. One of them, F. X. Winterhalter's *Florinda* (pl. 311), was bought by the Queen as a present for her husband. The *Times* counted eleven "female nymphs" in the large canvas (any other species is exceedingly rare), and hastened to add that "though warm in tone"—a characteristically cautious Victorian euphemism—it was "quite devoid of coarseness."[1]

Another of Southey's exotic poems, *Thalaba the Destroyer* (1801), figured in three paintings, each by a different artist, shown at the Royal Academy in 1845–46. His early ballad "Mary, the Maid of the Inn" was the subject of a painting by Samuel DeWilde, one of that artist's few nontheatrical pictures, in 1800. Mary, one more figure, though a minor one, in the poetic and artistic gallery of mad heroines, returned to the walls of the Royal Academy eighty years later, in a painting by J. R. Reid. Not that there was any revival of interest in Southey generally; as the *Times* pointed out, the ballad had been "of late resuscitated for penny readings,"[2] a familiar and innocuous kind of public entertainment that was responsible for keeping many favorite poems and "dramatic passages" in the popular repertory. The repeated portrayal, in 1807 (Mulready), 1853, 1858, and twice in 1865, of Old Kaspar and the inquisitive boy in Southey's "The Battle of Blenheim" ("'But what good came of it at last?' / Quoth little Peterkin. / 'Why, that I cannot tell,' said he; / 'But 'twas a famous victory.'") doubtless owed something to the poem's popularity as a recital piece as well as its presence in anthologies.

SCOTT

In 1828, when Sir Walter Scott attended the annual dinner of the Royal Academy for the first time after being elected Honorary Antiquary, Sir Thomas Lawrence, the president, toasted him in these words: "If *he* had been forgotten it had been as a gap in our great feast and all things unbecoming."[1] Lawrence might have chosen a more felicitous quotation from Shakespeare—the one he used had the inadvertent but sinister effect of casting him as Lady Macbeth and Scott as the doomed Banquo—but the Shakespearean gesture, like the occasion itself, was wholly appropriate, for Scott was at the time seriously thought to be Shakespeare's equal.[2] Besides, some formal recognition of Scott's service to the nation's artistic establishment was long overdue, for his poetry and novels had already given profitable employment to many painters. "How many pencils have already been employed," exclaimed the *Literary Gazette* three years later, "and how many will in future times be employed, in embodying the conceptions of that great writer!"[3] The retrospect and the prophecy were both true, especially the latter. In the ensuing two decades, pictures inspired by Scott would dominate the galleries; and their popularity, swelling the income of hundreds of artists, would continue to the very end of the century.[4] In 1881, Edwin Abbey reported that Sir James Dromgole Linton, who received 1,000 guineas apiece for his pictures, had "an order from a Manchester gentleman to paint two subjects and six single figures from each of Walter Scott's novels. These chaps," Abbey added, "are all aggravatingly prosperous"[5]—as they would continue to be so long as Manchester millionaires (to say nothing of prosperous and patriotic Scotsmen) wanted to be surrounded by pictures from Scott.

One of the earliest Scott paintings (pl. 312) was derived from almost the first work the Edinburgh advocate-antiquarian published, "The Fire-King," a melodramatic-supernatural ballad that he contributed to Matthew Gregory ("Monk") Lewis's "hobgoblin repast," a collection called *Tales of Wonder* (1801). It was a Gothick subject peculiarly adapted to the talents of Henry Fuseli, who was in fact the artist. In 1807, the first paintings from Scott appeared at the Royal Academy, two scenes from *The Lay of the Last Minstrel,* published two years earlier; one was by an artist

312. Henry Fuseli, *The Fire King Appears to Count Albert* (1801–10) (Victoria & Albert Museum, Crown Copyright). The first illustration of a published work by Sir Walter Scott, a ballad titled "The Fire King," in which a lapsed Christian crusader, Count Albert, descends into a demonic cave to obtain a magic sword.

313. Richard Bonington, *Amy Robsart and the Earl of Leicester* (ca. 1827) (Ashmolean Museum, Oxford). One of the few literary subjects undertaken by the artist, who died in 1828 at the age of twenty-seven. The earnestness, indeed the quiet amicability, of the two figures scarcely does justice to the tense and eventually tragic relationship that actually existed between Amy Robsart and her secret husband, the Earl of Leicester, in Scott's *Kenilworth.* For her fate, see pl. 41.

on the threshold of a prosperous career, Francis Philip Stephanoff. The next year, an equally promising Scots painter, John Watson (later Sir John Gordon-Watson), exhibited in Edinburgh a painting from the same poem, and another artist showed yet another scene, *The Minstrel on His Journey to the Mansion of the Duchess of Buccleuch and Monmouth,* at the Royal Academy. At the newly founded British Institution the following year (1809), there were no fewer than six paintings from *The Lay of the Last Minstrel.* Of the twenty paintings of literary subjects at the two London exhibitions in 1811, two were from *Marmion* (1808) and five from *The Lady of the Lake* (1810).

The Scott vogue was well under way, but it would not begin to approach its full magnitude until after the first Waverley novel appeared in 1814. It was in his fiction that Scott's descriptive powers became most amply apparent. His verbal pictures sometimes seemed actually to forestall graphic illustration; in 1819, Charles Leslie wrote to his fellow American, Washington Allston, "I have heard that you are making some designs from Sir Walter Scott's novels. They afford excellent material, though the picturesque scenes with which they abound are almost too highly finished by the author to leave anything for the painter to do but merely follow him, which is some disadvantage."[6] (Leslie soon came to terms with the disadvantage: two years later, he made designs for an edition of *Kenilworth.*)

As a pictorialist, with the minor exception of Ann Radcliffe, Scott had no illustrious predecessors among novelists, nor was he to have any peers in his time. He offered his readers, many painters among them, detailed portraits and figure studies, with antiquarianly accurate costume and accoutrement; meticulous interiors, ranging from cottages to castles, which constantly reminded critics of Dutch realistic paintings; a profusion of dramatic and pathetic scenes such as might be painted by history or narrative artists. Reviewers found it scarcely possible to discuss his romances without invoking painterly analogies. And when, in 1820, J. L. Adolphus argued at length that the Waverley novels, anonymously published, were from the same pen that had written and signed Scott's poems, among the evidence he offered was their common characteristic of strong pictorialism: "they seem to view Nature as through a Painter's eyes, selecting and combining features as a painter would."[7] In France, where Scott was almost as popular as he was in Britain, the perception of his pictorial gift was especially acute. Decades later, when Sainte-Beuve called him "an immortal painter," he was merely repeating what had long since become a platitude.[8] Contemporary French artists, most notably Delacroix, repeatedly took subjects from the Waverley romances.* At the Salon of 1830 alone, no fewer than thirty paintings from Scott were hung.

As we saw in chapter 3, from his first poetic romances onward, Scott gave a powerful impetus to landscape painting at large. In *Modern Painters,* Ruskin declared that "Scott's enjoyment of Nature is incomparably greater than that of any other poet I know," including Tennyson and Keats, and that "to give a complete analysis of all the feelings which appear to be traceable in Scott's allusions to landscape scenery . . . would require a volume." Scott, Ruskin said—his highest form of praise in such a context—was the Turner of verbal scenic artists.[9]

Scott had a gentleman's interest in painting.[10] He learned "the pleasure of looking at fine pictures," he said, when he visited Penicuik House in the company of a fellow law student, a scion of the Clerk family who owned

*What Delacroix called his "spiritual relation" with Scott began in the late 1820s, when he shared with his friend, the equally youthful English artist Richard P. Bonington, a strong enthusiasm for the novels, particularly *Quentin Durward.* (Bonington painted several subjects from Scott, including *Quentin Durward at Liège* and *Amy Robsart and the Earl of Leicester* [pl. 313]). Delacroix's *Guillaume de la Marck, surnommé le Sanglier des Ardennes,* was shown at the Royal Academy in 1830, under the title of *The Boar of Ardennes,* and at the Salon the following year, along with a small oil of Cromwell from *Woodstock.* After this burst of interest, which also resulted in a number of watercolors and lithographs, Delacroix did not draw further from Scott until 1846–50, when he did four *Ivanhoe* pictures, including two versions of *The Abduction of Rebecca,* one of which is now in the Louvre and the other at the Metropolitan Museum of Art. A list he made as late as 1860 of suitable literary subjects includes twenty-four from the same novel. (Douglas Cooper, "Bonington and *Quentin Durward,*" *Burlington Magazine* 88 [1946]: 112–17; Kemp, "Scott and Delacroix.")

the estate. Conspicuous among the paintings he would have seen there were Alexander Runciman's dozen scenes from Ossian. In his fiction, Scott constantly refers to painters, some three dozen in all, including Raphael, Rubens, Teniers, Salvator Rosa, Claude, Snyders, Wouvermans, Van Dyck; and he alludes to his fellow Scotsman David Wilkie in at least half a dozen of his novels. In his literary criticism as well as, inferentially, in his imaginative writing, he endorsed the concept of *ut pictura poesis.* Scott, however, was in no way a connoisseur. Visitors to Abbotsford, expecting to find him surrounded by art of a quality commensurate with his talent for painting word pictures, were disillusioned when they saw what he actually possessed. "He talked of scenery as he wrote of it—like a painter," recalled Leslie; "and yet for pictures, as works of art, he had little or no taste, nor did he pretend to any. . . . There were things hanging on the walls of his dining-room, which no eye possessing sensibility to what is excellent in art could have endured."[11]

314. Edwin Landseer, *Edie Ochiltree* (1829) (Private Collection). The blue gown beggar: "A slouched hat of huge dimensions; a long white beard which mingled with his grizzled hair; an aged but strongly marked and expressive countenance, hardened, by climate and exposure, to a right brickdust complexion; a long blue gown, with a pewter badge on the right arm; two or three wallets, or bags, slung across his shoulder, for holding the different kinds of meal, when he received his charity in kind from those who were but a degree richer than himself" (*The Antiquary,* chap. 4). This is one of the nine paintings Landseer made to be engraved for an edition of the Waverley novels.

By the time of Scott's death in 1832, the book illustration of his works had become a sizable industry.[12] The best-selling poems had been graced by engravings by Richard Westall, who also illustrated several of the early novels beginning with *Guy Mannering* and *The Monastery* in 1821. More than thirty artists, including Wilkie, Landseer, Leslie, Martin, Bonington, Mulready, and Stanfield, contributed to the so-called Magnum Opus edition of 1829–33. Each engraving was made from a small oil painting, some of which, Landseer's (pl. 314) and Wilkie's among them, were hung at the annual exhibitions. Turner prepared twenty-four designs for Robert Cadell's edition of Scott's poetry (1834) and forty for the companion edition of his nonfictional works in prose (1834–36); these were all pictures of localities associated with Scott's subjects or with Scott biography.[13] Cadell wanted Turner also to illustrate his edition of the novels, but various circumstances stood in the way.*

Collected editions of the novels appeared at the incredible average rate of one every two years, some with sets of freshly drawn illustrations, others with reused ones. These joined the portfolios of separate engravings that had begun to appear in the 1820s. A typical example was a portfolio of *Illustrations to Scott's Poetical Works* (1834) that contained forty plates, including three by Turner which were replicas of designs already found in his *Provincial Antiquities.* The taste of the time, which demanded galleries of Byron's and Shakespeare's "beauties" (in this case corporeal, not textual), encouraged the production of an album of *Portraits of the Principal Female Characters in the Waverley Novels* (1832–33) and the *Waverley Gallery* of the same (1840–42), not all of whose women—such was the variety of Scott's casts—were beauties by any definition. Beginning in 1865, the Scottish equivalent of the London Art Union, the Royal Association for the Promotion of the Fine Arts in Scotland, issued annual volumes of engravings, each devoted to scenes and characters from a single Scott novel (or sometimes, a Burns poem). In general magazines and the art press, meanwhile, appeared illustrated essays on the topography of the individual poems and novels. As late as 1887, the *Art Journal* ran a series of articles on "Sir Walter Scott's Country" with illustrations by John McWhirter.

Writing to her friend Sir William Elford, Mary Russell Mitford, the author best remembered for her sketches of country life, *Our Village,* praised the newly published *Ivanhoe* (1819): "I know nothing so rich, so

*Turner's *Fingal's Cave* (RA 1832) was exhibited with a quotation from Scott's verse romance *The Lord of the Isles.* Although that spectacular outcropping of basalt columns on the Isle of Staffa had long been known to artists, it was only after the poem was published in 1815 that it became a recurrent subject of "sublime" landscape painting.

splendid, so profuse, so like old painted glass or a Gothic chapel full of shrines, and banners, and knightly monuments." She went on to speak of "the melodramatic air, by which one feels almost as if the book were written for the accommodation of the artists of the Coburg and Surrey Theatres, with a tournament in act the first, a burning castle in act the second, a trial by combat in act the third—nothing for a dramatist to do but to cut out the speeches, and there is a grand spectacle ready made."[14]

In the course of the nineteenth century, Scott's poems and novels were adapted hundreds of times, as dramas, operas, burlesques, pantomimes, and ballets.[15]* Of the poems, *The Lady of the Lake* and *Marmion* were the most often dramatized, with eleven and four versions respectively; among the novels, *Kenilworth* held pride of place with thirty-eight adaptations recorded from 1821 to 1899, three of which were performed simultaneously in 1830. Runners-up were *Ivanhoe* with thirty-five adaptations, *The Heart of Mid-Lothian* with twenty-three, *The Bride of Lammermoor* with fifteen, and *Guy Mannering* with thirteen. The same qualities that recommended Scott's works to readers and picture-buyers appealed to theatrical managers and their clientele, as Miss Mitford intimated: the romantic settings, the exciting plots (reflected in the episodes chosen for painting), the uncomplicated, strongly portrayed characters. In addition, Scott's descriptions of exterior and interior settings were so detailed that they could be easily and faithfully realized in the scenery workshop. A few paintings were explicitly derived from these dramatizations in 1819–20: John Boaden's portrait of Thomas P. Cooke as Roderick Dhu in Dibdin's adaptation of *The Lady of the Lake,* G. H. Harlow's of Catherine Stephens as Diana Vernon in Pocock's opera *Rob Roy MacGregor,* and E. D. Leahy's of Mrs. Yates as Meg Merrilies in a staging of *Guy Mannering.* At mid-century, the American actress Charlotte Cushman also was painted as Meg Merrilies, her favorite role.

The influence these acting versions had on paintings was sometimes deplored. In 1832, for example, the *Athenaeum* said of a picture from *Rob Roy* that it was "a scene from the *Rob Roy* of the stage, but not from the living page of the great novelist. Has the painter ever read the romance?"[16] In this staging, Jarvie fought Allan Iverach not with the heroic "red-hot coulter of a plough" that Scott specified—a rather difficult property to supply from stock—but with a prosaic, easily portable poker. Possibly the most extensive protest against the theatrical treatment of a Scott novel in a painting was that lodged by Thackeray in 1844 against Robert Scott Lauder's *Claverhouse Ordering Merton to be Shot,* from *Old Mortality:*

> There sits Claverhouse in the centre in a Kean wig and ringlets, such as was never worn in any age of this world, except at the theatre in 1816, and he scowls with a true melo-dramatic ferocity; and he lifts a sign-post of a finger towards Morton, who forthwith begins to writhe and struggle into an attitude in the midst of a group of subordinate, cuirassed, buff-coated gentry. Morton is represented in tights, slippers, and a tunic . . . and he, too, must proceed to scowl and frown "with a flashing eye and a distended nostril," as they say in the novels,—as Gomersal scowls at Widdicumb before the combat between those two chiefs begins; and while they are measuring each other according to the stage wont from the toe of the yellow boot up to the tip of the stage-wig. There is a tragedy heroine in Mr. Lauder's picture, striking her attitude too, to complete the scene. It is entirely unnatural, theatrical. . . .[17]

*Isaac Pocock alone was responsible for at least nine such dramatizations. He was, in addition, an early minor link between painting and literature. He was the son of a marine artist, a pupil of Romney and, later, Sir William Beechey, and between 1803 and 1818 he exhibited many pictures at the Royal Academy and the British Institution. Among them were a number of familiar literary subjects, Sterne's Maria, Musidora, the Lady in *Comus,* and Prospero and Miranda. He was one of the very first illustrators of Scott: at the British Institution, he showed four designs from *The Lay of the Last Minstrel* (1809) and *The Death of Marmion* (1810). After inheriting some property from an uncle in 1818, he devoted most of his energies to writing for the stage, though none of his subsequent pieces matched the long-lasting popularity of his melodrama *The Miller and His Men* (1813).

In another connection, Thackeray later answered in effect the *Athenaeum*'s irritable question "Has the painter ever read the romance?". Whether or not he meant J. J. Ridley (in *The Newcomes*) to represent a large class of Victorian painters, in one respect Ridley was demonstrably typical, and the answer was "Yes." When Mr. Honeyman comes to live in the lodgings kept by Ridley's father, he "brings a set of Scott's novels, for which he subscribed when at Oxford; and young John James [who had already been illustrating Gothic novels which had fallen into his hands] . . . lights upon the volumes, and reads them with such a delight and passion of pleasure as all the delights of future days will scarce equal" (chapter 11). Thackeray implies that a young man of J. J.'s indifferently educated class ("his parents thought of apprenticing him to a tailor") would at least have read Scott. Even the Prince Consort painted scenes from the great novelist in his well-appointed studio.[18] Most Victorian artists* who left any record of their reading attested to their devotion to Scott, even though some happened never to illustrate his works in the course of their careers: the self-taught animal painter James Ward, the specialist in religious and allegorical subjects Joseph Noel Paton, the minor Liverpool artist Henry Liverseege, Dante Gabriel Rossetti—a diversified company indeed.[19] Burne-Jones reread *The Antiquary* alone no fewer than twenty-seven times, and urged others to do the same.[20] William Quiller Orchardson read the Waverley novels straight through as a boy, and though he never returned to them, his daughter averred that "he knew all about them, and in many instances could repeat the very words."[21]

George Frederic Watts's earliest inspiration, said his wife, came from the "Greek heroes" and the "knights and cavaliers" of the Waverley novels.[22] Looking grumpily back in old age to the literary attachments of his youth, Frith could "recall the bright pictures with which the Wizard of the North filled my imagination." He continued, "Why I did not, as a boy, try to reproduce Rebecca and Ivanhoe, or Jeanie Deans, or Madge Wildfire (I had enough of them afterwards), however imperfectly, is now a wonder to me."[23] The grounds of his interest in Scott eventually shifted from early enthusiasm to adult commercialism, as the tone of his parenthesis suggests and as we shall see below. A similar though more precocious sense of the market, exercised when he was still a boy painting at his family's house in Holborn, determined Holman Hunt's choice of a subject from *Woodstock* for what he hoped would be a vendible canvas: "It belonged to the class of pictures most popular, and so offered a fair chance of sale, as well as due exercise in serious inventiveness." When the picture was finished, he sold it for twenty pounds to a winner of that amount in the Art Union's lottery.[24]†

The recorded Scott pictures total in the neighborhood of one thousand. Of these, some eighty were of subjects from the three major narrative poems, *The Lay of the Last Minstrel, Marmion,* and *The Lady of the Lake.* As already noted, their popularity with the reading public was reflected at once in the exhibitions. But as Scott's career as a novelist advanced, pictures from the romances soon outnumbered those from the poems. The vogue of paintings from *The Lady of the Lake* ended as abruptly as it had begun, about 1819; and notwithstanding its initial popularity between 1813 and 1839, few later pictures from *The Lay of the Last Minstrel* are

*They were preceded by Sir Thomas Lawrence, who read Scott's books hot from the press. "Most of Walter Scott's works," wrote a longtime friend, "we had the delight of hearing from his lips, and I can never forget the charm of his reading 'Marmion' to us. They were all sent to him and a few other chosen friends by the author before they were published" ("Recollections of Sir Thomas Lawrence" by Elizabeth Croft, in *Sir Thomas Lawrence's Letter-Bag,* ed. George Somes Layard [New York, 1906], p. 245).

†The Scott experience of Philip Hamerton, etcher and prolific writer on art, was in a class by itself. "It is very remarkable," he wrote, "that for a long time I knew Scott thoroughly as a poet without having read a single novel by him. Having been invited by one of my school fellows to a country house not very far from Doncaster, I was asked by the lady of the house what authors I had read, and on mentioning Scott's poems was told that he was greater as a novelist than as a poet, and that the Waverley novels were certainly his finest works" (*Philip Gilbert Hamerton: An Autobiography 1834–1858* [London, 1897], pp. 54–55). Few schoolboys in that day, one imagines, would have been unaware of them.

315. John Faed, *Catherine Seyton and Roland Graeme* (Royal Scottish Academy, 1865, a sketch for the picture exhibited RA 1864) (Wolverhampton Art Gallery). The first meeting of the lovers. "She bent her beautiful eyes upon the work with which she was busied, and with infinite gravity sate out the two first turns of the matrons upon the balcony; but then, glancing her deep blue eyes a little towards Roland, and observing the embarrassment under which he laboured, now shifting in his chair, and now dangling his cap, the whole man evincing that he was perfectly at a loss how to open the conversation, she could keep her composure no longer, but after a vain struggle broke out into a sincere, though a very involuntary fit of laughing, so richly accompanied by the laughter of her merry eyes, which actually glanced through the tears which the effort filled them with, and by the waving of her rich tresses, that the goddess of smiles herself never looked more lovely than Catherine at that moment" (*The Abbot,* chap. 11).

recorded. Subjects from the poems did not participate in the great surge of Scott pictures during the early Victorian years, and only a handful were produced after 1860.

Despite the reading public's immediate and warm reception of Scott's first novel, *Waverley* (1814) was not represented by an exhibited picture until fourteen years had passed, during which time scores of paintings from eighteen of the subsequent novels had been shown. *The Bride of Lammermoor,* too, was a latecomer to the galleries; the first painting from it was shown nine years after its publication in 1819. Two other novels, *The Antiquary* and *The Black Dwarf* (both 1816), were first painted only after a lapse of five and ten years respectively. Portraits of Meg Merrilies, from *Guy Mannering* (1815), the second of the series, were hung at the British Institution the year after the book appeared; and once the popularity of Scott pictures was established, there was usually an interval of no more than a year or two between the publication of each novel and its advent in the exhibitions. Only *The Abbot* and *Redgauntlet* were delayed for as long as four years (1820–24 and 1824–28 respectively).*

The great age of Scott painting was the period 1830–50. During those two decades, well over 400 examples were exhibited, an average of more than twenty a year. In a typically productive year (1843), eight were to be seen at the Royal Academy, ten at the British Institution, seven at the Society of British Artists, and five at the Royal Scottish Academy. At the same exhibitions that year, there were only twenty-five paintings from Shakespeare; and even such other rivals in the regard of early Victorian art lovers as Goldsmith, Burns, and Byron were outnumbered. One easily understands why, when the Prince Consort arranged at that moment for the garden pavilion at Buckingham Palace to be decorated with frescoes from *Comus,* he had the two side rooms embellished by lesser artists with eight lunettes from Scott, incongruous as the juxtaposition may have seemed.

Pictures from Scott were the bread and butter of a whole succession of artists founded in the first years of the century by William Allan and

*Such time lags seldom were matched in the theater, where dramatizations in one form or another of many of the novels were performed only a month or two after publication. The only exceptions were *Waverley* (1814), first staged in 1822, and *Old Mortality* (1816), first staged in 1820. The scene painters' brushes obviously were much faster than those of their colleagues at the easel.

David Wilkie. Scott was one of the patrons of Allan, who illustrated *Tales of My Landlord* and several other novels in 1819–20. He was among the subscribers to one of the large paintings Allan brought back from several years' wandering in Russia and Turkey (*The Circassian Captives*), and the Waverley novels inspired a number of Allan's later pictures from Scottish history. Although Wilkie, in the aftermath of his popular scenes from Scottish rural life, was acclaimed as doing for Scotland what Sir Walter Scott was meanwhile doing in fiction, his personal links with Scott were less strong, possibly because he spent most of his time in London and on the Continent rather than in Edinburgh. His *The Reading of a Will* (RA 1820) was related to the scene of Lady Singleside's funeral in *Guy Mannering*, and he provided four illustrations for the Magnum Opus edition.*

The painters who were particularly associated with Scott themes included William Kidd, Robert Scott Lauder and his younger brother James Eckford Lauder, Thomas Duncan, Gourlay Steele, John Faed and his younger brother Thomas, Sam Bough, William Fettes Douglas, Robert Herdman, John Pettie, and Charles Martin Hardie, all born between 1790 and 1858. Several of the other popular Victorian subject painters repeatedly found ideas in Scott. Landseer painted scenes involving his dogs (in fiction and fact), among them a portrait (RA 1833) of the novelist himself seated at the bottom of the Rhymer's Glen (from *Minstrelsy of the Scottish Border*). Landseer's *Attachment* (RA 1830), derived from Scott's early poem "Helvellyn," on the loyalty of a terrier that guarded the body of its master for three months after he had fallen from the mountain, foreshadowed his more famous treatments of the same theme. At the same time, Landseer painted *A Visit to the Falconer's Nest*, in which a modern authority has found an amalgam of references to *The Abbot* and *The Betrothed*.[25] Two of Leslie's earliest commissions were his illustrations to *Kenilworth* (1821) and other Waverley novels (1823). For one patron,

316. William Allan, *The Black Dwarf* (ca. 1827) (National Gallery of Scotland). In addition to painting a number of illustrations from his friend Sir Walter Scott's novels, Sir William (as he later became) was the teacher of several younger Scottish artists who helped meet the demand for such pictures. In this scene, the Reiver of Westburnflat pulls up before the Black Dwarf's cottage as a storm gathers (*The Black Dwarf*, chap. 6).

*Wilkie was commissioned by the Duke of Wellington to draw the sketches for the program of *tableaux vivants* from Scott novels that the Marchioness of Salisbury presented at Hatfield House in 1833.

317. Robert Scott Lauder, *Maître Pierre, Quentin Durward, and Jacqueline* (National Institution for the Exhibition of Modern Art 1850) (Forbes Magazine Collection). From *Quentin Durward,* chap. 4. Like the brothers Faed, the brothers Lauder (James Eckford and Robert Scott) were among the most prominent and prolific illustrators of Scott's fiction. Both were pupils of William Allan, as was Thomas Faed.

318. James Eckford Lauder, *Bailie Duncan MacWheeble at Breakfast* (British Institution 1853) (National Gallery of Scotland). Scott's descriptions often supplied artists with all the details of staffage they needed, as in this Dutch-like portrait of Bradwardine's "prime minister": "Before him was a large bicker of oatmeal-porridge, and at the side thereof, a horn-spoon and a bottle of two-penny. Eagerly running his eye over a voluminous law-paper, he from time to time shovelled an immense spoonful of these nutritive viands into his capacious mouth. A pot-bellied Dutch bottle of brandy which stood by, intimated either that this honest limb of the law had taken his *morning* already, or that he meant to season his porridge with such digestive; or perhaps both circumstances might reasonably be inferred. His night-cap and morning-gown had whilome been of tartan, but, equally cautious and frugal, the honest Bailie had got them dyed black" (*Waverley,* chap. 66).

the Marquis of Lansdowne, he painted *Rebecca in Prison* (1821); for another, Lord Egremont, *Charles II and the Lady Bellenden,* from *Old Mortality* (pl. 319); for a third, *Jeanie Deans and Queen Caroline* (RA 1859).

Frith's numerous but seemingly not very enthusiastic contributions to Scott iconography spanned at least thirty years of his protracted career. His *Rebecca and Ivanhoe* (1840) had the distinction of being his only painting to be rejected for hanging (by the British Institution). This disappointment was balanced, however, by the acceptance of both this picture and his *Madge Wildfire and Jeanie Deans Entering Willingham Church* at the other minor exhibition, the Society of British Artists, where, in the preceding year, he had shown a scene from *The Lay of the Last Minstrel.* A *Kenilworth* scene (RA 1841) showed Amy Robsart and Leicester parting after one of his visits to Cumnor Place; perhaps because the details of the setting were copied from Knole, the picture, like his *Malvolio* of the year before, was hung in the Architecture Room of the Royal Academy. While he was working on his large *Ramsgate Sands* in 1853–54, Frith fell back on Scott subjects to keep his financial ship afloat. He painted four of them for an edition of the novels, and at the Royal Academy in 1854 exhibited *The Love Token* from *The Bride of Lammermoor* (pl. 320) and *The Poison Cup* from *Kenilworth,* sketches for a pair of pictures commissioned by a patron whom he looked back upon with distaste: "a grumbling ignoramus who could not see the faults that really existed, but discovered plenty of his own making. He grumbled during the progress of the pictures, and grumbled when they were finished; and when he sold them—as he did very shortly—for a great deal more than he had paid for them, he grumbled because he had not got enough."[26] Frith, however, was not so irremediably soured on Scott pictures as to be unable to relish the fact that a later one, a scene of the maid Janet dressing Amy Robsart prior to one of Leicester's visits, was the fourth of his canvases to need a railing to protect it from the overeager attention of visitors to the Royal Academy (1870).

319. Charles R. Leslie, *Charles II and Lady Bellenden* (RA 1837) (Petworth House). An elaboration of a few lines in *Old Mortality* (chap. 2): "On his route through the west of Scotland to meet Cromwell in the unfortunate field of Worcester, Charles the Second had actually breakfasted at the Tower of Tillietudlem—an incident which formed, from that moment, an important era in the life of Lady Margaret, who seldom afterwards partook of that meal, either at home or abroad, without detailing the whole circumstances of the royal visit, not forgetting the salutation which his Majesty conferred on each side of her face."

In the early 1830s, Mulready depicted at least five subjects from Scott's novels, including a pair from the seldom-painted *St. Ronan's Well* (RA 1832). In 1848, Maclise painted for Bulwer-Lytton *Chivalry in the Time of Henry VIII* (*The Combat of Two Knights*), from *Marmion.* A third artist, Augustus Egg, exhibited two Scott paintings, *Sir Percy Shafton and Mysie Happer* from *The Monastery* (RA 1843) and *Dame Ursula and Margaret* from *The Fortunes of Nigel* (RA 1854).

Millais painted his first Scott picture, from *Peveril of the Peak,* when he was only twelve years old (pl. 131). His other subjects from Scott were produced in the middle of his career. Two companion pieces, one portraying Effie Deans and George Staunton and the other Lucy Ashton and Edgar Ravenswood (pl. 321), were exhibited at the King Street Gallery in successive years, 1877–78.

One of Holman Hunt's first exhibited pictures (RA 1847), not to be confused with his juvenile *Woodstock* effort for which he got twenty pounds, was *Dr. Rochecliffe Performing Divine Service in the Cottage of Joceline Joliffe.* Another Pre-Raphaelite treatment of Scott was somewhat out of the ordinary: a utilitarian objet d'art rather than a gallery painting. In 1861, the architect John Dando Sedding designed a Gothic oak cabinet to hold his drawings and had it decorated by William Morris's firm. Shown the next year at the International Exhibition, it had four main panels, allegorizing Sculpture and Painting (both by Burne-Jones), Architecture by Ford Madox Brown and Music by Rossetti, "based on imaginary incidents in the honeymoon of King René of Anjou" in Scott's *Anne of Geierstein.*[27] One additional link between Scott and the painters of the Pre-Raphaelite–Aesthetic school was James McNeill Whistler's *Arrangement in Yellow and Gray: Effie Deans* (1876).

320. William P. Frith, *The Love Token* (RA 1854) (Victoria & Albert Museum, Crown Copyright). A scene from *The Bride of Lammermoor* (chap. 33): Lady Ashton cuts the love token from Lucy's neck and returns it to Ravenswood.

The novels differed widely in their popularity as subjects for paintings.* One hundred paintings from *Ivanhoe* are recorded, half of them produced in the heyday of Scott painting, 1830–50. Across the years, Rebecca was the subject of at least thirty-two canvases, including a number of her trial in the vaulted chamber. Isaac of York was often portrayed in his dungeon. There were tournament scenes, and pictures of Lady Rowena and of the swineherd Gurth and the jester Wamba. *The Heart of Mid-Lothian* and *The Bride of Lammermoor* were the sources of some eighty paintings apiece. Fifty-five of those from the former novel featured the Deans sisters. Jeanie was seen in numerous incidents, but most often visiting her sister in prison. Possibly the most famous of the surviv-

*Interestingly, the relative popularity of the novels in art does not coincide with the frequency with which they were adapted for the theater, as described above.

321. John Everett Millais, *The Bride of Lammermoor* (King St. Gallery 1878) (Bristol Museum and Art Gallery). "It represents Lucy Ashton, in a forest glade, leaning on the arm of her lover after he has saved her from the aggression of the wild bull. Her face—an exquisite piece of painting—is a marvellous study of girlish agitation, and that of the sombre young Master of Ravenswood is not less remarkable. . . . It would be hard to find a lovelier specimen of English girlish beauty than Lucy Ashton, or a more magnificent young man than her companion" (Henry James in the *Nation,* 6 June 1878; *The Painter's Eye,* p. 170).

ing *Heart of Mid-Lothian* paintings is James Drummond's *The Porteous Mob* (pl. 37), a dramatic night scene. Lucy Ashton appeared in at least half of the pictures from *The Bride of Lammermoor,* most often (fifteen times or more) visiting the mermaiden's fountain. The other favorite subject from the novel was Lucy and Ravenswood plighting their troth.

Old Mortality stood alone in the second range of popularity, accounting for about sixty paintings. These were dominated by the figure of Old Mortality himself, though even an approximate count is impossible because the many catalogue entries for "Old Mortality" may refer either to the character himself or to a scene from the novel. The many pictures of the Convenanters seen at the exhibitions, though essentially representations of historical events, were often linked in the catalogues with either *Old Mortality* or *The Heart of Mid-Lothian.*

Kenilworth, The Abbot, and *The Antiquary* were represented by approximately forty to fifty pictures each. The large majority of those from *Kenilworth* were of Amy Robsart with or without the Earl of Leicester, and often lying in a heap at the bottom of the fateful stairs at Cumnor Place (pl. 41). Queen Elizabeth's visit to Kenilworth was one of the several Scott subjects that attracted artists by the occasions they offered for colorful representations of sixteenth-century pageantry.* *The Abbot* was another novel that enabled painters to combine the mutually reinforcing appeals of history and Scottian romance; many of the pictures derived from it were of Mary Queen of Scots' abdication and escape from Loch Leven Castle (pl. 99). Of the novels so far mentioned, *The Antiquary* was the only exception to the general rule that, apart from the surge in 1830–50, their popularity was fairly constant from the time they first were taken up by artists until the close of the century. *The Antiquary*'s vogue in art began only about 1840, and fully half of the pictures drawn from it were exhibited after 1850.

The remaining novels were represented by fewer than forty paintings each, the bottom of the list being occupied by *St. Ronan's Well* and *The Black Dwarf,* each of which accounted for no more than a half-dozen canvases. Most of the pictures from *The Pirate* appeared during the flush decades, though there were twelve or so after that period. Minna and Brenda Troil and their father were the chief subjects, along with Norna relating her sad history. The popularity of *Rob Roy* was, for some reason, delayed; down to 1850, only about a dozen paintings are recorded, in the sixties there were a few, and in the period 1870–97 another dozen. Most of these depicted Diana Vernon, alone or with Frank Osbaldistone. In *Guy Mannering,* the artist's chief delight was Meg Merrilies the gypsy; Dominie Sampson, Ellangowan, and Julia Mannering were the other repeated figures. Alice Lee and Phoebe Mayflower among the fictional characters, and Charles II among the historical ones, were the central figures of paintings from *Woodstock.*

Although not painted as often, three novels—*Waverley, The Fair Maid of Perth,* and *A Legend of Montrose*—were represented more or less regularly from the time they were first drawn upon until the end of the century. The careers of the rest were erratic. *The Fortunes of Nigel* did not participate in the 1830–50 vogue; more than half of the recorded paintings were shown after 1850. *Peveril of the Peak* went unpainted for two decades (1848–68), then returned to mild favor. The relatively poor showing of three other novels evidently was due to their dropping out of favor in mid-Victorian times. After 1850, only seven paintings were made from

*One picture exhibited with a reference to *Kenilworth* illustrates how avid painters were for tie-ins with Scott, however tenuous. Frank Howard showed at the Society of British Artists in 1831 a picture entered in the catalogue as "The battle of the pigs. 'A country wedding at the time of Henry V. . . .' Vide Master Laneham's account of one of the pageants at the progress to Kenilworth. [Robert Laneham was an official at the Elizabethan court who left an eyewitness description of the festivities at Kenilworth in 1575.] It is remarkable that it is the only game unmentioned by Sir Walter Scott." Other artists similarly tried to enhance their pictures of old customs by alluding to Scott; the entry for a painting by John Gilbert (SBA 1839) read, "The feast of fools, a religious farce celebrated in the ancient Romish church. The scene represented more immediately refers to Sir Walter Scott's novel of *The Abbot.*" More famous pictures of the sort were Maclise's *Ordeal by Touch* (RA 1846) and Orchardson's *The Queen of the Swords* (pl. 323).

322. John Watson Nicol, *"For Better for Worse": Rob Roy and the Bailie* (RA 1886) (Sheffield City Art Galleries). Prosaic, cautious materialism (the cloth merchant Bailie Nicol Jarvie) and lawless romanticism (Rob Roy MacGregor) reach an understanding of sorts: "If ever I put my sons apprentice," says Rob Roy, "I will gie you the refusal o' them" (*Rob Roy,* chap. 34).

The Monastery, the last in 1862. With but one exception in each case, the exhibition records of *The Betrothed, The Talisman,* and *Quentin Durward* cease in 1847, 1851, and 1853 respectively.

A recent writer has enumerated the main reasons why Scott's novels were so popular: " . . . their humor, the earthiness and quaintness of the Scottish dialogue, the individuality of the characters, the melodrama, the sentiment, the good spirits, the 'sound' morality, the conventional

323. William Quiller Orchardson, *The Queen of the Swords* (RA 1877) (National Gallery of Scotland). An illustration of one of Scott's lengthy antiquarian footnotes, this one describing "the Sword-Dance . . . celebrated in general terms by Olaus Magnus. He seems to have considered it as peculiar to the Norwegians, from whom it may have passed to the Orkneymen and Zetlanders, with other northern customs," etc., etc. (*The Pirate,* chap. 15)

324. William Quiller Orchardson, *"Casus Belli"* (RA 1872) (Glasgow Art Gallery and Museum). Julian Peveril, escorting Alice Bridgenorth and Fenella along a London street, is chevied by two gallants. "That black-eyed sparkler looks as if she had a mind to run away from him," says one, in a loud voice. "Ay," answers the other, "and the blue-eyed trembler looks as if she would fall behind into my loving arms" (*Peveril of the Peak,* chap. 32).

love story and happy ending, the nature descriptions, the historical accounts, the thrilling battles. . . . "[28] Most of these were prominent among the subjects and qualities the average middle-class art-buyer in early and mid-Victorian times required in the canvases he bought, along with colorful costumes and imposing or humble but picturesque settings. Scott's heroines alone would have guaranteed his popularity among artists and their clientele. Either in figure studies or as central characters in tableaux, they constituted a gallery of women to the Victorian taste—sentimental, strong, humorous, pathetic, victimized, distraught, loyal: Lucy Ashton, the Glee Maiden, Meg Merrilies, Jeanie and Effie Deans, Madge Wildfire, Rebecca, Amy Robsart, Mysie Happer, Minna and Brenda Troil, Diana Vernon, Rose Bradwardine, Alice Lee, Phoebe Mayflower, Catherine Seyton, Flora MacIvor. Nowhere else except in Shakespeare could be found a wider assortment of characters and situations that lent themselves to the many moods of popular Victorian narrative and genre art—comedy, tragedy, pathos, melodrama, humor, family affection, madness—or the different but hardly less appealing spirit of history painting: spectacle and ceremony, combat, heroism, uprisings.

Scott's poetry and fiction not only constantly fed, but fundamentally affected, the art of Victorian England. The populous school of genre painters stemming from Allan and Wilkie found in Scott the lovingly described eccentrics, the burghers and cottagers, the domestic hearths and country lanes that suggested the themes for countless paintings of everyday life, however independent they might be of any specific literary inspiration. The most characteristic product of Victorian painting, the genre scene, owed more than can easily be estimated to Scott's popularity in literature and art.

BYRON

The popularity Byron's poetry enjoyed in the first half of the nineteenth century was amply apparent in the art exhibitions.[1] Subjects from

Byron were painted as often as subjects from those other two concurrent favorites, Burns and Scott (counting his poems only), and the number of scenes and figure studies bearing quotations from Byron but not directly related to his subjects was considerably greater than those from all other poets except Shakespeare, Thomson, and Tennyson. Although Byron's critical fortunes began to be reversed as early as the 1830s, his popularity among ordinary readers continued, and the market for pictures from his poems flourished accordingly. Only toward the end of the century did the demand for Byron subjects noticeably fade, just as the poet's critical reputation was slowly being reestablished on a more permanent basis.

The first of the two hundred recorded Byron paintings appeared at the Royal Academy in 1814, two from *The Corsair,* which was hot off the press; one of these was by Henry Singleton, the other by Henry Corbould, another popular artist of the day who favored literary subjects. At the Royal Academy show of 1817 were seen the first paintings from *Childe Harold's Pilgrimage,* the first three cantos of which had appeared in 1812–16, and in 1821, the first from *Don Juan*—a portrayal of Don Juan and Haidee from the brush of a rather improbable Byron illustrator, Lieutenant-Colonel (later General) Sir William Napier, a veteran of the Peninsular War, who after retiring from the army, had turned painter and sculptor, in which capacity he was made an honorary R.A. The following year (1822), the Academy saw paintings from both *Mazeppa* and *Manfred,* and the Byron boom in British art was well under way.

Fuseli, the last survivor of the Reynoldsian generation of artists, witnessed its early stage, and presumably approved; John Knowles, his early biographer, said that he "always read [Byron's] writings as soon as they were published, with great avidity."[2] The Princess of Wales asked him to paint for her any passage he wished from *The Corsair,* a request he seems not to have fulfilled. Byron's poetry, however, does not figure prominently among the books that significantly influenced the coming generation of Victorian artists. The exception was Ford Madox Brown, in whose "love-offering" to his favorite poets in the triptych *Chaucer Reading His*

325. Charles Eastlake, *Lord Byron's "Dream"* (RA 1829) (Tate Gallery, London). An illustration of a passage in Byron's poem (1816):

In the last he lay
Reposing from the noontide sultriness,
Couch'd among fallen columns, in the shade
Of ruin'd walls that had survived the names
Of those who rear'd them; by his sleeping side
Stood camels grazing, and some goodly steeds
Were fasten'd near a fountain; and a man
Clad in a flowing garb did watch the while,
While many of his tribe slumber'd around;
And they were canopied by the blue sky,
So cloudless, clear, and purely beautiful,
That God alone was seen to be in heaven.

326. David Wilkie, *The Maid of Saragossa* (RA 1829) (Royal Collection, Copyright Reserved). An episode in *Childe Harold's Pilgrimage,* canto 1: the "Maid of Saragossa," Maria Augustin, rallied the faltering Spanish troops during an engagement in the Peninsular Wars, thus joining the company of other heroines of revolutionary legend. Delacroix's celebrated picture *Liberty Leading the People,* which this resembles, was painted the following year.

Poems at the Court of Edward III (pl. 121), Byron was ranked with Shakespeare, Spenser, Milton, Pope, Burns, and Chaucer himself. Brown's first picture at the Royal Academy (1841) was *The Giaour's Confession,* and, more important, he returned time after time to Byronic themes, sometimes treating the subject first in watercolor and subsequently in one or more versions in oil. This was the case in the early 1870s when he made designs for William Michael Rossetti's edition of Byron's poetry: *The Dream (Byron and Mary Chaworth)* (pl. 129), *Haidee and Don Juan* (pl. 133), *The Younger Foscari (Jacopo Foscari),* and *The Dream of Sardanapalus.*

Wilkie drew from Byron only once, in his mid-career picture *The Maid of Saragossa* (pl. 326), from *Childe Harold.* Turner exhibited in the 1830s two major landscapes whose titles alluded to Byron, *Childe Harold's Pilgrimage—Italy* (pl. 327), and *The Bright Stone of Honor (Ehrenbreitstein) and the Tomb of Marceau,* also from *Childe Harold* (RA 1835); but neither canvas, like most of Turner's "literary" pictures, made any but a glancing reference to the poem itself.* Turner's book illustrations of Byron were considerably more numerous. He painted a total of twenty-six watercolors, mostly vignettes, to be engraved for various books: Murray's 1825 and 1832–34 editions of Byron's works and the Finden brothers' *Landscape and Portrait Illustrations to the Life and Works of Lord Byron* (1833–34).[3] The Findens were the most active of the several engraver-entrepreneurs who put together Byron picture books. Among these productions, in addition to the *Landscape and Portrait Illustrations,* were *The Byron Gallery* (1832) and *Findens' Byron Beauties; or, The Principal Female Characters in Lord Byron's Poems* (1836), all close kin to the keepsake annuals, at the peak of their popularity in those years, which featured similar scenes and portraits.

The disinclination of other leading British painters to take up Byronic subjects contrasts with the appeal they had to French artists, especially Delacroix, at a time when painting in France came under the influence of English literature as mediated especially by French editions and stage adaptations. At the Paris Salon between 1827 and 1849, Delacroix exhibited paintings from *Marino Faliero* (also British Institution 1828), *Sar-*

*The title of this painting, with its mistranslation of the German original, assimilated two contemporary literary references—to *Childe Harold,* canto 3, stanzas 55–58, and Kenelm Henry Digby's *The Broad Stone of Honour* (1822, with a number of subsequent editions and enlargements), a popular treatise on chivalry that did much to nurture the revived medievalism of Turner's time and beyond (see Mark Girouard, *The Return to Camelot* [New Haven, Conn., 1981], chap. 5).

danapalus, The Giaour, The Corsair, The Prisoner of Chillon, Don Juan, and *Lara.* He also drew subjects in various media from *The Bride of Abydos, Tasso, Mazeppa,* and *The Two Foscari.*[4]

Paintings from Byron acquired interest not only from the public's appetite for reading the actual text but also from the performance of a number of his dramas, which, unlike Scott's novels from which stage adaptations were made, had been intended for the theater from the beginning.[5] Of the plays most often represented in painting, *Sardanapalus* was performed some 186 times in the course of the century, *Manfred* 165, and *Marino Faliero* 52. (*The Two Foscari* and *Cain* lasted only through a few performances each; contrariwise, *Werner,* which was seldom painted, was performed 139 times.) The best-received plays had the advantage of celebrated actors like Macready (pl. 328) and Phelps in the leading roles. The qualities that made Byron's dramas successful in the theater (no other major Romantic poet had similar luck) were those that also won them places on the exhibition walls year after year: defiant heroes, melodramatic events, rugged landscapes, raging thunderstorms and other severe visitations of nature, roaring cataracts, raging fires—in short, the Martinesque sublime. Several productions of these plays were landmarks in the history of English stage spectacle. The first staging of *Sardanapalus* (Drury Lane 1834), with Macready in the role, was lavish enough, but it was outdone by Charles Kean at the Princess' Theatre in 1853–54. This production ran for ninety-three nights largely because of its imposing sets, inspired perhaps by Martin's architectural fantasies in pictures like *Belshazzar's Feast* and certainly, and more immediately, by the drawings accompanying Layard's recent and well-publicized account of his discovery of Assyrian monuments and palaces. *Manfred,* opening the same year

327. J. M. W. Turner, *Childe Harold's Pilgrimage—Italy* (RA 1832) (Tate Gallery, London). Classical landscapists had often peopled their scenes with spatially insignificant human figures whom they identified with a literary subject by the titles they gave the paintings. Turner worked in the same tradition, but in this case the literary association was no stronger than that supplied by his quotation from *Childe Harold's Pilgrimage,* canto 4: " . . . and now, fair Italy! / Thou art the garden of the world." The painting is as tenuously related to the poem as is Berlioz' *Harold in Italy;* except for the lines quoted, it might as well have been titled *Landscape with Picnickers.*

328. Daniel Maclise, *Macready as Werner* (RA 1851) (Victoria & Albert Museum, Crown Copyright). Macready first played Werner in 1830; this picture was exhibited the year he gave his last performance in the role.

as *Sardanapalus* but at Covent Garden, with Ellen Tree as the Witch of the Alps, was similarly celebrated for its pictorial splendor. Occasionally, one of Byron's so-called Turkish or Oriental tales, which had a different kind of appeal, was adapted for the stage, as was *The Bride of Abydos* in 1818 and 1847. Passages in *Don Juan* were staged in a melodrama (1822) and, six years later, both in a burletta and a romantic drama starring Ellen Tree, who was painted in her role of Haidee in a picture at the Royal Academy the same year.

In the selection of both dramatic and nondramatic Byronic subjects for art can be seen most of the elements that made the contemporary response a paradigm of Romantic sensibility, ranging from Oriental melodrama to erotic sentiment. The action typically occurred in the same glamorous locales—the Alps, Greece, Italy, and above all the Middle East—to which the Romantic imagination, particularly as expressed in nonliterary painting, was constantly returning. The moody, rebellious Byronic protagonist, the archetype of the Romantic hero, was captured in paint: "Everlasting protest, impetuous energy of will, melancholy and despondent reaction," wrote John Morley, looking back at the fashion from the vantage point of 1870. "Cain and Conrad; then Manfred and Lara and Harold."[6] Most buyers of pictures probably thought less about the political or philosophic implications of Byron's heroes than about the sheer glorious adventurousness they represented, along with their passionate relationships with beautiful women, who shared the billing.

The public evidently did not mind that diversity was not a distinctive quality of most of the painted representations of Byron's heroes and heroines. Macaulay's complaint serves as a miniature catalogue of Byronic art, distilling the essence of innumerable stylized tableaux and poses:

> All his characters,—Harold looking back on the western sky, from which his country and the sun are receding together,—the Giaour, standing apart in the gloom of the side-aisle, and casting a haggard scowl from under his long hood at the crucifix and the censer,—Conrad, leaning on his sword by the watch-tower,—Lara, smiling on the dancers,—Alp, gazing steadily on the fatal cloud as it passes before the moon,—Manfred, wandering among the precipices of Berne,—Azzo, on the judgement-seat,—Ugo, at the bar,—Lambro, frowning on the siesta of his daughter and Juan,—Cain, presenting his unacceptable offering,—are all essentially the same. The varieties are varieties merely of age, situation, and costume.[7]

"His women, like his men," Macaulay continued, "are all of one breed."

> Haidee is a half-savage and girlish Julia; Julia is a civilized and matronly Haidee. Leila is a wedded Zuleika—Zuleika a virgin Leila. Gulnare and Medora appear to have been intentionally opposed to each other. Yet the difference is a difference of situation only. . . . It is hardly too much to say, that Lord Byron could exhibit only one man and only one woman,—a man proud, moody, cynical,—with defiance on his brow, and misery in his heart; a scorner of his kind, implacable in revenge, yet capable of deep and strong affection;—a woman all softness and gentleness, loving to caress and to be caressed, but capable of being transformed by love into a tigress.

If one may judge from titles and such few canvases and (more) engravings as survive, this deadening monotony of treatment was most evident in pictures from the series of Oriental tales that began with *The Bride of Abydos* and *The Giaour* in 1813 and continued with *The Corsair* and its sequel *Lara* (both 1814). *The Bride of Abydos* inspired a dozen or so paintings, nearly all of which were portraits of Zuleika, the bride. Among them was William Allan's version (pl. 329). There was an equal number of pictures from *The Giaour,* all but one predating 1847; from the catalogue entries, it is impossible to pinpoint which episodes were chosen.

Of this early group of poems, the overwhelming favorite among artists was *The Corsair.* Pictures were painted from it the very year it was published, and, from then to the 1880s, some sixty "corsair" paintings made their appearance; this was one Byronic subject whose appeal lasted beyond mid-century. Corsairs (pirates) were a popular subject in Romantic painting, apart from the Byronic association, and on the stage as well.[8] There had been a play called *The Corsair* as early as 1801, and the publication of Byron's poem stimulated a corsair tradition in the theater that ran parallel to the one in the art gallery. In addition to corsairs pure and simple there was *The Corsair's Son; or, The Fall of Otranto* (1821), the title of which doubtless resulted from someone's notion that if an allusion to

329. William Allan, *The Bride of Abydos* (dated 1836) (Glasgow Art Gallery and Museum). An instance of the way artists drew from Byron's exotic poems subjects that would appeal to the current taste for Oriental genre. Allan was especially well qualified to do so because he had traveled extensively in Asia Minor early in the century.

Byron's poem could be relied on to lure playgoers, a tacked-on allusion to Walpole's Gothic novel would bring in twice as many. There were also a *Corsair's Bride* (1821), *The Corsair,* with music from Herold's *Zampa* (1836), and *The Corsair's Revenge* (three different productions in 1835–40). On the stage, the Byronic link was usually in name only; in art, painters made more explicit reference to the poem by naming their characters Conrad, Gulnare, and Medora, and by portraying situations found there—Medora awaiting Conrad's return, Gulnare's love for the Corsair being discovered by the Seyd, the parting of Conrad and Medora. Many of the paintings were simply of Medora herself.

Don Juan shares with *The Corsair* the distinction of being Byron's most-painted poem. Some fifty pictures from it are recorded, half of them from 1830 to 1850. Despite the poem's great length and kaleidoscopic variety, very few episodes were selected for treatment, decidedly the most popular being the love idyll of Don Juan and Haidee. Juan shipwrecked, Juan succored by Haidee (pl. 133), Juan separated from Haidee by her father and seized by pirates, were painted time after time, as was Haidee alone, the idealized Greek beauty (pl. 57). The only other recurring subject from the poem was Donna Julia, who turned up periodically between the 1830s and the 1860s.

From *Childe Harold's Pilgrimage,* the other long poem of Byron still read today, some fifteen paintings are recorded, all but three before 1850; these included the canvases by Wilkie and Turner mentioned above. No single theme predominated. The varied subjects included *The Maniac Visited by His Children, Harold at the Tomb of Cecilia Metella* (both canto 4), and, belatedly in 1868, Henry O'Neil's *The Night Before Waterloo* (canto 3).

Of Byron's shorter poems, the most painted was "The Prisoner of Chillon," the first three pictorial versions of which, surprisingly, did not appear until 1837, twenty-one years after the poem was published. Part of the theme's attraction was doubtless the opportunity it offered to emulate Reynolds's famous painting, from Dante, of Ugolino in the Tower. Ford Madox Brown's (pl. 97) is the most important surviving treatment of the poem.

330. Ford Madox Brown, *Manfred on the Jungfrau* (ca. 1841) (City Art Gallery, Manchester). One of the several pictures that reflect Brown's absorption in Byron's poetry in the very earliest years of his career (see also pl. 97). Here he represents, close up, the scene portrayed in rugged terrain in Martin's painting (pl. 331).

Brown's earlier picture from Byron, *Manfred on the Jungfrau* (pl. 330), was one of the two notable paintings taken from that poem, the other being Martin's dramatic portrayal (pl. 331) of the Faustian hero preparing to plunge from the Jungfrau into the illimitable lake below. The scenes chosen by the half-dozen other painters of subjects from the poem were Manfred and the chamois hunter, and Manfred and the Witch of the Alps. Presumably these were the subjects of the panels that Richard Dadd painted for Lord Foley's house in Grosvenor Square in 1841.

How many of the dozen nineteenth-century English paintings of the Mazeppa story were directly derived from Byron's treatment (1819) is open to question. The tale, of a nobleman who discovers his page Mazeppa to be his wife's lover and ties him to a wild horse for a night ride through a forest alive with packs of wolves, originated in Poland at the end of the seventeenth century; and a hundred years later, at least two portraits of the hero were painted on the Continent.[9] The first English Mazeppa paintings (1822) undoubtedly came from Byron, but those produced after 1824 may have had multiple sources, coming as they did in the wake not only of his poem but of Géricault's lithograph (1823), a play at the Royal Coburg theater in the same year, Horace Vernet's several

331. John Martin, *Manfred* (Society of British Artists 1826) (Birmingham City Museum and Art Gallery). A watercolor version (1837) of the lost original. Another watercolor by Martin depicted Manfred and the Witch of the Alps.

well-known paintings, and the stage adaptation made in 1831 for the celebrated equestrian-showman Andrew Ducrow, which became one of the most frequently performed of all nineteenth-century plays. The most notable surviving Mazeppa paintings by an English artist are John Frederick Herring's pair (1833), explicitly labeled as being "after Horace Vernet," and, like Vernet's, concentrating on the horses in one scene (pl. 93) and on the wolves in the other.

MOORE

Thomas Moore's career in English art in some ways resembled Byron's. The subjects of their poems enabled painters to exploit two extremely popular veins of Regency art, the sentimental female portrait and Oriental figures and scenes, a form of exotic genre. The poetry of both men was widely circulated in illustrated editions and volumes of "beauties" at the same time that paintings from the poems appeared in the galleries. Their popularity among painters and their clients reached its peak simultaneously in the 1840s and 1850s, when their critical reputations had sharply declined.[1] And though many scores of canvases bore subjects from Byron and Moore (the latter was represented by about seventy, as against Byron's two hundred), few were by the period's most accomplished or popular artists.* Probably for that reason, not many reviewers bothered to describe the pictures they looked at. As with Byron, remarkably few pictures from Moore, in proportion to the number produced, survive today, because they were of a kind particularly vulnerable to shifting popular taste, the first to be sent to jumble sales or sold to secondhand dealers for their frames when a household was cleared or redecorated in a newer fashion. But engravings and such descriptions as were printed suggest to the reluctant imagination what the paintings must have been like.

Lalla Rookh (1817) was the most painted of Moore's poems. Artists valued it more highly than did most reviewers, and for a good reason: the

*But more artists of stature contemplated subjects from Moore than actually painted them. Moore himself recorded in his journal on 4 June 1819 that he visited an exhibition of John Martin's pictures, including "Joshua bidding the sun stand still—one of the most magnificently conceived things I ever saw—poetry of the highest kind," and was told (by Martin himself?) that "he means to paint a subject from *Lalla Rookh*" (*The Journal of Thomas Moore,* ed. Wilfred S. Dowden [Newark, Del., 1983], 1: 182).

332. Daniel Maclise, *The Origin of the Harp* (RA 1842) (City Art Gallery, Manchester). "A bold attempt to embody in painting Moore's poetical idea of a female metamorphosed into the instrumental symbol of Green Erin, her hair falling over to form 'the golden strings'" (*Literary Gazette,* 7 May).

very qualities the critics deplored, above all the lush, cloying imagery, were those that the painters delighted in. Between its first appearance at the Royal Academy in 1819 and mid-century, it was represented by some thirty canvases, and fifteen more were painted in the next fifty years. The subjects were drawn from all four of the stories told by the young minstrel Feramorz as the wedding party of Lalla Rookh, daughter of an Indian mogul, moves from Delhi to Kashmir, where the princess is to marry the young king of Bukhara. Pictured most frequently was Nourmahal, the wife of the emperor Selim in the fourth tale ("The Light of the Haram"); she was seen as often as Byron's Haidee, posed in colorful costume against a background of Oriental ornaments and furniture. Of these many *Lalla Rookh* paintings, the only one of which substantial record survives—the picture itself is known only from a pencil study—was Daniel Maclise's melodramatic *Mokanna Revealing His Features to Zelica,* the climax of the first tale ("The Veiled Prophet of Khorassan"). After causing a sensation when it was first shown in Liverpool in 1832, it was brought to London and shown the following year at the British Institution.

Moore's other popular work, *Irish Melodies,* was published in 1807, with successive enlarged editions to 1834; that of 1824 contained six designs by Stothard. In the exhibitions, the collection was represented chiefly by pictures of Nora Creina, the subject of the song "Lesbia Hath a Beaming Eye". The popularity of this particular subject after mid-century was due to the wide circulation, in engraved form, of W. P. Frith's painting of Nora Creina (pl. 52), commissioned for an album of *The Beauties of Moore* (1846) to which Augustus Egg, Alfred Elmore, and E. M. Ward also contributed. Maclise's *The Origin of the Harp* (pl. 332), from *Irish Melodies,* is one of the few other identifiable paintings from Moore to survive.

SHELLEY

Shelley was not represented in exhibition catalogues during his lifetime, and when his poems eventually made their way there, it was oftener as sources of mottoes than as subjects of illustrations. The first paintings to be associated with him seem to have been two that were exhibited fully twenty years after his death. At the British Institution in 1842, two artists, Theodor von Holst and Thomas F. Marshall, showed pictures with identical titles and mottoes: *The Bride,* quoting Shelley's line "Ginevra from the nuptial altar went," in the poem describing a tragic story quite different from the one in which Samuel Rogers's heroine of the same name figures.

Artists probably entertained the same attitude toward Shelley that his early critics did.[1] One serious charge against him, compounded by his radical religious and political views, was his notoriously "immoral" character. Thanks to the great popularity of Byron's poetry, critics and artists alike managed to overlook similar failings in his case, but they were unable to do so in Shelley's. Reviewers, moreover, were too busy flaying him on personal grounds to say much about his artistry; and when they did, they merely used words like "imagery" without elaboration. Such small discussion of his imagery as did appear emphasized its indistinctness, the very opposite of the clear definition that normally recommended a poem to painters' attention. In 1821, for example, a writer in the *London Magazine* said: "He gives us for representations of things, rhapsodies of words. He does not lend the colours of imagination and the ornaments of styles to the objects of nature, but paints gaudy, flimsy, allegorical pictures on gauze, on the cobwebs of his own brain. . . . "[2]

The result was that most of the twenty or so paintings from Shelley came in the latter half of the century, when his infamy as a revolutionary thinker and violator of the marriage vows was slowly being replaced by celebrity as a poet. Only a handful of his poems figure in the list, and none more than three or four times. There were four paintings from *The Cenci,* the first of which (RA 1850) was greeted by the *Literary Gazette* as "a revolting subject, and quite unfit for art or exhibition."[3] But the subject was established in art long before Shelley took it up, in the celebrated painting of Beatrice Cenci, then attributed to Guido Reni, which the poet described in his preface to the play. In Shelley's mind as he conceived the character was Eliza O'Neill, the Regency actress who posed for a number of portraits; but although it is likely enough that the several artists who painted Shelley's Cenci were influenced by "Guido's" picture, none was old enough to have been affected by similar reminiscences of O'Neill.[4]

Although, as Hugh Honour has recently suggested, Turner's late *Queen Mab's Cave* (BI 1846) may be "directly related"[5] to Shelley's *Queen Mab,* the connection rests in the attitudes and symbolism the painter and poet shared rather than in any overt allusion to the text of the poem. The painting was exhibited with a supposed quotation from *A Midsummer Night's Dream,* "Frisk it, frisk it, by the Moonlight beam" (the line does not occur there) and another from Turner's own shadowy *Fallacies of Hope:* "Thy Orgies, Mab, are manifold." There was no reference to Shelley in the catalogue entry.[6] The two recorded paintings explicitly alluding to *Queen Mab* were typical mid-Victorian sentimental pictures of sleeping women named, for the occasion, Ianthe.

Not until 1936 was it discovered that an early work by John Martin, *Sadak in Search of the Waters of Oblivion* (pl. 36), illustrated at second hand a hitherto unidentified poem by Shelley.[7] The painting was exhibited in 1812 at the Royal Academy. Unsold there, it was subsequently bought at half price from the hard-up artist by a governor of the Bank of England. Its subject was typical Oriental claptrap—the story, taken from James Ridley's *Tales of the Genii* (1764), of Sadak, a Persian nobleman who was tricked by the Sultan, the abductor of his wife, to go on a quest for the Waters of Oblivion, with a sample of which the Sultan secretly planned to brainwash Sadak's wife. An engraving of the painting appeared in the *Keepsake* for 1828 in conjunction with an unsigned poem, "Sadak the Wanderer," which the index to the surviving manuscripts of contributions to that edition identified as Shelley's. Although Shelley may have seen Martin's picture, it is more likely that his source, like Martin's, was Ridley's tale.

KEATS

It has been said of Keats that he was "the most insistently pictorialist of any Romantic poet and one of the finest flowerings in any soil of the centuries-old and European-wide tradition of the Sister Arts."[1] He so steeped his imagination in graphic and plastic imagery from works of art he had seen as to require a whole book (Ian Jack's *Keats and the Mirror of Art*) to describe its effect on his poetry. More than any other major English poet, in the few years allotted to him he was a familiar figure in art circles and counted Haydon among his close friends. Perhaps this was why, although as yet he had few readers, his poems were represented in art exhibitions so quickly after his death in February 1821. In May of that year, Thomas Stothard showed at the Royal Academy a painting called

333. William Holman Hunt, *The Flight of Madeline and Porphyro during the Drunkenness Attending the Revelry* (RA 1848) (Guildhall Art Gallery, London). A pre-Pre-Raphaelite canvas: it was on the occasion of its display at the Academy that Hunt and Rossetti first met. Within a few months, they became close friends, and, attracting several like-minded young artists (who shared, among other enthusiasms, a love of Keats's poetry), formed the Pre-Raphaelite Brotherhood.

The Vintage, with a quotation from the "Ode to a Nightingale." (Stothard seems not to have acted on a hint, offered in a review of "Isabella, or the Pot of Basil" in the *Edinburgh Magazine* the preceding year, that he make a "beautiful picture" from the stanza in that poem beginning "And as he to the court-yard pass'd along.")[2] In 1828, a picture by another well-known artist of the day, William Hilton, bore the title "Amphitrite, Queen of Pearls" from the third book of *Endymion.*

During his lifetime, criticism of Keats was so polemic, controversial, and personal that the pictorial qualities of his poetry were not often mentioned.[3] One conspicuous exception was P.G. Patmore's review of *Endymion* in the *London Magazine* (1820) in which, anticipating the similar device Leigh Hunt, a close friend of Keats, would later apply to Spenser's verbal pictures, a garland of "beauties" from Keats was interspersed with art analogies: "The little cabinet gems which follow may take their place in any collection. The first might have been cut out of a picture by Salvator. . . . The next we can fancy to have formed part of one of Claude's delicious skies. . . . The third reminds us of a sublime picture of The Deluge, by Poussin. . . . The fourth picture has all the voluptuous beauty of Titian."[4]

In the quarter-century following his death, only three small editions of Keats's poems (1840, and two in 1841) were called for.[5] His fame was kept modestly alive by surviving friends and critics like Hunt, who wrote of "The Eve of St. Agnes" in 1835, "Could all the pomp and graces of aristocracy, with Titian's and Raphael's aid to boot, go beyond the rich religion of this picture, with its 'twilight saints,' and its 'scutcheons 'blushing with the blood of queens'?"[6] Nor was Keats wholly forgotten in the exhibitions. As early as 1832–33, treatments of the classical myth of Endymion—no newcomer to British art, bent as it was upon imitating the Renaissance masters; even Mulready had tried his hand at the subject in 1808, when Keats was only thirteen years old—were exhibited with quotations from the poem. Similarly, beginning with the version Joseph

Severn, Keats's best friend in his last illness, showed at the Royal Academy in 1840, treatments of the story of Isabella and the pot of basil were customarily associated with Keats's poem rather than the Boccaccian original. (G. F. Watts had another *Isabella* in the same show, but this bore a motto from Boccaccio rather than Keats.) The next year, Richard Dadd showed at the British Institution his early fairy painting, *Ever Let the Fancy Roam,* from "To Fancy." And the year after that (1842) C. H. Lear showed at the Royal Academy *Porphyria Discovered in the Hall of Madeline,* from "The Eve of St. Agnes."

But the turning point of Keats's fortunes in the world of art came when Dante Gabriel Rossetti assembled the Pre-Raphaelite Brotherhood, who shared, among other sympathies, an admiration of Keats's poetry. (William Bell Scott, an associate member, probably had been the first to discover Keats. In 1832, he had written an undergraduate poem in his memory.) The appearance of Holman Hunt's *The Flight of Madeline and Porphyro* (pl. 333) at the Royal Academy in 1848—significantly, the year that saw the publication of Richard Monckton Milnes's biography of the poet, which laid the foundation for his wider fame—occasioned the first meeting of Rossetti and Hunt, who had discovered Keats's poetry by way of a secondhand copy he bought for sixpence. At the exhibition, Rossetti went up to Hunt, "loudly declaring," Hunt recalled, "that my picture . . . was the best in the collection. Probably the fact that the subject was taken from Keats made him the more unrestrained, for I think no one had ever before painted any subject from this still little-known poet."[7] Hunt was wrong, of course, as we have just seen.

The three Keats poems that were most often illustrated were *Endymion,* "Isabella," and "The Eve of St. Agnes," from each of which some twenty pictures are recorded. All three occurred in the Pre-Raphaelites' oeuvres: Millais's *Isabella,* also known as *Lorenzo and Isabella* (pl. 334), which was at the center of the Pre-Raphaelite furor when it broke in 1849; Arthur

334. John Everett Millais, *Lorenzo and Isabella* (RA 1849) (Walker Art Gallery, Liverpool). A scene derived from the first lines of Keats's "Isabella; or, The Pot of Basil":

Fair Isabel, poor simple Isabel!
  Lorenzo, a young palmer in Love's eye!
They could not in the self-same mansion dwell
  Without some stir of heart, some malady;
They could not sit at meals but feel how well
  It soothed each to be the other by.

Isabella's wealthy brothers cannot abide the obvious romantic attachment between her and Lorenzo, their business associate, seen here offering her half of a blood-red orange. The displeasure of one of the brothers is expressed by kicking her dog. Eventually they will murder Lorenzo and plant his head in the pot of basil half-hidden at the end of the table.

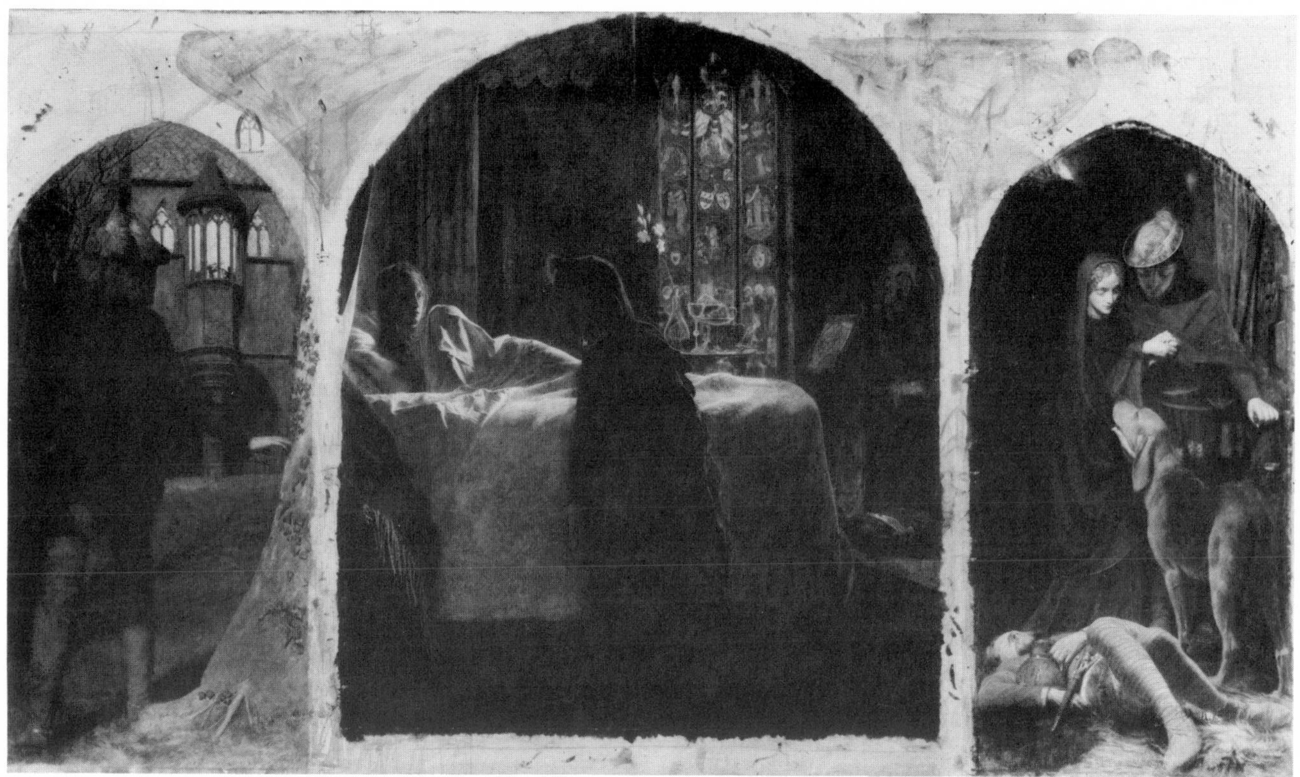

335. Arthur Hughes, *The Eve of St. Agnes* (RA 1856) (Tate Gallery, London). "The half-entranced, half-startled, face of the awaking Madeline is exquisite; but the lover's in both the centre and right-hand subjects very far from satisfactory. If, however, the reader knows the poem, he will be grateful for the picture" (Ruskin, *Academy Notes, Works,* 14: 70).

336. Daniel Maclise, *Madeline after Prayer* (RA 1868) (Walker Art Gallery, Liverpool). Although he never moved in the Pre-Raphaelite circle and had in any event established his reputation long before the movement got under way, Maclise's later style showed its influence.

Hughes's *The Eve of St. Agnes* (pl. 335); Millais's *The Eve of St. Agnes* (RA 1863), "the best abused picture of the season," according to the *Art Journal;*[8] Hunt's *Isabella and the Pot of Basil* (1868); and Hughes's *Endymion* (RA 1870).

After a comparative lull in the late sixties and the seventies, artists' interest in Keats revived, thanks in part to Moxon's sumptuous edition of the poems with six engravings from paintings by Edward Poynter. Between then and the end of the century, there were half a dozen new *Isabellas;* and "La Belle Dame Sans Merci," previously represented not at all, received some ten treatments. The most notable of these were Arthur Hughes's (Cosmopolitan Club 1863) and John William Waterhouse's (RA 1893)—a symptom of the increasing "Aesthetic" interest in the mysterious and baleful effect of the *femme fatale.*

HOOD

A popular humorist, editor, and poet in his day, Thomas Hood was represented in art mainly through at least fifteen paintings of work-worn seamstresses inspired by his "Song of the Shirt" (see Part One, above, chapter 5). But his other famous poem lamenting man's inhumanity to woman, "The Bridge of Sighs," was the subject of half a dozen paintings, and his ballad "The Dream of Eugene Aram," a favorite repertory number for platform and parlor elocutionists, was responsible for four more (1852–82). Bulwer-Lytton's novel on the same true murder story also was represented in a number of paintings. Altogether, some thirty recorded pictures came from Hood.

THE VICTORIAN ERA

TENNYSON

From 1850 to the end of the Victorian era, Alfred Tennyson, in collaboration with Shakespeare and Scott, largely supported the literary picture industry. In the decades of decline after 1870, when most authors' works gradually vanished from the exhibitions, paintings with subjects from Tennyson, or adorned with quotations from his poetry (only Shakespeare supplied more), were produced in quantity, year after year. The corpus of his poetry, still growing, offered a rich choice of subjects.[1] In the three hundred and more recorded paintings, about fifty poems were represented, some as many as forty times.

When Tennyson became laureate in 1850, he had been a published poet for two decades. As early as 1834, four years after the appearance of his first independent (and badly received) volume, *Poems, Chiefly Lyrical,* an obscure landscape artist named Henry F. Worsley showed at the British Institution a picture titled *The Water Mill, from Tennyson.* But it was not until after 1842, when the publication of a two-volume collection of his poetry laid the basis of his critical fame, that Tennyson began to be represented more or less regularly in the exhibitions. In 1843, James Eckford Lauder showed a *Mariana* at the Royal Scottish Academy; this did not bear an explicit reference to Tennyson's poem, though it is reasonable to assume that well-read spectators would have associated the two. In 1847, Richard Redgrave showed another *Mariana* at the British Institution, with a quotation from the poem. Tennyson's name seems to have first appeared in the Royal Academy's catalogue in 1849, when a painting "From Tennyson's ballad of the May Queen" was exhibited by Roger Fenton, an artist who was soon to abandon the studio for the darkroom as a pioneer photographer, part of whose experience in the new art was obtained in the Crimea. He would have been particularly well qualified to illustrate "The Charge of the Light Brigade," as other artists did from time to time.

Even before the turning point of 1842, Tennyson's name had been invoked in art criticism. The *Athenaeum* in its coverage of the 1841 season had said of Francis Danby's *The Enchanted Castle* that "it is a picture to which Tennyson might write a ballad—so rich an air of faëryism is diffused over it."[2] Conversely, his early reviewers repeatedly described his poetic art in terms of painting. One of the first, W. J. Fox, wrote of his 1830 volume, using a grotesque figure:

> He seems to obtain entrance into a mind as he would make his way into a landscape; he climbs the pineal gland as if it were a hill in the centre of the scene; looks around on all objects with their varieties of form, their movements, their shades of colour, and their mutual relations and influences; and forthwith produces as graphic a delineation in the one case as Wilson or Gainsborough could have done in the other, to the great enrichment of our gallery of intellectual scenery.[3]

In 1848, in the course of what was surely one of the most extravagant bouquets of praise tossed to any nineteenth-century poet, the "Ettrick Shepherd" (James Hogg) was inspired by Tennyson's "The Palace of Art" to declare, "You roam in restless wonder with this mighty painter, who combines the distinctive palpable power of individualizing and grouping possessed by Raphael, the grandeur of M. Angelo, and the richness of

337. William Maw Egley, *The Lady of Shalott* (British Institution 1858) (Sheffield City Art Galleries). "Flagrant Pre-Raphaelitism," said the *Athenaeum* (13 February), showing how widely the "disease" had spread in ten years. Critics who disliked the newly fashionable detailed style, whether or not the artist in question was associated with the Rossetti circle or avowed his sympathy with its ideals, found the label an ever handy form of castigation.

338. William Holman Hunt, *The Lady of Shalott* (1886) (City Art Gallery, Manchester). A sketch, based on one of Hunt's designs for the Moxon edition of Tennyson's poems (1857), for a painting that would be finished only in 1905. (It is now at the Wadsworth Athenaeum, Hartford, Connecticut.) Hunt wrote a long allegorical exegesis beginning "The parable [of the poem], as interpreted in this painting, illustrates the failure of a human Soul towards its accepted responsibility. The Lady typifying the Soul is bound to represent faithfully the workings of the high purpose of King Arthur's rule" (Bennett, *William Holman Hunt,* p. 57). Not all treatments of this familiar subject were so laden with systematic symbolism.

Titian's vehicle, together with the softness of Claude, through all the gradations and changes of nature's aspects."[4]

Despite this admiration of Tennyson's pictorialism, it was not until 1850 that artists generally began to realize the rich illustrative possibilities his poetry contained. By coincidence, two paintings bearing quotations, one from "The Gardener's Daughter" and the other from "The Mermaid," were hanging in the Royal Academy's summer exhibition at the moment *In Memoriam* was published on the first of June. Two others, from "Mariana" and "The Beggar Maid," had appeared at the British Institution in February. Thus, to the three major events of that wonderful year in the poet's life—the appearance of *In Memoriam,* which was to sell 60,000 copies within a few months and instantly establish Tennyson as the nation's favorite poet; his fortunate marriage; and his receiving, in November, the laureateship—may well be added a fourth, his decisive discovery by painters.

In Memoriam abounds with domestic scenes and images from nature, including landscapes, that would seem to have been ready-made to be transferred to Victorian canvases, but surprisingly few were actually chosen. The poem was represented in the exhibitions almost entirely by way of quotations appended to genre and anecdotal pictures dealing with death and remembrance in nonliterary contexts. Instead, during the 1850s the artists drew from the contents of the 1842 volumes, and their initial choice was to determine which of Tennyson's shorter poems the painters selected, and presumably the market demanded, as long as the Tennysonian vogue lasted. The two favorite poems, each represented by at least thirty-five recorded versions down to 1900, were "The Lady of Shalott" and "Mariana in the Moated Grange."

Between 1852 and 1859 alone, seven interpretations of "The Lady of Shalott" were painted, among the earliest being that by Tennyson's pas-

339. John W. Waterhouse, *The Lady of Shalott* (RA 1888) (Tate Gallery, London). One of Waterhouse's several treatments of the subject, and the biggest (60¼ × 78¾ inches). In 1894 the artist exhibited a painting of the scene previously depicted by Egley (pl. 337) and Hunt (pl. 338).

sionate admirer James Smetham, which was rejected by the Royal Academy and eventually found its way to a private collection in South Africa. Henry Darvall's was denounced as "a most injudicious choice of a subject, as provoking an unfavourable comparison between the present work and an exquisite version of the subject exhibited elsewhere last season,"[5] by which supposedly was meant Robert Scott Lauder's at the National Exhibition in Portland Place. William Maw Egley's version (pl. 337) was dismissed as "flagrant Pre-Raphaelitism"[6]—a risk of guilt-by-association every painter was to face after the publication the preceding summer of Moxon's Illustrated Edition, with its designs by, among other contributors, Rossetti, Millais, and Holman Hunt (chapter 11, above).* Arthur Hughes and Hunt (pl. 338) later painted oils of the same subject that can be jointly confronted in Manchester. Notwithstanding the reviewers' frequently expressed impatience and boredom, leading artists continued to paint those same trite scenes for forty years.

340. George Boughton, *The Road to Camelot* (RA 1898) (Walker Art Gallery, Liverpool). Most paintings from "The Lady of Shalott" portrayed the lady herself in the tower. This late example of Tennysonian art, however, shows what she saw in her mirror—"the red cloaks of market girls," "a troop of damsels glad," a "long-haired page in crimson clad," and "knights . . . riding two and two."

*In subsequent criticism of paintings from Tennyson, the Moxon illustrations were sometimes alluded to for purposes of comparison. For better or worse, because they appeared in an edition with which the poet was closely associated, they came to be regarded as "definitive" or at least (but erroneously) as author-approved. It would be interesting to know just how much effect they had on the pictures that came after.

The Lady of Shalott's close rival for the distinction of being the most banal Tennysonian subject in art was Mariana (in the Moated Grange). Probably the best-abused of the lot was one of the earliest, Millais's (RA 1851). The *Examiner*'s opinion was typical: "The figure is neither beautiful nor expressive of the sentiment: it is the weariness of the body, rather than of the soul, so well expressed in the lines, 'My life is dreary—He cometh not, she said.'"[7] The quotation itself quickly became a cliché in exhibition catalogues; it was attached to scores of portraits of—as a critic of one such picture put it in 1863—"that numerous class of young ladies found in all exhibitions, looking longingly into vacancy, and exclaiming in the words of Tennyson, after the approved fashion, 'He cometh not, she said!'"[8] Just as no radiantly expectant young woman in Victorian sentimental portraiture was without her line from *Romeo and Juliet,* so no disappointed one came on display without hers from Tennyson.

From the beginning of Tennyson's popularity among artists, he was valued for his poems for common life, the literary equivalent of genre paintings. It might almost be said that he was a genre painter *manqué.* As John Dixon Hunt has pointed out, numerous nonliterary Victorian paintings of incidents from domestic life might well be read as implicitly illustrating various passages in Tennyson's poems, particularly the group he called "English Idyls."[9] More pictures were specifically derived from these than from any other category except the Arthurian *Idylls.*

341. John A. Vinter, *The Miller's Daughter* (RA 1859) (Wolverhampton Art Gallery). Those who wished to do so were free to interpret this rural courtship scene as an illustration of Tennyson's poem of the same name; at least, in no detail did it conflict with the story (an aging man, the orphaned son of a squire, recalls his wooing of a girl from a lower social class). The lover's dejection may have sprung from his mother's remark that he "might have looked a little higher." In any case, the painting is an early genre work by an artist who was to exhibit at the Royal Academy for more than fifty years.

Among these studies of domestic life, two were favored above all others after 1850: "Dora" and "The Gardener's Daughter." "Dora," painted at least fifteen times between 1852 and 1885, was valued both for its adaptability to sentimental portraiture, as in William McTaggart's Royal Scottish Academy diploma picture (1868) of a mother crowning her little boy with a floral wreath, described in lines 78–82 of the poem, and for its pathetic Wordsworth-type incident. The three Dora paintings exhibited at the Royal Academy in a single year (1863) portrayed virtually the same moment in the poem.

As usual, a certain number of Dora pictures were female portraits, with no reference to Tennyson's poem apart from the exploitation of its title. Most of the pictures exhibited as "The Gardener's Daughter" must have been of the same kind. The full title of Tennyson's poem was "The Gardener's Daughter, or The Pictures," and its framing subject was two pictures, each painted by one of two artist friends who had been charmed by the lovely heroine. Hence the exhibited portraits of Rose, the gardener's daughter, may nominally have been realizations of the portraits in the poem, or at least of the model as first seen, standing at the door of her father's cottage, plucking roses from the arbor. But few of the thirty-odd recorded paintings called *The Gardener's Daughter* bore a credit line to Tennyson. One explanation might be that his poem was so well known that a picture bearing its title would automatically recall its story. Another is that many of the unattributed examples did not, in fact, have an intended reference to Tennyson, belonging instead to the large category of popular art that lay parallel to poetry of the kind exemplified by the English idyls. When he chose titles like "The Gardener's Daughter" and "The Miller's Daughter," Tennyson was not so much innovating as emulating—copying the current practice of run-of-the-mine Victorian genre illustrators. Rustic "daughters" of various sorts were well established as stock figures in sentimental portraiture by the time Tennyson came to write about them.

Some twenty pictures bore the title of his poem "The Miller's Daughter" (1832, much revised 1842), but few if any alluded explicitly to the poem itself. "Monk" Lewis, the celebrated writer of horror novels, wrote a ballad "The Miller's Daughter," a melancholy tale of a girl who drowned herself for love, which retained its popularity on the music racks in Victorian drawing rooms. Plays with that title were performed in 1804 and 1818. Tennyson's title was already generic when he chose it, and how many of the miller's daughter pictures actually came from his poem cannot be determined; most, as a matter of fact, were exhibited without specific reference to Tennyson. Insofar as they were anything more than sentimental portraits, which story line did they portray—Lewis's of the suicidal girl in the millstream or Tennyson's happier one? The poet's early critic, John Wilson Croker, wrote: "Miller's daughters, poor things, have been so generally betrayed by their sweethearts, that it is refreshing to find that Mr. Tennyson has united himself to *his* miller's daughter in lawful wedlock."[10] Tennyson's poem helped sustain the subject's—or at least the title's—popularity down to the end of the century. At the exhibition of the Society of British Artists as late as 1891, no fewer than four miller's daughters were on display.

342. George Jones, *Lady Godiva Preparing to Ride Through Coventry* (RA 1833) (Tate Gallery, London). This was one of the 221 works Jones exhibited at the Royal Academy over a span of sixty-seven years. Tennyson did not attend the exhibition that year, but, apart from the fact that in his poem, published in 1842, Lady Godiva undresses in "her inmost bower" before emerging to mount "her palfrey trapt / In purple blazoned with armorial gold," the painting may be regarded as a pre-illustration of the poem.

Lady Godiva, too, was a subject already known in art before Tennyson published his poetic version of the legend in 1842. In 1833 and 1836, George Jones had shown his companion pieces, *Lady Godiva Preparing to Ride through Coventry* (pl. 342) and *Lady Godiva's Return,* at the Royal Academy. Frederick Pickering's *Peeping Tom* was hung there, with a prose gloss, in 1842, just as the first reviews of Tennyson's collection were appearing. In 1846, the first Godiva picture to bear a quotation from the poem was presented to the public at the British Institution. It was doubtless merely an accident, with no direct bearing on Tennyson's poem, that in the same year, and again in 1848, a play called *Lady Godiva and Peeping Tom of Coventry* was seen in London, an obvious attempt to capitalize on the current vogue of *tableaux vivants,* which featured immobile groups of actors and actresses depicting famous paintings. The tight fleshings they wore came as close to nudity as the Victorian stage allowed.* And this, of course, remained the attraction of the Godiva theme. "Almost any semi-nude female study," commented the *Art Journal* when it reviewed A. J. Woolmer's canvas of 1856, "may be turned into a Godiva,"[11] especially, one might add, if a horse were included. (Godiva was shown in various stages of nudity. In Jones's picture of her preparing for her ride, she was letting her hair down and *about* to doff her filmy attire—the sort of titillating pose with which Victorian artists often evaded the conventions. Edmund Blair Leighton's fully clothed Godiva at the Royal Academy in 1892 would seem to have been rather pointless.) Few of the pictures of the Coventry heroine after the 1850s referred explicitly to Tennyson's poem, perhaps because his revered status discouraged associating him with what a critic of G. F. Watts's picture (RA 1900) called "the succession of commonplace nudities for which the story has afforded an excuse."[12]

Another poem in the 1842 collection made a similarly oblique contribution to the mid-Victorian fund of art subjects. The title of "The May Queen," lastingly notorious for its lines "You must wake and call me early, call me early, mother dear; . . . For I'm to be Queen o' the May, mother, I'm to be Queen o' the May," was given to some fifteen paintings. The first (1849) quoted from the poem, as did two or three others. But most pictures bearing the title seem not to have depicted the pathetic story told

*The leading producer of *tableaux vivants* at that time was one Madame Warton, whose Christmas program for 1847 was advertised as featuring a live-actress portrayal of Lady Godiva, "from Edwin Landseer R.A.'s forthcoming picture." This bit of art-world news was no casual show-business invention: Landseer was indeed working on a Godiva painting, but, learning a year or two later that several other pictures of the same subject were under way, he put his own aside (Oliver Beckett, *J. F. Herring & Sons* [London, 1981], p. 57). The picture, *Lady Godiva at Prayer* (which may or may not have been the pose in which Madame Warton's actress was seen), eventually was finished and found its way to the Academy exhibition of 1866.

343. Edward Burne-Jones, *King Cophetua and the Beggar Maid* (Grosvenor Gallery 1884) (Tate Gallery, London). Of the lady in this second version of the subject by Burne-Jones (the first was painted in 1862), the *Saturday Review* said (3 May), "[She] does not in any way answer to Tennyson's heroine." True: she was drawn from the beggar maid in the old ballad printed in Bishop Percy's collection rather than from Tennyson's poem, as the first had been. But most of the people who admired the picture at the Grosvenor Gallery would have seen it as an illustration of Tennyson rather than of an old ballad.

by the dying girl. Instead, they portrayed the humor and sentiment of the rural May Day celebration, as did Mrs. E. M. Ward's picture of the May Queen dressing near her window, her mother in attendance (RA 1856), and Eyre Crowe's "party of rough fellows, comprising one dressed as a clown, who lead an unlovely girl in a common cart" (RA 1879).[13] Tennyson's place in the ten or so treatments of King Cophetua and the beggar maid is difficult to determine. His poem "The Beggar Maid" (1842) was suggested, he said, by *Romeo and Juliet:* "Young Abraham Cupid, he that shot so true, / When King Cophetua loved the beggar-maid" (2.1.13–14), and the ballad Shakespeare alludes to is found in Percy's *Reliques of Ancient English Poetry.* Paintings of the subject therefore might have come from any of these three sources, or combined elements from them. For his version, Maclise worked independently, as he wrote in a letter in 1868: "The picture I have on my easel is one I have long wished to paint—'King Cophetua—Cophueta [*sic*]—and the Beggar Maid'—see Old Ballad and Tennyson; but I choose to invent the scene, and figure to myself a young king, with a few retainers grouped about him, under a tree, and *he,* seeing *her* pass by, loves her—weds her (as I hope)."[14] When the painting was exhibited the next year, it nevertheless bore the quotation from *Romeo and Juliet.* Burne-Jones produced two King Cophetuas.[15] The first (1862) illustrated Tennyson's poem, the second (pl. 343)—the artist's best-known work, which delighted Puvis de Chavannes and Gustave Moreau when it was hung at the Exposition Universelle in Paris in 1889—the Percy ballad.

One poem in the 1842 collection had strong artistic rather than literary resonances. The Ovidian judgment of Paris theme, a familiar one in Renaissance art, was chosen from time to time by British painters aspiring to the high style; in 1826, for example, William Etty exhibited his version (pl. 134) at the Royal Academy. Six years later, Tennyson published his poetic treatment under the title of "Oenone." Reprinted, much improved, in the 1842 collection, the poem's remembrance of artistic treatments of the judgment of Paris was immediately recognized. Leigh Hunt wrote that "Oenone lamenting the infidelity of Paris is as beautiful and graceful as if it had been painted by one of the Italian masters."[16] For the rest of the century, Tennyson's poem invited painters to revert to the classic theme under the auspices of English literature. A dozen paintings were titled simply *Oenone.* A few doubtless depicted the tableau of the judgment itself, but most seem to have been more or less sensuous portraits or figure studies of the wronged woman, against a lush background suggestive of Spenser and Keats. G. F. Watts painted the subject on three separate occasions late in the century (pl. 166).

Of the remaining poems in the 1842 collection, two, "The Talking Oak" and "The Lady Clare," inspired half a dozen pictures each; their Tennysonian origin is definite except insofar as one or two "Lady Clare" paintings may have referred to the character of the same name in Scott's *Marmion.* The indebtedness to Tennyson's poem of several pictures exhibited as "A Dream of Fair Women," two of them by Edward Armitage (RA 1872, 1874), may have extended no further than the title.

After 1850, Tennyson published hundreds of short and medium-length poems, only two of which, *Maud* (1855) and "Enoch Arden" (1864), were represented by more than one or two pictures; each inspired half a dozen. With only one or two exceptions, paintings from *Maud* evaded the story line (a frustrated lover driven to madness and finding his mental if not moral salvation in the Crimean War) and seized instead on the lyric "Come into the garden, Maud." One Enoch Arden painting, by William McTaggart (RA 1867), used the opening scene of the poem as a pretext for portraying three children building a sand castle on the beach.

In 1859, the first four *Idylls of the King* (*Enid, Vivien, Elaine,* and *Guinevere*) were published. Although, as we have seen, pictures from Tennyson were by no means lacking in the 1850s, it was with the appearance of the *Idylls* that he began to be a truly dominating presence in the exhibition rooms. Artists not previously attracted to Tennyson now discovered him; Swinburne later remembered how, when the first four poems appeared, "one of the greatest painters now [1886] living pointed out to me, with a brief word of rapturous admiration, the wonderful breadth of beauty and the perfect force of truth in a single verse of 'Elaine'—'And white sails flying on the yellow sea.'"[17]

Although Tennyson unquestionably was responsible for the wide popularity of the Arthurian stories in art, he was not the first to attract painters to them. As has been seen in chapter 8, Arthurian material was used in Dyce's allegorical frescoes in the Houses of Parliament beginning about 1849, and, more important, the Pre-Raphaelites, enchanted by Malory, had already painted a number of pictures from him, including the evanescent Oxford Debating Union frescoes (1857). (It is perhaps insufficiently appreciated how much Tennyson's decision to take up the matter of Arthur—a project he had contemplated early in his career and then dropped—may have been due to these developments in the 1850s.) The effect of the *Idylls* was to provide artists with an alternative source to Malory, whose developing popularity, far from being diminished, was in fact enhanced by that of Tennyson's narratives.

In the decade 1860–69 alone, fifty or sixty paintings of Arthurian subjects were presented to the public, eight of them—so instantaneous was the success of the first *Idylls*—in the year immediately following the book's publication, and another eight, five of which were at the Royal Academy, the next year (1861). All but ten or so were from Tennyson, most of them from the *Idylls* but a number from his earlier Arthurian poems, which had not hitherto been drawn upon: "The Morte d'Arthur" and "Sir Galahad," both first published in 1842. Among these paintings were Arthur Hughes's *The Knight of the Sun* (1860), and Watts's *Sir Galahad* (or *Sir Galahael,* as it was first called), of which he painted two versions in a single year (1862).*

The harvest of subjects from the first *Idylls* took two forms. One consisted of portraits of Enid and Elaine, the two "sympathetic" heroines among the four from whom the poems took their names. More precisely, it consisted of attaching the names to the usual female heads or figures, with no apparent effort to adhere to Tennyson's intent. "They are a good deal alike, and all tawdry," said a reviewer confronted by all four heroines painted by one artist, at the Society of British Artists show in 1862.[18] The remaining fast-multiplying pictures from the first *Idylls* were scenes from *Elaine,* either showing the ill-fated maiden tracing Sir Lancelot's history on the shield—there were competing versions in 1861, one at the Royal Academy, the other at the National Exhibition in Portland Place—or following her down the river to Camelot.[19] Repetition begot repletion, but still they came, down to the end of the century. No doubt there were more portrayals of Elaine going down the river than are evident in the record, because a number of pictures simply bearing her name may, in

*Watts, however, later asserted that at the time he painted the picture he had not read Tennyson's poem. When it was reshown at the Grosvenor Gallery in 1882, he "stated that he would like his picture to be illustrated by a rather different knight, Chaucer's young Squire from the prologue to the *Canterbury Tales*" (Maas, *Victorian Painters,* p. 29). But there is no question that the painting was *exhibited* as "Sir Galahad."

344. Sir John Gilbert, *Sir Launcelot du Lake* (RA 1887) (Guildhall Art Gallery, London). Like Burne-Jones's *Cophetua,* this representation of a subject the Victorians commonly associated with Tennyson was actually derived from a Percy ballad. "Such a picture," said the *Athenaeum* (21 May), "is an anachronism. . . . The picture would serve for Sir John's idea of Don Quixote quite as well as of Sir Lancelot."

fact, have been further versions of the scene. And to this total, whatever it may have been, must be added all the paintings of "The Lady of Shalott"; for though Tennyson derived that figure from an Italian source (he did not then [1832] know Malory's lily maid of Astolat), their story was the same. The distinguishing feature of some Lady of Shalott paintings is her mirror and "magic web," which are not in Malory but are a Tennysonian invention.

Although *Idylls of the King* expanded with successive batches of new books in 1870, 1872, and 1885, none of the poems Tennyson added to make up the final twelve proved as attractive to artists as the first four. Only one or two paintings were taken from *Pelleas and Ettarre* (1870) and seemingly none at all from *Balin and Balan* (1885). In this respect, the old order did not change, giving place to new; the tried-and-true subjects,

345. Arthur Hughes, *Sir Galahad: The Quest of the Holy Grail* (RA 1870) (Walker Art Gallery, Liverpool). This picture was exhibited five months after the publication of Tennyson's "The Holy Grail" (one of the *Idylls of the King*) late in 1869. The trio of censer-swinging angels, however, relates it to the poet's earlier "Sir Galahad" (1842).

346. Sophia Anderson, *Elaine* (RA 1870) (Walker Art Gallery, Liverpool). The title of the picture relates it more closely to Tennyson's "Elaine" (one of the *Idylls of the King,* published in 1859) than to "The Lady of Shalott," though Elaine was, in fact, "the lily maid of Astolat." The Paris-born artist spent some time in America as a portrait painter (1848–54); she began to exhibit at the Royal Academy soon after taking up residence in England in the latter year. This painting made such a favorable impression at the Academy in 1870 that it was immediately bought by the Walker Art Gallery—one of the very few literary pictures that went directly from exhibition to public gallery.

whose popularity was achieved in the 1860s, continued to dominate the selection. To those from *Elaine* were added Lancelot and Guinevere in their more chaste moments (the less chaste were taboo), Arthur dreaming in Avilion, Sir Galahad questing for the Holy Grail, and Tristram and Iseult, though toward the end of the century this last subject was no longer the virtual monopoly of Malory and Tennyson. A few Tristram and Iseult pictures were derived from Matthew Arnold and William Morris instead.

The most compelling reason why *Idylls of the King* was so popular with painters was Tennyson's successful "Victorianizing" of the *Morte Darthur.* Bringing Malory's characters and incidents into harmony with contemporary taste and morality, he transformed them into perfect subjects for drawing-room paintings, relieved of all the rude, barbarous strength they had in their original medieval literary setting. At the same time, the Arthurian materials gave Tennyson unlimited opportunity to do what he did best. The very suggestion of the word *idyll,* from the diminutive of the Greek word for "form," was pictorial, and pictorialism was Tennyson's forte, just as it had been Spenser's, Thomson's, and Keats's. On his verbal canvases, an array of colorfully costumed and suitably accoutered knights and ladies, described in careful Pre-Raphaelite detail, moved against backgrounds of equally colorful and detailed landscapes and interiors.[20] From their inception, the *Idylls of the King* demanded to be illustrated in paint, in all their heroism, pathos, idealism, and picturesqueness.

It was unfortunate that a term which critics repeatedly used to describe Tennyson's pictorial effects was "cabinet pictures," because this encouraged artists to regard the *Idylls* exclusively as a series of detached vignettes. (No matter that occasionally these swelled to heroic size, as did Edwin Abbey's *The Quest of the Holy Grail* series of five paintings [1895], each of which was designed to hang twelve or fourteen feet from the ground.) Like contemporary reviews of the poems, they did scant justice to the subtlety and complexity of Tennyson's intention. Concentrating as they did on individual characters at specific moments, the vignettes, detached from the broad tapestry, were unrelated to the grand scheme of the poem as an elaborately conceived and executed moral allegory. Critics and artists alike read the *Idylls* with oversimplifying eyes, treating characters and isolated tableaux and episodes as moral examples without regard for their function in the total design, an unavoidable reductiveness found also in art taken from another elaborate allegory, *The Faerie Queene*. Painters, in brief, were content to portray the surface flavor of what, in a famous phrase, Carlyle described to Emerson as superlative lollipops.[21] They spared their contemporaries the terrible truths so artfully concealed in the *Idylls*, truths that only recent criticism has fully recognized. Seldom does any intimation of such evil appear in the paintings from *Idylls of the King*. Probably the one major Arthurian picture that forthrightly conveys such an impression is Burne-Jones's *The Beguiling of Merlin* (pl. 88). But, significantly, its connection with either Tennyson or Malory is negligible, despite its Arthurian subject; it was based instead on a French medieval romance, translated in a volume of the *Early English Text Society*.

Given the sheer length of the *Idylls* and the number of paintings derived from them, it is remarkable how narrow was the range of subjects from which artists drew. Tennyson was highly selective to begin with, in his own quarrying of Malory, but the painters were even more so. Within the twelve narrative books, there were hundreds of potential vignettes, but the number they actually chose did not exceed a dozen or two.

So with Tennyson's poems at large. Although some fifty were represented in the galleries at one time or another, many of the poems that one would think would have been painted over and over were never, in fact, painted more than once or twice. The voluptuous classicism of "The Lotos Eaters" seems to have inspired only a handful of paintings. Neither the period flavor of *The Princess*, with its outdoor scenes from contemporary life, nor its intercalated lyrics such as "Tears, idle tears" and "Now sleeps the crimson petal, now the white," found their way into more than two or three paintings. The early "Palace of Art," itself a poetized saunter through an art gallery, was the subject of a single painting, more than sixty years after the poem appeared. There seems to be no record of any painting of "Ulysses" or "Tithonus" (both in the 1842 collection from which artists drew so many other poems) despite the profound philosophical statement each contains.

Notwithstanding such inexplicable omissions, Tennyson's poetry served Victorian painters well if not always wisely. Too often it supplied fresh impetus to the boudoir school of contemporary art: typically, "O swallow, flying from the golden woods" inspired Millais to paint what was described as "a modern idyl [showing] a young lady in a blue bodice, leaning her elbow upon a chair, standing at a window, and looking at a swallow which is without."[22] But such a cliché subject could be forgiven even an artist as admired as Millais had by then (1865) become; as the *Examiner* remarked, "though it is a thought better to be expressed in verse than in a richly-coloured picture . . . it is . . . English work upon an English theme."[23]

It is natural to think of Tennyson's poems as a long series of Victorian paintings, and one wonders to what extent his poetic imagination operated in terms of pictures already seen. He sometimes appears to have read popular taste through the mirror of the annual exhibitions and the engravings of the pictures shown there. Leigh Hunt suggested as much, as early as 1842. Tennyson's heroines, he wrote, "remind us too much of the fine young ladies in souvenirs and beauty-books, with rapturous eyes, dark locks and tresses, and all that. . . ."[24] It is perhaps not unfair to imagine a reciprocal arrangement between Tennyson and contemporary painters, whereby each party supplied the other with ready-made subjects. If innumerable female portraits and genre scenes were casually (but shrewdly) associated with Tennyson when they were exhibited, it is likely that many of the poems from which they were derived could have been traced in turn to female portraits and genre scenes already painted—the common coin of artistic production, widely familiar through both cabinet pictures and engravings.

THE BROWNINGS

Alexander Pope excepted, no English poet, of his own time or any other, had more varied connections with art than did Robert Browning.[1] Several of his greatest dramatic monologues are concerned with the practice, theory, and ideals of the painter's art. The dramatic monologue itself, which was his most characteristic poetic form and which he brought to perfection, may well have owed more than a little to the popularity of narrative paintings, in that they both portrayed single significant and revealing, if not necessarily crucial, moments in the lives of men and women. From childhood to old age he was a tireless gallerygoer, beginning with visits to the Dulwich Gallery across the fields from his home in Camberwell. At a time when his strongly individual genius was recognized by only a few, he replaced Scott and Byron in the admiration of Dante Gabriel Rossetti. Yet, in contrast to the hundreds of paintings inspired by Tennyson, Browning was invoked by a mere handful, even after he had belatedly achieved substantial popularity and his readers, one would think, had realized how many subjects in his colorful and dramatic poety cried out for pictorial treatment. Only a dozen or so of his poems were ever represented at exhibitions, and none by more than a few paintings apiece.

A brighter destiny might have been anticipated from the fact that despite its notorious unintelligibility, Browning's first long poem, *Paracelsus* (1835), was the subject of two paintings within five years of its publication, one by David Scott, which he sold to the Scottish Art Union (1839), the other by the popular genre painter Richard Redgrave, exhibited at the Royal Academy the following year.

The next inclusion of a Browning poem in an exhibition of art came about under unusual circumstances.[2] Near the end of 1841, Browning's friend John Forster "pressed me," he wrote in a letter, "into committing verse on the instant, not the minute" to accompany Daniel Maclise's "divine Venetian work," titled *A Serenade,* to the British Institution's next show. Browning obliged "on the instant" in Forster's rooms, without seeing the painting, and the resulting seven lines were duly printed in the catalogue:

I send my heart up to thee, all my heart
   In this my singing.
For the stars help me, and the sea bears part;
   The very night is clinging
Closer to Venice' streets to leave one space
   Above me, whence thy face
May light my joyous heart to thee its dwelling-place.

347. Dante Gabriel Rossetti, *"Hist! said Kate the Queen"* (1851) (Eton College). From Pippa's song in "Pippa Passes," part two:

"Hist!"—said Kate the Queen;
But "Oh!" cried the maiden, binding her tresses,
"'Tis only a page that carols unseen,
Crumbling your hounds their messes!"

A color sketch for an ambitious painting Rossetti never completed. A Leeds millionaire bought the sketch when it was still in Rossetti's studio.

"And now tell me," Browning asked, "is this below the average of Catalogue original poetry?" Forty years later, recounting the episode to F. J. Furnivall, Browning said, "When I did see it [the picture], I thought the Serenade too jolly somewhat for the notion I got from Forster—and I took up the subject in my own way" to the tune of 224 more lines, working up a self-contained and wholly original story. The poem, "In a Gondola," was published in its entirety in Browning's next collection of verse, *Dramatic Lyrics* (November 1842). Meanwhile, in May of that year, Browning had reversed the process by writing two poems for as yet nonexistent pictures. Willie Macready, the tragedian's oldest son who liked to draw, was ill with a bad cough, and Browning composed "The Cardinal and the Dog" and "The Pied Piper of Hamelin" for him to illustrate. The drawings are now in the Browning Collection at Baylor University; the poems were published alongside "In a Gondola" in *Dramatic Lyrics.*[3] "The Pied Piper" was probably illustrated more often than any other of Browning's poems; some eight versions are recorded (pl. 85).

Rossetti's enthusiasm for Browning was expressed chiefly in a scene from "Pippa Passes," *"Hist! said Kate the Queen"*. The painting was never finished and subsequently was cut up, but the color sketch, which Rossetti had first sold to his aunt Charlotte, was acquired by his early patron, a Leeds millionaire, and eventually went to Eton College (pl. 347). Another Pre-Raphaelite, Arthur Hughes, exhibited his *The King's Orchard* (RA 1859) with a quotation from "Pippa Passes."

There were a few other pictures from that poem and from "Childe Roland to the Dark Tower Came," as well as one or two from such poems as "Love Among the Ruins,"* "Saul," "Andrea del Sarto," "Caliban upon Setebos," and "A Toccata of Galuppi's"; but almost none are traced, nor were they often described in the press when exhibited. A rare exception is

*An important picture by Burne-Jones bears this title, and its subject—lovers meeting among the ruins of an ancient city—certainly is that of Browning's poem. But Burne-Jones is said to have derived it from one of the miniatures he painted for a manuscript of the *Rubáiyat of Omar Khayyám* that William Morris illuminated. The original gouache, exhibited at the New Gallery in 1873, had a rather unusual fate. Twenty years later, an employee of a French firm that was about to photograph the picture, unable to read the English inscription on the back that identified it as a watercolor, flooded it with egg white as he would have done with an oil painting. The result, as one of the artist's biographers observes, was disastrous (Malcolm Bell, *Edward Burne-Jones: A Record and Review,* 4th ed. [London, 1898], p. 50). Burne-Jones painted a replica in oil, which was exhibited at the New Gallery in 1894.

Hughes's *The Guarded Bower,* from "Count Gismond" (RA 1866), now at Bristol.

The half-dozen or so pictures from poems by Elizabeth Barrett Browning had a somewhat better survival rate. Four were painted from *Aurora Leigh,* including Hughes's *The Tryst* (pl. 170), whose subject, Aurora Leigh's dismissal of Romney, was identified only in 1964.[4] The wealthy patroness who commissioned the painting, a Miss Heaton (one of Ruskin's correspondents), was dissatisfied with it, but both Ruskin and Rossetti encouraged her to order another from Mrs. Browning's works. Hughes's subject this time was from her *Poems Before Congress*: *"That Was a Piedmontese"* (pl. 348).

BULWER-LYTTON

In the course of their travels in search of pictorial subjects, the artists Clive Newcome and J. J. Ridley, in Thackeray's novel *The Newcomes,* visit Pompeii.

> The young man [Clive] had read Sir Bulwer-Lytton's delightful story, which has become the history of Pompeii, before they came thither, and Pliny's description, *apud* the "Guide-Book." Admiring the wonderful ingenuity with which the English writer has illustrated the place by his text, as if the houses were so many pictures to which he had appended a story, Clive, the wag, who was always indulging his vein for caricature, was proposing that they should take the same place, names, people, and make a burlesque story: "What would be a better figure," says he, "than Pliny's mother, whom the historian describes as exceedingly corpulent, and walking away from the catastrophe holding cushions behind her, to shield her plump person from the cinders! Yes, old Mrs. Pliny shall be my heroine!" says Clive. A picture of her on a dark grey paper, and touched up with red at the extremities, exists in Clive's album to the present day. (Chap. 39)

Thackeray's biographers may be left to decide just how this sideswipe at Bulwer-Lytton fits in with his inveterate dislike of the man and his overwritten but popular novels. Clive and his friend, unlike other artists of the day, clearly had no high opinion of the famous catastrophe, with which Bulwer (as he then was) had become identified following the publication of *The Last Days of Pompeii* in 1834, as a subject for painting. Or perhaps, as is suggested by Clive's selection of the corpulent Mrs. Pliny as his heroine, they merely rejected Bulwer-Lytton's romantic treatment of the Pompeii theme.

In any case, the destruction of Pompeii and Herculaneum in 79 A.D. had become a well-established artistic subject long before Bulwer-Lytton used it as the setting for a romantic tale.[1] In the late eighteenth century, the Neapolitan painter Pierre-Jacques Volaire had made a veritable career of portraying the extinction of Pompeii; his numerous illustrations of the event still are scattered in galleries throughout Europe. In 1822, John Martin displayed at the Egyptian Hall his huge *Destruction of Pompeii and Herculaneum,* painted, as his "descriptive catalogue" boasted, after he had "sedulously consulted every source of information within his reach," including Mrs. Pliny's husband, Strabo, Diodorus Siculus, and the English archaeologist Sir William Gell.[2] It is rather surprising that although they were friends, and in his *England and the English,* published the year before *The Last Days of Pompeii* appeared, he had praised Martin as "the greatest, the most lofty, the most permanent, the most original genius of his age,"[3] Bulwer did not contrive an opportunity to mention him in the novel.

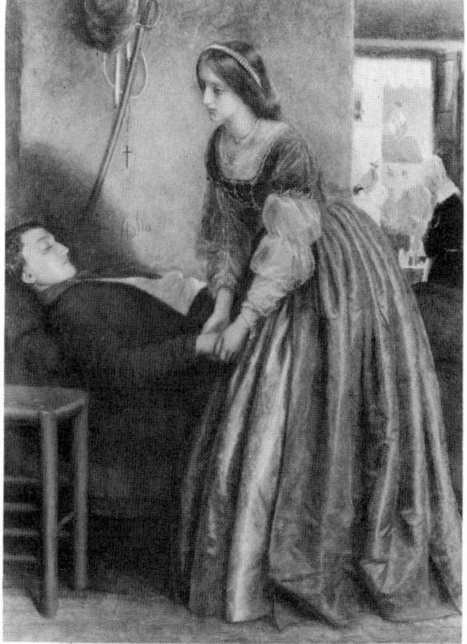

348. Arthur Hughes, *"That Was a Piedmontese"* (1862) (Tate Gallery, London). A scene from Elizabeth Barrett Browning's poem "A Court Lady" (*Poems Before Congress,* 1860): a "lady of Milan" pauses before a soldier wounded in the struggle for Italian independence. "Back he fell while she spoke. She rose to her feet with a spring— / 'That was a Piedmontese! and this is the Court of the King!'"

349. Edward J. Poynter, *Faithful unto Death* (RA 1865) (Walker Art Gallery, Liverpool). Like some other paintings by the Victorian classicists, Poynter's realization of a scene in Bulwer's *The Last Days of Pompeii* was widely reproduced in prints and textbooks, in this case to illustrate the ideal of stoic devotion to duty.

Instead, it has been shown that he derived some aspects of his Pompeiian setting from a then famous painting by the Russian artist Karl Bryullov, which was exhibited across the Continent in 1833–34.

The subject had entered literature with Madame de Staël's *Corinne* (1805), and it had affinities with the so-called school of catastrophe in contemporary English literature—the long, turgid poems by Henry H. Milman (*The Fall of Jerusalem,* 1820; *Belshazzar,* 1822), Edwin Atherstone (*The Last Days of Herculaneum,* 1821; *The Fall of Nineveh,* 1828–30), and James Montgomery (*The World Before the Flood* in ten cantos, 1813).[4] As Laurence Goldstein has shown, the subject of Pompeii had a dual symbolism: the idea of death (the end of the world, as far as the Pompeiians were concerned) and—unsettling to the pious, perhaps guilt-ridden Victorians—the notion of a materialistic, high-living society that virtually begged to be destroyed by an angry God, the Roman equivalent of Sodom, Gomorrah, and Babylon.[5]*

Thus the destruction of Pompeii had acquired a number of strong literary and artistic resonances by the time that Bulwer "humanized" the catastrophe by introducing a romantic plot in the midst of the Vesuvian ash and lava storm: the story of the young lovers Glaucus and Ione and the sacrifice of the blind slave girl Nydia, who, though hopelessly in love with Glaucus, leads the couple to safety and then commits suicide. The first Pompeii painting to be shown at the Royal Academy after the appearance of the novel was Joseph Severn's *The Witches' Cavern: Glaucus and Ione* (1840). In the next sixty years, during which the novel continued to be reprinted and read as a modern classic, well over thirty-five Pompeii paintings are recorded. (A few were exhibited without reference to Bulwer-Lytton, but every literate art lover could be relied upon to make the connection.) Of these, the best-known was Edward Poynter's *Faithful Unto Death* (pl. 349), suggested by the heroic sentry in the novel who was commemorated in a popular recitation piece by one Joseph Malins:

> What of the faithful sentinel?
> Undaunted still is he!
> There, lava pours, 'midst thunderous roars,
> Into the boiling sea;
> Here, clouds of burning ashes fall,
> And all in terror flee—
> Save one, whose grave doth round him rise;
> He stands unmoved; and standing—dies![6]

A rival picture at the 1865 Royal Academy was Paul Falconer Poole's *A Suburb of the Roman City of Pompeii, During the Eruption of 79 A.D.* Five years earlier, Poole had exhibited another scene from the novel, which the *Blackwood's* critic described in all too suitable language:

> The boat is speeding its swift escape from the devastated city, Glaucus and Ione recline in the soft dalliance of gentlest love, and the blind girl Nydia awakes her harp to music. A dream-like spell has softened all to harmony. It is a scene of poetic longing, or of languour, as of passion spent. The moon dances in silver footfalls upon the midnight sea; the harp-strings sound as the ripples play in the boat's gentle wake, while the soft joy of sadness floats the exiles from their ruined homes.[7]

But, the *Literary Gazette* had asked,

> What will Sir E. Bulwer-Lytton say . . . ? Just this, "They are none of mine." Did a more love-sea-sickened pair ever seek a flight o'er the ocean than these two lovers? They are painfully sentimental in their woe, and gentle Luna is

*Late in the Victorian era, when neo-academic artists were reviving Roman subjects to considerable acclaim, Alma-Tadema was rebuked for his suppression of this basic aspect of the Pompeii theme in a painting at the Royal Academy in 1896. Said the *Fortnightly Review* (n.s. 59: 968–69): ". . . A bevy of fair modern girls lie about, clad in not very archaeological costume. Girls like these, with these innocent naive faces, could not have existed in such a hot-bed of lust as Pompeii must have been. Painters who want to realise Roman women of the decadence should read Mr. Swinburne's 'Faustine' first."

> contributing everything that is bilious to their retching countenances. Mr. Poole is perfectly at home in plague-stricken horrors, and he then depicts with painful reality physiognomical suffering; but Glaucus and his lady-love were never intended to be sick, at least at sea, and even if they were, it was not the period for the artist to paint them.[8]

It seems likely that Poole, responding to this astringent criticism, omitted from the 1865 painting any narrative element, whether of seasick lovers or any other individual characters. His reviewers on this occasion compared the picture with his celebrated *Solomon Eagle Exhorting the People to Repentance* (pl. 286) during the indigenous English catastrophe of the plague, and said nothing about a story line.

If Bulwer-Lytton failed to mention Martin's painting in his novel, Martin in turn seems not to have alluded to the novel in his art. Instead, he drew upon Bulwer-Lytton's poem *King Arthur* (1848) for his painting of *Arthur and Aegle in the Happy Valley* (pl. 350), shown at the Royal Academy the next year. The poem, an ill-advised attempt to write the Arthurian epic Milton had once envisaged but failed to achieve, improbably brought the captive Arthur to a Shangri-La paradise founded by the Etruscans, where he falls in love with the queen. But, as the painting shows, the craggy Happy Valley is not exempt from time and catastrophe, and the lovers are brought face to face with mortality in the midst of one more depressingly sublime Martinesque landscape.

A total of about seventy-five paintings from Bulwer-Lytton is recorded. A dozen works in addition to *The Last Days of Pompeii* were represented, from *Eugene Aram* in 1832 (two sketches from this novel about a schoolmaster-murderer were shown at the Royal Academy within months of its appearance) to *What Will He Do With It?* in 1858. *Eugene Aram* was pictured some eight or ten times in all, the latest in 1876. One other subject from Bulwer-Lytton has a prominent place in the history of Victorian art. Although the story of Rienzi, "the last of the Romans" (a fourteenth-century Italian patriot), had previously been told by Mary Russell Mitford in her tragedy of 1828 (from which at least one painting, shown in 1831, was derived), it was his novel of 1835 that inspired Holman Hunt's *Rienzi Vowing to Obtain Justice for the Death of His Young Brother* (RA 1849).

350. John Martin, *Arthur and Aegle in the Happy Valley* (RA 1849) (Laing Art Gallery, Newcastle upon Tyne). Bulwer-Lytton's attempt at epic provided Martin with a contemporary source from which to derive one more portrayal of catastrophe and desolation.

DICKENS

The unprecedented popularity of Dickens's novels, particularly in the first half (1836–55) of his career, gave artists a large choice of subjects in the very years when anecdotal and narrative subjects were at the peak of their own popularity. Few members of the art-loving public were unacquainted with the scores of inimitable characters thus far introduced into the Dickens gallery or with the prodigal array of scenes fit for illustration. In 1855, one of Dickens's most perceptive contemporary critics, David Masson, praised his versatility as a painter of verbal backgrounds—rural scenes, sea pieces, cityscapes, the interiors of huts, drawing rooms, cathedrals—and as a Dutch-like delineator of details of dress and furniture.

> Take him, again, in the figure department [continued Masson]. Here he can be an animal-painter with Landseer when he likes, as witness his dogs, ponies, and ravens; he can be a historical painter, as witness his description of the Gordon riots; he can be a portrait-painter or a caricaturist like Leech; he can give you a bit of village or country life, like Wilkie; he can paint a haggard or squalid scene of low city-life, so as to remind one of some of the Dutch artists, Rembrandt included, or a pleasant family-scene, gay or sentimental, reminding one of Maclise or Frank Stone; he can body forth romantic conceptions of terror or beauty, that have risen in his own imagination; he can compose a fantastic fairy piece; he can even succeed in a powerful dream or allegory, where the figures are hardly human.[1]

But though Dickens may have been, even more than Scott, the Victorian artist's novelist just as Spenser was "the painter's poet," his novels placed prospective illustrators at a disadvantage unique in the history of English literature, because, at their first appearance in weekly or monthly numbers, most came equipped with a set of engraved illustrations.[2] Thus an iconographic tradition was instantaneously established, the more solidly because the illustrations accompanied the text to every reader. These engravings, by talented and experienced artists like Hablôt K. Browne ("Phiz") and George Cruikshank, who prepared them in close collaboration with Dickens himself, must have offered a certain amount of initial discouragement to artists ambitious to cash in on the lasting rage for Boz's fiction. Still, no set of illustrations, however skillful and however obedient to the author's intention, could be regarded as definitive; and, as with all literary works, there was still room for independent interpretation. Furthermore, unlike the initial illustrators, painters had the inestimable advantage of color at their disposal, so much more vivid and lifelike than the black-and-white designs to which the book engravings were confined.

The incidence of paintings from Dickens, as with those from Scott (there were some two hundred altogether), varied greatly from novel to novel and did not necessarily coincide with the novel's popularity. *Pickwick Papers* was seldom drawn from. Two versions of "The goblin that stole the sexton, Gabriel Grub"—from one of the interpolated tales, not from the Pickwick plot itself—were offered many years after Dickens's first novel appeared (1853, 1872); none seems to have been produced during the initial *Pickwick* craze (1836–37). This was in marked contrast to what happened when Dickens's next novels appeared. There was then no such lag between a novel's publication and the first paintings from it as occurred when the early Waverley novels appeared in their regular, stately sequence. Artists, indeed, were hardly less behindhand in exploiting Dickens's popularity than were the numerous playwrights who patched

351. Henry B. Roberts, *Oliver Twist's First Introduction to Fagin* (undated) (Walker Art Gallery, Liverpool). Roberts was a long-lived painter of genre subjects. Compared with Dickens's vivid description of Fagin and the room to which Jack Dawkins has brought Oliver (*Oliver Twist,* chap. 8) and with George Cruikshank's illustration of the same scene, this strikes one as a singularly bland—even laundered—translation of a Dickensian moment.

together stage adaptations of his current novel while it was still being written. The first painting from *Oliver Twist,* a picture of Rose Maylie by one Mrs. Battersby, was hung at the Royal Academy only two months after the serialization of the novel was completed in March 1839, although, to be sure, the whole book had been available in three volumes in the preceding October. From that time to the end of the century, some ten paintings from *Oliver Twist* are recorded, ranging from a mere topographical sketch "on the spot of Jacob's Island, Southwark, mentioned by Boz in *Oliver Twist*" exhibited at the Royal Academy in 1843, to the late *Oliver Twist: "He Walks to London"* (RA 1890).

Sir William Allan was the first to paint from *Nicholas Nickleby.* His *The Orphan and the Bird* was seen at the Royal Academy in 1840, six months after the serialization ended. There were half a dozen paintings from the novel in the next decade, and at least as many scattered across the forty years after that. The popular anecdotal painter Thomas Webster, who did not often draw from literary sources, painted two pictures from *Nicholas Nickleby.* One, seen at the Royal Academy in 1848, was titled *The Internal Economy of Dotheboys Hall* and portrayed Mrs. Squeers forcing brimstone and treacle, the well-known preventive panacea, down the throats of some thirty gagging pupil-victims. "The dame," remarked the *Literary Gazette,* "possesses all of her revolting attributes, and every child tells a tale of different distress and misery; fear, loathing, suffering fill the assembly, and yet there is *not a trait to wound the feelings of the spectator*" (emphasis added).[3] Webster's other (undated) picture, *The Interview Between Ralph Nickleby and His Niece Kate,* was sold at auction in 1867. Better known today is Edgar Bundy's riotous *Dotheboys Hall Breaks Up Forever,* which hangs in Dickens House, London.

Next came *The Old Curiosity Shop,* by a substantial margin the most popular of Dickens's novels as far as the art world was concerned. Of the approximately two hundred Dickens paintings recorded, more than forty

352. William Holman Hunt, *Little Nell and Her Grandfather* (British Institution 1846) (Sheffield City Art Galleries). "There was a pool of clear water in the field, in which the child laved her hands and face, and cooled her feet before setting forth to walk again. She would have the old man refresh himself in this way too, and making him sit down upon the grass, cast the water on him with her hands, and dried it with her simple dress" (*The Old Curiosity Shop,* chap. 15). Student work, painted when Hunt was nineteen years old. A number of other artists, including William Quiller Orchardson, treated this subject.

were from this novel, most of them, predictably, starring Little Nell either as a figure study or in a tableau, often with her undependable grandfather. As a student, Holman Hunt portrayed the pair lingering by a pond and looking back at the London they have lately left in order to escape Quilp's villainy (pl. 352). Robert Braithwaite Martineau's *Kit's Writing Lesson* (pl. 353) was bought by Mr. Mudie, the monarch of the circulating library business. Another portrait of Little Nell, exhibited at the Academy in 1881, was painted by Dickens's daughter Kate, the wife of the artist Charles Edward Perugini.

Barnaby Rudge, today one of Dickens's least-read novels, which followed *The Old Curiosity Shop,* was second only to that novel in the number of paintings it inspired—some twenty-five altogether. Its appearance was a crucial event in the life of Frith, who was just beginning his long career as an illustrator of English literary subjects. He recalled many years later:

> My inclination being strongly towards the illustration of modern life, I had read the works of Dickens in the hope of finding material for the exercise of any talent I might possess; but at that time the ugliness of modern dress frightened me, and it was not till the publication of "Barnaby Rudge," and the delightful Dolly Varden was presented to us, that I felt my opportunity had come, with the cherry-coloured mantle and the hat and pink ribbons.[4]

In 1842, a few months after the serialization of *Barnaby Rudge* was completed, Frith exhibited at the Society of British Artists a Dolly Varden portrait that was leagues removed from the insipidity of the keepsake school. Dickens saw it and wished to buy it, but the collector Joseph Gillott had already put in his claim, so Dickens commissioned another version, along with a scene from *Nicholas Nickleby* showing Kate Nickleby sewing a ball dress as her thoughts wander elsewhere. The two paintings remained in Dickens's possession throughout his life, and were sold after his death for the large sum of £1,360. Frith painted several more Dolly Varden pictures, showing the coquettish young woman in different attitudes and

353. Robert B. Martineau, *Kit's Writing Lesson* (RA 1852) (Tate Gallery, London). One of the best known paintings from Dickens, and a prime example of Victorian illustrations of the praiseworthy thirst for education, particularly in the lower ranks of society. Martineau captures the essence of the scene at the end of the third chapter of *The Old Curiosity Shop:* "He [Kit Nubbles] tucked up his sleeves and squared his elbows and put his face close to the copy-book and squinted horribly at the lines. . . . From the first moment of having the pen in his hand, he began to wallow in blots, and to daub himself with ink up to the very roots of his hair. . . . If he did by accident form a letter properly, he immediately smeared it out again with his arm in his preparations to make another"—all in the interests of Little Nell's "gentle wish to teach" and Kit's "anxious desire to learn."

with significant alterations of dress and accessories (pl. 354).[5] The original painting came to be known among artists as "the Dolly with the bracelet." The version Dickens acquired showed her looking flirtatiously back over her shoulder at Joe Willett as they pass in the woods. Still others had her delivering a letter from Edward Chester to Miss Haredale, and declaring, when taxed with a fondness for Joe Willett, that "she hoped she could do better than *that,* indeed!"[6] The success of these Dolly Varden pictures was promptly exploited. For fifteen years, from 1844 to 1860, Dolly Varden was Little Nell's constant rival in the annual exhibitions.*

354. William P. Frith, *Dolly Varden* (1842) (Tate Gallery, London). One of several versions Frith painted of this popular subject. There are at least two "Laughing Dollys," this one and another at the Victoria and Albert Museum.

Rather surprisingly, few painters derived subjects from Dickens's immensely popular Christmas books of the 1840s. There is evidently no record of a single painting from *A Christmas Carol* and only four or five, distributed at long intervals, from *The Chimes* and *The Cricket on the Hearth.* From the latter story was drawn a triad of theatrical portraits (RA 1846) showing Mr. and Mrs. Keeley and their daughter in one of the stage versions.

Martin Chuzzlewit stirred little enthusiasm among artists; two of the three recorded paintings date from much later (1860, 1875), and both depicted Sairey Gamp and Betsy Prig. By contrast, *Dombey and Son* evoked the speediest response of any of Dickens's novels. When the Royal Academy exhibition of 1847 opened, the serialization was less than half completed; the May number was the eighth of twenty-one. Yet no fewer than three *Dombey* paintings were shown: one of the death of little Paul Dombey, which had occurred in the February number, one of Walter Gay on board the *Son and Heir,* from the March number, and one of Captain Cuttle and Uncle Sol tracing the ship's course on their charts, from the very last page of that number. These were the first of some twenty paintings from the novel, most of which were concerned with the two sentimental foci, of Paul and his death as he kept wondering what the wild waves were saying, and of his—in effect—orphaned sister. The rest were genre scenes, presumably as full of quaint accessories as the Old Curiosity Shop, which depicted the snug interior of the Jolly Midshipman shop with its chaotic array of nautical equipment.

Dombey and Son was the last Dickens novel to appeal to many artists. Even *David Copperfield,* with its many possibilities for genre and sentimental work, inspired only half a dozen paintings. *Bleak House,* which repelled many readers because of its grim London scenes and its satiric assaults on such revered institutions as the law, religion, and philanthropy, accounted for scarcely more, among them—the first, 1853—a female portrait that an opportunistic artist named Rosa, for Lady Dedlock's maid. Much later, three artists ventured to depict the pathetic figure of Jo, the doomed crossing sweeper. One of these pictures (RA 1886) was of the actress Jenny Lee in the role of Jo in a dramatization of the novel.

There seem to have been no paintings from *Hard Times,* a novel set in a sooty manufacturing town that in general could not have supplied many subjects agreeable to current taste, although something could have been made out of Louisa Gradgrind's sad story and, in a different vein, Sleary's circus. *Little Dorrit* was represented by few pictures other than the two small oils that Frith painted to be engraved for the Library Edition of Dickens's works. Despite its chiaroscuro of melodrama and romance, *A Tale of Two Cities* attracted few painters apart from Henry Wallis, whose *The Devotion of Sidney Carton* was shown at the Royal Academy in 1876.

*When Dickens's effects were sold at auction immediately following his death, a women's magazine reported that the enthusiasm that greeted many items "culminated when the Dolly Varden was put up, and found vent in rounds of applause. The charming 'mist of coquettishness' environing this dainty figure, its beauty, its tripping, lightsome step, the innocent playfulness of the fair young face, took the room by storm." As a result, in the following year "Dolly Varden dresses," printed with a chintz pattern in pink, green, and mauve and enhanced by a matching straw hat, were all the fashion. They were worn at social occasions from flower shows to receptions for the Queen during her Irish visit, and popular songs were written about them:

Oh! have you seen my little girl,
She doesn't wear a bonnet
She's got a monstrous flip-flop hat
With cherry ribbons on it;
She dresses in bed furniture
Just like a flower garden
A blowin' and a growin'
And they call it Dolly Varden.

(Vanda Foster, "The Dolly Varden," *Dickensian* 73 [1977]: 19–24.)

355. William Maw Egley, *Florence Dombey in Captain Cuttle's Parlour* (ca. 1850) (Victoria & Albert Museum, Crown Copyright). The scene is either Captain Cuttle's lodgings near the India Docks (chap. 23) or his temporary quarters at the Wooden Midshipman (chaps. 48, 49). Only readers of the novel as well as of the painting would have realized the significance of certain details: the painting or engraving of a shipwreck (perhaps by Dickens's friend Clarkson Stanfield?), the ship model with its rigging awry, and the half-concealed map of the Cape of Good Hope—all referring to the feared fate of Walter Gay, Florence's unacknowledged lover. A painting and a ship model appear in "Phiz's" illustrations of both locales.

Associated with *Great Expectations* was a single painting, of Pip, Joe Gargery, and the convicts crossing the marsh early in the novel. From *Our Mutual Friend* came only half a dozen pictures, including two of Jenny Wren, the crippled doll's dressmaker; one of these (RA 1882) was by Kate Perugini.

In April 1870, the first number of Dickens's new novel *The Mystery of Edwin Drood* appeared. On the last day of the month, Dickens attended the banquet of the Royal Academy preceding the opening of the annual exhibition, on whose walls hung two of Luke Fildes's illustrations for *Edwin Drood.* In the presence of the Prince of Wales, Gladstone, and Disraeli, Dickens responded to the toast to literature:

> The literary visitors of the Royal Academy [of whom he was one] tonight desire to congratulate their hosts on a very interesting exhibition, in which risen excellence supremely asserts itself, and from which promise of a brilliant succession in time to come is not wanting. They naturally see with especial interest the writings and persons of great men—historians, philosophers, poets, and novelists—vividly illustrated around them here. And they hope they may modestly claim to have rendered some little assistance towards the production of many of the pictures in this magnificent gallery.[7]*

Dickens concluded by paying tribute to one of his longtime artist friends who had died three days earlier—Daniel Maclise, the illustrator of Shakespeare, Moore, Goldsmith, Milton, Bulwer-Lytton, Byron, Scott, Jonson, and Keats. This, as it turned out, was Dickens's last public appearance. Six weeks later, on 8 June, he had a stroke at his beloved country villa on the Rochester Road. By an ironic coincidence, the artist who of all Victorian painters loved literature most, James Smetham, was returning the next day from a holiday in Surrey. In a letter to his brother he wrote,

> At Rochester we learned from the verger of the Cathedral that Charles Dickens had been seized at dinner with a fit on Wednesday evening. On our way we had to pass his house at Gad's Hill—stopped opposite to it for a moment, and saw two physicians evidently in consultation at the bay window. This was at 4.30, and at that moment he was dying. He expired at 6 or soon after. It was affecting to see, for the first time, his country house under these circumstances. A few weeks ago I passed him as he walked in a weary sort of way, and wrapped in his own thoughts, from the Royal Academy Exhibition and down Piccadilly.[8]

THACKERAY

When he became a famous novelist, Thackeray, in contrast to Dickens, was seldom represented on the walls of the exhibitions he had once attended as a professional critic. Only one or two paintings are recorded from each of several novels, including *Vanity Fair, Pendennis,* and *The Virginians,* and half a dozen from *The Newcomes,* including at least two (1878 and 1886) of Colonel Newcome among the poor brethren in the Charterhouse. From *The History of Henry Esmond,* however, came ten or twelve pictures, the first at the Royal Academy the year following its publication in 1852. Of these, the most discussed was Augustus Egg's *Beatrix Knighting Henry Esmond* (pl. 356). Beatrix and Lady Castlewood were the favorite figures of the artists who chose *Esmond* subjects (see pl. 169). As late as 1898, visitors to the Royal Scottish Academy exhibition saw a canvas which depicted one of those scenes in literary history that should have happened even though they did not: Henry Esmond describing the Battle of Blenheim to Addison and Steele.

*Among the literature-related paintings hung that year were subjects from Tennyson, Sheridan, Shakespeare, Bulwer-Lytton, Burns, the *Spectator,* Scott, Fielding, Keats, Milton, Hood, Byron, Richardson, Bunyan, and Thackeray.

GEORGE ELIOT

Writing in the *Home and Foreign Review* in 1863, a perceptive critic said of George Eliot, "We are persuaded that the study of pictures has helped her as much as the study of living models. We should not be surprised if the famous scene at the Rainbow in *Silas Marner*—a scene compared by competent critics to Shakespeare's scenes at the Boar's Head—turned out to be one the like of which she has never witnessed except on the canvas of Teniers, seen through an atmosphere of Dickens, or of her own deep knowledge of rustic life."[1] Recent scholarship has confirmed the writer's guess.[2] Time after time in her novels, George Eliot applied her remembrance of paintings she had seen during her many visits with George Henry Lewes to art galleries in Britain and on the Continent. She regarded herself as a genre painter in words, and although critics during her lifetime alluded less often than might have been expected to the resemblances between her art and that of the Dutch school she so much admired, it is clear that one of the reasons for the popularity of *Adam Bede, The Mill on the Floss, Silas Marner, Felix Holt,* and to a somewhat lesser degree *Middlemarch* was the way Eliot imported into fiction the subjects and techniques of rural genre painting. They were praised in the same

356. Augustus Egg, *Beatrix Knighting Henry Esmond* (RA 1858) (Tate Gallery, London). Unlike Egg's other painting from *Henry Esmond,* exhibited the preceding year (pl. 169), this depicts an actual scene in the novel (bk. 2, chap. 15).

terms in which such pictures by contemporary artists were praised, for their sympathetic portrayal of the scenes and characters of country life. Apart from Scott a generation earlier (and possibly Dickens, who, however, used mostly urban material), she was the nineteenth-century novelist who brought literature into closest alliance with the tastes and topics of popular genre. In some respects, also, Eliot's fiction had an affinity with Goldsmith's; she mined the same vein that so many Victorian artists exploited in their scenes from *The Vicar of Wakefield.* One might say that the innumerable paintings from Goldsmith, along with all the similar subjects from nonliterary sources, helped sustain the taste for humble rural life in art until Eliot was ready to benefit from it.

Adam Bede was represented by a dozen or so paintings between 1861 and 1890, most of them being pictures of Hetty Sorrel, a latter-day Keepsake beauty discovered at the butter churn. Two of Edward Corbould's watercolors from the novel are in the royal collection: *Dinah Morris Preaching on Hayslope Green* and *Hetty and Captain Donnithorne in Mrs. Poyser's Dairy,* both painted in 1861.

The other novels from English life were seldom drawn upon, the only picture by a notable artist being Millais's *The Girlhood of St. Teresa* (RA 1893). A costume piece, it was suggested by "the lines in [the Prelude to] *Middlemarch* showing how the little girl walked forth one morning with her smaller brother, intent on seeking martyrdom in the country of the Moors. . . . The child here," said Millais's first cataloguer, "is clearly afflicted with religious mania, while her brother is indifferent to everything but the merits of his orange."[3]

Romola fared somewhat better. Frederic Leighton made thirty-eight drawings on wood for the first edition, and, possibly as a result of this impetus, between 1877 and 1892 nine paintings are recorded from the novel, two by another Leighton—Edmund Blair—*The Dying Copernicus* (RA 1880) and another simply titled *Romola* (RA 1887).

THE PRE-RAPHAELITES: ROSSETTI, MORRIS, SWINBURNE

The special link between poetry and painting represented by the Pre-Raphaelite group's work in both arts could be seen sometimes in the subjects taken from one man's poetry by other painters. But although Rossetti most conspicuously merged the sister arts, few of his poems were chosen, mainly because he was his own best illustrator.[1] It is likely, too, that his notoriety as the fomenter of the anti-Academic movement disqualified his poems as prospective sources for establishment painters to draw from. After 1871, in addition, his reputation as artist suffered indirectly from Robert Buchanan's attack on him, in the October number of the *Contemporary Review,* as the leader of "the fleshly school of poetry," far gone in libidinous abandon. In 1880, a review in the *Times* of a routine painting, *Thistledown Gatherer,* which quoted lines from Rossetti—"Gleaned by a girl in autumn of her youth, / Which one new year makes soft her marriage-bed,"—commented that Rossetti's poetry was "about as undesirable a source for inspiration as a young painter could resort to."[2] Such pictures as were derived from his poetry came from the easels of his associates and sympathizers.[3] Burne-Jones began a diptych of "The Blessed Damozel" in 1857 (and completed a watercolor of one half of the heaven/earth design); and Charles Fairfax Murray, Rossetti's studio assistant in the 1870s, painted a scene dimly inspired by "Love's Nocturn."

The Honorable John Collier showed *Lilith* at the Grosvenor Gallery in 1887, Gerald Moira painted *Willowwood* (from *The House of Life*) for the Academy show of 1894, and in the same years (1893–97) Byam Shaw displayed a series of pictures likewise titled from the poems: *Rose Mary, Silent Noon, The Blessed Damozel,* and *Love's Baubles.*

William Morris fared better with artists, largely because the long narrative poems that comprised his *Earthly Paradise* fitted in so well with the interests of the new classical school of Leighton, Poynter, and Alma-Tadema. Half a dozen paintings from *The Earthly Paradise,* most of them from the Psyche-Venus story, appeared at the Royal Academy and the Grosvenor Gallery between 1879 and 1894, including Spencer Stanhope's *Charon and Psyche* (1883). Poynter's *Atalanta's Race,* also known as *The Suppliant to Venus* (RA 1871), bore a quotation from Morris. Many of Burne-Jones's pictures came from the same source; the most ambitious was his series of eight paintings (four completed, the rest surviving as cartoons) of the Perseus myth, commissioned by Arthur Balfour for his house in Carlton Gardens and painted over a span of seventeen years.

Alma-Tadema took the title of his Royal Academy painting of 1891 from one Pre-Raphaelite poet and the motto from another: *An Earthly Paradise,* with a quotation from Swinburne. A handful of other pictures were exhibited with Swinburnian quotations, including Walter Crane's *Freedom* (Grosvenor Gallery 1885), but few if any actual subjects were taken from the poetry of the Victorian *enfant terrible.* He, too, located some of his most characteristic early poems in classic antiquity ("Faustine," "Hymn to Proserpine," "The Garden of Proserpine"). But in view of their "paganism", a convenient blur-word for blasphemy and deviant sexuality, it is easy to understand why the academic painters avoided them; the public demanded myths in which ancient Greeks and Romans, though their ladies were given to languishing in nude luxury in or alongside marble baths, were still somehow as respectable as themselves.

APPENDIXES

APPENDIX A

The Boydell Shakespeare Gallery

There are several conflicting accounts of how the Boydell Shakespeare Gallery (see Part One, chapter 2, above) originated. One that to my knowledge has not previously been pointed out occurs in John Adolphus's biography of the popular comedian John ("Jack") Bannister, briefly a pupil of Loutherbourg at the Royal Academy schools, and later a correspondent of Sir George Beaumont and a friend of Rowlandson, Morland, and Gainsborough. In his last years, he lived near Constable in Hampstead and bought from the artist, who described him as "a very fine creature . . . very sensible—*natural*—and a gentleman,"[1] the *Hampstead Heath* which is now in the Tate Gallery. Says Adolphus:

> He was a member of a select society, composed altogether of artists and theatrical performers, who were used to meet and dine at different coffee-houses, discussing at large whatever was interesting in their respective pursuits. At one of these meetings, the idea was started of an united effort to be made by the most celebrated painters for the formation of a combined tribute to the poet, who was justly the pride of the nation, and whose scenes and characters had so often furnished subjects for eminent artists. This project, after it had formed the subject of various discussions, was communicated to Alderman Boydell, who adopted it with eagerness, pursued it with alacrity and spirit, and finally rendered it a grand national object. A more lively interest was imparted to the public than had ever been created by a similar undertaking; an interest which was never intermitted, whether attention was directed to the exhibition of the pictures, the perfection of the engravings, or the progress of the work.
>
> Bannister bestowed on it a devoted attention. It has been asserted, that there was not a picture in the protracted series, of which he had not witnessed the rise and perfection. He was acquainted with the painters, enamoured of their art and of the subject, accurate in his notions of beauty and grace, and by his dramatic skill capable of supplying those personations, attitudes, and expressions of feature, which would so materially assist the imagination, and give life to the production.[2]

Devoid as it is of specifics, this account has little to recommend it as historical evidence, but it does suggest the prestige attached to the Boydell Gallery as late as the 1830s. To be alleged to have conceived the idea seemingly was a signal honor, even though the evidence might be no more than a thin wisp of hearsay.

APPENDIX B

Original Prices Paid for Nineteenth-Century Literary Paintings

Such small attention as has yet been given to the economics of art in nineteenth-century England has centered on the highest prices commanded by the most popular artists.*

*For the prices Boydell paid his Shakespeare Gallery artists, see Part One above, pp. 44–45, 45n, 48.

(See, for example, the long, fact-packed note in Oppé's "Art" [*Early Victorian England,* 2:117], from which a few representative instances have been given in chapter 4, and the table of "Some Notable Prices, 1859–1872" in Robertson, *Sir Charles Eastlake,* p. 209.) The following list of prices paid to the artist or his executors for literary paintings is probably typical of the range of prices paid for most kinds of paintings, regardless of subject. They were governed by the size of the canvas (from cabinet to larger-than-life), the reputation of the artist (whether he was at the beginning of his career or had established himself in the art market), the liberality of the purchaser (patrons may in some cases have paid more than a picture's probable market value for the sake of encouraging new talent), and, particularly after the 1830s, its desirability as a subject for engraving.

1801 Northcote's *Prospero, Miranda and Caliban.* Sold to Sir John Leicester for £100.[1]

1807 Opie's *Miranda.* Purchased by Sir John Leicester (from Mrs. Opie?) for £31.[2]

1807 Romney's *Titania, Puck and Changeling.* Purchased by Sir John Leicester at the Romney sale, £100.[3]

1807 Stothard's *The Canterbury Pilgrims.* Sold to Joseph Farington for £250.[4]

1808 Turner's *View of Pope's Villa at Twickenham.* Sold to Sir John Leicester for 200 guineas.[5]

1812 Martin's *Sadak in Search of the Waters of Oblivion.* Bought by William Manning, a governor of the Bank of England, for 50 guineas. (Martin had priced it at 100 guineas.)[6]

1813 Martin's *Adam's First Sight of Eve.* £73 10s.[7]

1814 Howard's *Sunrise* (from *Paradise Lost*). 200 guineas.[8]*

1817 Harlow's *The Court for the Trial of Queen Katherine* (*The Kemble Family*). 100 guineas (it could have been 500).[9]†

1818 Washington Allston's *The Angel Uriel.* Sold to the Marquis of Stafford for 150 guineas.[10]

1819 Fuseli's *Friar Puck.* Bought by Sir John Leicester for 100 guineas.[11]

*Three hundred, actually. Unsold at the Royal Academy, the painting was rehung at the British Institution, where it won 100 guineas as the second-best-in-show. When Howard protested that it deserved the first prize (200 guineas), the management admitted that his was the best picture in the exhibition, but "the prizes were not intended for artists of established reputation, but for students." Hearing this, the Marquis of Stafford asked Howard's price; two hundred, said Howard; wrap it up, said the Marquis in effect. So the artist kept his second prize and collected his asking price as well.

†Thereby hangs a tale of a different kind. The picture began as a portrait of Mrs. Siddons, commissioned by a gentleman named Welch. When it was completed in its greatly enlarged form, with eighteen figures, Welch insisted on paying Harlow one hundred guineas, but Harlow accepted only the twenty agreed upon. Soon afterward, the artist called on Welch to say that he would now take the full hundred: "Lord Darnley has seen the picture and has offered me five hundred, so that you shall sell him the picture, give me a hundred, and put the other four hundred in your own pocket." "I will do no such thing," replied Welch. "I am delighted that you permit me to relieve my conscience by giving you the hundred; but no Lord Darnley shall have the picture. I have no house fit to receive it, and shall therefore present it to the Green-room at Covent Garden Theatre."

1819 Leslie's *Sir Roger de Coverley Going to Church.* Commissioned by a Mr. Dunlap, a tobacco importer, for 100 guineas.[12]

1821 Etty's *Cleopatra's Arrival in Cilicia.* Commissioned by Sir Francis Freeling for 200 guineas, "although Gilchrist hints that a much lower sum was paid."[13]

1824 Leslie's *Anne Page and Master Slender* (replica?). Bought by Sir John Leicester for 60 guineas.[14]

1828 Etty's *Scene from Paradise Lost.* Sold to the Marquis of Stafford for £525.[15]

1831 Etty's *Sabrina.* 100 guineas.[16]

1831 Lawrence's *Satan Summoning His Legions.* Sold by his executors for £504.[17]

1832 Etty's *Phaedria and Cymocles.* Purchased by Wynne Ellis, M. P., for 100 guineas.[18]

1833 Etty's *Britomart Redeems Fair Amoret.* Sold to "Mr. L., Manchester," for £157.[19]

1839 David Scott's *Paracelsus.* Sold for £200 to the Scottish Art Union, which gave it to the National Gallery of Scotland.[20]

1843 Dyce's *Jessica (The Signal).* Bought from the Royal Academy wall by Gladstone for 30 guineas.[21]

1843 Frith's *The Merry Wives of Windsor.* Sold at the Liverpool exhibition for £100.[22]

1843 Frith's *Dolly Varden* and *Kate Nickleby.* Sold to Charles Dickens for £40 the pair.[23]

1845 Etty's *Circe and the Syrens Three* (from his ill-fated design for the summer pavilion at Buckingham Palace). Commissioned by Joseph Gillott for 350 guineas.[24]

1845 Etty's, Maclise's, and Eastlake's sketches for the same project. Sold for between £250 and £300.[25]

1845 Frith's *The Village Pastor* [*The Deserted Village*]. Commissioned by John Gibbons for £200.[26]

1845 Frith's *The Grisette's Pulse* [*A Sentimental Journey*]. £30.[27]

1845 Haydon's *Uriel and Satan.* £210.[28]

1846 Mulready's *Choosing the Wedding Gown* [*The Vicar of Wakefield*]. Commissioned by John Sheepshanks for £1,050.[29]

1847 Holman Hunt's *Scene from Woodstock.* Bought for £20 by a winner of that amount in the Art Union lottery.[30]

1848 Hunt's *The Eve of St. Agnes.* Bought for £60 by a winner of that amount in the Art Union lottery.[31]

1848 Frith's *Old Woman Accused of Witchcraft* [the *Spectator*]. Sold to Thomas Miller for 500 guineas.[32]

1849 Millais's *Lorenzo and Isabella.* Sold to a London tailor for £150 and a suit of clothes.[33]

1849 Hunt's *The Oath of Rienzi.* Sold to John Gibbons for £100, plus £5 for the frame.[34]

1850 Noel Paton's *The Quarrel of Oberon and Titania.* Bought for the National Gallery of Scotland by the Scottish Art Union. The price of £700 was the highest the union paid for a painting.[35]

1850 Millais's *Ferdinand and Ariel.* £150.[36]

1851 Landseer's *Titania and Bottom.* Commissioned by I. K. Brunel for 400 guineas.[37]

1852 Frith's *Pope Makes Love to Mary Wortley Montagu* (*The Rejected Poet*). 350 guineas.[38]

1853 H. S. Marks's *Dogberry Examining Conrade and Borachio.* £15.[39]

1857 Millais's *Sir Isumbras at the Ford.* Commissioned by the dealer Ernest Gambart for £800.[40]

1857 Cruikshank's *The Last Scene in The Merry Wives of Windsor.* 200 guineas.[41]

1858 Pettie's *Scene from The Fortunes of Nigel.* Sold to the Glasgow Association for the Promotion of Fine Arts for £15.[42]

1868 Frith's *At Boswell's Lodgings.* Bought by the dealer Agnew for £1,200.[43]

1868 Orchardson's "Shakespearean subject." £400.[44]

1870 Frith's *The Pulse, The Husband, Paris* [*A Sentimental Journey*]. £900.[45]

1872 F. M. Brown's *Haidee and Don Juan.* Bought before completion by Frederick Leyland for £420.[46]

1873 Landseer's *Lady Godiva's Prayer.* Sold by his executors for £3,360.[47]

1877 Yeames's *Amy Robsart.* Bought by the Chantrey Bequest committee for £1,000.[48]

1877 Orchardson's *The Queen of Swords.* £1,050.[49]

1890 Burne-Jones's *The Legend of the Briar Rose* (four pictures). Bought by Alexander Henderson, first Lord Faringdon, for £15,000.[50]

APPENDIX C

Reproductions of Literary Paintings

A selective listing, designed to facilitate access to photographs and engravings of paintings not reproduced in this book. Limited, with some exceptions, to exhibited oils. Omits engravings published separately or in collections such as gift books, in volumes devoted to illustrations from a single author or work (except Shakespeare and Milton), and in illustrated editions of individual works. Only a few theatrical paintings are included—representative scenes from "classic" English dramas.

There is a large collection of photographs of British paintings, with a computer-generated index, at the Yale Center for British Art. The Witt Library at the Courtauld Institute, London, has an extensive archive of reproductions, arranged by artist. The catalogues of the print collections in major libraries, such as the British Library and the Victoria and Albert Museum, are also valuable.

Unless prefixed by "p." (page), citations are to figure or plate number. Most of the abbreviated entries are amplified in the Bibliography. Others are:

Fuseli-Tate	*Henry Fuseli 1741–1825.* (Exhibition catalogue, Tate Gallery, 1975; text by Gert Schiff.)
Girouard	Mark Girouard, *The Return to Camelot* (New Haven, Conn., 1981).
Hardie-Pettie	Martin Hardie, *John Pettie R.A.* (London, 1908).

Hilton	Timothy Hilton, *The Pre-Raphaelites* (London, 1970).
Hobson	Anthony Hobson, *The Art and Life of J. W. Waterhouse* (London, 1980).
Manners	Lady Victoria Manners, *Matthew William Peters, His Life and Work* (London, 1913).
[Merchant	All "Merchant" references are to his *Shakespeare and the Artist.*]
Nicoll	John Nicoll, *The Pre-Raphaelites* (London, 1970).
Odell	George C. D. Odell, *Shakespeare from Betterton to Irving* (New York, 1920).
[Schiff	All "Schiff" references are to his *Johann Heinrich Füssli* (Zurich, 1973).]
Stone and Kahrl	George W. Stone, Jr., and George M. Kahrl, *David Garrick: A Critical Biography* (Carbondale, Ill., 1979).

PART TWO

Engravings of all the paintings in Boydell's Shakespeare Gallery are reproduced in Friedman and, in larger format, in a Benjamin Blom reprint (New York, 1968). A number are also reproduced in Hutton, Merchant, and Salaman. Photographs of the extant originals are designated by an asterisk.

THE COMEDIES

The Comedy of Errors

*Wheatley. *Shipwreck Scene.* Friedman 104; Webster 128.

The Taming of the Shrew

Dawe. *Catherine and Petruchio.* Waterhouse, *Dictionary,* p. 105.
Egg. *Katharina.* Salaman p. 107.
Hunt. *Bianca.* Ashton (2) 14.
Orchardson. *Induction, Scene 2.* Salaman p. 165; *Art Journal* 29 (1867): facing p. 212; *Art Annual* 1897, p. 22.
Watts. *Bianca. Magazine of Art* 17 (1894): p. 41.
*Wheatley. *Scene in Baptista's House.* Webster 119; Strong 38.

The Two Gentlemen of Verona

Abbey. *Sylvia. Edwin Austin Abbey (1852–1911)* (exhibition catalogue, Yale University Art Gallery, 1974), 4.
Elmore. *Subject from "The Two Gentlemen of Verona."* Ashton (2) 6; *Apollo* 89 (1969): p. 57.
*Kauffmann. *Valentine, Proteus, Sylvia, and Julia.* Friedman 51.

A Midsummer Night's Dream

Dadd. *The Contradiction of Oberon and Titania.* Allderidge 172 (color); Greysmith 89 (color).
———. *The Fairy Feller's Master-Stroke.* Allderidge 190 (color); Greysmith 90; Quennell p. [255] (color); Gaunt (3) 113; Maas p. 151; Reynolds (2) 18.
———. *Puck and the Fairies. Art Journal* 26 (1864): facing p. 130; Allderidge 58 (color); Greysmith 24.
———. *Titania Sleeping.* Allderidge 57 (color); Greysmith 25.
Fuseli. *Bottom Being Kissed by Titania.* Schiff 885; Gaunt (1) 110; Tomory 99; Fuseli-Tate 27.
———. *Cobweb.* Schiff 752; Fuseli-Tate 24.
———. *Oberon Squeezes the Flower on Titania's Eyelids.* Schiff 884a; Fuseli-Tate 25.
———. *Titania's Awakening.* Schiff 754 (color); Tomory 76; Fuseli-Tate 28 (color).
———. *Titania's Dream.* Schiff 923.
Hopley. *Puck and Moth.* Allen Staley, *The Pre-Raphaelite Landscape* (Oxford, 1973), 39a, b.
Huskisson. *Titania's Elves Robbing the Squirrel's Nest.* Maas p. 153.
Landseer (E.). *Titania and Bottom.* Ormond, *Landseer,* p. 190 (color); *Magazine of Art* 20 (1896): p. 178.
Paton. *The Indian Boy's Mother. Paintings, Water-Colours and Drawings from the Handley-Read Collection* (exhibition catalogue, Fine Art Society, 1974), 59.
———. *The Reconciliation of Oberon and Titania.* Maas p. 152; Irwin, *Scottish Painters,* 139.
Poynter. *Helena and Hermia.* Wood (2) p. 149.
Reynolds. *Robin Goodfellow (Puck).* Waterhouse, *Reynolds,* 294.
Scott. *Puck Fleeing Before the Dawn.* Stanley Cursitor, *Scottish Art to the Close of the Nineteenth Century* (New York, 1949), facing p. 78.
Turner. *Queen Mab's Cave.* Butlin and Joll 397 (color).
*Wheatley. *Theseus and Hippolyta Find the Lovers.* Webster 118.

Love's Labour's Lost

Jenkins. *The Princess of France.* Salaman p. 106.
*Hamilton. *"Love's Labour's Lost" 4.1.* Friedman 106.
Pickersgill. *Biron, Rosaline, and Others. Illustrated London News,* 24 May 1856, p. 569.
Wheatley. *"Love's Labour's Lost" 4.2.* Webster 124.
———. *"Love's Labour's Lost" 5.2.* Webster 125.

The Merchant of Venice

Alcock. *Portia and Shylock.* Ashton (2) 11.
Allston. *The Casket Scene.* W. H. Gerdts and T. E. Stebbins, Jr., *"A Man of Genius": The Art of Washington Allston* (exhibition catalogue, Boston Museum of Fine Arts, 1979), 18.
Alma-Tadema. *Portia. Burlington Magazine* 102 (January 1960): 53.
Boyne. *Macklin and Mrs. Pope as Shylock and Portia.* Odell 1: facing p. 370.
Dyce. *Jessica (The Signal).* Pointon, *Dyce,* 106.
Fildes. *Jessica. Art Annual* 1895, p. 9.
Smirke. *The Trial Scene.* Merchant 39b.
Stone (F.). *Bassanio Receiving the Letter Concerning Antonio. Art Journal* 18 (1856): p. 333.
Stoppelaer. *Shylock and Tubal.* Ashton (1) 153.
Turner. *Scene: A Street in Venice.* Butlin and Joll 479.
———. *Shylock: "Jessica, shut the window, I say."* Butlin and Joll 333; Quennell p. [52] (color).
Woods. *Portia.* Ashton (2) 32.

As You Like It

Bostock. *Celia.* Salaman p. 106.
Constable. *Jaques and the Wounded Stag.* Merchant 37a.

*Hodges. *The Forest of Arden.* Ashton (1) 85.
Maclise. *Wrestling Scene.* J. B. Priestley, *Victoria's Heyday* (London, 1972), p. 88 (color); *Illustrated London News,* 9 June 1855, p. 568; *Art Journal* 30 (1868): facing p. 4; Q. Bell 36.
Millais. *Rosalind, Celia, and Touchstone.* Millais 2: p. 3; Engen pp. 92–93.
Pettie. *Touchstone and Audrey.* Salaman p. 161.

Much Ado About Nothing

Fuseli. *Beatrice.* Schiff 1750.
———. *Beatrice Eavesdropping on Hero and Ursula.* Schiff 748, 749.
*Hamilton. *Hero Fainting in Church.* Friedman 108.
*Peters. *Beatrice Eavesdropping on Hero and Ursula.* Friedman 179; Salaman p. [61] (color); Manners IV.
Stone (M). *Claudio Accuses Hero. Illustrated London News,* 25 May 1861, p. 490; *Art Journal* 31 (1869): p. 35.

Twelfth Night

Abbey. *"O Mistress Mine."* Salaman p. 168.
Baxter. *Olivia.* Ashton (2) 1.
*Hamilton. *"Twelfth Night" 5.1.* Mander and Mitchenson 14; Ashton (1) 57.
Houghton. *Toby Belch, Viola, and Aguecheek.* Paul Hogarth, *Arthur Boyd Houghton* (London, 1981), p. 15.
Leighton. *Viola.* Hartmann p. 87.
Leslie. *Olivia Raising Her Veil. Art Journal* 25 (1863): facing p. 4.
Meadows. *Maria.* Salaman p. 103.
Sant. *"She never told her love." Illustrated London News,* 12 February 1853, p. 136.
Stothard. *Twelfth Night.* Mander and Mitchenson 20.
Waterhouse. *Miranda.* Hobson 18.
Wheatley. *The Duel in "Twelfth Night."* Webster 17; Salaman p. 74.

The Merry Wives of Windsor

Bonington. *Anne Page and Slender.* A. Dubuisson, *Richard Parkes Bonington* (London, 1924), facing p. 124; Hon. Andrew Shirley, *Bonington* (London, 1940), 95; Merchant 40a; Strong 105.
*Durno. *Falstaff in Disguise.* Friedman 187.
Farington and Smirke. *Falstaff in the Buck Basket.* Farington (I) 3:15.
———. *Falstaff at Herne's Oak.* Farington (1) 3:16.
Fuseli. *Falstaff in the Buck Basket.* Schiff 883; Tomory color plate VI.
———. *Mrs. Page.* Schiff 882.
Haytley. *Mrs. Woffington as Mrs. Ford.* Odell 1: facing p. 338.
Meadows. *Mrs. Ford.* Salaman p. 103.
*Peters. *Mrs. Page and Mrs. Ford Reading Falstaff's Letter.* Friedman 174; Salaman p. 57.
*———. *Mrs. Page and Mrs. Ford Tossing Falstaff in the Buck Basket.* Friedman 177; Manners, facing p. 48 (color).
*Smirke. *Sir Hugh Evans Examines William.* Friedman 237.
Stephanoff. *Falstaff at Herne's Oak.* Ashton (1) 152.

All's Well That Ends Well

*Wheatley. *" All's Well That Ends Well" 2.3.* Friedman 97; Webster 101.
*———. *"All's Well That Ends Well" 5.3.* Friedman 94; Webster 122.

Measure for Measure

Abbey. *Angelo and Isabella.* E. V. Lucas, *Edwin Austin Abbey* (London, 1921), I: facing p. 202.
———. *Friar Thomas and the Duke.* Lucas I: facing p. 200; Abbey catalogue (above, under *The Two Gentlemen of Verona*) 49.
Hamilton. *Claudio and Isabella.* Salaman p. 83.
*Kirk. *"Measure for Measure" 5.1.* Friedman 210.

THE HISTORY PLAYS

Henry VI

Abbey. *Gloucester Kills Henry VI.* Lucas (above, under *Measure for Measure*) 2: after p. 398.
Fuseli. *Cardinal Beaufort Terrified by the Ghost of Gloucester.* Schiff 1787; Fuseli-Tate 31.
———. *Warwick Taking the Oath Over Gloucester's Body.* Schiff 727.
*Hamilton. *Joan of Arc and the Furies.* Cummings and Staley 77; Friedman 119.
Herbert. *Queen Margaret of Anjou.* Salaman p. 110.
Orchardson. *Talbot and the Countess of Auvergne. Art Annual* 1897, p. 22.
Reynolds. *The Death of Cardinal Beaufort.* Friedman 17.

Richard III

Abbey. *Richard Duke of Gloucester and the Lady Anne.* Abbey catalogue (above, *The Two Gentlemen of Verona*), cover; Treble 1; Guise 178.
Clint. *Kean as Gloucester* (copy by another hand). Mander and Mitchenson 71; Odell 2: facing p. 128.
Fuseli. *Dighton and Forrest: The Murder of the Young Princes.* Schiff 728.
Halls. *Edmund Kean as Richard III.* J. B. Priestley, *The Prince of Pleasure* (London, 1969), p. 74 (color).
Hayman. *Garrick as Richard III.* Mander and Mitchenson 2.
Millais. *The Princes in the Tower.* Millais 2: p. 103; Bennett, *Millais,* 38; Strong, color plate VII.
*Northcote. *The Meeting of the Young Princes.* Friedman 69.

King John

Fuseli. *Lady Constance, Arthur, and Salisbury.* Schiff 722; Tomory 69; Fuseli-Tate 29. Another version, Schiff 1814.
*Northcote. *Hubert and Arthur.* Friedman 77.
Opie. *Arthur, Hubert, and the Executioners.* Hamlyn 37.
———. *The King, Arthur, and Hubert on the Battlefield.* Salaman p. 98.

Richard II

Gilbert. *Richard Resigning the Crown to Bolingbroke.* Salaman p. 136.
Northcote. *The Death of John of Gaunt.* Hamlyn 39.

Henry IV

Boaden. *John Philip Kemble as Hotspur.* Odell 2: facing p. 56.
*Boydell. *Prince Henry's Apology.* Salaman p. 80.
Elmore. *Hotspur and the Fop. Art Journal* 19 (1857): p. 113.
Gilbert. *King Henry IV. Illustrated London News,* 17 May 1845, p. 312.
Hayman. *Falstaff's Cowardice Detected.* Gowing 7.

Hogarth. *Falstaff Examines His Recruits.* Paulson, *Book and Painting* 20; Bindman 22; Frederick Antal, *Hogarth and His Place in European Art* (London, 1926), 19b.
Horsley. *Henry V When Prince of Wales. Art Journal* 19 (1857): p. 183.
Liverseege. *Falstaff and Bardolph.* Stuart Tave, *The Amiable Humorist* (Chicago, 1960), 6.
Marks. *Francis Feeble, the Lady's Tailor. Art Journal* 31 (1869): facing p. 372.
Orchardson. *Prince Henry, Poins, and Falstaff.* Salaman p. 163.
*Smirke. *The Carriers Outside the Inn at Rochester.* Friedman 240.
*———. *Scene at the Boar's Head Tavern.* Friedman 245.
*Westall. *The Conspiracy of Hotspur, Worcester, et al.* Friedman 143.

Henry VIII

Abbey. *The Trial of Queen Katherine.* Lucas (above, *Measure for Measure*) 2: facing p. 346.
Cope. *Wolsey at Leicester Abbey. Art Journal* 21 (1859): facing p. 264.
Gilbert. *The Disgrace of Cardinal Wolsey. Art Journal* 19 (1857): p. 243.
Fuseli. *Queen Katherine's Vision.* Schiff 729, 730.
Hogarth. *Henry VIII Leading Anne Boleyn to Court.* Antal (above, *Henry IV*) 17a; Paulson, *Hogarth: His Life, Art, and Times,* 59.
Leslie. *Queen Katherine and Her Maid.* Ashton (2) 16.
———. *Queen Katherine and Capuchius.* Cummings and Staley 164.
O'Neil. *Queen Katherine's Dream. Illustrated London News,* 7 May 1853, p. 348.
*Peters. *The Christening of Queen Elizabeth.* Salaman p. 59; Manners XV.
*———. *The Queen and Cardinals Wolsey and Campeius.* Friedman 182; Salaman p. 60; Manners XV.
Pott. *The Trial of Queen Katherine. Magazine of Art* 4 (1881): p. 25.

THE TRAGEDIES

Romeo and Juliet

Brown. *Romeo and Juliet.* Hueffer, facing p. [448].
Dicksee (F.). *Romeo and Juliet. Art Annual* 1905, p. 7.
Dicksee (T.F.). *Balcony Scene.* Ashton (2) 4.
Fuseli. *Balcony Scene.* Schiff 1815.
———. *Queen Mab.* Schiff 1496.
———. *Romeo and the Apothecary.* Schiff 1295 (Blake engraving).
———. *Romeo Contemplating Juliet in the Tomb.* Schiff 1207.
———. *Romeo Stabbing Paris in Juliet's Tomb.* Schiff 1206.
Grant. *Juliet and the Friar.* Ashton (2) 10.
Lehmann. *Helen Faucit as Juliet.* Ashton (2) 15.
Leighton. *Count Paris Comes to Claim His Bride.* Ormond, *Leighton,* 60.
———. *The Reconciliation of the Montagues and Capulets.* Ormond, *Leighton,* 44, 45.
Merritt. *Ellen Terry as Juliet, Mrs. Stirling as the Nurse.* Ashton (2) 25.
O'Connor. *Romeo and Juliet.* Crookshank and the Knight of Glin 258; *Connoisseur* 178 (1971): p. 234.
Peters. *Romeo and Juliet in the Crypt.* Salaman p. 56; Hamlyn 36.
Pettie. *Juliet and Friar Laurence.* Hardie-Pettie, facing p. 102 (color).
*Rigaud. *Romeo Taking Leave of Juliet.* Friedman 60.
Rossetti (Lucy). *Romeo and Juliet in the Tomb. Magazine of Art* 18 (1895): p. 342.
*Smirke. *Juliet and the Nurse.* Friedman 235.
Turner. *Juliet and Her Nurse.* Butlin and Joll 343 (color).
Van Haanen. *The Death of Juliet. Magazine of Art* 8 (1885): p. 464.
Wilson. *Garrick and Mrs. Bellamy as Romeo and Juliet.* Ashton (1) 162; Odell 1: facing p. 420; Stone and Kahrl p. 570.
———. *Garrick as Romeo.* Merchant 12b.
Wright. *The Tomb Scene.* Nicolson 305.

Hamlet

Abbey. *The Play Scene.* Abbey catalogue (above, *The Two Gentlemen of Verona*) 4 (color).
Dadd. *Hamlet and His Mother: The Closet Scene.* Ashton (1) 42.
Fuseli. *Hamlet, the Queen, and the Ghost.* Schiff 1747. Another version, Hamlyn 34.
Gordon. *Ophelia. Magazine of Art* 9 (1886): p. 164.
Hayman. *The Play Scene.* Merchant 8; Paulson, *Book and Painting,* 34.
Orchardson. *Hamlet and Ophelia.* Hardie, *Scottish Painting,* 30 (color); Salaman p. 164.
———. *Hamlet and the King. Art Annual* 1897, p. 21.
———. *Ophelia. Art Annual* 1897, p. 21.
Orpen. *The Play Scene.* Bruce Arnold, *Orpen: Mirror to an Age* (London, 1981), facing p. 65 (color).
Pettie. *"Dost know this waterfly?"* (Hardie-Pettie, facing p. 120 (color); *Magazine of Art* 4 (1881): p. 349.
Romney (attributed). *Hamlet and Polonius.* Mander and Mitchenson 16.
Stone (F.). *Ophelia and the Queen. Art Journal* 18 (1856): p. 336.
Stone (M.). *Ophelia. Magazine of Art* 3 (1880): p. 400.
Waterhouse. *Ophelia.* Hobson 74 (color). Another version, Hobson 79.
Watts. *The Madness of Ophelia (Ellen Terry). Burlington Magazine* 105 (1963): facing p. 486; Gaunt (3) 111.
Wilson. *Garrick as Hamlet.* Merchant 12a; Stone and Kahrl p. 546.

Othello

Egg. *Desdemona.* Salaman p. 101.
Hayter. *Desdemona.* Salaman p. 104.
Hillingford. *Othello Relating His Adventures to Desdemona.* Ashton (2) 13.
Rossetti. *Desdemona's Death Song. Victorian Poetry* 20, nos. 3–4 (1982): color plate I.

King Lear

Abbey. *Goneril and Regan.* Abbey catalogue (above, *The Two Gentlemen of Verona*) 12; *Harper's Magazine* 106 (1902–3): frontispiece (color).
———. *King Lear.* Abbey catalogue 1; Lucas (above, *Measure for Measure*) 2: facing p. 317.
Brown. *Cordelia Parting from Her Sisters. Victorian Studies* 21 (1978): p. 327.
Fuseli. *Edgar, Lear, and Kent.* Schiff 1734.
*———. *Lear Renouncing Cordelia.* Schiff 739; Tomory 240;

Irwin, *English Neoclassical Art,* 139.
———. *Lear's Awakening.* Schiff 741.
Joy. *Cordelia. Magazine of Art* 20 (1896–97): p. 58.
Newton. *Lear Attended by Cordelia and the Physician. Art Journal* 26 (1864): p. 14.
West. *Cordelia Making Herself Known to Her Father.* Engen p. 40.
———. *King Lear in the Storm.* Friedman 46; Grose Evans, *Benjamin West* (Carbondale, Ill., 1959), 57.
Wilson. *Garrick as Lear on the Heath.* Merchant 70b; Odell 1: facing p. 378; Stone and Kahrl p. 538.

Macbeth

Chalon. *Lady Macbeth.* Salaman p. 110.
Dawe. *Macbeth and the Witches.* Merchant 14a.
Fuseli. *Lady Macbeth Walking in Her Sleep.* Schiff 738; Fuseli-Tate 18.
———. *Macbeth Affrighted by the Severed Head.* Schiff 363.
———. *Macbeth Questions the Armed Head.* Schiff 881; Hamlyn 33.
———. *The Three Witches, Macbeth, and Banquo.* Schiff 1748.
———. *The Weird Sisters.* Schiff 733, 734, 735; Tomory 72; Fuseli-Tate 19.
Harlow. *Mrs. Siddons as Lady Macbeth* (letter scene). Joseph W. Donohue Jr., *Dramatic Character in the English Romantic Age* (Princeton, N.J., 1970), 37.
———. *Mrs. Siddons as Lady Macbeth* (sleepwalking scene). Donohue 39; Odell 2: facing p. 70.
Maclise. *Macbeth and the Weird Sisters.* Ormond, *Maclise* (exhibition catalogue) 69.
Reynolds. *Macbeth, Hecate, and the Witches.* Merchant 18b.
Sargent. *Ellen Terry as Lady Macbeth.* Ashton (2) 31a.

Antony and Cleopatra

Alma-Tadema. *Cleopatra.* Wood (2) p. 120.
Peters. *"Antony and Cleopatra" 1.2.* Salaman p. 55; Manners VII.
Prinsep. *The Death of Cleopatra.* Wood (1) p. [699]; Wood (2) p. 206.
Reynolds. *Kitty Fisher as Cleopatra.* Waterhouse, *Reynolds,* 59.

Coriolanus

Watts. *Coriolanus. The Victorian High Renaissance* (exhibition catalogue, Minneapolis Institute of Arts, 1979), 11.

THE ROMANCES

Cymbeline

Barry. *Iachimo Rising from the Chest in Imogen's Chamber.* Crookshank and the Knight of Glin, color plate 19; Pressly 97.
*Hoppner. *Imogen and Pisanio in the Wood.* Friedman 168.
Lawrenson. *William Smith as Iachimo.* Odell 1: facing p. 370.
Parris. *Imogen.* Salaman p. 109.

The Winter's Tale

Fuseli. *Mamillius in the Charge of a Lady of the Court.* Schiff 744; Fuseli-Tate 22.
———. *Perdita.* Schiff 745, 746, 747 (different scenes); Fuseli-Tate 23.
———. *Perdita Attended by Three Fairies.* Schiff 1749.
*Hamilton. *Leontes Looking at the Statue of Hermione.* Friedman 111.
Leslie. *Perdita.* Salaman p. 109.
Opie. *Antigonus and the Bear.* Hamlyn 38.
*Wheatley. *A Shepherd's Cot.* Friedman 90; Webster 120.
*Wright. *Antigonus in the Storm.* Nicolson 302. Another version, Leslie Parris, *Landscape in Britain* (London, 1973), 126; Nicolson 304.

The Tempest

Dadd. *"Come unto these yellow sands."* Allderidge 68 (color); Greysmith 26; Maas p. 150; Angus Wilson, *The World of Charles Dickens* (London, 1970), p. 125 (color).
Fuseli. *Ariel Riding on the Bat's Wing.* Schiff 1208.
Hayter. *Miranda.* Salaman p. 105.
Hoppner. *Mrs. Michaelangelo Taylor as Miranda.* William McKay and W. Roberts, *John Hoppner* (London, 1909), facing p. [250].
Houston. *Prospero and Miranda. Art Journal* 31 (1869): p. 69.
Hughes. *Ferdinand and Ariel.* Ironside and Gere 63.
Huskisson. *"Come unto these yellow sands."* Allderidge 248; Wood (1) p. [634].
Peters. *Prospero Dismissing Caliban.* Hamlyn 35.
Rolt. *Scene from "The Tempest." Illustrated London News,* 14 May 1853, p. 385.
Runciman (A.) and Brown. *Runciman and Brown in Dispute over a Passage in "The Tempest." Illustrated Souvenir of the Exhibition of Scottish Art, Royal Academy 1939,* p. 18.
Severn. *Ariel.* Lister, *British Romantic Art,* 97; Royal Academy of Arts Bicentenary Exhibition catalogue (1968–69), p. 61.
Stothard. *Prospero, Miranda, and Caliban.* Ashton (1) 154.
Ward. *Miranda and Caliban.* Merchant 37b.
*Wheatley. *Ferdinand and Maria Playing at Chess.* Webster 121.
*Wright. *Ferdinand, Prospero, and Miranda.* Nicolson 299.

Miscellaneous (allegorical, biographical, etc.)

Dawe. *The Downfall of Shakespeare. Burlington Magazine* 107 (September 1965): p. xxii.
Faed (J.). *Shakespeare and His Contemporaries.* Hartmann p. 23.
Fuseli. *The Nursery of Shakespeare.* Schiff 1202, 1203; Frederick Antal, *Fuseli Studies* (London, 1956), 37a; Lister, *British Romantic Art,* 23.
Hart. *An Early Reading of Shakespeare. Apollo* 89 (1969): p. 57.
Sant. *Shakespeare as a Boy of Twelve.* Hartmann p. 15.

PART THREE

THE MIDDLE AGES

Chaucer

Brown. *Chaucer at the Court of Edward III* (center panel). Wood (3) p. 47 (color); Strong 61 and color plates III, IV; Staley (above, *A Midsummer Night's Dream*) 6; Hilton 8.
Burne-Jones. *The Prioress' Tale.* Hilton 133; Harrison and

Waters 40.
Millais. *Design for a Picture of the Canterbury Pilgrims.* Millais 1: 59.
Mortimer. *The Devil, the Sompnour, and the Widow.* Tomory 162.

Malory and Arthurian Legend
(see also below, under Tennyson)

Archer. *King Arthur Obtains His Sword Excalibur. Art Journal* 33 (1871): p. 99.
Burne-Jones. *The Sleep of King Arthur in Avalon.* Harrison and Waters 253; Wood (3) p. 127 (color).
Dyce. *Religion: The Vision of Sir Galahad and His Company.* Robertson 96; Girouard 119.
Hughes. *The Death of Arthur (The Knight of the Sun).* Wood (3) p. 55 (color); Gaunt (3) 102 (color); *Burlington Magazine* 112 (1970): facing p. 452; Staley (above, *A Midsummer Night's Dream*) 42b.
Paton. *Morte d'Arthur. Art Journal* 31 (1869): p. 1.
Stephens. *Mort d'Arthur.* Nicoll 23.

THE ELIZABETHAN ERA

Spenser

Cosway (M.). *The Duchess of Devonshire as Cynthia. Marsyas* 20 (1979–80): XX. (Subsequent references are to this same issue.)
Frost. *Una. Art Journal* 22 (1860): facing p. 4.
Fuseli. *Amoret Delivered by Britomart.* Schiff 1494.
———. *The Vision of Prince Arthur.* Schiff 721; Tomory 157; Boase, "Macklin and Bowyer," p. 155; *Marsyas* XVI.
Hilton. *Sir Calepine Rescuing Serena. Art Journal* 17 (1855): p. 253.
———. *Una Seeking Shelter in the Cottage of Corceca.* Engen p. 45.
Opie. *The Freeing of Amoret. Marsyas* XVI.
Pickersgill. *Britomart Unarming. Illustrated London News,* 9 June 1855, p. 561.
———. *The Golden Girdle: Britomart Unveiling Amoret. Illustrated London News,* 10 June 1848, p. 378.
Reynolds. *Una and the Lion. Marsyas* XIX.
Strudwick. *Acrasia the Enchantress.* Girouard 128.
Turner. *The Cave of Despair.* Butlin and Joll 452.
Uwins. *Sir Guyon Destroys the Enchantments That Have Kept His Companions from Their Duty* (sketch). *Connoisseur* 158 (1965): p. 241.
Watts. *The Dream of Britomart. Marsyas* XXII.
West. *The Cave of Despair. Burlington Magazine* 110 (1965): facing p. 677.
———. *Una and the Lion.* Robert C. Alberts, *Benjamin West* (Boston, 1978), section of plates following p. 78; Evans (above, *King Lear*) 30; Marsyas XVIII.

Jonson

Fuseli. *Scene from "Every Man in His Humour."* Schiff 886; Antal (above, Shakespeare: Miscellaneous) 54a.
Reynolds. *Garrick as Kitely.* Waterhouse, *Reynolds,* 122.
Zoffany. *Garrick as Abel Drugger.* Stone and Kahrl p. 491; Lady Victoria Manners and G. C. Williamson, *Johann Zoffany* (London, 1920), facing p. 26.

THE SEVENTEENTH CENTURY

Walton

Boughton. *Izaak Walton and the Milkmaids. Christmas Art Annual* 1904, p. 22.

Milton

More than two hundred engravings of pictures from Milton, including some from oil paintings, are in Pointon, *Milton and English Art.* Additional book illustrations are reproduced in Collins Baker's article in *The Library* (1948).

PICTURES IN THE MILTON GALLERY

For engravings of pictures in Fuseli's Milton Gallery, see Schiff's two-volume catalogue of Fuseli's oeuvre and his monograph on the gallery (Zurich, 1973; cited as "MG"). The following list is confined to reproductions of the original paintings and copies thereof. For nos. 4, 7, 11, 12, 17, 25, 30, and 45, see also Fuseli-Tate, pp. 87–91.

1. *Satan Rising from the Flood.* Schiff 889; MG 6.
2. *Satan Calling His Legions.* Schiff 890; MG 9.
4. *The Shepherd's Dream.* Schiff 1762; MG 42; Tomory color plate VII.
5. *Satan Encountering Death.* Schiff 891; MG 14.
7. *Sin Pursued by Death.* Schiff 892.
11. *Satan Bursts from Chaos.* Schiff 893; MG 22.
12. *Odysseus Between Scylla and Charybdis.* Schiff 894; MG 23.
16. *Eve's Dream.* Schiff 896.
17. *The Creation of Eve.* Schiff 897; MG 31.
22. *Death and Sin Bridging the Waste of Chaos.* Schiff 899; MG 19.
25. *The Vision of the Deluge.* Schiff 901; MG 35; Pointon 99.
26. *Noah's Dream.* Schiff 902; MG 41.
30. *Faery Mab.* Schiff 909, 910.
33. *Silence.* Schiff 915.
37. *Solitude. Twilight.* Schiff 905; MG 43.
39. *Milton as a Youth.* Schiff 918; MG 58.
40. *Milton Dictating to His Daughter.* Schiff 921; MG 62.
45. *Euphrosyne.* Schiff 907; MG 46.

OTHER PICTURES FROM MILTON

Paradise Lost

Allston. *The Angel Uriel.* Gerdts and Stebbins (above, *The Merchant of Venice*), p. 41 (color); Jared Flagg, *Life and Letters of Washington Allston* (New York, 1892), facing p. 424.
Barry. *The Temptation of Adam.* Pressly, color plate I; Irwin, *English Neoclassical Art,* 19.
Fuseli (pictures painted before or after the Milton Gallery period, 1791–1800).
———. *The Expulsion from Paradise,* Schiff 1214; MG 34.
———. *The Fall of Satan.* Schiff 1216; Tomory 90.
———. *The Messiah Triumphant.* Schiff 1213.
———. *Satan on the Burning Lake.* Schiff 1209.
———. *Satan, Sin, and Death.* Schiff 1210.
———. *Satan Starting from the Touch of Ithuriel's Spear.* Schiff 1212 (color); MG 28.
———. *Sin Intervening Between Satan and Death.* Schiff 891; Tomory 94.
———. *The Temptation of Eve.* Schiff 1215; MG 30; Tomory, color plate X.

———. *Uriel Observes Satan on His Flight to Earth.* Schiff 1211.
Haydon. *Uriel and Satan. Illustrated London News,* 7 June 1845, p. 363.
Hayman (?). *Fairies Dancing on the Green by Moonlight.* Gowing 2; *Apollo* 109 (1979): p. 208.
Horsley. *Satan Touched by Ithuriel's Spear.* Robertson 163.
Lawrence. *Satan Calling His Legions.* MG 7.
Martin. *Adam and Eve Entertaining the Angel Raphael.* Feaver 38.
———. *The Celestial City and River of Bliss.* Feaver 125.
———. *The Creation of Light.* Feaver 62.
———. *The Deluge.* Christopher Johnstone, *John Martin* (London, 1974), p. [72] (color).
———. *The Eve of the Deluge.* Feaver 121; Johnstone p. 73.
———. *The Expulsion of Adam and Eve.* Feaver, color plate II; Johnstone p. 39.
———. *The Judgment of Adam and Eve* (watercolor version). Feaver 139.
———. *Pandemonium.* Feaver 124; Johnstone p. 92.
Runciman (A.). *The Detection of Satan by Ithuriel.* Pressly 9.
West. *The Expulsion from Paradise.* John Dillenberger, *Benjamin West* (San Antonio, Texas, 1977), 36.

Comus

Eastlake. *Comus.* Robertson 39.
Etty. *Circe, Syrens, and Naiads.* Farr 80.
———. *The Gardens of Hesperus.* Pointon, *Milton,* 186; Farr 81; William Gaunt and F. Gordon Roe, *Etty and the Nude* (Leigh-on-Sea, 1943), 52.
———. *"Venus now wakes, and wakens love."* Farr 27b.
Frost. *Chastity. Art Journal* 19 (1857): p. 5; 28 (1866): facing p. 76.
———. *Nymphs Dancing (Sabrina).* Treble 16.
———. *The Syrens. Art Journal* 19 (1857): p. 6.
Maclise. *Sabrina Releasing the Lady from the Enchanted Chair.* Ormond, *Maclise* (exhibition catalogue), 90.
Richmond. *Comus.* Raymond Lister, *George Richmond* (London, 1981), XIII.
Wheatley. *Anthony Webster as Comus.* Webster E10.

L'Allegro and Il Penseroso

Fuseli. *Euphrosyne.* Schiff 1813.
———. *Fairy Mab.* Schiff 909, 1498.
———. *L'Allegro.* Schiff 907; Pointon 93.
Hicks. *Il Penseroso and L'Allegro.* Engen p. 76; Guise 170a, b.
Reynolds. *Mrs. Hale as Euphrosyne.* Waterhouse, *Reynolds,* 90.
Runciman (A.). *Landscape from "L'Allegro."* Irwin, *Scottish Painters,* 48; Parris (above, *The Winter's Tale*) 91.
Sidley. *L'Allegro.* Wood (1) p. [721].
Webster. *Il Penseroso. Art Journal* 17 (1855): p. 295.

Biographical

Brown. *Cromwell Discussing the Protection of the Vaudois with Milton and Marvell.* Strong 169; Hueffer facing p. 313.
Crowe. *Milton Visiting Galileo in Prison. Art Journal* 26 (1864): p. 206.
Fuseli. *Milton's Dream of His Second Wife.* Schiff 920; MG 60.
———. *The Return of Milton's First Wife.* Schiff 919; MG 59.
Romney. *Milton Dictating "Paradise Lost" to His Daughter.* MG 63.

The Diarists: Evelyn and Pepys

Elmore. *The Wife's Portrait. Art Journal* 28 (1866): facing p. 204.
Frith. *Charles II and Lady Castlemaine.* Noakes p. [111].
———. *King Charles II's Last Sunday.* Noakes p. [113]; Strong 128.

Butler

LePiper. *The Combat of Hudibras and Cerdon.* Bindman 15.

Bunyan

Gilbert. *Christiana at the House of Gaius. Art Journal* 29 (1867): facing p. 120.
Harvey. *John Bunyan and His Daughter at the Door of Bedford Jail. Art Journal* 20 (1858): p. 75.
Pickersgill. *Christiana in the Valley of Humiliation. Art Journal* 26 (1864): facing p. 184.

Dryden

Fuseli. *Theodor and Honoria.* Schiff 755.
Millais. *Cymon and Iphigenia.* Nicoll 1; Hilton 14.
Reynolds. *Cymon and Iphigenia.* Oliver Millar, *Late Georgian Pictures in the Collection of H. M. the Queen* (London, 1969), 103.

THE EIGHTEENTH CENTURY

Defoe

Crowe. *Defoe in the Pillory. Art Journal* 30 (1868): facing p. 27.

Swift

Penny. *A Scene from Swift's Description of a City Shower.* Waterhouse, *Dictionary,* p. 274.

The Spectator

Crowe. *Sir Richard Steele Writing to His Wife. Art Journal* 26 (1864): p. 205.
Frith. *Sir Roger de Coverley and the Perverse Widow.* Noakes p. [82].
Fuseli. *The Rosicrucian Cavern.* Schiff 1217; Tomory 233.
Gilbert. *Brunetta and Phillis. Illustrated London News,* 30 March 1844, p. 197.
Solomon. *Academy for the Instruction of the Discipline of the Fan. Illustrated London News,* 26 May 1849, p. 345.

Gay

Frith. *Polly Peachum.* Noakes p. [36].
Landseer (E.). *The Monkey Who Had Seen the World.* Ormond, *Landseer,* p. 56 (color).
Opie. *Hobnelia, or The Spell.* Ada Earland, *John Opie* (London, 1911), facing p. 196.
Newton. *Captain Macheath Upbraided by Polly and Lucy. Art Journal* 26 (1864): p. 13.
Ward. *The Council of Horses. Art Journal* 14 (1852): facing p. 332.

Ramsay

Johnston. *Roger and Jenny. Illustrated London News,* 17 February 1849, p. 105.

———. *Scene from "The Gentle Shepherd." Art Journal* 19 (1857): p. 59; Guise 48.

Pope

(Halsband, *"The Rape of the Lock,"* reproduces numerous engravings from illustrated editions of the poem.)
Crowe. *Pope's Introduction to Dryden. Art Journal* 26 (1864): p. 207.
Fradelle. *Belinda at Her Toilette.* Halsband 34.
Fuseli. *Belinda's Awakening.* Halsband plate V (color); Schiff 1751.
———. *The Cave of Spleen.* Halsband 23; Schiff 945; Tomory, color plate VIII.
Graham. *Scene from "The Rape of the Lock."* Halsband 16.
Hamilton. *The Rape of the Lock.* Halsband, frontispiece (color).
Morland. *Belinda Billet Doux.* Sir Walter Gilbey and E. D. Cuming, *George Morland* (London, 1907), facing p. 16 (color).
Peters. *Miss Bampfylde as Belinda.* Halsband 15; Manners, facing p. 16.
Sharpe. *Belinda.* Halsband 33.
Turner. *Pope's Villa at Twickenham.* Brownell 30; Finley p. 41; Butlin and Joll 60 (color).

Thomson

(Cohen, *The Art of Discrimination,* reproduces a number of book illustrations from *The Seasons.*)
Fuseli. *Celadon and Amelia.* Schiff 1218; Tomory 108.
———. *The Dying Shepherd.* Schiff 1315; Cohen 21; Tomory 144.
Hamilton, William. *Celadon and Amelia.* Cohen 20.
———. *Palemon and Lavinia.* Cohen 24–26.
Hughes. *Musidora.* Raymond Watkinson, *Pre-Raphaelite Art and Design* (London, 1970), 79.
Kirk. *Musidora.* Cohen 34.
Westall. *The Dying Shepherd.* Cohen 22.
Wilson. *Celadon and Amelia (A Summer Storm).* Cohen 20a; W. G. Constable, *Richard Wilson* (Cambridge, Mass., 1953), 24b.

Gray

Corbould. *The Bard. Apollo* 84 (1966): August supplement, p. 1.
Jones. *The Bard.* J. D. Hunt, *The Figure in the Landscape,* 51; Parris (above, *The Winter's Tale*) 94; *National Library of Wales Journal* 14 (1965–66): XIV.8.

Richardson

Hayman. *Scene in "Pamela."* Gowing 27.
Highmore. *Illustrations to "Pamela".* Nos. 2, 12, *Fitzwilliam Museum: Catalogue of the Paintings: Vol. III, British School* (Cambridge, 1977), 7; nos. 3, 4, *The First Hundred Years of the Royal Academy* (London, 1951), pp. 95–96; no. 6, Webster, *Wheatley,* 70; no. 8, Burke, *English Art 1714–1800,* 47b; no. 9, Gaunt (1) 44.

Sterne

Carter. *The Shepherd.* Gordon (3) IV.
Gaugain. *Maria.* Waterhouse, *Dictionary,* p. 144.
Gilbert. *My Uncle Toby and Corporal Trim. Magazine of Art* 2 (1879): p. 157
Hurlstone. *Maria.* Gordon (3) VIII.
Kauffmann. *Maria near Moulines.* Gordon (3) IX.
Mortimer. *The Captive.* Gordon (3) V.
Reinagle. *The Fair Maria.* Tomory 193.
Romney. *Dr. Slop in Mr. Shandy's Parlor.* Tave (above, *Henry IV*) 7.
Ward. *La Fleur's Departure from Montreuil. Art Journal* 17 (1855): p. 46.
West. *The Pilgrim and His Dead Ass.* Dillenberger (above, *Paradise Lost*) 19.
Wright. *Maria.* Nicolson 220; Gordon (3) XI.
———. *Maria and Her Dog Sylvio.* Nicolson 184; Gordon (3) X.
———. *Sterne's Captive.* Nicolson 162; Ronald Paulson, *Emblem and Expression* (London, 1975), 126; Gordon (3) VII.

Goldsmith

Baxter. *Olivia and Sophia. Illustrated London News,* 3 April 1852, p. 277; *Art Journal* 26 (1864): p. 145.
Brown. *The Vicar of Wakefield.* W. H. Hunt, 1: 117.
Faed (J.). *Goldsmith in His Study. Magazine of Art* 3 (1880): p. 432.
Faed (T.). *Sophia and Olivia. Illustrated London News,* 14 May 1853, p. 377.
Frith. *Back to Back.* Noakes p. [42].
———. *The Village Pastor.* Mario Praz, *The Hero in Eclipse* (London, 1956), facing p. 336.
Martin. *Edwin and Angelina.* Johnstone, *Martin* (above, *Paradise Lost*), p. 48; Parris (above, *The Winter's Tale*) 275.
Mulready. *Burchell and Sophia (Haymaking).* Heleniak 137.
———. *The Whistonian Controversy.* Heleniak 135.
Newton. *The Vicar of Wakefield and His Family. Art Journal* 26 (1864): p. 15.
Solomon. *An Awkward Position. Illustrated London News,* 14 June 1851, p. 550.
Ward. *Goldsmith as a Wandering Musician. Art Journal* 17 (1855): p. 48.
Wheatley. *The Deserted Village.* Webster E112.

Ossian

Kauffmann. *Trenmore and Imbaca.* Irwin, *English Neoclassical Art,* 117.
MacWhirter. *Ossian's Grave. Art Annual* 1903, p. 24.
Runciman (A.). *Ossian Singing* (ceiling picture at Penicuik, sketch). Irwin, *Scottish Painters,* 43.
———. *The Death of Oscar* (sketch). Irwin, *English Neoclassical Art,* 115.
Trumbull. *Lamderg and Gelchossa.* Helen A. Cooper, *John Trumbull: The Hand and Spirit of a Painter* (exhibition catalogue, Yale University Art Gallery, 1982), 104, 156 (two versions).

Sheridan

Pettie. *Charles Surface Selling His Ancestors.* Hardie-Pettie, facing p. 126 (color).
———. *Lady Teazle: A Cup of Tea.* Hardie-Pettie, facing p. 96 (color).

Cowper

Barker. *Crazy Kate.* Tomory 191.
Fuseli. *Illustrations to "The Task."* Schiff 1229–1236 (1230 and

1232 in color); Fuseli-Tate 134 (color); Tomory 142, 190; Antal (above, Shakespeare: Miscellaneous) 54b, 55b.

Burns

Fraser. *Tam o' Shanter in the Smiddie.* Caw [14].
Ibbetson. *Hallowe'en.* Rotha M. Clay, *J. C. Ibbetson* (London, 1948), 97.
———. *Tam o' Shanter.* Clay 98.

THE ROMANTIC ERA

Wordsworth

Joy. *Laodamia. Magazine of Art* 20 (1896–97): p. 58.

Coleridge

Dyce. *Christabel.* Pointon, *Dyce,* 108; Staley (above, *A Midsummer Night's Dream*) 92b.

Scott

Allan. *Scott at Shakespeare's Tomb.* S. Schoenbaum, *Shakespeare's Lives* (Oxford, 1970), after p. 552.
Beavis. *March of the Men of Buccleuch.* Gordon (2) 29.
Boaden. *Cooke as Roderick Dhu in "The Lady of the Lake."* Mander and Mitchenson 70.
Bonington. *Quentin Durward at Liège. Burlington Magazine* 88 (1946): facing p. 112.
Cattermole. *Wordsworth and Scott at Newark Castle.* James Reed, *Sir Walter Scott: Landscape and Locality* (London, 1980), 1.
Danby. *The Escape of Mary Queen of Scots.* Gordon (2) 14.
Drummond. *The Fiery Cross.* Gordon (2) 4.
Douglas. *The Invasion of the Sanctum Sanctorum.* Gordon (2) 20.
Faed (J.). *Catherine Seyton and Roland Graeme* (sketch). Gordon (2) 11.
Frith. *Amy Robsart and Janet.* Noakes p. [39].
——. *Catherine Seyton.* See Landseer (E.), below.
——. *Madge Wildfire and Jeanie Deans.* Gordon (4) 5.
Gavin. *Phoebe Mayflower. Art Journal* 28 (1866): facing p. 12.
Hay. *Caleb Blunderstone's Ruse* (sketch). Gordon (2) 5.
Herdman. *Interview Between Jeanie and Effie Deans in Prison.* Gordon (2) 23; Gordon (4) 6.
Howard. *The Rescue of Roland Graeme.* Gordon (4) 4.
Johnson. *The Swineherd, Gurth, Son of Beowulf. Magazine of Art* 2 (1879): facing p. 163.
Landseer (C.). *The Dying Warrior.* Gordon (2) 12.
Landseer (E.). *Attachment.* Ormond, *Landseer,* p. 103 (color).
——. *The Bride of Lammermoor.* Ormond, *Landseer,* p. 115.
——. *Catherine Seyton Looking from the Battlements of Loch Leven* (formerly attributed to Frith). Gordon (2) 9.
——. *A Visit to the Falconer's Nest.* Ormond, *Landseer,* p. 117.
Lauder (R.S.). *The Bride of Lammermoor.* Gordon (2) 16.
——. *The Glee Maiden.* Hardie, *Scottish Painting,* 12.
——. *The Gow Chrom Conducting the Glee Maiden to a Place of Safety.* Gordon (2) 18.
——. *Meg Merrilies and the Dying Smuggler. Illustrated London News,* 4 April 1857, p. 318.
——. *The Trial of Effie Deans.* Gordon (2) 25; McKay, facing p. 224; Caw [17]; Guise 134.
Maclise. *The Combat of Two Knights.* Crookshank and the Knight of Glin, 232.
Millais. *The Bride of Lammermoor.* Guise 62.
———. *Diana Vernon.* Millais 2: p. 167
———. *Effie Deans.* Millais 2: p. 99; Gordon (2) 32; Guise 61.
Mulready. *Mr. Peregrine Touchwood Breaking in on the Rev. Josiah Cargill.* Heleniak 115
Nash. *Amy Robsart and Janet.* Strong 24.
Pettie. *The Appearance of the Countess of Derby in the Golden Room.* Hardie-Pettie, facing p. 144 (color); Gordon (2) 33.
———. *The Chieftain's Candlesticks.* Hardie-Pettie, facing p. 128 (color).
———. *Jacobites 1745.* Hardie-Pettie, facing p. 72 (color).
———. *Scene in Hal of the Wynd's Smithy.* Gordon (2) 17; *Magazine of Art* 4 (1881): 13.
Phillip. *Catherine Glover and Father Clement.* Gordon (2) 15.
Rossetti. *King René's Honeymoon.* Surtees 255.
Severn. *The Abdication of Mary Queen of Scots.* Gordon (2) 13.
Trumbull. *The Knighting of DeWilton by the Earl of Angus.* Gordon (1) p. 46; Cooper (above, Ossian) 98 (color).
Turner. *Staffa (Fingal's Cave).* Butlin and Joll 329 (color).
Westall. *Two Scenes from "Marmion."* Gordon (4), 2, 3.
Wilkie. *Julian Peveril and Sir Geoffrey Hudson.* Gordon (2) 7.
Windus. *Morton Before Claverhouse.* Gordon (2) 26; Reynolds, *Victorian Painting,* 45.

Byron

Allan. *Byron Reposing in the House of a Turkish Fisherman. Connoisseur* 186 (1974): facing p. 93 (color).
Brown. *The Young Foscari. Magazine of Art* 20 (1896–97): p. 260.
Etty. *The Corsair.* Farr 86.
O'Neill. *Zuleika. Illustrated London News,* 8 April 1848, p. 231.
Turner. *The Bright Stone of Honour.* Butlin and Joll 335 (color).

Moore

Maclise. *Mokanna Revealing His Features to Zelica* (pencil study). Ormond, *Maclise* (exhibition catalogue) 66.

Shelley

Severn. *Shelley Composing "Prometheus Unbound" in the Baths of Caracalla.* Quennell p. 151.
Wilson. *Asia.* Percy H. Bate, *The English Pre-Raphaelite Painters,* 3d ed. (London, 1905), facing p. 66.

Keats

(The Keats-Shelley Memorial Souvenir Issue of the [London] *Bookman,* 42 [1912], cited as "KS", contains several book illustrations of Keats's poems.)
Crane. *La Belle Dame sans Merci.* KS p. 13.
Dicksee. *La Belle Dame sans Merci.* Hobson 62.
Hughes. *La Belle Dame sans Merci. Burlington Magazine* 112 (1970): facing p. 455.
Hunt. *Isabella and the Pot of Basil.* Bennett, *William Holman Hunt,* 2; Wood (3) p. 105 (color); W. H. Hunt, 2: facing p. 255; KS p. 40.
Millais. *The Eve of St. Agnes.* Millais 1: 375; Nicoll 3.
Rae. *Isabella.* KS p. 35.
Rheam. *La Belle Dame sans Merci.* KS p. 17.
Scott. *Keats's Grave in the Old Protestant Cemetery at Rome.* Wood (1) p. [716].
Southall. *Isabella.* KS p. 41.

Strudwick. *Isabella*. Bate (above, Shelley), after p. 110.
Waterhouse. *La Belle Dame sans Merci*. Hobson 58 (color); Wood (3) p. 143 (color).
———. *Lamia*. Hobson 80 (color). Another version, Hobson 81 (color).
Watts. *Endymion*. KS p. 34.

Hood

Blunden. *The Song of the Shirt*. *Victorian Studies* 23 (1980): p. 191.
Holl. *The Song of the Shirt*. Wood (4) 131.
Redgrave. *The Sempstress*. Forbes, *Royal Academy*, 57; Treble 47; *Victorian Studies* 23 (1980): p. 187.
Smallfield. *First Love*. Maas p. 238.

THE VICTORIAN ERA

Tennyson

Archer. *Arthur and Guinevere*. *Apollo* 51 (1950): cover of April issue, where erroneously ascribed to Hughes.
Breakspeare. *"He cometh not."* Handley-Read (above, *A Midsummer Night's Dream*) 13.
Burne-Jones. *The Legend of the Briar Rose*. *Connoisseur* 161 (1966): 5 (color); Hilary Beck, *Victorian Engravings* (London, 1973), 48–51; Staley (above, *A Midsummer Night's Dream*) 49b.
———. *Sir Galahad*. Nicoll 117.
Dicksee. *The Passing of Arthur*. *Art Annual* 1905, p. 12
———. *Yseult*. *Art Annual* 1905, p. 26.
Gilbert. *Sir Lancelot du Lake*. *Magazine of Art* 16 (1893): p. 358.
Grimshaw. *Elaine*. Wood (3) p. 133 (color).
Hughes. *Enid and Geraint (The Brave Geraint)*. Wood (3) p. 57 (color); Nicoll 100; Hilton 78; *Burlington Magazine* 112 (1970): facing p. 452.
Leighton. *A King and a Beggar Maid*. Wood (1) p. 649.
———. *Lady Godiva*. Engen p. 53.
MacNab. *The Lady of Shalott*. *Magazine of Art* 10 (1887): p. 291.
McTaggart. *Enoch Arden*. *Magazine of Art* 4 (1881): p. 104.
Millais. *"She only said, My life is dreary. . . ." (Mariana)*. Wood (3) p. 31 (color); Maas p. 139; Hilton 36; Nicoll 29; Millais 1: 107.
Paton. *Hesperus*. Wood (3) p. 76 (color).
———. *Sir Galahad's Vision of the Holy Grail*. Girouard color plate XVIII.
Sandys. *Mariana in the Moated Grange*. *Apollo* 82 (1965): p. 399 (color).
Shaw. *The Lady of Shalott*. Handley-Read (above, *A Midsummer Night's Dream*) 70.
Smetham. *The Rose of Dawn*. [Edward Malins and Morchard Bishop,] *James Smetham and Francis Danby: Two Nineteenth Century Romantic Painters* (London, 1974), 14.
Strudwick. *Elaine*. *Magazine of Art* 14 (1891): p. 263.
Waterhouse. *The Lady Clare*. Hobson 96.
———. *The Lady of Shalott*. Hobson 64 (color); Wood (3) 141 (color).
———. *Mariana in the South*. Hobson 71 (color).
———. *St. Cecilia*. Hobson 63 (color); Harrison and Waters 267.
Watts. *Sir Galahad*. Maas p. 29; Handley-Read (above, *A Midsummer Night's Dream*) 95; *Burlington Magazine* 105 (1963): facing p. 480.

Browning

Hughes. *The Guarded Bower*. *Anthology of Victorian and Edwardian Paintings* (exhibition catalogue, Bristol City Art Gallery, 1975), 20.
Scott. *Scene from "Paracelsus."* Thompson, *Art for Scotland*, 44.

Bulwer-Lytton

Hunt. *Rienzi Vowing to Obtain Justice*. Wood (3) p. 13; Nicoll 24; Hilton 17; Gaunt (3) 74; Bennett, *Holman Hunt*, 14; Cummings and Staley 215.

Dickens

Chapman. *Little Nell and Her Grandfather*. Wood (1) p. [568].
Millais. *Little Nell and Her Grandfather*. Millais 2: 377.

Rossetti

Moira. *Willowwood*. *Victorian Poetry* 20, nos. 3–4 (1982): 22.
Murray. *Love's Nocturn*. Ibid., 18.
Shaw. *The Blessed Damozel*. Wood (3) p. 152 (color).

NOTES

Full bibliographical information concerning most of the references given in these notes in abbreviated form will be found in the Bibliography. Full citations for the rest are given on their first occurrence in each chapter. Additional cue terms:

Constable	*John Constable's Correspondence,* ed. R. B. Beckett, vols. 1–6 (Suffolk Records Society, 1962–68).
Hazlitt	*The Complete Works of William Hazlitt,* ed. P. P. Howe, 21 vols. (London, 1930–34).
JWCI	*Journal of the Warburg and Courtauld Institutes.*
Ruskin	*The Works of John Ruskin: Library Edition,* ed. E. T. Cook and A. D. O. Wedderburn, 39 vols. (London, 1902–12).
V & A Scrapbook	*Press Cuttings from English Newspapers on Matters of Artistic Interest, 1686–1835,* 6 vols. (Victoria and Albert Museum Library)
Yale Walpole	*Yale Edition of the Correspondence of Horace Walpole,* ed. W. S. Lewis et al. 48 vols. (New Haven, Conn., 1937–83).

Part One

INTRODUCTION

1. Fuseli in the *Analytical Review,* June 1788, quoted in Mason, *The Mind of Fuseli,* p. 204.
2. Quoted in Edgar Johnson, *Charles Dickens: His Tragedy and Triumph* (New York, 1952), 2:796.
3. Alexander Gilchrist, *Life of William Blake,* ed. Ruthven Todd, Everyman ed. (London, 1942), p. 83.
4. *The Complete Poetry and Prose of William Blake,* ed. David V. Erdman (Berkeley, Cal., 1982), p. 530.
5. W. M. Rossetti, *Ruskin; Rossetti; Preraphaelitism,* quoted in Brian and Judy Dobbs, *Dante Gabriel Rossetti: An Alien Victorian* (London, 1977), p. 126.
6. *Memorial Catalogue of the Burns Exhibition Held in the Galleries of the Royal Glasgow Institute . . . 1896* (Glasgow, 1898), pp. 5–90.
7. See especially C. R. Parsons, "Eugène Delacroix and Literary Inspiration," *University of Toronto Quarterly* 33 (1964): 164–77; Philippe Verdier, "Delacroix and Shakespeare," *Yale French Studies,* no. 33 (1964), pp. 37–45; and Esther Gordon Dotson, "English Shakespeare Illustrations and Eugène Delacroix," *Essays in Honor of Walter Friedlaender* (New York, 1965), pp. 40–61. Specialized studies of Delacroix's use of subjects from Scott and Byron will be cited in the notes to Part Three.
8. *The Spectacular Career of Clarkson Stanfield, 1793–1867* (exhibition catalogue, Tyne and Wear County Council Museums, 1979), p. 35.
9. Gerald Reitlinger, *The Economics of Taste: The Rise and Fall of Picture Prices, 1760–1960* (London, 1961), p. 92.
10. Balston, *John Martin,* pp. 244–48.
11. Farington (1), 3:1051 (29 August 1798).
12. Allderidge, *The Late Richard Dadd,* p. 82.
13. Balston, p. 36.
14. Graves, *The Society of Artists,* p. 142.
15. *Literary Gazette,* 23 May 1835, p. 330.
16. *Athenaeum,* 5 July 1862, p. 23.
17. James, *The Painter's Eye,* p. 203. (Originally in the *Atlantic Monthly,* August 1882.)

CHAPTER ONE

1. Quoted in Moore, *Hogarth's Literary Relationships,* p. 22.
2. See *Thirty Different Likenesses: David Garrick in Portrait and in Performance* (exhibition catalogue, Buxton Museum and Art Gallery, 1981), and a fuller study by Kalman A. Burnim, "Looking upon His Like Again: Garrick and the Artist," in Shirley Strum Kenny, ed., *British Theatre and the Other Arts, 1660–1800* (Washington, D.C., 1984), pp. 182–218.
3. See Bertelsen, "Garrick and English Painting."
4. George Winchester Stone, Jr., and George M. Kahrl, *David Garrick: A Critical Biography* (Carbondale, Ill., 1979), pp. xvi, 46. The whole of chapter 14 is devoted to Garrick as a patron of the arts.
5. The most abundant sources on these pictures are Adams, *Catalogue of Pictures in the Garrick Club,* and Mander and Mitchenson, *Guide to the Maugham Collection.*
6. See Moore, *Hogarth's Literary Relationships.*
7. See T. C. Duncan Eaves, "Graphic Illustration of the Novels of Samuel Richardson, 1740–1810," *Huntington Library Quarterly* 14 (1951): 349–83.
8. See Gowing, "Hogarth, Hayman, and the Vauxhall Decorations," and Paulson, *Hogarth: His Life, Art, and Times,* 1:347–50.
9. See Alastair Smart, "Hogarth or Hayman? Another Look at the *Fairies Dancing on the Green by Moonlight,*" *Apollo* 109 (1979): 208–12.
10. John Ingamells and Robert Raines, "A Catalogue of the Paintings, Drawings and Etchings of Philip Mercier," *Walpole Society* 46 (1976–78): 45.
11. T. C. Duncan Eaves, "'The Harlowe Family' by Joseph Highmore: A Note on the Illustration of Richardson's *Clarissa,*" *Huntington Library Quarterly* 7 (1943): 89–96.
12. Quoted from *Works of James Barry* (1809) in Burke, *English Art, 1714–1800,* p. 253.
13. The fullest discussions of the ramifications and implica-

tions of *ut pictura poesis* are Davis, "Ut pictura poesis"; Lee, "Ut pictura poesis"; and Hagstrum, *The Sister Arts.*

14. Letter quoted in Mason, *The Mind of Fuseli,* pp. 110–11.

15. "Memoirs of Thomas Jones," *Walpole Society* 32 (1946–48): 33–34.

16. Sandby, *History of the Royal Academy,* 2:412–13.

17. Quoted in Witemeyer, *George Eliot and the Visual Arts,* p. 33.

18. The Garrick Club pictures are catalogued in Adams, and those at the National Theatre in Mander and Mitchenson. See also *The DeWildes* (exhibition catalogue, Northampton Museums and Art Gallery, 1971; text by Ian Mayes) and Mayes's "John Bell, *The British Theatre* and Samuel De Wilde," *Apollo* 113 (1981): 100–103.

19. See Eichholz, "William Kent's Career as Literary Illustrator," and Michael I. Wilson, *William Kent: Architect, Designer, Painter, Gardener, 1685–1748* (London, 1984), pp. 67–73, 148–53, 203–7.

20. See Strong, *Recreating the Past,* pp. 17–22.

21. Anthony Blunt, *The Art of William Blake* (New York, 1959), p. 7 n.

22. Boase, "Macklin and Bowyer," pp. 174–76.

23. Northcote, *Conversations,* p. 195.

24. Cunningham, *Lives,* 1:253.

25. See J. L. Nevinson, "Vandyke Dress," *Connoisseur* 157 (1964): 166–71.

26. Northcote, *Reynolds,* 2:88.

27. Cunningham, *Lives,* 1:192.

28. Leslie, *Reynolds,* 1:354–55, 434.

29. Hazlitt, 18:58. (Originally in the *Champion,* 30 October 1814.)

30. See Sacheverell Sitwell, *Conversation Pieces,* and Williamson, *English Conversation Pictures.*

31. Quoted in Luke Herrmann, *British Landscape Painting of the Eighteenth Century* (London, 1973), p. 19.

32. Whitley (1), 2:379.

33. See Cohen, *The Art of Discrimination,* chap. 4.

34. Leslie Parris, *Landscape in Britain ca. 1750–1850* (exhibition catalogue, Tate Gallery, 1973), p. 75. This passage is indebted also to J. D. Hunt, *The Figure in the Landscape,* passim.

35. See Lynne Epstein, "Mrs. Radcliffe's Landscapes: The Influence of Three Landscape Painters on Her Nature Descriptions," *Hartford Studies in Literature* 1 (1969): 107–20.

36. Nathan Drake, *Literary Hours* (1798), quoted in Lindsay, *The Sunset Ship,* p. 26.

37. Quoted ibid., p. 17.

38. See Jean Hamilton, *The Sketching Society, 1799–1851* (Victoria and Albert Museum, 1971), and David Winter, "Girtin's Sketching Club," *Huntington Library Quarterly* 37 (1974): 123–29.

39. Quoted in Sitwell and Barton, "Taste," 2:4.

40. Ibid., 2: 9.

CHAPTER TWO

1. The most detailed gathering of information on illustrated editions in the period is Hammelmann, *Book Illustrators in Eighteenth-Century England.* A briefer account is Williams, "English Book-Illustration, 1700–1775."

2. See Montague Summers, "The First Illustrated Shakespeare," *Connoisseur* 102 (1938): 305–9.

3. Bertelsen, "Garrick and English Painting," p. 316.

4. Halsband, *"The Rape of the Lock,"* p. 4.

5. Muir, *Victorian Illustrated Books,* p. 1.

6. Halsband, *"The Rape of the Lock,"* p. 7.

7. See W. M. Merchant, "Francis Hayman's Illustrations of Shakespeare," *Shakespeare Quarterly* 9 (1958): 141–47; and Marcia Allentuck, "Sir Thomas Hanmer Instructs Francis Hayman: An Editor's Notes to His Illustrator (1744)," ibid., 27 (1976): 288–315. On Hayman, see also Hammelmann, "Eighteenth Century English Illustrators: Francis Hayman, R. A."

8. W. Jackson Bate, *The Burden of the Past and the English Poet* (Cambridge, Mass., 1970), pp. 87–88.

9. Leigh Hunt, *Autobiography* (New York, 1855), 1:91–92.

10. Quoted in Mrs. [Anna Eliza] Bray, *Life of Thomas Stothard, R.A.* (London, 1851), p. 229. For a reasonably full catalogue of Stothard's works, see A. C. Coxhead, *Thomas Stothard, R.A.: An Illustrated Monograph* (London, 1906).

11. Hazlitt, 18:29. (Originally in the *Champion,* 26 June 1814.)

12. W. B. Scott, *Memoir of David Scott, R. S. A.* (Edinburgh, 1850; rpt. New York, 1975), p. 21.

13. W. B. Scott, *Autobiographical Notes,* 1:14–15.

14. See Edward C. J. Wolf, *Rowlandson and His Illustrations of Eighteenth Century English Literature* (Copenhagen, 1945).

15. *The Poems of Thomas Gray, William Collins, and Oliver Goldsmith,* ed. Roger Lonsdale (London, 1969), pp. 397, 399.

16. Background information on Shakespeare's fame, here and in later contexts, is from Louis Marder, *His Exits and His Entrances: The Story of Shakespeare's Reputation* (Philadelphia, 1963) as well as other sources mentioned in these notes.

17. On Pine, see William Dunlap, *A History of the Rise and Progress of the Arts of Design in the United States* (Boston, 1918), 1: 375–80; Strong, *Recreating the Past,* pp. 17–18; *Dictionary of National Biography; Dictionary of American Biography.*

18. Newspaper clippings hand-dated 17 May 1781 and [no date] 1782, respectively, in V & A Scrapbook, 1: 197, 218.

19. See Dotson, "English Shakespeare Illustrations and Eugène Delacroix" (see above, Introduction, n. 7).

20. The main authorities on Boydell's Shakespeare Gallery are Friedman, *Boydell's Shakespeare Gallery* (the most detailed treatment, though not without errors); Boase, "Illustrations of Shakespeare's Plays," especially pp. 94–107; Hutton, *Alderman Boydell's Shakespeare Gallery;* and Thompson, "The Boydell Shakespeare."

21. These pamphlets were reviewed and quoted in the *Monthly Review* 79 (1788): 81, and 80 (1789): 362–63.

22. *Monthly Review* 2d ser. 4 (1791): 332–34.

23. Newspaper clipping dated 1789, in V & A Scrapbook, 2: 509.

24. Yale Walpole, 33:546–47.

25. *Letters of Sir Joshua Reynolds,* ed. Frederick Whiley Hilles (Cambridge, 1929), p. 174. For the dispute over the price of the *Macbeth* picture, see *Portraits by Sir Joshua Reynolds,* ed. Frederick Whiley Hilles (New York, 1952), pp. 179–84.

26. Northcote, *Reynolds,* 2:227–28.

27. For much information on Romney's illustrations of Shakespearean subjects, see Elizabeth Johnson, *George Romney, Paintings and Drawings* (exhibition catalogue, Kenwood House, 1961).

28. Boydell's prospectus, quoted in Friedman, p. 67.

29. Charles Beecher Hogan, *Shakespeare in the Theatre, 1701–1800* (Oxford, 1952–57), 2:716–19.

30. Farington (1), 9:3407 (24 February 1809).

31. *The Private Letter-Books of Sir Walter Scott,* ed. Wilfred Partington (New York, 1930), pp. 248–49.

32. Yale Walpole, 15:206.

33. Northcote, *Conversations,* pp. 115–16.

34. Ibid., p. 114.

35. Hazlitt, 5:234. (Originally in the *Examiner,* 23 July 1815.)

36. *Magazine of Art* 9 (1886): 219; Farington (1), 7:2796 (25 June 1806); Farington (2), 6:81 n.

37. *Letters of Charles Lamb,* ed. E. V. Lucas (New Haven, Conn., 1935), 3:394.

38. Lamb, "Detached Thoughts on Books and Reading."

39. Review of John Leech's *Pictures of Life and Character, Quarterly Review* 96 (1854): 75.

40. C. R. Smith, "Pictorial Illustrations of Shakespeare," pp. 459–60.

41. Scott, *Autobiographical Notes,* 1:16–17.

42. Whitley (3), p. 5.

43. Dotson, "English Shakespeare Illustrations and Eugène Delacroix," p. 47 n.

44. The definitive treatment of the Woodmason Gallery is Hamlyn, "An Irish Shakespeare Gallery."

45. The little that is known—or has been collected—about the Poet's Gallery is in Boase. "Macklin and Bowyer," pp. 148–55.

46. The magisterial work on Fuseli is Gert Schiff, *Johann Heinrich Füssli,* where all the artist's works mentioned in the present book are described and illustrated. There are several other book-length studies of Fuseli, by Arnold Federmann (Zurich, 1927), Paul Ganz (Berne, 1947), Eudo C. Mason (London, 1951), Frederick Antal (1956), and Peter Tomory (London, 1972). A more recent discussion is in Peter Conrad, *Shandyism: The Character of Romantic Irony* (Oxford, 1978), chaps. 6 and 7. On Fuseli as a book illustrator, see Hammelmann, "Eighteenth-Century English Illustrators: Henry Fuseli, R. A." Finally, there is Schiff's book devoted to the Milton Gallery: *Johann Heinrich Füsslis Milton-Galerie.*

47. Farington (1), 5:1942 (6 December 1802).

48. Quoted in C. R. Smith, "Pictorial Illustrations of Shakespeare," pp. 460–61.

49. *The Letters and Prose Writings of William Cowper,* ed. James King and Charles Ryskamp (Oxford, 1979–), 3:572 (14 September 1791).

50. *Collected English Letters of Fuseli,* p. 61 (17 August 1790). (The whole troubled ten-year history of the gallery can be intimately followed in these letters; see the Index.)

51. Ibid., p. 74 (22 October 1791).

52. Ibid., p. 86 (15 January 1793).

53. Ibid., p. 90 (26 February 1794).

54. Ibid., p. 138 (14 August 1795).

55. Ibid., p. 135 (21 June 1795).

56. Ibid., p. 153 (15 June 1796).

57. Ibid., p. 154 (9 August 1796).

58. Ibid., p. 212 (18 June 1800).

59. Ibid., pp. 217–18 (11 August 1800).

60. Ibid., p. 224 (4 December 1800).

61. Ibid., p. 572.

62. Alfred Beaver, "Fuseli's Milton Gallery," *Magazine of Art* 14 (1891): 167–68.

63. Jared B. Flagg, *The Life and Letters of Washington Allston* (New York, 1892), p. 39; William H. Gerdts and Theodore E. Stebbins, Jr., *"A Man of Genius": The Art of Washington Allston* (exhibition catalogue, Boston Museum of Fine Arts, 1979), p. 27.

64. Blake's annotation in his copy of *The Works of Sir Joshua Reynolds* (*The Complete Poetry and Prose of William Blake,* ed. David Erdman [Berkeley, Cal., 1982], p. 636).

65. Haydon, *Painting and the Fine Arts,* pp. 212–13.

66. Farington (1), 10:3685 (3 July 1810).

CHAPTER THREE

1. On the fortunes of *ut pictura poesis* in the Romantic period, see Park, "'Ut pictura poesis': The Nineteenth-Century Aftermath," and the same author's *Hazlitt and the Spirit of the Age,* chap. 5; Hagstrum, "The Sister Arts: From Neoclassic to Romantic"; and Jack, *Keats and the*

Mirror of Art, pp. 53–57.

2. Barry, *Lectures on Painting,* pp. 113–14.
3. Fuseli in the *Analytical Review,* November 1794, quoted in Mason, *The Mind of Fuseli,* p. 206.
4. Opie, *Lectures on Painting,* p. 273.
5. *Letters of Samuel Taylor Coleridge,* ed. Earl Leslie Griggs (Oxford, 1956–71), 1:511.
6. "A Gallery of Pictures from Spenser," *Imagination and Fancy* (New York, 1846), p. 72.
7. See Hamilton and Winter (above, chap. 1, n. 38), and *A Memoir of Thomas Uwins, R. A.,* by Mrs. Uwins (London, 1858; rpt. Wakefield, Yorkshire, 1978), 1:163–207.
8. Leslie, *Autobiographical Recollections,* p. 194.
9. George Dunlop Leslie, *The Inner Life of the Royal Academy* (London, 1914), p. 21.
10. *Athenaeum,* 10 May 1834, p. 356.
11. Strong, *Recreating the Past,* p. 36.
12. "The Exhibition at Paris," *Times,* 5 April 1838, p. 5.
13. Frederick Hardman, "The Pictures of the Season," *Blackwood's Magazine* 68 (1850): 83.
14. See Frank Simpson, "Dutch Paintings in England before 1760," *Burlington Magazine* 95 (1953): 39–42.
15. Mrs. Bray, *Life of Stothard* (London, 1851), pp. 192–93.
16. Edward Bulwer-Lytton, *England and the English,* ed. Standish Meacham (Chicago, 1970), pp. 345–46.
17. Hazlitt, 19: 53. (Originally in the *London Magazine,* May 1821.)
18. *Crabbe: The Critical Heritage,* ed. Arthur Pollard (London, 1972), p. 144.
19. Ibid., pp. 150–51. The subsequent course of the debate, not pursued here, may be traced in the ensuing pages of this volume.
20. Preface to *Joseph Andrews.*
21. Coleridge, *Table Talk,* 4 August 1833; *The Complete Works of Samuel Taylor Coleridge,* ed. W. T. G. Shedd (New York, 1863–64), 6: 472–73.
22. John Gibson Lockhart, *Memoirs of the Life of Sir Walter Scott, Bart.* (Boston, n.d.), 1: 66.
23. See Finley, *Landscapes of Memory,* and Holcomb, "Scott and Turner."

CHAPTER FOUR

1. *Memoir of Thomas Uwins* (London, 1858), 2: 261–62.
2. On various aspects of this development, see Francis Haskell, *Rediscoveries in Art: Some Aspects of Taste, Fashion, and Collecting in England and France* (Ithaca, N.Y., 1976), chap. 5 ("Spreading the News"), and Landow, "There Began to be a Great Talking About the Fine Arts."
3. George Spater, *William Cobbett: The Poor Man's Friend* (Cambridge, 1982), 1:169.
4. Robert Bernard Martin, *Tennyson: The Unquiet Heart* (Oxford, 1980), p. 16.
5. Quoted in a letter from William Bell Scott, 23 March 1858, in Raleigh Trevelyan, *A Pre-Raphaelite Circle* (London, 1978), p. 118.
6. Allen Staley in Forbes, *The Royal Academy Revisited,* p. 3; Graves, *The British Institution,* Preface; [Royal Society of British Artists,] *Works Exhibited . . . ,* Introduction.
7. Hutchison, *History of the Royal Academy,* p. 104; E. V. Lucas, *Edwin Austin Abbey: Royal Academician* (London, 1921), 2:347.
8. Thomas Smith, *Recollections of the British Institution,* passim.
9. *Athenaeum,* 24 March 1832, p. 195; 3 April 1858, p. 438.
10. Leslie, *Autobiographical Recollections,* p. 191.
11. *Athenaeum,* 19 February 1842, p. 171.
12. Marcus B. Huish, "Ten Years of British Art," *Nineteenth Century* 27 (1890): 109. (The 6.5-to-1 ratio is based on Lucas, *Abbey,* 2:347.) Additional figures on the number of works exhibited can be found in the various histories of the exhibiting institutions. The reviews of the annual shows in the periodicals often began with such statistics.
13. George, *Life and Death of Haydon,* p. 231 n.
14. See Evelyn Joll, "Painter and Patron: Turner and the Third Earl of Egremont," *Apollo* 105 (1977): 374–79.
15. Andrew Shirley, in Leslie, *Constable,* p. xxv. For the collection itself, see Douglas Hall, "The Tabley House Papers," *Walpole Society* 38 (1960–62): 59–122.
16. Gerald Reitlinger, *The Economics of Taste* (London, 1961), pp. 101–2.
17. This list is based on the roll of Turner's patrons (all of whom bought the work of other British artists as well) in the "Biographical Index of Correspondents" in *Collected Correspondence of J. M. W. Turner,* ed. John Gage (Oxford, 1980), pp. 239–302. It omits, of course, the not inconsiderable number of collectors, particularly those active after 1830, who could not abide the style of the later Turner. Only one of the dozen collectors described in Frank Davis, *Victorian Patrons of the Arts: Twelve Famous Collections and Their Owners* (London, 1963) was a notable collector of literary pictures—John Sheepshanks.
18. Leslie, *Autobiographical Recollections,* Appendix.
19. Ormond, *Landseer,* p. 189.
20. L. T. C. Rolt, *Isambard Kingdom Brunel* (Harmondsworth, 1970), p. 135; I. Brunel, *The Life of Isambard Kingdom Brunel,* quoted in Ashton (2), p. 14.
21. *Athenaeum,* 12 May 1849, p. 494.
22. These prices for paintings with no literary associations are from the list in Oppé, "Art," 2:117 n. Another list, for a shorter period of time, is in Robertson, *Eastlake,* p. 209.
23. Wilkie, "Remarks on Painting" (1836?) in Cunningham, *Wilkie,* 3:148.
24. *Athenaeum,* 20 May 1843, p. 492.

25. Quoted in Redgrave, *Century of British Painters,* p. 2.

26. Boase, "The Decoration of the New Palace of Westminster," p. 324.

27. John Callcott Horsley, *Recollections of a Royal Academician,* ed. Mrs. Edmund Helps (London, 1903), pp. 256–57.

28. *Letters of James Smetham,* ed. Sarah Smetham and William Davies (London, 1902), pp. 271–72.

29. Bulwer-Lytton, *England and the English* (Chicago, 1970), pp. 340–41.

30. Martin, *Tennyson,* p. 403.

31. *The Letters of Edward FitzGerald,* ed. Alfred McKinley Terhune and Annabelle Burdick Terhune (Princeton, N.J., 1978–80), 2:471.

32. Redgrave, *Century of British Painters,* p. 288.

33. J. B. Atkinson in *Blackwood's Magazine* 82 (1857): 167–68.

34. Wilkie, "Remarks on Painting," p. 144.

35. Leslie, *Autobiographical Recollections,* p. xviii.

36. *Edinburgh Review* 54 (1831): 166.

37. See Maurice Willson Disher, *Victorian Song from Dive to Drawing Room* (London, 1955), and J. S. Bratton, *The Victorian Popular Ballad* (London, 1975).

38. Hazlitt, 10:8. (Originally in *Sketches of the Principal Picture-Galleries in England,* 1824.)

39. John Barrell, *The Dark Side of the Landscape: The Rural Poor in English Painting, 1730–1840* (Cambridge, 1980), pp. 90, 122, 174.

40. See Guise, *Great Victorian Engravings;* Hunnisett, *Steel-Engraved Book Illustration;* and two books by Engen, *Victorian Engravings* and *Dictionary of Victorian Engravers.*

41. Guise, p. 9.

42. The chief printed sources on the Art Union are Anthony King, "George Godwin and the Art Union of London, 1837–1911," *Victorian Studies* 8 (1964): 101–30; Elizabeth Aslin, "The Rise and Progress of the Art Union of London," *Apollo* 85 (1967): 12–16; and Hunnisett, *Steel-Engraved Book Illustration,* pp. 173–77. There is also a lengthy Ph.D. dissertation by Lyndel I. S. King, "The Art Union of London 1837–1912" (University of Minnesota, 1982).

43. Grigson, "English Painting from Blake to Byron," p. 267.

44. *Recollections of the Table-Talk of Samuel Rogers,* ed. Morchard Bishop (Lawrence, Kans., 1953), p. 112.

45. "May Gambols," *Fraser's Magazine* 29 (1844): 701.

46. See Thompson, *Pictures for Scotland,* especially pp. 56–62.

47. Irwin, *Scottish Painters,* pp. 285–86.

48. This subject is inseparable from that of book illustration, for which see the books listed in the bibliography under Harvey, Hodnett, Houfe, Hunnisett, Muir, Ray, Reid, and White.

49. See Harvey, *Victorian Novelists and Their Illustrators.*

50. Newspaper clipping in V & A Scrapbook, 4:1028.

51. For a concise summary of the keepsake phenomenon, see Hunnisett, *Steel-Engraved Book Illustration,* pp. 139–52.

52. "Caricatures and Lithography in Paris," *The Paris Sketch Book, Works of William Makepeace Thackeray,* Charterhouse ed. (London, 1901), 16:173–75.

53. Reynolds, *Victorian Painting,* p. 30.

54. *Art Journal* 26 (1864): 88.

55. *Times,* 8 May 1865, p. 8.

56. See *Art Journal* 51 (1889): 95–96, and Mowbray Morris, "Reflections in a Picture-Gallery," *Macmillan's Magazine* 57 (1888): 440–47.

57. *Art Journal* 51 (1889): 95–96.

CHAPTER FIVE

1. Marillier, *The Liverpool School of Painters,* p. 19.

2. Allderidge, *The Late Richard Dadd,* p. 15.

3. William Vaughan, *German Romanticism and English Art* (New Haven, Conn., 1979), pp. 142–44.

4. For the contents of the Vernon collection, see *Vernon Heath's Recollections* (London, 1892), pp. 342–48. (Heath was Vernon's nephew.) For the contents of Sheepshanks's collection, see Algernon Graves, *Summary of and Index to Waagen [Treasures of Art in Great Britain, 1854–57]* (London, 1912; rpt. London, 1970), Index. (The literary pictures in the Sheepshanks collection are now brought together in a single room in the Sir Henry Cole wing of the Victoria and Albert Museum.) A good idea of the incidence of literary paintings in mid-Victorian collections at large can be obtained from a series of articles, "Private Galleries of the British School," *Art Journal* 19 (1857)–20 (1858).

5. Francis T. Palgrave, "How to Form a Good Taste in Art," *Cornhill Magazine* 18 (1868): 170. (A lecture delivered before the Royal Institution.)

6. Raymond Watkinson, *Pre-Raphaelite Art and Design* (London, 1970), p. 165.

7. "A Pictorial Rhapsody," *Fraser's Magazine* 21 (1840): 725.

8. Edgar Breitenbach, "The Bibliography of Illustrated Books: Notes with Two Examples from English Book Illustration of the Nineteenth Century," *Library Association Record* 4th ser. 2 (1935): 177–83. See also Cohen, *The Art of Discrimination,* pp. 402–4.

9. Gulliver: *Literary Gazette,* 9 May 1835, p. 298; Lady Macbeth: *Athenaeum,* 31 March 1838, p. 241; Sterne: *Literary Gazette,* 9 February 1850, p. 111; Beatrix: *Art Journal* 19 (1857): 171; Falstaff: *Times,* 9 May 1867, p. 7.

10. *Richard Redgrave: A Memoir Compiled from His Diary,* ed. F. M. Redgrave (London, 1891), pp. 131–32.

11. Constable, 3:25.

12. *Memoir of Thomas Uwins* (see above, chap. 3, n. 7), 1:125.

13. Frith, *Autobiography,* 3:208.

14. "A Second Lecture on the Fine Arts," *Fraser's Magazine* 19 (1839): 745.

15. *Literary Gazette,* 20 May 1848, pp. 345–46.

16. *Athenaeum,* 22 May 1847, p. 552.

17. Vaughan, *German Romanticism and English Art,* p. 103.

18. W. H. Hunt, *Pre-Raphaelitism,* 1:114.

19. *Examiner,* 27 February 1814, p. 139.

20. *Literary Gazette,* 23 May 1846, p. 478.

21. *Literary Gazette,* 22 April 1848, p. 283.

22. For this picture and its progeny, see T. J. Edelstein, "They Sang 'The Song of the Shirt': The Visual Iconology of the Seamstress," *Victorian Studies* 23 (1980): 183–210. See also Susan P. Cateras, *The Substance or the Shadow: Images of Victorian Womanhood* (exhibition catalogue, Yale Center for British Art, 1982), pp. 31–32.

23. "May Gambols," *Fraser's Magazine* 29 (1844): 704.

24. Arthur B. Chamberlain, *George Romney* (London, 1910), pp. 99, 123–26, 386–89.

25. Morchard Bishop, *Blake's Hayley* (London, 1951), pp. 331–32.

26. *Art Journal* 21 (1858): 161.

27. [Jane Ellen Panton,] *Leaves from a Life* (London, 1908), p. 29.

28. Ian Jack, *English Literature, 1815–1832* (Oxford, 1963), p. 405.

29. Wordsworth, "Essays upon Epitaphs III," *The Prose Works of William Wordsworth,* ed. W. J. B. Owen and Jane Worthington Smyser (Oxford, 1974), 2:84. See also Edmund Blunden, *"Elegant Extracts," Essays on the Eighteenth Century Presented to David Nichol Smith* (Oxford, 1945; rpt. New York, 1963), pp. 225–37.

30. W. H. Hunt, *Pre-Raphaelitism,* 1:xi.

31. "Recollections of Sir Thomas Lawrence" by Elizabeth Croft, in *Sir Thomas Lawrence's Letter-Bag,* ed. George Somes Layard (New York, 1906), p. 246; M. S. Watts, *George Frederic Watts,* 1:15.

32. *Jane Austen's Letters,* ed. R. W. Chapman (Oxford, 1923), 2:468–69.

33. *Jane Austen: The Critical Heritage,* ed. B. C. Southam (London, 1968), p. 266.

34. *The Life of Mary Russell Mitford,* ed. Rev. A. G. K. L'Estrange (New York, 1870), 2:157–58.

35. See N. John Hall, *Trollope and His Illustrators* (London, 1980).

36. *Athenaeum,* 20 March 1869, p. 399.

37. *Letters of Edward FitzGerald,* ed. Terhune (Princeton, N.J., 1978–80), 4:98.

38. Ibid., 4:330.

CHAPTER SIX

1. The major book-length studies of the use of old pictorial motifs in Victorian art and literature are two by Landow—*Victorian Types, Victorian Shadows* and *Images of Crisis*—and Sussman, *Fact into Figure.*

2. Maas, *Victorian Painters,* chap. 10.

3. On dreams in Romantic art, see Honour, *Romanticism,* pp. 314–18, and in nineteenth-century English literature, John R. Reed, *Victorian Conventions* (Athens, Ohio), pp. 448–52.

4. See Adeline R. Tintner, "The Sleeping Woman: A Victorian Fantasy," *Pre-Raphaelite Review* 2 (1978): 12–26.

5. On madness in Romantic art, see Honour, *Romanticism,* pp. 271–75, and Reed, *Victorian Conventions,* chap. 9.

6. See Mario Praz's overdogmatic and indiscriminate but suggestive *The Hero in Eclipse in Victorian Fiction,* trans. Angus Davidson (London, 1956).

7. Stuart M. Tave, *The Amiable Humorist: A Study in the Comic Theory and Criticism of the Eighteenth Century* (Chicago, 1960).

8. Ibid., pp. viii, 43–44.

9. On the theme of love in Romantic art, see Honour, *Romanticism,* pp. 302–9.

10. For a comprehensive treatment of the occurrence of this subject in British art, see Strong, *Recreating the Past,* pp. 119–21.

11. See especially Nina Auerbach, *Woman and the Demon: The Life of a Victorian Myth* (Cambridge, Mass., 1982); Cateras (see above, chap. 5, n. 22); and Helene E. Roberts, "Marriage, Redundancy or Sin: The Painter's View of Women in the First Twenty-Five Years of Victoria's Reign," *Suffer and Be Still,* ed. Martha Vicinus (Bloomington, Ind., 1972), pp. 45–76. On the various types of women represented in English nineteenth-century literature, see Reed, *Victorian Conventions,* chap. 2.

12. On artistic treatments of Lady Jane Grey and Mary Queen of Scots, see Strong, *Recreating the Past,* pp. 122–26 and 128–35 respectively.

13. On the femme fatale, see Cateras, pp. 42–44.

14. See Praz, *The Hero in Eclipse,* p. 60, and Cateras, pp. 12–13.

15. Alexander Welsh, *The Hero of the Waverley Novels,* Yale Studies in English 154 (New Haven, Conn., 1963), pp. 71–76.

16. Clark, *The Romantic Rebellion,* p. 64.

17. M. F. A. Husband, *A Dictionary of the Characters in the Waverley Novels* (London, 1910), Introductory Note.

18. *Art Journal* 33 (1871): 150.

19. *Times,* 1 July 1833, p. 3.

20. *Saturday Review* 21 (1866): 592.

21. T. S. R. Boase, "Shipwrecks in English Romantic Painting," *JWCI* 22 (1959): 332–46. See also Landow, *Images of Crisis,* chap. 2.

22. *Athenaeum,* 14 February 1846, p. 179.

23. Boase, "Shipwrecks," pp. 335–36.

24. Lorenz Eitner, "Cages, Prisons, and Captives in Eighteenth-Century Art," Kroeber and Walling, *Images of Romanticism,* pp. 13–38.

CHAPTER SEVEN

1. See Robert Rosenblum, "The Origin of Painting: A Problem in the Iconography of Romantic Criticism," *Art Bulletin* 39 (1957): 279–90, and addenda by George Levitine, ibid., 10 (1958): 329–31.

2. So far as European painting is concerned, this topic is covered in Honour, *Romanticism,* pp. 258–62; Francis Haskell, "The Old Masters in Nineteenth-Century French Painting," *Art Quarterly* 34 (1971): 55–58; and Michael Levey, *The Painter Depicted: Painters as a Subject in Painting* (London, 1981). An adequate study of the subject in nineteenth-century British art remains to be done.

3. See Leonée Ormond, "Browning and Painting."

4. Hazlitt, 6:29. (Originally in *Lectures on the English Comic Writers,* 1819.)

5. See the introduction to *Minor Lives: A Collection of Biographies by John Nichols,* ed. Edward L. Hart (Cambridge, Mass., 1971), pp. xv–xviii. A wider discussion of the developing popular interest in literary biography can be found in Richard D. Altick, *Lives and Letters: A History of Literary Biography in England and America* (New York, 1965), chaps. 2–4.

6. Fuseli in the *Analytical Review,* May 1795, quoted in Mason, *The Mind of Fuseli,* p. 196.

7. See Martha Winburn England, *Garrick's Jubilee* (Columbus, Ohio, 1964).

8. Quoted in Cunningham, *Lives,* 2:178.

9. See David Piper, "The Development of the British Literary Portrait up to Samuel Johnson," *Proceedings of the British Academy* 54 (1968): 51–72, and the same author's "The Chesterfield House Library Portraits," *Evidence in Literary Scholarship: Essays in Memory of James Marshall Osborn,* ed. René Wellek and Alvaro Ribiero (Oxford, 1979), pp. 179–95.

10. See Morchard Bishop, *Blake's Hayley* (London, 1951), pp. 265–67.

11. S. Schoenbaum, *Shakespeare's Lives* (Oxford, 1970), p. 279. Most of the following material, not otherwise attributed, on Shakespeare's popular fame is from this copious and valuable source.

12. *Athenaeum,* 9 May 1863, p. 623.

13. *Examiner,* 11 July 1863, p. 439.

14. W. B. Scott, *Memoir of David Scott* (Edinburgh, 1850), p. 218.

15. *Examiner,* 19 May 1877, pp. 630–31.

16. *Saturday Review* 3 (1857): 476.

17. Johnson, "Life of Milton," *Lives of the Poets,* World's Classics edition (London, 1936), 1:100.

18. "A Pictorial Rhapsody: Concluded," *Fraser's Magazine* 22 (1840): 122.

19. David Masson, *The Life of John Milton,* new and revised ed. (London, 1881; rpt. New York, 1946), 1:188.

20. *The Diary of Ford Madox Brown,* pp. 1–2.

21. *Times,* 8 May 1862, p. 8.

22. *Saturday Review* 13 (1862): 593.

23. Frith, *Autobiography,* 1:221, 224.

24. On Swift's fame at the time, see Donald M. Berwick, *The Reputation of Jonathan Swift, 1781–1882* (Philadelphia, 1941), parts 2 and 3.

25. Frith, *Autobiography,* 2:213–14; *Saturday Review* 51 (1881): 559–60.

26. *Literary Gazette,* 13 May 1854, p. 448.

27. "Picture Gossip," *Fraser's Magazine* 31 (1845): 722.

28. *Boswell's Life of Johnson,* ed. G. B. Hill and L. F. Powell (Oxford, 1934–50), 2:120.

29. *Times,* 2 May 1868, p. 11.

30. Frith, *Autobiography,* 1:389.

31. *Boswell's Life of Johnson,* 2:405–6.

32. *Art Journal* 25 (1863): 111 (quoting the catalogue).

33. Washington Irving, *Oliver Goldsmith: A Biography* (1849), ed. Elsie Lee West (Boston, 1979), pp. 232–33.

34. Mentioned by E. H. W. Meyerstein, *A Life of Thomas Chatterton* (New York, 1930; rpt. New York, 1972), p. 490. Meyerstein saw only the engraving, "a wretched picture—I have not seen the original, nor know where it is."

35. Ibid., p. 490; *Dictionary of National Biography; John Constable: Further Documents and Correspondence* (Suffolk Records Society 18 [1975]), pp. 195–96, 199–201.

36. On the progress of Chatterton's fame, see, in addition to Meyerstein, Linda Kelly, *The Marvellous Boy: The Life and Myth of Thomas Chatterton* (London, 1971), part 3.

37. *Literary Gazette,* 17 May 1856, p. 284.

38. Ruskin, 14:60.

39. Farington (1), 10:3697 (26 July 1810).

40. Maurice Lindsay, *Robert Burns: The Man, His Work, The Legend* (London, 1979), pp. 105–6.

41. Ruskin, 14:69.

42. For Scott's relations with art, see the sources listed in the notes to Part Three.

43. Ford Madox Hueffer's note in the catalogue of the exhibition of Brown's works at the Leicester Galleries, 1909.

CHAPTER EIGHT

1. Quoted in Frederick Whiley Hilles, *The Literary Career of*

Sir Joshua Reynolds (Cambridge, 1936), p. xvi. The rest of the paragraph is based on the same source.

2. *The Letters of Thomas Gainsborough,* ed. Mary Woodall (Greenwich, Conn., 1961), p. 53.

3. Ibid., p. 11.

4. William Hayley, *The Life of George Romney, Esq.* (Chichester, 1809), p. 131.

5. Ibid., p. 114.

6. Lambourne, *An Introduction to Victorian "Genre" Painting,* pp. 7–9. See also J. T. Nettleship, *George Morland and the Evolution from Him of Some Later Painters,* Portfolio Monographs on Artistic Subjects 39 (London, 1898), p. 1.

7. Reynolds, *Discourses on Art,* p. 117.

8. Ada Earland, *John Opie and His Circle* (London, 1911), p. 23.

9. *Lectures on Painting,* p. 272.

10. *The Letters of William and Dorothy Wordsworth,* ed. Ernest de Selincourt, vol. 2, 2d ed. rev. by Mary Moorman (Oxford, 1969), p. 518.

11. Cunningham, *Wilkie,* 1:148.

12. Haydon, *Autobiography,* 2:652.

13. *John Constable: Further Documents* (see above, chap. 7, n. 35), pp. 39–44.

14. Constable, 5:77.

15. Farington (1), 8:3164 (12 December 1807).

16. Constable, 6:61.

17. The chief sources for Turner's knowledge of poetry are those that deal with his own poetic productions: Lindsay, *The Sunset Ship;* Ziff, "J. M. W. Turner on Poetry and Painting"; the same author's "John Langhorne and Turner's 'Fallacies of Hope'," *JWCI* 27 (1964): 340–42; and Ann Livermore, "J. M. W. Turner's Unknown Verse-Book," *Connoisseur Year Book 1957,* pp. 78–86. Other references are scattered through the recent literature on Turner.

18. *Collected Correspondence of J. M. W. Turner,* ed. John Gage (Oxford, 1980).

19. "Doings in Fresco," *Fraser's Magazine* 25 (1842): 672.

20. Robertson, *Eastlake,* p. 113.

21. "Doings in Fresco," p. 672.

22. W. B. Scott, *Autobiographical Notes,* 1:13–14.

23. Frith, *Autobiography,* 1:6, 152.

24. Cunningham, *Wilkie,* 1:41.

25. Mrs. E. M. Ward, *Memories of Ninety Years,* 2d ed. (New York, [1925]), p. 42.

26. Charles Henry Cope, *Reminiscences of Charles West Cope, R. A.* (London, 1891), p. 23.

27. Henry Stacy Marks, *Pen and Pencil Sketches* (London, 1894), 1:50–51.

28. See Spender, "The Pre-Raphaelite Literary Painters."

29. *Some Reminiscences of William Michael Rossetti,* 1:31, 57.

30. Burne-Jones, *Memorials of Burne-Jones,* 1:58.

31. See Gordon (2), pp. 6–7.

32. W. H. Hunt, *Pre-Raphaelitism,* 1:23.

33. *Letters of James Smetham* (London, 1892); see also *The Literary Works of James Smetham* (London, 1893), containing his essays on Reynolds, Blake, Alexander Smith, and Gerrit Dou, originally published in the *London Quarterly Review.* There are two appreciations of Smetham as man and artist: Geoffrey Grigson, "James Smetham," *Cornhill Magazine* 163 (1948): 332–46, and Morchard Bishop, "Some Reflections on the Career of James Smetham," in [Edward Malins and Morchard Bishop], *James Smetham and Francis Danby: Two Nineteenth Century Romantic Painters* (London, 1974), pp. 15–38.

34. On the persistence of Reynolds's doctrines down to the 1830s, see Van Akin Burd, "Background to *Modern Painters:* The Tradition and the Turner Controversy," *PMLA* 74 (1959): 254–67.

35. Farington (1), 4:1198 (13 April 1799).

36. Salaman, *Shakespeare in Pictorial Art,* p. 30.

37. Waagen, *Works of Art and Artists in England,* passim. Waagen's *Treasures of Art in Great Britain,* trans. Lady Rigby (London, 1854; supplementary volume, 1857) incorporates the results of his inspection of fifty-four additional collections in 1850. The contents of the 1854–57 volumes are indexed in Algernon Graves, *Summary of and Index to Waagen* (London, 1912). For a description of this "kunsthistorischer Pickwick," see Frank Herrmann, "Collecting Classics: 1. Dr. Waagen's *Works of Art and Artists in England,*" *Connoisseur* 161 (1966): 173–77.

38. Farr, *William Etty,* pp. 49–50.

39. See Edward S. LeComte, *Endymion in England: The Literary History of a Greek Myth* (New York, 1944), especially chapter 6.

40. On Etty's indebtedness to the Italian masters, see R. W. Alston, "William Etty, R. A.," *Nineteenth Century* 134 (1943): 70–76.

41. Walpole, *Anecdotes of Painting,* quoted in Burke, *English Art, 1714–1800,* p. 208.

42. See Edgar Wind, "'Borrowed Attitudes' in Reynolds and Hogarth," *JWCI* 2 (1938): 182–85; Frederick Antal, *Hogarth and His Place in European Art* (London, 1962); Paulson's writings on Hogarth, passim; and Tomory, *The Life and Art of Fuseli,* chaps. 3 and 4.

43. *Times,* 4 May 1836, p. 5; *Literary Gazette,* 14 May 1836, p. 314.

44. *Art Journal* 32 (1870): 169.

45. *Art Journal* 15 (1853): 136.

46. The best account of the Westminster fresco competition is Boase, "The Decoration of the New Palace of Westminster." See also Boase, *English Art, 1800–1870,* pp. 209–18. Additional details are in Robertson, *Eastlake,* Appendix D, and in the biographies of the artists involved.

47. "Doings in Fresco," *Fraser's Magazine* 25 (1842): 671–72.
48. Robertson, *Eastlake,* p. 336.
49. *New Monthly Magazine* 71 (1844): 551.
50. Dyce's involvement is described in Pointon, *William Dyce,* pp. 81–92, 100–106, 110–18.
51. Reynolds, *Victorian Painting,* p. 35.

CHAPTER NINE

1. On typology in nineteenth-century British art and literature, see the books listed above, chap. 6, n. 1.
2. Solomon's alteration of the composition was first pointed out in Reynolds, *Painters of the Victorian Scene,* p. 65, and amplified in Reynolds's *Victorian Painting,* p. 113. Both versions are reproduced in Wood, *Victorian Panorama,* pls. 225, 226.
3. *Times,* 3 May 1879, p. 5.
4. *Saturday Review* 37 (1874): 654.
5. Campbell Lennie, *Landseer: The Victorian Paragon* (London, 1976), pp. 201–3.
6. *Saturday Review* 58 (1882): 632.
7. *Athenaeum,* 27 March 1841, p. 245.
8. *Fraser's Magazine* n.s. 8 (1873): 82.
9. *Literary Gazette,* 12 May 1860, p. 586.
10. E. Rimbault Dibdin, "The Art of Frank Dicksee, R. A.," *Christmas Art Annual 1905,* p. 18.
11. *Art Journal* 18 (1856): 180.
12. *Athenaeum,* 23 May 1857, p. 667.
13. *Saturday Review* 37 (1874): 654.
14. *Spectator* 47 (1874): 692.
15. *Saturday Review* 37 (1874): 621.
16. *Further Extracts from the Note-Books of Samuel Butler,* ed. A. T. Bartholomew (London, 1934), p. 336.
17. Bliss, *Sir Walter Scott and the Visual Arts,* p. 22.
18. Quoted in Treble, *Great Victorian Pictures,* p. 92.
19. David Piper, *The English Face* (London, 1957), p. 75.
20. Knowles, *Fuseli,* 1:236.
21. Fuseli, *Lectures on Painting,* p. 435.
22. Northcote, *Conversations with James Ward,* pp. 117–19.
23. See Michael Wheeler, *The Art of Allusion in Victorian Fiction* (London, 1979), pp. 14–16.
24. Ibid., pp. 23–24.
25. Tom Burns Haber, "The Chapter-Tags in the Waverley Novels," *PMLA* 45 (1930): 1140–49.
26. J. R. Tye, "George Eliot's Unascribed Mottoes," *Nineteenth-Century Fiction* 22 (1967): 235–49; David Leon Higdon, "George Eliot and the Art of the Epigraph," ibid. 25 (1970): 127–51.
27. George P. Landow, *The Aesthetic and Critical Theories of John Ruskin* (Princeton, N.J., 1971), pp. 45–46.
28. Butlin and Joll, *The Paintings of Turner,* 1:169.
29. Finberg, *Turner,* pp. 157–58; Butlin and Joll, *The Paintings of Turner,* 1:56; Ann Livermore, "J. M. W. Turner's Unknown Verse-Book," *Connoisseur Year Book 1957,* pp. 78–79, 85–86.
30. Quennell, *Romantic England,* p. 199.
31. Jerrold Ziff, "John Langhorne and Turner's 'Fallacies of Hope'," *JWCI* 27 (1964), 340–42.
32. *Punch* 6 (1844): 200.
33. "Picture Gossip," *Fraser's Magazine* 31 (1845): 720–21.
34. Graham Reynolds, *Turner* (London, 1969), p. 36.
35. Peter Conrad, *Shandyism* (Oxford, 1978), p. 152.
36. *John Constable's Discourses,* ed. R. B. Beckett (Suffolk Records Society 14 [1970]), pp. 1–27.
37. See Stephen Sartin, *Thomas Sidney Cooper, C. V. O., R. A., 1803–1902* (Leigh-on-Sea, 1976), pp. 28–29.
38. Haber (see above, n. 25), pp. 1143, 1146.
39. Hilda Orchardson Gray, *The Life of Sir William Quiller Orchardson, R. A.* (London, 1930), p. 35.
40. *Art Journal* 22 (1860): 171.
41. Graham Reynolds, *Constable, the Natural Painter* (New York, 1965), p. 107.
42. *Athenaeum,* 19 May 1855, p. 591.
43. *Thackeray: The Critical Heritage,* ed. Geoffrey Tillotson and Donald Hawes (London, 1968), p. 266.
44. Hazlitt, 18:94. (Originally in the *Champion,* February 1815.)
45. "The Exhibitions of 1860," *Fraser's Magazine* 61 (1860): 878. The author is unidentified.
46. O'Neil, *Lectures on Painting,* p. 15.
47. Jack, *Keats and the Mirror of Art,* chap. 13.
48. See Shackford, *Wordsworth's Interest in Painters and Pictures.*
49. Russell Noyes, *Wordsworth and the Art of Landscape* (Bloomington, Ind., 1968), pp. 81, 124–26.
50. This topic is discussed to the point of exhaustion in *Dante Gabriel Rossetti and the Double Work of Art,* ed. Maryan Wynn Ainsworth (exhibition catalogue, Yale University Art Gallery, 1976). See also Wolfgang Lottes, "'Take out the Picture and Frame the Sonnet': Rossetti's Sonnets and Verses for His Own Works of Art," *Anglia* 96 (1978): 108–35.

CHAPTER TEN

1. "A Pictorial Rhapsody," *Fraser's Magazine* 21 (1840): 720–21.
2. Sidney Colvin, "Art and Criticism," *Fortnightly Review* n.s. 26 (1879): 211.
3. Helene E. Roberts, "Art Reviewing in Early Nineteenth-

Century Art Periodicals," *Victorian Periodicals Newsletter* [now *Victorian Periodicals Review*], no. 19 (March 1973), p. 10; Treble, *Great Victorian Pictures*, p. 14.

4. *Examiner,* 17 September 1809, p. 605.

5. The most extensive survey of the personnel of the art-journalism world at the time is Christopher Kent, "Periodical Critics of Drama, Music, and Art, 1830–1914: A Preliminary List," *Victorian Periodicals Review*, vol. 13, nos. 1–2 (Spring-Summer 1980), pp. 31–54. See also Roberts, "Art Reviewing"; and, by the same author, "Exhibition and Review: The Periodical Press and the Victorian Art Exhibition System," *The Victorian Periodical Press: Samplings and Soundings*, ed. Joanne Shattock and Michael Wolff (Leicester, 1982), pp. 79–108.

6. See R. W. Peattie, "William Michael Rossetti's Art Notices in the Periodicals, 1850–1878: An Annotated Checklist," *Victorian Periodicals Newsletter* 8 (June 1975): 79–92.

7. Gwenllian F. Palgrave, *Francis Turner Palgrave: His Journals and Memories of His Life.* (London, 1899; rpt. New York, 1971), pp. 78, 111.

8. "The Suffolk Street Exhibition," *Fraser's Magazine* 3 (1831): 680.

9. *Athenaeum,* 18 May 1861, p. 666; *Art Journal* 30 (1868): 86: *Athenaeum,* 19 February 1853, p. 233.

10. On Thackeray's aesthetics, see Helene E. Roberts, "'The Sentiment of Reality': Thackeray's Art Criticism," *Studies in the Novel* 13 (1981): 21–39; and Judith L. Fisher, "The Aesthetic of the Mediocre: Thackeray and the Visual Arts," *Victorian Studies* 26 (1982): 65–82.

11. "Picture Gossip," *Fraser's Magazine* 31 (1845): 715; *Morning Chronicle,* 11 May 1846 (*Thackeray's Contributions to the "Morning Chronicle,"* ed. Gordon N. Ray [Urbana, Ill., 1955]), p. 150.

12. *Academy Notes* are collected in the Cook and Wedderburn edition of Ruskin's works, vol. 14.

13. For the survival of *ut pictura poesis* into Victorian times, see Landow, *The Aesthetic and Critical Theories of John Ruskin* (above, chap. 9, n. 27), chap. 1 ("Ruskin's Theory of the Sister Arts"); Wendell Stacy Johnson, "'The Bride of Literature': Ruskin, the Eastlakes, and Mid-Victorian Theories of Art," *Victorian Newsletter,* no. 26 (Fall 1964), pp. 23–28; Findlay, "Aspects of Analogy"; and Elizabeth K. Helsinger, *Ruskin and the Art of the Beholder* (Cambridge, Mass., 1982), pp. 50–54.

14. Haydon, *Lectures on Painting and Design,* 1:299–331.

15. Howard, *A Course of Lectures on Painting,* pp. 17, 53–54.

16. Ruskin, 5:31.

17. Sidney Colvin, "Some Phases of Art under George the Third," *Fortnightly Review* n.s. 15 (1874): 667.

18. Kester Svendsen, "John Martin and the Expulsion Scene of *Paradise Lost,*" pp. 72–73.

19. Peter Conrad, *Shandyism* (London, 1978), p. 152.

20. Allan and/or Peter Cunningham, "Doings in Fresco," *Fraser's Magazine* 25 (1842): 672–73.

21. W. M. Rossetti, *Fine Art,* p. 257.

22. O'Neil, *Lectures on Painting,* p. 53.

23. *Athenaeum,* 12 May 1832, p. 309.

24. "The Somerset House Annual," *Fraser's Magazine* 12 (1835): 57.

25. Haydon, *Autobiography,* 1:48–49.

26. O'Neil, *Lectures on Painting,* p. 68.

27. *Athenaeum,* 14 May 1842, p. 435.

28. *Examiner,* 2 June 1811, pp. 348–49.

29. *Examiner,* 13 June 1819, p. 382.

30. *Times,* 23 May 1835, p. 6.

31. *Literary Gazette,* 21 May 1831, p. 331; *Times,* 6 May 1831, p. 4; cf. *Examiner,* 15 May 1831, p. 309.

32. Ruskin, 14:38.

33. *Examiner,* 13 May 1854, p. 294.

34. *Athenaeum,* 6 May 1854, p. 560.

35. *Athenaeum,* 11 February 1832, p. 98.

36. *Athenaeum,* 6 May 1837, p. 330.

37. *Literary Gazette,* 20 May 1837, p. 332.

38. W. M. Rossetti in *Saturday Review* 5 (1858): 502.

39. *Times,* 19 May 1869, p. 5.

40. *Art Journal* 21 (1859): 166.

41. *Literary Gazette,* 21 May 1859, p. 618.

42. *Literary Gazette,* 19 February 1853, p. 185.

43. *Art Journal* 33 (1871): 214.

44. *Literary Gazette,* 16 February 1850, p. 130.

45. The phrase is the *Times*'s, quoted in Whitley (3), p. 191.

46. *Blackwood's Magazine* 40 (1836): 551.

CHAPTER ELEVEN

1. O'Neil, *Lectures on Painting,* p. 69.

2. Quoted in Tomory, *The Life and Art of Fuseli,* p. 15. On the origins of pictorial dramaturgy in England, see Meisel, *Realizations,* chap. 3 ("Speaking Pictures: The Drama").

3. Park, *Hazlitt and the Spirit of the Age,* p. 140.

4. Leslie, *Reynolds,* 2:489, 514–15.

5. Tomory, *Fuseli,* p. 15.

6. *The Reminiscences of Solomon Alex. Hart,* ed. Alexander Brodie (privately printed, 1882), pp. 20–21.

7. *Correspondance Générale de Eugène Delacroix,* ed. André Joubin (Paris, 1935–38), 1:162–63, 166.

8. *Letters of Edward FitzGerald,* ed. Terhune (Princeton, N.J., 1978–80), 3:624.

9. The best source on the theater at this time is Joseph Donohue, *Theatre in the Age of Kean* (Oxford, 1975).

10. Helen O. Borowitz, "'King Lear' in the Art of Ford Madox Brown," *Victorian Studies* 21 (1978): 309–24.

11. This development is traced in Strong, *Recreating the Past,* pp. 49–60.

12. Merchant, *Shakespeare and the Artist,* pp. 89–90.

13. *The Letters of Sir Walter Scott,* ed. H. J. C. Grierson (London, 1932–37), 2:321.

14. Ibid., 3:227.

15. Balston, *John Martin,* p. 51.

16. See Michael R. Booth, *Victorian Spectacular Theatre, 1850–1910* (London, 1981), especially pp. 8–14, 18–20.

17. Ibid., p. 41.

18. Allardyce Nicoll, *A History of English Drama, 1660–1900,* rev. ed. (Cambridge, 1952–59), vol. 4 (*1800–1850*).

19. Winton Tolles, *Tom Taylor and the Victorian Drama* (New York, 1940), p. 75. For much useful detail on the development of pictorial allusion in the theater, including the actual dramatization of paintings, see Meisel, *Realizations,* chaps. 6–7.

20. Quoted from Northcote's article in *The Artist* (1807) in Park, *Hazlitt and the Spirit of the Age,* p. 140.

21. Farington (1), 8:2912 (20 November 1806).

22. Letter of 23 March 1807: Haydon, *Autobiography,* 1:48–49.

23. Frith, *Autobiography,* 3:199–200.

24. "The Suffolk Street Exhibition," *Fraser's Magazine* 3 (1831), 679.

25. *Times,* 9 May 1843, p. 6.

26. W. H. Hunt, *Pre-Raphaelitism,* 1:51.

27. Arthur Colby Sprague, *Shakespearian Players and Performances* (Cambridge, Mass., 1953), p. 54.

28. "The Drama," *Blackwood's Magazine* 79 (1856): 220.

29. *Times,* 14 May 1845, p. 6; *Examiner,* 10 May 1845, p. 293.

30. *Saturday Review* 33 (1872): 696.

31. *Athenaeum,* 11 May 1872, p. 597.

32. *Illustrated London News,* 6 June 1846, p. 376.

33. *Literary Gazette,* 26 February 1848, p. 153.

34. *Literary Gazette,* 21 February 1852, p. 187.

35. *Saturday Review* 5 (1858): 190.

36. *Art Journal* 26 (1864): 153.

37. *Athenaeum,* 11 May 1867, p. 629.

38. Yale Walpole, 17:339.

39. Frith, *Autobiography,* 1:185.

40. Mary McKerrow, *The Faeds: A Biography* (Edinburgh, 1982), p. 22.

41. *Art Journal* 28 (1866): 163.

42. *Examiner,* 5 May 1866, p. 279.

43. *Athenaeum,* 12 May 1855, p. 558; 19 May 1855, p. 591.

44. Harry Quilter, "Notes on the Royal Academy Exhibition," *Contemporary Review* 41 (1882): 950.

45. *Times,* 3 May 1842, p. 5.

46. *Literary Gazette,* 10 May 1851, p. 33.

47. *Times,* 3 May 1851, p. 8.

48. *Athenaeum,* 7 May 1853, p. 567.

49. *Athenaeum,* 2 April 1859, p. 457.

50. *Literary Gazette,* 2 April 1859, p. 438.

51. *Art Journal* 22 (1860): 168.

52. *Athenaeum,* 6 February 1841, p. 117.

53. *Examiner,* 10 June 1832, p. 373.

54. W. B. Scott, *Autobiographical Notes,* 1:15–16.

55. *New Monthly Magazine* 74 (1845): 197.

56. "Picture Gossip," *Fraser's Magazine* 74 (1845): 719.

57. *Times,* 9 May 1850, p. 5.

58. *Literary Gazette,* 31 May 1856, p. 331. The other naysayers were the *Times*, 3 May 1856, p. 9 (" . . . What can be the meaning of those absurd Cupids on the ground and hovering in the air we cannot imagine, save to show how badly this artist can draw"); and the *Examiner,* 31 May 1857, p. 341 (" . . . What of the little Cupids in the air?").

59. *Art Journal* 19 (1857): 172.

60. Redgrave, *Century of British Painters,* p. 301. Smetham shared this opinion: see *Letters of James Smetham* (London, 1892), pp. 147–48.

61. F. T. Palgrave, *Gems of English Art* (London, 1869), pp. 9–10.

62. Wood, *The Pre-Raphaelites,* p. 46.

63. Christine Poulson, "A Checklist of Pre-Raphaelite Illustrations of Shakespeare's Plays," *Burlington Magazine* 122 (1980): 244–50.

64. The story is told by R. B. Martin, *Tennyson* (Oxford, 1980), pp. 414–18, and in more detail by Richard L. Stein, "The Pre-Raphaelite Tennyson," *Victorian Studies* 24 (1981): 279–301.

65. On the wider topic of artists' illustration of contemporary literature, see, in addition to the books listed above (chap. 4, n. 48), Jane R. Cohen, *Charles Dickens and His Original Illustrators* (Columbus, Ohio, 1980); N. John Hall, *Trollope and His Illustrators* (London, 1980); two articles in the *Victorian Periodicals Newsletter,* vol. 9, no. 2 (June 1976), pp. 39–68: Sybille Pantazzi, "Author and Illustrator: Images in Confrontation," and Allan R. Life, "The Periodical Illustrations of John Everett Millais and Their Literary Interpretation"; and Arlene M. Jackson, *Illustration and the Novels of Thomas Hardy* (Totowa, N.J., 1981).

66. "The Royal Academy Exhibition," *Fraser's Magazine* 67 (1863): 787.

67. *Art Journal* 25 (1863): 108–9.

68. *Athenaeum,* 2 May 1868, p. 631.

69. Bernard Cracroft, "Mr. Holman Hunt's 'Isabel'" [*sic*], *Fortnightly Review* n.s. 3 (1868): 654–55.

70. *Art Journal* 30 (1868): 97.

CHAPTER TWELVE

1. Ruskin, 14:107.

2. *Saturday Review* 3 (1857): 452; *Athenaeum*, 9 May 1857, p. 602. The whole critical hubbub is described in Millais, *Life and Letters*, 1:311–14.

3. Richard Ormond, "Private Life of a Victorian Painter," *Country Life* 140 (1966): 462.

4. Catalogues of the Grosvenor Gallery exhibitions in the Victoria and Albert Museum Library.

5. See [Royal Society of Artists,] *Works Exhibited at the Royal Society of Artists . . . and the New English Art Club.*

6. See White, *English Illustration*, and Reid, *Illustrators of the Sixties*, as well as the wider treatments of English illustration by Bland, Muir, and Ray.

7. R. St. John Tyrwhitt, "Pictures of the Year," *Contemporary Review* 11 (1869): 363.

8. Colvin, "Art and Criticism," *Fortnightly Review* n.s. 26 (1879): 211.

9. Edward J. Poynter, *Ten Lectures on Art* (London, 1880), pp. 43–44.

10. Taine, *Notes sur l'Angleterre*, trans. Edward Hyams (London, 1957), pp. 262–63.

11. James, *The Painter's Eye*, p. 148. (Originally in the *Galaxy*, August 1877.)

12. Harrison, "A Few Words about Picture Exhibitions," *Nineteenth Century* 24 (1888): 43–44.

13. Ibid., pp. 35–36.

14. *Times*, 4 May 1857, p. 9.

15. *Athenaeum*, 17 February 1844, p. 157.

16. *Scott: The Critical Heritage*, ed. John O. Hayden (London, 1970), p. 394.

17. *Times*, 25 November 1889, p. 10.

18. *Times*, 1 May 1890, p. 18.

19. *Saturday Review* 33 (1872): 696. The comment was pre-echoed in the *Times*, 27 May, p. 5.

20. Smith, "Pictorial Illustrations of Shakespeare," p. 475.

21. *Spectator* 48 (1875): 661.

22. James, *The Painter's Eye*, p. 90. (Originally in the *Galaxy*, July 1875.)

23. Harrison (see above, n. 12), p. 43.

24. Wood (3), p. 139.

25. See E. K. Helsinger, *Ruskin and the Art of the Beholder* (Cambridge, Mass., 1982), part 2.

26. Quoted in Frederick Antal, *Fuseli Studies* (London, 1956), p. 137.

27. Svendsen, "John Martin and the Expulsion Scene of *Paradise Lost*," p. 64.

28. *Examiner*, 3 May 1840, p. 278; 21 June 1840, p. 387.

29. Cohen, *The Art of Discrimination*, p. 251. Recent examples of the way illustrations can deepen and perhaps clarify literary interpretation are two articles by Stephen Leo Carr and Peggy A. Knapp, "Verbal-Visual Relationships: Zoffany's and Fuseli's Illustrations of *Macbeth*," *Art History* 3 (1980): 375–87, and "Seeing through *Macbeth*," *PMLA* 96 (1981): 837–47.

30. Jerome Meckier, "Dickens and King Lear: A Myth for Victorian England," *South Atlantic Quarterly* 71 (1972): 75–90.

Part Two

INTRODUCTION

1. Walter Frith, "Small Talk with My Father," *Cornhill Magazine* n.s. 23 (1907), 803–4.

2. Previous discussions and catalogues of Shakespeare in art include: Ashton (1) and (2); Boase, "Illustrations of Shakespeare's Plays in the Seventeenth and Eighteenth Centuries"; Hartmann, *Shakespeare in Art;* Merchant, *Shakespeare and the Artist* and *Shakespeare in Art* (exhibition catalogue); Royal Shakespeare Theatre Picture Gallery, *Catalogue of Pictures and Sculptures;* Salaman, *Shakespeare in Pictorial Art;* Smith, "Pictorial Illustrations of Shakespeare"; and Woodward, "Shakespeare in English Painting." A useful, though incomplete, listing is Studing and Merlo, "Shakespeare in Art: A Bibliography."

3. For Shakespeare's fame in the eighteenth century, see R. W. Babcock, *The Genesis of Shakespeare Idolatry, 1766–1799* (Chapel Hill, N.C., 1931; rpt. New York, 1964) and Louis Marder, *His Exits and His Entrances* (Philadelphia, 1963).

4. See David Nichol Smith, *Shakespeare in the Eighteenth Century* (Oxford, 1928), pp. 82–85.

5. Joseph W. Donohue, Jr., *Dramatic Character in the English Romantic Age* (Princeton, N. J., 1970), p. 190.

6. See Donohue, "John Hamilton Mortimer and Shakespearean Characterization," *Princeton University Library Chronicle* 29 (1968): 193–207.

7. *Portraits by Sir Joshua Reynolds*, ed. F. W. Hilles (New York, 1952), pp. 131–33.

8. Newspaper clipping hand-dated 11 May 1781, in V & A Scrapbook, 1:197.

9. Material on adaptations is drawn from two books by Hazelton Spencer, *Shakespeare Improved: The Restoration Versions in Quarto and on the Stage* (Cambridge, Mass., 1927) and *The Art and Life of William Shakespeare* (New York, 1940).

10. See, for example, the use made of iconographic evidence in Dennis Bartholomeuz, *"Macbeth" and the Players* (Cambridge, 1969).

11. George C. D. Odell, *Shakespeare from Betterton to Irving* (New York, 1920), 2:15–19, 49–50, 53–54.

12. For these paintings, see Simon, "Hogarth's Shakespeare."

13. See Charles Beecher Hogan, *Shakespeare in the Theatre, 1701–1800* (Oxford, 1952–57), 2:217–19; and Arthur

H. Scouten, "The Increase in Popularity of Shakespeare's Plays in the Eighteenth Century," *Shakespeare Quarterly* 7 (1956): 189–202.

14. Newspaper clipping hand-dated 1790 in V & A Scrapbook, 2:542.

THE COMEDIES

The Taming of the Shrew

1. All material on the stage history of Shakespeare's plays is from Spencer, *The Art and Life of William Shakespeare,* and Odell, *Shakespeare from Betterton to Irving* (both cited above, nn. 9, 11); Ernest Bradlee Watson, *Sheridan to Robertson: A Study of the Nineteenth-Century London Stage* (Cambridge, Mass., 1926); and Arthur Colby Sprague, *Shakespearian Players and Performances* (Cambridge, Mass., 1953).

The Two Gentlemen of Verona

1. *Athenaeum,* 26 May 1849, p. 548.

2. *Art Journal* 13 (1851): 160.

3. *Examiner,* 7 June 1851, pp. 358–59.

A Midsummer Night's Dream

1. Friedman, *Boydell's Shakespeare Gallery,* p. 123.

2. Gerald Reitlinger, *The Economics of Taste* (London, 1961), p. 77.

The Merchant of Venice

1. Spencer, *The Art and Life of Shakespeare,* p. 248.

2. *Athenaeum,* 5 June 1830, p. 347.

3. *Literary Gazette,* 29 May 1830, p. 353.

4. *Athenaeum,* 5 June 1830, p. 357.

5. Whitley (3), p. 192.

6. Ibid.

7. Clair Hughes, "Zoffany's Trial Scene from *The Merchant of Venice,*" *Burlington Magazine* 123 (1981): 290–94.

As You Like It

1. Constable, 2:292.

2. See Arthur H. R. Fairchild, *Shakespeare and the Arts of Design* (University of Missouri Studies 12, no. 1 [1937]), p. 28; and Samuel C. Chew, *The Pilgrimage of Life* (New Haven, Conn., 1962), pp. 153–73.

3. "Strictures on Pictures," *Fraser's Magazine* 17 (1838): 760.

4. *Times,* 1 February 1830, p. 2.

Much Ado About Nothing

1. Newspaper clipping in V & A Scrapbook, 2:329.

2. *Gentleman's Magazine* n.s. 22 (1829): 249.

3. *Examiner,* 18 May 1850, p. 309.

The Merry Wives of Windsor

1. *Athenaeum,* 15 May 1875, p. 661.

Measure for Measure

1. *Examiner,* 7 May 1853, p. 294.

THE HISTORY PLAYS

Henry VI

1. *Leigh Hunt's Dramatic Criticism, 1808–1831,* ed. Lawrence Huston Houtchens and Carolyn Washburn Houtchens (New York, 1949), pp. 181–82. (Originally in the *Examiner,* 28 December 1817.)

2. Leslie, *Autobiographical Recollections,* p. 196.

Richard III

1. See Alice Wood, *The Stage History of Shakespeare's "King Richard the Third"* (New York, 1909), chaps. 4–5.

2. See Strong, *Recreating the Past,* pp. 119–21.

3. Quoted in George Rowell, *Queen Victoria Goes to the Theatre* (London, 1978), p. 85.

4. F. T. Palgrave, *Essays on Art* (London, 1866), p. 54.

King John

1. Hazlitt, 18:92. (Originally in the *Champion,* February 1815.)

2. *Spectator* 55 (1882): 723.

Henry IV

1. See Stuart M. Tave, *The Amiable Humorist* (Chicago, 1960), pp. 121–34.

2. Hazlitt, 4:278. (Originally in *Characters of Shakespeare's Plays,* 1817.)

3. Farington (1), 1:172 (21 [actually 22] March 1794).

4. *Athenaeum,* 10 May 1851, p. 504.

5. *Literary Gazette,* 12 February 1859, p. 213.

Henry VIII

1. For the significance of this subject in the drama of the time, see Andrew Sanders, *Charles Dickens, Resurrectionist* (London, 1982), pp. 21–22.

2. Quoted in Rowell (see above, *Richard III,* n. 3), p. 56.

THE TRAGEDIES

Romeo and Juliet

1. *Examiner,* 4 June 1809, pp. 366–67.

2. *London Magazine* n.s. 1 (1825): 261–62.

3. *Examiner,* 7 April 1833, p. 214.

4. *Athenaeum,* 9 May 1863, p. 622.
5. *Blackwood's Magazine* 40 (1836): 551.
6. *Times,* 6 May 1836, p. 3. For more on this controversial picture, see Whitley (3), pp. 318–19. The painting is minutely explicated in Paulson, *Book and Painting,* pp. 142–51.
7. Hueffer, *Ford Madox Brown,* p. 230.
8. James, *The Painter's Eye,* p. 250. (Originally in *Harper's Weekly,* 20 February 1897.)
9. *Times,* 3 May 1884, p. 4.
10. Constable, 2:8–9.
11. "The Royal Academy," *Blackwood's Magazine* 119 (1876): 768.
12. Quoted in Odell, *Shakespeare from Betterton to Irving,* 1:346.
13. *Examiner,* 17 March 1811, pp. 171–72.

Hamlet

1. On Ophelia in art, see Dotson, "English Shakespeare Illustrations and Eugène Delacroix" (above, Introduction to Part One, n. 7) pp. 56–60, and Landow, *Images of Crisis,* pp. 214–15.
2. *Examiner,* 7 February 1808, p. 94.
3. Quoted in Arthur B. Chamberlain, *George Romney* (London, 1910), p. 232.
4. *Life and Letters of Millais,* 1:146.
5. *Athenaeum,* 22 May 1852, p. 581.
6. *Art Journal* 14 (1852): 174.
7. *Times,* 14 May 1852, p. 6.
8. "An Exhibition Gossip," *Ainsworth's Magazine* 1 (1842): 321.
9. *Athenaeum,* 7 May 1842, p. 410.
10. Ruskin, 3:82.
11. Ibid., 3:619.
12. *Times,* 31 May 1878, p. 4.
13. *Athenaeum,* 2 May 1874, p. 600, and 30 May 1874, p. 738.
14. *Saturday Review* 37 (1874): 621.
15. *Athenaeum,* 2 May 1868, p. 633.

Othello

1. *Examiner,* 28 July 1839, p. 469.
2. *Literary Gazette,* 25 May 1839, p. 332.
3. *Fraser's Magazine* 51 (1855): 711.

King Lear

1. *Five Restoration Adaptations of Shakespeare,* ed. Christopher Spencer (Urbana, Ill., 1965), p. 273.
2. A. C. Sprague, *Shakespearian Players and Performances* (Cambridge, Mass., 1953), p. 185.
3. *Athenaeum,* 12 May 1855, p. 557.
4. See the important discussion in Merchant, *Shakespeare and the Artist,* chap. 12.
5. *Examiner,* 24 May 1851, p. 326; *Illustrated London News,* 10 May 1851, p. 384.
6. *Saturday Review* 41 (1876): 649.
7. See Borowitz, "'King Lear' in the Art of Ford Madox Brown," *Victorian Studies* 21 (1978): 309–34.
8. *Times,* 9 May 1850, p. 5.
9. Newspaper clipping in V & A Scrapbook, 1:103.

Macbeth

1. On Fuseli and *Macbeth* in general, see Paulson, *Book and Painting,* pp. 127–37. Details of all of Fuseli's pictures from *Macbeth* (and other Shakespearean plays) are in Schiff, *Johann Heinrich Füssli.*
2. Quoted in Mason, *The Mind of Fuseli,* pp. 289–90.
3. Knowles, *Fuseli,* 1:189–90.
4. *Henry Crabb Robinson on Books and Their Writers,* ed. Edith J. Morley (London, 1938), 1:34.
5. Hazlitt, 18:59. (Originally in the *Champion,* 6 November 1814.)
6. *The Diaries of William Charles Macready, 1833–1851,* ed. William Toynbee (London, 1912), 1:268
7. *Blackwood's Magazine* 40 (1836): 550.
8. *London Magazine* 1 (1820): 310. The painting was described at great length in the *New Monthly Magazine* 13 (1820): 468–70.
9. *Athenaeum,* 2 May 1868, p. 631.
10. *Examiner,* 16 February and 14 June 1812, pp. 107, 380.
11. *Letters of James Smetham* (London, 1892), pp. 271–72.
12. *Macready's Reminiscences,* ed. Sir Frederick Pollock (New York, 1875), p. 467.
13. *Examiner,* 3 May 1840, p. 278.
14. "A Pictorial Rhapsody: Concluded," *Fraser's Magazine* 22 (1840): 113–15; *Blackwood's Magazine* 48 (1840): 379. See also Ormond, "Daniel Maclise," p. 690.
15. The story of the picture is told in Roger Manvell, *Ellen Terry* (London, 1968), pp. 198–202, 261, using Terry's notes.
16. Quoted in Whitley (1), 2:377.
17. *Athenaeum,* 31 March 1838, p. 241.
18. Fuseli, *Collected Letters,* pp. 366–67.
19. Rowell, *Queen Victoria Goes to the Theatre* (London, 1978), p. 56.

Antony and Cleopatra

1. *Saturday Review* 69 (1890): 569.
2. Leslie, *Reynolds,* 1:13.
3. Michael R. Booth, *Victorian Spectacular Theatre* (London, 1981), p. 57.

Coriolanus

1. See the extensive discussion in Merchant, *Shakespeare and the Artist,* chap. 11.

THE ROMANCES

Cymbeline

1. C. H. Cope, *Reminiscences of Charles West Cope* (London, 1891), p. 23.
2. *Art Journal* 19 (1857): 71.

The Winter's Tale

1. Booth, *Victorian Spectacular Theatre,* pp. 49–50.
2. *Saturday Review* 2 (1856): 79.
3. *Literary Gazette,* 10 May 1856, p. 259.

The Tempest

1. See Mary M. Nilan, "Shakespeare, Illustrated: Charles Kean's 1857 Production of *The Tempest,*" *Shakespeare Quarterly* 26 (1975): 196–204.
2. Cunningham, *Lives,* 2:170.
3. Ibid., 2:183.
4. *Gentleman's Magazine* 98 (1828): 448.
5. W. B. Scott, *Memoir of David Scott* (Edinburgh, 1850), pp. 206–7.
6. *Athenaeum,* 1 June 1850, p. 591.
7. *Times,* 9 May 1850, p. 5.
8. *Examiner,* 25 May 1850, p. 326.
9. Anna Eliza Bray, "Reminiscences of Stothard," *Blackwood's Magazine* 39 (1836): 684.

PART THREE

INTRODUCTION

1. See Jonathan Lawson, *Robert Bloomfield* (Boston, 1980).
2. Hazlitt, 5:95. (Originally in *Lectures on the English Poets,* 1818.)
3. Farington (1), 6:2270 (21 March 1804).
4. Rotha Mary Clay, *Julius Caesar Ibbetson, 1759–1817* (London, 1948), pp. 93–94.
5. Cunningham, *Wilkie,* 1:206.
6. Constable, 2:299, 335, 345.

THE MIDDLE AGES

Chaucer

1. Mrs. Bray, *Life of Stothard* (London, 1851), p. 140.
2. *Athenaeum,* 7 May 1859, p. 617.
3. For Griselda as a Victorian type-figure, see J. R. Reed, *Victorian Conventions* (Athens, Ohio), pp. 40–44.
4. *Examiner,* 31 May 1812, p. 346.

Malory and Arthurian Legend

1. The fluctuating fame of Malory and "the matter of Arthur" to the beginning of the Victorian era is traced by James Douglas Merriman, *The Flower of Kings: A Study of the Arthurian Legend in England between 1485 and 1835* (Lawrence, Kans., 1973). This is supplemented by Barry Gains, "The Editions of Malory in the Early Nineteenth Century," *Papers of the Bibliographical Society of America* 68 (1974): 1–17, and Mark Girouard, *The Return to Camelot: Chivalry and the English Gentleman* (New Haven, Conn., 1981), chaps. 1–7 and 12. Most of the material in the following paragraphs is derived from these sources. There is also a recent 842-page Ph.D dissertation: Debra N. Mancoff, "The Arthurian Revival in Victorian Painting" (Northwestern University, 1982). Also helpful is the "Chronology of Significant Arthurian Publications in the Nineteenth Century" in J. Philip Eggers, *King Arthur's Laureate: A Study of Tennyson's "Idylls of the King"* (New York, 1971), pp. 215–32.
2. Burne-Jones, *Memorials of Burne-Jones,* 1:116–17.
3. The story of the Oxford Union frescoes has been told, at various lengths, by every biographer of each participant. Additional details and illustrations are in Rosalie Mander, "Rossetti and the Oxford Murals, 1857," *Pre-Raphaelite Papers,* ed. Leslie Parris (London, 1984), pp. 170–83. The list of subjects given here is from Harrison and Waters, *Burne-Jones,* p. 35.
4. Scott, *Autobiographical Notes,* 2:41.
5. *Memorials of Burne-Jones,* 2:333.
6. See Robin Gibson, "Arthur Hughes: Arthurian and Related Subjects of the Early 1860's," *Burlington Magazine* 112 (1970): 451–66. Gibson points out that no specific source for *The Knight of the Sun* has been identified.
7. *Athenaeum,* 14 May 1864, p. 682.

THE ELIZABETHAN ERA

Spenser

1. Joseph Spence, *Observations, Anecdotes, and Characters of Books and Men,* ed. James M. Osborn (Oxford, 1966), 1:182.
2. For opposing opinions of this commonplace, see Jefferson B. Fletcher, "The Painter of the Poets," *Studies in Philology* 14 (1917): 153–66, and Rudolf Gottfried, "The Pictorial Element in Spenser's Poetry," *That Soueraine Light: Essays in Honor of Edmund Spenser,* ed.

William R. Mueller and Don Cameron Allen (Baltimore, 1952), pp. 123–33.

3. Hazlitt, 20:240. (Originally in the *Monthly Magazine*, July 1829.)

4. *Art Journal* 17 (1855): 170.

5. A full study of Spenserian subjects in art is being written by Professor Norman K. Farmer, Jr.

6. Bradley, "Eighteenth-Century Paintings and Illustrations of Spenser's *Faerie Queene*," contains a convenient list of *Faerie Queene* paintings exhibited at the Royal Academy.

7. Walpole to George Montagu, 13 June 1751: Yale Walpole, 9:116.

8. Mrs. Bray, *Life of Stothard* (London, 1851), p. 120.

9. Newspaper clipping dated 1820 in V & A Scrapbook, 5:1210.

10. *New Monthly Magazine* 38 (1833): 161–62.

11. "The British School of Painting," *Blackwood's Magazine* 40 (1836): 83.

12. Hazlitt, 5:38. (Originally in *Lectures on the English Poets*, 1818.)

13. For a comprehensive statement of the qualities mid- and late-Victorian readers (and viewers) would have found in Spenser's women, see Edward Dowden, "Heroines of Spenser," *Cornhill Magazine* 39 (1879): 663–80.

14. *Letters of Edward FitzGerald*, ed. Terhune (Princeton, N.J., 1978–80), 1:173.

15. *Illustrated London News*, 9 June 1855, p. 562.

Jonson

1. G. W. Stone, Jr., and G. M. Kahrl, *David Garrick* (Carbondale, Ill., 1979), pp. 462–63.

2. Quoted in Whitley (1), 2:377.

3. *Examiner*, 10 May 1812, p. 302.

THE SEVENTEENTH CENTURY

Walton

1. See Peter Oliver, *A New Chronicle of "The Compleat Angler"* (New York, 1936); Bernard S. Horne, *"The Compleat Angler," 1653–1967* (Pittsburgh, 1970), especially pp. 325–29; and Raoul Granqvist, "Isaak Walton's *Lives* in the Nineteenth and the Early Twentieth Century: A Study of a Cult Object," *Studia Neophilologica* 54 (1982): 247–61.

Milton

1. The widest-ranging account of illustrations of Milton, including paintings, is Pointon, *Milton and English Art*. Paulson, *Book and Painting*, discusses the eighteenth-century phase. See also n. 3 below.

2. See John Walter Good, "Studies in the Milton Tradition," University of Illinois Studies in Language and Literature 1, nos. 3–4 (1915).

3. This is one aspect of English literary art that has been extensively canvassed. See, in addition to Baker, Pointon, Svendsen, and Wittreich, Stephen C. Behrendt, *The Moment of Explosion: Blake and the Illustration of Milton* (Lincoln, Neb., 1983), chap. 4 ("The Tradition of *Paradise Lost* Illustration" down to Blake.) A slighter treatment is J. D. Hunt, "Milton's Illustrators."

4. *Writings and Speeches of Edmund Burke*, World's Classics edition (London, 1906), 1:217–18.

5. Reynolds, *Discourses on Art*, p. 164.

6. Waagen, *Works of Art and Artists in England*, 2:127–28.

7. The painting is discussed at length in David Bindman, "Hogarth's 'Satan, Sin and Death' and Its Influence," *Burlington Magazine* 112 (1970): 153–58. See also Peter Conrad, *Shandyism* (Oxford, 1978), pp. 123–29.

8. Johnson, *Lives of the Poets*, World's Classics edition (London, 1936), 1:127.

9. Whitley (1), 1:284.

10. Pressly, *James Barry*, pp. 152–67.

11. Waagen, *Works of Art*, 2:128.

12. The Miltonic presence—or at least that of *Paradise Lost*—in the Victorian era is described in James G. Nelson, *The Sublime Puritan: Milton and the Victorians* (Madison, Wis., 1963).

13. See Arthur Barker, "' . . . And on His Crest Sat Horror': Eighteenth Century Interpretations of Milton's Sublimity and His Satan," *University of Toronto Quarterly* 11 (1942): 421–36.

14. Nelson, *Sublime Puritan*, pp. 44–47.

15. See Muir, *Victorian Illustrated Books*, pp. 75–78, and Ray, *The Illustrator and the Book in England*, pp. 44–45.

16. Cunningham, *Lives*, 3:37.

17. Whitley (3), p. 183.

18. Farington (1), 3:825 (19 April 1797).

19. Ibid., 3:825, 1029 (7 July 1798).

20. Whitley (1), 2:213.

21. *Times*, 31 March 1853, p. 5.

22. *Times*, 29 April 1848, p. 3.

23. See Svendsen, "John Martin and the Expulsion Scene of *Paradise Lost*," and Hughes, "Some Illustrators of Milton."

24. Haydon, *Lectures on Painting and Design*, 2:27.

25. *Times*, 6 May 1845, p. 6.

26. "Picture Gossip," *Fraser's Magazine* 31 (1845): 715.

27. J. B. Flagg, *Life and Letters of Washington Allston* (New York, 1892), p. 73; *Letters of John Keats*, ed. Hyder Edward Rollins (Cambridge, Mass., 1958), 1:236.

28. *Examiner*, 8 February 1818, p. 91.

29. "Memoir" prefixed to Howard, *A Course of Lectures on Painting*, p. lxiii.

30. *London Magazine* 7 (1823): 701.

31. Howard, "Memoir," p. lxii.

32. Richard D. Altick, *The Shows of London* (Cambridge, Mass., 1978), pp. 364–65.

33. David H. Stevens, *Reference Guide to Milton from 1800 to the Present Day* (Chicago, 1930), pp. 43–44.

34. See *Index to "The London Stage, 1660–1800"*, ed. Ben Ross Schneider, Jr. (Carbondale, Ill., 1979), p. 572.

35. Balston, *John Martin*, p. 54.

36. Constable, 6:236.

37. *Times*, 4 February 1828, p. 3.

38. *Examiner*, 12 February 1832, p. 100.

39. The story of the Buckingham Palace pavilion frescoes has been told in a number of places, in most detail by Farr, *William Etty*, pp. 95–98. Other sources are listed in the following notes.

40. Robertson, *Eastlake*, p. 336.

41. George Rowell, *Queen Victoria Goes to the Theatre* (London, 1978), p. 40.

42. *Journals and Correspondence of Lady Eastlake*, ed. Charles Eastlake Smith (London, 1895; rpt. New York, 1975), 1:117–18.

43. "May Gambols," *Fraser's Magazine* 29 (1844): 706.

44. "Picture Gossip," *Fraser's Magazine* 31 (1845): 719.

45. Haydon, *Correspondence*, 2:213.

46. *The Letters of Robert Browning and Elizabeth Barrett, 1845–1846*, ed. Elvan Kintner (Cambridge, Mass., 1969), 2:739, 741.

47. "Picture Gossip," *Fraser's Magazine* 31 (1845): 719–20.

48. Ibid., p. 719.

49. *Art Journal* 11 (1849): 172.

50. Raymond D. Havens, *The Influence of Milton on English Poetry* (Cambridge, Mass., 1922; rpt. New York, 1961), p. 469.

51. *Art Journal* 13 (1851): 74.

52. *Literary Gazette*, 16 August 1851, p. 564.

53. Ruskin, 14:20.

54. *Examiner*, 18 July 1863, p. 456.

55. *Athenaeum*, 13 May 1865, p. 658.

56. *Times*, 18 May 1865, p. 6.

57. Marion H. Spielmann, *Millais and His Works, with Special Reference to the Exhibition at the Royal Academy, 1898* (London, 1898), p. 139.

The Diarists: Evelyn and Pepys

1. *The Diary of John Evelyn*, ed. E. S. de Beer (Oxford, 1955), 3:567, 572.

2. Ibid., 3:573.

3. Mrs. E. M. Ward, *Memories of Ninety Years* (New York, 1925), p. 47.

4. Frith, *Autobiography*, 1:372, 374.

5. Evelyn, *Diary*, 4:413–14.

6. *Athenaeum*, 4 May 1867, p. 593.

7. Henry Blackburn, *Academy Notes* (London, 1875), p. 50.

8. *Examiner*, 10 May 1851, p. 294.

Butler

1. Hazlitt, 6:62. (Originally in *Lectures on the English Comic Writers*, 1819.)

2. Hunt, *Autobiography* (New York, 1855), 1:94.

3. James T. Hillhouse, *The Waverley Novels and Their Critics* (Minneapolis, 1936), p. 121.

4. Charles Cowden Clarke, quoted in Richard D. Altick, *The Cowden Clarkes* (London, 1948), p. 111.

5. See Moore, "Hogarth as Illustrator," pp. 195–97.

6. *New Monthly Magazine* 13 (1820): 468.

Bunyan

1. Monica Furlong, *Puritan's Progress* (New York, 1975), pp. 180–87, and Lynn Veach Sadler, *John Bunyan* (Boston, 1979), pp. 133–34, are the sources of evidence on Bunyan's popularity in the following paragraphs.

2. Frank Mott Harrison, "Some Illustrators of *The Pilgrim's Progress* (Part One): John Bunyan," *Library* 4th ser. 17 (1936): 241–63; John Brown, *John Bunyan: His Life, Times, and Work*, rev. by Frank Mott Harrison (London, 1928), pp. 386, 441–50.

THE EIGHTEENTH CENTURY

Defoe

1. The history of the illustrated editions has been sketched in M. H. Spielmann, "The New 'Robinson Crusoe'," *Magazine of Art* 15 (1892): 47–51, and George Somes Layard, "Robinson Crusoe and Its Illustrators," *Bibliographica* 2 (1896): 181–203.

2. *Blackwood's Magazine* 54 (1843): 189.

3. *Pictorial Times*, 13 May 1843, in Thackeray, *Strayed Papers . . . Being Stories, Reviews, Verses, and Sketches*, ed. Lewis Melville (Philadelphia, 1901; rpt. New York, 1971), p. 217.

4. Treble, *Great Victorian Pictures*, pp. 68–69.

Swift

1. See David S. Lenfest, "A Checklist of Illustrated Editions of 'Gulliver's Travels'," *Papers of the Bibliographical Society of America* 62 (1968): 85–123.

2. See A. C. Sewter, "Four English Illustrative Pictures," *Burlington Magazine* 74 (1939): 122–27, and Elizabeth Duthie, "Gulliver Art," *Scriblerian* 10 (1978): 127–31.

3. *Athenaeum*, 16 May 1835, p. 379; *Fraser's Magazine* 12 (1835): 59.

The Spectator

1. See "[The *Spectator*'s] Reputation in the Eighteenth Cen-

tury—and After," *The Spectator,* ed. Donald F. Bond (Oxford, 1965), 1:xcvi–cvi.

2. *Boswell's London Journal, 1762–1763,* ed. Frederick A. Pottle (New York, 1950), e.g., pp. 62, 188.

3. *Literary Gazette,* 9 April 1831, p. 233.

Gay

1. See William Eben Schultz, *Gay's "Beggar's Opera": Its Content, History, and Influence* (New York, 1923; rpt. New York, 1967)—an exhaustive study that leaves but one stone unturned: nothing is said of *The Beggar's Opera*'s career in art.

2. Ibid., p. 92.

3. See William Henry Irving, *John Gay, Favorite of the Wits* (Durham, N.C., 1940), pp. 221–22, 312.

Ramsay

1. See Burns Martin, *Allan Ramsay: A Study of His Life and Works* (Cambridge, Mass., 1931), pp. 83–96.

2. William Bayne, *Sir David Wilkie, R. A.* (London, 1903), pp. 6–7, 29–30.

Pope

1. Pope's multifarious relations with the visual arts have been examined in several studies: Robert J. Allen, "Pope and the Sister Arts," in *Pope and His Contemporaries: Essays Presented to George Sherburn,* ed. James L. Clifford and Louis A. Landa (Oxford, 1949; rpt. New York, 1978), pp. 78–88; Norman Ault, "Mr. Alexander Pope: Painter," *New Light on Pope* (London, 1949; rpt. Hamden, Conn., 1967), chap. 5; Hagstrum, *The Sister Arts,* chap. 8; Sambrook, "Pope and the Visual Arts"; Brownell, *Alexander Pope and the Arts of Georgian England;* and Halsband, *"The Rape of the Lock" and Its Illustrations.*

2. Ault, "Mr. Alexander Pope," p. 82.

3. See Oscar Maurer, Jr., "Pope and the Victorians," *Studies in English* (University of Texas) 24 (1944): 211–38.

4. Halsband's treatment is searching but less than comprehensive.

5. Halsband, *"The Rape of the Lock,"* p. 32.

6. Whitley (2), p. 234.

7. Letter to Peter Murray, 3 December 1830: *Letters of Washington Irving,* ed. Ralph M. Aderman et al. (Boston, 1979–82), 2:566.

8. *Athenaeum,* 6 May 1854, p. 560.

9. Ruskin, 14:38.

10. *Fraser's Magazine* 51 (1855): 711–12.

Thomson

1. Cohen, *The Art of Discrimination,* p. 381; Hilbert H. Campbell, *James Thomson* (Boston, 1979), p. 143. Cohen's chapter 5 is devoted to book illustrations of *The Seasons;* see also the formidable list of illustrated editions, pp. 472–507.

2. Hazlitt, 17:120. (Originally in the *Liberal,* April 1823.)

3. Quoted by J. R. Watson, *Picturesque Landscape and English Romantic Poetry* (London, 1970), p. 34.

4. See, for example, Hagstrum, *The Sister Arts,* pp. 257–58, and Campbell, *Thomson,* pp. 105–6.

5. Hagstrum, *The Sister Arts,* pp. 250–51; Kenneth Clark, *Landscape into Art,* rev. ed. (London, 1976), p. 135.

6. Cohen, *The Art of Discrimination,* p. 250.

7. *The Prose Works of William Wordsworth* (see above, pt. 1, chap. 5, n. 29), 3:74.

8. Musidora's career in book illustrations is described in Cohen, *The Art of Discrimination,* pp. 291–96.

9. Quoted ibid., p. 293.

10. Haydon, *Autobiography,* 2:437.

11. *Literary Gazette,* 9 February 1850, p. 112.

Gray

1. The subject is covered by Bell, "Thomas Gray and the Fine Arts."

2. *Correspondence of Thomas Gray,* ed. Philip Toynbee and Leonard Whibley (Oxford, 1935), 2:476–77.

3. Hagstrum, *The Sister Arts,* pp. 296–301.

4. On Gray's popularity, see Alastair Macdonald, "Gray and His Critics," *Fearful Joy: Papers from the Thomas Gray Bicentenary Conference at Carleton University,* ed. James Downey and Ben Jones (Montreal, 1974), pp. 172–97.

5. See F. I. McCarthy, "*The Bard* of Thomas Gray: Its Composition and Its Use by Painters," *National Library of Wales Journal* 14 (1965): 105–12.

6. Quoted ibid., p. 110.

7. Arthur S. Marks, "The Source of John Martin's 'The Bard'," *Apollo* 84 (1966), August supplement, pp. 1–2.

8. Quoted in Whitley (3), p. 234.

Richardson

1. See T. C. Duncan Eaves, "Graphic Illustration of the Novels of Samuel Richardson" (see above, pt. 1, chap. 1, n. 7), pp. 349–83.

2. "Richardson's Illustrators," *Times Literary Supplement,* 16 December 1920, p. 864.

3. Gowing, "Hogarth, Hayman, and the Vauxhall Decorations," p. 11.

4. All material in this paragraph is from Eaves, "Graphic Illustration," pp. 369–72. See also his earlier article, "'The Harlowe Family' by Joseph Highmore" (above, pt. 1, chap. 1, n. 11).

5. *Athenaeum,* 12 May 1866, p. 639.

6. *Athenaeum,* 9 May 1874, p. 638.

Fielding

1. Fielding's reputation in the second half of the eighteenth century and the whole of the nineteenth is traced by Frederic T. Blanchard, *Fielding the Novelist: A Study in Historical Criticism* (New Haven, Conn., 1926). *Henry*

Fielding: The Critical Heritage, ed. Ronald Paulson and Thomas Lockwood (London, 1969), is a collection of Fielding criticism during his lifetime only.

2. *Art Journal* 19 (1857): 169.

Sterne

1. The vicissitudes of Sterne's reputation are described in Alan B. Howes, *Yorick and the Critics: Sterne's Reputation in England, 1760–1868,* Yale Studies in English 139 (New Haven, Conn., 1958), and documented in *Sterne: The Critical Heritage,* ed. Howes (London, 1974). See also John H. Hicks, "The Critical History of *Tristram Shandy,*" *Boston University Studies in English* 2 (1956): 65–84.
2. See R. F. Brissenden, "Sterne and Painting," *Of Books and Humankind: Essays and Poems Presented to Bonamy Dobrée,* ed. John Butt (London, 1965), pp. 93–108.
3. See William Holtz, "Pictures for Parson Yorick: Laurence Sterne's London Visit of 1760," *Eighteenth-Century Studies* 1 (1967): 169–84.
4. *Letters of Laurence Sterne,* ed. L. P. Curtis (Oxford, 1935), pp. 99–100.
5. T. C. Duncan Eaves, "George Romney: His *Tristram Shandy* Paintings and Trip to Lancaster," *Huntington Library Quarterly* 7 (1944): 321–26.
6. Hazlitt, 6:121. (Originally in *Lectures on the English Comic Writers,* 1819.)
7. Quoted in Cunningham, *Lives,* 2:151.
8. On paintings from *Tristram Shandy* and *A Sentimental Journey,* see Gordon (3).
9. *Sterne: The Critical Heritage,* p. 257.
10. Ibid., p. 350.
11. *Joseph Wright of Derby* (exhibition catalogue, Corporation Art Gallery, Derby, 1934); Gordon (3), p. 53.
12. *Works of Thackeray* (Charterhouse edition), 23:321, 325.
13. Leslie, *Autobiographical Recollections,* p. xli.
14. Morse's letter to his brothers, 21 September 1832: *Samuel F. B. Morse: His Letters and Journals,* ed. Edward Lind Morse (Boston, 1914), 1:433.
15. *Athenaeum,* 26 May 1849, p. 548.
16. *Times,* 5 May 1866, p. 9; *Examiner,* 5 May 1866, p. 279.
17. *Times,* 28 June 1880, p. 5.
18. Palgrave, *Gems of English Art of This Century* (London, 1869), p. 13.

Goldsmith

1. Farington (2), 8:208 n.
2. Quoted in *Goldsmith: The Critical Heritage,* ed. G. S. Rousseau (London, 1974), p. 276.
3. Haydon's journal, 29 April 1828: *Autobiography,* 2:444.
4. *Literary Gazette,* 1 June 1839, p. 348.
5. *Athenaeum,* 8 May 1841, p. 368.
6. On the long-lived Mulready edition, see Heleniak, *Mulready,* p. 138.
7. Leslie, *Autobiographical Recollections,* p. xli.
8. "May Gambols," *Fraser's Magazine* 29 (1844): 706.
9. *Punch* 8 (1845): 246.
10. "May Gambols," p. 706.
11. *Times,* 9 May 1850, p. 5.
12. *Art Journal* 12 (1850): 166; *Examiner,* 18 May 1850, p. 310.
13. "The Pictures of the Season," *Blackwood's Magazine* 68 (1850): 79.
14. *Athenaeum,* 28 May 1842, p. 482.
15. Leslie, *Reynolds,* 1:400 n.
16. "Picture Gossip," *Fraser's Magazine* 31 (1845): 718.

Ossian

1. A scholarly, fully illustrated account of the Ossian phenomenon in art is *Ossian und die Kunst um 1800* (exhibition catalogue, Kunsthalle, Hamburg, 1974); there is a French version, somewhat abbreviated, prepared for the same exhibition when shown at the Grand Palais, Paris. This supersedes Henry Okun, "Ossian in Painting," *JWCI* 30 (1967): 327–56 (very incomplete on the British side). A good idea of the extent and duration of the Ossian craze in print is provided by George F. Black, "Macpherson's *Ossian* and the Ossianic Controversy: A Contribution towards a Bibliography," *Bulletin of the New York Public Library* 30 (1926): 424–39, 508–24, supplemented by John J. Dunn, ibid., 75 (1971): 465–73.
2. Nicoll, *History of English Drama* (see above, pt. 1, chap. 11, n. 18), 3:72.
3. Yale Walpole, 31:221–22.
4. Burne-Jones, *Memorials of Burne-Jones,* 1:18; 2:42.
5. See Susan Booth, "The Early Career of Alexander Runciman and His Relations with Sir James Clerk of Penicuik," *JWCI* 32 (1969): 332–43.

Sheridan

1. Michael R. Booth, *Victorian Spectacular Theatre* (London, 1981), p. 23.

Cowper

1. Norma Russell, *A Bibliography of William Cowper to 1837* (Oxford, 1963), p. xvi. On Cowper's interest in art, see Desai, "William Cowper and the Visual Arts." On his reputation, see Lodwick Hartley, "'The Stricken Deer' and His Contemporary Reputation," *Studies in Philology* 36 (1939): 637–50.
2. Constable, 2:78.
3. Leigh Hunt, *Autobiography* (New York, 1855), 1:224.
4. Haydon, *Painting and the Fine Arts,* p. 214.
5. John Gilpin was a favorite subject for illustration. See H. T. Kirby, "John Gilpin in Picture: Some Illustrators of of Cowper's Famous Poem," *Bookman* (London) 81 (1931): 189–200, and the same author's "John Gilpin: A Note on the Pictorial History of a Famous Horseman," *Print Collector's Quarterly* 23 (1936): 167–86.

Crabbe

1. See Walter E. Broman, "Factors in Crabbe's Eminence in the Early Nineteenth Century," *Modern Philology* 51 (1953): 42–49; *Crabbe: The Critical Heritage,* ed. Arthur Pollard (London, 1972); and John O. Hayden, *The Romantic Reviewers, 1802–1824* (Chicago, 1968), pp. 232–39.
2. Letter of 15 September 1817: *Byron's Letters and Journals,* ed. Leslie A. Marchand (London, 1973–82), 5:266.
3. Broman, "Factors in Crabbe's Eminence," p. 46; *The Letters of William and Dorothy Wordsworth,* 2d ed., vol. 5, rev. by Alan G. Hill (Oxford, 1979), p. 692.
4. *Crabbe: The Critical Heritage,* p. 211. (Originally in the *Pamphleteer,* 1815.)
5. Ibid., pp. 315–16. (Originally in the *Quarterly Review,* January 1834.)

Rogers

1. On Rogers's career as a poet, see J. R. Hale, "Samuel Rogers the Perfectionist," *Huntington Library Quarterly* 25 (1961): 61–67, and P. W. Clayden, *Rogers and His Contemporaries* (London, 1889), 2:1–7.
2. Farington (1), 11:4094–95 (18 March 1812).
3. A. C. Coxhead, *Thomas Stothard, R. A., An Illustrated Monograph* (London, 1906), pp. 129–30.
4. See Adele M. Holcomb, "A Neglected Classical Phase of Turner's Art: His Vignettes to Rogers's *Italy,*" *JWCI* 32 (1969): 405–10; Harry Rycroft, "Samuel Rogers, His Illustrators, J. M. W. Turner and Thomas Stothard, and Other Friends," *Book Handbook,* no. 3 (1947), pp. 198–218; and *Turner and the Poets: Engravings and Watercolours from His Later Period* (exhibition catalogue, Greater London Council, 1975; text by Mordechai Omer).
5. Quoted in F. T. Palgrave, *Gems of English Art* (London, 1869), p. 18.
6. Ruskin, 35:29.
7. Hale, "Samuel Rogers," p. 61.
8. *Letters of Sir Walter Scott,* ed. Grierson (London, 1932–37), 9:460; Clayden, 2:88.
9. Hale, "Samuel Rogers," p. 62.

Burns

1. Lockhart, *Memoirs of Scott* (see above, pt. 1, chap. 3, n. 22), 1:167.
2. See Robert Rosenblum, "Sources of Two Paintings by Joseph Wright of Derby," *JWCI* 25 (1962): 135–36.
3. Maurice Lindsay, *The Burns Encyclopedia,* 3d ed. (London, 1980), p. 7; *Letters of Robert Burns,* ed. J. DeLancey Ferguson (Oxford, 1931), 2:300–301.
4. On the progress of Burns's reputation to 1837, see *Robert Burns: The Critical Heritage,* ed. Donald A. Low (London, 1974). The large topic of Burns subjects in art awaits intensive study; so far as I know, the only treatment to date is H. C. Shelley, "Burns in Art," in *Burnsiana: A Collection of Literary Odds and Ends Relating to Robert Burns,* ed. John D. Ross (Paisley and London, 1897), 4:16–23.
5. *Burns: The Critical Heritage,* p. 345.
6. Ibid., p. 69.
7. Ibid., p. 361. (Originally in the *Edinburgh Review,* December 1828.)
8. Hazlitt, 18:169. (Originally in the *Scotsman,* 20 April 1822.)
9. *Punch* 6 (1844): 200.
10. *Burns: The Critical Heritage,* p. 310. (Originally in *Blackwood's Magazine,* February 1819.)
11. Quoted in R. M. Clay, *Julius Caesar Ibbetson* (London, 1948), pp. 91–92.
12. *Literary Gazette,* 14 February 1852, p. 162.
13. *Literary Gazette,* 21 February 1818, p. 123.

THE ROMANTIC ERA

Wordsworth

1. See Shackford, *Wordsworth's Interest in Paintings and Pictures.* Wordsworth's relations with Constable have been dealt with by several writers, including J. R. Watson, "Wordsworth and Constable," *Review of English Studies* n.s. 13 (1962): 361–67; R. F. Storch, "Wordsworth and Constable," *Studies in Romanticism* 5 (1966): 121–38; R. B. Beckett (Constable, 5:73–78); Karl Kroeber, *Romantic Landscape Vision: Constable and Wordsworth* (Madison, Wis., 1975); and Mark L. Reed, "Constable, Wordsworth, and Beaumont: A New Constable Letter in Evidence," *Art Bulletin* 64 (1982): 481–83. See also Russell Noyes, *Wordsworth and the Art of Landscape* (Bloomington, Ind., 1968).
2. See Cummings and Staley, *Romantic Art in Britain,* p. 323. On Inchbold's use of Wordsworth's poetry in general, see Allen Staley, *The Pre-Raphaelite Landscape* (Oxford, 1973), pp. 113–15.

Coleridge

1. On Coleridge's own interest in art, see Carl Woodring, "What Coleridge Thought of Pictures," Kroeber and Walling, *Images of Romanticism,* pp. 91–106.
2. *Examiner,* 24 May 1812, p. 328.
3. W. B. Scott, *Memoir of David Scott* (Edinburgh, 1850), p. 150.
4. *Letters of Samuel Taylor Coleridge,* ed. Griggs (Oxford, 1956–71), 6:1058.
5. Irwin, *Scottish Painters,* p. 265. See also Irwin, "David Scott," pp. 462–63.
6. Ruskin, 14:19.

Southey

1. *Times,* 1 May 1852, p. 8.
2. *Times,* 18 May 1880, p. 4.

Scott

1. Farington (2), 8:208 n.
2. The best sources on Scott's reputation are James T. Hillhouse, *The Waverley Novels and Their Critics* (Minneapolis, 1936); *Scott: The Critical Heritage*, ed. John O. Hayden (London, 1970); and John Henry Raleigh, "What Scott Meant to the Victorians," *Victorian Studies* 7 (1963): 7–34.
3. *Literary Gazette*, 23 March 1831, p. 266.
4. See three discussions by Gordon: "The Illustration of Sir Walter Scott," "Scott's Impact on Art," and *The Lamp of Memory*.
5. E. V. Lucas, *Edwin Austin Abbey* (London, 1921), 1:111.
6. J. B. Flagg, *Life and Letters of Washington Allston* (New York, 1892), pp. 157–58.
7. Bliss, *Sir Walter Scott and the Visual Arts*, p. 8.
8. Kemp, "Scott and Delacroix," p. 227.
9. The *locus classicus* for Ruskin on Scott and the art of landscape is *Modern Painters* III, pt. 4, chap. 16 ("Of Modern Landscape"), *Works*, 5: especially pp. 339–53.
10. This many-sided subject is covered by Bliss, *Scott and the Visual Arts*, and Murdoch, "Scott, Pictures, and Painters."
11. Leslie, *Autobiographical Recollections*, pp. 62–63.
12. See, in addition to Gordon's articles listed above, Muir, *Victorian Illustrated Books*, pp. 74–75, 85–86.
13. Holcomb, "Scott and Turner" (an expanded version of "Turner and Scott," *JWCI* 34 [1971]: 386–97), and Finley, *Landscapes of Memory*.
14. Letter dated 24 January 1820: *Life of Mary Russell Mitford* (New York, 1870), 1:322–23.
15. These are discussed in Nicoll, *History of English Drama* (see above, pt. 1, chap. 11, n. 18), 4:91–95, and in more detail by Henry Adelbert White, *Sir Walter Scott's Novels on the Stage*, Yale Studies in English 76 (New Haven, Conn., 1927). The fullest list of adaptations to the end of the nineteenth century is Richard Ford, *Dramatisations of Scott's Novels: A Catalogue*, Oxford Bibliographical Society Occasional Publications 12 (1979).
16. *Athenaeum*, 11 February 1832, p. 99.
17. "May Gambols," *Fraser's Magazine* 29 (1844): 709.
18. John Callcott Horsley, *Recollections of a Royal Academician* (London, 1903), p. 136.
19. Alfred T. Story, "Sir Noel Paton: His Life and Work," *Art Journal* 57 (1895): 118; George Richardson, *The Works of Henry Liverseege, with a Memoir* (London, 1875), pp. 11–12; W. M. Rossetti, *Some Reminiscences*, 1:57.
20. Burne-Jones, *Memorials of Burne-Jones*, 2:329.
21. Hilda Orchardson Gray, *Life of Sir William Quiller Orchardson* (London, 1930), p. 29.
22. Watts, *G. F. Watts*, 1:15.
23. Frith, *Autobiography*, 1:6–7.
24. W. H. Hunt, *Pre-Raphaelitism*, 1:64, 72.
25. Ormond, *Landseer*, p. 117.
26. Frith, *Autobiography*, 1:225.
27. Surtees, *The Paintings and Drawings of Rossetti*, 1:101. See also John P. Seddon, "The 'King René's Honeymoon' Cabinet," *Magazine of Art* 20 (1897): 323–24.
28. Raleigh, "What Scott Meant to the Victorians," p. 10.

Byron

1. The course of Byron's reputation is described in Samuel C. Chew, *Byron in England: His Fame and After-Fame* (New York, 1924), and documented in *Byron: The Critical Heritage*, ed. Andrew Rutherford (London, 1970).
2. Knowles, *Fuseli*, 1:359.
3. See *Turner and the Poets* (above, Rogers n. 4).
4. This topic is thoroughly covered by George Heard Hamilton, "Eugène Delacroix and Lord Byron," *Gazette des Beaux Arts* 6th ser. 23 (1943): 99–110; "Hamlet or Childe Harold? Delacroix and Byron," ibid., 26 (1944): 365–86; "Delacroix, Byron, and the English Illustrators," ibid., 36 (1949): 261–78; and "Delacroix's Memorial to Byron," *Burlington Magazine* 94 (1952): 257–61. See also Lee Johnson, "Delacroix and *The Bride of Abydos*," *Burlington Magazine* 114 (1972): 579–85, and Frank Anderson Trapp, *The Attainment of Delacroix* (Baltimore, 1970), passim.
5. See Samuel C. Chew, *The Dramas of Lord Byron: A Critical Study* (Baltimore, 1915), and Boleslaw Taborski, *Byron and the Theatre*, Salzburg Studies in English Literature (1972).
6. *Byron: The Critical Heritage*, p. 399.
7. Ibid., pp. 309, 311. (Originally in the *Edinburgh Review*, June 1831.)
8. See the handlist of plays in Nicoll (above, pt. 1, chap. 11, n. 18), vol. 4.
9. See Hubert F. Babinski, *The Mazeppa Legend in European Romanticism* (New York, 1974), especially the appendix, "Ivan Mazeppa in Works of Art and Literature (1688–1840)."

Moore

1. A concise summary of Moore's contemporary reputation is in J. O. Hayden, *The Romantic Reviewers* (Chicago, 1968), pp. 217–25.

Shelley

1. See Sylva Norman, *Flight of the Skylark: The Development of Shelley's Reputation* (Norman, Okla., 1954); Newman I. White, *The Unextinguished Hearth: Shelley and His Contemporary Critics* (Durham, N.C., 1938); and *Shelley: The Critical Heritage*, ed. James E. Barcus (London, 1975). A full account of the poet's knowledge of Italian art is Frederic S. Colwell, "Shelley and Italian Painting," *Keats-Shelley Journal* 29 (1980): 43–66.
2. *London Magazine* 3 (1821): 370.
3. *Literary Gazette*, 1 June 1850, p. 378.
4. See Joseph W. Donohue, Jr., *Dramatic Character in the*

English Romantic Age (Princeton, N.J., 1970), pp. 163–69.

5. Honour, *Romanticism,* p. 100.
6. Butlin and Joll, *The Paintings of Turner,* 1:239.
7. Davidson Cook, "'Sadak the Wanderer': An Unknown Shelley Poem," *Times Literary Supplement,* 16 May 1936, p. 424. See also Feaver, *The Art of John Martin,* pp. 16–17.

Keats

1. Hagstrum, "The Sister Arts: From Neoclassic to Romantic," p. 190.
2. *Keats: The Critical Heritage,* ed. G. M. Matthews (London, 1971), p. 214.
3. On Keats's critical reputation, see, in addition to the Critical Heritage volume just cited, George H. Ford, *Keats and the Victorians,* Yale Studies in English 101 (New Haven, Conn., 1944).
4. *London Magazine* 4 (1820): 385–86.
5. The first illustrated edition appeared in 1854. See Helen E. Haworth, "'A Thing of Beauty is a Joy Forever?': Early Illustrated Editions of Keats's Poetry," *Harvard Library Bulletin* 21 (1973): 88–103. *The Bookman Keats-Shelley Memorial Souvenir* (a special number of the [London] *Bookman,* 1912) reproduces a number of illustrations of Keats's poems.
6. *Keats: The Critical Heritage,* pp. 278–79. (Originally in [Leigh Hunt's] *London Journal,* 21 January 1835.)
7. W. H. Hunt, *Pre-Raphaelitism,* 1:105–6.
8. *Art Journal* 25 (1863): 108–9.

THE VICTORIAN ERA

Tennyson

1. Tennyson's critical reputation is documented in *Tennyson: The Critical Heritage,* ed. J. D. Jump (London, 1967). George Wesley Whiting, *The Artist and Tennyson,* Rice University Studies 50 (1964), collects, without significant comment, some reviews of various pictures of Tennysonian subjects.
2. *Athenaeum,* 5 June 1841, p. 443.
3. *Tennyson: The Critical Heritage,* p. 26. (Originally in the *Westminster Review,* January 1831.)
4. "Alfred Tennyson," *Eclectic Magazine* (New York) 13 (1848): 290.
5. *Art Journal* 17 (1855): 139.
6. *Athenaeum,* 13 February 1858, p. 214.
7. *Examiner,* 7 June 1851, p. 359.
8. *Art Journal* 25 (1863): 47.
9. J. D. Hunt, "'Story Painters and Picture Writers'," passim.
10. *Tennyson: The Critical Heritage,* p. 72. (Originally in the *Quarterly Review,* April 1833.)
11. *Art Journal* 18 (1856): 135.
12. H. Heathcote Statham, "At the Royal Academy," *Fortnightly Review* n.s. 67 (1900): 1023–24.
13. *Athenaeum,* 31 May 1879, p. 702.
14. W. J. O'Driscoll, *Memoir of Daniel Maclise* (London, 1871), p. 222.
15. On these, see W. S. Taylor, "King Cophetua and the Beggar Maid," *Apollo* 97 (1973): 148–55.
16. *Tennyson: The Critical Heritage,* p. 131. (Originally in the *Church of England Quarterly Review,* October 1842.)
17. Ibid., p. 347. (Originally in Swinburne's *Miscellanies,* 1886.)
18. *Athenaeum,* 29 March 1862, p. 434.
19. Elaine is interpreted as "the ideal Pre-Raphaelite: poet and painter in one" by Catherine Barnes Stevenson, "How It Struck a Contemporary: Tennyson's 'Lancelot and Elaine' and Pre-Raphaelite Art," *Victorian Newsletter,* no. 60 (Fall 1981), pp. 8–14.
20. Particularly relevant to the study of Tennyson's imagery in the *Idylls* are John D. Rosenberg, *The Fall of Camelot: A Study of Tennyson's "Idylls of the King"* (Cambridge, Mass., 1973), chap. 4 ("Landscape"), and J. P. Eggers, *King Arthur's Laureate* (New York, 1971), pp. 65–70.
21. *The Correspondence of Emerson and Carlyle,* ed. Joseph Slater (New York, 1964), p. 553.
22. *Athenaeum,* 29 April 1865, p. 592.
23. *Examiner,* 13 May 1865, p. 296.
24. *Tennyson: The Critical Heritage,* p. 130.

The Brownings

1. The subject is well treated in Leonée Ormond, "Browning and Painting."
2. The story is told in William Clyde DeVane, *A Browning Handbook,* 2d ed. (New York, 1955), pp. 114–16.
3. Ibid., pp. 127–28.
4. Rosalie Mander, "'The Tryst' Unravelled," *Apollo* 79 (1964): 221–23.

Bulwer-Lytton

1. See Honour, *Romanticism,* pp. 206–12, and Alexandra R. Murphy, *Visions of Vesuvius* (exhibition catalogue, Boston Museum of Fine Arts, 1978).
2. Feaver, *The Art of John Martin,* p. 55.
3. Bulwer-Lytton, *England and the English* (Chicago, 1970), p. 343.
4. See Curtis Dahl, "Bulwer-Lytton and the School of Catastrophe," *Philological Quarterly* 32 (1953): 428–42.
5. Laurence Goldstein, "The Impact of Pompeii on the Literary Imagination," *Centennial Review* 23 (1979): 227–41.
6. J. S. Bratton, *The Victorian Popular Ballad* (London, 1975), p. 64.
7. *Blackwood's Magazine* 88 (1860): 78–79.

8. *Literary Gazette,* 19 May 1860, p. 615.

Dickens

1. *Dickens: The Critical Heritage,* ed. Philip Collins (London, 1971), pp. 255–56. (Originally in the *North British Review,* May 1851.)
2. The most authoritative treatment of this much-discussed topic is J. R. Cohen, *Charles Dickens and His Original Illustrators* (Columbus, Ohio, 1980).
3. *Literary Gazette,* 6 May 1848, p. 316.
4. Frith, *Autobiography,* 1:101–2.
5. See A. G. Temple, *The Art of Painting in the Queen's Reign,* pp. 150–51.
6. Frith, 1:102.
7. *The Speeches of Charles Dickens,* ed. K. J. Fielding (Oxford, 1960), p. 421.
8. *Letters of James Smetham* (London, 1892), p. 207.

George Eliot

1. *George Eliot: The Critical Heritage,* ed. David Carroll (London, 1971), pp. 235–36.
2. See Witemeyer, *George Eliot and the Visual Arts.*
3. M. H. Spielmann, *Millais and His Works* (London, 1898), p. 97.

The Pre-Raphaelites

1. The relations between Rossetti's art and his poetry are most extensively canvassed in *Dante Gabriel Rossetti and the Double Work of Art* (see above, pt. 1, chap. 9, n. 50). Details of all his pictures with literary subjects are in Surtees, *The Paintings and Drawings of Rossetti.*
2. *Times,* 13 May 1880, p. 8.
3. The following list is derived from Steven Kolsteren, "Rossetti's Writings as a Source of Inspiration for Victorian Artists," *Victorian Poetry* 20, nos. 3–4 (Autumn–Winter 1982): 113–43.

Appendix A

1. Constable, 6:231. See also p. 211.
2. John Adolphus, *Memoirs of John Bannister, Comedian* (London, [1839]), 1:292–93.

Appendix B

1. Douglas Hall, "The Tabley House Papers," *Walpole Society* 38 (1960–62): 117.
2. Ibid., p. 118.
3. Ibid., pp. 89, 119.
4. Farington (1), 10:3675 (26 June 1810).
5. Hall, "The Tabley House Papers," pp. 93, 120.
6. Feaver, *The Art of John Martin,* p. 16; Mary L. Pendered, *John Martin, Painter: His Life and Times* (New York, 1934), pp. 79–80.
7. Gerald Reitlinger, *The Economics of Taste* (London, 1961), p. 381.
8. Memoir prefixed to Howard, *A Course of Lectures on Painting,* pp. lxix–lxx.
9. Mary Russell Mitford, letter to Sir William Elford, 23 May 1817: *Life of Mary Russell Mitford* (New York, 1870), 1:266.
10. J. B. Flagg, *Life and Letters of Washington Allston* (New York, 1892), p. 72.
11. Hall, "The Tabley House Papers," p. 114.
12. Flagg, *Allston,* p. 147.
13. Farr, *Etty,* p. 141.
14. Hall, "The Tabley House Papers," p. 116.
15. Reitlinger, *The Economics of Taste,* p. 141.
16. Farr, *Etty,* p. 153.
17. Reitlinger, *The Economics of Taste,* p. 363.
18. Farr, *Etty,* p. 151.
19. Ibid., p. 140.
20. Thompson, *Pictures for Scotland,* p. 56.
21. Pointon, *Dyce,* p. 58.
22. Frith, *Autobiography,* 1:100.
23. Ibid., 1:105.
24. Farr, *Etty,* p. 141.
25. Robertson, *Eastlake,* p. 270.
26. Frith, *Autobiography,* 1:113–14.
27. Ibid., 2:13–14.
28. Haydon, *Diary,* 5:599.
29. Treble, *Great Victorian Pictures,* p. 62.
30. W. H. Hunt, *Pre-Raphaelitism,* 1:72.
31. William Vaughan, *German Romanticism and English Art* (New Haven, Conn., 1979), p. 58.
32. Frith, *Autobiography,* 1:155.
33. Hunt, *Pre-Raphaelitism,* 1:177. Augustus Hare recorded the same incident, related to him by Holman Hunt, but which he misconstrued to have happened to Frederic Leighton (*In My Solitary Life,* ed. Malcolm Barnes [London, 1953], p. 289—an abridgement of the last three volumes of Hare's *The Story of My Life*).
34. Hunt, *Pre-Raphaelitism,* 1:182–83.
35. Thompson, *Pictures for Scotland,* p. 60.
36. W. M. Rossetti, *The P. R. B. Journal,* p. 60.
37. Campbell Lennie, *Landseer* (London, 1976), p. 153.
38. Frith, *Autobiography,* 1:222.
39. Henry Stacy Marks, *Pen and Pencil Sketches* (London, 1894), 1:50–51.
40. Reitlinger, *The Economics of Taste,* p. 389.

41. Ashton (1), p. 14.

42. Martin Hardie, *John Pettie, R.A.* (London, 1908), p. 23.

43. Frith, *Autobiography,* 1:389.

44. Reitlinger, *The Economics of Taste,* p. 404.

45. Frith, *Autobiography,* 2:14.

46. W. M. Rossetti, *Diary,* p. 152.

47. Reitlinger, *The Economics of Taste,* p. 359.

48. Bevis Hillier, "The St. John's Wood Clique," *Apollo* 79 (1964): 491.

49. Reitlinger, *The Economics of Taste,* p. 404.

50. *Burne-Jones Talking: His Conversations, 1895–1898, Preserved by His Studio Assistant, Thomas Rooke,* ed. Mary Lago (Columbia, Mo., 1981), p. 105.

BIBLIOGRAPHY

Limited, in general, to basic books on the history of British art (1760–1900), major books on painters prominent in this study, the more important books and articles devoted to the illustration of English literary works (the remainder are cited at appropriate places in the source notes), and other items referred to more than three or four times in the notes. Of the many scores of exhibition catalogues examined, only a few—the most important for present purposes—are included here.

Adams, C. K. *A Catalogue of the Pictures in the Garrick Club.* Privately printed, 1936.

Allderidge, Patricia. *The Late Richard Dadd, 1817–1886.* (Exhibition catalogue, Tate Gallery, 1974.)

[Ashton, Geoffrey.] (1) *Shakespeare and British Art.* (Exhibition catalogue, Yale Center for British Art, 1981.)

______. (2) *Shakespeare's Heroines in the Nineteenth Century.* (Exhibition catalogue, Buxton Museum and Art Gallery, 1980.)

Aubrat, Odette, *La Peinture de genre en Angleterre, de la mort de Hogarth (1764) au PréRaphaélisme (1850).* Paris, 1934.

Baker, C. H. Collins. "Some Illustrators of Milton's *Paradise Lost.*" *Library* 5th ser. 3 (1948): 1–21, 101–19.

Balston, Thomas. *John Martin, 1798–1854: His Life and Works.* London, 1947.

Barry, James. *Lectures on Painting.* In Wornum (below), pp. 56–236.

Beckett, R. B. "Constable as an Illustrator." *Connoisseur* 134 (1954): 79–84.

Bell, C. F. "Thomas Gray and the Fine Arts." *Essays and Studies by Members of the English Association* 30 (1944): 50–81.

Bell, Quentin. *Victorian Artists.* London, 1975.

Bennett, Mary. "A Checklist of Pre-Raphaelite Pictures Exhibited at Liverpool, 1846–67, and Some of Their Northern Collectors." *Burlington Magazine* 105 (1963): 486–95.

______. *Ford Madox Brown, 1821–1893.* (Exhibition catalogue, Walker Art Gallery, 1964.)

______. *Millais, P.R.B., P.R.A.* (Exhibition catalogue, Walker Art Gallery and the Royal Academy, 1967.)

______. *William Holman Hunt.* (Exhibition catalogue, Walker Art Gallery and Victoria and Albert Museum, 1969.)

Bertelsen, Lance. "David Garrick and English Painting." *Eighteenth-Century Studies* 11 (1978): 308–24.

Bindman, David. *Hogarth.* London, 1981.

Bland, David. *A History of Book Illustration.* 2d rev. ed. Berkeley, Cal., 1969.

Bliss, Douglas Percy. *Sir Walter Scott and the Visual Arts.* (David Cargill Lecture, Glasgow School of Art, 1970.) Glasgow, 1971.

Boase, T. S. R. "The Decoration of the New Palace of Westminster, 1841–1863." *Journal of the Warburg and Courtauld Institutes* (hereafter cited as *JWCI*) 17 (1954): 319–58.

______. *English Art, 1800–1870.* Oxford History of English Art, Vol. 10. Oxford, 1959.

______. "Illustrations of Shakespeare's Plays in the Seventeenth and Eighteenth Centuries." *JWCI* 10 (1947): 83–108.

______. "Macklin and Bowyer." *JWCI* 26 (1963): 148–77.

Bradley, Laurel. "Eighteenth-Century Paintings and Illustrations of Spenser's *Faerie Queene:* A Study in Taste." *Marsyas* (New York University Institute of Fine Arts) 20 (1979–80): 31–51.

Brion, Marcel. *Art of the Romantic Era: Romanticism, Classicism, Realism.* New York, 1966.

Brown, Ford Madox. *The Diary of Ford Madox Brown.* Ed. Virginia Surtees. New Haven, Conn., 1981.

Brownell, Morris R. *Alexander Pope and the Arts of Georgian England.* Oxford, 1978.

Burke, Joseph. *English Art, 1714–1800.* Oxford History of English Art, Vol. 9. Oxford, 1976.

Burne-Jones, Georgiana. *Memorials of Edward Burne-Jones.* 2 vols. London, 1904.

Butlin, Martin, and Evelyn Joll. *The Paintings of J. M. W. Turner.* 2 vols. New Haven, Conn., 1977.

Caw, James L. *Scottish Painting, Past and Present, 1620–1908.* Edinburgh, 1908. Rpt. Bath, 1975.

Clark, Kenneth. *The Romantic Rebellion: Romantic versus Classic Art.* New York, 1973.

Clement, Clara E., and Laurence Hutton. *Artists of the Nineteenth Century and Their Works.* 3d ed., rev. 2 vols. Boston, 1885. (Originally published London, 1879.)

Cohen, Ralph. *The Art of Discrimination: Thomson's "The Seasons" and the Language of Criticism.* London, 1974.

Conrad, Peter. *The Victorian Treasure-House.* London, 1973.

Crookshank, Anne, and the Knight of Glin. *The Painters of Ireland c. 1600–1920.* London, 1978.

Cummings, Frederick J., and Allen Staley. *Romantic Art in Britain: Paintings and Drawings, 1760–1860.* (Exhibition catalogue, Detroit Institute of Arts and Philadelphia Museum of Art, 1968.)

Cunningham, Allan. *The Life of Sir David Wilkie.* 3 vols. London, 1843.

______. *The Lives of the Most Eminent British Painters.* Annotated and continued by Mrs. Charles Heaton. 3 vols. London, 1879–80. (Originally published London, 1829–33.)

Davies, Cicely. "Ut pictura poesis." *Modern Language Review* 30 (1935): 159–69.

Desai, Rupin W. "William Cowper and the Visual Arts." *Bulletin of the New York Public Library* 72 (1968): 359–72.

Donohue, Joseph W. Jr. "John Hamilton Mortimer and Shakespearean Characterization." *Princeton University Library Chronicle* 29 (1968): 193–207.

[Dyce.] *Centenary Exhibition of the Work of William Dyce.* (Catalogue, Aberdeen Art Gallery and Thomas Agnew & Sons, 1964.)

Eichholz, Jeffrey P. "William Kent's Career as Literary Illustrator." *Bulletin of the New York Public Library* 70 (1966): 620–46.

Engen, Rodney K. *Dictionary of Victorian Engravers, Print Publishers, and Their Works.* Cambridge, 1979.

———. *Victorian Engravings.* London, 1975.

[Etty.] *An Exhibition of Paintings by William Etty.* (Catalogue, Arts Council, 1955.)

Farington, Joseph. (1) *The Diary of Joseph Farington.* Ed. Kenneth Garlick et al. 16 vols. New Haven, Conn., 1978–84.

———. (2) *The Farington Diary.* Ed. James Greig. 8 vols. London, 1923–28.

Farr, Dennis. *English Art, 1870–1940.* Oxford History of English Art, Vol. 11. Oxford, 1978.

———. *William Etty.* London, 1958.

Fawcett, Trevor. *The Rise of English Provincial Art.* Oxford, 1974.

Feaver, William. *The Art of John Martin.* Oxford, 1975.

Finberg, A. J. *The Life of J. M. W. Turner, R.A.* 2d ed. Oxford, 1961.

Findlay, L. M. "Aspects of Analogy: The Changing Role of the Sister Arts Tradition in Victorian Criticism." *English Studies in Canada* 3 (1977): 51–68.

Finley, Gerald. *Landscapes of Memory: Turner as Illustrator to Scott.* London, 1980.

Forbes, Christopher. *The Royal Academy (1837–1901) Revisited: Victorian Paintings from the Forbes Magazine Collection.* (Exhibition catalogue, Metropolitan Museum of Art and Princeton University Art Museum, 1975.)

[*Forbes Magazine.*] *The Art and Mind of Victorian England: Paintings from the Forbes Magazine Collection.* (Exhibition catalogue, University of Minnesota Art Gallery, 1974.)

Fredeman, William E. *Pre-Raphaelitism: A Bibliocritical Study.* Cambridge, Mass., 1965.

Friedman, Winifred H. *Boydell's Shakespeare Gallery.* New York, 1976. (Ph.D. dissertation, Harvard University, 1974.)

Frith, William Powell. *My Autobiography and Reminiscences.* 3 vols. London, 1887–88.

Fuseli, Henry. *The Collected English Letters of Henry Fuseli.* Ed. David H. Weinglass. Millwood, N.Y., 1982.

———. *Lectures on Painting.* In Wornum (below), pp. 337–560.

Gaunt, William. (1) *A Concise History of English Painting.* London, 1964.

———. (2) *The Great Century of English Painting: Hogarth to Turner.* 2d ed. London, 1978.

———. (3) *The Restless Century: Painting in Britain, 1800–1900.* 2d ed. London, 1978.

———. (4) *Victorian Olympus.* London, 1952.

Gent, Lucy. *Picture and Poetry, 1560–1620: Relations Between Literature and the Visual Arts in the English Renaissance.* Leamington Spa, 1981.

George, Eric. *The Life and Death of Benjamin Robert Haydon.* 2d ed. Oxford, 1967.

Gordon, Catherine. (1) "The Illustration of Sir Walter Scott: Nineteenth Century Enthusiasm and Adaptation." *JWCI* 34 (1971): 297–317.

———. (2) *The Lamp of Memory: Scott and the Artist.* (Exhibition catalogue, Buxton Museum and Art Gallery, 1979.)

———. (3) " 'More Than One Handle': The Development of Sterne Illustration, 1760–1820." *Words: Wai-te-Ata Studies in Literature* (New Zealand), no. 4 (January 1974), pp. 47–58.

———. (4) "Scott's Impact on Art." *Apollo* 98 (1973): 36–39.

Gowing, Lawrence, "Hogarth, Hayman, and the Vauxhall Decorations." *Burlington Magazine* 95 (1953): 4–19.

Graves, Algernon. *Art Sales from Early in the Eighteenth Century to Early in the Twentieth Century.* 3 vols. London, 1918–21. Rpt. Bath, 1973.

———. *The British Institution, 1806–1867. A Complete Dictionary of Contributors and Their Work.* London, 1875. Rpt. Bath, 1969.

———. *A Century of Loan Exhibitions, 1813–1912.* 5 vols. London, 1913–15. Rpt. New York, n.d.

———. *A Dictionary of Artists Who Have Exhibited Works in the Principal London Exhibitions from 1760 to 1893.* 3d ed. London, 1901. Rpt. Bath, 1973.

———. *The Royal Academy of Arts: A Complete Dictionary of Contributors and Their Work from Its Foundation in 1769 to 1904.* 8 vols. London, 1905–6.

———. *The Society of Artists of Great Britain, 1760–1791 / The Free Society of Artists, 1761–1783 / A Complete Dictionary of Contributors and Their Work from the Foundation of the Societies to 1791.* London, 1907.

Greysmith, David. *Richard Dadd: The Rock and Castle of Seclusion.* London, 1973.

Grigson, Geoffrey. "English Painting from Blake to Byron." In *From Blake to Byron* (Pelican Guide to English Literature, Vol. 5: Harmondsworth, England, 1957), pp. 258–72.

Grundy, Joan. *Hardy and the Sister Arts.* London, 1979.

Guise, Hilary. *Great Victorian Engravings: A Collector's Guide.* London, 1980.

Hagstrum, Jean H. "The Sister Arts: From Neoclassic to Romantic." In *Comparatists at Work: Studies in Comparative Literature,* ed. Stephen G. Nichols, Jr., and Richard B. Vowles (Waltham, Mass., 1968), pp. 169–94.

———. *The Sister Arts: The Tradition of Literary Pictorialism and English Poetry from Dryden to Gray.* Chicago, 1958.

Halsband, Robert. *"The Rape of the Lock" and Its Illustrations, 1714–1896.* Oxford, 1980.

Hamlyn, Robin. "An Irish Shakespeare Gallery." *Burlington Magazine* 120 (1978): 515–29.

Hammelmann, Hanns. *Book Illustrators in Eighteenth-Century*

England. Ed. and completed by T. S. R. Boase. New Haven, Conn., 1975.

———. "Eighteenth-Century English Illustrators: Francis Hayman, R. A." *Book Collector* 2 (1953): 116–32.

———. "Eighteenth-Century English Illustrators: Henry Fuseli, R. A." *Book Collector* 6 (1957): 350–60.

Hardie, William. *Scottish Painting, 1837–1939.* London, 1976.

———. *Sir William Quiller Orchardson, R. A.* (Exhibition catalogue, Scottish Art Council, 1972.)

Harrison, Martin, and Bill Waters. *Burne-Jones.* New York, 1973.

Hartmann, Sadakichi. *Shakespeare in Art.* Boston, 1901.

Harvey, J. R. *Victorian Novelists and Their Illustrators.* New York, 1971.

Haydon, Benjamin Robert. *The Autobiography and Memoirs of Benjamin Robert Haydon.* Ed. Tom Taylor. New ed. 2 vols. New York, [1926].

———. *Benjamin Robert Haydon: Correspondence and Table-Talk.* 2 vols. London, 1876.

———. *The Diary of Benjamin Robert Haydon.* Ed. Willard Bissell Pope. 5 vols. Cambridge, Mass., 1960–63.

———. *Lectures on Painting and Design.* 2 vols. London, 1844–46.

———. *Painting and the Fine Arts.* Edinburgh, 1838.

Heleniak, Kathryn Moore. *William Mulready.* New Haven, Conn., 1980.

Hemstedt, Geoffrey. "Painting and Illustration." In *The Victorians,* ed. Laurence Lerner (New York, 1978), pp. 139–52.

Hodnett, Edward. *Image and Text: Studies in the Illustration of English Literature.* London, 1982.

Holcomb, Adele M. "Scott and Turner." In *Scott Bicentenary Essays,* ed. Alan Bell (Edinburgh, 1973), pp. 199–212.

Honour, Hugh. *Romanticism.* New York, 1979.

Houfe, Simon. *The Dictionary of British Book Illustrators and Caricaturists, 1800–1914.* Woodbridge, England, 1978.

Howard, Henry. *A Course of Lectures on Painting, Delivered at the Royal Academy of Fine Arts.* London, 1848.

Hudson, Derek. *Sir Joshua Reynolds: A Personal Study.* London, 1958.

Hueffer, Ford M. *Ford Madox Brown: A Record of His Life and Work.* London, 1896.

Hughes, Merritt Y. "Some Illustrators of Milton: The Expulsion from Paradise." *Journal of English and Germanic Philology* 60 (1961): 670–79.

Hunnisett, Basil. *Steel-Engraved Book Illustration in England.* London, 1980.

Hunt, John Dixon, ed. *Encounters: Essays on Literature and the Visual Arts.* London, 1971.

———. *The Figure in the Landscape: Poetry, Painting, and Gardening during the Eighteenth Century.* Baltimore, 1976.

———. "Milton's Illustrators." In *John Milton: Introductions,* ed. John Broadbent (Cambridge, 1973), pp. 208–25.

———. "'Story Painters and Picture Writers': Tennyson's Idylls and Victorian Painting." In *Tennyson,* ed. D. J. Palmer (Athens, Ohio, 1973), pp. 180–202.

Hunt, William Holman. *Pre-Raphaelitism and the Pre-Raphaelite Brotherhood.* 2 vols. New York, 1905–6.

Hutchison, Sidney C. *The History of the Royal Academy, 1768–1968.* London, 1968.

Hutton, Richard W. *Alderman Boydell's Shakespeare Gallery: An Exhibition of the Engravings.* (Catalogue, David and Alfred Smart Gallery, University of Chicago, 1978.)

Ironside, Robin, and John Gere. *Pre-Raphaelite Painters.* London, 1948.

Irwin, David. "David Scott: Illustrations of Mysticism and the Supernatural." *Studies in Romanticism* 15 (1976): 461–67.

———. *English Neoclassical Art: Studies in Inspiration and Taste.* London, 1966.

———, and Francina Irwin. *Scottish Painters at Home and Abroad, 1700–1900.* London, 1975.

Irwin, Michael. *Picturing: Description and Illusion in the Nineteenth-Century Novel.* London, 1979.

Jack, Ian. *Keats and the Mirror of Art.* Oxford, 1967.

James, Henry. *The Painter's Eye: Notes and Essays on the Pictorial Arts.* Ed. John L. Sweeney. Cambridge, Mass., 1956.

Kemp, Martin. "Scott and Delacroix, with Some Assistance from Hugo and Bonington." In *Scott Bicentenary Essays,* ed. Alan Bell (Edinburgh, 1973), pp. 213–27.

Knowles, John. *The Life and Writings of Henry Fuseli.* 3 vols. London, 1831.

Kroeber, Karl, and William Walling, eds. *Images of Romanticism: Verbal and Visual Affinities.* New Haven, Conn., 1978.

Lambourne, Lionel. *An Introduction to "Victorian" Genre Painting from Wilkie to Frith.* London, 1982. (A Victoria and Albert Museum Guide.)

Landow, George P. *Images of Crisis: Literary Iconology, 1750 to the Present.* London, 1982.

———. "There Began to be a Great Talking About the Fine Arts." In *The Mind and Art of Victorian England,* ed. Josef Altholz (Minneapolis, 1976), pp. 124–45.

———. *Victorian Types, Victorian Shadows: Biblical Typology in Victorian Literature, Art, and Thought.* Boston, 1980.

Lee, Rensselaer W. "*Ut pictura poesis:* The Humanistic Theory of Painting." *Art Bulletin* 22 (1940): 197–269. Rpt. separately, New York, 1969.

Leslie, Charles Robert. *Autobiographical Recollections by the Late Charles Robert Leslie, R. A.* Boston, 1860. (Prefatory essay by Tom Taylor, pp. xiii–lviii.)

———. *Life and Times of Sir Joshua Reynolds.* Continued and concluded by Tom Taylor. 2 vols. London, 1865.

———. *Memoirs of the Life of John Constable, R.A.* Ed. and enlarged by the Hon. Andrew Shirley. London, 1937. (Originally published London, 1843.)

Lindsay, Jack, ed. *The Sunset Ship: The Poems of J. M. W. Turner.* Lowestoft, England, 1966.

Lipking, Lawrence. *The Ordering of the Arts in Eighteenth-Century England.* Princeton, N.J., 1970.

Lister, Raymond. *British Romantic Art.* London, 1973.

———. *Victorian Narrative Paintings.* New York, 1966.

Maas, Jeremy. *Victorian Painters.* London, 1969.

MacColl, Dugald S. *Nineteenth-Century Art.* Glasgow, 1902.

McKay, William D. *The Scottish School of Painting.* London, 1906.

Mander, Raymond, and Joe Mitchenson. *Guide to the Maugham Collection of Theatrical Paintings.* (Catalogue, National Theatre, 1980.)

Marillier, Henry Currie. *The Liverpool School of Painters.* London, 1904.

Mason, Eudo C. *The Mind of Henry Fuseli.* London, 1951.

Meisel, Martin. *Realizations: Narrative, Pictorial, and Theatrical Arts in Nineteenth-Century England.* Princeton, N.J., 1983.

Merchant, W. Moelwyn. "Blake's Shakespeare." *Apollo* 79 (1964): 318–25.

———. *Shakespeare and the Artist.* London, 1959.

———. *Shakespeare in Art: Paintings, Drawings and Engravings Devoted to Shakespearean Subjects.* (Exhibition catalogue, Arts Council, 1964.)

Millais, John Guille. *The Life and Letters of Sir John Everett Millais.* 2 vols. New York, 1899.

Mitchell, Charles. "The History-Picture in English Art." *Listener* 43 (1950): 918–21.

Moore, Robert E. "Hogarth as Illustrator." *Art in America* 36 (1948): 193–204.

———. *Hogarth's Literary Relationships.* Minneapolis, 1948.

Muir, Percy. *Victorian Illustrated Books.* New York, 1971.

[Mulready.] *William Mulready, 1786–1863.* (Exhibition catalogue, Bristol City Art Gallery, 1964.)

Murdoch, J. D. W. "Scott, Pictures, and Painters." *Modern Language Review* 67 (1972): 31–43.

Murdoch, John. "English Realism: George Eliot and the Pre-Raphaelites." *JWCI* 37 (1974): 313–29.

Nicolson, Benedict. *Joseph Wright of Derby: Painter of Light.* 2 vols. London, 1968.

Noakes, Aubrey. *William Frith: Extraordinary Victorian Painter.* London, 1978.

Northcote, James. *Conversations of James Northcote, R.A., with James Ward, on Art and Artists.* Ed. Ernest Fletcher. London, 1901.

———. *The Life of Sir Joshua Reynolds.* 2d ed. 2 vols. London, 1819.

Olmsted, John Charles, ed. *Victorian Painting: Essays and Reviews.* Volume 1: 1832–1848; Volume 2: 1849–1860. New York, 1980, 1983.

O'Neil, Henry Nelson. *Lectures on Painting Delivered at the Royal Academy.* London, 1866.

Opie, John. *Lectures on Painting.* In Wornum (below), pp. 237–336.

Oppé, A. J. "Art." In *Early Victorian England, 1830–1865,* ed. G. M. Young (London, 1934), 2: 101–76.

Ormond, Leonée. "Browning and Painting." In *Robert Browning,* ed. Isobel Armstrong (London, 1974), pp. 184–210.

———, and Richard Ormond. *Lord Leighton.* New Haven, Conn., 1975.

Ormond, Richard. "Daniel Maclise." *Burlington Magazine* 110 (1968): 685–93.

———. *Daniel Maclise, 1806–1870.* (Exhibition catalogue, National Portrait Gallery and National Gallery of Ireland, 1972.)

———. *Sir Edwin Landseer.* New York, 1981. (Exhibition catalogue, Philadelphia Museum of Art and Tate Gallery.)

Palgrave, Francis Turner. *Essays on Art.* London, 1866.

Park, Roy. *Hazlitt and the Spirit of the Age: Abstraction and Critical Theory.* Oxford, 1971.

———. "'Ut pictura poesis': The Nineteenth-Century Aftermath." *Journal of Aesthetics and Art Criticism* 28 (1969): 155–64.

Passavant, M. *Tour of a German Artist in England.* Trans. Elizabeth Rigby. 2 vols. London, 1836. Rpt. Wakefield, Yorkshire, 1978.

Paulson, Ronald. *Book and Painting: Shakespeare, Milton and the Bible: Literary Texts and the Emergence of English Painting.* Knoxville, Tenn., 1982.

———. *Hogarth: His Life, Art, and Times.* 2 vols. New Haven, Conn., 1971.

Piper, David, ed. *The Genius of British Painting.* London, 1975.

———. *The Image of the Poet: British Poets and Their Portraits.* Oxford, 1982.

Pointon, Marcia R. *Milton and English Art.* Manchester, 1970.

———. *William Dyce, 1806–1864: A Critical Biography.* Oxford, 1979.

Praz, Mario. *Conversation Pieces: A Survey of the Informal Group Portrait in Europe and America.* University Park, Pa., 1971.

———. *Mnemosyne: The Parallel Between Literature and the Visual Arts.* Princeton, N.J., 1970.

[Pre-Raphaelites.] *Paintings and Drawings of the Pre-Raphaelites and Their Circle.* (Exhibition catalogue, Fogg Art Gallery, 1948.)

The Pre-Raphaelite Brotherhood. (Exhibition catalogue, Birmingham Art Gallery, 1947.)

The Pre-Raphaelite Brotherhood, 1848–1948. A Centenary Exhibition. (Catalogue, Tate Gallery, 1948.)

The Pre-Raphaelites and Their Associates in the Whitworth Art Gallery. (Exhibition catalogue, 1972.)

The Pre-Raphaelites and Their Circle in the National Gallery of Victoria. (Exhibition catalogue, 1978.)

Pressly, William L. *The Life and Art of James Barry.* New

Haven, Conn., 1981.

Quennell, Peter. *Romantic England: Writing and Painting, 1717–1851.* New York, 1970.

Ray, Gordon N. *The Illustrator and the Book in England from 1790 to 1914.* New York, 1976.

Redgrave, Richard, and Samuel Redgrave. *A Century of British Painters.* Ed. Ruthven Todd. London, 1947. (Originally published London, 1866.)

Reid, Forrest. *Illustrators of the Sixties.* London, 1953.

Reynolds, Graham. *Painters of the Victorian Scene.* London, 1953.

______. *Victorian Painting.* London, 1966.

______. *Victorian Paintings.* (Exhibition catalogue, Arts Council, 1962.)

Reynolds, Sir Joshua. *Discourses on Art.* Ed. Robert R. Wark. San Marino, Cal., 1959.

Rinder, Frank. *The Royal Scottish Academy, 1826–1916.* Glasgow, 1917.

Robertson, David. *Sir Charles Eastlake and the Victorian Art World.* Princeton, N.J., 1978.

Rosenblum, Robert. "The Dawn of British Romantic Painting, 1760–1780." In *The Varied Pattern: Studies in the Eighteenth Century,* ed. Peter Hughes and David Williams (Toronto, 1971), pp. 189–210.

______. *Transformations in Late Eighteenth Century Art.* Princeton, N.J., 1967.

Rossetti, William Michael. *The Diary of William Michael Rossetti, 1870–1873.* Ed. Odette Bornand. Oxford, 1977.

______. *Fine Art, Chiefly Contemporary: Notices Re-Printed, with Revisions.* London, 1867.

______. *The P. R. B. Journal: William Michael Rossetti's Diary of the Pre-Raphaelite Brotherhood, 1849–1853.* Ed. William E. Fredeman. Oxford, 1975.

______. *Some Reminiscences of William Michael Rossetti.* 2 vols. London, 1906.

Royal Shakespeare Theatre Picture Gallery. *Catalogue of Pictures and Sculptures.* 6th ed. Stratford-on-Avon, 1970.

[Royal Society of British Artists.] *Works Exhibited at the Royal Society of British Artists, 1824–1893, and the New English Art Club, 1888–1917.* [Woodbridge, England,] 1975.

Salaman, Malcolm C. *Shakespeare in Pictorial Art.* Ed. Charles Holme. *Studio* Special Number, Spring 1916.

Sambrook, James. "Pope and the Visual Arts." In *Alexander Pope,* ed. Peter Dixon (London, 1972), pp. 143–71.

Sandby, William. *The History of the Royal Academy of Arts from Its Foundation in 1768 to the Present Time.* London, 1862.

Schiff, Gert. *Johann Heinrich Füssli, 1741–1825.* 2 vols. Zurich, 1973.

______. *Johann Heinrich Füsslis Milton-Galerie.* Zurich, 1963.

Scott, William Bell. *Autobiographical Notes of the Life of William Bell Scott.* Ed. W. Minto. 2 vols. New York, 1892.

Shackford, Martha H. *Wordsworth's Interest in Painters and Pictures.* Wellesley, Mass., 1945. Rpt. New York, 1976.

Shirley, Hon. Andrew. "Painting and Engraving." In *Johnson's England,* ed. A. S. Turberville (Oxford, 1933), 2: 41–71.

Simon, Robin. "Hogarth's Shakespeare." *Apollo* 109 (1979): 213–20.

Sitwell, Osbert, and Margaret Barton. "Taste." In *Johnson's England,* ed. A. S. Turberville (Oxford, 1933), 2: 1–40.

Sitwell, Sacheverell. *Conversation Pieces: A Survey of English Domestic Portraits and Their Painters.* London, 1937.

______. *Narrative Pictures: A Survey of English Genre and Its Painters.* London, 1937.

[Smith, C. R.] "Pictorial Illustrations of Shakespeare." *Quarterly Review* 142 (1876): 457–79.

Smith, Thomas. *Recollections of the British Institution . . . 1805–1859.* London, 1860.

Spender, Stephen. "The Pre-Raphaelite Literary Painters." *New Writing and Daylight* 6 (1945): 123–51.

Stein, Richard L. *The Ritual of Interpretation: The Fine Arts as Literature in Ruskin, Rossetti, and Pater.* Cambridge, Mass., 1975.

Strong, Roy. *Recreating the Past.* New York, 1978. (British edition: *"And When Did You Last See Your Father?"*)

Studing, Richard, and Carolyn Merlo. "Shakespeare in Art: A Bibliography." *Shakespeare Newsletter* 28 (1978): 42–43.

Surtees, Virginia. *The Paintings and Drawings of Dante Gabriel Rossetti . . . A Catalogue Raisonné.* 2 vols. Oxford, 1971.

Sussman, Herbert L. *Fact into Figure: Typology in Carlyle, Ruskin, and the Pre-Raphaelite Brotherhood.* Columbus, Ohio, 1979.

Svendsen, Kester. "John Martin and the Expulsion Scene of *Paradise Lost.*" *Studies in English Literature* 1 (1961): 63–73.

Temple, Alfred G. *The Art of Painting in the Queen's Reign.* London, 1897.

Thompson, Colin. *Pictures for Scotland: The National Gallery of Scotland and Its Collections: A Study of the Changing Attitude to Painting since the 1820s.* Edinburgh, 1972.

Thompson, Lawrance. "The Boydell Shakespeare: An English Monument to the Graphic Arts." *Princeton University Library Chronicle,* 1, no. 2 (1940), pp. 17–24.

Tinker, Chauncey Brewster. *Painter and Poet: Studies in the Literary Relations of English Painting.* Cambridge, Mass., 1938.

Tomory, Peter. *The Life and Art of Henry Fuseli.* London, 1972.

[Treble, Rosemary.] *Great Victorian Pictures: Their Paths to Fame.* (Exhibition catalogue, Arts Council [Royal Academy], 1978.)

Vaughan, William. *Romantic Art.* London, 1978.

Waagen, G. F. *Works of Art and Artists in England.* Trans. H. E. Lloyd. 3 vols. London, 1838.

Waldfogel, Melvin. "Narrative Painting." In *The Mind and Art of Victorian England,* ed. Josef Altholz (Minneapolis, 1976), pp. 159–74.

Waterhouse, Ellis K. *The Dictionary of British Eighteenth Cen-*

tury Painters in Oils and Crayons. Woodbridge, England, 1981.

———. "English Painting and France in the Eighteenth Century." *JWCI* 15 (1952): 122–35.

———. "The First Royal Academy Exhibition, 1769." *Listener* 43 (1950): 944–46.

———. *Painting in Britain 1530 to 1790.* Pelican History of Art. 4th ed. Harmondsworth, England, 1978.

———. *Reynolds.* London, 1941.

———. *Three Decades of British Art, 1740–1770.* (Memoirs of the American Philosophical Society 63.) Philadelphia, 1965.

Watts, Mary S. *George Frederic Watts: The Annals of an Artist's Life.* 2 vols. London, 1913. (Vol. 3: *His Writings.*)

Webster, Mary. *Francis Wheatley.* London, 1970.

———. *Johann Zoffany, 1733–1810.* (Exhibition catalogue, National Portrait Gallery, 1976.)

Wendorf, Richard, ed. *Articulate Images: The Sister Arts from Hogarth to Tennyson.* Minneapolis, 1983.

[Wheatley.] *Francis Wheatley, R.A.* (Exhibition catalogue, Aldeburgh Festival and City Art Gallery, Leeds, 1965.)

White, Gleeson. *English Illustration: "The Sixties": 1855–70.* London, 1906.

Whitley, William T. (1) *Artists and Their Friends in England, 1700–1799.* 2 vols. Cambridge, 1928. Rpt. New York, 1968.

———. (2) *Art in England, 1800–1820.* Cambridge, 1928. Rpt. New York, 1975.

———. (3) *Art in England, 1821–1837.* Cambridge, 1930. Rpt. New York, 1973.

Williams, Iolo A. "English Book-Illustration, 1700–1775." *Library* 4th ser. 17 (1936): 1–21.

Williamson, George C. *English Conversation Pictures of the Eighteenth and Early Nineteenth Centuries.* London, 1932. Rpt. New York, 1975. (Title of New York 1931 edition: *Intimate Paintings of the Georgian Period.*)

Wind, Edgar. "The Revolution of History Painting." *JWCI* 2 (1938): 116–27.

Witemeyer, Hugh. *George Eliot and the Visual Arts.* New Haven, Conn., 1979.

Wittreich, Joseph A., Jr. "Illustrators." In *A Milton Encyclopedia* (Lewisburg, Pa., 1978), 4: 55–78.

Wood, Christopher. (1) *The Dictionary of Victorian Painters.* 2d ed. Woodbridge, England, 1978.

———. (2) *Olympian Dreamers: Victorian Classical Painters, 1860–1914.* London, 1983.

———. (3) *The Pre-Raphaelites.* New York, 1981.

———. (4) *Victorian Panorama: Paintings of Victorian Life.* London, 1976.

Woodward, John. "Shakespeare and English Painting." *Listener* 43 (1950): 1017–18, 1030.

Wornum, Ralph N., ed. *Lectures on Painting, by the Royal Academicians Barry, Opie, and Fuseli.* London, 1848.

Ziff, Jerrold. "J. M. W. Turner on Poetry and Painting." *Studies in Romanticism* 3 (1964): 193–215.

Periodicals

Files of *Apollo, Art Journal, Athenaeum, Burlington Magazine, Connoisseur, Examiner, Illustrated London News, Literary Gazette, Saturday Review, Spectator, Times.*

The three volumes thus far published of the *Wellesley Index to Victorian Periodicals* (1966–) list some 300 articles dealing with contemporary British art, including reviews of current exhibitions.

INDEX

Principal references are in **boldface** *type. Characters in literary works are included in the title entries. Titles of works by* BURNS, BYRON, DICKENS, MILTON, SCOTT, SHAKESPEARE, *and* TENNYSON *are entered under author. Additional information in the picture captions is indicated by parentheses enclosing the plate number.*